TCL /TK
TOOLS

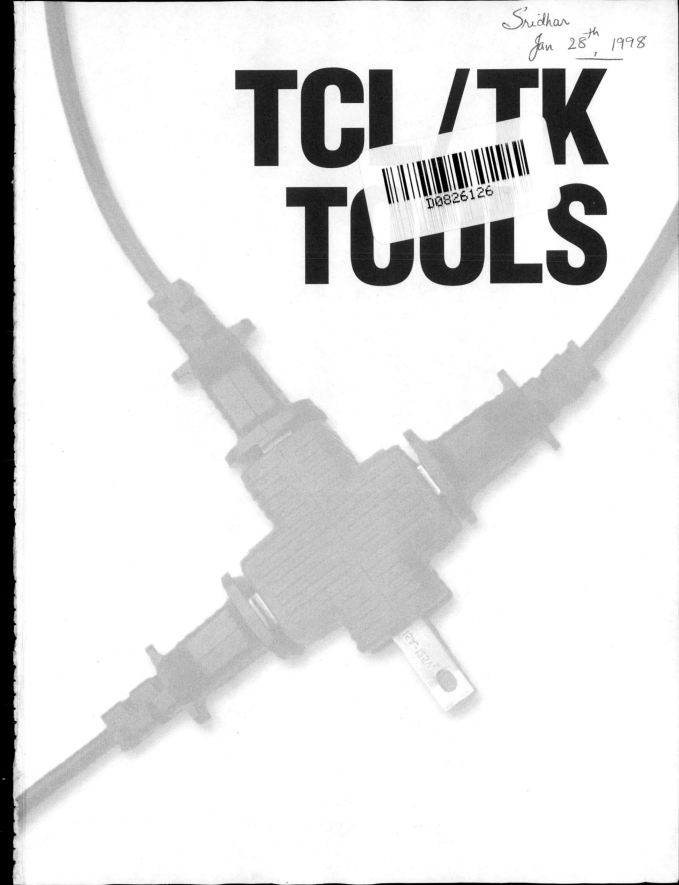

TCL/TK TOOLS

Mark Harrison
with other contributors, including Allan Brighton, De Clarke,
Charles Crowley, Mark Diekhans, Saul Greenberg, D. Richard
Hipp, George A. Howlett, Ioi Lam, Don Libes, Michael
McLennan, John Ousterhout, Tom Poindexter, Mark Roseman,
Lawrence A. Rowe, Brian Smith, and Mark Ulferts

O'REILLY™

Cambridge • Köln • Paris • Sebastopol • Tokyo

Tcl/Tk Tools
by Mark Harrison and other contributors

Copyright © 1997 O'Reilly & Associates, Inc. All rights reserved.

Editor: Andy Oram

Production Editor: John Files

Editorial and Production Services: Benchmark Productions, Inc., Boston, MA

Printing History:

  August 1997:   First Edition.

ISBN: 1-56592-218-2

Table of Contents

Foreword

by John Ousterhout

This book describes a collection of extensions, tools, and applications that have played an essential role in the success of the Tcl scripting language and the Tk toolkit. When I designed Tcl, I intended for it to be used as a glue language. That is, I didn't expect people to build things from scratch in Tcl. Instead, I expected people to use Tcl primarily for connecting together powerful components built in other languages like C or C++. I didn't really know what the components would look like or where they would come from, but I knew that they must exist in order for Tcl to be successful.

Components began to appear almost immediately once Tcl became available. For example, Don Libes wrote Expect within a few weeks of hearing the first Tcl paper at USENIX in 1990. Expect provided a neat set of Tcl extensions for automating things that would normally have to be typed by a user at a terminal; users could then write Tcl scripts that solved a variety of system administration and other problems. For quite a while, the download rate for Expect was greater than the download rate for Tcl! Other component sets, like Mark Diekhans' and Karl Lehenbauer's TclX package, appeared shortly after that.

The facilities described in this book have made my early dreams for Tcl into a reality. Tcl became popular because it provided rapid application development, but it could do this only because of the rich set of components that were available. I suspect that most Tcl developers use at least one of the facilities in this book, whether it is Michael McLennan's [INCR TCL] package for object-oriented programming, George Howlett's BLT widget package, Tom Poindexter's Sybtcl and Oratcl packages for database access, or one of the other fine packages described here.

This book represents not only the most important code in the Tcl world but also many of the key people in the Tcl world. People like Mark Harrison, Mark Diekhans, George Howlett, Karl Lehenbauer, Don Libes, Michael McLennan,Tom

Poindexter, and Larry Rowe were among the earliest users of Tcl and Tk. They shaped the development of Tcl not only with the tools and components they created, but also with the advice they have given me over the years. Many of the features that are now in the Tcl core were suggested or influenced by these people. In some cases, the features in an extension, like the file I/O facilities of TclX, were so universally compelling that we moved them into the Tcl core.

I hope that this book provides you not only with useful information for developing Tcl applications, but also a glimpse into the history of Tcl and the minds of the people who have influenced its evolution.

John Ousterhout
February 15, 1997

Preface

How This Book Came to Be

Like many other people, I was first exposed to Tcl and Tk at the 1990 Winter Usenix Conference, when John Ousterhout presented his paper on Tk (Tcl had been presented the previous year). At the time I was an enthusiastic Awk programmer, and my first response was "This is great: It's Awk, with graphics!" It also filled an immediate need, as my employer at the time was in the process of replacing our ASCII terminals with workstations (200 of them), and we were in the process of converting a lot of programs from character interfaces to graphical interfaces. It did not take a lot of experience with Xt and the Athena widgets (the original widget set from MIT) to convince me that this was going to be a lot of hard work. Being able to do this in Tcl and Tk was a very attractive option, and it saved a lot of time.

In 1992 I moved to DSC Communications Corporation to work on Intelligent Network systems, bringing my enthusiasm for Tcl and Tk with me. I immediately started to figure out how to evangelize my new colleagues about this great language and its GUI toolkit. In the beginning, it was not an easy sell. Commercial toolkits like OpenLook and Motif had by this time displaced the Athena widget set, and the marketing departments of many powerful and well-known companies were putting forth a lot of effort to ensure that their particular toolkit would prevail as "The Standard." It didn't seem that a free toolkit from a professor at Berkeley would stand much of a chance against that onslaught.

It took a bit of effort, but I was gradually able to demonstrate the overall soundness of both Tk as a GUI toolkit and Tcl as an embedded command language.

In addition to Tcl and Tk being overall excellent packages, one of the things that helped to convince people that this approach was a good solution for our work was

---

the availability of some really good extension sets. [INCR TCL], which adds a C++-like class system to Tcl, allowed us to build larger applications. Tcl-DP, which adds commands to do distributed processing over TCP/IP connections, allowed us to quickly code distributed applications. The BLT toolkit provided a nice set of GUI widgets, allowing us to provide interfaces with a much more polished look and feel. The facilities provided by Extended Tcl (TclX) and Expect allowed us to write a number of useful programs that probably would have gone unwritten if we would have had to code these programs from scratch.

So, in some cases, the extension sets helped to drive the acceptance of Tcl. Someone would come by and say "I'm looking for an easy way to write some socket programs," and they would become an immediate Tcl-DP convert. Someone else would come by and say "We've got a pretty large GUI program to write, and we want to start by encapsulating some program behavior in an object system." They would try [INCR TCL] and be off and running. (The end results of one of these trials became the [INCR WIDGETS] toolchest).

Tcl and Tk became so popular that I started to distribute nicely bound copies of the man pages. In addition, I started to put together what I called the "Tk Supplemental Reference," which was a collection of man pages, conference papers, slide presentations, and anything else I could get my hands on that discussed the extension sets we were using.

There was a problem, however. While all the packages were extremely well done and professionally put together, most of them suffered from what I started to call the "man page syndrome." Almost all of the packages had complete and comprehensive references in the form of Unix manual pages (TclX alone was more than 100 pages long), but there was a shortage of introductory or overview material. I really wanted to have something that would say "Here's the philosophy behind this package, and here are some examples of how to use it effectively." This need became especially apparent when the number of Tcl programmers at DSC grew from a handful to dozens to well over one hundred.

So it was a fortuitous thing when my editor, Andy Oram, contacted me with the idea of writing a Nutshell Handbook on Tcl and Tk. We didn't want an introductory or tutorial book—both Ousterhout* and Brent Welch† have done a fine job covering that angle. After a little thought, it became obvious what to write—the book on extensions that I wanted so desperately. Additionally, it seemed that this would mesh well with the O'Reilly approach to books. In addition to a long history of supporting freely available software, they have a good track record of producing collaborative works that still maintain consistency and coherence among the various contributing authors.

I knew immediately which extensions I wanted to write about—the ones we used every day! But, there were problems. Some of the extension sets are pretty big (Don Libes managed to write over 500 pages on Expect), and there was no way that I would be able to comprehensively cover all the extension sets I wanted to write about in a timely manner—by the time I finished, the book would be out of date, and I would have to start over! In addition, I didn't know the plans the extension

---

* Ousterhout, John K. Tcl and the Tk Toolkit, Addison-Wesley, 1994.

† Welch, Brent, Practical Programming in Tcl and Tk, Prentice-Hall, 1995.

authors had for future enhancements and extensions, so I wouldn't be able to cover future directions very well. Finally, I was worried about what the extension authors themselves might think about my efforts. What if these people (whose work I admired so much) thought I did a bad job of explaining their extensions? What if they went around telling everyone, "Mark Harrison ruined my extension with his crummy examples!"

With all these factors in consideration, Andy and I came to the conclusion that it would be a good idea to get the extension authors themselves to write chapters covering their own extensions. It would shorten the total cycle time, and it would make this book truly "authoritative" concerning the extension sets covered.

In addition to providing coverage on the extension sets, I wanted to cover other sundry topics such as configuration management (not a glamorous topic, but one that can make or break projects), miscellaneous development and debugging tools, security, and instructions for getting further information and assistance. In short, everything I wanted to give to my colleagues whenever they asked for help on a topic related to Tcl.

Typographical Conventions

The following typographic conventions are used in this book:

Italic is used for Unix commands, file names, and for program names.

Courier is used for listings and the output from programs. It is also used for elements of code that appear in the text, such as Tcl commands.

Bold Courier is used to show user input that should be typed literally by the user. In some code examples, it is used to highlight code that is new.

Further Information

The most up-to-date information on Tcl is usually found in the Usenet newsgroup *comp.lang.tcl*. In addition to the usual questions, answers, and commentary, there is a Frequently Asked Questions (FAQ) list, and pointers to Tcl-related Web and FTP sites.

We will keep a page on the O'Reilly Web site that has links to current versions of the extensions, any extension home pages, and other interesting Tcl links. Check it out at *http://www.ora.com/info/tcltk*.

If you have questions or comments on this book, please feel free to send them to *tcl-extensions@ora.com*. In particular, if you have or know of a good extension that you feel would benefit the Tcl community, please let us know!

You Can Help!

Tcl is continuing to grow at an incredible pace. Between the time this project started and wrapped up, Tcl has been ported to both Microsoft Windows and the Macintosh, and features like built-in networking and dynamically loadable modules have been introduced. In addition, new extensions continue to be written, and existing extensions are upgraded.

It is our goal to update and revise this book regularly to add coverage for more extensions, and to keep up with the latest features in existing extensions. If you know of an extension set that meets the standards outlined earlier (or especially if you have written one) and are interested in writing about it, please let us know!

Acknowledgments

First, of course, all Tcl programmers owe a debt of gratitude to John Ousterhout. Without his vision and boundless energy there wouldn't be anything to write about.

Second, I would like to thank the extension authors who have contributed to this book. Tcl has attracted a large number of extremely talented individuals, and we have all benefited from their skill and hard work.

I would also like to thank some of my colleagues at DSC Communications Corporation who made this book both necessary and possible. Raj Rao first had the vision that there was a better way to program GUIs. Mark Ulferts took up the challenge, and not only demonstrated that it was possible to produce high quality Tcl GUIs, but went on to create the [INCR WIDGETS] package. A really great management team saw the value of what we were doing and encouraged us every step of the way: Mahesh Shah, Sandra Au, Gil Stevens, Carlos Macia, Cliff Johnson, and Allen Adams all provided the backing necessary to make our Tcl effort a success. Cliff deserves to be thanked twice, since he originally sent me to Usenix when we were both at our previous employer.

Michael McLennan of AT&T provided the training for well over 100 engineers—his boundless enthusiasm and energy helped push us over the top.

Thanks to Dave Beazley, Sean Kelley, and Brent Welch, who provided valuable comments on various portions of the manuscript.

Carol A. Block performed valuable formatting work on the Tcl-DP chapter.

Our series editor Andy Oram deserves special praise, not only for doing an excellent job but for doing much of it while recovering from an incident involving one of the motorists for which Boston is so famous. Thanks also to the Most Excellent staff at O'Reilly who shepherded this book through the various stages of design and production.

And finally, I must give my sincerest thanks to my wife Ellen and children Allegra and Alexander for the many hours in which they allowed me to work on this book. Without their patience and support, this book would have never seen the light of day.

1

Introduction

This book is about Tcl Extensions. If you're a Tcl user, you already know that it's a powerful and flexible language. If you use Tk, you already know that it's one of the highest quality and best engineered GUI toolkits available.

Both packages are suited to a wide range of tasks, from serving as an embedded control language to controlling NASA's most advanced spacecraft. Tens of thousands of programmers use these tools daily to produce high-quality, mission-critical applications in a timely, cost-effective manner.

But that's only part of the story. Tcl's extensible architecture has encouraged many talented programmers to develop new packages of commands, commonly known as *extensions*. These extensions make developing Tcl applications even easier and more pleasurable. Some of them are simply libraries of useful Tk widgets, while others extend Tcl to handle things as diverse as database access, Web programming, object-oriented programming, and multithreading. Most of them are released under the same liberal licensing policy as Tcl and Tk, allowing you to economically incorporate them into your applications without worrying about any restrictive copyright restrictions.

In this book I've chosen the extensions that I think the largest group of Tcl programmers will find helpful (I'll describe my criteria later in this chapter). All of them can save literally hundreds of hours of development time. Many of them allow you to write programs you would otherwise probably never attempt.

If you are not familiar with Tcl, it is probably best to briefly review a bit of Tcl history and see where the idea of extensions came from and why they are important.

The Origin of Tcl

Tcl (the "tool command language," pronounced "tickle") was written by John Ousterhout in the spring of 1988. He and his team at the University of California at Berkeley had been building tools for circuit design and found themselves "spending a lot of time writing bad command languages.*" If he could write a general purpose command language that could be linked into an application and extended with application-specific commands, he could free up the effort that each team member spent writing his or her own command language. In addition, since everyone was using the same core language, there would be no need to learn a new syntax for each application, and improvements to the core language would enhance the functionality of the applications at no extra cost. In addition, it meant that libraries of Tcl commands could be packaged together and reused by application programs.

Tk (Tcl's graphical toolkit, pronounced "tee-kay") was done as a follow-on to this work. Ousterhout followed the strategy of using the core Tcl language, and adding the graphics functionality as a set of Tcl commands. He provided a standalone interpreter (*wish*, the "windowing shell"), enabling people to write graphical applications at the script level.

The Birth of Extensions

At the same time, others were starting to write their own Tcl extensions. Two of the earliest extensions were Expect and Extended Tcl (TclX). These were well received, and demonstrated the value of building on an existing core language. You could concentrate on adding the functionality you were interested in without wasting time worrying about language design issues. When you were finished, people could easily integrate your work into their applications using their existing Tcl infrastructure. Additionally, they would already know the basic syntax—all they would have to learn would be the functionality of the new commands you had provided.

Fueled by both the success of *wish* (for writing script-level GUI programs) and Expect (which rapidly became a staple in the system adminstrator's toolbox), Tcl started to grow at a very rapid rate. As this happened, people started sharing extensions they had written for their own use. Many of these extensions were well-written, production-quality packages used in demanding, mission-critical applications.

As I recounted in the Preface, it became obvious that there was a demand for more documentation on these extensions than what was available. Most of the extensions weren't big enough to fill an entire book, but all of them could benefit from at least a chapter's worth of material.

How This Book Is Arranged

The first part of this book contains the information related to developing and maintaining Tcl programs. This includes configuration management, combining extensions, and managing multiple versions of Tcl. In addition, it covers some of the various development and debugging tools that have been contributed to the Tcl archives.

The remainder of the book (which has continued to grow and dwarf the original planned sections of the book) covers the extension sets. Not everything is a "pure" extension set, however. "Embedded Tk" is a package for doing Tk programming at the C or C++ level, and "TkReplay" is a program that lets you capture and replay

---

* Ousterhout, John K., *Tcl and the Tk Toolkit*, Addison-Wesley, 1994: xvii.

Tk sessions. These packages are so useful to Tcl programmers, however, that I really thought they should be covered, without being too concerned that these packages were not "pure" extension sets.

To get the most bang for the buck, we restrict our information to what's specific in Tcl. For example, we don't cover how sockets work in the Tcl-DP chapter, or how to write SQL in the Sybtcl and Oratcl chapters. There are plenty of other books on these topics. Similarly, we don't offer a Tcl Primer. Both the Ousterhout and Welch books do a fine job on that.

How did I pick the particular packages included in this book? There were several criteria that I followed:

- First, the package needed to be generally useful. Our own experience at DSC was a good starting point; in addition, reading the Usenet newsgroup *comp.lang.tcl* provided good feedback as to packages that were well received or well thought of.
- Second, the package had to be of production quality. One of the most pleasant things about being a Tcl programmer is the incredibly high standard of quality that Ousterhout has established, and which most Tcl packages come close to. I don't want to waste my time or risk my projects by using some unreliable, off-the-cuff extension, and I'm sure you don't either.
- Finally, the author should have some long-term plans for supporting or maintaining the extension. This was the easy part—someone who wasn't interested in continuing to work on an extension surely wouldn't be interested in taking the time to write about it.

Extensions Covered

Here's a quick overview of the packages that we cover.

Language Related Extensions

[INCR TCL]—Object-Oriented Tcl Programming

[INCR TCL] is an object system for Tcl, providing the same type of object model as C++. Objects are organized into classes with identical characteristics, and classes can inherit functionality from one another. This helps you organize your code into modules that are easier to understand and maintain, so you can build larger Tcl/Tk applications. The name is a pun: "[INCR TCL]" means the same thing in Tcl that "C++" does in C.

Embedded Tk (ET)—Tools for Mixing Tcl/Tk with C/C++ Code

Embedded Tk is not a extension in the usual sense. It is a tool to simplify writing programs that combine C or C++ with Tcl/Tk. Using Embedded Tk (also called ET), you can include bits of Tcl/Tk in the middle of a C or C++ routine and vice versa. This allows the user interface to be coded in Tcl/Tk, but speed-critical or compute-intensive code to be written in C or C++. ET programs compile into standalone executables which are able to run on machines that do not have Tcl/Tk installed.

Tk Graphics Widgets

TSIPP—3D Graphics with the SIPP (Simple Polygon Processor) Library

TSIPP (Tcl TSIPP) is a 3D image specification and rendering toolkit. It is based on SIPP, the SImple Polygon Processor, a library for creating three-dimensional scenes and rendering them using a scan-line z-buffer algorithm. Tcl commands are used to specify surfaces, objects, scenes, and rendering options. Scenes may be rendered to files in the PPM or Utah Raster Toolkit RLE formats. Additionally, interactive applications can render directly to a Tk photo image.

TkTree—A Widget for Displaying Dynamic Trees

The Tree widget draws trees in a Tk canvas. The nodes can be made up of any number of canvas items or even other Tk widgets. The Tree widget will optimally lay out the tree elements to take up the minimum amount of space required on the screen. The tree can be displayed horizontally or vertically.

Widget Toolsets

[INCR TK]—An Object-Oriented Mega-Widget Framework for Tk

[INCR TK] is a framework for building mega-widgets using the [INCR TCL] object system. Mega-widgets are high-level widgets like a file browser, a combo box, or a tabbed notebook. They look like ordinary Tk widgets, but they are constructed using the Tk widgets as component parts, allowing you to create a new kind of mega-widget in just a few hours without having to write any C code. With a large catalog of prefabricated parts, your Tcl applications can come together in a fraction of the usual time.

Tix—A Library of Over 40 Mega-Widgets

The Tix library has a collection of over 40 mega-widgets, including Hierarchical Listbox, Directory List/Tree View, SpreadSheet, Tabular Listbox, ComboBox, File Selection Box, and more. Tix also comes with several new image types and has an object-oriented framework for rapid development of new mega-widgets.

[INCR WIDGETS]—An Extensible Mega-Widget Set Based on [INCR TK]

This is a nicely featured widget set built on top of [INCR TK]. It features a variety of useful and attractive widgets. Since it is built on top of [INCR TK], you can easily extend the widgets with the standard [INCR TK] constructs.

BLT—Bacon, Lettuce, and Tomatoes: Advanced Tk Widgets

The "Bacon, Lettuce, and Tomatoes" toolkit features graphing, geometry management, and a number of other useful widgets.

Programming Tools

Oratcl—Access the Oracle Database

Oratcl and Sybtcl Oratcl are extensions that provide access to Sybase and Oracle database servers. These packages add commands that log in to a SQL Server, send SQL code, fetch return results, and so on. They can also read and write text/image columns, execute store procedures, and access metadata, such as column names and datatypes from returned rows. If you use either of these databases you should be using these extensions!

Sybtcl—Access the Sybase Database

(See Oratcl)

Groupkit—Build Real-Time Groupware Applications

GroupKit is a groupware toolkit developed at the University of Calgary. It is used for developing real-time conferencing applications. These are groupware applications like drawing tools, editors, and meeting tools that are shared simultaneously among several users. The distribution includes not only the core toolkit but over 30 example groupware tools.

TclX—Commands for Unix System Programming

One of the first Tcl extension sets, TclX provides access to most Posix (Unix) functions, keyed data types, and an assortment of other useful commands.

Tcl-DP—Distributed Internet Tcl Programming

Tcl-DP adds TCP, UDP, and IP-multicast connection management, remote procedure call (RPC), distributed object protocols, and a name server to Tcl. A C interface to the RPC primitives is also provided.

Development Tools

Expect—An Extension for Automating Interactive Applications

Expect allows you to automate Telnet, FTP, passwd, rlogin, and hundreds of other applications that normally require human interaction. Using Expect to automate these applications will let you speed up tasks and, in many cases, solve new problems that you never would have even considered before.

For example, you can use Expect to test interactive programs with no changes to their interfaces. Or wrap interactive programs with Motif-like frontends to control applications by buttons, scrollbars, and other graphic elements with no recompilation of the original programs. You don't even need the source code! Expect works with remote applications, too. Use it to tie together Internet applications including Telnet, Archie, FTP, Gopher, and Mosaic.

This application allows you to record and play back a Tk session. The recorded scripts can be easily edited and combined. In addition to its main use for regression testing GUI applications, it is also useful for running demonstration programs.

How the CD Is Arranged

Finally, there is a companion CD to this book. In addition to the source code for all of these extensions, it has these packages ported to popular Unix platforms. The CD is arranged like this:

```
/
README
distributions/
binaries/
       solaris/
               bin/
               include/
               lib/
               man/
       linux/
               bin/
               include/
               lib/
               man/
src/
       blt2.3
       Tix4.1.0
       ...
```

The directory */src* contains the unconfigured source code for Tcl, Tk, and each of the extensions. The directory */distributions* contains the standard distributions of each package, in the form of compressed tar files.

There is one directory under */binaries* for each of the supported platforms. Each of these directories has the usual directories created during the installation process (*bin*, *lib*, *include*, and *man*). The extensions have been configured with a prefix of */usr/local*.*

The file *README* contains information on installing and running the software.

---

* See Chapter 17, *Configuration Management*.

2

Object-Oriented Programming with [incr Tcl]

by Michael McLennan

Copyright 1997 Lucent Technologies, Inc.

Tcl/Tk applications come together with astounding speed. You can write a simple file browser in an afternoon, or a card game like Solitaire within a week. But as applications get larger, Tcl code becomes more difficult to understand and maintain. You get lost in the mass of procedures and global variables that make up your program. It is hard to create data structures, and even harder to make reusable libraries.

[INCR TCL] extends the Tcl language to support object-oriented programming. It wasn't created as an academic exercise, nor to be buzzword-compatible with the latest trend. It was created to solve real problems, so that Tcl could be used to build large applications.

[INCR TCL] is fully backward-compatible with normal Tcl, so it will run all of your existing Tcl/Tk programs. It simply adds some extra commands which let you create and manipulate objects.

It extends the Tcl language in the same way that C++ extends the base language C. It borrows some familiar concepts from C++,* so many developers find it easy to learn. But while it resembles C++, it is written to be consistent with the Tcl language. This is reflected in its name, which you can pronounce as "increment tickle" or "inker tickle." This is the Tcl way of saying "Tcl++."

---

* Stanley B. Lippman, C++ Primer (2nd edition), Addison-Wesley, 1991; and Bjarne Stroustrup, *The Design and Evolution of C++,* Addison-Wesley, 1994.

This chapter shows how [INCR TCL] can be used to solve common programming problems. As an example, it shows how a tree data structure can be created and used to build a file browser. Along the way, it illustrates many important concepts of object-oriented programming, including encapsulation, inheritance, and composition.

Objects and Classes

I won't go on for pages about object-oriented programming. You have probably read about it in other contexts, and there are some really good texts* that explain it well. But the basic idea is that you create *objects* as building blocks for your application. If you are building a kitchen, for example, you might need objects like toasters, blenders, and can openers. If you are building a *large* kitchen, you might have many different toasters, but they all have the same characteristics. They all belong to the same *class*, in this case a class called `Toaster`.

Each object has some data associated with it. A toaster might have a certain heat setting and a crumb tray that collects the crumbs that fall off each time it toasts bread. Each toaster has its *own* heat setting and its *own* crumb count, so each `Toaster` object has its own variables to represent these things. In object speak, these variables are called *instance variables* or *data members*. You can use these instead of global variables to represent your data.

You tell an object to do something using special procedures called *methods* or *member functions*. For example, a `Toaster` object might have a method called `toast` that you use to toast bread, and another method called `clean` that you use to clean out the crumb tray. Methods let you define a few strictly limited ways to access the data in a class, which helps you prevent many errors.

Everything that you need to know about an object is described in its *class definition*. The class definition lists the instance variables that hold an object's data and the methods that are used to manipulate the object. It acts like a blueprint for creating objects. Objects themselves are often called *instances* of the class that they belong to.

Variables and Methods

Let's see how objects work in a real-life example. Suppose you want to use the Tk canvas widget to build a file browser. It might look something like the one shown in Figure 2-1. Each entry would have an icon next to the file name to indicate whether the file is an ordinary file, a directory, or an executable program. Aligning each icon with its file name is ordinarily a lot of work, but you can make your job much simpler if you create an object to represent each icon and its associated file name. When you need to add an entry to the file browser, you simply create a new object with an icon and a text string, and tell it to draw itself on the canvas.

We will create a class `VisualRep` to characterize these objects. The class definition is contained in the file *itcl/tree/visrep.itcl* on the CD-ROM that accompanies this book, and it appears in Example 2-1.

---

* For example: Grady Booch, *Object-Oriented Design*, 1991; Benjamin/Cummings and Timothy Budd, *An Introduction to Object-Oriented Programming*, Addison-Wesley, 1991.

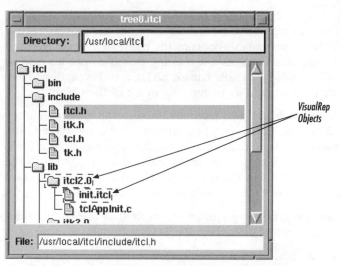

Figure 2-1: Using VisualRep Objects to Build a File Browser

Example 2-1: The Class Definition for VisualRep Objects

```
image create photo default -file default.gif

class VisualRep {
    variable canvas
    variable icon
    variable title


    constructor {cwin ival tval} {
        set canvas $cwin
        set icon $ival
        set title $tval
    }
    destructor {
        erase
    }

    method draw {x y} {
        erase
        $canvas create image $x $y -image $icon -anchor c -tags $this
        set x1 [expr $x + [image width $icon]/2 + 4]
        $canvas create text $x1 $y -text $title -anchor w -tags $this
    }
    method erase {} {
        $canvas delete $this
    }
}
```

All of the [INCR TCL] keywords in Example 2-1 are in bold type. You use the class command to define a new class of objects. Inside the class definition is a series of statements that define the instance variables and the methods for objects that belong to this class. In this example, each `VisualRep` object has three variables: `canvas`, `icon,` and `title`. The `canvas` variable contains the name of the canvas widget that will display the object. The `icon` variable contains the name of a Tk image used as the icon. And the `title` variable contains a text string that is displayed next to the icon. Each object also has a built-in variable named `this`, which you don't have to declare. It is automatically defined, and it contains the name of the object.

Each `VisualRep` object responds to the two methods listed in the class definition. You can ask the object to `draw` itself at an (x,y) coordinate on the canvas, and the icon will be centered on this coordinate. You can also ask the object to `erase` itself. Notice that all of the canvas items created in the `draw` method are tagged with the name of the object, taken from the built-in `this` variable. This makes it easy to erase the object later by deleting all canvas items tagged with the object name.

The `constructor` and `destructor` are special methods that are called automatically when an object is created and destroyed. We'll talk more about these later.

The methods and variables in one class are completely separate from those in another. You could create a `Book` class with a `title` variable, or a `Chalkboard` class with `draw` and `erase` methods. Since these members belong to different classes, they will not interfere with our `VisualRep` class. It is always obvious which methods and variables you can use if you think about which object you are manipulating. Because classes keep everything separate, you don't have to worry so much about name collisions, and you can use simpler names in [INCR TCL] code than you would in ordinary Tcl code.

Methods look a lot like ordinary Tcl procedures. Each method has a name, a Tcl-style argument list, and a body. But unlike procedures, methods automatically have access to the variables defined in the class. In the `draw` method, we talk to the canvas widget using the name stored in the `canvas` variable. We access the icon using `$icon`, and the title string using `$title`. There is no need to declare these variables with anything like the Tcl `global` statement. They have been declared once and for all in the class definition.

The same thing holds true for methods. Within one method, we can treat the other methods as ordinary commands. In the destructor, for example, we call the `erase` method simply by using the command `erase`. In effect, we are telling this object (whichever one is being destroyed) to erase itself. In the code outside of a class, we have to be more specific. We have to tell a particular object to erase itself.

Having defined the class `VisualRep`, we can create an object like this:

```
VisualRep vr1 .canv default "Display this text"
```

The first argument (`vr1`) is the name of the new object. The remaining arguments (`.canv default "Display this text"`) are passed along to the constructor to initialize the object. This might look familiar. It is precisely how you would create a Tk widget:

```
button .b -background red -text "Alert"
```

Here, the first argument (`.b`) is the name of the new widget, and the remaining arguments (`-background red -text "Alert"`) are used to configure the widget. This similarity is no accident. [INCR TCL] was designed to follow the Tk paradigm. Objects can even have configuration options just like the Tk widgets. We'll see this later, but for now, we'll stick with simple examples.

Once an object has been created, you can manipulate it using its methods. You start by saying which object you want to manipulate. You use the object name as a command, with the method name as an operation, and the method arguments as additional parameters. For example, you could tell the object vr1 to draw itself like this:

```
vr1 draw 25 37
```

or to erase itself from the canvas like this:

```
vr1 erase
```

Again, this might look familiar. It is precisely how you would use a Tk widget. You might tell a button to configure itself like this:

```
.b configure -background blue -foreground white
```

or to flash itself like this:

```
.b flash
```

Putting all of this together, we can use VisualRep objects to create the drawing shown in Figure 2-2.

Figure 2-2: Simple Drawing Composed of VisualRep Objects

We need to create five VisualRep objects for this drawing. The first object has a directory folder icon and the message [incr Tcl] has:. The remaining objects have file icons and various message strings. We can create these objects and tell each one to draw itself on the canvas using the handful of code in Example 2-2.

Example 2-2: Code Used to Produce Figure 2-2

```
canvas .canv -width 150 -height 120 -background white
pack .canv

image create photo dir1 -file dir1.gif
image create photo file -file file.gif

VisualRep title .canv dir1 "\[incr Tcl\] has:"
title draw 20 20
```

```
VisualRep bullet1 .canv file "Objects"
bullet1 draw 40 40

VisualRep bullet2 .canv file "Mega-Widgets"
bullet2 draw 40 60

VisualRep bullet3 .canv file "Namespaces"
bullet3 draw 40 80

VisualRep bullet4 .canv file "And more..."
bullet4 draw 40 100
```

Constructors and Destructors

Let's take a moment to see what happens when an object is created. The following command:

```
VisualRep bullet1 .canv file "Objects"
```

creates an object named `bullet1` in class `VisualRep`. It starts by allocating the variables contained within the object. For a `VisualRep` object, this includes the variables `canvas`, `icon`, and `title`, as well as the built-in `this` variable. If the class has a `constructor` method, it is automatically called with the remaining arguments passed as parameters to it. The constructor can set internal variables, open files, create other objects, or do anything else needed to initialize an object. If an error is encountered within the constructor, it will abort, and the object will not be created.

Like any other method, the constructor has a Tcl-style argument list. You can have required arguments and optional arguments with default values. You can even use the Tcl `args` argument to handle variable-length argument lists. But whatever arguments you specify for the constructor, you must supply those arguments whenever you create an object. In class `VisualRep`, the constructor takes three values: a canvas, an icon image, and a title string. These are all required arguments, so you must supply all three values whenever you create a `VisualRep` object. The constructor shown in Example 2-1 simply stores the three values in the instance variables so they will be available later when the object needs to draw itself.

The constructor is optional. If you don't need one, you can leave it out of the class definition. This is like having a constructor with a null argument list and a null body. When you create an object, you won't supply any additional parameters, and you won't do anything special to initialize the object.

The `destructor` method is also optional. If it is defined, it is automatically called when an object is destroyed to free any resources that are no longer needed. An object like `bullet1` is destroyed using the `delete object` command like this:

```
delete object bullet1
```

This command can take multiple arguments representing objects to be deleted. It is not possible to pass arguments to the destructor, so as you can see in Example 2-1, the destructor is defined without an argument list.

Instance variables are deleted automatically, but any other resources associated with the object should be explicitly freed. If a file is opened in the constructor, it should be closed in the destructor. If an image is created in the constructor, it should be deleted in the destructor. As a result, the destructor usually looks like the inverse of the constructor. If an error is encountered while executing the destructor, the `delete object` command is aborted and the object remains alive.

For the `VisualRep` class, the destructor uses the `erase` method to erase the object from its canvas. Whenever a `VisualRep` object is deleted, it disappears.

Pointers

Each object must have a unique name. When we use the object name as a command, there is no question about which object we are talking to. In effect, the object name in [INCR TCL] is like the memory address of an object in C++. It uniquely identifies the object.

We can create a "pointer" to an object by saving its name in a variable. For example, if we think of the objects created in Example 2-2, we could say:

```
set x "bullet1"
$x erase
```

The variable x contains the name `bullet1`, but it could just as easily have the name `bullet2` or `title`. Whatever object it refers to, we use the name $x as a command, telling that object to erase itself.

We could even tell all of the objects to erase themselves like this:

```
foreach obj {title bullet1 bullet2 bullet3 bullet4} {
    $obj erase
}
```

One object can point to another simply by having an instance variable that stores the name of the other object. Suppose you want to create a tree data structure. In ordinary Tcl, this is extremely difficult, but with [INCR TCL] you simply create an object to represent each node of the tree. Each node has a variable `parent` that contains the name of the parent node, and a variable `children`, that contains a list of names for the child nodes. The class definition for a `Tree` node is contained in the file *itcl/tree/tree1.itcl*, and it appears in Example 2-3.

Example 2-3: The Class Definition for a Simple Tree Data Structure

```
class Tree {
    variable parent ""
    variable children ""

    method add {obj} {
        $obj parent $this
        lappend children $obj
    }
    method clear {} {
        if {$children != ""} {
            eval delete object $children
        }
        set children ""
    }
```

```
    method parent {pobj} {
        set parent $pobj
    }

    method contents {} {
        return $children
    }
}
```

Notice that when we declared the **parent** and **children** variables, we included an extra **""** value. This value is used to initialize these variables when an object is first created, before calling the constructor. It is optional. If a variable does not have an initializer, it will still get created, but it will be undefined until the constructor or some other method sets its value. In this example, we do not have a constructor, so we are careful to include initializers for both of the instance variables.

The **Tree** class has four methods: the **add** method adds another **Tree** object as a child node; the **parent** method stores the name of a parent **Tree** object; the **contents** method returns a list of immediate children, and is used to traverse the tree; and the **clear** method destroys all children under the current node.

Notice that in the **clear** method we used the Tcl **eval** command. This lets us delete all of the children in one shot. The **eval** command flattens the list **$-children** into a series of separate object names, and the **delete object** command deletes them. If we had forgotten the **eval** command, the **delete object** command would have misinterpreted the value **$children** as one long object name, and it would have generated an error.

We can create a series of **Tree** objects to represent any tree information that exists as a hierarchy. Consider the tree shown in Figure 2-3. We can create the root object "henry" like this:

```
    Tree henry
```

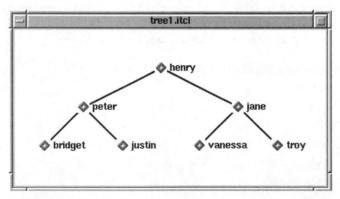

Figure 2-3: Diagram of a Family Tree

This allocates memory for the object and initializes its **parent** and **children** variables to the null string. In effect, it has no parent and no children. Since there is no constructor for this class, construction is over at this point, and the object is ready to use.

We can add children to this node by creating them:

```
Tree peter
Tree jane
```

and by adding them in:

```
henry add peter
henry add jane
```

Each of these calls to the **add** method triggers a series of other statements. We could draw the flow of execution as shown in Figure 2-4. Each object is drawn with a piece broken off so that you can see the **parent** and **children** variables hidden inside of it. When we call **henry add peter**, we jump into the context of the **henry** object (meaning that we have access to its variables), and we execute the body of the **add** method. The first statement tells **peter** that its parent is now **henry**. We jump into the context of the **peter** object, execute its **parent** method, and store the name **henry** into its **parent** variable. We then return to **henry** and continue on with its **add** method. We append **peter** to the list of **henry**'s children, and the add operation is complete. Now **henry** knows that **peter** is a child, and **peter** knows that **henry** is its parent.

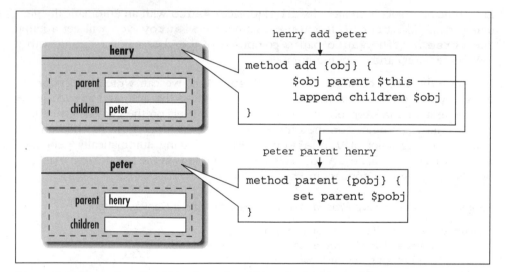

Figure 2-4: Execution Can Flow from One Object Context to Another

This simple example shows the real strength of [INCR TCL]: *encapsulation*. The variables inside each object are completely protected from the outside world. You cannot set them directly. You can only call methods, which provide a controlled interface to the underlying data. If you decide next week to rewrite this class, you can change the names of these variables or you can eliminate them entirely. You will have to fix the methods in the class, but you won't have to fix any other code. As long as you don't change how the methods are used, the programs that rely on this class will remain intact.

We can create the rest of the tree shown in Figure 2-3 as follows:

```
peter add [Tree bridget]
peter add [Tree justin]

jane add [Tree vanessa]
jane add [Tree troy]
```

We have shortened things a bit. The `Tree` command returns the name of each new `Tree` object. We capture the name with square brackets and pass it directly to the `add` method.

Generating Object Names

If you are creating a lot of objects, you may not want to think of a name for each one. Sometimes you don't care what the name is, as long as it is unique. Remember, each object must have a unique name to identify it. [INCR TCL] will generate a name for you if #auto is included as all or part of the object name. For example, we could add 10 more children to the `jane` node like this:

```
for {set i 0} {$i < 10} {incr i} {
    jane add [Tree #auto]
}
```

Each time an object is created, [INCR TCL] replaces #auto with an automatically generated name like tree17. If you use a name like x#autoy, you will get a name like xtree17y. The #auto part is composed of the class name (starting with a lowercase letter) and a unique number.

If we use the `Tree` class together with `VisualRep`, we can write a procedure to draw any tree on a canvas widget. We simply traverse the tree, and at each node, we create a `VisualRep` object and tell it to draw itself on the canvas. Of course, we also draw some lines on the canvas connecting each parent to its children. We will be creating a lot of `VisualRep` objects, so having automatically generated names will come in handy. A complete code example is in the file *itcl/tree/tree1.itcl*, but the drawing part appears in Example 2-4.

Example 2-4: A Recursive Procedure Draws the Tree onto a Canvas Widget

```
proc draw_node {canvas obj x y width} {
    set kids [$obj contents]
    if {[llength $kids] == 1} {
        set x0 $x
        set delx 0
    } else {
        set x0 [expr $x-0.5*$width]
        set delx [expr 1.0*$width/([llength $kids]-1)]
    }
    set y0 [expr $y+50]

    foreach o $kids {
        $canvas create line $x $y $x0 $y0 -width 2
        draw_node $canvas $o $x0 $y0 [expr 0.5*$delx]

        set x0 [expr $x0+$delx]
```

```
        }
        set visual [VisualRep #auto $canvas default $obj]
        $visual draw $x $y
    }

    canvas .canv -width 400 -height 200 -background white
    pack .canv

    draw_node .canv henry 190 50 200
```

We create the canvas and pack it, and then we call draw_node to draw the tree
starting at node henry. Inside draw_node, we use the contents method to get
a list of children for the current node. If there is only one child, we draw it directly
below the current node. Otherwise, we divide up the available screen width and
place the children starting at the x-coordinate $x0, with $delx pixels between
them. We draw a line down to each child's position, and we draw the child by calling draw_node recursively. This will draw not only the child, but all of the children below it as well. We finish up by creating a VisualRep for the current node.
The default argument says to use the default (diamond) icon, and the $obj argu-
ment sets the title string to the object name. We need to tell this VisualRep to
draw itself on the canvas, so we capture its automatically generated name in the
visual variable, and we use this as a pointer to the object.

A Real Application

We can use our Tree class to build a real application, like a file browser that helps
the user find wasted disk space. The Unix du utility reports the disk usage for a
series of directories, given a starting point in the file system. Its output is a long list
of sizes and directory names that looks like this:

```
$ du -b /usr/local/itcl
29928      /usr/local/itcl/lib/tcl7.4
...
36343      /usr/local/itcl/man/man1
812848     /usr/local/itcl/man/man3
1416632    /usr/local/itcl/man/mann
2274019    /usr/local/itcl/man
11648898   /usr/local/itcl
```

The -b option says that directory sizes should be reported in bytes.

It is much easier to understand this output if we present it hierarchically, as shown
in Figure 2-5. If we are looking at the *usr/local/itcl* directory, for example, we can
see that it has four subdirectories, and of these, *bin* is the biggest. We could double-
click on this directory to see a listing of its contents, or double-click on *BACK UP*
to move back to the parent directory.

We can use a tree to organize the output from the du command. Each node of the
tree would represent one directory. It would have a parent node for its parent directory and a list of child nodes for its subdirectories. The simple Tree class shown
in Example 2-3 will handle this, but each node must also store the name and the
size of the directory that it represents.

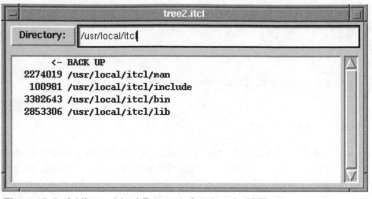

Figure 2-5: A Hierarchical Browser for the du Utility

We can modify the Tree class to keep track of a name and a value for each node as shown in Example 2-5.

Example 2-5: Tree Class Updated to Store Name/Value Pairs

```
class Tree {
    variable name ""
    variable value ""
    variable parent ""
    variable children ""

    constructor {n v} {
        set name $n
        set value $v
    }
    destructor {
        clear
    }

    method add {obj} {
        $obj parent $this
        lappend children $obj
    }
    method clear {} {
        if {$children != ""} {
            eval delete object $children
        }
        set children ""
    }
    method parent {pobj} {
        set parent $pobj
    }

    method get {{option -value}} {
        switch -- $option {
            -name    { return $name }
```

```
            -value   { return $value }
            -parent { return $parent }
        }
        error "bad option \"$option\""
    }
    method contents {} {
        return $children
    }
}
```

We simply add **name** and **value** variables to the class. We also define a constructor, so that the name and the value are set when each object is created. These are
required arguments, so when we create a **Tree** node, the command must look
something like this:

```
Tree henry /usr/local/itcl 8619141
```

Actually, the name and value strings could be anything, but in this example, we are
using **name** to store the directory name, and **value** to store the directory size.

We have also added a destructor to the **Tree** so that when any node is destroyed,
it clears its list of children. This causes the children to be destroyed, and their
destructors cause their children to be destroyed, and so on. So destroying any node
causes an entire sub-tree to be recursively destroyed.

If we are moving up and down the tree and we reach a certain node, we will probably want to find out its name and its value. Remember, variables like **name** and
value are kept hidden within an object. We can't access them directly. We can tell
the object to do something only by calling one of its methods. In this case, we
invent a method called **get** that will give us access to the necessary information. If
we have a **Tree** node called **henry**, we might use its **get** method like this:

```
puts "directory: [henry get -name]"
puts "     size: [henry get -value]"
```

The **get** method itself is defined in Example 2-5. Its argument list looks a little
strange, but it is the standard Tcl syntax for an optional argument. The outer set of
braces represents the argument list, and the inner set represents one argument: its
name is **option**, and its default value (if it is not specified) is **-value**. So if we
simply want the value, we can call the method without any arguments, like this:

```
puts "     size: [henry get]"
```

The **get** method merely looks at its **option** flag and returns the appropriate information. We use a Tcl **switch** command to handle the various cases. Since the
option flag will start with a -, we are careful to include the -- argument in the
switch command. This tells the switch that the very next argument is the string to
match against, not an option for the **switch** command itself.

With a new and improved **Tree** class in hand, we return to building a browser for
the Unix **du** utility. If you are not used to working with tree data structures, this
code may seem complicated. But keep in mind that it is the example itself—not
[INCR TCL]—that adds the complexity. If you don't believe me, try solving this same
problem without [INCR TCL]!

We create a procedure called `get_usage` to load the disk usage information for any directory. This is shown in Example 2-6.

Example 2-6: Disk Usage Information Is Stored In a Tree

```
set root ""
proc get_usage {dir} {
    global root

    if {$root != ""} {
        delete object $root
    }
    set parentDir [file dirname $dir]
    set root [Tree #auto $parentDir ""]
    set hiers($parentDir) $root

    set info [split [exec du -b $dir] \n]
    set last [expr [llength $info]-1]

    for {set i $last} {$i >= 0} {incr i -1} {
        set line [lindex $info $i]

        if {[scan $line {%d %s} size name] == 2} {
            set hiers($name) [Tree #auto $name $size]

            set parentDir [file dirname $name]
            set parent $hiers($parentDir)
            $parent add $hiers($name)
        }
    }
    return $root
}
```

We simply pass it the name of a directory, and it runs the du program and creates a tree to store its output. We use the Tcl exec command to execute the du program, and we split its output into a list of lines. We traverse backward through this list, starting at the root directory, and working our way downward through the file hierarchy because the du program puts the parent directories after their children in its output. We scan each line to pick out the directory name and size, ignoring any lines that have the wrong format. We create a new Tree object to represent each directory. We don't really care about the name of the Tree object itself, and we don't want to make up names like "henry" and "jane," so we use #auto to get automatically generated names. Once each Tree node has been created, we add it into the node for its parent directory.

Finding the node for the parent directory is a little tricky. We can use the Tcl file dirname command to get the name of the parent directory, but we must figure out what Tree object represents this directory. We could scan through the entire tree looking for it, but that would be horribly slow. Instead, we create a lookup table using an array called hiers that maps a directory name to its corresponding Tree object. As we create each object, we are careful to store it in this array so it can be found later when its children are created. Figure 2-6 shows the array and how the values relate to the directory structure we started with.

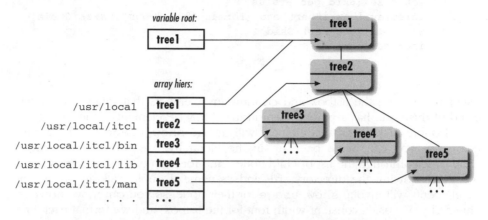

Figure 2-6: Finding Directories in a Tree of Disk Usage Information

Since we traverse backward through the du output, parent `Tree` nodes will always be created and entered into the `hiers` array before their child nodes. The only exception is the parent for the very first node. It will not appear in the output from du, so we have to create it ourselves to get everything started. We call this the *root node*, and we save its name in a global variable called `root`. The next time we call `get_usage`, we can destroy the old tree simply by destroying the root node, and then start a new tree by creating a new root node.

We can put all of this together in an application like the one shown in Figure 2-5. A complete example appears in the file *itcl/tree/tree2.itcl*, so I will not show all of the code here. But it works something like this. When the user types a directory name at the top of this application, we call the procedure `get_usage` to execute du and build a tree containing the output. We then call another procedure `show_usage` to display the root object in a listbox. The code for `show_usage` appears in Example 2-7.

Example 2-7: The Contents of Any Tree Node Can Be Displayed in a Listbox

```
proc show_usage {obj} {
    global root lbox

    catch {unset lbox}
    .display.lbox delete 0 end
    .display.lbox selection clear 0 end

    set counter 0

    if {[$obj get -parent] != ""} {
        .display.lbox insert end "          <- BACK UP"
        set lbox($counter) [$obj get -parent]
        incr counter
    }
```

```
    foreach kid [$obj contents] {
        set name [$kid get -name]
        set size [$kid get -value]
        .display.lbox insert end [format "%9d %-50s" $size $name]
        set lbox($counter) $kid
        incr counter
    }
}
```

We start by clearing the listbox and clearing any elements that might have been selected. If this node has a parent, we add the *BACK UP* element at the top of the listbox. Double-clicking on this element will invoke `show_usage` for the parent directory, so you can move back up in the hierarchy. We use the `contents` method to scan through the list of child nodes, and for each of these nodes we add an element showing the directory size and its name. Double-clicking on any of these elements will invoke `show_usage` for their node, so you can move down in the hierarchy. We use a constant-width font for the listbox, and we format each line with the Tcl `format` command to make sure that size and name fields align properly as two columns.

Notice that as we create each element, we are careful to build an array called `lbox` which maps the element number to a `Tree` node. Later on when we get a double-click, we can use this array to figure out which `Tree` node to show. We simply add a binding to the listbox like this:

```
bind .display.lbox <Double-ButtonPress-1> {
    set index [.display.lbox nearest %y]
    show_usage $lbox($index)
    break
}
```

When the double-click occurs, the `%y` field is replaced with the y coordinate of the mouse pointer, and the listbox `nearest` operation returns the number of the element nearest this position. We convert this to the corresponding `Tree` object using the `lbox` array, and then use `show_usage` to display the information for that node. Normally, the double-click would also be handled as another ordinary button press event, but we are careful to avoid this by breaking out of any further event processing.

Without the `Tree` class, this application would have been considerably more difficult to write. [INCR TCL] solves the problem by providing a way to create new data structures. Data structures are encapsulated with a well-defined set of methods to manipulate them. This naturally supports the creation of libraries. A generic component like the `Tree` class can be written once and reused again and again in many different applications.

Interface Versus Implementation

As classes get more complicated, and as method bodies get longer, the class definition becomes more difficult to read. Finding important information, like the method names and argument lists, is like looking for a needle in a haystack of [INCR TCL] code. But a method body does not have to be included with the method declaration. Class definitions are much easier to read if the bodies are defined elsewhere,

using the body command. For example, our `Tree` class can be rewritten as shown
in Example 2-8.

Example 2-8: Separating the Tree Class Interface from Its Implementation

```
class Tree {
    variable name ""
    variable value ""
    variable parent ""
    variable children ""

    constructor {n v} {
        set name $n
        set value $v
    }
    destructor {
        clear
    }

    method add {obj}
    method clear {}
    method parent {pobj}
    method get {{option -value}}
    method contents {}
}

body Tree::add {obj} {
    $obj parent $this
    lappend children $obj
}
body Tree::clear {} {
    if {$children != ""} {
        eval delete object $children
    }
    set children ""
}
body Tree::parent {pobj} {
    set parent $pobj
}

body Tree::get {{option -value}} {
    switch -- $option {
        -name    { return $name }
        -value   { return $value }
        -parent  { return $parent }
    }
    error "bad option \"$option\""
}
body Tree::contents {} {
    return $children
}
```

Since the `body` commands appear outside of the class definition, we cannot use simple method names like `add`. Remember, we could have other classes that also have an `add` method. Outside of the class, we must use a full name like `Tree::add` to identify the method. A class name followed by `::` characters is called a *scope qualifier*. You can add this to any method name or variable name to clear up ambiguities.

The class definition establishes once and for all what methods are available, and how they are used. Whatever arguments you give when you declare a method, you must use the same arguments later when you define the method body. For example, when we declared the `Tree::add` method, we said that it takes one argument named `obj`. Later, when we defined the body, we used the same argument list. When we declared the `Tree::contents` method, we gave it a null argument list. Again, when we defined the body, we repeated the null argument list. If you make a mistake and the argument lists do not match, the `body` command will report the error.

It turns out that the argument lists don't have to match letter for letter, but they must match in meaning. The argument names can change, but the argument lists must have the same number of required arguments, and all optional arguments must have the same default values. For example, when we declared the `Tree::get` method, we said that it has one argument named `option` with a default value `-value`. When we define the body we must still have one argument with a default value `-value`, but its name could be anything, like this:

```
body Tree::get {{new -value}} {
    switch -- $new {
        ...
    }
}
```

If you use the special `args` argument when you declare a method, you can replace it with other arguments when you define the method body. The `args` argument represents variable argument lists, so it acts like a wildcard when the argument lists are compared by the `body` command.

If you want to completely suspend this consistency check, you can simply leave the argument list off when you declare the method in the class definition. The `body` command will have no argument list to compare against, so it will use whatever argument list you give it.

Since the constructor and destructor declarations have a slightly different syntax, their bodies *must* be included in the class definition. However, you can declare them with null bodies, and redefine the bodies later using the `body` command. If you do this, the argument list for the constructor must match whatever appears in the class definition, and the argument list for the destructor must always be null.

The `class` command defines the *interface* for a class, and subsequent `body` commands define the *implementation*. Separating the interface from the implementation not only makes the code easier to read, but as we will soon see, it also supports interactive development.

Protection Levels: Public and Private

Usually, the class methods are the public part of an object, and the class variables are kept hidden inside. But what if you want to keep a method hidden for internal use? In our `Tree` class, for example, the `parent` method is used internally to tell a child that it has a new parent. If it is exposed, someone using the `Tree` class might be tempted to call it, and they could destroy the integrity of the tree. Or consider the opposite problem: What if you want to allow access to a variable? In our `Tree` class, the `name` and `value` variables are kept hidden within an object. We added a `get` method so that someone using the class could access these values, but there is a better way to handle this.

You can use the `public` and `private` commands to set the protection level for each member in the class definition. For example, we can use these commands in our `Tree` class as shown in Example 2-9.

Example 2-9: Adding Protection Levels to the Tree Class

```
class Tree {
    public variable name ""
    public variable value ""

    private variable parent ""
    private variable children ""

    constructor {args} {
        eval configure $args
    }
    destructor {
        clear
    }

    public method add {obj}
    public method clear {}
    private method parent {pobj}

    public method back {}
    public method contents {}
}
```

Any member can be accessed by methods within the same class, but only the public members are available to someone using the class. Since we declared the `parent` method to be private, it will not be visible to anyone outside of the class.

Each class has built-in `configure` and `cget` methods that mimic the behavior of Tk widgets. The `configure` method provides access to an object's attributes, and the `cget` method returns the current value for a particular attribute. Any variable declared to be public is treated as an attribute that can be accessed with these methods. Just by declaring the `name` and `value` variables to be public, for example, we can say:

```
Tree henry
henry configure -name "Henry Fonda" -value "great actor"
puts " name: [henry cget -name]"
puts "value: [henry cget -value]"
```

Just like Tk, the attribute names have a leading – sign, so if the variable is called name, the attribute is –name.

You can also set the attributes when you create an object, as long as you define the constructor as shown in Example 2-9. For example, we can say:

```
Tree henry -name "Henry Fonda" -value "great actor"
```

The extra arguments are captured by the args argument and passed along to the configure method in the constructor. The eval command is needed to make sure that the args list is not treated as a single argument, but as a list of option/value pairs. It is a good idea to write your constructor like this. It mimics the normal Tk behavior, and it lets someone using the class set some of the attributes, and leave others with a default value.

Now that we know about the built-in cget method, our get method is obsolete. We have removed it from the class definition in Example 2-9, in favor of a back method that can be used to query the parent for a particular node.

Since anyone can change a public variable by configuring it, we need a way to guard against bad values that might cause errors. And sometimes when an option changes, we need to do something to update the object. Public variables can have some extra code associated with them to handle these things. Whenever the value is configured, the code checks for errors and brings the object up to date. As an example, suppose we add a -sort option to the Tree class, to indicate how the contents of each node should be sorted. Whenever the -sort option is set, the code associated with it could reorder the child nodes. We could update the Tree class to handle sorting as shown in Example 2-10.

Example 2-10: Tree Class with a -sort Option

```
class Tree {
    public variable name ""
    public variable value ""

    public variable sort ""
    private variable lastSort ""

    private variable parent ""
    private variable children ""

    constructor {args} {
        eval configure $args
    }
    destructor {
        clear
    }
```

```
        public method add {obj}
        public method clear {}
        private method parent {pobj}

        public method back {}
        public method contents {}
        private method reorder {}
    }


    . . .


    body Tree::add {obj} {
        $obj parent $this
        lappend children $obj
        set lastSort ""
    }
    body Tree::contents {} {
        reorder
        return $children
    }

    body Tree::reorder {} {
        if {$sort != $lastSort} {
            set children [lsort -command $sort $children]
        }
        set lastSort $sort
    }

    configbody Tree::sort {
        reorder
    }
```

We add a -sort option simply by adding a public variable called sort. Its initial
value is "", which means that by default, sorting is turned off. We can add some
code to this variable in the class definition, right after its default value. Or we can
define it later with a configbody command. The configbody command is just
like the body command, but it takes two arguments: the name of the variable and
the body of code. There is no argument list for a variable, as you would have for
a method. In this example, we use the configbody command near the end to
define the code for the sort variable. Whenever the -sort option is configured,
we call the reorder method to reorder the nodes.

If there are a lot of nodes, reordering them can be expensive, so we try to avoid
sorting whenever possible. We have a variable called lastSort that keeps track
of the last value for the -sort option, which is the name of some sorting procedure, as we'll see later on. We can call the reorder method as often as we want,
but it will reorder the nodes only if the -sort option has really changed.

We also set things up so that the nodes will be reordered properly if a new node
is added. We could just reorder the list each time a node is added, but that would
be expensive. Instead, we reorder the list when someone tries to query it via the

contents method. Most of the time, the list will already be sorted, and the reorder method will do nothing. Whenever we add a node in the add method, we reset the value of lastSort to "", so that the next call to contents will actually reorder the nodes.

The configure method automatically guards against errors that occur when an option is set. For example, if we say:

```
Tree henry
henry configure -sort bogus_sort_proc -value 1
```

the configure method finds the public variable sort and sets it to the value bogus_sort_proc. Then it looks for code associated with this variable and executes it. In this case, it calls the reorder method to reorder the nodes using the procedure bogus_sort_proc. If this causes an error, the variable is automatically reset to its previous value, and the configure command aborts, returning an error message. Otherwise, it continues on with the next option, in this case handling the -value option.

Let's take a look at how the -sort option is actually used. In the reorder method, the sort value is given to the Tcl lsort command to do the actual sorting. The lsort command treats this as a comparison function. As it is sorting the list, it calls this function again and again, two elements at a time, and checks the result. The function should return +1 if the first element is greater than the second, "1" if the first is less than the second, and "" if they are equal. The lsort command orders the two elements accordingly.

For example, if we want an alphabetical listing of Tree objects, we could write a function like this to compare the -name options:

```
proc cmp_tree_names {obj1 obj2} {
    set val1 [$obj1 cget -name]
    set val2 [$obj2 cget -name]
    return [string compare $val1 $val2]
}
```

and we could tell a particular Tree object like henry to use this:

```
henry configure -sort cmp_tree_names
```

Its children would then be listed alphabetically. If we wanted a value-ordered list, we could write a function like cmp_tree_values to compare the -value attributes, and use that function as the -sort option.

We can put all of this together in a new and improved du browser, as shown in Figure 2-7. A complete code example appears in the file *itcl/tree/tree5.itcl*, but it works like this. When the user clicks on a radiobutton to change the sorting option, we configure the -sort option for the node being displayed, query its children, and update the listbox.

Common Variables and Procedures

Sometimes it is necessary to have variables that do not belong to any particular object, but are shared among all objects in the class. In C++ they are referred to as *static data members*. In [INCR TCL], they are called *common variables*.

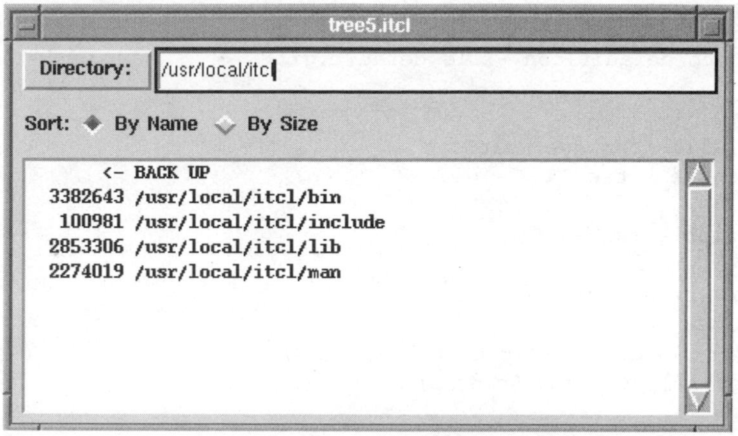

Figure 2-7: An Improved du Browser with Radiobuttons to Control Sorting

We can see the need for this in the following example. Suppose we improve our du application to have a graphical display like the one shown in Figure 2-8. Each file name has an icon next to it. We could use a canvas widget in place of a listbox, and draw each entry on the canvas with a `VisualRep` object, as we did in Example 2-2.

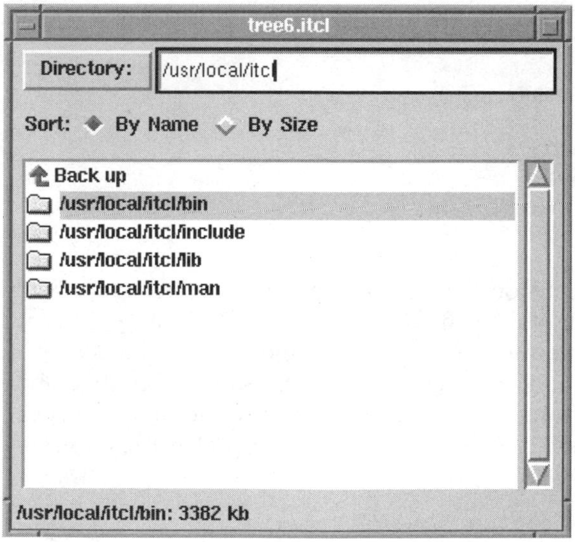

Figure 2-8: An Improved du Browser with a graphical display.

In this example, we will take things one step further. We set up the browser so that when you click on a file, it becomes selected. It is highlighted with a gray rectangle, and its usage information is displayed in a label at the bottom of the application.

We can fix up our `VisualRep` class to do most of the work for us. We will add `select` and `deselect` methods, so that each `VisualRep` object will know whether or not it is selected, and will highlight itself accordingly. A complete code example appears in the file *itcl/tree/tree6.itcl*, but the `VisualRep` class itself appears in Example 2-11.

Example 2-11: An Improved VisualRep Class with select/deselect Methods

```
image create photo defaultIcon -file default.gif

class VisualRep {
    public variable icon "defaultIcon"
    public variable title ""

    private variable canvas ""

    constructor {cwin args} {
        set canvas $cwin
        if {![info exists selectedObjs($canvas)]} {
            set selectedObjs($canvas) ""
        }
        eval configure $args
    }
    destructor {
        deselect
        $canvas delete $this
    }

    public method draw {ulVar midVar}
    public method select {}
    public method deselect {}

    public method canvas {args}

    private common selectedObjs
    public proc clear {canv}
    public proc selected {canv}
}
```

We have made a lot of improvements on the `VisualRep` class presented in Example 2-1. We still need to keep track of the canvas containing the `VisualRep`, so we still have a private `canvas` variable. But we have added the public variables `icon` and `title` so that we can treat the icon image and the title string as configuration options. We also changed the constructor so that the canvas widget must be specified, but everything else is optional. If we create a `VisualRep` object like this:

```
canvas .display.canv
VisualRep vr1 .display.canv -title "/usr/local/lib"
```

we get the default icon with the title `/usr/local/lib`. The constructor saves the canvas name in the `canvas` variable, does something with the `selectedObjs` array that we'll talk more about later on, and then does the usual `eval config-ure $args` to handle the configuration options.

We also changed the way we use the `draw` method. We won't show the implementation here—you can check file *tree/tree6.itcl* for details—but this is how it works. Instead of a simple (x,y) coordinate, we pass in the names of two variables. These are used by the `draw` method and then modified to return some drawing information. The first argument is an array representing the upper-left corner for the

VisualRep object. If we have a `VisualRep` object called `vr1` and we want its upper-left corner at the coordinate (25,37), we might call the `draw` method like this:

```
set ul(x) 25
set ul(y) 37
vr1 draw ul midpt
```

Before it returns, the `draw` method modifies the `y` coordinate in the `ul` array so that it points to the next position, immediately below the `VisualRep` object that we have just drawn. This makes it easy to draw a list of `VisualRep` objects on the canvas, even if their icons are different sizes. The `draw` method also stores the `x` and `y` coordinates for the midpoint of the icon in the `midpt` variable. This will come in handy for another example that we'll see later in this chapter.

As we said before, we have also added `select` and `deselect` methods to support file selection. When you click on a file in the browser, we call the `select` method for its `VisualRep`. Thus, if you click on a file that has a `VisualRep` named `vr1`, we call its `select` method like this:

```
vr1 select
```

the object would be highlighted with a gray rectangle. If we call the `deselect` method like this:

```
vr1 deselect
```

it would go back to normal. In theory, we could select as many objects as we want simply by calling their `select` methods. This might be useful in a file browser that allows many files to be moved, copied, or deleted at once.

When multiple objects can be selected, we need to keep a list of all the `VisualRep` objects that are selected. But each `VisualRep` object keeps track of itself, and knows nothing about other objects in the class. Somewhere we have to keep a master list of selected objects. We want something like a global variable, but we want to keep it protected within the class, where it is actually used. In this case, we want a *common* variable.

We create a common variable called `selectedObjs`, as shown near the bottom of Example 2-11. We declare it to be private so that it can be accessed only within the class. Instead of keeping one master list with all the `VisualRep` objects that are selected, we keep a separate list for each canvas. That way, we can find out later what objects are selected on a particular canvas. To do this, we treat the `selected-Objs` variable as an array, with a different slot for each canvas. Whenever we create a `VisualRep` object, we make sure that a slot exists for its associated canvas and, if not, we create one. This is handled by some code in the constructor.

We handle the selection of a `VisualRep` object like this:

```
body VisualRep::select {} {
    $canvas itemconfigure $this-hilite -fill LightGray

    if {[lsearch $selectedObjs($canvas) $this] < 0} {
        lappend selectedObjs($canvas) $this
    }
}
```

The first statement turns on the gray rectangle on the canvas. In the `draw` method, we make an invisible rectangle tagged with the name `$this-hilite`, so when we want it to appear, we simply change its fill color. Next, we check to see if this object appears on the list of selected objects for its canvas. If not, we add it to the list.

Notice that we can access the `selectedObjs` variable without declaring it with anything like the Tcl `global` command. It has already been declared in the class definition, so it is known by all methods in the class.

We handle the de-selection like this:

```
body VisualRep::deselect {} {
    $canvas itemconfigure $this-hilite -fill ""

    set i [lsearch $selectedObjs($canvas) $this]
    if {$i >= 0} {
        set selectedObjs($canvas) [lreplace \
            $selectedObjs($canvas) $i $I]
    }
}
```

We turn off the gray rectangle by making its fill color invisible. Then we find the object on the list of selected objects and we remove it from the list.

At this point, we know which `VisualRep` objects are selected, but we still haven't answered our question: What if someone using the class wants to get a list of all the `VisualRep` objects that are selected? Remember, the `selectedObjs` variable is private. It cannot be accessed outside of the class. We did this on purpose to prevent anyone else from tampering with it.

One way to solve this problem is to add a method called `selected` which returns a list of objects that are selected on a particular canvas. After all, a method has access to things inside the class. This would work, but then each time we wanted to use the method we would need to find an object to talk to. For example, we might ask an object named `vr1` like this:

```
set objlist [vr1 selected .display.canv]
```

This is awkward, and there is a better way to handle it. We need a function that belongs to the class as a whole. In C++, this is called a *static member function*. In [INCR TCL], it is called a *procedure* or *proc*. Class procedures are just like ordinary Tcl procedures, but they reside within the class, so their names won't conflict with other procedures in your application.

A procedure is declared with the `proc` command, as shown at the bottom of Example 2-11. In many respects, it looks like a method. But a procedure belongs to the class as a whole. It doesn't know about any specific object, so it doesn't have access to instance variables like `icon`, `title`, and `canvas`. It has access only to common variables.

The advantage of using a procedure is that it can be called like this:

```
set objlist [VisualRep::selected .display.canv]
```

Since we are calling this from outside of the class, we have to use the full name `VisualRep::selected`. But we do not have to talk to a specific object. In effect, we are talking to the class as a whole, asking for the objects that are selected on a particular canvas. The implementation of this procedure is fairly trivial:

```
body VisualRep::selected {canv} {
    if {[info exists selectedObjs($canv)]} {
        return $selectedObjs($canv)
    }
    return ""
}
```

We simply look for a value in the `selectedObjs` array, and return that list.

Procedures are also useful when you want to operate on several objects at once, or perhaps on the class as a whole. For example, we can add a `clear` procedure to deselect all of the `VisualRep` objects on a particular canvas. We might use the procedure like this:

```
VisualRep::clear .display.canv
```

and it is implemented like this:

```
body VisualRep::clear {canv} {
    if {[info exists selectedObjs($canv)]} {
        foreach obj $selectedObjs($canv) {
            $obj deselect
        }
    }
}
```

It simply finds the list of objects that are selected on the canvas, and tells each one to deselect itself.

Inheritance

Object-oriented systems provide a way for one class to borrow functionality from another. One class can *inherit* the characteristics of another, and add its own unique features. The more generic class is called a *base class*, and the more specialized class is called a *derived class*. This technique leads to a style of programming-by-differences, and helps to organize code into cohesive units. Without inheritance, object-oriented programming would be little more than a data-centric view of the world.

Single Inheritance

We can use our `Tree` class to build a regular file browser like the one shown in Figure 2-9. You enter a directory name at the top of the browser, and it lists the files and directories at that location. Directories are displayed with a trailing / character, and files are displayed along with their size in bytes. If you double-click on a directory name, the browser displays that directory. If you double-click on *BACK UP*, you go back to the parent directory.

We could build a tree to represent all of the files on the file system and display it in this browser, just like we did for the du application. But instead of spending a lot of time to build a complete tree, we should start with a single node. When the user asks for the contents of a directory, we will look for files in that directory and

```
┌─────────────────────────────────────────────────────────┐
│ ─                          tree7.itcl                   □ │
├─────────────────────────────────────────────────────────┤
│  ┌──────────┐  ┌───────────────────────────────────────┐│
│  │Directory:│  │/usr/local/itcl                        ││
│  └──────────┘  └───────────────────────────────────────┘│
│                                                           │
│  Sort: ◆ By Name ◇ By Size                                │
│                                                           │
│  ┌─────────────────────────────────────────────────┬──┐ │
│  │        <- BACK UP                                 │▲ │ │
│  │        /usr/local/itcl/lib/itcl2.0/               │  │ │
│  │        /usr/local/itcl/lib/itk2.0/                │  │ │
│  │        /usr/local/itcl/lib/iwidgets2.0/           │  │ │
│  │ 81884  /usr/local/itcl/lib/libitcl2.0.a           │  │ │
│  │ 36728  /usr/local/itcl/lib/libitk2.0.a            │  │ │
│  │428186  /usr/local/itcl/lib/libtcl7.4.a            │  │ │
│  │620118  /usr/local/itcl/lib/libtk4.0.a             │  │ │
│  │        /usr/local/itcl/lib/tcl7.4/                │  │ │
│  │        /usr/local/itcl/lib/tk4.0/                 │▼ │ │
│  └─────────────────────────────────────────────────┴──┘ │
└─────────────────────────────────────────────────────────┘
```

Figure 2-9: A Simple File Browser Built with the FileTree Class

add some nodes to the tree. With this scheme, we can bring up the file browser quickly and populate the tree as we go along.

We could add a little extra functionality to our **Tree** class to support the file system queries, but having a generic **Tree** class is useful for many different applications. Instead, it is better to create a separate **FileTree** class to represent the file system, and have it inherit the basic tree behavior from **Tree**. Inheritance relationships are often described as *is-a* relationships. If **FileTree** inherits from **Tree**, then a **FileTree** *is-a* **Tree**, but with a more specialized behavior. The relationship between these classes can be diagrammed using the OMT notation* as shown in Figure 2-10.

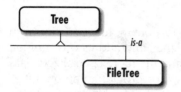

Figure 2-10: Relationship Between the Tree Base Class and Its FileTree Specialization

The file *itcl/tree/tree7.itcl* contains a complete code example for the file browser, but the **FileTree** class is shown in Example 2-12. The **inherit** statement brings in all of the characteristics from the base class **Tree**. Because of this statement, the **FileTree** automatically acts like a tree. It keeps track of its parent and its children, and it has all of the usual **Tree** methods including **add**, **contents**, **back**, and **clear**. It also has the configuration options **-name**, **-value**, and **-sort**.

───────────────────────────

* James Rumbaugh, Michael Blaha, William Premerlani, Frederick Eddy, and William Lorensen, *Object-Oriented Modeling and Design*, Prentice-Hall, 1991.

Example 2-12: The FileTree Class Inherits from Tree

```
class FileTree {
    inherit Tree

    public variable procreate ""

    private variable file ""
    private variable mtime 0

    constructor {fname args} {
        if {![file exists $fname]} {
            error "file not found: $fname"
        }
        set file $fname
        eval configure $args
    }

    public method contents {}
    private method populate {}
}

body FileTree::populate {} {
    if {[file mtime $file] != $mtime} {
        clear
        foreach f [glob -nocomplain $file/*] {
            add [uplevel #0 $procreate $f]
        }
        set mtime [file mtime $file]
    }
}
body FileTree::contents {} {
    populate
    return [Tree::contents]
}
```

In the `FileTree` class, we redefine the `contents` method. When you ask for the contents of a `FileTree` node, we invoke another method called `populate` which automatically scans the file system and creates child nodes. After we have populated the node, we use the usual `Tree::contents` method to return the list of children.

Notice that we are careful to say `Tree::contents`. Whenever the base class and the derived class both have a method with the same name, you need to include a scope qualifier like this to avoid ambiguity. If you use a simple, unqualified name like `contents`, you will get the most specific implementation for the object. For a `FileTree` object, the name `contents` means `FileTree::contents`. If you want some other version of the method, you must use a qualified name like `Tree::contents`.

When an object gives you the most specific implementation of a method, the method is said to be *virtual*. This is a fundamental feature of object-oriented programming. It lets you treat all the objects in a class the same way, but it lets specialized objects react in their own specialized manner. For example, all `Tree` objects have a `contents` method that returns a list of child nodes, so you can get the contents of either an ordinary `Tree` object or a `FileTree` object. When you get the contents of an ordinary `Tree` object, it simply returns a list of object names. But when you get the contents of a `FileTree` object, it will look for files and automatically create the child nodes before returning their names. You don't have to remember what kind of tree object you're talking to. You simply call the `contents` method, and each object does the right thing.

This is true even when you call a method from a base class context. Suppose for a moment that we had defined the `clear` method in the `Tree` base class like this:

```
body Tree::clear {} {
    set objs [contents]
    if {$objs != ""} {
        eval delete object $objs
    }
    set children ""
}
```

Instead of using the `children` variable directly, we have used the `contents` method to query the list of children. When you clear an ordinary `Tree` object, it would use `Tree::contents` to get the list of children. This simply returns `$-children`, so it looks as though nothing has changed. But when you clear a `FileTree` object, it would use `FileTree::contents` to get the list of children. It would look for files and automatically create the child nodes, and then turn right around and delete them. In this case, using the `contents` method may be a dumb idea. But it does illustrate an important point: The methods that you call in a base class use the specialized behaviors that you provide later on for derived classes. Again, each object does the right thing depending on its type.

We set up the constructor so that you cannot create a `FileTree` object without saying what file or directory it represents. You might create a `FileTree` object like this:

```
FileTree barney /usr/local/lib -name "local libraries"
```

The first argument (`/usr/local/lib`) is assigned to the `fname` parameter. The constructor makes sure that the file exists, and then copies the name to the `file` variable. If the file is not found, the constructor returns an error, and the object creation is aborted.

The remaining arguments (`-name "local libraries"`) are treated as configuration options. They are absorbed by the `args` parameter, and they are applied by calling the `configure` method at the bottom of the constructor. Remember, a `FileTree` *is-a* `Tree`, so it has options like `-name` and `-value`.

When we query the contents of a `FileTree` node, it is automatically populated. The `populate` method treats the file name as a directory and uses the `glob` command to query its contents. We create a new `FileTree` object for each file in the directory and add it to the tree using the `add` method. Once a node has been populated, we save the modification time for its file in the `mtime` variable. We can call `populate` as often as we like, but the node will not be re-populated unless the modification time changes.

Each `FileTree` object populates itself by adding new `FileTree` objects as child nodes. We'll call this process *procreation*. We could create the offspring directly within the `populate` method, but this would make it hard to use the same `FileTree` in lots of different file browsers. For example, one file browser might set the `-value` option on each `FileTree` object to store the size of the file, so files could be sorted based on size. Another might set the `-value` option to store the modification time, so files could be sorted by date. We want to allow for both of these possibilities (and many more) when we create each `FileTree` object.

One solution is to add a procreation method to the `FileTree` class. The `populate` method would call this whenever it needs to create a `FileTree` object. We could have lots of different derived classes that overload the procreation method and create their offspring in different ways. This approach works fine, but we would probably find ourselves creating lots of new classes simply to override this one method.

Instead, let's think for a moment about the Tk widgets. You may have lots of buttons in your application, but they all do different things. Each button has a `-command` option that stores some code. When you push a button, its `-command` code gets executed.

In the same manner, we can add a `-procreate` option to the `FileTree` class. Whenever a `FileTree` object needs to procreate, it calls whatever procedure you specify with the `-procreate` option, passing it the file name for the child object. This is what we do in the `populate` method, as you can see in Example 2-12.

Whenever you have an option that contains code, you have to be careful how you execute the code. We could use the `eval` command to execute the procreation code, but it might be more than just a procedure name. For all we know, it could be a whole script of code. If it sets any variables, we don't want to affect variables inside the `populate` method by accident. Instead, we use `uplevel #0` to evaluate the command at the global scope, outside of the `FileTree` class. If it accidentally sets a variable like `file`, it will be a global variable called `file`, and not the private variable `file` that we can access inside the `populate` method. We will explore scoping issues like this in more detail later in this chapter. But for now, just remember to use `uplevel #0` to evaluate any code passed in through a configuration option.

We can tell a `FileTree` object like `barney` to procreate with a custom procedure like this:

```
barney configure -procreate create_node
```

When `barney` needs to procreate, it calls `create_node` with the child's file name as an argument. This in turn creates a `FileTree` object for the file, configures options like `-name`, `-value`, and `-sort`, and returns the name of the new object. For example, we could use a procedure like this to set the file modification time as the value for each node:

```
proc create_node {fname} {
    set obj [FileTree #auto $fname -name "$fname"]
    $obj configure -value [file mtime $fname]
    return $obj
}
```

We can use all of this to build the file browser shown in Figure 2-9. Again, the file *itcl/tree/tree7.itcl* contains a complete code example, but the important parts are shown in Example 2-13.

Example 2-13: A Simple File Browser Built with the FileTree Class

```
set root ""
proc load_dir {dir} {
    global root

    if {$root != ""} {
        delete object $root
    }
    set root [FileTree #auto $dir -procreate create_node]
    return $root
}

proc create_node {fname} {
    if {[file isdirectory $fname]} {
        set obj [FileTree #auto $fname -name "$fname/"]
    } else {
        set obj [FileTree #auto $fname -name $fname]
        $obj configure -value [file size $fname]
    }
    $obj configure -procreate create_node

    return $obj
}
```

When you enter a directory name at the top of the browser, we call the `load_dir` procedure to build a new file tree. If there is an existing tree, we destroy it by destroying its root node. Then, we create a new root object to represent the tree. At some point, we use another procedure called `show_dir` (not shown here) to display the contents of this node in a listbox. When you double-click on a directory, we call `show_dir` for that node. When you double-click on *BACK UP*, we call `show_dir` for the parent node. Whenever we call `show_dir`, it asks for the contents of a node, and the node populates itself as needed.

The root object uses the `create_node` procedure to procreate. When its child nodes are created, directory names are given a trailing /, and regular files are given a value that represents their size. All child nodes are configured to procreate using the same `create_node` procedure, so each node expands the same way.

Multiple Inheritance

Suppose we want to create a file browser with a graphical display like the one shown in Figure 2-11.

We have all of the pieces that we need. We can use the `FileTree` class to store the file hierarchy, and the `VisualRep` class to draw file elements on a canvas.

But how do we combine these elements together? One solution is to use inheritance. We might create a class `VisualFileTree` to represent each file on the dis-

```
┌─────────────────────────────────────────┐
│ ▣            tree8.itcl                 ▣ │
├─────────────────────────────────────────┤
│ ┌──────────┐ ┌──────────────────────────┐│
│ │Directory:│ │/usr/local/itcl▏          ││
│ └──────────┘ └──────────────────────────┘│
│ ┌───────────────────────────────────┐ ┌┐ │
│ │ 📁 itcl                            │ │▲│ │
│ │  ├─📁 bin                          │ │ │ │
│ │  ├─📁 include                      │ │ │ │
│ │  │   ├─📄 itcl.h                   │ │ │ │
│ │  │   ├─📄 itk.h                    │ │ │ │
│ │  │   ├─📄 tcl.h                    │ │ │ │
│ │  │   ├─📄 tk.h                     │ │ │ │
│ │  ├─📁 lib                          │ │ │ │
│ │  │   ├─📁 itcl2.0                  │ │ │ │
│ │  │   │   ├─📄 init.itcl            │ │ │ │
│ │  │   │   └─📄 tclAppInit.c         │ │ │ │
│ │  📁 itk2.0                         │ │▼│ │
│ └───────────────────────────────────┘ └┘ │
│ ┌──────────────────────────────────────┐ │
│ │File: /usr/local/itcl/include/itcl.h   │ │
│ └──────────────────────────────────────┘ │
└───────────────────────────────────────────┘
```

Figure 2-11: A File Browser with a Graphical Display

play. We could say that VisualFileTree *is-a* FileTree, since it represents a node in the file hierarchy, and VisualFileTree *is-a* VisualRep, since it will be drawn on a canvas. In this case, VisualFileTree needs to inherit from two different base classes. This is called *multiple inheritance*. A diagram of these relationships is shown in Figure 2-12.

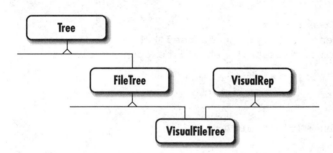

Figure 2-12: Diagram of Class Relationships with Multiple Inheritance

The file *itcl/tree/tree8.itcl* contains a complete code example for the file browser, but the VisualFileTree class itself is shown in Example 2-14.

Example 2-14: VisualFileTree Class Used for the File Browser Shown in Figure 2-11

```
class VisualFileTree {
    inherit FileTree VisualRep

    public variable state "closed"
    public variable selectcommand ""

    constructor {file cwin args} {
        FileTree::constructor $file
        VisualRep::constructor $cwin
```

```
    } {
        eval configure $args
    }

    public method select {}
    public method toggle {}

    public method draw {ulVar midVar}
    public method refresh {}
}

body VisualFileTree::select {} {
    VisualRep::clear $canvas
    VisualRep::select
    regsub -all {%o} $selectcommand $this cmd
    uplevel #0 $cmd
}

body VisualFileTree::toggle {} {
    if {$state == "open"} {
        set state "closed"
    } else {
        set state "open"
    }
    refresh
}

configbody VisualFileTree::state {
    if {$state != "open" && $state != "closed"} {
        error "bad value \"$state\": should be open or closed"
    }
    refresh
}

body VisualFileTree::draw {ulVar midVar} {
    upvar $ulVar ul
    upvar $midVar mid

    VisualRep::draw ul mid
    $canvas bind $this <ButtonPress-1> "$this select"
    $canvas bind $this <Double-ButtonPress-1> "$this toggle"

    set lr(x) [expr $ul(x) + 2*($mid(x)-$ul(x))]
    set lr(y) $ul(y)

    if {$state == "open"} {
        foreach obj [contents] {
            $obj draw lr mid2
            set id [$canvas create line \
                $mid(x) $mid(y) $mid(x) $mid2(y) $mid2(x) $mid2(y) \
                -fill black]
```

```
                    $canvas lower $id
            }
        }
        set ul(y) $lr(y)
    }

    body VisualFileTree::refresh {} {
        set root $this
        while {[$root back] != ""} {
            set root [$root back]
        }

        set oldcursor [$canvas cget -cursor]
        $canvas configure -cursor watch
        update
        $canvas delete all

        set ul(x) 5
        set ul(y) 5
        $root draw ul mid
        set bbox [$canvas bbox all]
        $canvas configure -cursor $oldcursor -scrollregion $bbox
    }
```

Each class can have only one `inherit` statement, but it can declare several base classes, which should be listed in their order of importance. First and foremost, `VisualFileTree` is a `FileTree`, but it is also a `VisualRep`. This means that any methods or variables that are not defined in `VisualFileTree` are found first in `FileTree`, and then in `VisualRep`. When base classes have members with the same name, their order in the `inherit` statement can affect the behavior of the derived class.

Notice that we added a `-state` option to `VisualFileTree`, and we redefined the draw method to handle it. When we draw a node that has `-state` set to `open`, we also draw the file hierarchy underneath it. First, we call `VisualRep::draw` to draw the file name and its icon on the canvas. Then, if this object is in the `open` state, we scan through the list of child nodes and tell each one to draw itself in the space below. If a child is also in the `open` state, it will tell its children to draw themselves, and so on.

It is easy to arrange things on the canvas. The `draw` method does all of the hard work. As you will recall from Example 2-11, we use the `ul` array to pass in the (x,y) coordinate for the upper-left corner of the icon. When we call `VisualRep::draw`, it draws only a file name and an icon, and it shifts `ul(y)` down below them. When we call `VisualFileTree::draw`, it draws a file name and an icon, and perhaps an entire file tree below it. But again, it shifts `ul(y)` down so we are ready to draw the next element.

The `draw` method also returns the midpoint of the icon via the `midVar` argument. This makes it easy to draw the connecting lines between a parent icon and each of the child icons. In the `VisualFileTree::draw` method, for example, we capture the parent coordinate in the `mid` array. When we call the `draw` method for the

---

child, it returns the child coordinate in the mid2 array. We then draw the lines connecting these two points.

As we draw each file entry, we add some bindings to it. If you click on a file, we call the select method to select it. If you double-click on a file, we call the toggle method to toggle it between the open and closed states.

We redefined the select method for a VisualFileTree object to support a -selectcommand option. This is a lot like the -command option for a button widget. It lets you do something special each time a VisualFileTree object is selected. When we call the select method, it first calls VisualRep::clear to deselect any other files, and then calls the base class method VisualRep::select to highlight the file. Finally, it executes the code stored in the -selectcommand option. We use uplevel #0 to execute this code at the global scope, so it doesn't change any variables within the select method by accident.

If the -selectcommand code contains the string %o, we use regsub to replace it with the name of the VisualFileTree object before the code is executed. This is similar to the way the Tk bind command handles fields like %x and %y. This feature lets us use the same -selectcommand for all of our VisualFileTree objects, but each time it is executed, we know which object was selected.

The toggle method toggles the -state option between open and closed, and refreshes the drawing on the canvas. In effect, this opens or closes a folder in the file hierarchy.

The refresh method should be called whenever anything changes that would affect the drawing on the canvas. Whenever the -state option changes, for instance, we need to refresh the drawing to expand or collapse the file tree at that point. The configbody for the state variable first checks to see if the new state is valid, and then calls refresh to update the drawing. The refresh method searches up through the hierarchy to find the root of the tree. It clears the canvas and then tells the root object to draw itself at the coordinate (5,5). If the root is open, then its children will be drawn, and if they are open, their children will be drawn, and so forth. The entire drawing is regenerated with just one call to refresh.

Protection Levels: Protected

So far, we have discussed two protection levels. Private class members can be accessed only in the class where they are defined. Public members can be accessed from any context. When one class inherits another, therefore, the inherited members that are public can be accessed from the derived class context. The private members are completely private to the base class.

Some members sit in the gray area between public and private. They need to be accessed in derived classes, but they should not be exposed to anyone using the class. For example, in the VisualRep base class shown in Example 2-11, we defined a canvas variable to store the name of the canvas used for drawing. Since this is a private variable, a derived class like VisualFileTree does not have access to it. The methods shown in Example 2-14 like VisualFileTree::draw and Visual-FileTree::select will fail, claiming that canvas is an undefined variable.

Like C++, [INCR TCL] provides a third level of protection that falls between public and private. When members need to be shared with derived classes but shielded from anyone using the class, they should be declared *protected*. We can fix the Visual-Rep class to use a protected variable as shown in Example 2-15.

Example 2-15: "Protected" Members Can Be Accessed in Derived Classes

```
class VisualRep {
    public variable icon "default"
    public variable title ""

    protected variable canvas ""

    ...
}

class VisualFileTree {
    inherit FileTree VisualRep
    ...
    public method select {}
    ...
}

body VisualFileTree::select {} {
    VisualRep::clear $canvas
    VisualRep::select
    regsub -all {%o} $selectcommand $this cmd
    uplevel #0 $cmd
}
```

As a rule, it is better to use public and private declarations for most of your class members. Public members define the class interface, and private members keep the implementation details well hidden. Protected members are useful when you are creating a base class that is meant to be extended by derived classes. A few methods and variables may need to be shared with derived classes, but this should be kept to a minimum. Protected members expose implementation details in the base class. If derived classes rely on these details, they will need to be modified if the base class ever changes.

Constructors and Destructors

Each class can define one constructor and one destructor. However, a class can inherit many other constructors and destructors from base classes.

When an object is created, all of its constructors are invoked in the following manner. First, the arguments from the object creation command are passed to the most specific constructor. For example, in the command:

```
VisualFileTree #auto /usr/local/lib .canv -icon dirIcon
```

the arguments /usr/local/lib .canv -icon dirIcon are passed to Visual-FileTree::constructor. If any arguments need to be passed to a base class constructor, the derived constructor should invoke it using a special piece of code

---

called an *initialization statement*. This statement is sandwiched between the constructor's argument list and its body. For example, the `VisualFileTree` class shown in Example 2-14 has an initialization statement that looks like this:

```
FileTree::constructor $file
VisualRep::constructor $cwin
```

The `file` argument is passed to the `FileTree::constructor`, and the `cwin` argument is passed to the `VisualRep::constructor`. The remaining arguments are kept in the `args` variable, and are dealt with later.

After the initialization statement is executed, any base class constructors that were not explicitly called are invoked without arguments. If there is no initialization statement, all base class constructors are invoked without arguments. This guarantees that all base classes are fully constructed before we enter the body of the derived class constructor.

Each of the base class constructors invoke the constructors for their base classes in a similar manner, so the entire construction process is recursive. By default, an object is constructed from its least specific to its most specific class. If you're not sure which is the least specific and which is the most specific class, ask an object to report its heritage. If we had a `VisualFileTree` object named `fred`, we could query its heritage like this:

```
% fred info heritage
VisualFileTree FileTree Tree VisualRep
```

This says that `VisualFileTree` is the most specific class and `VisualRep` is the least specific. By default, the constructors will be called in the order that you get by working backward through this list. Class `VisualRep` would be constructed first, followed by `Tree`, `FileTree`, and `VisualFileTree`. Our initialization statement changes the default order by calling out `FileTree::constructor` before `VisualRep::constructor`.

Objects are destroyed in the opposite manner. Since there are no arguments for the destructor, the scheme is a little simpler. The most specific destructor is called first, followed by the next most specific, and so on. This is the order that you get by working forward through the heritage list. `VisualFileTree` would be destructed first, followed by `FileTree`, `Tree`, and `VisualRep`.

Inheritance Versus Composition

Inheritance is a way of sharing functionality. It merges one class into another, so that when an object is created, it has characteristics from both classes. But in addition to combining classes, we can also combine objects. One object can contain another as a component part. This is referred to as a *compositional* or *has-a* relationship.

For example, suppose we rewrite our `VisualFileTree` class so that a `VisualFileTree` *is-a* `FileTree`, but *has-a* `VisualRep` as a component part. Figure 2-13 shows a diagram of this design.

The code for this `VisualFileTree` class is quite similar to Example 2-14, but we have highlighted several important differences in bold type. Whenever we create a `VisualFileTree` object, we create a separate `VisualRep` object to handle inter-

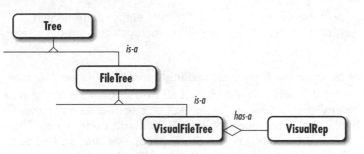

Figure 2-13: VisualFileTree Class has-a VisualRep Component

actions with the canvas. We create this component in the constructor, and save its name in the variable `vis`. We delete this component in the destructor, so that when a `VisualFileTree` object is deleted, its `VisualRep` component is deleted as well. If we didn't do this, the `VisualRep` components would hang around indefinitely, and we would have a memory leak.

With inheritance, all of the public members from the base class are automatically integrated into the derived class, becoming part of its interface. With composition, nothing is automatic. If you need to access a method or a configuration option on the component, you must write a *wrapper* in the containing class. For example, the `VisualRep` component has `-icon` and `-title` options that control its appearance. If we want to be able to set `-icon` and `-title` for the `VisualFileTree` object, we must explicitly add these variables, and include configbody code to propagate any changes down to the `VisualRep` component.

With inheritance, we have access to protected data members defined in the base class. With composition, we have access only to the public interface for the component part. Since the `VisualRep` is now a separate object, we cannot access its `canvas` variable from `VisualFileTree`, but we can call its `canvas` method to query the name of its canvas. (We were smart enough to add this back in Example 2-11, although we hardly mentioned it at the time.) We use this in the `select` method to clear other `VisualRep` objects on the same canvas before selecting a new one.

Inheritance and composition are like two sides of the same coin. Sometimes inheritance leads to a better solution, sometimes composition. Many problems are solved equally well using either approach. Knowing whether to use inheritance or composition is a matter of experience and judgement, but I can give you a few simple guidelines here.

- Use inheritance to create layers of abstraction.

  For example, the code for a `VisualFileTree` is neatly abstracted into three classes: `VisualFileTree` *is-a* `FileTree`, which *is-a* `Tree`. Now suppose that we have a problem with the `VisualFileTree`. We won't have to search through all of the code to find the bug. If the problem has to do with the tree, we look in the `Tree` class. If it has to do with the file system, we look in the `FileTree` class. And so on.

- Use inheritance to build a framework for future enhancements.

  We can extend our tree library at any point by adding new classes into the hierarchy. For example, we might create a class `WidgetTree` that *is-a* `Tree`, but adds code to query the Tk widget hierarchy. We might create a class `SourceFileTree` that *is-a* `FileTree`, but adds methods to support source code control.

- Use composition when you catch yourself making exceptions to the *is-a* rule.

  With inheritance, all of the public variables and all of the methods in the base class apply to the derived class. For example, `FileTree` *is-a* `Tree`, so we can treat it exactly like any other `Tree` object. We can add nodes to it, reorder the nodes, clear the nodes, and set the `-name`, `-value`, and `-sort` options. If you catch yourself making exceptions to this, then you are no longer talking about inheritance.*

  Suppose you're thinking that `FileTree` is like a `Tree`, except that you can't clear it, and it doesn't have the `-value` option. In that case, you should add the tree behavior using composition instead of inheritance. You could say that `FileTree` *has-a* `Tree` within it to maintain the actual data. The `Tree` would be completely hidden, but you could wrap the methods and the options that you want to expose.

- Use composition when the relationships between classes are dynamic.

  Again, with inheritance `FileTree` *is-a* `Tree`, once and for all time. Suppose you wanted to have `FileTree` switch dynamically between a tree representation and a flat list of files. In that case, you would be better off using composition to support interchangeable parts. You could say that `FileTree` *has-a* `Tree`, or that `FileTree` *has-a* `List`, depending on its mode of operation.

- Use composition when a single object must have more than one part of the same type.

  When we first presented class `VisualFileTree`, for example, we said that `VisualFileTree` *is-a* `VisualRep`, which appears on a canvas. But suppose that you wanted a single `VisualFileTree` object to appear on many different canvases. You could support this using composition. You could say that `VisualFileTree` *has-a* `VisualRep` component for each canvas that it appears on.

- Use composition to avoid deep inheritance hierarchies.

  With inheritance, each class builds on the one before it. At first, this seems like an exciting way to reuse code. But it can easily get out of hand. At some point, it becomes impossible to remember all the details that build up in a series of base classes. Most programmers reach their limit after something like five levels of inheritance. If you trade off some of your inheritance relationships for composition, you can keep your hierarchies smaller and more manageable.

- If you can't decide between inheritance and composition, favor composition.

  Inheritance lets you reuse code, but it is white-box reuse. Each base class is exposed—at least in part—to all of its derived classes. You can see this in

---

* C++ lets you suppress certain things coming from a base class through private inheritance. This evil feature is not supported by [INCR TCL].

Example 2-15. The `VisualFileTree` class relies on the `canvas` variable coming from the `VisualRep` base class. This introduces coupling between the two classes and breaks encapsulation. If we ever change the implementation of `VisualRep`, we may have to revisit `VisualFileTree`.

On the other hand, composition supports black-box reuse. The internal workings of each object are completely hidden behind a well-defined interface. In Example 2-16, we modified the `VisualFileTree` class to use a `VisualRep` component. Instead of relying on its internal `canvas` variable, we used a well-defined method to interact with its canvas. Therefore, `VisualFileTree` is completely shielded from any changes we might make inside `VisualRep`.

Example 2-16: VisualFileTree Class Which Brings in VisualRep Using Composition Instead of Inheritance

```
class VisualFileTree {
    inherit FileTree

    public variable state "closed"
    public variable selectcommand ""

    public variable icon "" {
        $vis configure -icon $icon
    }
    public variable title "" {
        $vis configure -title $title
    }

    private variable vis ""

    constructor {file cwin args} {
        FileTree::constructor $file
    } {
        set vis [VisualRep #auto $cwin -icon $icon -title $title]
        eval configure $args
    }
    destructor {
        delete object $vis
    }

    public method select {}
    public method toggle {}

    public method draw {ulVar midVar}
    public method refresh {}
}

body VisualFileTree::select {} {
    VisualRep::clear [$vis canvas]
    $vis select
```

```
        regsub -all {%o} $selectcommand $this cmd
        uplevel #0 $cmd
    }

    ...
```

Neither inheritance nor composition should be used exclusively. Using only one or the other is like using only half of the tools in a toolbox. The choice of tool should be based on the problem at hand. Realistic designs have many different classes with a mixture of both relationships.

Namespaces

A *namespace* is a collection of commands, variables, and classes that is kept apart from the usual global scope. It provides the extra packaging needed to create reusable libraries that plug-and-play with one another.

For example, suppose we want to reuse our file browser code in other applications. We need to include our classes, along with procedures like `load_dir` and `create_node` shown in Example 2-13. But if an application happens to have procedures named `load_dir` or `create_node`, adding the file browser code will break it. If an application already uses a global variable named `root`, calling the `load_dir` procedure will corrupt its value.

Name collisions like this make it difficult to construct large Tcl/Tk applications. They cause strange errors that are difficult to debug, and they are a barrier to code reuse. But when commands, variables, and classes are packaged in their own namespace, they are shielded from the rest of an application. Libraries can be used freely, without fear of unwanted interactions.

Creating Namespaces

We can turn our file browser code into a file browser library by packaging it in a namespace. A complete code example appears in the file *itcl/tree/tree10.itcl*, but the important parts are shown in Example 2-17. Variables and procedures are added to a namespace in much the same way that they are added to a class. Procedures are defined using the usual `proc` command. Variables are defined using the `variable` command, which may include an initialization value. These are not instance variables like you would have in a class. These variables act like ordinary "global" variables, but they reside within the namespace, and not at the usual global scope. Defining a variable causes it to be created, but unlike a class, the variable is not automatically available in the procedures in the namespace. You must declare each variable with the Tcl `global` command to gain access to it.

Example 2-17: Namespace for the File Browser Library

```
namespace filebrowser {
    variable roots

    proc load_dir {cwin dir {selcmd ""}} {
        global roots
```

```
        if {[info exists roots($cwin)]} {
            delete object $roots($cwin)
        }
        set roots($cwin) [create_node $cwin $selcmd $dir]
        $roots($cwin) configure -state open
        $roots($cwin) refresh

        return $roots($cwin)
    }

    proc create_node {cwin selcmd fname} {
        ...
    }

    proc cmp_tree {option obj1 obj2} {
        ...
    }
}
```

Within the context of the namespace, commands and variables can be accessed using simple names like load_dir and roots. All of the procedures defined in a namespace execute in that context, so within the body of load_dir, we can access things like create_node and roots without any extra syntax. In another context, names must have an explicit namespace qualifier. For example, an application could use the load_dir procedure like this:

```
filebrowser::load_dir .display.canv /usr/local/lib
```

This is just how we would call a class procedure, and the similarity is no accident. A class is a namespace, but with a little extra functionality to create and manage objects. Classes are also more rigid. Once the class interface is defined, it cannot be modified unless the class is deleted. But a namespace can be updated on the fly to create, redefine, or delete commands and variables.

We can add another procedure to the filebrowser namespace with another namespace command, like this:

```
namespace filebrowser {
    proc all {} {
        global roots
        return [array names roots]
    }
}
```

This activates the filebrowser context, and then executes the proc command within it, defining the new procedure. Another way of creating the procedure is to define it with an ordinary proc command, but include the namespace context in its name:

```
proc filebrowser::all {} {
    global roots
    return [array names roots]
}
```

The procedure can be deleted like this:

```
namespace filebrowser {
    rename all ""
}
```

or like this:

```
rename filebrowser::all ""
```

An entire namespace can be deleted using the **delete** command, like this:

```
delete namespace filebrowser
```

This deletes all commands and variables in the namespace, and removes all trace of the namespace itself.

The namespace containing a command or variable is part of the identity for that command or variable. Elements with the same name in another namespace are totally separate. Suppose we wrap our du browser in a namespace, as shown in Example 2-18.

Example 2-18: Namespace for the du Browser Library

```
namespace diskusage {
    variable roots

    proc load_dir {twin dir} {
        global roots

        set parentDir [file dirname $dir]
        set roots($twin) [Tree ::#auto -name $parentDir]
        set hiers($parentDir) $roots($twin)

        set info [split [exec du -b $dir] \n]
        set last [expr [llength $info]-1]

        for {set i $last} {$i >= 0} {incr i -1} {
            ...
        }
        show_dir $twin $roots($twin)
        ...
    }

    proc show_dir {twin obj} {
        ...
    }

    proc add_entry {twin line obj} {
        ...
    }

    proc cmp_tree {obj1 obj2} {
        ...
    }
}
```

The `diskusage` namespace also contains a `load_dir` command and a `roots` variable, but they are completely separate from those in the `filebrowser` namespace. This is obvious when we try to use them. An application could load a directory into the file browser like this:

```
filebrowser::load_dir .display.canv /usr/local/lib
```

and display the usage information for a directory like this:

```
diskusage::load_dir .textwin /usr/local/lib
```

The explicit namespace qualifiers remove the ambiguity between these two commands.

One namespace can contain another namespace inside it, so one library can have its own private copy of another library. For example, we could include the `diskusage` library within the `filebrowser` library like this:

```
namespace filebrowser {
    namespace diskusage {
        variable roots
        proc load_dir {twin dir} {
            ...
        }
        ...
    }
}
```

Within the `filebrowser` namespace, the usage information for a directory could be displayed as shown earlier:

```
namespace filebrowser {
    diskusage::load_dir .textwin /usr/local/lib
}
```

Outside of `filebrowser`, the complete namespace path must be specified:

```
filebrowser::diskusage::load_dir .textwin /usr/local/lib
```

Every interpreter has a global namespace called `::` which contains all of the other namespaces. It also contains the usual Tcl/Tk commands and global variables. Each Tcl/Tk application starts off in this namespace, which I call the *global context*. When you define other namespaces and call their procedures, the context changes.

Name Resolution

Qualified names are like file names in the Unix file system, except that a `::` separator is used instead of `/`. Any name that starts with `::` is treated as an absolute reference from the global namespace. For example, the command

```
::filebrowser::diskusage::load_dir .textwin /usr/local/lib
```

refers to the `load_dir` command in the `diskusage` namespace, in the `filebrowser` namespace, in the global namespace.

If a name does not have a leading `::`, it is treated relative to the current namespace context. Lookup starts in the current namespace, then continues along a search path. Each namespace has an *import* list that defines its search path. When a namespace is added to the import list, all of the commands and variables in that namespace can be accessed with simple names.

For example, we could import the `filebrowser` namespace into the global namespace like this:

```
import add filebrowser
```

We could then use the `load_dir` command in the global namespace without an explicit qualifier, like this:

```
load_dir .display.canv /usr/local/lib
```

The `load_dir` command is not found directly in the global namespace, but resolution continues along the import path to the `filebrowser` namespace, where the `filebrowser::load_dir` command is found.

It is okay to import other namespaces that have the same command or variable names. We could import the `diskusage` namespace, even though it also has a `load_dir` procedure. The first command or variable found along the import path is the one that gets used.

If you have any questions regarding name resolution, they can be answered by using the `info which` command. This command returns the fully qualified name for any command, variable, or namespace in the current context. In this example, the command:

```
info which -command load_dir
```

would return the fully qualified name `::filebrowser::load_dir`.

By default, each namespace imports its parent, so commands and variables in the global namespace are automatically accessible. Other import relationships should be used sparingly. After all, if the global namespace imported all of the others, we would be back to one big pot of commands and variables, and there wouldn't be much point to having namespaces.

Using Objects Outside of Their Namespace

If you create an object within a namespace, you'll have trouble referring to it outside of the namespace. Suppose you create a `VisualFileTree` object within the `filebrowser` namespace like this:

```
namespace filebrowser {
    VisualFileTree fred /usr/local/lib .display.canv
}
```

and then you try to add a node to it in another namespace like this:

```
namespace diskusage {
    VisualFileTree wilma /usr/local/bin .display.canv
    fred add wilma
}
```

This will fail. Since the `fred` object was created in the `filebrowser` namespace, the `fred` command is local to that namespace. We will not be able to find a `fred` command in `diskusage` unless the `filebrowser` namespace is somewhere on its import path.

Usually, this is a good thing. Namespaces are doing their job of keeping the two packages separate, and protecting the elements inside them. But from time to time, you will want to share objects between packages. This problem all has to do with naming, and it can be solved through proper naming, too.

One solution is to use the full name of an object when you are referring to it in another namespace. For example, we could say:

```
namespace diskusage {
    VisualFileTree wilma /usr/local/bin .display.canv
    ::filebrowser::fred add wilma
}
```

You may have noticed that an object's `this` variable reports the full name of the object, including its namespace path. The reason is this: If you use `$this` as a command, you will be able to find the object from any context. When you use the full name, you leave nothing to chance in command resolution.

Another solution is to create the object in some namespace that all of your packages naturally import. For example, all namespaces import the global `::` namespace. You can create an object in the global namespace like this:

```
namespace filebrowser {
    uplevel #0 VisualFileTree fred /usr/local/lib .display.canv
}
```

or like this:

```
namespace filebrowser {
    namespace :: { VisualFileTree fred /usr/local/lib .display.canv }
}
```

or like this:

```
namespace filebrowser {
    VisualFileTree ::fred /usr/local/lib .display.canv
}
```

In the first case, we use the `uplevel #0` command to transition to the 0th call frame, which is the global context, and we create the object there. In the second case, we use the `namespace` command to get the same effect. In the third case, we execute the `VisualFileTree` command in the `filebrowser` namespace, but we give the object a name that belongs to the global namespace. The effect is the same. We create an object named `fred` that we can access from the global namespace and, therefore, we can access it from any namespace in the application.

Instead of putting an object all the way out in the global namespace, you may want to put it in a more restricted namespace that only certain packages have access to. Remember, namespaces can be nested, and each namespace automatically imports things from its parent. We could wrap the `filebrowser` and the `diskusage` namespace in another namespace called `filestuff`, for example, and put all of the shared objects in `filestuff`:

```
namespace filestuff {
    namespace filebrowser {
        ...
        VisualFileTree ::filestuff::fred /usr/local/lib .display.canv
    }
    namespace diskusage {
        ...
        VisualFileTree ::filestuff::wilma /usr/local/bin .display.canv
        fred add wilma
    }
}
```

That way, these objects can still be shared across `filebrowser` and `diskusage`, but they won't interfere with any other packages.

Sometimes it is easy to forget that other classes need access to an object. When the `Tree` class adds an object to a tree, for example, it needs to talk to that object to set its parent. If all of our `Tree` objects are sitting in the `filestuff` namespace, but the `Tree` class itself is sitting one level up in the global namespace, we will again have problems. As much as possible, keep all of the code related to a package together in the same namespace. If the `Tree` class is needed only for the `filebrowser` package, put it in the `filebrowser` namespace. If it needs to be shared across both the `filebrowser` and the `diskusage` packages, put it above them in the `filestuff` namespace.

Classes can be defined within a namespace like this:

```
namespace filestuff {
    class Tree {
        ...
    }
    class FileTree {
        ...
    }
    ...
}
```

or like this:

```
class filestuff::Tree {
    ...
}
class filestuff::FileTree {
    ...
}
...
```

In either case, the classes are completely contained within the `filestuff` namespace, so if an application has another `Tree` class, it will not interfere with the one in the `filestuff` namespace. More importantly, since the `Tree` class now resides within `filestuff`, it automatically has access to the objects in `filestuff`.

Protection Levels

Just as you can have public, private, and protected elements in a class, you can have public, private, and protected elements in a namespace. This helps to document your interface, so that someone using your library knows which variables and procedures they can access, and which ones they should leave alone. For example, look at the filebrowser library shown in Example 2-19. It is obvious that `load_dir` procedure is the only thing that you need to use to access a file browser. Everything else is private to the `filebrowser` namespace.

Example 2-19: File Browser Library with Public/Private Declarations

```
namespace filebrowser {
    private variable roots

    public proc load_dir {cwin dir {selcmd ""}} {
        global roots

        if {[info exists roots($cwin)]} {
            delete object $roots($cwin)
        }
        set roots($cwin) [create_node $cwin $selcmd $dir]
        $roots($cwin) configure -state open
        $roots($cwin) refresh

        return $roots($cwin)
    }

    private proc create_node {cwin selcmd fname} {
        ...
    }

    private proc cmp_tree {option obj1 obj2} {
        ...
    }
}
```

If you don't specify a protection level, everything is public by default, including your variables. This makes namespaces backward-compatible with the rest of Tcl/Tk, but it also makes them different from classes. In classes, methods are public by default, but variables are protected.

Namespaces are also a little different when it comes to protected elements. In a class, protected elements can be accessed in any derived class. But there is no "derived" namespace. The closest equivalent is a nested namespace. If you create a protected element in one namespace, you can access the element in any of the other namespaces nested within it. You might create a protected variable in a namespace like `filestuff` and share it among the namespaces like `filebrowser` and `diskusage` nested within it.

On the other hand, a private element is completely private to the namespace that contains it. If you create a private variable in `filestuff`, it will not show up in any other context, including nested namespaces like `filebrowser` and `diskusage`.

Using Classes and Namespaces

There are some strong similarities between classes and namespaces, but they play different roles in your application. Classes are data structures. They let you create objects to represent the data in your application. For example, we used Visual-FileTree objects to represent each of the files in our file browser. On the other hand, namespaces are a way of organizing things. We used the filebrowser namespace to wrap up the variables and procedures for our file browser library. There is one variable roots and one procedure load_dir for the file browser, but instead of floating around at the global scope, they are grouped together in the filebrowser namespace.

You can use namespaces to organize classes. For example, we grouped Tree, FileTree and VisualFileTree into the filestuff namespace. Again, instead of floating around at the global scope, these classes reside with the rest of the file browser library, where they are needed.

You can also use namespaces to organize other namespaces. For example, we grouped the filebrowser namespace and the diskusage namespace into the same filestuff namespace. We can add the filestuff library to any of our applications, and access the separate filebrowser and diskusage utilities within it.

Scoped Commands and Variables

Classes and namespaces are really good at protecting the elements within them. But suppose you want something to be private or protected, but there is one other class—or perhaps one other object—that needs to have access to it. This may be a completely separate class with no inheritance relationship, so we can't rely on "protected" access to solve the problem. And we don't want to open things up for "public" access. In C++, you can declare certain classes and functions as *friends*, thereby granting them special access privileges. In [INCR TCL], we handle this in a different manner, but the effect is the same.

You can see the problem more clearly in the following example. Suppose we have a folder::create procedure that creates a checkbutton with an associated file folder icon. We might use this procedure like this:

```
set counter 0

foreach dir {/usr/man /usr/local/man /usr/X11/man} {
    set name ".dir[incr counter]"
    folder::create $name $dir
    pack $name -fill x
}
```

to create the checkbuttons shown in Figure 2-14. When you toggle one of these checkbuttons, it changes the indicator box, and it also opens or closes the folder icon.

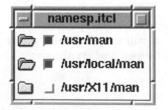

Figure 2-14: Some Checkbuttons Created by folder::create

The `folder::create` procedure is shown in Example 2-20. Each time we call it, we create a frame with a label and a checkbutton. Each checkbutton needs a variable to keep track of its state. If we use an ordinary global variable, it might conflict with other variables in the application. Instead, we create a `modes` variable inside the `folder` namespace, and we make it private so that no one else can tamper with it. We treat this variable as an array, and we give each folder assembly a different slot within it. Whenever the checkbutton is invoked, it toggles this variable and calls the `redisplay` procedure to update the icon.

Example 2-20: Using the code and scope Commands to Share Command and Variable References

```
namespace folder {
    private variable images
    set images(open)   [image create photo -file dir1.gif]
    set images(closed) [image create photo -file dir2.gif]

    private variable modes

    public proc create {win name} {
        frame $win
        label $win.icon
        pack $win.icon -side left

        checkbutton $win.toggle -text $name \
            -onvalue "open" -offvalue "closed" \
            -variable [scope modes($win)] \
            -command [code redisplay $win]

        pack $win.toggle -side left -fill x
        $win.toggle invoke
    }

    public proc get {win} {
        global modes
        return $modes($win)
    }

    private proc redisplay {win} {
        global modes images
        set state $modes($win)
        $win.icon configure -image $images($state)
    }
}
```

The checkbutton is clearly a key player in the `folder` library. We want it to have access to the `modes` variable and to the `redisplay` procedure, but we also want to keep these things private. No one else should really be using them. Unless we do something special, the checkbutton will be treated as an outsider and it will be denied access to these elements.

The problem is that options like `-command` and `-variable` are being set inside the `folder` namespace, but they are not evaluated until much later in the program.

It is not until you click on a checkbutton that it toggles the variable and invokes the command. This happens in another context, long after we have left the `folder::create` procedure.

There are two commands that let you export part of a namespace to a friend. The `scope` command lets you export a variable reference, and the `code` command lets you export a code fragment. Both of these commands are used on a case-by-case basis. When we create the checkbutton and set the `-variable` option, for example, we enclosed the `modes` variable in the `scope` command. This gives the checkbutton access to just this variable.* If we set the `-variable` option to a different variable name, it will lose access to the `modes` variable. Similarly, when we set the `-command` option, we enclosed the code fragment in the `code` command. This lets the checkbutton execute the `redisplay` command. But if we set the `-command` option to something else, again, it will lose access to `redisplay`.

The `code` and `scope` commands work by capturing the namespace context. They preserve it in such a way that it can be revived again later. So when the checkbutton needs to access its variable, it actually jumps back into the `folder` namespace and looks for the `modes` variable. When the checkbutton needs to invoke its command, again, it jumps back into the `folder` namespace and looks for the `redisplay` command. Since it accesses things from within the `folder` namespace, it bypasses the usual protection levels. In effect, we have given the checkbutton a "back door" into the namespace.

You can see how this works if you query back the actual `-command` or `-variable` string that the checkbutton is using. For example, we created the checkbutton with a command like this:

```
checkbutton $win.toggle ... -command [code redisplay $win]
```

But if we query back the `-command` string, it will look like this:

```
@scope ::folder {redisplay .dir1}
```

This string is the result of the `code` command, and is called a *scoped value*. It is really just a list with three elements: the `@scope` keyword, a namespace context, and a value string. If this string is executed as a command, it automatically revives the `::folder` namespace, and then executes the code fragment `redisplay .dir1` in that context.

Note that the `code` command does not execute the code itself. It merely formats the command so that it can be executed later. We can think of [`code` ...] as a new way of quoting Tcl command strings.

When the `code` command has multiple arguments, they are formatted as a Tcl list and the resulting string becomes the "value" part of the scoped value. For example, if you execute the following command in the `folder` namespace:

```
set cmd [code $win.toggle configure -text "empty folder"]
```

it produces a scoped value like this:

```
@scope ::folder {.dir1.toggle configure -text {empty folder}}
```

---

* Actually, to just one slot in the array.

Notice how the string "empty folder" is preserved as a single list element. If it were not, the command would fail when it is later executed.

The `code` command can also be used to wrap up an entire command script like this:

```
bind $win.icon <ButtonPress-1> [code "
    $win.toggle flash
    $win.toggle invoke
"]
```

In this case, we combined two commands into one argument. There are no extra arguments, so the code paragraph simply becomes the "value" part of the scoped value that is produced.

The `scope` command works the same way as the `code` command, except that it takes only one argument, the variable name. For example, we created the check-button like this:

```
checkbutton $win.toggle ... -variable [scope modes($win)]
```

But if we query back the `-value` string, it will look like this:

```
@scope ::folder modes(.dir1)
```

This entire string represents a single variable name. If we try to get or set this variable, the `@scope` directive shifts us into the `folder` namespace, and looks for a variable named `modes` in that context.

If you forget to use the `code` and `scope` commands, you'll get the normal Tk behavior—your commands and variables will be handled in the global context. For example, if we created the checkbutton like this:

```
checkbutton $win.toggle -text $name \
    -onvalue "open" -offvalue "closed" \
    -variable modes($win) \
    -command "redisplay $win"
```

then it would look for a variable named `modes` in the global namespace, and it would try to execute a command called `redisplay` in the global context. In some cases this is okay, but more often than not you will need to use the `code` and `scope` commands to get things working properly.

You should use the `code` and `scope` commands whenever you are handing off a reference to something inside of a namespace. Use the `code` command with configuration options like `-command`, `-xscrollcommand`, `-yscrollcommand`, *etc.*, and with Tk commands like `bind`, `after`, and `fileevent`. Use the `scope` command with options like `-variable` and `-textvariable`, and with Tk commands like `tkwait variable`.

But although you should use these commands, you should not abuse them. They undermine a key feature of object-oriented programming: encapsulation. If you use these commands to break into a class or a namespace where you don't belong, you will pay for it later. At some point, details inside the class or the namespace may change, and your code will break miserably.

Interactive Development

[INCR TCL] has many features that support debugging and interactive development. Each class has a built-in `info` method that returns information about an object, so you can query things like an object's class or its list of methods on the fly. This is not possible in C++, but it is quite natural in a dynamic language like Tcl.

Suppose we have defined classes like `Tree` and `FileTree`, and we create a `FileTree` object by typing the following command at the `%` prompt:

```
% FileTree henry /usr/local -procreate "FileTree #auto"
henry
```

We get the result `henry` which tells us that an object was created successfully.

If someone hands us this object and we want to determine its class, we can use the `info class` query:

```
% henry info class
FileTree
```

This says that `henry` was created as a `FileTree` object, so its most specific class is `FileTree`. You can get a list of all the classes that `henry` belongs to using the `info heritage` query:

```
% henry info heritage
FileTree Tree
```

This says that first and foremost, `henry` is a `FileTree`, but it is also a `Tree`. The classes are visited in this order whenever a method or a variable reference needs to be resolved.

When you want to know if an object belongs to a certain class, you can check its heritage. You can also use the built-in `isa` method to check for base classes. You give `isa` a class name, and it returns nonzero if the class can be found in the object's heritage. For example:

```
% henry isa Tree
1
% henry isa VisualRep
0
```

This says that `henry` belongs to class `Tree`, but not to class `VisualRep`.

The `info function` query returns the list of class methods and procs. This includes the built-in methods like `configure`, `cget`, and `isa` as well:

```
% henry info function
FileTree::populate FileTree::contents FileTree::constructor
Tree::configure Tree::reorder Tree::cget Tree::isa Tree::constructor
Tree::destructor Tree::add Tree::back Tree::parent Tree::contents
Tree::clear
```

Each function is reported with its full name, like `Tree::add`. This helps clarify things if you inherit methods from a base class. You can retrieve more detailed information if you ask for a particular function:

```
% henry info function contents
public method FileTree::contents {} {
    populate
    return [Tree::contents]
}
```

The info variable query returns the list of variables, which includes all instance variables and common variables defined in the class, as well as the built-in this variable:

```
% henry info variable
FileTree::mtime FileTree::file FileTree::this FileTree::procreate
Tree::lastSort Tree::sort Tree::children Tree::value Tree::name
Tree::parent
```

Again, you can retrieve more detailed information if you ask for a particular variable:

```
% henry info variable mtime
private variable FileTree::mtime 0 0
```

The last two elements represent the initial value and the current value of the variable. In this case, they are both 0. But suppose we query the contents of the file tree like this:

```
% henry contents
fileTree0 fileTree1 fileTree2 fileTree3 fileTree4 fileTree5 file-
Tree6 fileTree7 fileTree8 fileTree9 fileTree10 fileTree11 file-
Tree12 fileTree13 fileTree14 fileTree15
```

The populate method creates a series of child nodes, and saves the modification time for this directory in the mtime variable, as a reminder that the file system has been checked. If we query mtime again, we can see that it has changed:

```
% henry info variable mtime
private variable FileTree::mtime 0 845584013
```

You can obtain other high-level information via the usual Tcl info command. You can ask for the list of classes in the current namespace like this:

```
% info classes
VisualFileTree FileTree Tree VisualRep
```

and for the list of objects in the current namespace like this:

```
% info objects
fileTree11 fileTree2 fileTree7 fileTree9 fileTree12 fileTree1
fileTree6 fileTree15 henry fileTree13 fileTree3 fileTree14 file-
Tree0 fileTree5 fileTree8 fileTree10 fileTree4
```

This introspection facility is extremely useful for debugging, and it could support the construction of a class browser or an interactive development environment.

As you are testing your code and finding bugs, you may want to fix things in a class. You can use the body command to redefine the body of any method or proc. You can also use the configbody command to change the configuration code for a public variable.

This is particularly easy to do in the `tcl-mode` of the Emacs editor. You simply load an [INCR TCL] script into Emacs, and tell Emacs to run it. As you are testing it and finding bugs, you can make changes to your script and test them out immediately. You don't have to shut down and start over. Bodies can be changed on the fly. You simply highlight a new `body` or `configbody` definition and tell Emacs to send it off to the test program.

If you don't use Emacs, you can keep your body definitions in a separate file, and you can use the Tcl `source` command to load them into a test program again and again, as bugs are found and corrected.

Although the bodies may change, the class interface cannot be defined more than once. This prevents collisions that would otherwise occur if two developers chose the same class name by accident. But you can delete a class like this:

```
delete class Tree
```

This deletes all objects that belong to the class, all derived classes which depend on this class, and then deletes the class itself. At that point, you can source in your script to redefine the class, and continue debugging.

Autoloading

Tcl provides a way to create libraries of procedures that can be loaded as needed in an application. This facility is called *autoloading*, and it is supported by [INCR TCL] as well.

To use a class library that has been set up for autoloading, you simply add the name of the directory containing the library to the `auto_path` variable:

```
lappend auto_path /usr/local/oreilly/itcl/lib
```

The first time that a class is referenced in a command like this:

```
Tree henry -name "Henry Fonda"
```

the class definition is loaded automatically. The autoloading mechanism searches each directory in the `auto_path` list for a special *tclIndex* file. This file contains a list of commands defined in the directory, along with the script file that should be loaded to define each command. When a command like `Tree` is found in one of the *tclIndex* files, it is automatically loaded, and the command is executed. The next time that this command is needed, it is ready to use.

To create an autoloadable class library, you simply create a directory containing all of the code for the library. Put each class definition in a separate file. These files typically have the extension *.itcl* or *.itk*, but any naming convention can be used. Finally, generate a *tclIndex* file for the directory using the `auto_mkindex` command like this:

```
auto_mkindex /usr/local/oreilly/itcl/lib *.itcl
```

This scans all of the files matching the pattern *.itcl* in the directory */usr/local/oreilly/itcl/lib* and creates a *tclIndex* file in that directory. Once the index file is in place, the library is ready to use. Of course, the index file should be regenerated whenever the source code for the library changes.

Adding C Code to [INCR TCL] Classes

With a little extra C code, we can extend the Tcl/Tk system to have new commands and capabilities.* This is easy to do, and it is one area where Tcl/Tk outshines other packages. C code can also be integrated into [INCR TCL] classes, to implement the bodies of class methods and procs.

For example, suppose we write a C implementation for the **add** method in our **Tree** class, shown in Example 2-21. Instead of specifying the body as a Tcl script, we use the name **@tree-add**. The leading @ sign indicates that this is the symbolic name for a C procedure.

Example 2-21: Tree Class with a C Implementation for the add Method

```
class Tree {
    variable parent ""
    variable children ""

    method add {obj} @tree-add

    method clear {} {
        if {$children != ""} {
            eval delete object $children
        }
        set children ""
    }
    method parent {pobj} {
        set parent $pobj
    }
    method contents {} {
        return $children
    }
}
```

Somewhere down in the C code for our **wish** executable, we have a Tcl-style command handler for the **add** method. We must give the command handler a symbolic name by registering it with the **Itcl_RegisterC** procedure. We do this in the **Tcl_AppInit** procedure, which is called automatically each time the **wish** executable starts up. You can find the **Tcl_AppInit** procedure in the standard Tcl/Tk distribution, in a file called *tclAppInit.c* (for building **tclsh**) or *tkAppInit.c* (for building **wish**). Near the bottom of this procedure, we add a few lines of code like this:

```
if (Itcl_RegisterC(interp, "tree-add", Tree_AddCmd) != TCL_OK) {
    return TCL_ERROR;
}
```

This gives the symbolic name **tree-add** to the C procedure **Tree_AddCmd**. This procedure will be called to handle any class method or class proc that has the body **@tree-add**.

---

* For details, see John K. Ousterhout, Tcl and the Tk Toolkit, Addison-Wesley, 1994.

Example 2-22 shows the implementation for the `Tree_AddCmd` procedure. It takes the usual arguments for a Tcl-style command handler: The first argument is required but not used: `interp` is the interpreter handling a Tcl command; `argc` is the number of arguments on the Tcl command line; and `argv` is the list of Tcl argument strings.

Example 2-22:Implementation for the Tree_AddCmd Handler

```c
#include <tcl.h>
int
Tree_AddCmd(dummy, interp, argc, argv)
    ClientData dummy;            /* unused */
    Tcl_Interp *interp;          /* current interpreter */
    int argc;                    /* number of arguments */
    char **argv;                 /* argument strings */
{
    char *val;
    Tcl_DString buffer;

    if (argc != 2) {
        Tcl_AppendResult(interp, "wrong # args: should be \"",
            argv[0], " treeObj\"", (char*)NULL);
        return TCL_ERROR;
    }

    /*
     *  Build a command string like "treeObj parent $this" and
     *  execute it.
     */
    Tcl_DStringInit(&buffer);
    val = Tcl_GetVar(interp, "this", TCL_LEAVE_ERR_MSG);
    if (val == NULL) {
        Tcl_DStringFree(&buffer);
        return TCL_ERROR;
    }
    Tcl_DStringAppendElement(&buffer, argv[1]);
    Tcl_DStringAppendElement(&buffer, "parent");
    Tcl_DStringAppendElement(&buffer, val);
    val = Tcl_DStringValue(&buffer);

    if (Tcl_Eval(interp,val) != TCL_OK) {
        Tcl_DStringFree(&buffer);
        return TCL_ERROR;
    }
    Tcl_ResetResult(interp);

    /*
     *  Add the specified object to the "children" list.
     */
    val = Tcl_SetVar(interp, "children", argv[1],
        TCL_LEAVE_ERR_MSG | TCL_LIST_ELEMENT | TCL_APPEND_VALUE);

    if (val == NULL) {
```

```
        Tcl_DStringFree(&buffer);
        return TCL_ERROR;
    }

    Tcl_DStringFree(&buffer);
    return TCL_OK;
}
```

This procedure has to mimic our **add** method. It takes the name of another **Tree** object, and adds it to the list of children for the current node. Whenever **Tree_AddCmd** is called, therefore, we should have two argument strings: the command name **add** (stored in **argv[0]**), and the name of the child object (stored in **argv[1]**). We first check to make sure that this is true, and if not, we immediately return an error.

Next, we build the command string **$obj parent $this** in a dynamic string buffer. This command notifies the child that it has a new parent. We query the value of the **this** variable using **Tcl_GetVar**. We build the command string in a **Tcl_DString** buffer, and then use **Tcl_Eval** to execute the command.

The name of the child object is then appended to the **children** list using **Tcl_SetVar**.

This implementation is identical to the Tcl version shown in Example 2-3, although it requires many more C language statements to perform the same task. In this case, the result is no better. The C version is not much faster, and the Tcl version was considerably easier to write.

But the interesting part of this example is the interface between the C code and the [INCR TCL] class. When the command handler is executed, class variables can be accessed as ordinary variables. Class methods can be invoked as ordinary commands. [INCR TCL] handles this automatically by setting up the object context before the handler is invoked. Because of this, we were able to access the **children** variable and the built-in **this** variable with ordinary **Tcl_GetVar** and **Tcl_SetVar** calls.

Therefore, a single class can have some parts written in C code, and others written in Tcl. The Tcl parts can be migrated to C for better performance as the need arises.

Tcl is an excellent "glue" language. It stitches C code blocks together with Tcl statements to form applications. [INCR TCL] takes the glue to a higher level. Bits of Tcl and C code can be mixed together to create classes. These high-level building blocks provide better support for building larger applications.

Summary

Extension:	[INCR TCL]—Object-Oriented Programming for Tcl
Author:	Michael J. McLennan Bell Labs Innovations for Lucent Technologies mmclennan@lucent.com
Other Contributors:	Jim Ingham Lee Bernhard …and many others listed on the Web site

Platforms Supported:	All major Unix platforms Linux Windows 95 (release itcl2.2 and beyond) Macintosh (release itcl2.2 and beyond)
Web Site:	`http://www.tcltk.com/itcl`

Mailing List (bug reports):	`mail -s "subscribe" itcl-request@tcltk.com`
	to subscribe to the mailing list
	
	`mail itcl@tcltk.com`
	to send mail

Quick Reference

Classes

```
class className {
    inherit baseClass ?baseClass...?
    constructor args ?init? body
    destructor body
    method name ?args? ?body?
    proc name ?args? ?body?
    variable varName ?init? ?configBody?
    common varName ?init?
    set varName ?value?
    array option ?arg arg ...?
    public command ?arg arg ...?

    protected command ?arg arg ...?

    private command ?arg arg ...?
```

`}`		Defines a new class of objects.
`body`	`className::function args body`	Redefines the body for a class method or proc.
`configbody`	`className::varName body`	Redefines the body of configuration code for a public variable or a mega-widget option.
`delete`	`class name ?name...?`	Deletes a class definition and all objects in the class.
`info`	`classes ?pattern?`	Returns a list of all classes, or a list of classes whose names match pattern.

Objects

`className`	`objName ?arg arg ...?`	Creates an object that belongs to class className.
`objName`	`method ?arg arg ...?`	Invokes a method to manipulate an object.

delete	object *objName ?objName...?* Deletes one or more objects.
info	objects *?-class className? ?-isa className? ?pattern?* Returns a list of all objects, or a list of objects in a certain class *className*, whose names match *pattern*.

Namespaces

```
namespace namespaceName {
    variable varName ?value?
    proc cmdName args body
    private command ?arg arg ...?
    protected command ?arg arg ...?
    public command ?arg arg ...?
    command ?arg arg ...?
```

}	Finds an existing namespace or creates a new namespace and executes a body of commands in that context. Commands like **proc** and **variable** create Tcl commands and variables that are local to that namespace context.

namespaceName::cmdName ?arg arg ...?
namespaceName::namespaceName::...::cmdName ?arg arg ...?
Invokes a procedure that belongs to another namespace.

code	*command ?arg arg ...?* Formats a code fragment so it can be used as a callback in another namespace context.
delete	*namespace namespaceName ?namespaceName...?* Deletes a namespace and everything in it.
import	add *name ?name...? ?-where pos...?* all *?name?* list *?importList?* remove *name ?name...?* Changes the import list for a namespace.
info	context Returns the current namespace context.
info	namespace all *?pattern?* namespace children *?name?* namespace parent *?name?* Returns information about the namespace hierarchy.
info	namespace qualifiers *string* namespace tail *string* Parses strings with :: namespace qualifiers.
info	protection *?-command? ?-variable? name* Returns the protection level (public/protected/private) for a command or variable.

info	which ?-command? ?-variable? ?-namespace? *name* Searches for a command, variable, or namespace and returns its fully qualified name.
scope	*string* Formats a variable name so it can be accessed in another namespace context.

3

Building Mega-Widgets with [INCR TK]

by Michael McLennan

Copyright 1997 Lucent Technologies, Inc.

Tk lets you create objects like buttons, labels, entries, and so forth, but it is not truly object-oriented. You can't create a new widget class like HotButton and have it inherit its basic behavior from class Button. So you really can't extend the Tk widget set unless you tear apart its C code and add some of your own.

[INCR TK] lets you create brand new widgets, using the normal Tk widgets as component parts. These *mega-widgets* look and act like ordinary Tk widgets, but you can create them without writing any C code. Instead, you write an [INCR TCL] class to handle each new type of mega-widget.

If you read Chapter 4 on the [INCR WIDGETS] library, you can see what great results you'll get using [INCR TK]. [INCR WIDGETS] has more than 30 new widget classes including Fileselectionbox, Panedwindow, Canvasprintbox, Option-menu, and Combobox, and they were all built with the [INCR TK] framework.

You can understand the essence of a mega-widget simply by looking at one of these widgets. For example, the *Spinint* widget shown in Figure 3-1 is created like this:

```
spinint .s -labeltext "Repeat:" -width 5 -range {1 10}
pack .s
```

It has an entry component that holds a numeric value, and a pair of buttons for adjusting that value. Whenever you create a Spinint widget, all of these internal components are created and packed automatically. When you set the -labeltext option, a label appears. You can set the -range option to control the range of integer values. If you use the arrow buttons and bump the number beyond this range, it will wrap around to the other end of the scale.

A Spinint can be configured like a normal Tk widget. It has many internal components, but they all work together as one widget. All of their configuration options

---

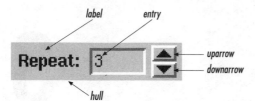

Figure 3-1: A `Spinint` Mega-Widget Has Many Component Parts

are merged together into a single list called the *master option list*. When you set master configuration options like this:

```
.s configure -background tan -textbackground white
```

the effects propagate down to all of the internal components. Setting the `-background` option changes the background of the `hull`, `label`, `uparrow`, and `downarrow` components. Setting the `-textbackground` option changes the background of the entry component.

A Spinint also has options to control the layout of its components. You can rearrange the buttons like this:

```
.s configure -arroworient horizontal
```

and reposition the label like this:

```
.s configure -labelpos nw
```

You can even query the current option settings like this:

```
set bg [.s cget -background]
```

Of course, you can add all of these settings to the options database, so that Spinint widgets will have these values by default:

```
option add *Spinint.background tan
option add *Spinint.textBackground white
option add *Spinint.arrowOrient horizontal
option add *Spinint.labelPos nw
```

A Spinint widget has a well-defined set of operations or *methods* to manipulate it. You can load a new integer into the text area like this:

```
.s clear
.s insert 0 "10"
```

and you can programmatically bump up the value like this:

```
.s up
```

When you destroy the widget:

```
destroy .s
```

all of its internal components are destroyed automatically.

Mega-widgets have all of the characteristics that we would expect from a Tk widget. But since they do not require any C code or X library programming, they are considerably easier to implement.

Overview

To understand [INCR TK], you have to understand how a mega-widget handles its component parts and their configuration options. In this section, we'll explore [INCR TK] from a conceptual standpoint. Later on, we'll look at real code examples.

Class Hierarchy

To create a new type of mega-widget, you simply derive a new [INCR TCL] class from one of the existing [INCR TK] base classes. The [INCR TK] class hierarchy is shown in Figure 3-2. All of these classes reside in the `itk` namespace, so they will not interfere with the rest of your application.

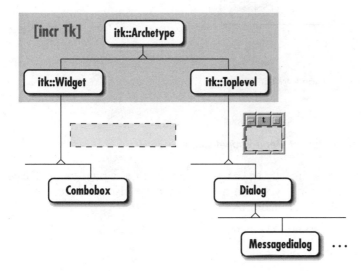

Figure 3-2: Mega-Widgets Are Created by Extending One of the Base Classes in [INCR TK]

There are basically two different kinds of mega-widgets, so there are two [INCR TK] base classes that you use to build them. If you want a mega-widget to pop up in its own top-level window, then have it inherit from `itk::Toplevel`. This lets you build dialog widgets like the `Fileselectiondialog`, `Messagedialog`, and `Canvasprintdialog` in the [INCR WIDGETS] library. Otherwise, if you want a mega-widget to sit inside of some other top-level window, then have it inherit from the `itk::Widget` class. This lets you build things like the `Optionmenu`, `Combobox`, and `Panedwindow` in the [INCR WIDGETS] library.

Suppose we were starting from scratch to create the `Spinint` class. Spinint widgets are the kind that sit inside of other top-level windows, so we should use the `itk::Widget` class as a starting point.

Both `itk::Widget` and `itk::Toplevel` inherit the basic mega-widget behavior from `itk::Archetype`. This class keeps track of the mega-widget components and their configuration options.

Class Definition

If we wanted to implement the Spinint widget, we would write a class definition that looks something like the one shown in Figure 3-3.*

```
class Spinint {
    inherit itk::Widget

    constructor {args} {
```

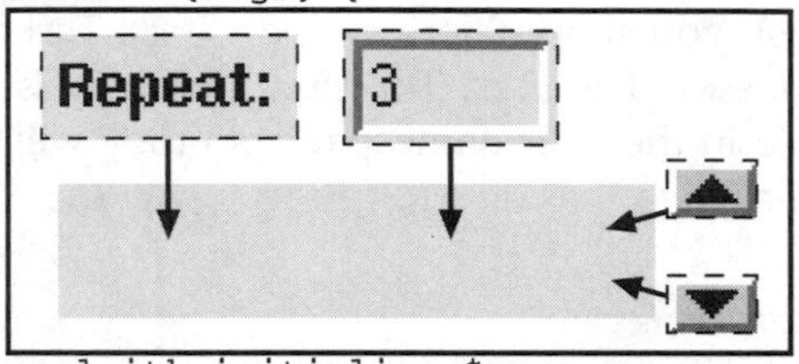

```
        eval itk_initialize $args

    }

    public method clear {}
    public method insert {index value}

    public method up {}
    public method down {}
}
```

Figure 3-3: Conceptual View of Spinint Mega-Widget Class

Notice that we use a class name like `Spinint` that starts with a capital letter. This is a rule in Tk. For the time being, you can assume that we also have to create mega-widgets with a capitalized command like this:

Spinint .s -labeltext "Repeat:" -width 5 -range {1 10}

Later on, I will show you how to get around this.

Inside the class definition, we start off with an `inherit` statement that brings in the `itk::Widget` base class. As we will soon see, this automatically gives us a container for the mega-widget called the *hull*. We write a constructor to create all of the component widgets and pack them into the hull. Instead of including the actual code, we simply illustrated this process in the constructor shown in Figure 3-3.

Notice that the constructor uses the `args` argument to handle any configuration options that might be specified when a widget is created, like this for example:

Spinint .s **-labeltext "Number of Copies:" -background red**

But instead of handling these arguments with:

eval configure $args

as we would for an ordinary [INCR TCL] class, we use:

eval itk_initialize $args

You must call `itk_initialize` instead of `configure` for all of your [INCR TK] mega-widgets. This is a protected method that belongs to the `itk::Archetype` base class. It not only applies the configuration changes, but it also makes sure that

---

* The `Spinint` class in the [INCR WIDGETS] library is a little more complicated, but this example will give you the basic idea.

all mega-widget options are properly initialized. If you forget to call it for a particular class, some of the configuration options may be missing whenever you create a mega-widget of that class.

Near the bottom of the class definition we include some methods to handle the operations for this mega-widget. As I said before, you can load a new value into a Spinint widget like this:

```
.s clear
.s insert 0 "10"
```

So we have a method `clear` to clear the entry, and a method `insert` to insert some new text. We also have a method called `up` to increment the value, and a method called `down` to decrement it. We can add more operations to the `Spinint` class simply by defining more methods.

Notice that we didn't define a destructor. The `itk::Archetype` base class keeps track of the component widgets and destroys them for you when the mega-widget is destroyed. You won't need a destructor unless you have to close a file or delete some other object when the mega-widget is destroyed.

Mega-Widget Construction

Let's take a moment to see what happens when a mega-widget is constructed. For example, suppose we create a Spinint widget like this:

```
Spinint .s -labeltext "Starting Page:" -range {1 67}
```

When [INCR TCL] sees this command, it creates an object named `.s` in class `Spinint`, and calls its constructor with the remaining arguments. But before it can actually run the `Spinint::constructor`, all of the base classes must be fully constructed. This process is illustrated in Figure 3-4.

The constructor for the least specific class `itk::Archetype` is called first. It initializes some internal variables that keep track of the component widgets and their configuration options. Next, the `itk::Widget` constructor is called. It creates the hull frame that acts as a container for the component widgets. The name of this frame widget is stored in a protected variable called `itk_interior`. We will use this name later on as the root for component widget names. Finally, the `Spinint` constructor is called. It creates the `label`, `entry`, and `uparrow` and `downarrow` components, and packs them into the hull.

As each component is created, its configuration options are merged into a master list of options for the mega-widget. We will see precisely how this is done in the next section, but we end up with a mega-widget that has an overall list of configuration options. Near the end of the `Spinint` constructor, we call `itk_initialize` to finalize the list and apply any configuration changes.

Creating Component Widgets

Let's look inside the constructor now and see how we create each of the mega-widget components. Normally, when we create a Tk widget, we use a simple command like this:

```
label .s.lab
```

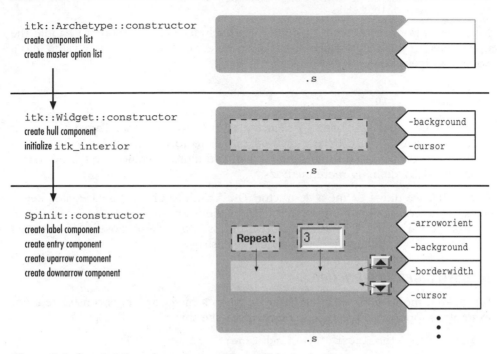

Figure 3-4: Construction of a Spinint *Mega-Widget*

This says that we have a frame called .s and we want to put a label named lab inside it. For a mega-widget, we can't hard-code the name of the containing frame. It will be different for each widget that gets created. If we create a Spinint named .s, it will have a hull named .s, and the label should be called .s.lab. But if we create a Spinint named .foo.bar, it will have a hull named .foo.bar, and the label should be called .foo.bar.lab. Instead of hard-coding the name of a frame, we use the name in the itk_interior variable, like this:

```
label $itk_interior.lab
```

We also have to do something special to let the mega-widget know that this is a component. We wrap the widget creation command inside an itk_component command like the one shown in Figure 3-5.

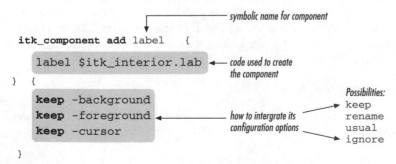

Figure 3-5: Syntax of the itk_component Command

This command executes the code that you give it to create the component, and saves the name of the resulting widget. It stores this name in a protected array called `itk_component`, using the symbolic name as an index. When you want to refer to the component later on, you can look it up in this array using its symbolic name. For example, in Figure 3-5 we created a label with the symbolic name `label`. We can pack this component using its symbolic name, like this:

```
pack $itk_component(label) -side left
```

The expression `$itk_component(label)` expands to a real widget path name like `.s.lab` or `.foo.bar.lab`. We can use this in any of the methods in the `Spinint` class to refer to the label component.

You can also use symbolic component names outside of the mega-widget class, but you do it a little differently. The `itk::Archetype` class provides a method called `component` that you can use to access components. If you call this method without any arguments:

```
% Spinint .s
.s
% .s component
hull label entry uparrow downarrow
```

it returns a list of symbolic component names. You can also use this method to reach inside the mega-widget and talk directly to a particular component. For example, we might configure the label to have a sunken border like this:

```
.s component label configure -borderwidth 2 -relief sunken
```

Using symbolic names insulates you from the details inside of a mega-widget class. Suppose we decide next week to rearrange the components, and we change the name of the actual label widget from `$itk_interior.lab` to `$itk_interior.box.l1`. Code inside the class like:

```
pack $itk_component(label) -side left
```

and code outside the class like:

```
.s component label configure -borderwidth 2 -relief sunken
```

will not have to change, since we used the symbolic name in both places.

The `itk_component` command does one other important thing. As you add each component, its configuration options are merged into the master list of options for the mega-widget. When you set a master option on the mega-widget, it affects all of the internal components. When you set the master `-background` option, for example, the change is propagated to the `-background` option of the internal components, so the entire background changes all at once.

You can control precisely how the options are merged into the master list by using a series of commands at the end of the `itk_component` command. We will explain all of the possibilities in greater detail later, but in Figure 3-5 we used the `keep` command to merge the `-background`, `-foreground`, and `-cursor` options for the label into the master list.

All of the master configuration options are kept in a protected array called `itk_option`. You can use this in any of the methods to get the current value for a configuration option. It will save you a call to the usual `cget` method. For example, if we were in some method like `Spinint::insert`, we could find out the current background color using either of these commands:

```
set bg [cget -background]        ;# a little slow
set bg $itk_option(-background)  ;# better
```

But if you want to change an option, you can't just set the value in this array. You must always call the `configure` method, as shown here:

```
set itk_option(-background) red  ;# error!  color does not change
configure -background red        ;# ok
```

As you can see, there is a close relationship between the `itk_component` command and the `itk_component` and `itk_option` arrays. Whenever you add a new component, its symbolic name is added to the `itk_component` array, and its configuration options are merged into the `itk_option` array. This relationship is summarized in Figure 3-6.

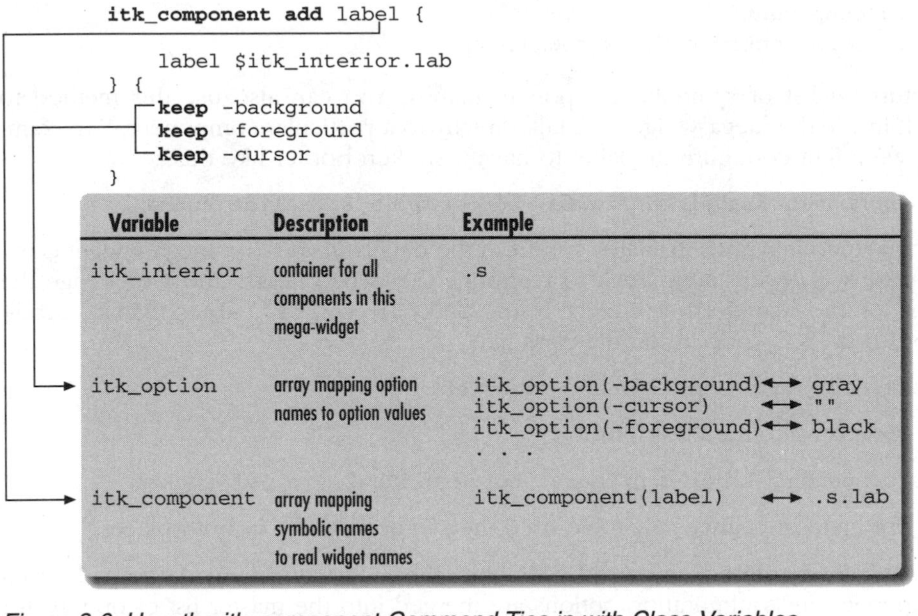

Figure 3-6: How the itk_component Command Ties in with Class Variables

Keeping Configuration Options

Each mega-widget has a master list of configuration options. When you set a master option, it affects all of the internal components that are tied to that option. For example, if we have a Spinint mega-widget named `.s` and we configure its master background option:

```
.s configure -background green
```

the change is automatically propagated down to the `hull`, `label`, `uparrow`, and `downarrow` components. In effect, the overall background turns green with one simple command. This is what you would naively expect, since a mega-widget is supposed to work like any other Tk widget. But [INCR TK] has special machinery under the hood that allows this to take place.

When you create a component widget, you can specify how its configuration options should be merged into the master list. One possibility is to add component options to the master list using the `keep` command. When you keep an option, it appears on the master list with the same name. For example, in Figure 3-7 we show two different `Spinint` components being created. The `label` component keeps its `-background`, `-foreground`, and `-cursor` options, so these options are added directly to the master list. The `entry` component keeps these same options, and keeps the `-borderwidth` option as well.

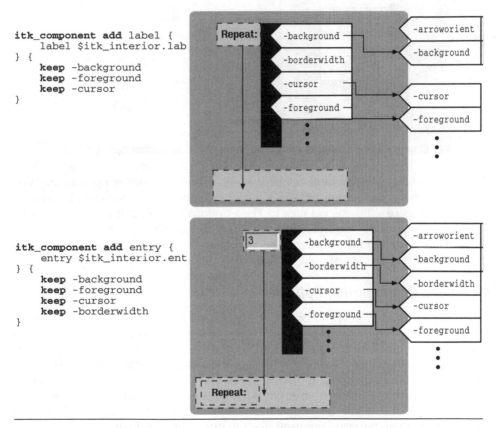

```
itk_component add label {
    label $itk_interior.lab
} {
    keep -background
    keep -foreground
    keep -cursor
}
```

```
itk_component add entry {
    entry $itk_interior.ent
} {
    keep -background
    keep -foreground
    keep -cursor
    keep -borderwidth
}
```

Figure 3-7: Keeping Component Options on the Master Option List

When we configure a master option for the mega-widget, the change is propagated down to all of the components that kept the option. This process is shown in Figure 3-8.

When we configure the `-background` option, both the label and the entry are updated, but when we configure `-borderwidth`, only the entry is updated. Since we did not keep `-borderwidth` for the label, it is not affected by a change in border width.

```
.s configure -background tan - borderwidth 2
```

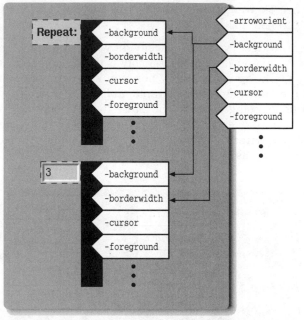

Figure 3-8: Configuration Changes Are Propagated Down to Component Widgets

You must include a `keep` statement for each of the component options that you want to access on the master list. The rest of the component options will be ignored by default. It is usually a good idea to keep options like `-background`, `-foreground`, `-font`, and `-cursor`, which should be synchronized across all components in the mega-widget. Options like `-text` or `-command`, which are different for different components, should be ignored.

Renaming Configuration Options

Suppose you want to keep an option on the master list, but you want to give it a different name. For example, suppose you want to have an option named `-textbackground` for the Spinint mega-widget that changes the background color of the entry component. Having a separate option like this would let you highlight the entry field with a contrasting color, so that it stands out from the rest of the mega-widget. We want to keep the `-background` option for the entry component, but we want to tie it to a master option with the name `-textbackground`. We can handle this with a `rename` command like the one shown in Figure 3-9.

We could create another component and rename its `-background` option to `-textbackground` as well. If we did, then both of these components would be controlled by the master `-textbackground` option. We could even create a component and rename its `-foreground` option to `-textbackground`. Again, any change to a master option like `-textbackground` is propagated down to all of the component options that are tied to it, regardless of their original names.

When you rename an option, you need to specify three different names for the option: an option name for the `configure` command, along with a resource name,

```
itk_component add entry {
    entry $itk_interior.ent
} {
    rename -background -textbackground textBackground Background
    keep -foreground
    keep -cursor
    keep -borderwidth
}
```

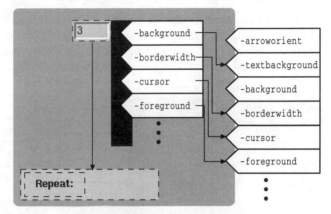

Figure 3-9: Renaming Component Options on the Master Option List

and a resource class for the options database. In Figure 3-9, we renamed the entry's
-background option, giving it the name -textbackground, the resource name
textBackground, and the resource class Background. Each of these names can
be used as follows.

We can use the option name to configure the entry part of a Spinint mega-widget
like this:

```
.s configure -textbackground white
```

We can use the resource name in the options database to give all of our Spinint
mega-widgets this value by default:

```
option add *Spinint.textBackground white
```

Instead of setting a specific resource like textBackground, we could set a more
general resource class like Background:

```
option add *Spinint.Background blue
```

This affects all of the options in class Background, including both the regular
-background option and the -textbackground option. In this case, we set
both background colors to blue.

"Usual" Configuration Options

If you have to write keep and rename statements for each component that you
create, it becomes a chore. You will find yourself typing the same statements again
and again. For a label component, you always keep the -background, -fore-
ground, -font, and -cursor options. For a button component, you keep these

same options, along with -activebackground, -activeforeground, and -disabledforeground.

Fortunately, the keep and rename statements are optional. If you don't include them, each widget class has a default set of keep and rename statements to fall back on. These defaults are included in the [INCR TK] library directory, and they are called the *usual option-handling code*. You can change the "usual" code or even add "usual" code for new widget classes, as we'll see later on.

You can ask for the "usual" options one of two ways, as shown in Figure 3-10. You can either include the usual command in the option-handling commands passed to itk_component, or you can leave off the option-handling commands entirely. As you can see, the second way makes your code look much simpler.

```
itk_component add label {
    label $itk_interior.lab
} {
    usual
}
```

or

```
itk_component.add label {
    label $itk_interior.lab
}
```

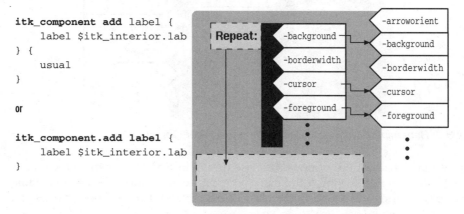

Figure 3-10: Adding a Component with the "Usual" Option-Handling Code

Having the usual command is useful if you want to have most of the "usual" options, but with a few changes. For example, suppose we are adding the entry component to a Spinint. We can get all of the "usual" options, but then override how the -background option is handled. We can rename the -background option to -textbackground like this:

```
itk_component add entry {
    entry $itk_interior.ent
} {
    usual
    rename -background -textbackground textBackground Background
}
```

This is much better than the code shown in Figure 3-9. There are many entry widget options like -insertbackground and -selectbackground that we had ignored earlier. The "usual" code for an entry handles these properly, without any extra work.

Ignoring Configuration Options

In addition to the keep, rename, and usual commands, you can also ask for certain options to be ignored using the ignore command. In most cases, this is not really needed. If you include any option-handling code at all, it will start by assuming that all options are ignored unless you explicitly keep or rename them. But the ignore command is useful when you want to override something in the "usual" code.

Suppose the "usual" option-handling code keeps an option like -foreground, and you really want that option to be ignored for a particular component. You can use the usual command to bring in the "usual" code, and then ignore a particular option like this:

```
itk_component add entry {
    entry $itk_interior.ent
} {
    usual
    ignore -foreground
}
```

Setting Widget Defaults

As we saw earlier, you can establish a default value for any mega-widget option using the options database. For example, suppose we are creating an application, and we set the following resources:

```
option add *Spinint.background blue
option add *Spinint.textBackground white
```

The *Spinint part says that these values apply to all Spinint widgets in the application, regardless of their name or where they appear in the window hierarchy. The .background and .textBackground parts access specific resources on each Spinint widget.

Remember, a master option like -background may be tied to many component widgets that kept or renamed that option. In this case, the -background option of a Spinint is tied to the -background option of the hull, label, up, and down components. The default value for the Spinint background is automatically propagated down to each of these components.

As a mega-widget designer, it is your responsibility to make sure that all of the options in your mega-widget have good default values. It's a good idea to include settings like these just above each mega-widget class:

```
option add *Spinint.textBackground white widgetDefault
option add *Spinint.range "0 100" widgetDefault
option add *Spinint.arrowOrient horizontal widgetDefault
option add *Spinint.labelPos nw widgetDefault
```

All of these settings are given the lowest priority widgetDefault, so that you can override them later on. You might add other option statements to customize a particular application. On Unix platforms, the user might add similar resource settings to a .Xdefaults or .Xresources file.

If you don't provide a default value for an option, then its initial value is taken from the component that first created the option. For example, we did not include a default value for the background resource in the preceding statements. If there is no other setting for `background` in the application, then the default value will be taken from the `hull` component, which was the first to keep the `-background` option. The hull is a frame, and its default background is probably gray, so the default background for the Spinint will also be gray. Many times, the default values that come from components work quite well. But when they do not, you should set the default explicitly with an `option` statement.

Simple Example

Now that we understand how the components fit into a mega-widget, we can see how everything works in a real example. In the previous chapter, we saw how [INCR TCL] classes could be used to build a file browser. We wrote classes to handle the file tree and its visual representation. We even wrote a few procedures so that we could install a file tree on any canvas widget.

Now we can take this idea one step further. Instead of grafting our file tree onto an external canvas, we can wrap the canvas and the file tree code into a Fileviewer mega-widget. When we are done, we will be able to create a Fileviewer like this:

```
Fileviewer .viewer -background LightSlateBlue -troughcolor NavyBlue
pack .viewer -expand yes -fill both -pady 4 -pady 4
```

and have it display a file tree like this:

```
.viewer display /usr/local/lib
```

This will create a widget that looks like the one shown in Figure 3-11. It has a canvas to display the file tree, and a built-in scrollbar to handle scrolling. If you click on a file or a folder, it becomes selected with a gray rectangle. If you double-click on a folder, it expands or collapses the file hierarchy beneath it.

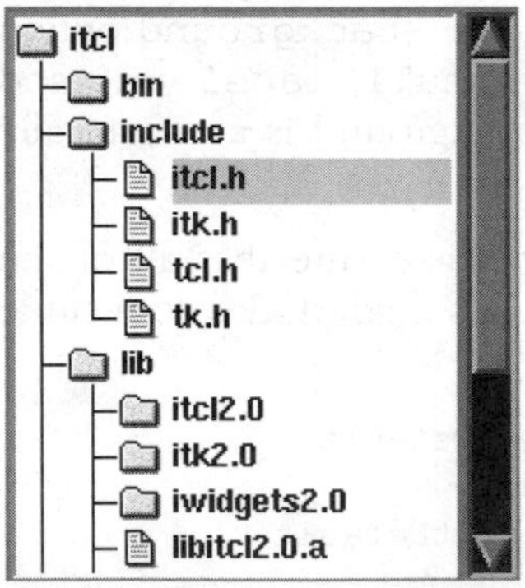

Figure 3-11: Fileviewer Mega-Widget

Now, we'll write the `Fileviewer` class.

Fileviewer Construction

A complete code example appears in the file *itcl/itk/fileviewer1.itk*, but the `Fileviewer` class itself is shown below in Example 3-1.

Example 3-1: Class Definition for the Fileviewer Mega-Widget

```
option add *Fileviewer.width 2i widgetDefault
option add *Fileviewer.height 3i widgetDefault

class Fileviewer {
  inherit itk::Widget

  constructor {args} {
    itk_component add scrollbar {
      scrollbar $itk_interior.sbar -orient vertical \
        -command [code $itk_interior.canv yview]
    }
    pack $itk_component(scrollbar) -side right -fill y

    itk_component add display {
      canvas $itk_interior.canv -borderwidth 2 \
        -relief sunken -background white \
        -yscrollcommand [code $itk_interior.sbar set]
    } {
      keep -cursor -height -width
      keep -highlightcolor -highlightthickness
      rename -highlightbackground -background background Background
    }
    pack $itk_component(display) -side left -expand yes -fill both

    eval itk_initialize $args
  }

  private variable root ""

  public method display {dir}

  private method createNode {dir}
  private proc cmpTree {option obj1 obj2}
}
```

We start off by inheriting the basic mega-widget behavior from itk::Widget. This means that the Fileviewer will be the kind of widget that sits inside of another top-level window, so we can use a Fileviewer component in many different styles of file selection dialogs.

In the constructor, we create the components within each Fileviewer, and pack them into the hull. We create a scrollbar component named scrollbar like this:

```
itk_component add scrollbar {
  scrollbar $itk_interior.sbar -orient vertical \
    -command [code $itk_interior.canv yview]
}
```

As we saw in Figure 3-6, we use $itk_interior as the root of the component widget name. If we create a Fileviewer mega-widget named .fv, then $itk_interior will also be .fv, and the scrollbar will be named .fv.sbar.

Since we didn't include any `keep` or `rename` statements, we will get the "usual" option-handling code for scrollbars. This automatically adds options like `-back-ground` and `-troughcolor` to the master options for a Fileviewer. The "usual" code ignores options like `-orient` and `-command` that are probably unique to each scrollbar component. We really don't want anyone using a Fileviewer to change these options. We just set them once and for all when the scrollbar is first created.

Notice that we used the `code` command to wrap up the code for the `-command` option. This isn't absolutely necessary, but it is a good idea for the reasons that we discussed in the previous chapter. If you do something like this:

```
itk_component add scrollbar {
    scrollbar $itk_interior.sbar -orient vertical \
        -command "$itk_interior.canv yview"
}
```

it will still work, but the scrollbar command will take longer to execute. Each time it tries to talk to the canvas widget, it will start looking for it in the global namespace. Since the canvas is created in the Fileviewer constructor, its access command is buried inside of the Fileviewer namespace, and it will take a little longer to find.* The `code` command wraps up the scrollbar command so that when it is needed later on, it will be executed right in the Fileviewer namespace, so the canvas will be found immediately. Whenever you are configuring a component widget, you should always use a `code` command to wrap up code fragments for options like `-command` or `-yscrollcommand`. Likewise, you should also use a `scope` command to wrap up variable names for options like `-variable`.

Once the scrollbar has been created, we can use its symbolic name in the `itk_component` array to refer to it later on. For example, we pack the scrollbar like this:

```
pack $itk_component(scrollbar) -side right -fill y
```

We create a canvas component called display in a similar manner. But instead of getting the "usual" configuration options, we include explicit `keep` and `rename` statements to merge its options into the master list:

```
itk_component add display {
    canvas $itk_interior.canv -borderwidth 2 \
        -relief sunken -background white \
        -yscrollcommand [code $itk_interior.sbar set]
} {
    keep -cursor -height -width
    keep -highlightcolor -highlightthickness
    rename -highlightbackground -background background Background
}
```

You can list all of the options in a single `keep` statement, or you can include lots of different `keep` statements. In this case, we used two different `keep` statements to make the code more readable. We did not keep the `-background`, `-borderwidth`,

---

* If this were an ordinary object, it wouldn't be found at all. But there is some special code in the Tcl unknown proc that finds widgets no matter where they are in the namespace hierarchy.

or `-relief` options. We simply fix their values when the canvas is created. If you configure the `-background` option of a Fileviewer, the rest of the widget will change, but the canvas background is not tied in, so it will always remain white.

Notice that we renamed the `-highlightbackground` option to `-background`. Whenever we configure the master `-background` option, the `-highlight-background` option on the canvas component will be updated as well. If you don't do this, you will see a problem as soon as you change the master `-back-ground` option. Most of the background will change, but the focus highlight rings inside the mega-widget will remain a different color. This rename trick fixes the problem. It is such a good trick that it is part of the "usual" option-handling code that you normally get by default.

Fileviewer Methods

The `Fileviewer` class in Example 3-1 has one public method. If we have created a Fileviewer named `.viewer`, we can tell it to display a certain directory by calling the `display` method:

```
.viewer display /home/mmc
```

The `createNode` method and the `cmpTree` proc are there only to help the `display` method, so we make them private. We'll see how they are used in a moment.

A Fileviewer mega-widget works just like the file browser that we created in Example 2-14. If you have forgotten all about `VisualFileTree` objects and how we built the file browser, you should take a moment to remind yourself.

The implementation for the `Fileviewer::display` method is shown in Example 3-2.

Example 3-2: Implementation for the Fileviewer::display Method

```
body Fileviewer::display {dir} {
    if {$root != ""} {
        delete object $root
    }
    set root [createNode $dir]
    $root configure -state open
    $root refresh
}
```

Each Fileviewer maintains a tree of `VisualFileTree` objects that represent the files on its display. We use the private `root` variable to store the name of the root object for the tree. Whenever we call the `display` method, we destroy the existing file tree by destroying the root node, and then we start a new file tree by creating a new root node. We configure the root node to the "open" state, so that when it draws itself, it will display other files and folders below it. Finally, we tell the root node to refresh itself, and it draws the entire file tree onto the canvas.

Whenever we need to create a `VisualFileTree` node for the `Fileviewer`, we call the `createNode` method, giving it the name of the file that we want to represent. The implementation of this method is shown in Example 3-3.

Example 3-3: Implementation for the Fileviewer::createNode Method

```
body Fileviewer::createNode {fname} {
    set obj [VisualFileTree ::#auto $fname $itk_component(display)]

    $obj configure -name $fname \
        -sort [code cmpTree -name] \
        -procreate [code $this createNode]

    if {[file isdirectory $fname]} {
        $obj configure -icon dirIcon
    } elseif {[file executable $fname]} {
        $obj configure -icon programIcon
    } else {
        $obj configure -icon fileIcon
    }
    $obj configure -title [file tail $fname]

    return $obj
}
```

We start by creating a `VisualFileTree` object. Remember, its constructor demands two arguments: the file that it represents, and the canvas that will display it. We use the `display` component that we created for this `Fileviewer` as the display canvas. We get the real window path name for this component from the `itk_component` array, and we pass it into the `VisualFileTree` constructor. We create the `VisualFileTree` object with the name `::#auto` so we will get an automatically generated name like `::visualFileTree12`. As I discussed earlier in the section "Using Objects Outside of Their Namespace" in Chapter 2, this puts the object in the global namespace, so we can share it with other classes like `Tree` that will need to access it.

We configure the `-name` and `-sort` options so that all files will be sorted alphabetically by name. We use the `Fileviewer::cmpTree` procedure as the comparison function for `lsort`. If we were calling this procedure right now in the context of `Fileviewer`, we could use a simple command like `cmpTree`. But we are giving this command to a completely separate `VisualFileTree` object, and it will be used later in the `Tree::reorder` method. In that context, there is no command called `cmpTree`. Therefore, we cannot use a simple command like `cmpTree -name`. We must wrap it up with the `code` command like `[code cmpTree -name]`. Roughly translated, this means that the `Fileviewer` is telling the `VisualFileTree` object: "When you need to compare two `VisualFileTree` objects later on, come back to the current (`Fileviewer`) context and call the `cmpTree` procedure. Since we're friends, I'm giving you access to my namespace and letting you use my private procedure."

We also configure the `-procreate` option so that all child `VisualFileTree` nodes are created by the `Fileviewer::createNode` method. Remember, we start with a single root node and build the file tree gradually, as needed. When you double-click on a folder in the display, you open it and ask it to display its contents. If it hasn't already done so, the `VisualFileTree` object will scan the file system at that point, and automatically create child nodes for the files within it.

Whatever command we give for the `-procreate` option will be executed by the `VisualFileTree` object in a completely different context. Again, we must be careful to use the `code` command. But in this case, `createNode` is not just a procedure, it is a method, so we must do something extra. We use the command `[code $this createNode]`. Roughly translated, the `Fileviewer` is telling the `VisualFileTree` object: "When you need to create a node later on, talk to me. My name is `$this`, and you can use my `createNode` method. This is usually a private method, but since we're friends, I'm letting you back in to the current (`Fileviewer`) namespace, and you can access `createNode` from there."

Near the end of the `createNode` method, we configure the `VisualFileTree` object to display the file name and an icon that indicates whether the file is a directory, a program, or an ordinary file. When we are done configuring the object, we return its name as the result of the `createNode` method.

Each node uses the `Fileviewer::cmpTree` procedure when sorting its child nodes. This is a standard `lsort`-style procedure. It takes the names of two `VisualFileTree` objects, compares them, and returns +1 if the first goes after the second, -1 if the first goes before the second, and 0 if the order does not matter. The implementation of the `cmpTree` procedure is shown in Example 3-4.

Example 3-4: Implementation for the Fileviewer::cmpTree Procedure

```
body Fileviewer::cmpTree {option obj1 obj2} {
    set val1 [$obj1 cget $option]
    set val2 [$obj2 cget $option]
    if {$val1 < $val2} {
        return -1
    } elseif {$val1 > $val2} {
        return 1
    }
    return 0
}
```

We have made this procedure general enough that we can use it to sort based on any option of the `VisualFileTree` object. If we want an alphabetical listing, we use `-name` for the `option` argument.* If we want to sort based on file size, we use `-value` for the `option` argument, and we set the `-value` option to the file size when each `VisualFileTree` object is created.

Fileviewer Creation Command

You create a Fileviewer widget like any other [INCR TCL] object—by using the class name as a command:

```
Fileviewer .viewer -background tan
```

Unfortunately, all of the other Tk widget commands have lowercase letters. If we want to follow the Tk convention, we should really have a command called `fileviewer` to create a Fileviewer widget.

---

* This is what we did in the `createNode` procedure shown above.

You might wonder: Why not just change the class name to `fileviewer`? We could do this, but Tk has a convention that all widget class names start with a capital letter. You should follow this same convention in [INCR TK]. If you don't, you'll have trouble accessing defaults in the options database, and you'll have trouble with class bindings.

We simply need to add a `fileviewer` procedure that acts as an alias to the real `Fileviewer` command, like this:

```
proc fileviewer {pathName args} {
    uplevel Fileviewer $pathName $args
}
```

This procedure takes a window path name and any option settings, and passes them along to the `Fileviewer` command. Notice that `pathName` is a required argument, so if you forget to specify a window path name, you'll get an error. We use the `uplevel` command so that the widget is created in the context of the caller. After all, the caller wants ownership of whatever widget we create. If we didn't do this, the widget would be created in the namespace that contains the `fileviewer` proc, and in some cases,* this can cause problems.

Defining New Configuration Options

So far, all of the configuration options for a mega-widget like Fileviewer have been added by keeping or renaming options from its component widgets. But what if you want to add a brand-new option that doesn't belong to any of the components?

For example, suppose we want to add a `-selectcommand` option to the `Fileviewer`. This is something like the `-command` option for a Tk button. It lets you configure each `Fileviewer` to do something special whenever you select a node in its file tree.

As a trivial example, we could create a `Fileviewer` that prints out a message when each file is selected, like this:

```
fileviewer .fv -selectcommand {puts "selected file: %n"}
pack .fv
```

We will set things up so that any `%n` fields in the command string will be replaced with the name of the selected file. This mimics the Tk `bind` command, and it makes it easy to know which file was selected whenever the command is executed.

Having this feature opens the door for more interesting applications. We might use it to create an image browser for a drawing program. Whenever you click on a file in a recognized image format like gif, tiff, or jpeg, the selection command could load a thumbnail image that you could preview before clicking *OK*.

The `-selectcommand` option is not kept or renamed from a component widget. It is a brand-new option that we are adding to the `Fileviewer` class itself. If this were an ordinary [INCR TCL] class, we would add a configuration option by defining

---

* Suppose we put the `fileviewer` proc in a namespace called `utilities`. Without the `uplevel` command, the `Fileviewer` widgets that it creates would have their access commands added to the `utilities` namespace. This would make it harder to access these widgets, and therefore slow down the application.

a public variable. You can do this for a mega-widget too, but if you do, the option won't be tied into the options database properly. Remember, public variables have one name, but each widget option has three names: an option name, a resource name, and a resource class.

Instead, when you define an option in a mega-widget class, you should use the `itk_option define` command with the syntax shown in Figure 3-12. Believe it or not, this looks a lot like a public variable declaration. It includes the three names for the option, an initial value, and some code that should be executed whenever the option is configured. Like a public variable, the configuration code is optional, and you can specify it outside of the class definition using a `configbody` command.

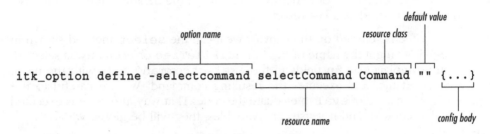

Figure 3-12: Syntax of the itk_option define Command

We can add the `-selectcommand` option to the `Fileviewer` class as shown in Example 3-5. You can find the complete code example in the file *itcl/itk/fileviewer2.itk*. We have also added a `select` method to the `Fileviewer` class. We'll see in a moment how the `-selectcommand` option and the `select` method work together.

Example 3-5: Adding the -selectcommand Option to the Fileviewer Mega-Widget

```
class Fileviewer {
    inherit itk::Widget

    constructor {args} {
        ...
    }

    itk_option define -selectcommand selectCommand Command ""

    private variable root ""

    public method display {dir}
    public method select {node}

    private method createNode {dir}
    private proc cmpTree {option obj1 obj2}
}

...
```

```
body Fileviewer::select {node} {
    set name [$node cget -name]
    regsub -all {%n} $itk_option(-selectcommand) $name cmd
    uplevel #0 $cmd
}
```

Notice that the `itk_option define` statement appears outside of the constructor, at the level of the class definition. Again, think of it as a public variable declaration. It defines something about the class.

The `-selectcommand` option has the resource name `selectCommand` and the resource class `Command` in the options database. Whenever a Fileviewer widget is created, the options database is used to determine the initial value for this option. If a value cannot be found for either of these names, the default value (in this case, the null string) is used as a last resort.

Whenever a file is selected on the canvas, we'll call the `select` method shown in Example 3-5, giving it the name of the `VisualFileTree` object that was selected. This method replaces all `%n` fields in the `-selectcommand` code with the name of the selected file, and executes the resulting command. We are careful to use `uplevel #0` instead of `eval` to evaluate the code. That way, the code is executed in the global context, and if it uses any variables, they will be global variables.

You might wonder how we know when a file has been selected. As you will recall from Example 2-14, each `VisualFileTree` object has its own `-selectcommand` option that is executed whenever a file is selected. We simply tell each `Visual-FileTree` node to call the `Fileviewer::select` method when a node is selected. We do this when each `VisualFileTree` node is created, as shown in Example 3-6.

Example 3-6: VisualFileTree Nodes Notify the Fileviewer of Any Selections

```
body Fileviewer::createNode {fname} {
    set obj [VisualFileTree ::#auto $fname $itk_component(display)]

    $obj configure -name $fname \
        -sort [code cmpTree -name] \
        -procreate [code $this createNode] \
        -selectcommand [code $this select %o]
    ...
}
```

When you click on a file, the entire chain of events unfolds like this. Your click triggers a binding associated with the file, which causes the `VisualFileTree` object to execute its `-selectcommand` option. This, in turn, calls the `select` method of the Fileviewer, which executes its own `-selectcommand` option. In effect, we have used the primitive `-selectcommand` on each `VisualFileTree` object to support a high-level `-selectcommand` for the entire `Fileviewer`.

As another example of a brand-new option, suppose we add a `-scrollbar` option to the `Fileviewer`, to control the scrollbar. This option might have three values. If it is `on`, the scrollbar is visible. If it is `off`, the scrollbar is hidden. If it is `auto`, the scrollbar appears automatically whenever the file tree is too long to fit on the canvas.

Example 3-7 shows the `Fileviewer` class with a `-scrollbar` option. You can find a complete code example in the file *itcl/itk/fileviewer3.itk*.

Example 3-7: Adding the -scrollbar option to the Fileviewer Mega-Widget

```
class Fileviewer {
    inherit itk::Widget

    constructor {args} {
        ...
    }

    itk_option define -selectcommand selectCommand Command ""

    itk_option define -scrollbar scrollbar Scrollbar "on" {
        switch -- $itk_option(-scrollbar) {
            on - off - auto {
                fixScrollbar
            }
            default {
                error "bad value \"$itk_option(-scollbar)\""
            }
        }
    }

    private variable root ""

    public method display {dir}
    public method select {node}

    private method createNode {dir}
    private proc cmpTree {option obj1 obj2}

    private method fixScrollbar {args}
    private variable sbvisible 1
}
```

In this case, we have added some configuration code after the default on value. Whenever the `configure` method modifies this option, it will execute this bit of code to check the new value and bring the widget up to date. In this case, we check the value of the `-scrollbar` option to make sure that it is on or off or auto. You can always find the current value for a configuration option in the `itk_option` array. If the value looks good, we use the `fixScrollbar` method to update the scrollbar accordingly. If it does not have one of the allowed values, we signal an error, and the `configure` method sets the option back to its previous value, and then aborts with an error.

We must also call `fixScrollbar` whenever any conditions change that might affect the scrollbar. Suppose the scrollbar is in auto mode. If we shorten the widget, we might need to put up the scrollbar. If we lengthen the widget, we might need to take it down. If we double-click on a file and expand or collapse the file tree, again, we might need to fix the scrollbar. All of these conditions trigger a change in the view associated with the canvas. To handle them, we must make sure that `fixScrollbar` gets called whenever the view changes. We do this by hijacking the normal communication between the canvas and the scrollbar, as shown in Example 3-8.

Example 3-8: Using fixScrollbar to Handle Changes in the Canvas View

```
class Fileviewer {
    inherit itk::Widget

    constructor {args} {
        ...
        itk_component add display {
            canvas $itk_interior.canv -borderwidth 2 \
                -relief sunken -background white \
                -yscrollcommand [code $this fixScrollbar]
        } {
            ...
        }
        pack $itk_component(display) -side left -expand yes -fill both
        eval itk_initialize $args
    }
    ...
}
```

Each time the view changes, the canvas calls its `-yscrollcommand` to notify the scrollbar. In this case, it calls our `fixScrollbar` method instead, which checks to see if the scrollbar should be visible, and updates it accordingly. The `fixScroll-bar` method then passes any arguments through to the scrollbar, so the normal canvas/scrollbar communication is not interrupted.

The `fixScrollbar` method is implemented as shown in Example 3-9.

Example 3-9: Implementation for the Fileviewer::fixScrollbar Method

```
body Fileviewer::fixScrollbar {args} {
    switch $itk_option(-scrollbar) {
        on  { set sbstate 1 }
        off { set sbstate 0 }

        auto {
            if {[$itk_component(display) yview] == "0 1"} {
                set sbstate 0
            } else {
                set sbstate 1
            }
        }
    }
    if {$sbstate != $sbvisible} {
        if {$sbstate} {
            pack $itk_component(scrollbar) -side right -fill y
        } else {
            pack forget $itk_component(scrollbar)
```

```
            }
            set sbvisible $sbstate
        }

        if {$args != ""} {
            eval $itk_component(scrollbar) set $args
        }
    }
```

First, we check the `-scrollbar` option and determine whether or not the scroll-bar should be visible, saving the result in the variable `sbstate`. If the scrollbar is `on` or `off`, the answer is obvious. But if it is `auto`, we must check the current view on the `display` canvas. If the entire canvas is visible, then the view is `0 1`, and the scrollbar is not needed.

We then consult the `sbvisible` variable defined in Example 3-7 to see if the scrollbar is currently visible. If the scrollbar needs to be put up, it is packed into the hull. If it needs to be taken down, then the `pack forget` command is used to unpack it.

Finally, we pass any extra arguments on to the `set` method of the scrollbar component. Normally, there are no arguments, and this does nothing. But having this feature lets the `fixScrollbar` method be used as the `-yscrollcommand` for the canvas, without disrupting the normal communication between the canvas and the scrollbar.

Defining "Usual" Options

When you add a component to a mega-widget, you must keep, rename, or ignore its configuration options. As we saw earlier, each of the Tk widget classes has a default set of `keep` and `rename` statements to handle its configuration options in the "usual" manner. There is even a `usual` statement to request the "usual" option-handling code.

But what happens if you use a mega-widget as a component of a larger mega-widget? What if you use a `Fileviewer` as a component within a larger Fileconfirm mega-widget? Again, you must keep, rename, or ignore the configuration options for the `Fileviewer` component. And what if someone asks for the "usual" option-handling code for a `Fileviewer` component? It is your job as the mega-widget designer to provide this.

The option-handling commands for a new widget class are defined with a `usual` declaration, like the one shown in Example 3-10.

Example 3-10: Defining the "Usual" Options for a Fileviewer Component

```
option add *Fileviewer.width 2i widgetDefault
option add *Fileviewer.height 3i widgetDefault
option add *Fileviewer.scrollbar auto widgetDefault

class Fileviewer {
    ...
}
```

```
usual Fileviewer {
    keep -activebackground -activerelief
    keep -background -cursor
    keep -highlightcolor -highlightthickness
    keep -troughcolor
}

proc fileviewer {pathName args} {
    uplevel Fileviewer $pathName $args
}
```

Here, the `keep` commands refer to the overall options for a Fileviewer mega-widget. Suppose you use a `Fileviewer` as a component in a Fileconfirm mega-widget, and you ask for the "usual" options. Each of the options shown above would be kept in the `Fileconfirm` option list. For example, if you set the master -background option on a `Fileconfirm`, it would propagate the change to the -background option of its `Fileviewer` component, which in turn would propagate the change to the -background option on its scrollbar and the -highlightbackground option on its canvas.

It is best to write the "usual" declaration at the last moment, after you have put the finishing touches on a mega-widget class. You simply examine the master configuration options one by one, and decide if they should be kept, renamed, or ignored.

Only the most generic options should be kept or renamed in the "usual" declaration for a widget class. If we had two `Fileviewer` components within a Fileconfirm mega-widget, both of them might be tied to the `Fileconfirm` option list in the "usual" way. Which options should they have in common? Options like -background, -foreground, -cursor, and -font are all good candidates for the `keep` command. On the other hand, options like -text, -bitmap, and -command are usually unique to each component, so options like these should be ignored.

Inheritance and Composition

Mega-widgets can be used to build even larger mega-widgets. Like the Tk widgets, mega-widgets support composition. One mega-widget can be used as a component within another. But mega-widgets also support inheritance. One mega-widget class can inherit all of the characteristics of another, and add its own specializations. You are no longer limited to what a class like `Fileviewer` provides. You can derive another class from it and add your own enhancements. So a mega-widget toolkit can be extended in a way that transcends the standard Tk widgets.

In this section, we explore how inheritance and composition can be used to build mega-widgets. These relationships become even more powerful when combined.

Designing a Base Class

Suppose we plan to build many different kinds of confirmation windows. We may build a Messageconfirm mega-widget, which prompts the user with a question and requests a *Yes/No* or *OK/Cancel* response. We may build a Fileconfirm mega-widget, which gives the user a file browser to select a file, and requests a *Load/Cancel* or *Save/Cancel* response.

Both of these mega-widgets have a common abstraction. They pop up in their own top-level window, they have *OK/Cancel* buttons at the bottom, and they prevent the application from continuing until the user has responded. When mega-widgets share a common abstraction like this, we can design a mega-widget base class to handle it. In this case, we will create a base class called `Confirm` which provides the basic functionality for a confirmation dialog.

A Confirm mega-widget looks like the one shown in Figure 3-13. It has an empty area called the "contents" frame at the top, which can be filled in with messages, file browsers, or whatever information is being confirmed. A separator line sits between this frame and the *OK* and *Cancel* buttons at the bottom of the dialog. This dialog always pops up on the center of the desktop, and it locks out the rest of the application until the user has pressed either *OK* or *Cancel*.

Figure 3-13: Generic Confirm Mega-Widget

The class definition for a Confirm mega-widget is shown in Example 3-11. A complete code example appears in the file *itcl/itk/confirm.itk*.

Example 3-11: The Class Definition for a Confirm Mega-Widget

```
class Confirm {
  inherit itk::Toplevel

  constructor {args} {
    itk_component add contents {
      frame $itk_interior.contents
    }
    pack $itk_component(contents) -expand yes -fill both -padx 4 -pady 4

    itk_component add separator {
      frame $itk_interior.sep -height 2 \
        -borderwidth 1 -relief sunken
    }
    pack $itk_component(separator) -fill x -padx 8

    private itk_component add controls {
      frame $itk_interior.cntl
    }
    pack $itk_component(controls) -fill x -padx 4 -pady 8

    itk_component add ok {
      button $itk_component(controls).ok -text "OK" \
```

```
      -command [code $this dismiss 1]
  }
  pack $itk_component(ok) -side left -expand yes

  itk_component add cancel {
    button $itk_component(controls).cancel -text "Cancel" \
      -command [code $this dismiss 0]
  }
  pack $itk_component(cancel) -side left -expand yes

  wm withdraw $itk_component(hull)
  wm group $itk_component(hull) .
  wm protocol $itk_component(hull) \
    WM_DELETE_WINDOW [code $this dismiss]

  after idle [code $this centerOnScreen]
  set itk_interior $itk_component(contents)

  eval itk_initialize $args
}

private common responses

public method confirm {}
public method dismiss {{choice 0}}

protected method centerOnScreen {}
}
```

The Confirm class inherits from the itk::Toplevel base class, so each Confirm widget pops up with its own top-level window. We create a frame component called contents to represent the "contents" area at the top of the window. We use another frame component called separator to act as a separator line, and we add two button components called ok and cancel at the bottom of the window. Note that the ok and cancel components sit inside of a frame component called controls. This frame was added simply to help with packing.

When you have a component like controls that is not an important part of the mega-widget, you can keep it hidden. You simply include a protected or private declaration in front of the itk_component command. This is the same protected or private command that you would normally use in a namespace to restrict access to a variable or procedure. It simply executes whatever command you give it, and it sets the protection level of any commands or variables created along the way. When a mega-widget component is marked as protected or private, it can be used freely within the mega-widget class, but it cannot be accessed through the built-in component method by anyone outside of the class.

Once we have created all of the components, we do a few other things to initialize the Confirm widget. Since this is a top-level widget, we use the wm command to tell the window manager how it should handle this window. We ask the window manager to withdraw the window, so that it will be invisible until it is needed. We group it with the main window of the application. Some window managers use the group to iconify related windows when the main application window is iconified. We also set the "delete" protocol, so that if the window manager tries to delete the window, it will simply invoke the `dismiss` method, as if the user had pressed the *Cancel* button.

In all of these commands, we are talking to the window manager about a specific top-level window—the one that contains our Confirm mega-widget. Remember, the container for any mega-widget is a component called the `hull`, which in this case is created automatically by the `itk::Toplevel` base class. The window manager won't understand a symbolic component name like `hull`, so we give it the real window path name stored in `itk_component(hull)`.

When the Confirm mega-widget appears, we want it to be centered on the desktop. We have a method called `centerOnScreen` that determines the overall size of the dialog, and uses the `wm geometry` command to position it on the desktop. You can find the implementation of this method in the file *itcl/itk/confirm.itk*. The details are not particularly important. We should call this method once, when the widget is first created. But we can't call it directly in the constructor. At this point, we haven't finished building the `Confirm` dialog. As we'll see shortly, more widgets need to be created and packed into the "contents" frame. If we call `centerOnScreen` too early, the dialog will be centered based on its current size, and when more widgets are added, it will appear to be off-center.

This situation arises from time to time—you want something to happen *after* construction is complete. You can handle this quite easily with the Tk `after` command. Normally, you give `after` a command and a certain time interval, and the command is executed after that much time has elapsed. In this case, we don't care exactly when `centerOnScreen` is called, so instead of using a specific time interval, we use the key word `idle`. This tells `after` to execute the command at the first opportunity when the application is idle and has nothing better to do. Again, since the `centerOnScreen` method will be called in another context, long after we have returned from the constructor, we are careful to include the object name `$this`, and to wrap the code fragment with the `code` command.

As always, we finish the construction by calling `itk_initialize` to initialize the master option list and apply any option settings.

A Confirm widget can be created and packed with a label like this:

```
confirm .ask
set win [.ask component contents]
label $win.message -text "Do you really want to do this?"
pack $win.message
```

Although we did not explicitly create options for the labels on the *OK/Cancel* buttons, we can still change them like this:

```
.ask component ok configure -text "Yes"
.ask component cancel configure -text "No"
```

Sometimes it is better to access individual components like this, instead of adding more options to the master option list. If a mega-widget has too many options, it is difficult to learn and its performance suffers.

Whenever a confirmation is needed, the `confirm` method can be used like this:

```
if {[.ask confirm]} {
    puts "go ahead"
} else {
    puts "abort!"
}
```

The `confirm` method pops up the `Confirm` window, waits for the user's response, and returns 1 for *OK* and 0 for *Cancel*. The `if` statement checks the result and prints an appropriate message.

The `confirm` method is implemented as shown in Example 3-12.

Example 3-12: Implementation for the Confirm::confirm Method

```
body Confirm::confirm {} {
    wm deiconify $itk_component(hull)
    grab set $itk_component(hull)
    focus $itk_component(ok)

    tkwait variable [scope responses($this)]

    grab release $itk_component(hull)
    wm withdraw $itk_component(hull)

    return $responses($this)
}
```

First, we ask the window manager to pop up the window using the `wm deiconify` command, and we set a grab on the window. At this point, all other windows in the application will be unresponsive, and the user is forced to respond by pressing either *OK* or *Cancel*. The default focus is assigned to the *OK* button, so the user can simply press the space bar to select *OK*.

The `tkwait` command stops the normal flow of execution until the user has responded. In this case, we watch a particular variable that will change as soon as the user presses either *OK* or *Cancel*. Each Confirm widget should have its own variable for `tkwait`. Normally, we would use an object variable for something like this, but there is no way to pass an object variable to a command like `tkwait`. The `scope` operator will capture the namespace context for a variable, but not the object context. So the `scope` command works fine for common class variables, but not for object variables. We can use the following trick to get around this problem: We define a common array called `responses`, and we assign each widget a slot with its name `$this`. As long as we wrap each slot `responses($this)` in the `scope` command, we have no trouble passing it along to `tkwait`.

Thanks to the `-command` option of the `ok` and `cancel` components, pressing *OK* invokes the `dismiss` method with the value 1, and pressing *Cancel* invokes the

Chapter 3: Building Mega-Widgets with [INCR TK]

`dismiss` method with the value 0. The `dismiss` method itself is quite trivial. Its body is shown in Example 3-13.

Example 3-13: Implementation for the Confirm::dismiss Method

```
body Confirm::dismiss {{choice 0}} {
    set responses($this) $choice
}
```

It simply stores whatever value you give it in the `responses` array. But if we're sitting at the `tkwait` instruction in the `confirm` method, this is just what we're looking for. Setting this variable causes `tkwait` to return control, and execution resumes within the `confirm` method. We release the grab, hide the dialog, and return the user's response.

The Confirm mega-widget is useful in its own right, but it can be even more useful as the basis of other mega-widget classes. Derived classes like `Messageconfirm` and `Fileconfirm` can inherit most of the basic functionality, and simply add a few components into the `contents` frame.

But how do derived classes know that they are supposed to use the `contents` frame? We use the variable `itk_interior` to track this. In the `itk::Widget` or `itk::Toplevel` base class, `itk_interior` is set to the window path name of the `hull` component. In the `Confirm` base class, we create components in this interior, and then change `itk_interior` to the window path name of the `contents` frame. Derived classes create components in this interior, and perhaps change `itk_interior` to their own innermost window. If all classes use `itk_interior` like this, making classes work together becomes a simple matter of changing their `inherit` statements.

Using Inheritance

We can continue with the example just described, using inheritance to create a Messageconfirm mega-widget like the one shown in Figure 3-14. A `Messageconfirm` *is-a* Confirm, but it has an icon and a text message in the `contents` frame.

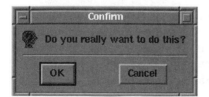

Figure 3-14: A Messageconfirm Mega-Widget

The class definition for Messageconfirm is shown in Example 3-14. A complete code example appears in the file *itcl/itk/messageconfirm.itk*.

Example 3-14: Class Definition for a Messageconfirm Mega-Widget

```
class Messageconfirm {
    inherit Confirm
```

```
constructor {args} {
    itk_component add icon {
        label $itk_interior.icon -bitmap questhead
    } {
        usual
        rename -bitmap -icon icon Bitmap
    }
    pack $itk_component(icon) -side left

    itk_component add message {
        label $itk_interior.mesg -wraplength 3i
    } {
        usual
        rename -text -message message Text
    }
    pack $itk_component(message) -side left -fill x

    eval itk_initialize $args
}
}
```

By inheriting from the Confirm class, Messageconfirm automatically has its own top-level window with a contents frame, a separator line, and *OK* and *Cancel* buttons. It has confirm and dismiss methods, and it automatically comes up centered on the desktop.

It has the same basic configuration options as well, but it does not inherit any default settings from the base class. If you have defined some resource settings for the Confirm class, like this:

```
option add *Confirm.background blue widgetDefault
option add *Confirm.foreground white widgetDefault
```

you will have to repeat those settings for the derived class:

```
option add *Messageconfirm.background blue widgetDefault
option add *Messageconfirm.foreground white widgetDefault
```

In its constructor, the Messageconfirm adds an icon component, which represents the bitmap icon to the left of the message. We use the usual command in the option-handling commands for this component to integrate most of its options in the "usual" manner, but we rename the -bitmap option, calling it -icon in the master list. This is a better name for the option, since it indicates which bitmap we are controlling.

The Messageconfirm also adds a message component, which represents the message label. Again, we use the usual command to integrate most of its options, but we rename the -text option, calling it -message in the master list.

As always, we create these two component widgets with the root name $itk_interior. But in this case, $itk_interior contains the name of the contents frame that we created in the constructor for base class Confirm. So these new components automatically sit inside of the `contents` frame, as explained earlier.

We might create a Messageconfirm widget like this:

```
messageconfirm .check -background tomato -icon warning \
    -message "Do you really want to do this?"
```

and use it like this:

```
if {[.check confirm]} {
    puts "go ahead"
} else {
    puts "abort!"
}
```

With a simple `inherit` statement and just a few lines of code, we have created a very useful widget.

Mixing Inheritance and Composition

Inheritance is a powerful technique, but so is composition. Many good designs use both relationships. For example, suppose we create a Fileconfirm mega-widget like the one shown in Figure 3-15. A `Fileconfirm` *is-a* `Confirm`, and *has-a* `Fileviewer` component packed into the `contents` frame. It also *has-a* entry component packed into the `contents` frame. When the user selects a file, its name is automatically loaded into the entry component. Of course, the user can also edit this name, or type an entirely different name into the entry component.

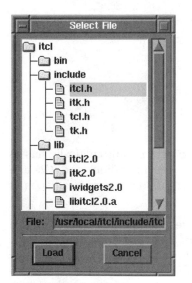

Figure 3-15: A Fileconfirm Mega-Widget

The class definition for Fileconfirm is shown in Example 3-15. A complete code example appears in the file *itcl/itk/fileconfirm.itk*.

Example 3-15: Class Definition for a Fileconfirm Mega-Widget

```
class Fileconfirm {
    inherit Confirm

    constructor {args} {
        itk_component add fileTree {
            fileviewer $itk_interior.files \
                -selectcommand [code $this select %n]
        }
        pack $itk_component(fileTree) -expand yes -fill both

        itk_component add fileLabel {
            label $itk_interior.flabel -text "File:"
        }
        pack $itk_component(fileLabel) -side left -padx 4

        itk_component add fileEntry {
            entry $itk_interior.fentry
        }
        pack $itk_component(fileEntry) -side left -expand yes -fill x

        eval itk_initialize $args
    }

    itk_option define -directory directory Directory "" {
        $itk_component(fileTree) display $itk_option(-directory)
    }

    public method get {} {
        return [$itk_component(fileEntry) get]
    }
    protected method select {name} {
        $itk_component(fileEntry) delete 0 end
        $itk_component(fileEntry) insert 0 $name
    }
}
```

Again, by inheriting from the `Confirm` class, `Fileconfirm` automatically has its own top-level window with a `contents` frame, a separator line, and *OK* and *Cancel* buttons. It has `confirm` and `dismiss` methods, and it automatically comes up centered on the desktop.

In its constructor, `Fileconfirm` adds a `Fileviewer` component. It also adds a *File:* label and an entry component at the bottom of the `contents` frame. These are three separate components, but they interact within the `Fileconfirm` in the following manner. When the user selects a file, the `Fileviewer` executes its `-selectcommand` code, which calls the `Fileconfirm::select` method with the selected file name substituted in place of `%n`. The `select` method then loads the file name into the entry component. Whatever name is sitting in the entry component is treated as the official file selection. At any point, you can use the `Fileconfirm::get` method to get the file name sitting in the entry component.

The -directory option controls the top-level directory in the Fileconfirm. Whenever it is configured, it automatically invokes the display method of the Fileviewer to update the display.

We might create a Fileconfirm widget like this:

```
fileconfirm .files -directory $env(HOME)
```

and use it like this:

```
if {[.files confirm]} {
    puts "selected file: [.files get]"
} else {
    puts "abort!"
}
```

We use the confirm method to pop up the dialog and wait for the user to select a file and press *OK* or *Cancel*. If he or she pressed *OK*, we use the get method to get the name of the selected file, and we print it out.

We leveraged the Confirm class with inheritance, and the Fileviewer class with composition. Together, these two techniques produce a complex widget with just a little extra code.

Reviving Options

Sometimes a derived class needs to override the way a base class handles its configuration options. For example, suppose we want to define the -width and -height options of a Fileviewer widget so that they represent the overall width and height, including the scrollbar. Previously, we kept the -width and -height options from the canvas component, so the overall width was a little bigger when the scrollbar was visible. Instead, we need to keep the -width and -height options from the hull component. But the hull component is created in the itk::Widget base class, and we can't modify that code.

Options that belong to a base class component can be revived in a derived class using the itk_option add command. You simply tell the mega-widget to add an option that was previously ignored back into the master list. A complete code example appears in the file *itcl/itk/fileviewer4.itk*, but the important parts are shown in Example 3-16.

Example 3-16: Options Can Be Revived Using itk_option add

```
option add *Fileviewer.width 2i widgetDefault
option add *Fileviewer.height 3i widgetDefault
option add *Fileviewer.scrollbar auto widgetDefault

class Fileviewer {
    inherit itk::Widget

    constructor {args} {
        itk_option add hull.width hull.height
        ...
        itk_component add display {
```

```
                    canvas $itk_interior.canv -borderwidth 2 \
                        -relief sunken -background white \
                        -yscrollcommand [code $this fixScrollbar] \
                        -width 1 -height 1
            } {
                keep -cursor
                keep -highlightcolor -highlightthickness
                rename -highlightbackground -background background \
                        Background
            }
            pack $itk_component(display) -side left -expand yes \
                -fill both

            eval itk_initialize $args

            pack propagate $itk_component(hull) 0
            bind $itk_component(display) <Configure> [code $this \
                    fixScrollbar]
        }
        ...
    }
```

The itk_option add command is different from the itk_option define command that we saw earlier. You use itk_option define as part of a class definition to define a new configuration option. On the other hand, you use itk_option add in the constructor (or in any other method) to reinstate a configuration option that already exists but was ignored by a base class. The itk_option add command can appear anywhere in the constructor, but it is normally included near the top. It should be called before itk_initialize, since options like -width and -height might appear on the args list.

Each option is referenced with a name like *component*.*option* if it comes from a component, or with a name like *class*::*option* if it comes from an itk_option define command. In either case, *option* is the option name without the leading - sign. In this example, we are reviving the -width and -height options of the hull component, so we use the names hull.width and hull.height. Fileviewer widgets will behave as if these options had been kept when the component was first created.

Now that we have reinstated the -width and -height options, we must make sure that they work. Frames normally shrink-wrap themselves around their contents, but we can use the pack propagate command to disable this, so the hull will retain whatever size is assigned to it. We also set the width and height of the canvas to be artificially small, but we pack it to expand into any available space.

Suppressing Options

Options coming from a base class can be suppressed using the itk_option remove command. But this command should be used carefully. A derived class like Fileviewer should have all of the options defined in its base class itk::Widget. After all, a Fileviewer *is-a* Widget. An option should be suppressed in the base class only if it is being redefined in the derived class.

For example, suppose we want to change the meaning of the -cursor option in the Fileviewer widget. We set things up previously so that when you configure the master -cursor option, it propagates the change down to all of the components in the Fileviewer. Suppose instead that we want the -cursor option to affect only the display component. That way, we could assign a special pointer for selecting files, but leave the scrollbar and the hull with their appropriate default cursors.

To do this, we must keep the -cursor option on the display component, but avoid keeping it on the scrollbar and hull components. A complete code example appears in the file *itcl/itk/fileviewer5.itk*, but the important parts are shown below in Example 3-17.

Example 3-17: Options Can Be Suppressed Using itk_option remove

```
option add *Fileviewer.width 2i widgetDefault
option add *Fileviewer.height 3i widgetDefault
option add *Fileviewer.scrollbar auto widgetDefault
option add *Fileviewer.cursor center_ptr widgetDefault

class Fileviewer {
    inherit itk::Widget

    constructor {args} {
        itk_option add hull.width hull.height
        itk_option remove hull.cursor

        itk_component add scrollbar {
            scrollbar $itk_interior.sbar -orient vertical \
                -command [code $itk_interior.canv yview]
        } {
            usual
            ignore -cursor
        }
        ...

        eval itk_initialize $args
        component hull configure -cursor ""

        pack propagate $itk_component(hull) 0
        bind $itk_component(display) <Configure> \
            [code $this fixScrollbar]
    }
    ...
}
```

Since we create the scrollbar component in class Fileviewer, we can simply fix its option-handling code to suppress the -cursor option. We integrate its options in the "usual" manner, but we specifically ignore its -cursor option. The hull component, on the other hand, is created in the itk::Widget base class, and we can't modify that code. Instead, we use the itk_option remove command to disconnect its -cursor option from the master list. We create the display component just as we did before, keeping its -cursor option. Having done all this, we can configure the master -cursor option, and it will affect only the display component.

We might even add a default cursor like this:

```
option add *Fileviewer.cursor center_ptr widgetDefault
```

Whenever we create a new Fileviewer widget, its -cursor option will be center_ptr by default, so the file area will have a cursor that is more suitable for selecting files.

At this point, the example should be finished. But there is one glitch that keeps this example from working properly. Unfortunately, when you set a resource on a class like Fileviewer, it affects not only the master Fileviewer options, but also the options on the hull component that happen to have the same name. We were careful to disconnect the hull from the master -cursor option, but unless we do something, the hull will think its default cursor should be center_ptr. Even though it is not connected to the master option, it will accidentally get the wrong default value.

We can counteract this problem by explicitly configuring the hull component in the Fileviewer constructor like this:

```
component hull configure -cursor ""
```

So the hull will indeed get the wrong default value, but we have explicitly set it back to its default value, which is the null string.* This problem is rare. It occurs only when you try to suppress one of the hull options like -cursor, -border-width, or -relief, and yet you set a class resource in the options database. It is easily fixed with an explicit configuration like the one just shown.

Building Applications with Mega-Widgets

Using mega-widgets as building blocks, applications come together with astonishing speed. Consider the widgetree application shown in Figure 3-16, which is modeled after the hierquery program.† It provides a menu of Tcl/Tk applications that are currently running on the desktop. When you select a target application, its widget hierarchy is loaded into the main viewer. You can double-click on any widget in the tree to expand or collapse the tree at that point. If you select a widget and press the *Configure* button, you will get a panel showing its configuration options. You can change the settings in this panel and immediately apply them to the target application. This tool is a great debugging aid. It lets you explore an unfamiliar Tk application and quickly make changes to its appearance.

The widgetree application was built with a handful of mega-widgets and about 100 lines of Tcl/Tk code. Most of the mega-widgets came off-the-shelf from the [INCR WIDGETS] library, described in Chapter 4. The application menu is an Optionmenu widget. The panel of configuration options is a Dialog with an internal Scrolledframe containing Entryfield widgets, which represent the various configuration options.

---

* In Tk, widgets with a null cursor inherit the cursor from their parent widget.
† David Richardson, "Interactively Configuring Tk-based Applications," Proceedings of the Tcl/Tk Workshop, New Orleans, LA, June 23–25, 1994.

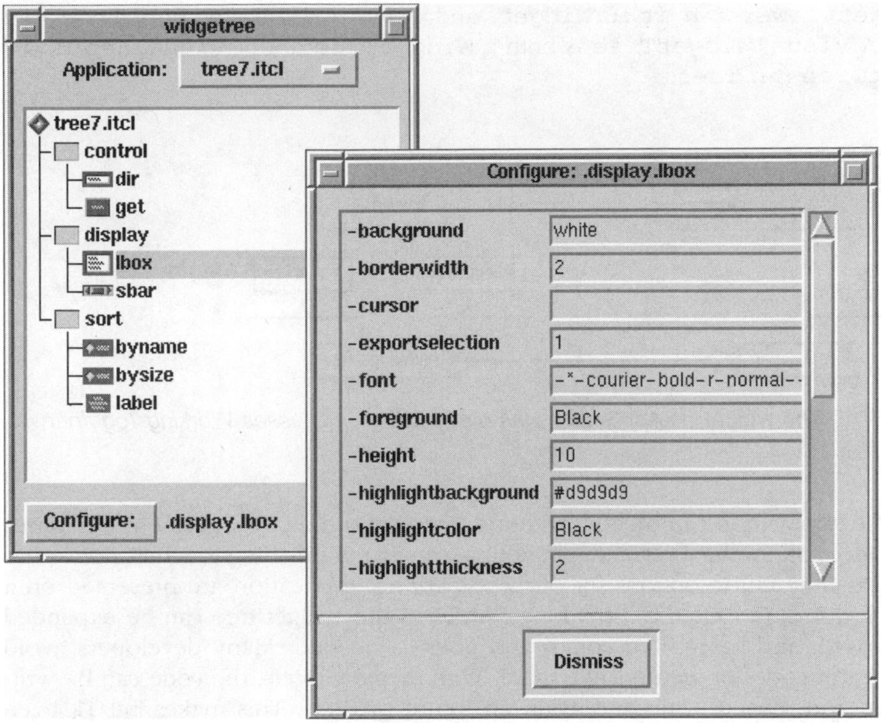

Figure 3-16: The widgetree Application Lets You Explore Any Tk Application

We developed one customized mega-widget for this application: a `Widgetviewer` class to manage the widget tree. You can find the code for the `Widgetviewer` class in the file *itcl/widgetree/widgetviewer.itk*. The details are not all that important. As you might have noticed, the `Widgetviewer` looks suspiciously like a `Fileviewer`. It has a `display` component and a `scrollbar` component, and it stores its data using `VisualWidgetTree` objects. Like the `VisualFileTree` class, the `VisualWidgetTree` class inherits from the `Tree` and `VisualRep` classes developed in the previous chapter. But instead of populating itself with nodes that represent files, each `VisualWidgetTree` object populates itself with nodes that represent child widgets. When you expand a `VisualWidgetTree` node on the display, you trigger a call to its `contents` method and the node populates itself. It sends the `winfo children` command to the target application, gets a list of child widgets, and creates other `VisualWidgetTree` objects to represent the children.

The `widgetree` application has many different classes that all contribute to its operation. You can find the code for this application in the file *itcl/widgetree/widgetree*. Rather than present the code here, we will simply comment on the way that these classes were used to structure the code.

The relationships between these classes are a mixture of inheritance and composition. They can be diagrammed using the OMT notation* as shown in Figure 3-17.

---

* James Rumbaugh, Michael Blaha, William Premerlani, Frederick Eddy, and William Lorensen, *Object-Oriented Modeling and Design*, Prentice-Hall, 1991.

A `Widgetviewer` *is-a* `itk::Widget`, and it *has-a* `VisualWidgetTree` root object. A `VisualWidgetTree` *is* both a `WidgetTree` and a `VisualRep`, and a `WidgetTree` *is-a* `Tree`.

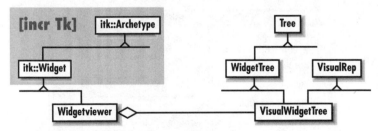

Figure 3-17: The widgetree Application Has Many Different Classes Working Together

The same application can be built without objects and mega-widgets, but it requires more code, and the final result might not have as many finishing touches. For example, the configuration options for our `widgetree` application are presented on a scrollable form, in case the list is long. Nodes in the widget tree can be expanded or collapsed, and a scrollbar comes and goes as needed. Many developers avoid writing extra code for features like these. With mega-widgets, the code can be written once and reused again and again on future projects. This makes Tcl/Tk even more effective for building large applications.

Summary

Extension: [INCR TK]—Mega-Widget Framework

Author: Michael J. McLennan
Bell Labs Innovations for Lucent Technologies
mmclennan@lucent.com

*Other
Contributors:*   Mark L. Ulferts
Jim Ingham
...and many others listed on the web site

*Platforms
Supported:*   All major Unix platforms
Linux
Windows 95 (release itcl2.2 and beyond)
Macintosh (release itcl2.2 and beyond)

Web Site: http://www.tcltk.com/itk

*Mailing List
(bug reports:)*   `mail -s "subscribe" itcl-request@tcltk.com`
   to subscribe to the mailing list

   `mail itcl@tcltk.com`
   to send mail

Quick Reference

Public Methods

The following methods are built into all mega-widgets. If you have created a mega-widget with the Tk name *pathName*, you can access these methods as follows:

pathName   `cget` *-option*
       Returns the current value for any mega-widget option. Works just like the usual `cget` method in Tk.

pathName   `component` *?symbolicName? ?command arg arg ...?*
       Provides access to well-known components within a mega-widget.

pathName   `configure` *?-option? ?value -option value ...?*
       Used to query or set mega-widget options. Works just like the usual `configure` method in Tk.

Protected Methods

The following methods are used within a mega-widget class as part of its implementation:

```
itk_component add symbolicName {
    widget pathName ?arg arg...?
}
```

or

```
itk_component add symbolicName {
    widget pathName ?arg arg...?
} {
    ignore -option ?-option -option ...?
    keep -option ?-option -option ...?
    rename -option -newName resourceName resourceClass
    usual ?tag?
}
```

       Creates a widget and registers it as a mega-widget component. The extra `ignore`, `keep`, `rename`, and `usual` commands control how the configuration options for this component are merged into the master option list for the mega-widget.

`itk_option`   `add` *optName ?optName optName...?*
       where *optName* is *component.option,* or *className::option.* Adds an option that was previously ignored back into the master option list.

`itk_option`   `remove` *optName ?optName optName...?*
       where *optName* is *component.option* or *className::option.* Removes an option that was previously merged into the master option list.

itk_option	*define -option resourceName resourceClass init ?configBody?*
	Defines a new configuration option for a mega-widget class.
itk_initialize	*?-option value -option value...?*
	Called when a mega-widget is constructed to initialize the master option list.

Protected Variables

The following variables can be accessed within a mega-widget class:

itk_component(*symbolicName*)

> Contains the Tk window path name for each component named *symbolicName*.

itk_interior

> Contains the name of the top-level or frame within a mega-widget which acts as a container for new components.

itk_option(-option)

> Contains the current value for any configuration option.

Auxiliary Commands

The following commands are available outside of a mega-widget class. They provide useful information about all Tk widgets:

usual	*tag ?commands?*
	Used to query or set "usual" option-handling commands for a widget in class *tag*.
winfo	*command window*
	Returns the access command for any widget, including its namespace qualifiers.
winfo	*megawidget window*
	Returns the name of the mega-widget containing the widget named *window*.

4

[incr Widgets]

by Mark Ulferts

A Mega-Widget Set

Tcl/Tk GUI development is filled with patterns. Programmers usually find themselves creating the same portions of code over and over again. The problem is that the Tk widget set is fairly basic. Repetitiously, we add labels to our entry widgets and scrollbars to listboxes, canvases, and text widgets. In fact, those are relatively simple examples—consider the amount of code we replicate making various dialogs like file selection and prompt dialogs. These are much more complicated and definitely more error prone. Seasoned coders try and bundle up these code segments by centralizing the functionality and creating composite widgets in a set of functional procedures. This strategy gets the job done, but it's clunky and inflexible, lacking the encapsulation and cohesiveness of a standard Tk widget. Absent also is the Tk framework of commands such as `configure` and `cget`. The end result just doesn't seem like a Tk widget.

With the introduction of the [INCR TCL] and [INCR TK] extensions, this process has been made much easier. The extensions allow Tk widgets to be combined into patterns of higher level building blocks called "Mega-Widgets." [INCR TCL] allows us to move away from the object-based model of Tcl/Tk and into an object-oriented paradigm similar to that of C++, complete with inheritance. Data and commands can be encapsulated; implementation can be hidden. The [INCR TK] extension goes even further, providing the Tk framework of configuration options and basic widget commands like `configure` and `cget`. These are the kind of features that make prototyping really easy and allow you to create code quicker. In the simplest of terms, each mega-widget based on [INCR TCL] and [INCR TK] seamlessly blends with the standard Tk widgets. They look, act, and feel like Tk widgets.

[INCR WIDGETS] is a set of mega-widgets based on [INCR TCL] and [INCR TK]. It delivers many general purpose widgets like option menus, selection boxes, and various dialogs whose counterparts are found in Motif and Windows. These mega-widgets

---

replace many of the most common patterns of widget combinations with higher level abstractions, blending with the standard Tk widgets and making it easier to consistently develop well-styled applications. [INCR WIDGETS] is also distinguished by its consistent use of style, built-in intelligence, high degree of flexibility, ease of extension, and object-oriented implementation. Its use results in increased productivity, reliability, and style guide adherence. This chapter details the [INCR WIDGETS] mega-widget set and illustrates its innovative concepts.

[INCR WIDGETS] Programming Advantages

[INCR WIDGETS] lets you create complex interfaces in substantially fewer lines of code. Not only can you work faster, but the resulting code is more readable and therefore easier to maintain. Let's take a look at a specific example, comparing the construction of a typical data entry interface using just Tcl/Tk, and then using [INCR WIDGETS].

Using Tcl/Tk, an entry form for name, address, and phone number would be constructed using combinations of frames, labels, and entry widgets. The frames would be needed to organize each entry field. The code would be like that shown in Example 4-1 and look like Figure 4-1.

Example 4-1: Tcl/Tk Data Entry Interface Code

```
wm title . Form

frame .name
pack .name -fill x
label .name.label -text Name:
pack .name.label -side left
entry .name.entry
pack .name.entry -fill x

frame .address
pack .address -fill x
label .address.label -text Address:
pack .address.label -side left
entry .address.entry
pack .address.entry -fill x

frame .citystate
pack .citystate -fill x
label .citystate.label -text "City, State:"
pack .citystate.label -side left
entry .citystate.entry
pack .citystate.entry -fill x

frame .phone
pack .phone -fill x
label .phone.label -text Phone:
pack .phone.label -side left
entry .phone.entry
pack .phone.entry -fill x
```

Figure 4-1: Tcl/Tk Data Entry Interface

The coupling of label and entry widgets to provide an entry field is probably the most redundant pattern seen in your typical Tcl/Tk program. [INCR WIDGETS] provides an entry field mega-widget that is much simpler and cleaner. The same entry form can be coded using the [INCR WIDGETS] entryfield in less than half the amount of code without all the extra frames.

```
entryfield .name -labeltext Name:
entryfield .address -labeltext Address:
entryfield .citystate -labeltext "City, State:"
entryfield .phone -labeltext Phone:

pack .name -fill x
pack .address -fill x
pack .citystate -fill x
pack .phone -fill x
```

Now we'll turn up the heat a little and add on some more requirements. Let's say we want to have the phone number field do some input verification, accepting only numbers and the – character. We also want the labels aligned and the background of the entry widgets to be different from the rest of the form. The [INCR WIDGETS] entryfield widget provides for all of these needs with a couple of additional options. Thus, with the addition of a few more lines of code we can make the example meet the requirements and improve its appearance.

```
option add *textBackground white

entryfield .name -labeltext Name:
entryfield .address -labeltext Address:
entryfield .citystate -labeltext "City, State:"
entryfield .phone -labeltext Phone: \
    -width 12 -fixed 12 \
    -validate {validate_number %P}

Labeledwidget::alignlabels \
    .name .address .citystate .phone

pack .name -fill x
pack .address -fill x
pack .citystate -fill x
pack .phone -fill x

proc validate_number {number} {
    return [regexp {^[-0-9]*$} $number]
}
```

When we created the phone widget, we used the -validate option to indicate that the input would be checked by the validate_number procedure as the user entered it. Further down, we define validate_number, which returns either 1 (true) or 0 (false). What it actually returns is the value returned by a regexp call, which just determines whether the input consists of digits and hyphens using a regular expression. The final result appears in Figure 4-2.

Figure 4-2: [INCR WIDGETS] Data Entry Interface

[INCR WIDGETS] Basics

Certain general operations work the same for all widgets. By learning about them at the start, you can more easily understand the activities of particular widgets later in the chapter.

Construction, Destruction, and Commands

Creation of an [INCR WIDGETS] mega-widget is exactly like that of a standard Tk widget; you invoke the class name as a command. The first argument is the path name of the new mega-widget, and succeeding arguments are option-value pairs. The following command creates an instance of a scrolled listbox with a constant vertical scrollbar and a horizontal scrollbar that appears on demand.

```
scrolledlistbox .slb -vscrollmode static \
    -hscrollmode dynamic
pack .slb
```

Once the mega-widget has been created, a new object exists whose name is the mega-widget path name. Now a new set of commands that are specific to the object's class can be invoked. For example, the scrolled listbox provides commands that support insertion and deletion of entries in the list.

```
.slb insert 0 Linux SunOS Solaris HP/UX Windows
.slb delete Windows
```

All the standard Tk commands that take a widget path name as an argument work as expected. For example, if you want to know the class of an [INCR WIDGETS] mega-widget, use the standard winfo class command:

```
% winfo class .slb
Scrolledlistbox
```

Finally, to destroy an [INCR WIDGETS] mega-widget, use the same Tk destroy command you normally would.

```
destroy .slb
```

Configuration

Just like Tk widgets, [INCR WIDGETS] mega-widgets keep a set of configuration options that mirror their current state. They may be used when creating a mega-widget and modified subsequently using the `configure` command. In addition, many of these options affect the physical layout of the mega-widget, allowing the visual appearance to be dynamically tweaked. [INCR WIDGETS] provides this capability under the principle that flexibility yields reuse. If you'd rather have the label for the entry field on top rather than the side, no problem; the option has been included. If you want scrollbars on demand for your scrolled listbox, you got it. Each mega-widget has been designed to allow exactly this sort of modification of the visual aspects of the components through a rich option suite. In addition, default option values may be specified in the option database.

This type of dynamic configuration is a very useful quality. The fact that Tcl/Tk is interpretive accentuates this virtue, allowing interactive interface design. Programs can be built that change appearance on-the-fly based on user input or program needs. An application that demands multiple flavors of a message dialog like confirmation and warning dialogs, with different messages, can create one instance and change the options between uses to create different appearances. This can be much more efficient than creating separate dialogs, since construction time is much more costly than the time required to modify and map the widget.

Consider an application that must confirm user exit requests prior to leaving an application. Should the user respond "Yes," then we'll need to ask if he or she would like to save any changes. To illustrate, the following code segment creates the initial message dialog and configures the message to ask "Are you sure ?" The dialog is then activated, which pops it on the display. Should the user respond positively, then the message is changed to "Would you like to save changes ?" and displayed a second time. This eliminates the need for two message dialogs with different messages when one would be more efficient. The message dialog configurations are shown in Figure 4-3.

Figure 4-3: Confirmation Dialog Configuration

```
messagedialog .md -modality application \
    -title Confirmation -bitmap questhead \
    -text "Are you sure ?"
.md buttonconfigure OK -text "Yes"
.md buttonconfigure Cancel -text "No"
.md hide Help
```

```
    if {[.md activate]} {
        .md configure \
            -text "Would you like to save changes ?"

        if {[.md activate]} {
            #
            # Save changes
            #
        }

        exit
    }
```

We can change much more than just the message text. This same message dialog can be configured on-the-fly into an error dialog. Since all the options can be dynamically changed, it is possible to change not only the bitmap but its location as well. Furthermore, we can modify the text of the buttons and make the dialog modeless.

Now let's make a change after the dialog has been activated. The `activate` command shows the dialog to the user, mapping it to the display. With the dialog visible, we'll change the orientation and position of the buttons to be vertical along the right-hand side. It is important to realize that no new message dialog has been created. Instead, one message dialog has been configured differently a total of four times. Also note that configuration options may be modified at any time, regardless of the current mapped status of the mega-widget. The error dialog configurations are displayed in Figure 4-4.

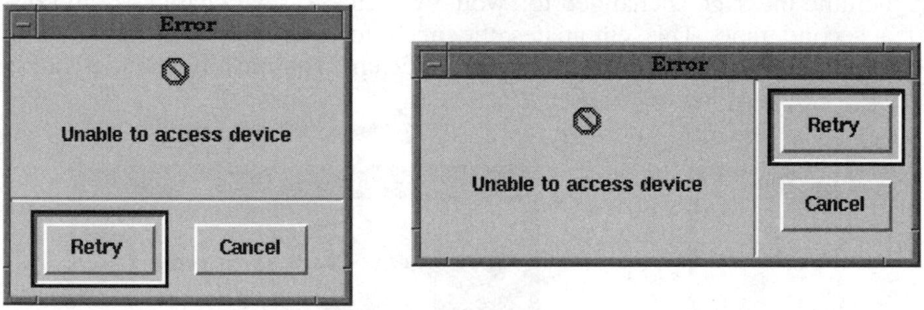

Figure 4-4: Error Dialog Configuration

```
    .md configure -bitmap error -imagepos n \
        -text "Unable to access device" \
        -modality none -title Error
    .md buttonconfigure OK -text Retry
    .md buttonconfigure Cancel -text Cancel

    .md activate

    .md configure -buttonboxpos e
```

Childsites

Childsites are an integral and innovative concept in the [INCR WIDGETS] mega-widget set. Basically, a childsite is a placeholder. Let me explain with a concrete example.

The dialog mega-widget may provide, for example, some buttons like "OK" and "Cancel" for operations you embed. What you provide in the body of the dialog may vary widely from application to application. It may be a scrolledtext widget in one case, a set of entryfields in another, and so on. So a lot of the [INCR WIDGETS] mega-widgets offer a general place—a childsite—to insert whatever you want. The contents can be any widgets or mega-widgets you choose.

In terms of implementation, a childsite is actually a standard Tk frame widget. You acquire the widget path of this frame via the `childsite` command. With the path in hand, you can start packing in other widgets with the childsite as the parent, filling your application's needs.

Now let's illustrate the use of childsites by making an RGB color selection dialog. We'll create a dialog and grab the childsite path, stuffing it into a variable. Next, we'll create three scales, one for red, green, and blue, within the dialog's childsite using this variable. We'll use the scale's `-to` option to limit the range to 255. Finally, we'll make the dialog active, appearing like the one shown in Figure 4-5.

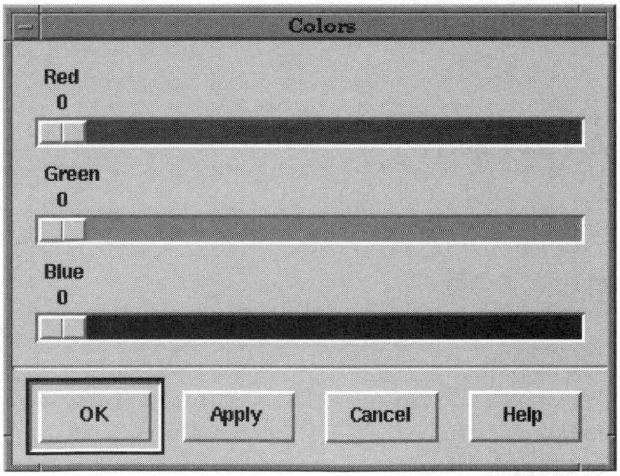

Figure 4-5: Colors Dialog Using a Dialog Childsite

```
dialog .rgb -title Colors
set cs [.rgb childsite]

scale $cs.red -orient horizontal \
    -label Red -to 255 -troughcolor Red
pack $cs.red -fill x

scale $cs.green -orient horizontal \
    -label Green -to 255 -troughcolor Green
pack $cs.green -fill x
```

```
scale $cs.blue -orient horizontal \
    -label Blue -to 255 -troughcolor Blue
pack $cs.blue -fill x
.rgb activate
```

One more quick example. The childsite of the entryfield mega-widget can be useful when you need a units label or a button that invokes a procedure. For example, let's create an entry field for file name entry and alternatively provide a button that can be used to select a file using a file selection dialog. We'll create an entry field and fill its childsite with a button labeled "..." We'll also create a file selection dialog and use it in a procedure tied to the button. Upon selection of the button, the procedure activates the dialog and waits for a response. If the user selects the OK button, the filename in the entry field is replaced with the one from the file selection dialog. Our file selection entry field would look like the one shown in Figure 4-6.

Figure 4-6: File Entry Field Using an Entryfield Childsite

```
fileselectiondialog .fsd -modality application
proc SelectFileProc {} {
    if {[.fsd activate]} {
        .filename delete 0 end
        .filename insert end [.fsd get]
    }
}


entryfield .filename -labeltext File:


set childsite [.filename childsite]


button $childsite.button -text "..." \
    -padx 5 -command SelectFileProc
pack $childsite.button -padx 5


pack .filename -padx 10 -pady 10 \
    -fill x -expand yes
```

[INCR WIDGETS] Hierarchy

The [INCR WIDGETS] class hierarchy is derived from several base classes provided by [INCR TK]. Figure 4-7 depicts the [INCR WIDGETS] inheritance hierarchy. They provide option management, standard commands, and a parent for components called the hull widget. The hull is just like a childsite. It is a placeholder for widgets, which [INCR TK] refers to as components. In addition, the hull's path is stored in a protected class variable named itk_interior.

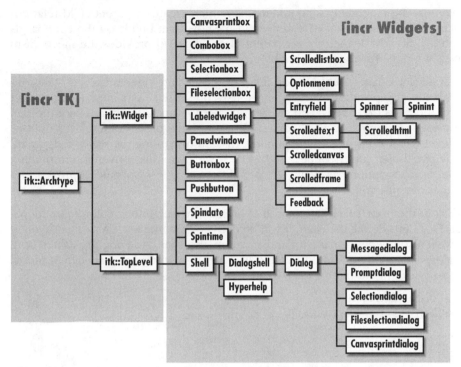

Figure 4-7: [INCR WIDGETS] Inheritance Hierarchy

Many mega-widgets within [INCR WIDGETS] successively maintain the hull variable in the hierarchy, passing it along from parent to child. When a mega-widget is constructed, new components are built off the hull's path. As mega-widgets are derived one from another, they may wish to redefine the hull. To do this, the mega-widget constructs a frame which it would now like to call the hull, setting the `itk_interior` variable to this new hull's path. This allows for the hull to change from parent to child as each mega-widget sees fit.

For example, the [INCR TK]'s top-level class defines a hull that is filled by the [INCR WIDGETS]'s `Dialogshell` class with a buttonbox for push buttons, a separator, and a frame on top. The Dialogshell redefines the hull to be this frame and adds a `childsite` command to provide access for composition purposes. The `Dialog` class is derived from `Dialogshell`, adding specific buttons and leaving the hull just as it was defined by the `Dialogshell` class to be the area above the separator. The `Selectiondialog`, next in the hierarchy, is derived from the `Dialog` class, filling the hull with a scrolledlistbox, an entryfield, and a frame. It changes the hull to now be this frame and provides a new `childsite` access command as well. Thus, you can see that the definition of the hull may change throughout the hierarchy. Each mega-widget passes it along, defining it as needed for the next class and narrowing its focus.

Creating New Mega-Widgets

Thus far, the childsite examples presented have extended an [INCR WIDGETS] mega-widget by just sticking widgets or even other mega-widgets inside one another using the `childsite` command—a technique known as composition. Mega-wid-

---

gets may also be extended using inheritance which creates a parent-child relation-ship between mega-widgets. The new child mega-widget builds on the commands and options already defined in our parent class. [INCR TK] provides the mechanism and [INCR WIDGETS] furnishes the hooks.

To illustrate, let's make a colordialog mega-widget using inheritance that will con-trast with the composition example previously presented. As a new mega-widget we'll call the class `Colordialog`. We'll also take the opportunity to make the col-ordialog less hard-wired to RGB values. Since we have more control over options at this level, we'll keep them more generic. Instead of naming the scales red, green, and blue, we'll use value1, value2, and value3. We'll use this convention in naming the label and to options as well. The benefits to this less specific approach will become apparent later.

Let's look at the [INCR TK] code required to create a more generic colordialog mega-widget. First, let's define the class. It will be derived from the [INCR WIDGETS] `Dialog` class. We'll also need a constructor and a `get` method for retrieving the values from our scales. This method should be able to query the value for a specific scale or default to returning all three values in a list.

```
class Colordialog {
    inherit iwidgets::Dialog

    constructor {args} {}

    public method get {{which all}}
}
```

Now we'll need to specify the body for our constructor. It will need to create three scales as components using `itk_component add`. Each will have the hull as its parent, which is stored in the `itk_interior` variable. The result is that the scales are created in the dialog's childsite. We'll keep specific options offered by the scale widget, renaming those which might otherwise conflict by prefixing the scale's name to the `-to`, `-label`, and `-troughcolor` options. This will make them unique and allow each to be independently modified. The last thing the construc-tor will need to do is evaluate any option arguments.

```
body Colordialog::constructor {args} {
    itk_component add value1 {
        scale $itk_interior.value1 \
            -orient horizontal
    } {
        keep -activebackground -background \
          -cursor -font -foreground \
          -highlightbackground -highlightcolor \
          -highlightthickness -repeatdelay \
          -repeatinterval -showvalue

        rename -to -value1to value1To To
        rename -label -value1label \
            value1Label Label
        rename -troughcolor -value1troughcolor \
            value1TroughColor TroughColor
```

```
        }
        pack $itk_component(value1) -fill x
```

Similarly for value2 and value3 scales ...

```
        eval itk_initialize $args

        hide Help
    }
```

Next, we'll define the body of the `get` method. It will take a default argument of "all" and allow individual scale values to be retrieved. We'll also install an error check for invalid arguments.

```
    body Colordialog::get {{which all}} {
        switch -regexp -- $which {
            value[1-3] {
                return [$itk_component($which) get]
            }
            all {
                return [list \
                [$itk_component(value1) get] \
                [$itk_component(value2) get] \
                [$itk_component(value3) get]]
            }
            default {
                error "bad get argument \
                \"$which\",should be:\
                value1, value2, value3, or all"
            }
        }
    }
```

Currently, construction of a new colordialog would require us to use the uppercase class name. This doesn't really follow the Tk model of lowercase commands. So, we'll provide a bit of syntactic sugar to remedy this.

```
    proc colordialog {args} {
        uplevel Colordialog $args
    }
```

This completes the code required for our `colordialog` class implementation. Next, we'll make use of the option database to define defaults that will map to our previous example. Mega-widgets, when created, consult the option database for option values not defined at construction. We'll define default values for the scale labels setting them to "Red," "Green," and "Blue." We'll also default the scale's `-to` options to be 255.

```
    option add *Colordialog.title \
        "Color Dialog" widgetDefault
    option add *Colordialog.value1Label \
        Red widgetDefault
    option add *Colordialog.value2Label \
```

```
        Green widgetDefault
option add *Colordialog.value3Label \
        Blue widgetDefault

option add *Colordialog.value1To \
        255 widgetDefault
option add *Colordialog.value2To \
        255 widgetDefault
option add *Colordialog.value3To \
        255 widgetDefault
```

The example presented earlier can now be created much more directly, using a much simpler syntax.

```
colordialog .cd
.cd activate
```

The [INCR TK] base classes enable the colordialog to act exactly like a standard Tk widget. Commands like `configure` and `cget` work as expected. Other typical Tk commands work as well.

```
% .cd configure -value1troughcolor Red \
        -value2troughcolor Green \
        -value3troughcolor Blue
% winfo class .cd
Colordialog
```

This version of the colordialog is much more versatile than before. We can easily create a colordialog for entering HSV (Hue Saturation Value) values by changing the scale label and `-to` option values as seen in Figure 4-8.

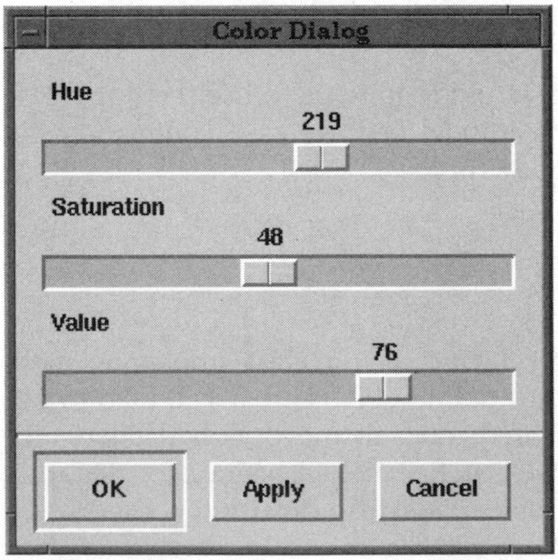

Figure 4-8: Colordialog Mega-Widget

```
colordialog .cd -value1label Hue -value1to 360 \
    -value2label Saturation -value2to 100 \
    -value3label Value -value3to 100
.cd activate
```

[INCR WIDGETS] Tour

The [INCR WIDGETS] mega-widget classes can be divided into widgets, scrolled widgets, managers, and dialogs. Each of these will be detailed in separate sections.

General Characteristics

The widgets that allow textual input or selection maintain an additional option called textbackground. This is independent of the background option and enables the user to specify a separate color for the text area as opposed to the complete background. The entryfield, scrolledlistbox, and scrolledtext widgets all provide the textbackground option. For example, Figure 4-9 depicts two scrolled listboxes, the first one with a standard background of gray and the second with a text background of GhostWhite.

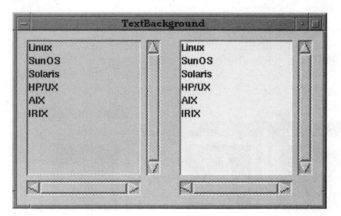

Figure 4-9: Textbackground Option

```
scrolledlistbox .grey
scrolledlistbox .gwhite -textbackground GhostWhite

pack .grey -side left -padx 10 -pady 10
pack .gwhite -side left -padx 10 -pady 10

set OSs [list Linux SunOS Solaris HP/UX AIX IRIX]

foreach item $OSs{
    .grey insert end $item
    .gwhite insert end $item
}.
```

The use of -textbackground produces a much more aesthetically pleasing interface. So rather than duplicate it for every example, we'll just put it into our default X resource file and use it implicitly throughout the rest of this chapter, taking advantage of its visual affect. Typically, this file is called *Xdefaults* or *Xresources* depending on your system.

```
*textBackground: GhostWhite
```

Widgets

[INCR WIDGETS] widgets represent the most basic of mega-widgets. Tk widgets are combined and enhanced, expanding the command and option suites, and providing a simpler means of creating typical Tk widget patterns.

Labeledwidget

The labeledwidget is the most primitive widget in the [INCR WIDGETS] set, providing label support for many of the other classes. The class contains a label, a margin, and a childsite that can be filled with other widgets of your choice. The options provide the ability to position the label around the childsite, modify the font, and adjust the margin distance. Valid locations for label position follow the notation established by Tk: n, ne, e, se, s, sw, w, and nw. It should also be noted that labels for labeledwidgets are not just limited to text strings; both bitmaps and images are supported as well.

The following example creates a labeledwidget with a canvas widget in the childsite. The label is set to `Canvas` and initially located south of the childsite. Next, the label is moved around the childsite while the margin is set to various distances as seen in Figure 4-10.

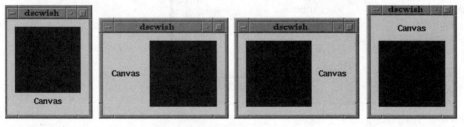

Figure 4-10: Labeledwidget Label Positions

```
labeledwidget .lw -labeltext "Canvas" -labelpos s
set childsite [.lw childsite]
canvas $childsite.c -relief raised -width 100 \
    -height 100 -background black

pack $childsite.c
pack .lw -fill both -expand yes -padx 10 -pady 10

update; after 1000
.lw configure -labelpos w -labelmargin 10

update ;after 1000
.lw configure -labelpos e -labelmargin 5

update; after 1000
.lw configure -labelpos n -labelmargin 7
```

A typical problem with a set of labeled widgets is alignment. You'll feel the need for this whenever you pack together a group of widgets, such as entryfields, with labels of different lengths. The `labeledwidget` class solves this problem by providing a command—`alignlabels`—that performs alignment by adjusting the margins so the fields all start at the same position. This command is actually a class command, global to all instances of `labeledwidget` and any other classes based on `labeledwidget`. As a class command, it has an unusual syntax in that the class name precedes the `alignlabels` command. The command takes as parameters the widgets to be aligned, which must be all derived from `labeledwidget`. In order for alignment to work, you must pack the widgets using the `-fill` option. Example 4-2 creates a second canvas with a longer label text than the previous example and aligns the labels. The result is pictured in Figure 4-11.

Example 4-2: Aligning labels.

```
.lw configure -labelpos w -labelmargin 1

labeledwidget .lw2 -labeltext "Another Canvas" \
    -labelpos w
set childsite [.lw2 childsite]
canvas $childsite.c2 -relief raised -width 100 \
    -height 100 -background white

pack $childsite.c2
pack .lw2 -fill both -expand yes -padx 10 -pady 10

Labeledwidget::alignlabels .lw .lw2
```

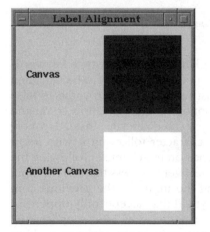

Figure 4-11: Labeledwidget Label Alignment

Entryfield

The `entryfield` class associates a label with an entry widget for text entry. The combination has been further enhanced by providing length control and validation capabilities. Since the class is based on the `labeledwidget` class, all the options and commands for labeledwidgets are supported in entryfields. Also, the commands for the standard Tk entry widget have been included such as `insert`, `delete`, `get`, and `scan` to name a few.

Anyone who has worked significantly with the standard Tk entry widget has become aware of its limitations. The entry widget lacks any restrictions on length and provides no simple means for input validation. [INCR WIDGETS] provides a remedy. The entryfield widget furnishes a -fixed option, which limits the number of characters allowed to be entered in the widget. Once this character limit has been reached, input is discarded and the user is alerted via the bell. The entryfield widget lets you restrict input to particular types of data through the -validate option. Character input can be limited to alphabetic, numeric, alphanumeric, integer, hexadecimal, and real.

The default action that occurs following the reception of invalid input is to ignore the character and ring the bell. Should more drastic action be warranted, include the -invalid option and the name of a procedure that is to be called whenever user input fails to meet your requirements. To illustrate, the following example shown in Figure 4-12 creates an entryfield for hexadecimal entry. By the way, should the user enter invalid characters, an error message is written out to standard error.

Figure 4-12: Hexadecimal Entryfield Validation

```
entryfield .hex -labeltext Hex: \
    -validate hexadecimal \
    -invalid {puts stderr "Invalid Hex Character"}
pack .hex -padx 10 -pady 10
```

Input can also be restricted to a finer level of granularity. Besides the type keywords previously given, the -validate option accepts a command script to be executed upon detection of character input. The script must return a Boolean value. A false value triggers the execution of the -invalid option. If the validation command contains any % characters, the script will not be executed directly. Instead, a new script is generated by replacing each % and the character following it with information from the entryfield. The replacement depends on the character following the %. These substitution characters allow scripts to selectively process the current input character, the contents of the entryfield following the input, or the previous contents. For example, let's suppose we want an entryfield that accepts only uppercase alphabetic characters and the _ character. We can use the -validate option and %c to specify a command procedure to take the current input character as an argument. The procedure then uses a regular expression to validate the argument, returning a Boolean result.

```
proc RegExpValidate {inputChar} {
    return [regexp {[A-Z_]} $inputChar]
}

entryfield .e -labeltext "Restricted Input:" \
    -validate {RegExpValidate %c}
pack .e -padx 10 -pady 10
```

Pushbutton

The `pushbutton` class augments the Tk button widget, adding default button display using a recessed ring. The primary use for the pushbutton is as components of the `buttonbox` class. In addition to furnishing the commands and options that the push-button gets from the Tk button widget, the pushbutton provides options for enabling or disabling the display of the default ring. The amount of padding within the default ring is adjustable using the `-defaultringpad` option. The following code segment creates a pushbutton with the default ring displayed as shown in Figure 4-13.

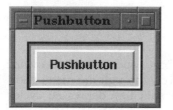

4-13: Pushbutton

```
pushbutton .pb -text Pushbutton \
    -defaultring yes -defaultringpad 4
pack .pb -padx 12 -pady 12
```

Optionmenu

The `Optionmenu` class allows users to select one item from a set. Only the selected item is displayed until the user selects the option menu button and a pop-up menu appears with all the choices available. Once a new item is chosen, the currently selected item is replaced and the pop-up is removed from the display. The [INCR WIDGETS] `optionmenu` class is based on the `labeledwidget` class and therefore supports label specification, position, and alignment.

The best way to understand the capabilities of the optionmenu widget is by example. The following creates a labeled optionmenu of various flavors of operating systems as depicted in Figure 4-14. It also associates a command procedure with the selection that will print out the selection. The procedure is called only upon change in current selection.

Figure 4-14: Optionmenu

```
proc SelectOSProc {} {
    puts "The best OS is : [.om get]"
}
```

```
optionmenu .om -command SelectOSProc \
    -labeltext "Operating Systems:" \
    -items {SunOS HP/UX AIX OS/2 Windows DOS}
pack .om -padx 10 -pady 10
```

Widget commands for manipulating the menu list contents have also been included
such as insert, delete, select, disable, enable, and sort.

```
.om insert end Linux VMS
.om disable DOS
.om delete 1 2
.om sort ascending
.om select Linux
.om configure -cyclicon true
```

Cyclic item selection is offered as an extension to the basic operations of standard
option menus. This allows the right mouse button to cycle through the menu without displaying the pop-up. The right mouse with the shift key depressed cycles
though the items in the reverse order.

Combobox

The [INCR WIDGETS] combobox provides an enhanced entryfield widget with an
optional label and a scrolledlistbox. When an item is selected in the list area of a
combobox its value is then displayed in the entry field text area. Functionally similar to an optionmenu, the combobox adds optional list scrolling and the ability to
edit and insert items.

There are two basic styles of comboboxes: dropdown and simple. The dropdown
style adds an arrow button to the right of the entry field, which when selected pops
up the scrolledlistbox beneath the entryfield widget. The simple, non-dropdown,
combobox permanently displays the listbox beneath the entry field and has no
arrow button. Both styles provide an optional label. Example 4-3 and Figure 4-15
illustrate the various flavors of comboboxes.

Example 4-3: Comboboxes

```
#
# Non-editable dropdown combobox
#
set monthList \
    {Jan Feb Mar Apr May June \
     Jul Aug Sept Oct Nov Dec}

combobox .noneditcb -labeltext Month: \
    -editable false -items $monthList
pack .noneditcb -padx 10 -pady 10 -fill x


#
# Editable dropdown
#
combobox .editablecb -fliparrow true \
    -popupcursor hand1 -listheight 100 \
```

```
        -items {Linux HP-UX SunOS Solaris Irix} \
        -labeltext "Operating Systems:"
pack .editablecb -padx 10 -pady 10 -fill x


#
# Empty editable dropdown
#
combobox .numericcb -unique true -labelpos nw \
        -validate numeric -labeltext "Numeric Combo:"
pack .numericcb -padx 10 -pady 10 -fill x


#
# Simple combobox
#
combobox .simplecb -dropdown false -textfont 9x15 \
        -labelpos nw -labeltext "Font:" \
        -items [exec xlsfonts] -listheight 220
pack .simplecb -padx 10 -fill both -expand yes
```

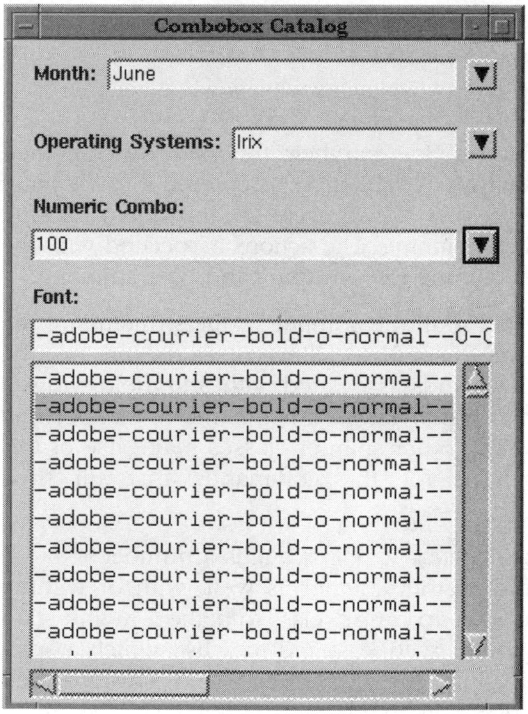

Figure 4-15: Comboboxes

Feedback

The feedback mega-widget is a simple progress indicator. It has commands for stepping along and resetting the indicator. Options enable the width, height, and color of the status bar to be configured. Its application can be seen in the hyperhelp

---

mega-widget, which displays a feedback widget during html rendering. For a more simple example, we'll cycle through a loop and update our progress once a second. A snapshot of the feedback widget in action can be seen in Figure 4-16.

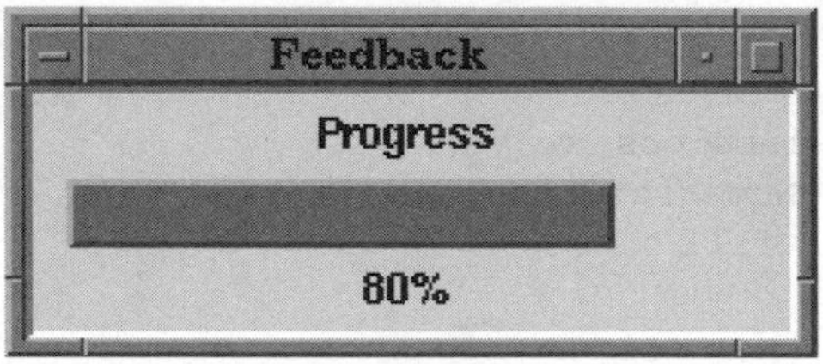

Figure 4-16: Feedback

```
feedback .gauge -steps 10 -labeltext Progress
pack .gauge

for {set i 0} {$i < 10} {incr i} {
    after 1000
    .gauge step
}
```

Spinners

Spinners constitute a set of widgets that provide entryfield functionality combined with increment and decrement arrow buttons. A value may be entered into the entry area explicitly or the buttons may be pressed, which cycle up and down through the choices. This latter behavior is called spinning. The actions associated with the arrow buttons vary from class to class, offering integer, time, and date spinning.

Spinner. The spinner class is the basis for all the spinner widgets, including the more specialized spinint, spintime, and spindate. Since it is based on the entryfield class, all the options and commands associated with entryfield widgets are provided, as well as additional options that enable a command to be specified for increment and decrement actions. The other spinner classes make use of this capability and have predefined actions for the commands that fill their functionality.

The `spinner` class is simple and generic. [INCR WIDGETS] builds a number of fancy classes from it, and you can develop a custom spinner as well, with or without using inheritance. For example, let's use the `spinner` class to make a month spinner as depicted in Figure 4-17. The months will be stored in a list, which a spinMonth procedure cycles through. The Spinner `-increment` and `-decrement` options invoke this procedure with a direction argument of either `1` or `-1`.

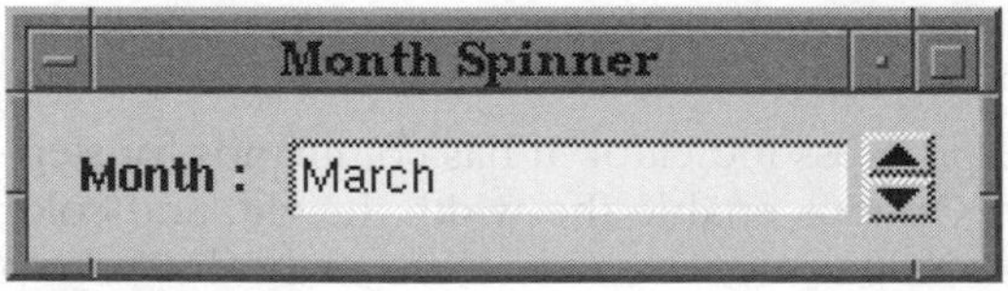

Figure 4-17: Spinner

```
set months {January February March April \
    May June July August September \
    October November December}
proc spinMonth {direction} {
    global months

    set index [expr [lsearch $months [.sm get]] \
        + $direction]

    if {$index < 0} {set index 11}
    if {$index > 11} {set index 0}

    .sm delete 0 end
    .sm insert 0 [lindex $months $index]
}

spinner .sm -labeltext "Month : " \
    -fixed 10 -validate {return 0} \
    -decrement {spinMonth -1} \
    -increment {spinMonth 1}
.sm insert 0 January
pack .sm -padx 10 -pady 10
```

The default orientation of the spinner arrows is vertical, but this can be modified by the -orient option that allows for a side-by-side, horizontal presentation as well. The previously created month spinner can be configured to illustrate this option as shown in Figure 4-18.

Figure 4-18: Spinner Arrow Orientation

```
.sm configure -arroworient horizontal
```

Spinint. Integers are the most common data type needing a spinning behavior. The spinint class offers this capability. Additional options are provided for step and range values that vary and limit the cycling. You can include the Boolean -wrap option to let the user go straight from the maximum value to the minimum, or vice versa.

The following code segment creates a water temperature integer spinner widget labeled appropriately and pictured in Figure 4-19. The widget limits the range of values to be between freezing and boiling, and specifies a step value of two.

```
spinint .temp -labeltext "Water Temperature:" \
    -fixed 5 -range {32 212} -step 2
pack .temp -padx 10 -pady 10
```

Figure 4-19: Spinint

Spintime. The `spintime` class provides a set of spinners for entering various units of time. The set includes an hour, minute, and second spinner widget. Options allow each spinner to be hidden or shown. Also, the format of the time is configurable between military and normal display. Figure 4-20 depicts a sample spintime widget.

Figure 4-20: Spintime

```
spintime .st
pack .st -padx 10 -pady 10
```

Spindate. The `spindate` class supports date value entry. Just as with the `spintime` class, the display of each spinner can be separately controlled. The format of the month display may also be varied between text and integer display. The spindate widget looks like the one shown in Figure 4-21.

Figure 4-21: Spindate

```
spindate .sd -monthformat string
pack .sd -padx 10 -pady 10
```

Scrolled Widgets

Another common pattern in typical Tk scripts is the attachment of scrollbars to those Tk widgets that support scrolling. Sometimes you want just a vertical scrollbar, other times just a horizontal one, and sometimes both. These combinations were a prime candidate for replacement by [INCR WIDGETS], which provides a scrolled listbox, text, canvas, and frame.

Each of the [INCR WIDGETS] widgets that support scrolling offer wide-ranging control of scrollbar display and appearance. Figure 4-22 presents the four basic visual formats of scrolled widgets. Both the vertical and horizontal scrollbars can be separately configured for three different modes of display: static, dynamic, and none. In static mode, the scrollbar is displayed at all times. Dynamic mode displays the scrollbar as required, and none disables scrollbar display. The default is static. The width of the scrollbars and the margins between the bars and the widget being scrolled can also be adjusted via options.

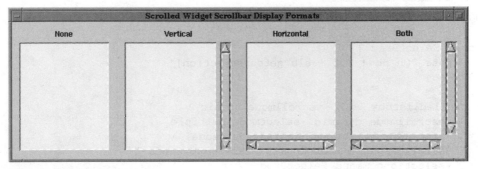

Figure 4-22: Scrollbar Positioning

Each of the [INCR WIDGETS] scrolled widgets provides **-width** and **-height** options for geometry specification. These dimensions apply to the widget as a whole, inclusive of the other components: label, margins, and scrollbars. Any additional space required to display these components comes from the space allocated to the primary widget to be scrolled. The dimensions are fixed in that the values given apply to the overall frame.

The scrolledlistbox and scrolledtext widgets offer an alternative method of geometry specification. Both of these widgets provide a **-visibleitems** option that specifies the width in characters and height in lines for the listbox or text widget. The dimensions of the listbox or text widget become fixed. The outer frame expands as needed to display the label, margins, and scrollbars. This option is effective only if the **-width** and **-height** options are both set to zero. Otherwise, the **-visibleitems** option applies by default.

Scrolledlistbox

The scrolledlistbox extends the standard Tk listbox widget with vertical and horizontal scrollbars and a label. The set of options has been expanded to let you specify list items and bind single- and double-click selections to procedures.

The following example, pictured in Figure 4-23, shows a multiple selection scrolledlistbox of common weeds, which exist in my yard. The widget has a statically displayed vertical scrollbar and a horizontal one that appears on demand. A command procedure has been associated with the single select action to print the item.

Figure 4-23: Scrolledlistbox

```
proc SelectProc {} {
    puts "Oh no ! Not [.slb getcurselection]"
}

scrolledlistbox .slb -vscrollmode static \
    -hscrollmode dynamic -selectmode multiple
    -items {Crabgrass Dallisgrass Nutsedge} \
    -scrollmargin 5 -labelpos n -labeltext weeds \
    -selectioncommand SelectProc
pack .slb -padx 10 -pady 10 -fill both -expand yes
```

The standard listbox commands have been amended with ones for sorting the list contents and a shortcut for getting the current selection. The `getcurselection` command combines the actions of the `curselection` and `get` commands so that the text of a selected item may be retrieved in a single action.

```
.slb insert 2 Sandbur Goosegrass Barnyardgrass
.slb insert end Chickweed Johnsongrass Puncturevine
.slb sort ascending
```

Scrolledtext

The scrolledtext widget provides all the functionality of the standard Tk text widget, along with scrollbar and label control. The commands have been extended to include file import and export. To illustrate, we'll create a scrolled-text widget that imports the password file from my Linux machine. The result is depicted in Figure 4-24.

```
scrolledtext .st -labeltext "passwd" -wrap none \
    -visibleitems 80x10

pack .st -padx 10 -pady 10 -fill both -expand yes

.st import /etc/passwd
.st yview end
```

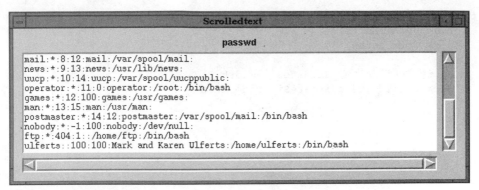

Figure 4-24: Scrolledtext

Scrolledframe

The scrolledframe combines the functionality of scrolling with that of a standard Tk frame widget, yielding a clipable viewing area whose visible region may be modified with the scrollbars. This allows the construction of visually larger areas than could normally be displayed, containing a heterogenous mix of widgets.

Once a scrolledframe has been created, the childsite can be accessed and filled with widgets. One ideal usage is for tables. For example, using the childsite as a parent for the combination of labels and entry widgets, we can create a simple checkbook as seen in Figure 4-25.

Scrolledframe

CheckBook

Date	Num	Payee	Payment	Deposit	Bala
3/3/96	1001	American Express	350.00		1912
3/21/96	1002	Morgage Company	1200.00		712.(
3/29/96		Pay Check		1450.00	2162

Figure 4-25: Scrolledframe

```
scrolledframe .sf \
    -vscrollmode static -hscrollmode static \
    -labeltext CheckBook -width 7i -height 2i

set childsite [.sf childsite]

frame $childsite.f
pack $childsite.f
label $childsite.f.date -text Date -width 8 -bd 4
pack $childsite.f.date -side left

...
```

```
for {set i 0} {$i < 30} {incr i} {
    frame $childsite.f$i
    pack $childsite.f$i

    entry $childsite.f$i.date$i -width 8
    pack $childsite.f$i.date$i -side left

    ...

}

pack .sf -expand yes -fill both
```

Scrolledcanvas

The scrolledcanvas applies scrollbars and display options to a Tk canvas widget. All the usual canvas commands and options have been kept. A new option, -autoresize, has been added, allowing automatic resizing of the scrolled region to be the bounding box covering all the items. The region is adjusted continuously as items are created and destroyed via the canvas commands, affecting the display of the scrollbars. Figure 4-26 shows the Tk floorplan demo script modified to use a scrolledcanvas.

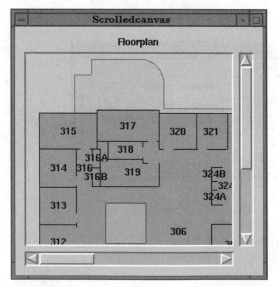

Figure 4-26: Scrolledcanvas

```
scrolledcanvas .sc -labeltext Floorplan \
    -width 300 -height 300
.sc create line 386 129 398 129 -fill black
.sc create line 258 355 258 387 -fill black
...
```

Managers

[INCR WIDGETS] manager widgets include buttonbox, radiobox, toolbar, panedwindow, and tabbednotebook classes. Each acts as a container, providing geometry management for its children. This entails arranging the relative positions of the widgets placed inside, and adjusting the size of the container that holds them.

Buttonbox

The buttonbox performs geometry management for pushbuttons. Commands allow the user to add new pushbuttons, define the default button, control their display, and manage pushbutton configuration. The primary tasks of a buttonbox are to equally distribute the visible pushbuttons and maintain their widths consistently. When another pushbutton is added that has a much longer text than those which are currently displayed, the widths of all the buttons are adjusted, making them of equal size. This class is used to manage the buttons for all the dialogs in the [INCR WIDGETS] widget set.

When you create a buttonbox it initially contains no buttons. Add them through the add command, which accepts a tag name and a series of options to be applied to the pushbutton. The tag can later be used in other commands that employ an index as a reference to the button. Indexes may be specified numerically, using keywords, or a pattern that is matched against the tags. For example, the following code segment creates a buttonbox, adds buttons, and specifies the default using a numerical index. For simplicity, we'll initially keep the text the same as the tags. Figure 4-27 shows the final product.

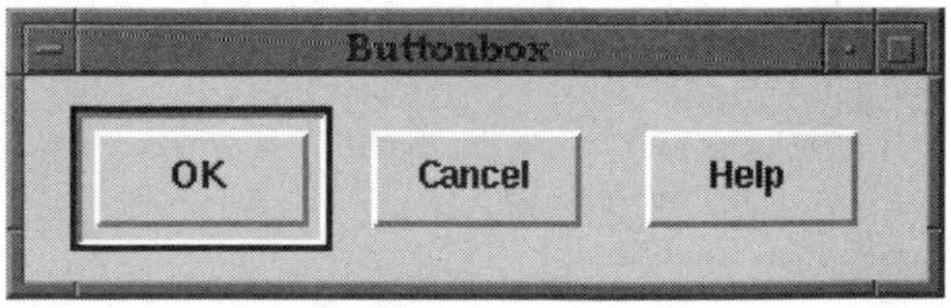

Figure 4-27: Buttonbox add Command

```
buttonbox .bb -padx 10 -pady 10

.bb add OK -text OK -command {puts OK}
.bb add Cancel -text Cancel -command {puts Cancel}
.bb add Help -text Help -command {puts Help}
.bb default 0

pack .bb -expand yes -fill both
```

The add command appends pushbuttons to the end of the buttonbox. Another command, insert, allows pushbuttons to be placed before another pushbutton. The command takes as arguments the index of an existing pushbutton, followed by a tag, and finally the options to be applied to the new pushbutton. For example, we can place an Apply pushbutton between the OK and Cancel pushbuttons using the tag of the Cancel button as the index as seen in Figure 4-28.

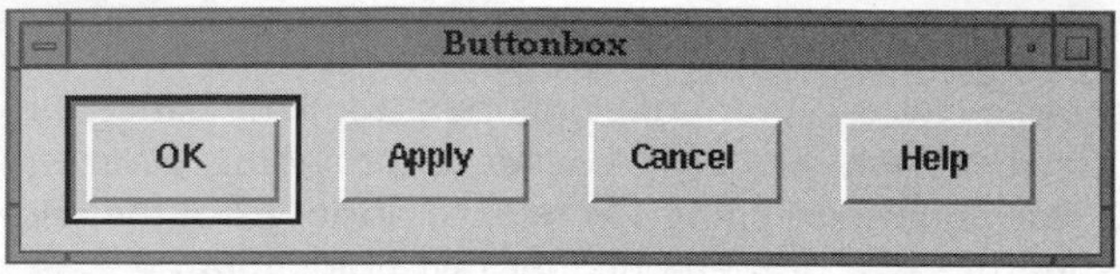

![Buttonbox window with buttons OK, Apply, Cancel, Help]

Figure 4-28: Buttonbox insert Command

```
.bb insert Cancel Apply -text Apply
```

Commands have also been included to `hide`, `show`, or `delete` a pushbutton. In addition, the options for a tagged pushbutton can be configured using the `button-configure` command. Now we'll take our buttonbox and hide the Help button, and change the text of the button tagged OK to be Commit as illustrated in Figure 4-29.

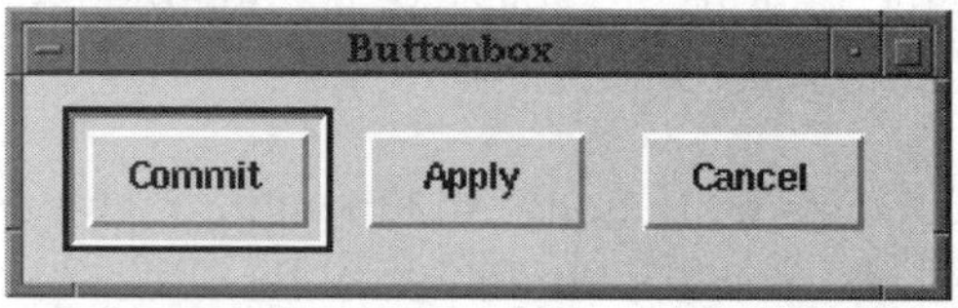

![Buttonbox window with buttons Commit, Apply, Cancel]

Figure 4-29: Buttonbox buttonconfigure Command

```
.bb hide Help
.bb buttonconfigure OK -text Commit
```

The orientation of the buttonbox, and the distance between the buttons and the perimeter may also be modified through options. For example, the buttonbox can be made horizontal with additional padding using the `-orient`, `-padx`, and `-pady` options. The result is pictured in Figure 4-30.

Figure 4-30: Buttonbox orient and pad Options

```
.bb configure -orient vertical -padx 20 -pady 20
```

Radiobox

The [INCR WIDGETS] radiobox manages radiobuttons, encapsulating the global variable needed for Tk radiobutton usage. Once the radiobox has been created, radiobuttons are added with a tag using the `add` command. The tag can be used in other commands such as `insert, delete, select, deselect,` and `invoke`. The current setting can be obtained using the `get` command. A `buttonconfigure` command allows the options associated with a tagged radiobutton to be modified and queried. The radiobox is based on the `labeledwidget` class, so all the options for label management are available. Let's create a font radiobox like the one in Figure 4-31, demonstrating command and option usage.

Figure 4-31: Radiobox

```
radiobox .rb -labeltext Fonts -relief raised

.rb add times -text Times
.rb add helvetica -text Helvetica

.rb insert times courier -text Courier
.rb insert 2 symbol -text Symbol

pack .rb -padx 20 -pady 20 -fill both -expand yes

.rb buttonconfigure times -command {puts Times}
.rb select times
.rb get
```

Toolbar

A toolbar makes for a very nice addition to any application's main window. It displays a collection of widgets like buttons, radiobuttons, or optionmenus, offering quick access to a set of commonly needed functions for user convenience. The toolbar can also be used as a mousebar. Placed horizontally beneath a menubar, you get a toolbar; oriented vertically and placed on the side, you have a mousebar. As an extra feature, the `toolbar` class offers string and balloon help for each widget that it manages. This comes in quite handy when filling a toolbar with buttons that are labeled with bitmaps. It allows the user to see a simple help string associated with the item the mouse happens to be positioned over prior to selecting it.

The following example shown in Figure 4-32 illustrates these features of the toolbar, creating an instance containing buttons with various bitmaps. The toolbar is created with a `help` variable, which is a global variable. As each button is added, a help string and balloon help value are associated with the component. The buttons use the standard @ syntax in the `-bitmap` option to locate the bitmap file. Finally, a Tk entry widget is added for displaying help strings using its `-textvariable` option. As the mouse passes over each toolbar component, the help string is written to the entry widget. Should the mouse pause over a button, the balloon help pops up.

Figure 4-32: Toolbar

```
toolbar .tb -helpvariable statusVar

.tb add button line -helpstr "Draw a line" \
    -bitmap @line.xbm -balloonstr "Line" \
    -command {puts LINE}
.tb add button box -helpstr "Draw a box" \
    -bitmap @box.xbm -balloonstr "Box" \
    -command {puts BOX}
.tb add button oval -helpstr "Draw an oval" \
    -bitmap @oval.xbm -balloonstr "Oval" \
    -command {puts OVAL}
.tb add button points -helpstr "Draw poly points" \
    -bitmap @points.xbm -balloonstr "Points" \
    -command {puts POINTS}
.tb add frame filler -borderwidth 1 \
    -width 10 -height 10
.tb add button text -bitmap @text.xbm \
    -helpstr "Enter text" -balloonstr "Text" \
    -command {puts TEXT}

pack .tb -side top -anchor nw -fill x

entry .e -textvariable statusVar
pack .e -side top -anchor nw -fill x
```

Panedwindow

Most of the [INCR WIDGETS] classes contain at most one childsite. The panedwindow is unique in that it manages multiple childsites. The mega-widget is composed of panes, separators, and sashes for adjustment of the separators. The sash is the little button used to grab the separator running beneath it and change the size of the pane. Each pane is a childsite whose path may be obtained using the `childsite` command. Once the paths have been acquired, you may fill them with widget combinations.

Once a panedwindow has been created, panes can be added and inserted using the `add` and `insert` commands. Each pane is assigned a unique tag identifier. Other commands like `hide`, `show`, and `delete` take the tag as an argument. The viewable percentage of each pane can be modified using the `fraction` command. To illustrate, the following example creates a panedwindow with three panes, assigning a viewable percentage, and fills the childsites with scrolledlistboxes. Figure 4-33 depicts the results.

Figure 4-33: Panedwindow

```
panedwindow .pw -width 400 -height 500
.pw add top
.pw add bottom -margin 10
.pw insert bottom middle -minimum 70

.pw fraction 50 30 20

pack .pw -fill both -expand yes

foreach pane [.pw childsite] {
    scrolledlistbox $pane.slb \
        -vscrollmode static -hscrollmode static
    pack $pane.slb -fill both -expand yes
}
```

As new panes are added, options may be specified that apply to the individual pane. These options include −margin and −minimum. The margin is the distance between the pane and the actual childsite. The `-minimum` option sets the minimum size in pixels that a pane's contents may reach. The `paneconfigure` command allows modification of the option values previously specified in an `add` or `insert` command.

Once visible, the separators on the panedwindow can be adjusted by selecting the square sash button and, with the mouse button held down, moving the separator to the desired location. When the user releases the mouse button, the size of the panes will be updated. One feature of the panedwindow that is evident with three or more panes is that separator movement is allowed to bump and move other separators. Any minimum value previously set is maintained at all times.

The panedwindow offers significant control over its presentation through a rich set of options. The option set allows specification of the orientation, separator thickness, dimensions, sash position, and sash cursor. The `-sashindent` option specifies the placement of the sash button as an offset. Positive values offset the sash relative to the near (left/top) side, whereas negative values denote an offset from the far (right/bottom) side.

Now, let's take this same panedwindow previously created and highlight some more of the commands and options we just talked about. We'll hide the center pane which was tagged "middle" and configure the minimum size of the top pane to be 100 pixels. Also, we'll change the orientation to be vertical using the `-orient` option. The `-sashindent`, `-sashheight`, `-sashwidth`, `-sashcursor`, and `-thickness` options will be used to alter the appearance of the sash and separator. The final product is shown in Figure 4-34.

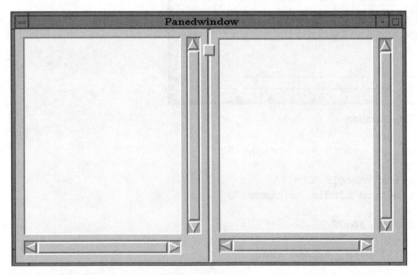

Figure 4-34: Panedwindow Configuration

```
.pw configure -orient vertical \
    -sashindent 20 -sashheight 15 \
    -sashwidth 15 -thickness 5 -sashcursor gumby

.pw hide middle
.pw paneconfigure top -minimum 100
```

Tabnotebook

The tabnotebook mega-widget is one of the stars in the [INCR WIDGETS] parade. Its unique presentation allows users to organize their interface as a set of tabbed pages, displaying one page at a time. When created, tabnotebooks have no pages. The add command allows pages to be affixed to the notebook. Additional widget commands support page deletion and configuration. Each tabnotebook page contains a single childsite that serves as a container for user-defined widgets. Tabs are shown on the page borders, serving as page selectors and identifying each page with a label. As a tab is selected, the contents of the associated page are displayed. Visually, the selected tab maintains a three-dimensional effect, making it appear to float above the other tabs.

Tabs themselves are quite configurable. The richness of the option suite permits a wide variety of styles and appearances, including Microsoft, Borland property, or Borland Delphi styles. Positionally, tabs may be located along the north, south, east, or west sides of the notebook. North and south tabs may appear angled, square, or beveled. West and east tabs may be square or beveled. Additional tab options allow specification of their gap, margin, internal padding, font, and label. To illustrate, we'll take a page from Quicken, no pun intended, and create a tabnotebook like that pictured in Figure 4-35 for bank, credit, investment, and other general types of accounts. Each page will contain a set of more specific accounts using scrolledlistboxes. We'll give the initial size of the tabnotebook using the -width and -height options. The -angle option specifies the angle of all the tabs.

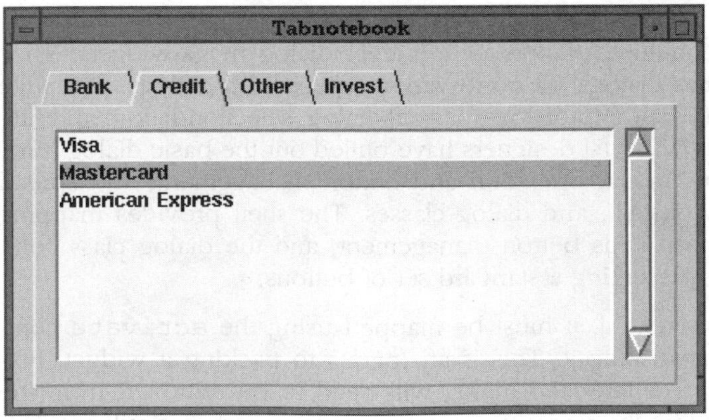

Figure 4-35: Tabnotebook

```
tabnotebook .tn -tabpos n -angle 15\
    -width 400 -height 200

.tn add -label "Bank"
.tn add -label "Credit"
.tn add -label "Other"
.tn add -label "Invest"

scrolledlistbox [.tn childsite "Bank"].bank \
    -hscrollmode none \
```

```
       -items {"Joint Checking" "Savings"}
pack [.tn childsite "Bank"].bank \
    -fill both -expand yes -padx 10 -pady 10

scrolledlistbox [.tn childsite "Credit"].credit \
    -hscrollmode none \
    -items {"Visa" "Mastercard" "American Express"}
pack [.tn childsite "Credit"].credit \
    -fill both -expand yes -padx 10 -pady 10

scrolledlistbox [.tn childsite "Other"].other \
    -hscrollmode none
pack [.tn childsite "Other"].other \
    -fill both -expand yes -padx 10 -pady 10

scrolledlistbox [.tn childsite "Invest"].invest \
    -hscrollmode none -items {"Stocks" "Bonds"}

pack [.tn childsite "Invest"].invest \
    -fill both -expand yes -padx 10 -pady 10

pack .tn -fill both -expand yes -padx 10 -pady 10

.tn select 0
```

Dialogs

[INCR WIDGETS] provides multiple flavors of top-level dialog mega-widgets. They range from the bare-bones dialogshell up to various specialized dialogs. The suite includes the Motif favorites: promptdialog, messagedialog, selectiondialog, and file-selectiondialog. The [INCR WIDGETS] designers have pulled out the basic dialog functional requirements, like modal operation and button management, and spread them over the shell, dialogshell, and dialog classes. The shell provides mapping capabilities. The dialogshell adds button management, and the dialog class completes the feature set by presenting a standard set of buttons.

Once a dialog has been created, it must be mapped using the `activate` command when you want to display it. This is analogous to packing a widget. Following activation, sooner or later the dialog will need to be removed from the display. This is facilitated by the `deactivate` command, which is similar to Tk's `pack forget` command.

Modal dialog levels include global, application, and none; the difference being the degree of blocking. Global modal dialogs block all applications, whereas application modal dialogs block the current application. This allows the program to retrieve dialog contents easily as a return value from the dialog after it is deactivated. Modeless dialogs are of the modal type `none`. They are non-blocking, enabling the application to continue. In this case, the actions attached to the buttons should perform all processing of the dialog contents, including deactivation of the dialog itself. The default modal type is none.

The desired modal level is specified via the `-modality` option in the command creating the dialog and it takes effect upon activation. For application and global modal dialogs, the `activate` command does not immediately return. Instead, it waits until the dialog is deactivated. The more specific dialogs, like messagedialog, promptdialog, selectiondialog, and fileselectiondialog, are deactivated automatically upon selection of the OK or Cancel buttons. In this case, the OK button returns the value of 1 and Cancel of 0 to the waiting `activate` command. This feature comes in quite handy when you wish to wait for the user response to a dialog and process it only if they selected OK. For example, we can create a promptdialog like the one shown in Figure 4-36, making it application modal. Following activation, we'll wait for a value of 1 to be returned, signifying the user selected OK. Next, we can process the prompted value retrieved via the `get` command.

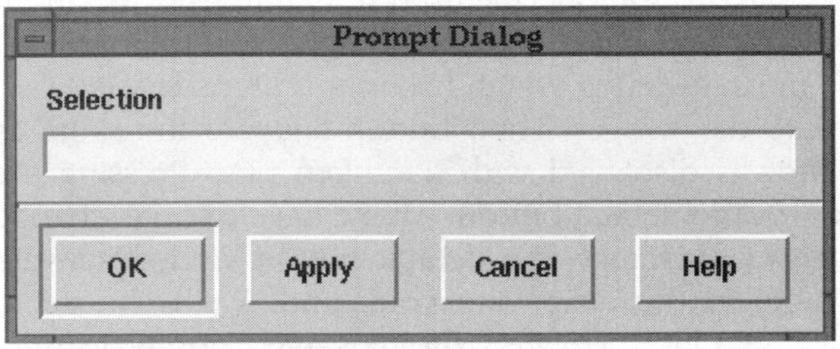

Figure 4-36: Dialog Activation

```
promptdialog .pd -modality application

if {[.pd activate]} {
    set response [.pd get]
    #
    # Process response
    #
}
```

Sometimes we may want to catch the selection of OK or Cancel and not just let the dialog deactivate automatically. Consider the promptdialog again. Let's say we want to `deactivate` the promptdialog only if the user has non-blank input in the entry field. In this case, we'll need to modify the behavior of the OK button to invoke a procedure that can check for this. The `buttonconfigure` command will allow us to modify the -command option associated with the OK button through the button's tag. By default, the tag for the OK button is OK. So now let's take our promptdialog example and add a checkInput procedure that uses promptdialog's `get` command combined with a regular expression test to make sure the input isn't just blank. If the input is acceptable, we'll deactivate the dialog and process the input.

```
promptdialog .pd -modality application
.pd buttonconfigure OK -command checkInput

proc checkInput {} {
    if {[regexp {[^ \t]} [.pd get]]} {
        .pd deactivate
        #
        # Process response
        #
```

```
        }
    }

    .pd activate
```

The `buttonconfigure` command is capable of configuring all the options associated with the buttons, including the labels. The `deactivate` command accepts an optional argument that will be returned as a result of the `activate` command for global and application modal dialogs. This allows control over status notification. By default, OK returns 1 and Cancel returns 0 to the `activate` command, but this can easily be modified.

Let's consider a messagedialog similar to the one pictured in Figure 4-37 that notifies the user of impending doom and requests a response of ignore, retry, or abort. To implement this, we'll use the messagedialog which has four buttons labeled OK, Apply, Help, and Cancel built into the widget. Their button tags are the same as their labels, and the default button is displayed with a sunken ring. Pressing the return key within the dialog invokes the default button. All we have to do is change the labels of the buttons via the tags, change the default button, and deactivate explicitly, passing the button label to the deactivate command. We'll choose to make the abort button be the default. Once activated, the messagedialog waits until deactivated, reacting to the argument passed to the `deactivate` command.

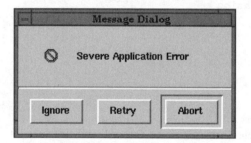

Figure 4-37: Dialog Deactivation

```
messagedialog .doom -bitmap error \
    -text "Severe Application Error" \
    -modality global

.doom show Apply
.doom hide Help
.doom default Cancel

.doom buttonconfigure OK -text Ignore \
    -command {.doom deactivate ignore}
.doom buttonconfigure Apply -text Retry \
    -command {.doom deactivate retry}
.doom buttonconfigure Cancel -text Abort \
    -command {.doom deactivate abort}

switch [.doom activate] {
    ignore {
        # Process ignore ...
```

```
    }
    retry {
        # Process retry ...
    }
    abort {
        # Process abort ...
    }
}
```

Dialogshell

The dialogshell is the most primitive of the [INCR WIDGETS] dialogs, composed of a buttonbox and childsite. It provides modal operation, button management support, and a childsite that lies above a separator. Button management includes the ability to add, insert, delete, hide, show, and configure buttons based on a tag. Since no buttons exist by default, deactivation must be explicitly handled in any buttons added to the dialogshell.

Even given only the basics, many dialogs can be constructed using the `dialogshell` class. For example, let's create the database login dialog shown in Figure 4-38. We need to add buttons for opening a new or existing database and for exiting the dialog. The command associated with each button will deactivate the dialog and pass its label back to the **activate** command. The childsite will be filled with entryfield prompts for name, password, and database. The code looks like this.

Figure 4-38: Dialogshell

```
dialogshell .dblogin \
    -title "Database Login" -modality global

.dblogin add New -text New \
    -command {.dblogin deactivate new}
.dblogin add Open -text Open \
    -command {.dblogin deactivate open}
.dblogin add Exit -text Exit \
    -command {.dblogin deactivate exit}

.dblogin default New

set childsite [.dblogin childsite]
```

```
entryfield $childsite.name \
    -labeltext Name:
pack $childsite.name -fill x
entryfield $childsite.password \
    -labeltext Password: -show \267
pack $childsite.password -fill x
entryfield $childsite.database \
    -labeltext Database:
pack $childsite.database -fill x

Labeledwidget::alignlabels $childsite.name \
    $childsite.password $childsite.database

if {[set type [.dblogin activate]] != "exit"} {
    switch $type {
        new {
            # Open new database
        }
        open {
            # Open existing database
        }
    }
}
```

Dialog

The [INCR WIDGETS] `dialog` class is basically a dialogshell with several predefined buttons. They include the standard OK, Apply, Cancel, and Help. The command options for both the OK and Cancel buttons have also been preset. The OK command is `deactivate 1`, and the Cancel command is `deactivate 0`.

The labels and commands for the default dialog buttons are not cast in stone. They can easily be configured to meet our needs. Let's revisit the database login example again. This time, we'll create the same effect using a dialog widget, but instead of adding buttons like we did before with the dialogshell, we'll just make use of the dialog's existing buttons, configuring their labels and commands using the `buttonconfigure` command and the button tags.

```
dialog .dblogin \
    -title "Database Login" -modality application

.dblogin hide Help

.dblogin buttonconfigure OK -text New \
    -command {.dblogin deactivate new}
.dblogin buttonconfigure Apply -text Open \
    -command {.dblogin deactivate open}
.dblogin buttonconfigure Cancel -text Exit \
    -command {.dblogin deactivate exit}

.dblogin default OK

...
```

Messagedialog

The [INCR WIDGETS] messagedialog combines the display of an image and text together with dialog behavior. The option set allows the image to be located at various locations relative to the text: n, s, e, and w. Padding options have been included to provide extra space surrounding the text. Since the messagedialog is a dialog, all the button management commands from the buttonbox class are also available.

Many examples of typical messagedialog usage have been previously illustrated. A more unusual example is that of a copyright like the one depicted in Figure 4-39. The following code segment creates this copyright dialog and activates it. The dialog is non-modal and unnecessary buttons have been hidden, leaving only the OK button.

Figure 4-39: Messagedialog

```
messagedialog .cr -title "Copyright" \
    -bitmap @ora.xbm -imagepos n \
    -text "Copyright 1996\nAll rights reserved"

.cr hide Apply
.cr hide Cancel
.cr hide Help

.cr activate
```

By default, selection of the OK button will deactivate the copyright dialog. Yet, if this were the first dialog for our application, forcing the user to explicitly remove it repeatedly would be quite annoying. As a matter of fact, it would be user hostile. A better approach would be to display the copyright for a finite period of time and then deactivate it ourselves. The Tk `after` command could be used to create this effect. This would provide two means by which the copyright notice may be removed: user action or timer.

```
after 10000 {.cr deactivate}
```

Promptdialog

The [INCR WIDGETS] promptdialog mirrors the appearance of the Motif prompt dialog. It is a dialog whose childsite contains an entryfield widget. All the entryfield options

---

are available, along with the buttonbox button management commands. For example, a password prompt can quickly be created which looks like the one in Figure 4-40. It inhibits the display of the input text by setting the -show option to display asterisks in place of each character entered in the entryfield.

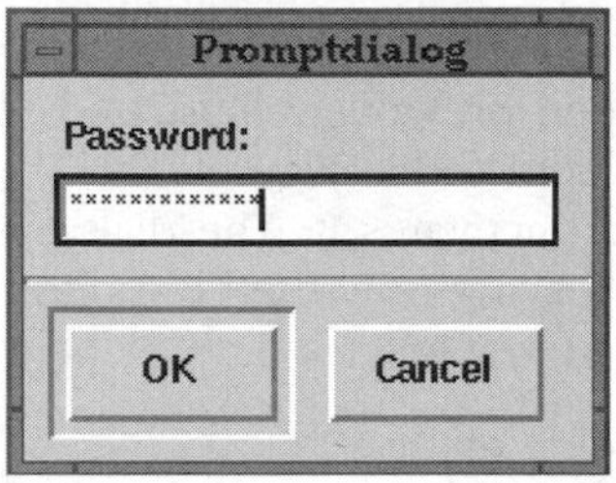

Figure 4-40: Promptdialog

```
promptdialog .pd -modality global -show * \
    -title Promptdialog -labeltext Password:
.pd hide Apply
.pd hide Help

if {[.pd activate]} {
    puts "Password entered: [.pd get]"
} else {
    puts "Password prompt cancelled"
}
```

Selectiondialog

The selectiondialog class combines a scrolledlistbox of items, an editable entryfield for the selected item, and a pair of labels, allowing the user to select or enter one item from a list of alternatives. It is a dialog-based extension of the [INCR WIDGETS] selectionbox class. The selectiondialog also provides a childsite and an option to control its position. This enables the widget to be extended by placing other widgets in the childsite, specializing the functionality.

The selectiondialog includes a wide assortment of options. Since both the scrolledlistbox and the entryfield component widgets have labels, their position control options have been kept. Options have also been included to hide each of the two major components.

Let's consider an application that requires an icon selection dialog, visually displaying the icon as the textual name is selected from the list. We'll use the childsite in the selectiondialog, filling it with a canvas for icon display. We'll also modify the default behavior of the selection command for the items list to place the icon bitmap in the canvas. Finally, we'll force the user to select icons from the list rather than type them, by turning off the display of the selection entryfield. The final product is illustrated in Figure 4-41.

```
selectiondialog .icons -title "Icon Selector" \
    -itemslabel Icons -itemscommand SelectProc \
    -selectionon no -items [exec ls]
```

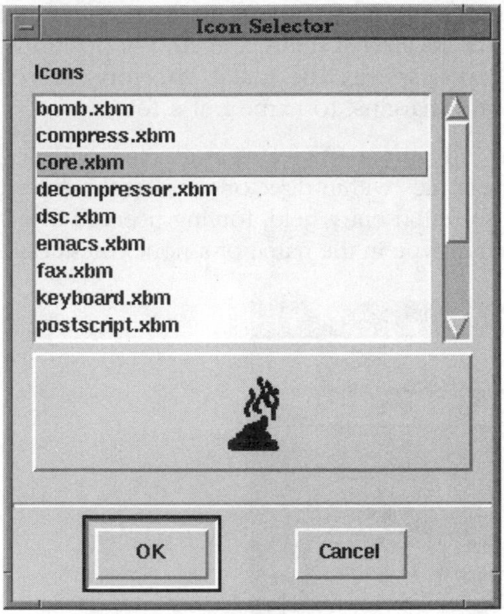

Figure 4-41: Selectiondialog

```
.icons hide Help
.icons hide Apply

set cs [.icons childsite]
pack $cs -fill x

canvas $cs.canvas -height 70 \
    -relief raised -borderwidth 2
pack $cs.canvas -fill x -expand yes

proc SelectProc {} {
    global cs

    .icons selectitem

    $cs.canvas delete all
    $cs.canvas create bitmap \
        [expr [winfo width $cs.canvas] / 2] \
        [expr [winfo height $cs.canvas] / 2] \
        -bitmap @[.icons get]
}

.icons activate
```

Fileselectiondialog

The [INCR WIDGETS] fileselectiondialog combines the `fileselectionbox` and `dialog` classes to achieve a Motif-style file selection dialog. It consists of a file and directory list as well as a filter and a selection entry widget. The display of each of these components can be controlled through options. A childsite has been provided along with a position option. The site can be located at the n, s, e, and w positions. The option set is quite extensive, letting you specify the initial directory, search commands, filter mask, no-match string, and margins, to name but a few.

To illustrate, the following example shown in Figure 4-42 creates a fileselectiondialog for selection of C language source and header files within directories using the -mask option. It also turns off the display of the selection entry field, forcing users to select only existing files, rather than allowing them to type in the name of a nonexistent one.

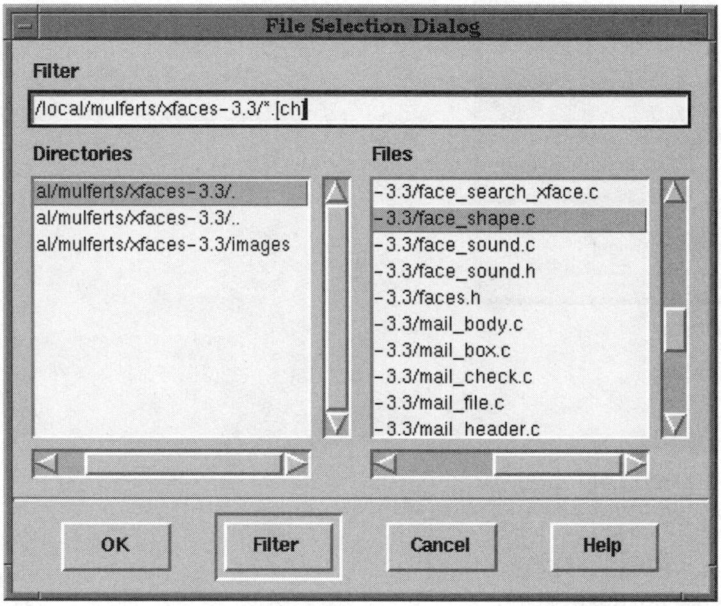

Figure 4-42: Fileselectiondialog

```
fileselectiondialog .fsd -selectionon no \
    -mask "*.\[ch\]"

.fsd activate
```

A file selection widget is now offered by the TK core, but the [INCR WIDGETS] widget is still useful if you want a non-modal widget.

Canvasprintdialog

[INCR WIDGETS] provides a handy dialog for preformatting the postscript output of a Tk canvas widget. This dialog displays a shrunken copy of a canvas in a stamp area. It supports configuration of the page size, orientation, and print command. The output may be posterized or, in other words, spread out over MxN pages, and even stretched to fit on your selected page size. In addition, the widget provides a command for easy computation of typical paper sizes. This can be quite useful when constructing your input canvas size.

The basic functionality of the canvasprintdialog is contained in a separate mega-widget called canvasprintbox. Structurally, the canvasprintdialog is a dialog mega-widget containing a canvasprintbox. Since the canvasprintdialog is dialog-based, all the dialog commands for controlling button display and their callback commands are available.

The canvasprintdialog layout contains option menus for output, paper size, and orientation. The stamp appears centered in the dialog above the checkbuttons for posterization and stretching. File output selection demands filename input, whereas printer output requires a printer command. So, if you've chosen to go with one output mode versus the other, the label of the entry field is modified appropriately.

The following example code creates the canvasprintdialog depicted in Figure 4-43, displaying a source canvas filled with various geometric shapes. The actual code required to produce the shapes has been left to your imagination.

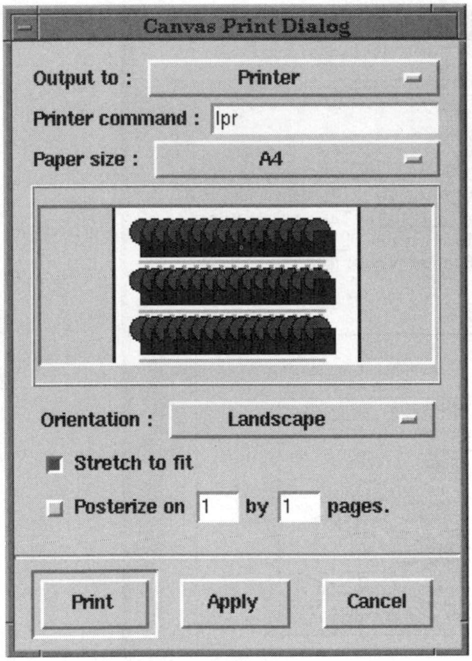

Figure 4-43: Canvasprintdialog

```
canvas .c
pack .c -expand 1 -fill both

# Fill canvas with shapes.

Canvasprintdialog .pcd -modality application \
    -pagesize A4

.pcd setcanvas .c

if {[.pcd activate]} {
    .pcd print
}
```

Hyperhelp

The [INCR WIDGETS] hyperhelp widget is a HTML hypertext help viewer. HTML is not only the language of the Web; it has become one of the more common formats for help files. At the time of this writing, the hyperhelp widget is able to process HTML 1.0 codes. Support for the more advanced codes is forthcoming.

The hyperhelp interface is simple. Help files are displayed in a scrolled region below a menubar containing topic and navigate pulldowns. The topic menu lists the configured topics. As they are selected, the associated HTML help file is rendered in the scrolled area. The navigate menu lets the user move through the help file history. Figure 4-44 shows a typical hyperhelp example.

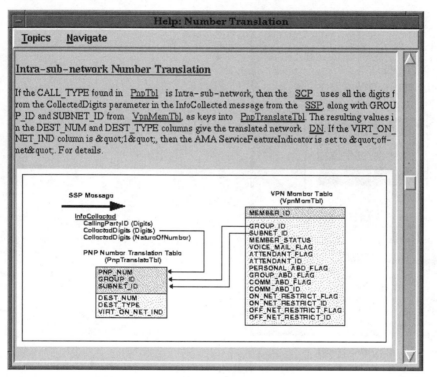

Figure 4-44: Hyperhelp

From a programming perspective, the hyperhelp mega-widget is similar to other dialogs. The widget supports modal blocking, activation, and deactivation. In addition, a `showtopic` command is provided to initialize or change the current topic. Topics are directly mapped to HTML help files. The option set enables the help file source directory and topic list to be configured.

Sample Application

Thus far, each [INCR WIDGETS] mega-widget has been presented separately. In this section, we'll put it all together and illustrate the use of [INCR WIDGETS] in the construction of a complete application. We'll build a multi-file text editor, capable of splitting the screen either vertically or horizontally. All in all, we'll do the whole thing in less than 170 lines of Tcl code, illustrating the use of dialogs, panedwindows, and scrolledtext mega-widgets.

The main window for the editor will contain a menubar and panedwindow. We'll create scrolledtext widgets on demand as children of the panes. The menubar will house the actions available. The following code segment creates our main window and sets the dimensions using the option database.

```
option add *edit.width 6i startupFile
option add *edit.height 6i startupFile

frame .mbar -borderwidth 2 -relief raised
pack .mbar -side top -fill x

panedwindow .edit
pack .edit -expand yes -fill both
```

The menubar needs a file menu for loading and saving files. The actions will activate dialogs for file selection and possible error notification. We'll also need a means for quitting the application. The following code adds the file menu to the menubar and binds the accelerators (keys that invoke the commands when pressed) to the window. The procedures for loading, saving, and clearing the text areas will be defined later.

```
menubutton .mbar.file -text "File" \
    -underline 0 -menu .mbar.file.menu
pack .mbar.file -side left -padx 4

menu .mbar.file.menu
.mbar.file.menu add command -label "Load..." \
    -accelerator "  ^L" -underline 0 \
    -command file_load
bind . <Control-KeyPress-l> \
    { .mbar.file.menu invoke "Load..." }

.mbar.file.menu add command -label "Save As..." \
    -accelerator "  ^S" -underline 0 \
    -command file_save_as
bind . <Control-KeyPress-s> \
    { .mbar.file.menu invoke "Save As..." }

.mbar.file.menu add separator

.mbar.file.menu add command -label "Quit" \
    -accelerator "  ^Q" -underline 0 \
    -command {clear_text; exit}
bind . <Control-KeyPress-q> \
    { .mbar.file.menu invoke Quit }
```

Next, we'll add menubar commands for splitting the screen and changing the orientation under a view menu. The changing of orientation requires us to configure the -orient option of the panedwindow appropriately. The procedure for splitting the window comes later.

```
menubutton .mbar.view -text "View" \
    -underline 0 -menu .mbar.view.menu
pack .mbar.view -side left -padx 4

menu .mbar.view.menu
.mbar.view.menu add command -label "Split" \
    -underline 0 -command split_view
.mbar.view.menu add separator
.mbar.view.menu add command -label "Horizontal" \
    -command {.edit configure -orient horizontal} \
    -underline 0
.mbar.view.menu add command -label "Vertical" \
    -command {.edit configure -orient vertical} \
    -underline 0
```

We'll be needing a couple of messagedialogs for error reporting and exit confirmation. The type of errors we need to report include not being able to write out the file to disk. Exit confirmations request the user to save changes prior to exiting. Since both these dialogs will need to vary their text message to include the filename, we'll create the dialogs now and activate them later whenever we need to, configuring the text as appropriate. Figure 4-45 shows the message dialogs as they will appear with their text messages configured.

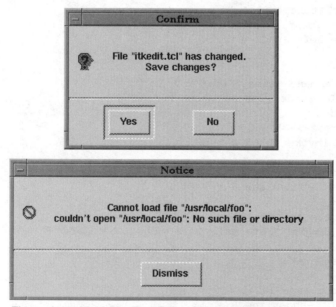

Figure 4-45: Multi-File Text Editor Message Dialogs

```
messagedialog .notice -title "Notice" \
    -bitmap info -modality application
.notice hide OK
.notice hide Help
.notice buttonconfigure Cancel -text "Dismiss"
```

```
messagedialog .confirm -title "Confirm" \
    -bitmap questhead -modality application
.confirm hide Help
.confirm buttonconfigure OK -text "Yes"
.confirm buttonconfigure Cancel -text "No"
```

We'll need a means of selecting files for loading or saving. The straight out-of-the-box [INCR WIDGETS] fileselectiondialog almost fits the bill, but not quite. When users select a file to be loaded, they also need to select a pane to place it in. What we need is a fileselectiondialog with an embedded optionmenu for pane selection. Fortunately, the fileselectiondialog can easily be extended using the childsite provided for just this sort of situation. We'll just stick an optionmenu in its childsite and fill the menu with the list of available panes, adjusting the contents with each split of the editor. Since we'll have to access the optionmenu later in various procedures, we'll save its widget path name in a variable. Our fileselectiondialog will look similar to the one shown in Figure 4-46.

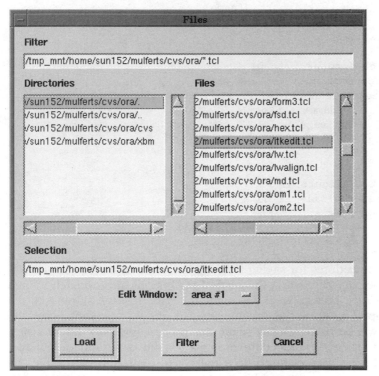

Figure 4-46: Multi-File Editor File Selection Dialog

```
fileselectiondialog .files -title "Files" \
    -childsitepos s -modality application
.files hide Help

set PaneMenu "[.files childsite].panes"
optionmenu $PaneMenu -labeltext "Edit Window:"
pack $PaneMenu -pady 6
```

All that is left is to write a few procedures. First, we need the procedure to load a file into a selected pane. It will be tied to the load menu option and needs to activate the fileselectiondialog, waiting for a selection. Once a file has been chosen, we'll retrieve it from the dialog and get the selected pane from the option menu. Next, we'll clear the desired pane and import the file. Should an error occur during loading, we'll use the notification messagedialog to alert the user of the problem. Finally, we'll set the title for the scrolledtext widget to be the filename.

```
proc file_load {} {
    global FileName PaneMenu

    .files buttonconfigure OK -text "Load"

    if {[.files activate]} {
        set fname [.files get]
        set pane [$PaneMenu get]
        set win [.edit childsite $pane]
        set cmd {$win.text import $fname}

        clear_text $win

        if {[catch $cmd err] != 0} {
            .notice configure -bitmap error \
                -text "Cannot load file\
                    \"$fname\":\n$err"
            .notice activate
            return
        }

        $win.text configure \
            -labeltext "file: $fname"
        set FileName($win) $fname
    }
}
```

Similarly, we need procedures for saving files. We'll use the same fileselectiondialog that was used before, configuring the label of the buttons appropriately. When the user selects the save button, we'll determine the pane to save along with the filename and attempt to perform the operation. Again, should problems occur, the notification dialog will be used. We'll separate this process into two different procedures. The file_save_as procedure prompts for the pane and output filename, and the file_save procedure does the actual exporting of the file. By dividing the work, we can reuse the file_save procedure later when we need to save changes as we clear the text. This way, we won't need to repeatedly prompt when saving multiple files.

These two procedures and the file_load proc use a couple of global variables. The first variable, FileName, is an array that associates panewindow childsites with the filename occupying the space. Since the "file save as" action allows the user to change filenames, we'll need this array to hold all the names associated with different panes. In order to remember where the user has made changes since the last save, we'll associate the array of panes with an array of dirty flags (Boolean values that are cleared when the file is saved and set when a keystroke is made).

```
proc file_save_as {} {
    global FileName PaneMenu

    .files buttonconfigure OK -text "Save"

    if {[.files activate]} {
        set pane [$PaneMenu get]
        set win [.edit childsite $pane]
        set FileName($win) [.files get]

        file_save $win
    }
}

proc file_save {win} {
    global FileName FileChanged

    set cmd {$win.text export $Filename($win)}

    if {[catch $cmd err] != 0} {
        .notice configure -bitmap error \
            -text "Cannot save file\
                \"$FileName($win)\":\n$err"
        .notice activate
        return
    }

    set FileChanged($win) 0
    $win.text configure \
        -labeltext "file: $FileName($win)"
}
```

Another procedure we'll need is one to clear a pane and save any pending changes. We'll also add in some versatility. The **areas** parameter will take the childsite of the pane to be cleared as a argument. Should one not be provided, then we'll set it to all the panes using the `childsite` command. This allows us to kill two birds with one stone. We can use this procedure to clear a single pane as we load in new files and also to clear out all the panes during cleanup prior to exiting.

```
proc clear_text {{areas ""}} {
    global FileName FileChanged FileWindows

    if {$areas == ""} {
        set areas [.edit childsite]
    }

    foreach win $areas {
        if {$FileChanged($win)} {
            set fname \
```

```
          [file tail $FileName($win)]
      .confirm configure \
        -text "File \"$fname\"\
          has changed.\
            \nSave changes?"
      if {[.confirm activate]} {
        file_save $win
      }
    }

    $win.text clear
    set FileChanged($win) 0
  }
}
```

Last, we'll need a procedure that splits the screen, adding a new pane on the bottom and filling its childsite with a scrolledtext widget. We'll also initialize our global variables used for tracking changes and associating filenames with panes. In addition, we'll update the contents of our optionmenu in the fileselectiondialog to include the new pane and do the dirty flag binding.

```
proc split_view {} {
  global FileName FileChanged FileWindows PaneMenu

  set pane "area #[incr FileWindows]"
  .edit add $pane -minimum 100
  $PaneMenu insert end $pane

  set win [.edit childsite $pane]
  set FileName($win) untitled.txt
  set FileChanged($win) 0

  scrolledtext $win.text -wrap none \
    -labeltext "file: $FileName($win)" \
    -hscrollmode none -vscrollmode dynamic
  pack $win.text -expand yes -fill both

  bind [$win.text component text] <KeyPress> \
    "set FileChanged($win) 1"
}
```

With our procedures defined, we need one last bit of initialization to kick-start our editor. We'll need to set our global variable that tracks the number of panes to 0 and then split the screen the first time. This adds our first pane and scrolled text area, producing the screen layout illustrated in Figure 4-47.

```
set FileWindows 0
split_view
```

Now as we use it, splitting the screen and loading new files, it would look like the one shown in Figure 4-48. Not a bad little split-screen editor for 170 lines of code.

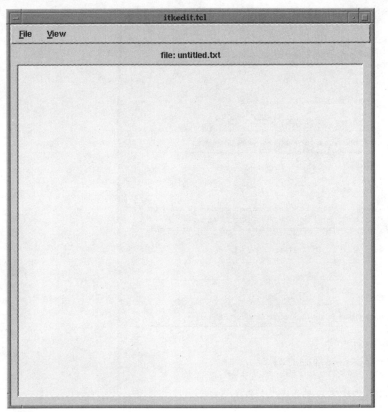

Figure 4-47: Multi-File Text Editor Initial Layout

Contributing to [INCR WIDGETS]

[INCR WIDGETS] is a continuing effort. We have many new mega-widgets currently under development, and contributions are greatly appreciated. [INCR WIDGETS] is a good start in the direction of establishing a strong set of object-oriented mega-widgets, but I swear that every time I go back and look at the source I see an even better of doing something. Should anybody within the Tcl/Tk community come upon a good improvement, a great enhancement, or an awesome new mega-widget altogether, please don't hesitate to send it to the author listed in the source file header or to myself, *mulferts@austin.dsccc.com,* as moderator. Any members of the development team are always available via email for a technical interchange of ideas. You'll also find us lurking about the *comp.lang.tcl* newsgroup.

The [INCR WIDGETS] distribution is moderated. Contributed mega-widgets must be of good quality and complete with documentation, tests, and demonstrations. Please follow the coding style found in the distribution source. This includes man page and test script formats as well. The languages and extensions on which [INCR WIDGETS] is based are of high standards. [INCR WIDGETS] strives to attain this same level.

The mega-widgets we are looking for include but are not limited to the following list. Should you be interested in signing up for any of those listed here, please send

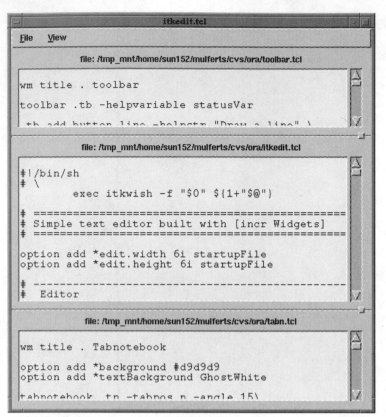

Figure 4-48: Multi-File Text Editor with Several Files Opened

email to *mulferts@spd.dsccc.com*. Also, should you have any ideas on others not listed, please send email to the same.

[INCR WIDGETS] Distribution

The [INCR WIDGETS] distribution is included with [INCR TCL] version 2.0 and greater. It is available via ftp at *ftp.neosoft.com/languages/tcl/NEW*. Consult the included release documentation for installation notes. For the latest in distribution information, consult our Web site: *http://www.tcltk.com/iwidgets*.

The [INCR TCL] distribution will always include the most current release of [INCR WIDGETS] possible at the time of its release. It is anticipated that [INCR WIDGETS] will change more rapidly than [INCR TCL]. This being the case, in between [INCR TCL] releases, the latest version of [INCR WIDGETS] is also separately available via ftp at the same location as well as the Web site.

The version number of [INCR WIDGETS] tracks the release of [INCR TCL], identifying its compatibility. The version numbering system for [INCR WIDGETS] includes an extra number. For example, Version 2.0.3 of [INCR WIDGETS] is compatible with [INCR TCL] 2.0. As the minor number of [INCR TCL] increases the second digit of the [INCR WIDGETS] version varies. This makes for easy release compatibility identification.

Acknowledgments

Thanks to the original development team, comprised of Mark Ulferts, Bret Schuhmacher, Sue Yockey, Alfredo Jahn, John Sigler, and Bill Scott. Also thanks to Mark Harrison for his influence, confidence, and ideas. Much credit goes to Michael McLennan, creator of [INCR TCL] and [INCR TK], for providing beta copies, training, assistance, and his infectious enthusiasm.

Thanks also to DSC Communications for picking up the copyright and supporting the public release of this software. I would specifically like to mention, Allen Adams, Larry Sewell, and Gil Stevens. In addition, numerous directors and managers have allowed me to work on this effort, cutting time out of my already full schedule for [INCR WIDGETS] development. They include Mahesh Shah, Rick Ross, Kevin Gallagher, Jack Davenport, and most notably, Pete Kielius and Pardeep Kohli.

Thanks to our many individual contributors—Ken Copeland for enhancing the panedwindow, smoothing out the scrolling and making panes bumpable; Tako Schotanus for contributing the canvasprintdialog mega-widget; Kris Raney who provided the Hyperhelp and Feedback mega-widgets based on Sam Shen's work with tkinspect; Tom Tromey for his endless supply of suggestions and bug reports which always include the necessary patch; and Tony Parent who did a great job of augmenting the fileselectionbox with a style option.

Thanks to John P. Davis for creating the [INCR WIDGETS] "Flaming Toaster" logo that can be seen at the [INCR WIDGETS] home page *http://www.tcltk.com/iwidgets* and to WebNet Technologies, *http://www.wn.com/*, for their assistance is designing the [INCR WIDGETS] Web site, as well as hosting it.

Special thanks to my wife Karen for supporting this effort and to our two girls, Katelyn and Bailey, who occasionally shared the PC with me. Also, thanks to my Discman and its relentless power supply as well as my CD collection. No tunes—no mega-widgets.

5

Tix Mega-Widgets

by Ioi Lam

The acronym Tix stands for Tk Interface Extension. Tix is different things for different people.

If you are a GUI application programmer, that is, if you earn a living by building graphical applications, you will appreciate Tix as a library of *mega-widgets*: widgets made out of other widgets. To use a crude analogy, if the widgets in the standard Tk library are bricks and mortar for a builder, the mega-widgets in the Tix library are walls, windows, or even pre-built kitchens. Of course, these "bigger components" are themselves made of bricks and mortar, but it will take much less effort to put them together than planting bricks on top of each other.

The Tix widgets not only help you speed up the development of your applications, they also help you in the design process. Since the standard Tk widgets are primitive, they force you to think of your house as, by using the same analogy, millions of bricks. With the help of the Tix mega-widgets, you can design your application in a more structural and coherent manner.

Moreover, the Tix library provides a rich set of widgets. Figure 5-1 shows all Tix widgets—there are more than 40 of them! Although the standard Tk library has many useful widgets, they are far from complete. The Tix library provides most of the commonly needed widgets that are missing from standard Tk: FileSelectBox, ComboBox, Control (a.k.a. SpinBox), and an assortment of scrollable widgets. Tix also includes many more widgets that are generally useful in a wide range of applications: NoteBook, FileEntry, PanedWindow, MDIWindow, and others.

With all these new widgets, you can introduce new interaction techniques into applications, creating more useful and more intuitive user interfaces. You can design your application by choosing the most appropriate widgets to match the special needs of your application and users.

On the other hand, if you are a widget developer, Tix provides an object-oriented programming environment carefully designed for the development of mega-widgets. If you have developed widgets in C, you know how slow and painful such a process can be. In recognition of the difficulties in widget development, the Tix Intrinsics includes many tools that dramatically cut down the efforts required to develop new widgets. With the Tix Intrinsics, the rapid prototyping/development of widgets is finally feasible; you can write a new mega-widget in a matter of hours or even minutes.

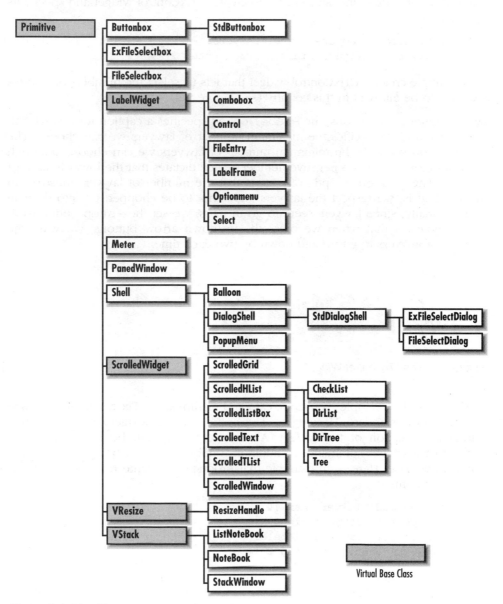

Figure 5-1: The Class Hierarchy of Tix Widgets

Getting Started: The TixControl Widget

Before delving into the deep philosophy of the Tix widgets, let us first have a quick example to demonstrate their usefulness and convenience. The TixControl widget is basically an entry widget plus two arrow buttons. The user can enter a value directly or press the buttons to change the value.

Creating a TixControl Widget

The following code demonstrates how to create a TixControl widget and specify its options:

```
tixControl .lawyers -label Lawyers: -max 10 -min 0
.lawyers configure -integer true -step 2
```

This example creates a TixControl widget that lets us select the numbers of lawyers we wish to be allowed in this country (see Figure 5-2).

Let us examine the options: the -label option specifies a caption for this widget. The -max option specifies the maximum number of lawyers we can choose. The -min option specifies the minimum number of lawyers we can choose; although we would love to enter a negative number, reality dictates that the lower limit must be zero. The -integer option indicates that the number of lawyers must be an integer; that is, we respect the lawyers' rights not to be chopped up into decimal points. Finally, since lawyers seem to go in pairs, we set the -step option to 2, which indicates that when we press the up/down arrow buttons, we want the number of lawyers to go up and down by two each time.

Figure 5-2: The TixControl Widget

As shown in the example, you can create and manipulate a Tix widget in the same manner as the standard Tk widgets. The options of the widget can be specified during the creation of the widget. Alternatively, they can be changed by the configure widget command. In addition, options can also be specified in the options database. Here is an example that produces the same result as the previous code fragment:

```
option add *lawyers.max 10
option add *lawyers.min 0
tixControl .lawyers -label Lawyers: -integer true
.lawyers configure -step 2
```

In Figure 5-3 you can see the composition of TixControl; it is made out of a label widget, an entry widget, and two button widgets.

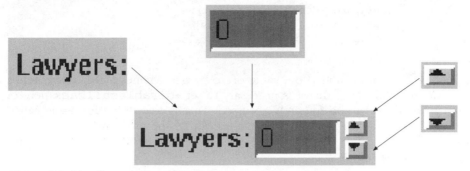

Figure 5-3: The Composition of TixControl

Accessing the Value of a TixControl Widget

The TixControl widget allows the user to input a value. There are several ways to read this value in your program. First of all, TixControl stores the current value in the `-value` option. You can query the `-value` option by calling the command

```
.c cget -value
```

This command will return the current value of the tixControl widget `.c`. The following command sets the value of the widget to a new number (100):

```
.c configure -value 100
```

The second way to access the value of TixControl is to use the `-variable` option. This option instructs the TixControl widget to store the value into a global variable so that you can read it at any time. Also, by assigning a new value to this global variable, you can change the value of the TixControl widget. Here is an example:

```
.c configure -variable myvar
set myvar 100
```

In some situations, you may want to be informed immediately when the value of the TixControl widget changes. To accomplish this, you can supply a Tcl *callback* script to the `-command` option. The following line causes the TCL procedure `valueChanged` to be called whenever the value of `.c` changes:

```
tixControl .c -command valueChanged
```

Disabling Callbacks Temporarily

The callback script you supply with the `-command` option is called whenever the widget's value changes, regardless of whether the user changed it or the program itself. If the callback script changes the value, then it will be recursively called again, which is probably not a good idea.

To overcome this problem, the callback script can temporarily disable callbacks by using the `-disablecallback` option. Here is an example:

```
tixControl .c -command addOne
proc addOne {value} {
```

```
        .c configure -disablecallback true
        .c configure -value [incr value]
        .c configure -disablecallback false
    }
```

The procedure addOne adjusts the value of .c by one whenever the user enters a new value into .c. Notice that it is necessary to set -disablecallback here or otherwise addOne will be infinitely recursed! That is because addOne is called *every time* the value changes, either by the user or by the program.

Validating User Inputs

Sometimes it may be necessary to check the user input against certain criteria. For example, you may want to allow only even numbers in a TixControl widget. To do this, you can use the -validatecmd option, which specifies a Tcl command to call whenever the user enters a new value. Here is an example:

```
tixControl .c -value 0 -step 2 -validatecmd evenOnly
proc evenOnly {value} {
    return [expr $value - ($value %2)]
}
```

The value parameter to evenOnly is the new value entered by the user. The evenOnly procedure makes sure that the new value is even by returning a modified, even number. The Tcl command specified by the -validatecmd must return a value which it deems valid, and this value will be stored in the -value option of the TixControl widget.

Accessing the Components Inside Mega-Widgets

As we have seen, the TixControl widget is composed of several widgets: one label widget, one entry widget, and two button widgets. These "widgets inside mega-widgets" are called *subwidgets* in the Tix terminology. You will often have to access these subwidgets. For example, sometimes you need to change the configuration options of the subwidgets. In other cases, you may need to interact with the subwidgets directly.

Subwidget Names

Each subwidget inside a mega-widget is identified by a *subwidget name*. Naturally, the label and entry subwidgets inside a TixSelect widget are called label and entry, respectively. The two button widgets are called incr and decr because they are used to increment and decrement the value inside the TixControl widget (see Figure 5-4).

The subwidget Method

While it's convenient to throw together many widgets and handle them as one large mega-widget, you don't want to lose the ability to manipulate the smaller widgets individually. All Tix mega-widgets support the subwidget method. This method takes at least one argument, the name of a subwidget. When you pass only one argu-

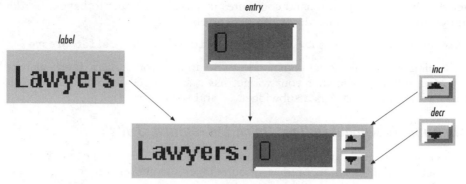

Figure 5-4: Subwidgets Inside the TixControl Widget

ment to this method, it returns the pathname of the subwidget which is identified by that name. For example, if `.c` is the pathname of a TixControl widget, the command:

```
.c subwidget entry
```

returns the pathname of the `entry` subwidget, which is `.c.frame.entry` in this case.

If you call the `subwidget` method with additional arguments, the widget command of the specified subwidget will be called with these arguments. For example, if `.c` is, again, the pathname of a TixControl widget, the command:

```
.c subwidget entry configure -bg gray
```

will cause the widget command of the `entry` subwidget of `.c` to be called with the arguments `configure -bg gray`. So actually, this command will be translated into the following call:

```
.c.frame.entry configure -bg gray
```

which calls the configure method of the entry subwidget with the arguments `-bg gray` and changes its background color to gray.

You can call the `subwidget` method with other types of arguments to access different methods of the specified subwidget. For example, the following call:

```
.c subwidget entry icursor end
```

calls the `icursor` method of the `entry` subwidget with the argument `end`, thus setting the insert cursor of the `entry` subwidget to the end of its input string.

Chaining the subwidget Method

Some Tix mega-widgets may have subwidgets that in turn contain subwidgets. For example, the TixExFileSelectDialog widget contains a TixExFileSelectBox subwidget called `fsbox`, which in turn contains a TixComboBox subwidget called `dir`. If you want to access the `dir` subwidget, you can just "chain" the `subwidget` method. For example, if you have a TixExFileSelectDialog called `.file`, the following command will return the pathname of the `dir` subwidget of the `fsbox` subwidget of `.file`:

```
.file subwidget fsbox subwidget dir
```

Moreover, the following command configures the `dir` subwidget to have a border of the groove type with a border width of 2 pixels:

```
.file subwidget fsbox subwidget dir configure -bd 2 -relief groove
```

The chaining of the subwidget command can be applied for as many levels as necessary, depending on whether your widget has a subwidget that has a subwidget that has a subwidget that has a subwidget. . . and so on.

Configuring Subwidget Options Using the -options Switch

As shown earlier, you can use commands like `subwidget` *name* `configure` `...` to set the configuration options of subwidgets. However, this can get quite tedious if you want to configure many options of many subwidgets.

There is a more convenient and terse way to configure the subwidget options without using the `subwidget` method: the `-options` switch. All Tix mega-widgets support the `-options` switch, which can be used during the creation of the mega-widget.

The use of the `-options` switch is illustrated in Example 5-1 , which creates two TixControl widgets for the user to enter his income and age. Because of the different sizes of the labels of these two widgets, if we create them haphazardly, the output may look like Figure 5-5(a) .

Example 5-1: Using the -options Switch

```
tixControl .income -label "Income: " -variable income -options {
    label.width       8
    label.anchor      e
    entry.width       10
    entry.borderWidth 3
}
tixControl .age     -label "Age: "    -variable age    -options {
    label.width       8
    label.anchor      e
    entry.width       10
    entry.borderWidth 3
}
pack .income .age -side top
```

(a) Unaligned labels   *(b) Aligned labels*

Figure 5-5: Using the -options Switch

To avoid this problem, we set the width of the label subwidgets of the .income and .age widgets to be the same (8 characters wide) and set their -anchor option to e (flushed to right), so that the labels appear to be well-aligned. Example 5-1 also does other things like setting the entry subwidgets to have a width of 10 characters and a border width of 3 pixels so that they appear wider and deeper. A better result is shown in Figure 5-5(b). As we can see from Example 5-1, the value for the -options switch is a list of one or more pairs of

```
subwidget-option-spec value ..
```

subwidget-option-spec is in the form *subwidget-name.option-name*. For example, label.anchor identifies the anchor option of the label subwidget, entry.width identifies the width option of the entry subwidget, and so on.

Notice we must use the *name* of the option, not the *command-line switch* of the option. For example, the option that specifies the border width of the entry subwidget has the command-line switch -borderwidth but its name is borderWidth (notice the capitalization on the name but not on the command-line switch). Therefore, we have used the capitalized version of entry.borderWidth 3 in Example 5-1 and not entry.borderwidth 3. To find out the names of the options of the respective subwidgets, please refer to their manual pages.

Configuring Subwidget Options Using the Tk Option Database

The -options switch is good if you want to specify subwidget options for one or a few mega-widgets. If you want to specify the subwidget for many mega-widgets, it is easier to use the Tk Option Database.

Options in the Tk Option Database can be specified using the option command and the pathname of the widget. For all the Tix mega-widgets, the pathnames of their subwidgets are guaranteed to end with the *name* of the subwidgets. For example, if we have a mega-widget called .a.b.megaw and it has a subwidget whose name is subw, then the pathname of the subwidget will be something like:

```
.a.b.megaw.foo.bar.subw
```

Therefore, if we want to specify options for it in the Option Database, we can issue commands like:

```
option add *a.b.megaw*subw.option1 value1
option add *a.b.megaw*subw.option2 value2
```

Notice that it will be wrong to issue the commands as:

```
option add *a.b.megaw.subw.option1 value1
option add *a.b.megaw.subw.option2 value2
```

because in general we will not know if the subwidget is an immediate child window of .a.b.megaw.*

---

* Such a decision is left to the mega-widget implementor and may vary in different versions of the same mega-widget. The rules of parsing the options database: a period means that the names are right next to each other in the hierarchy, the first lying right above the second; an asterisk allows other items to lie between them in the hierarchy.

Example 5-2 demonstrates how the Tk Option Database can be used to achieve the same effect as in Example 5-1.

Example 5-2: Using the Tk Option Database in Place of the -options Switch

```
option add *TixControl*label.width        8
option add *TixControl*label.anchor       e
option add *TixControl*entry.width        10
option add *TixControl*entry.borderWidth 3
tixControl .income -label "Income: " -variable income
tixControl .age    -label "Age: "    -variable age
pack .income .age -side top
```

Caution: Restricted Access

In the current implementation of Tix, there are no limits on how you can access the options of the subwidgets. However, many options of the subwidgets may already be used by the mega-widget in special ways. For example, the -textvariable option of the entry subwidget of TixControl may be used to store some private information for the mega-widget. Therefore, you should access the options of the subwidgets with great care. In general, you should access only those options that affect the appearance of the subwidgets (such as -font or -foreground) and leave everything else intact.*

Another Tix Widget: TixComboBox

The *TixComboBox* widget is very similar to the combobox widgets available in MS Windows and Motif 2.0. A TixComboBox consists of an entry widget and a listbox widget. Usually, the ComboBox contains a list of possible values for the user to select. The user may also choose an alternative value by typing it in the entry widget. Figure 5-6 shows two ComboBoxes for the user to choose fonts and character sizes. You can see from the figure that a listbox drops down and lists fonts that the user can choose from.

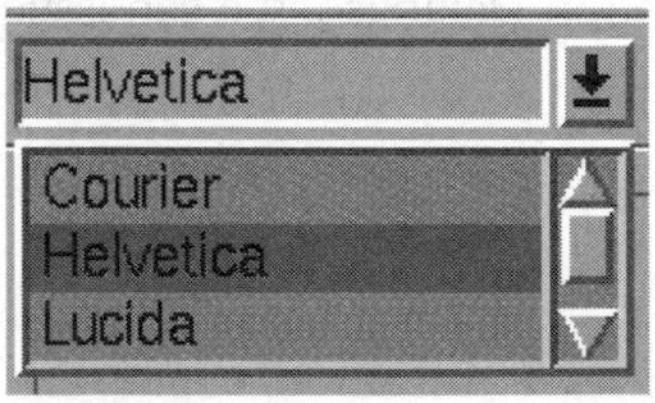

Figure 5-6: The TixComboBox Widget

Creating a TixComboBox Widget

In Example 5-3, we set up a ComboBox .c for the user to select an animal to play with. The user could just press the arrow button and select a predesignated animal

---

* In future versions of Tix, there will be explicit restrictions on which subwidget options you can access. Errors will be generated if you try to access restricted subwidget options.

like "dog." However, if she wants to try something new, she could type "micky" or "sloth" into the entry widget and she will get to play with her favorite animal.

Example 5-3: Creating a ComboBox

```
tixComboBox .c -label "Animal:" -editable true
.c insert end cat
.c insert end dog
.c insert end pig
```

Of course, sometimes we don't want too many sloths around us and we want to limit the range of the user's selections. In this case, we can do one of two things: First, we can set the -editable option to false so that the user cannot type in the entry widget at all. Second, we can use the -validatecmd option to check the input.

Controlling the Style of the TixComboBox

The TixComboBox widget can appear in many different styles. If we set the -dropdown option to true (which is the default), the listbox will appear only when the user presses the arrow button. When -dropdown is set to false, the listbox is always shown and the arrow button will disappear because it is not needed anymore.

There is also an option called -fancy. It is set to false by default. When set to true, a tick button and a cross button appear next to the entry widget. The tick button allows you to reselect the value that's already in the ComboBox. If you press the cross button, the entry widget will be cleared.

Static Options

The -dropdown and -fancy options are so-called "static options." They can be set only during the creation of the ComboBox. Hence, this code is valid:

```
tixComboBox .c -dropdown true
```

But the following code will generate an error because it attempts to set the -dropdown option *after* the ComboBox has already been created.

```
TixComboBox .c
.c configure -dropdown true
```

The restrictions of the static options, although annoying, nevertheless make sense because we don't want our interface to suddenly change its style. If sometimes a button is there and sometimes it disappears all by itself, that will certainly create a lot of confusion and make the user wonder why he should buy our software.

Accessing the value of the ComboBox is very similar to accessing the value of the TixControl widget. The ComboBox has four options, which we discussed earlier: -value, -variable, -command, and -validatecmd. You can use these four options to access the user input and respond to user actions in exactly the same way as previously discussed.

Monitoring the User's Browsing Actions

When the user drags the mouse pointer over the listbox, the listbox item under the pointer is highlighted and a "browse event" is generated. If you want to keep track of what items the user browses through, you can use the `-browsecmd` option. Here is an example:

```
tixComboBox .c -browsecmd mybrowse
....
proc mybrowse {item} {
    puts "user has browsed $item"
}
```

When the Tcl command specified by the `-browsecmd` option is called, it will be called with one parameter—the current item that the user has highlighted.

The `-browsecmd` is useful because it gives the user the possibility of temporarily seeing the results of several choices before committing to a final choice. For example, we can list a set of image files in a ComboBox. When the user single-clicks on an item on the ComboBox, we want to show a simplified view of that image. After the user has browsed through several images, he can finally decide on which image he wants by double-clicking on that item in the listbox.

The following is some pseudo Tcl code that does this. Please notice that the `-browsecmd` procedure is called every time the user single-clicks on an item or drags the mouse pointer in the listbox. The `-command` procedure is called only when the user double-clicks on an item.

```
tixComboBox .c -dropdown false -browsecmd show_simple \
-command load_fullsize
.c insert end "/pkg/images/flowers.gif"
.c insert end "/pkg/images/jimmy.gif"
.c insert end "/pkg/images/ncsa.gif"
proc show_simple {filename} {
    # Load in a simplified version of $filename
}
proc load_fullsize {filename} {
    # Load in the full size image in $filename
}
```

As we shall see, all Tix widgets that let us do some sort of selections have the `-browsecmd` option. This option allows us to respond to user events in a simple, straight-forward manner. Of course, you can do the same thing with the Tk `bind` command, but you don't want to do that unless you are very fond of things like: `<Control-Shift-ButtonRelease-1>` and `"%x %X $w %W %w"`.

The TixSelect Widget

The TixSelect widget shown in Figure 5-7 provides the same kind of facility that is available with the Tk radiobutton and checkbutton widgets. That is, TixSelect allows the user to select one or more values out of many choices. However, TixSelect is

Figure 5-7: The TixSelect Widget

superior because it allows you to layout the choices in much less space than is required by the Tk radiobutton widgets. Also, TixSelect supports complicated selection rules. Because of these reasons, TixSelect is a primary choice for implementing toolbar buttons, which often have strict space requirements and complicated selection rules.

Example 5-4 shows how to create a TixSelect widget. At line 1 of Example 5-4, we create a TixSelect using the the `tixSelect` command.

Example 5-4: Creating a TixSelect Widget

```
tixSelect .fruits -label "Fruits: " -orientation horizontal
   .fruits add apple  -text Apple  -width 6
   .fruits add orange -text Orange -width 6
   .fruits add banana -text Banana -width 6
   pack .fruits
```

Label and Orientation

As shown in Example 5-4, the `-label` option puts a label as the caption of the TixSelect widget. We can also control the layout of the button subwidgets using the `-orientation` option. The `-orientation` option can have two values: `horizontal` (the default value) or `vertical`. The buttons are lined up accordingly. The output of Example 5-4 is shown in Figure 5-8. This figure also shows the output of a TixSelect widget whose `-orientation` is set to `vertical`.

Figure 5-8: TixSelect in Alternative Orientations

Creating the Button Subwidgets and Configuring Their Appearance

After we have created the TixSelect widget, we can create the button subwidgets inside the TixSelect widget by the `add` widget command (lines 2–4 of Example 5-4).

The first argument to the `add` command is the name of the button subwidget. Additional arguments can be given in *option-value* pairs to configure the appearance of the button subwidget. These *option-value* pairs can be any of those accepted by a normal Tk button widget. As shown in Example 5-4, we use the `-text` option to put appropriate text strings over the three button subwidgets.

Notice that we also set the `-width` option of all the button subwidgets to 6 characters. This way, the three buttons will have the same width. If we didn't set the `-width` option for the button widgets, they would have different widths, depending on their text string, and the result would look less esthetically pleasing than buttons with same widths.

Accessing the Button Subwidgets

We have already seen the concept of subwidgets and how they can be accessed—when we create a Tix mega-widget, some subwidgets are created automatically, for example, the label and entry subwidgets inside a TixControl widget. We can access these subwidgets in a multitude of ways, including the use of the `subwidget` method.

One thing about the subwidgets we saw is that they are "static," meaning they are created when the mega-widget is created and they remain there for the whole lifetime of the mega-widget.

The TixSelect widget takes us to a new concept: *dynamic subwidgets*, which are subwidgets that can be created on-the-fly. After we add a new button into the TixSelect widget, we get a new subwidget. The name of this new subwidget is given by the first parameter passed to the `add` method. As Example 5-5 demonstrates, we can access this new subwidget using the `subwidget` method.

Example 5-5: Creating the Button Subwidgets Using the add Widget Command

```
tixSelect .s
.s add apple  -text Apple
.s add orange -text Orange
#   Mmmm..., let's make the widget look more educated
#   by using French words
.s subwidget apple  configure -text Pomme
.s subwidget orange configure -text Orange
```

Specifying Selection Rules

For simple selection rules, you can use the `-allowzero` and `-radio` options. The `-allowzero` option specifies whether the user can make an empty selection inside the TixSelect widget. If this option is set to false, the user must select at least one choice. The `-radio` option controls how many buttons can be selected at once: When set to true, the user can select only one button at a time; when set to false, the user can select as many buttons as he desires.

With these two options, we can write a program using two TixSelect widgets for little Jimmy to fill up his lunch box. On the Sandwich side, we set `-radio` to true and `-allowzero` to `false`. That means Jimmy can select one and only one sandwich among beef, cheese, or ham sandwiches. On the Veggie side, we want to encourage Jimmy to consume as much vegetables as possible, so we set the `-radio` option to `false`. We also set the `-allowzero` option to `false` so that Jimmy cannot get away with eating none of the vegetables (see Example 5-6).

Example 5-6: Specifying Simple Selection Rules

```
tixSelect .sandwich -allowzero false -radio true -label "Sandwich :"
.sandwich add beef    -text Beef
.sandwich add cheese -text Cheese
.sandwich add ham     -text Ham
tixSelect .vegie -allowzero false -radio false -label "Vegetable :"
.vegie add bean      -text Bean
.vegie add carrot   -text Carrot
.vegie add lettuce -text Lettuce
```

Accessing the Value of a TixSelect Widget

The *value* of a TixSelect widget is a list of the names of the button subwidgets that are currently selected. For example, in Example 5-4, if the user has selected the apple button, then the value of the TixSelect widget is `apple`. If the user has selected both the apple and the orange buttons, then the value is the list `"apple orange"`.

The TixSelect widget allows you to access its value through the same set of options as the the TixControl widget. The `-value` option stores the current value, which can be queried and modified using the `cget` and `configure` methods. You can also use the `-variable` option to specify a global variable to store the value of the TixSelect widget. The `-command` option specifies a Tcl command to be called whenever the user changes the selection inside a TixSelect widget. This command is called with one argument: the new value of the TixSelect widget. Don't forget the `-disablecallback` option, which you can use to control whether the command specified by the `-command` option should be called when the value of the TixSelect changes.

Specifying Complex Selection Rules

If you want to have more complex selection rules for the TixSelect widget, you can use the `-validatecmd` option. This option works the same as the `-validatecmd` option of the TixControl widget: it specifies a command to be called every time the user attempts to change the selection inside a TixSelect widget.

In Example 5-7, the procedure `TwoMax` will be called every time the user tries to change the selection of the fruits widget. `TwoMax` limits the maximum number of fruits to two by always truncating the value of the TixSelect widget so it has no more than two items. If you run this program, you will find out that you can never select a third fruit after you have selected two fruits.

Example 5-7: Specifying More Complex Selection Rules

```
tixSelect .fruits -label "Fruits: " -radio false -validatecmd TwoMax
    .fruits add apple  -text Apple  -width 6
    .fruits add orange -text Orange -width 6
```

```
.fruits add banana -text Banana -width 6
pack .fruits
proc TwoMax {value} {
    if {[llength $value] > 2} {
        return [lrange $value 0 1]
    } else {
        return $value
    }
}
```

Container Widgets

In addition to providing some nice-looking interface elements, Tix offers useful ways to organize the elements that you create. It does this by providing *container widgets*, which are widgets designed to contain whatever you want to put into them.

Different container widgets have different policies for arranging the widgets inside them. In this section, we'll talk about TixNoteBook, which arranges its subwidgets using a notebook metaphor; TixPanedWindow, which arranges its subwidgets in non-overlapping horizontal or vertical panes; and a family of "Scrolled Widgets," which attach scrollbars to their subwidgets.

TixNoteBook

When your need to put a lot of information into your interface, you may find out that your window has to grow intolerably big in order to hold all the information. Having a window that's 10,000 pixels wide and 5000 pixels high doesn't seem to be the perfect solution. Of course, you can "chop up" your big window into a set of smaller dialog boxes, but the user will most likely find it impossible to manage 20 different dialog boxes on their desktop.

The TixNoteBook (Figure 5-9) widget comes to the rescue. It allows you to pack a large interface into manageable "pages" using a notebook metaphor. It contains multiple pages with anything you want on them, displays one page at a time, and attaches a tab to each page so the user can bring it forward with a single click on the tab.

Adding Pages to a TixNoteBook

The sample program in Example 5-8 creates the TixNoteBook widget shown in Figure 5-9. In the first three lines, we create the notebook widget and two pages inside it. While we create the pages, we also set the labels on the tabs associated with each page, and use the −underline option to indicate the keyboard accelerator for each page.

Each time we create a page in the notebook using the add method, a frame subwidget is created automatically. This frame subwidget has the same name as the page (the first parameter passed to the add method). We can use the subwidget method to find out the pathname of this frame subwidget and pack everything we want to display on the page into this frame widget. Lines 4–10 of Example 5-8 shows how to create the widgets inside the "Hard Disk" page. Creating the widgets inside the "Network" page will be similar.

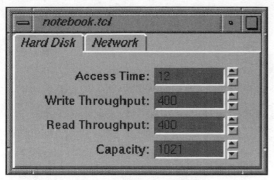

Figure 5-9: The TixNoteBook Widget

Example 5-8: Using the TixNoteBook Widget

```
tixNoteBook .n
.n add hd  -label "Hard Disk" -underline 0
.n add net -label "Network"   -underline 0

set frame [.n subwidget hd]
tixControl $frame.access   -label "Access Time:"
tixControl $frame.write    -label "Write Throughput:"
tixControl $frame.read     -label "Read Througput:"
tixControl $frame.capacity -label "Capacity:"
pack $frame.access $frame.write $frame.read $frame.capacity
    -side top -fill x
```

Note that in lines 2–3 of Example 5-8, we have indicated the keyboard accelerators for the two pages using the -underline option. The value of this option is the position of the character to be underlined in the string, where zero represents the first character. When the user presses Alt-N or Meta-N the "Network" page will be activated; on the other hand, if he presses Alt-H or Meta-H the "Hard Disk" page will be activated. The TixNoteBook widget will automatically create the keyboard bindings for these accelerators, in a way similar to what the menu widget does, so there is no need to set the keyboard bindings ourselves.

Delaying the Creation of New Pages

If your notebook contains many complicated pages, it may take quite a while to create all widgets inside these pages and your program will probably freeze for a few seconds when it pops up the notebook for the first time. To avoid embarrassing moments like this, we can use the "delayed page creation" feature of the TixNoteBook widget.

When we create a page using the add method, we can specify the optional parameter -createcmd so that we need to create the page only when the user wants to see it. This is illustrated in Example 5-9.

Example 5-9: Delayed Page Creation

```
tixNoteBook .n
.n add hd  -label "Hard Disk" -underline 0 -createcmd CreateHd
```

```
.n add net -label "Network"     -underline 0 -createCmd CreateNet

proc CreateHd {frame} {
    tixControl $frame.access    -label "Access Time:"
    tixControl $frame.write     -label "Write Throughput:"
    tixControl $frame.read      -label "Read Througput:"
    tixControl $frame.capacity -label "Capacity:"
    pack $frame.access $frame.write $frame.read $frame.capacity
        -side top -fill x
}

proc CreateNet {frame} {
    ...
}
```

In line 2 of Example 5-9, we use the `-createcmd` option to specify that the procedure `CreateHd` should be called when the "Hard Disk" page needs to be created. `CreateHd` takes one argument, the frame subwidget of the page. As we can see, Example 5-9 is not very different from Example 5-8, except now we can issue fewer commands during the setup of the NoteBook widget and the interface can be started up more quickly.

Changing Page Tabs and Deleting Pages

To change the information in the tabs of the pages, we can use the `pageconfigure` method. For example, the following command:

```
.nb pageconfigure hd -label "Fixed Disk"
```

changes the label from "Hard Disk" to "Fixed Disk." To delete a page, we can use the `delete` method.

You should avoid using `pageconfigure` and `delete`. Your users will just feel annoyed if the interface changes all the time and notebook pages appear and disappear every now and then.

PanedWindow

The TixPanedWindow widget arranges its subwidgets in non-overlapping panes. As we can see in Figure 5-10, the PanedWindow widget puts a resize handle between the panes for the user to manipulate the sizes of the panes interactively. The panes can be arranged either vertically or horizontally.

Each individual pane may have upper and lower limits of its size. The user changes the sizes of the panes by dragging the resize handle between two panes.

Adding Panes Inside a TixPanedWindow Widget

You can create a TixPanedWindow widget using the `tixPanedWindow` command. After that, you can add panes into this widget using the `add` method (see Example 5-10).

When you use the `add` method, several optional parameters let you control the size of each of the panes. The `-min` parameter controls the minimum size of the pane

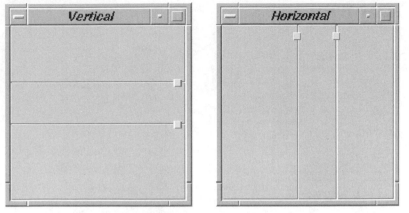

Figure 5-10: The TixPane Widget

and the **−max** parameter controls its maximum size. These two parameters control how much the user can expand or shrink a pane. If neither is specified, then the pane can be expanded or shrunk without restrictions.

In addition, the **−size** parameter specifies the initial size of the pane. If it is not specified, then the initial size of the pane is its natural size.

In Example 5-10, we set the initial size of **pane1** to 100 pixels using the **−size** parameter. We don't set the **−size** parameter for **pane2**, so it will appear in its natural size. However, we use the **−max** option for **pane2** so that the user can never expand the size of **pane2** to more than 300 pixels.

Example 5-10: Adding Panes into a TixPanedWindow Widget

```
tixPanedWindow .p
.p add pane1 -size 100
.p add pane2 -max 300

set p1 [.p subwidget pane1]
button $p1.b1 -text Button1
button $p1.b2 -text Button2
pack $p1.b1 $p1.b2 -side left -expand yes

set p2 [.p subwidget pane2]
button $p2.b -text "Another Button"
pack $p2.b -side left -expand yes -fill both

pack .p -expand yes -fill both
```

Each pane we have created using the **add** method is essentially a frame widget. After we have created the panes, we can put widgets inside them. As shown in Example 5-10, we can use the **subwidget** method to find out the name of the pane sub-widgets. Then we can just create new widgets as their children and pack these new widgets inside the panes. The output of Example 5-10 is shown in Figure 5-11.

Usually, when you create a new pane, it is added to the bottom or right of the list of panes. If you want to control the order in which the panes appear inside the Tix-

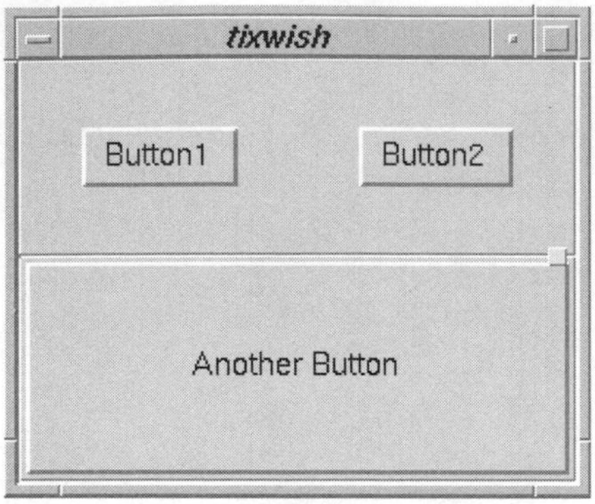

Figure 5-11: Output of Example 5-10

PanedWindow widget, you can use the optional parameters –before and –after in the add method. For example, the call:

```
.p add pane2 -after pane1
```

places the new pane immediately after pane1. The call:

```
.p add pane2 -before pane1
```

places the new pane immediately in front of pane1.

If you want to change the sizes of the existing panes or change their maximum/minimum size constraints, you can use the paneconfigure method. For example, the following code changes the size of pane2 to 100 pixels and adjusts its minimum size constraint to no less than 10 pixels:

```
.p paneconfigure pane2 -size 100 -min 10
```

Notice that after you call the paneconfigure method, the PanedWindow may jitter and that may annoy the user. Therefore, use this method only when it is necessary.

The Family of Scrolled Widgets

With plain Tcl/Tk, the widgets do not automatically come with scrollbars. If you want to use scrollbars with the text, canvas, or listbox widgets, you need to create scrollbars separately and attach them to the widgets. This can be a lot of hassle because you would almost always need scrollbars for these widgets. Sometimes you will wonder why you need to write the same boring code again and again just to get the scrollbars to work.

The Tix scrolled widgets are here to make your life easier. With a single command such as tixScrolledListBox or tixScrolledText, you can create a listbox or text widget that comes automatically with scrollbars attached.

Another advantage of the Tix scrolled widgets is that you can specify their scrolling policy so that the scrollbars appear only when they are needed. This feature is especially useful if you are displaying a lot of widgets and running out of screen real estate.

You can create a scrolled listbox widget using the `tixScrolledListBox` command. Notice that the widget created by the `tixScrolledListBox` command is not itself a listbox widget. Rather, it is a frame widget that contains two scrollbar subwidgets: one is called hsb (the horizontal scrollbar) and the other is called vsb (the vertical scrollbar). Similarly, the listbox being scrolled is also a subwidget which is appropriately called listbox. Therefore, if we need to put things into the listbox (as we always do!), we can use the `subwidget` method. As shown in Example 5-11, we first find the pathname of the listbox subwidget by calling `.sl subwidget listbox`. Then, we insert some items into the listbox subwidget.

Example 5-11: Scrolled Listbox Widget

```
tixScrolledListBox .sl -scrollbar auto
set listbox [.sl subwidget listbox]

for {set x 0} {$x < 6} {incr x} {
    $listbox insert end "This is item $x"
}

pack .sl -side left -expand yes -fill both
```

Also, as seen in the first line of Example 5-11, we use the `-scrollbar` option to control the scrolling policy of the TixScrolledListBox widget. Usually, we'll set it to `auto`: the scrollbars are displayed only if they are needed. Other possible values are:

- `both`: the two scrollbars are always displayed.
- `x`: the horizontal scrollbar is always displayed, while the vertical scrollbar is always hidden.
- `y`: the opposite of `x`.
- `none`: the two scrollbars are always hidden.

The result of Example 5-11 is shown in Figure 5-12.

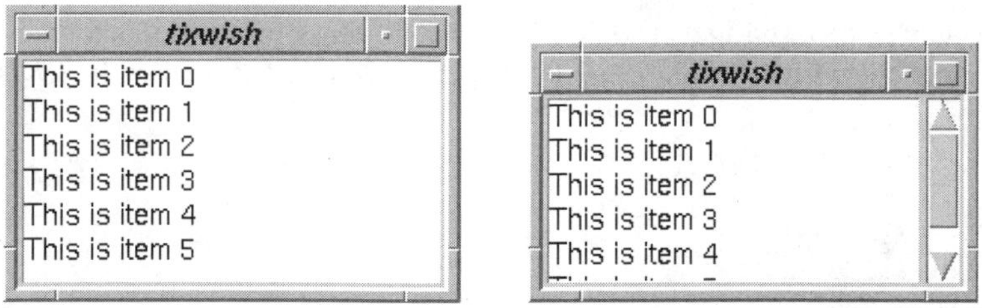

Figure 5-12: Scrolled ListBox with Automatic Scrollbars

The TixScrolledText widget is very similar to the TixScrolledListBox widget, except that it scrolls a text subwidget, which is called text. One problem with the TixScrolledText widget, though, is that its `-scrollbar` option doesn't work in the **auto** mode. This is due to a bug in Tk that doesn't report the width of the text subwidget correctly. Until this bug is fixed in Tk, the auto mode will behave the same way as the both mode for the TixScrolledText widget.

Another scrolled widget is TixScrolledWindow. Sometimes you have a large number of widgets that can't possibly be shown on the screen all at once and your application doesn't allow you to divide the widgets into several pages of a TixNoteBook. In this case, you can use TixScrolledWindow. It contains a frame subwidget called window. You can just create all the widgets you need as children of the window subwidget. An example is shown in Example 5-12, which uses the TixScrolledWindow widget to implement a "cheap" spreadsheet application. The boxes of the spreadsheet are just entry widgets and they are packed inside the window subwidget. The user will be able to scroll to different parts of the spreadsheet if it is too large to fit on one screen.

Example 5-12: Cheap Spreadsheet Application with TixScrolledWindow

```
tixScrolledWindow .sw -scrollbar auto
set f [.sw subwidget window]

for {set x 0} {$x < 10} {incr x} {
    frame $f.f$x
    pack  $f.f$x -side top -expand yes -fill both
    for {set y 0} {$y < 10} {incr y} {
        entry $f.f$x.e$y -width 10
        pack $f.f$x.e$y -side left -fill x
    }
}

pack .sw -side left -expand yes -fill both
```

There are two more scrolled widgets in the Tix library: TixScrolledTList scrolls a TixTList widget and TixScrolledHList scrolls a TixHList widget. The subwidgets that they scroll are called tlist and hlist, respectively. The TList and HList widgets are described in the coming section.

tixTList—The Tix Tabular Listbox Widget

TixTList is the Tabular Listbox widget. It displays a list of items in a tabular format. For example, the TixTList widget in Figure 5-13 displays files of a directory in rows and columns.

Figure 5-13: Files Displayed in a TixTList Widget in a Tabular Format

TixTList does essentially the same thing as the standard Tk listbox widget, i.e., it displays a list of items. However, TixTList is superior to the listbox widget in many respects. First, TixTList allows you to display the items in a two-dimensional format. This way, you can display more items at a time. Usually, the user can locate the desired items much faster in a two-dimensional list than the one-dimensional list displayed by the Tk listbox widget.

In addition, while the Tk listbox widget can display only text items, the TixTList widget can display a multitude of types of items: text, images, and widgets. Also, you can use many different fonts and colors in a TixTList widget. In Figure 5-12, we use graphical images inside a tixTList widget to represent file objects. In Figure 5-14, we display the names of all employees of a hypothetical company. Notice the use of a bold font to highlight all employees whose first name is Joe.

Figure 5-14: Employee Names Displayed in a TixTList Widget

Display Items

Before we rush to discuss how to create the items inside a TixTList widget, let's first spend some time on a very important topic about the Tix library: the relationship between the display items and the widgets that display them.

We can better define the terms by taking a quick preview of the TixHList widget, which will be covered in detail in the next section. Take a look at the item that shows the {usr} directory in the TixTList widget on the left and the TixHList widget on the right. They both display images next to text names; the only difference is how these items are arranged.

With this observation in mind, we can see a separation of tasks between the widgets and the items they display. We call the TixHList and TixTList widgets in Figure 5-15 *host widgets*: their task is to arrange the items according to their particular rules. However, they don't really care what these items display; they just treat the items as rectangular boxes. In contrast, these items, which are called *display items* in Tix terminology, control the visual information they display, like the images, text strings, colors, fonts, and so on. However, they don't really care where they will appear on the host widget.

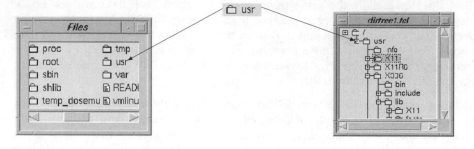

Figure 5-15: Same Type of Items Displayed in a TixTList (Left) and a TixHList (Right)

Advantages of Display Items

It is easy to see the advantages of separating the display items from their host widgets. First, the display items are easy to learn, since they are the same across different types of widgets. Once you learn about types of display items, you will know how to use them in all Tix widgets that support display items (currently these include TixHList, TixTList, and the spreadsheet widget TixGrid, but the number is growing). In contrast, if you want to create a text item for the Tk widgets, you will find out that the listbox, text, canvas, and entry widgets each have a different method of creating and manipulating text items.

Second, the hosts widgets that use display items are extensible. Because of the separation of task, the host widgets are not involved in the implementation details of the display items. Therefore, if you add a new type of display items, such as an `animation` type that displays live video, the host widgets will gladly take them in and display them. You don't need to modify the existing host widgets at all. In contrast, if you want to display graphical images in the existing Tk listbox widget, you'd better set aside 100 hours to rewrite it completely!

Third, display items are good for developers of host widgets, because now they just need to implement the arrangement policy of the host widgets. They don't need to worry about drawing at all because it is all handled by the display items. This is a significant saving in code because a widget that does not use display items has to spend 30% of its C code to do the drawing.

Display Items and Display Styles

The appearance of a display item is controlled by a set of attributes. For example, the `text` attribute controls the text string displayed on the item and the `font` attribute specifies what font should be used.

Usually, each of the attributes falls into one of two categories: *individual* or *collective*. For example, each of the items inside a TixTList widget may display a different text string; therefore, we call the text string an *individual attribute*. However, in most cases, the items share the same color, font, and spacing, and we call these *collective attributes*.

One question concerns where we keep the collective attribute for the display items. Certainly, we can keep a `font` attribute for each item, but this is not really an efficient solution. In fact, if all the items have the same font, we would be keeping a copy of the same font for each of the items we create. Since a host widget may have many thousands of items, keeping thousands of copies of the same font, or any other collective attribute, would be very wasteful.

To avoid the unnecessary duplication of resources, Tix stores the collective attributes in special objects called *display styles*. The relationship between display items and their styles is depicted in Figure 5-16. Each item holds its own copy of the individual attributes, such as `text`. In addition, each item has a special `style` attribute that tells it which style it should use. In Figure 5-16, therefore, since items *a* and *b* are assigned the same style, they share the same font and color. Item *c* is assigned a different style, so it uses a different font than *a* and *b*.

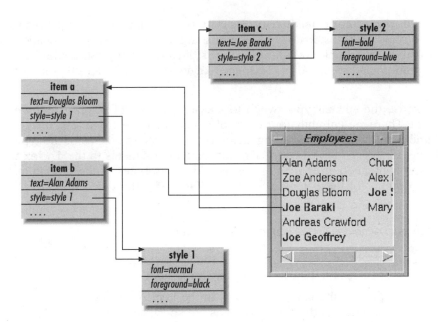

Figure 5-16: Relationship Between Display Items and Display Styles

Configuring and Deleting the Items

You can configure the individual attributes of the items using the `entryconfigure` method. There is also the `entrycget` method for querying the attributes of the items. To delete the items, you can use the `delete` method. In the following example, we use these two methods to change the first and third items to display the text strings One and Two and to change the third item to use the style `$style2`. Then we delete the second item using the `delete` command.

```
.t entryconfigure 0 -text One
.t entryconfigure 2 -text Two
.t delete 1
```

Using Display Items in the TixTList Widget

Now it's time to put our knowledge about host widgets, display items, and display styles into practice. The following example code creates two items in a TixTList widget using the `insert` method:

```
tixTList .t
pack .t

.t insert end -itemtype text -text "First Item"  -underline 0
.t insert end -itemtype text -text "Second Item" -underline 0

set picture [image create bitmap -file picture.xbm]
.t insert end -itemtype image -image $picture
```

As we can see, the `insert` method of TixTList is very similar to the `insert` method of the standard Tk listbox widget. The first argument it takes is the location of the new item. For example, 0 indicates the first location in the list, 1 indicates the second location, and so on. Also, the special keyword `end` indicates the end of the list.

Then, we can use the `-itemtype` switch to specify the type of display item we want to create. There are currently four types of items to choose from: text, image, imagetext, and window. In the preceding example, we create two items of the type `text` and one item of the type `image`. The subsequent arguments to the `insert` method set the configuration options of the individual attributes of the new item. The available options for these items are listed in Tables 5-1 through 5-7.

Table 5-1: Individual Attributes for the imagetext Display Item

Option	Meaning
-bitmap	Specifies the bitmap to display in the item.
-image	Specifies the image to display in the item. When both the -bitmap and -image options are specified, only the image will be displayed.
-style	Specifies the display style to use for this item.
-showimage	A Boolean value that specifies whether the image/bitmap should be displayed.
-showtext	A Boolean value that specifies whether the text string should be displayed.
-text	Specifies the text string to display in the item.
-underline	Specifies the integer index of a character to underline in the text string in the item. 0 corresponds to the first character of the text displayed in the widget, 1 to the next character, and so on.

Table 5-2: Individual Attributes for the text Display Item

Option	Meaning
-style	Specifies the display style to use for this item.
-text	Specifies the text string to display in the item.
-underline	Specifies the integer index of a character to underline in the text string in the item. 0 corresponds to the first character of the text displayed in the widget, 1 to the next character, and so on.

Table 5-3: Individual Attributes for the image Display Item

Option	Meaning
-style	Specifies the display style to use for this item.
-image	Specifies the image to display in the item.

Table 5-4: Individual Attributes for the window Display Item

Option	Meaning
-style	Specifies the display style to use for this item.
-window	Specifies the widget to display in the item.

Table 5-5: Collective Attributes for the imagetext and text Display Items

-activebackground	-activeforeground	-anchor
-background	-disabledbackground	-disabledforeground
-foreground	-font	-justify
-padx	-pady	-selectbackground
-selectforeground	-wraplength	

Table 5-6: Collective Attributes for the window Display Item

-anchor	-padx	-pady

Table 5-7: Collective Attributes for the image Display Item

-activebackground	-activeforeground	-anchor
-background	-disabledbackground	-disabledforeground
-foreground	-padx	-pady
-selectbackground	-selectforeground	

Setting the Styles of the Display Items

Note that in the preceding example, if we want to control the foreground color of the text items, we cannot issue commands like:

```
.t insert end -itemtype text -text "First Item" -foreground black
```

because −foreground is not an individual attribute of the text item. Instead, it is a collective attribute and must be accessed using a display style object. To do that, use the command tixItemStyle to create display styles, as shown in the following example:

```
set style1 [tixDisplayStyle text -font 8x13]
set style2 [tixDisplayStyle text -font 8x13bold]

tixTList .t; pack .t

.t insert end -itemtype text -text "First Item"  -underline 0
    -style $style1
.t insert end -itemtype text -text "Second Item" -underline 0
    -style $style2
.t insert end -itemtype text -text "Third Item"  -underline 0
    -style $style1
```

The first argument of tixDisplayStyle specifies the type of style we want to create. Each type of display item needs its own type of display styles. Therefore, for example, we cannot create a style of type text and assign it to an item of type image. The subsequent arguments to tixDisplayStyle set the configuration options of the collective attributes defined by this style. A complete list of the configuration options of each type of the display style has been shown earlier.

The tixDisplayStyle command returns the names of the newly created styles to us; we use the variables style1 and style2 to store these names. We can then assign the styles to the display items by using the names of the styles. As shown in Figure 5-17(a), by passing these two styles to the −style option of the display items, we assigned a medium-weight font to the first and third item and a bold font to the second item.

(a) Three text items in a TixTList   (b) The text items with fonts switched

Figure 5-17: Two Display Styles with Different Fonts

The name of the style returned by tixDisplayStyle is also the name of a command that we can use to control the style. For example, we can use the following commands to switch the fonts in the two styles we created in the preceding example:

Chapter 5: Tix Mega-Widgets

```
$style1 configure -font 8x13bold
$style2 configure -font 8x13
```

After the execution of this command, the font in the second item in the TixTList widget becomes medium-weight and the font in the first and third items becomes bold, as shown in Figure 17(b).

Choosing the Orientation and Number of Rows or Columns

There are three options that control the layout of the items in the TixTList widget. The -orientation option can be set to either vertical or horizontal. When -orientation is set to vertical, the items are laid out vertically from top down and wrapped to the next column when the bottom is reached (see Figure 5-18(a)). The opposite layout policy is chosen if -orientation is set to horizontal (see Figure 5-18(b)).

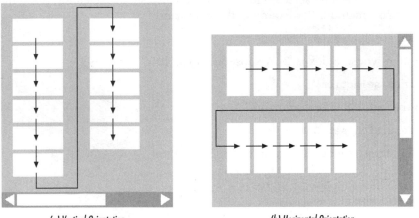

(a) Vertical Orientation   (b) Horizontal Orientation

Figure 5-18: The -orientation option of the TixSelect Widget

When the -orientation option is set to vertical, normally the number of columns displayed depends on the number of items in the TixTList widget; the more items there are, the more columns will there be. However, we can use the -columns option to control the number of columns. The items will be wrapped in a way so that the number of columns produced will be exactly as dicated by the -columns option.

One use of the -columns option is to specify the same layout policy as that of the standard Tk listbox widget. We can do this by setting -orientation to vertical and -columns to 1. This way we can get a replacement listbox widget that can display multiple fonts and colors and graphics!

The counterpart of the -columns option is the -rows option, which is used for the same purpose when the -orientation option is set to horizontal.

Event Handling

You can handle the events in a TList widget using the -browsecmd and -command options. The meanings of these two options are similar to their meanings in other Tix widgets such as the ComboBox. Usually, the command specified by -browsecmd is called when the user clicks or drags the mouse over the items or presses the arrow keys. The command specified by -command is called when the user double-clicks or presses the Return key. These commands are called with one extra argument—the index of the currently "active" item, which is usually the item under the mouse cursor.

The -selectmode option controls how many items the user can select at one time. In the single and browse modes, the user can select only one item at a time. In the multiple and extended modes, the user can select multiple items; the extended mode allows disjoint selections while the multiple mode does not.

Normally, the user selects the items using the mouse or the keyboard. You can find out which items the user has selected with the info selection method, which returns a list of the currently selected items. You can also set the selection using the selection set method. For example, the command

    .tlist selection set 3

selects the item whose index is 3. A subsequent call to

    .tlist info selection

will return the index 3. The command

    .tlist selection set 2 10

selects all the items at index 2 through 10. The method

    selection clear

empties the selection.

Hierarchical Widgets

Some very sophisticated relationships can be displayed through a hierarchical listbox or tree structure.

TixHList—The Tix Hierarchical Listbox Widget

TixHList is the Tix Hierarchical Listbox Widget. You can use it to display any data that have a hierarchical structure. For example, the HList widget in Figure 5-19(a) displays a Unix file system directory tree; the HList widget in Figure 5-19(b) displays the corporate hierarchy of a hypothetical company. As shown in these two figures, the entries inside the TixHList widget are indented and can be optionally connected by branch lines according to their positions in the hierarchy.

Creating a Hierarchical List

A TixHList widget can be created by the command tixHList. However, you probably want to create a TixHList with scrollbars attached. Therefore, you usually use the tixScrolledHList command to create a scrolled hierarchical listbox (line 1

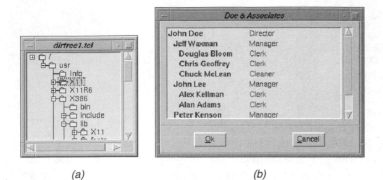

| (a) | (b) |

Figure 5-19: Examples of the TixHList Widget

in Example 5-13). The `tixScrolledHList` command is very similar to the `TixScrolledListBox` command we saw earlier. It creates a TixHList subwidget with the name hlist and attaches two scrollbars to it.

As shown in the first five lines in Example 5-13, we create a scrolled TixHList widget, using the `-options` switch to set several options for the `hlist` subwidget (we'll talk about these options shortly). Then, we can access the HList subwidget widget using the `subwidget hlist` method (line 7 in Example 5-13). The output of Example 5-13 is shown in Figure 5-20.

Example 5-13: Creating Entries in an Hlist Widget

```
tixScrolledHList .sh -options {
    hlist.itemType text
    hlist.drawBranch false
    hlist.indent      8
}
pack .sh -expand yes -fill both
set hlist [.sh subwidget hlist]

$hlist add foo           -text "foo"
$hlist add foo.bar       -text "foo's 1st child"
$hlist add foo.bor       -text "foo's 2nd child"
$hlist add foo.bar.bao   -text "foo's 1st child's 1st child"
$hlist add foo.bar.kao   -text "foo's 1st child's 2nd child"
$hlist add dor           -text "dor, who has no child"
```

Creating Entries in an HList Widget

Each entry in an HList widget has a unique name, called its *entry-path*, which determines each entry's position in the HList widget. The entry-paths of the HList entries are very similar to the pathnames of Unix files. Each entry-path is a list of string names separated by a *separator character*. By default, the separator character is the period character (`.`), but it can be configured using the `-separator` option of the HList widget.

In Example 5-13, we add several new entries `foo`, `foo.bar`, `foo.bor`, `foo.bar.bao`, .. etc., into the HList widget using the `add` method. The relationship between the entries is signified by their names, similar to how Unix denotes

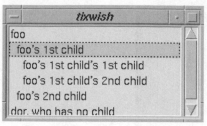

Figure 5-20: Output of Example 5-13

directories and subdirectories. For example, `foo` is the *parent* of `foo.bar` and `foo.bor`; `foo.bar` is the parent of `foo.bar.bao`, and so on. As far as the terminology goes, we also say that `foo.bar` is a *child* of `foo`; `foo` is an *ancestor* of `foo.bar.bao` and `foo.bar.bao` is a *descendant* of `foo`.

The output of Example 5-13 is shown in Figure 5-20. As we can see, the entries are displayed under their parents with the amount of indentation controlled by the `-indent` option of the HList widget: `foo.bar.bao` and `foo.bar.kao` are display under `foo.bar`, which is in turn is displayed under `foo`.

Entries with no parents, for example, `foo` and `dor` in Example 5-13, are called *top-level entries*. Top-level entries are usually entries with no immediate superiors in a hierarchy, for example, the owner of a company, the principle of a school, or the root directory of a Unix file system. Top-level entries are displayed with no indentation.

As evident from Example 5-13, all entries whose entry path does not contain a separator character are top-level entries. The only exception is the separator character itself, which is also a top-level entry. This makes it easy to display Unix file and directory names inside the HList widget, as shown in Example 5-14. The output of Example 5-14 is Figure 5-21.

Example 5-14: Displaying Directories in an Hlist Widget

```
set folder [tix getimage folder]
tixScrolledHList .sh -options {
    hlist.separator       /
    hlist.itemType        imagetext
    hlist.drawBranch      true
    hlist.indent          14
    hlist.wideSelection false
}
pack .sh -expand yes -fill both
set hlist [.sh subwidget hlist]

foreach directory {/ /usr /usr/bin /usr/local /etc /etc/rc.d} {
    $hlist add $directory -image $folder -text $directory
}
```

Each entry is associated with a display item. We can use the `itemType` option of the HList subwidget to specify the default type of display item. In Examples 5-13 and 5-14, using the `-options` switch, we set the default type by setting the `itemType` option to `imagetext`. We can also specify alternative types using the `-itemtype` option for the `add` method.

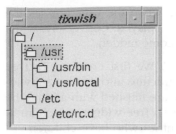

Figure 5-21: Output of Example 5-14

Controlling the Layout of the Entries

There are two options to control the layout of the entries: the `-showbranch` option specifies whether branch lines should be drawn between parent entries and their children; and the `-indent` option controls the amount of relative indentation between parent and child entries. Notice that the `-drawbranch` option is turned on in Example 5-14 but turned off in Example 5-13. Usually, we need to set a bigger indentation when the branches are shown—we used an indentation of 14 pixels in Example 5-14 compared to 8 pixels in Example 5-13.

Handling the Selection and User Event

The handling of the selection and user events for the HList widget is very similar to the TList widget, except that for the HList widget all the operations are based on entry-paths, not list indices. The methods `info selection`, `selection set`, and `selection clear` can be used to query, set, or clear the selection. The following example checks whether the current selection is the entry `/`. If so, it clears the selection and selects the entries `/usr/bin` and `/usr/local`.

```
if {[$hlist info selection] == "/"} {
    $hlist selection clear
    $hlist selection set /usr/bin
    $hlist selection set /usr/local
}
```

In addition, the option `-selectmode` controls how many entries can be selected at a time; the options `-browsecmd` and `-command` can be used to specify a command to be called to handle user events.

There is one more option worth mentioning: the `-wideselection` option. When set to `true`, the selection highlight is drawn across the whole HList widget (see Figure 5-20). When set to false, selection highlight is drawn as wide as the selected entry (see Figure 5-21). Normally, you would set `-wideselection` to `false` when you use `imagetext` items inside (see Example 5-14).

Creating Collapsible Tree Structures with TixTree

The TixTree widget is based on the TixScrolledHList widget; you can use it to create a collapsible hierarchical structure so that the user can conveniently navigate through a large number of list entries. As shown in Figure 5-22, the TixTree puts little + and – icons next to the branches of an HList entry that has descendants. These two icons

---

Creating Collapsible Tree Structures with TixTree   **195**

are known as the open and close icons, respectively. When the user presses the open icon next to an entry, its immediate children are displayed. Conversely, when the user presses the close icon, the entry's children become hidden.

Example 5-15 shows how to create a collapsible tree. We first create a TixTree widget. Then we add the entries in your hierarchical structure into its hlist subwidget using the add method of this subwidget. When we are finished with adding the entries, we just call the autosetmode method of the TixTree widget, which automatically adds the open and close icons next to the entries who have children.

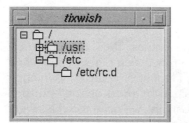

Figure 5-22: Output of Example 5-15

Example 5-15: Creating a Collapsible Hierarchy

```
set folder [tix getimage folder]
tixTree .tree -command Command -options {
    hlist.separator   /
    hlist.itemType    imagetext
    hlist.drawBranch  true
    hlist.indent      18
}
pack .tree -expand yes -fill both
set hlist [.tree subwidget hlist]

foreach directory {/ /usr /usr/bin /usr/local /etc /etc/rc.d} {
    $hlist add $directory -image $folder -text $directory
}
.tree autosetmode

proc Command {entry} {
    puts "you have selected $entry"
}
```

After studying Example 5-15 for a while, you may discover that both the TixTree widget and its hlist subwidget support an option called -command. When you want to handle events in the TixTree widget, which one of these two options should you use?

For the sake of clarity, let's call these two options TixTree.command and Tix-Tree.hlist.command. When an event happens, TixTree.hlist.command gets called first, which invokes an event handler in TixTree. Depending on the type of the event, this event handler may open the branches or highlight entries. When the event handler finishes processing the event, it calls TixTree.command. Therefore, you should use `TixTree.command` to define your own event handlers, as we did in Example 5-15. If you change the `-command` option of the `hlist` widget by mistake, you will find out that the TixTree no longer opens its branches! In general, if both a mega-widget and its subwidget have options of the same name, you would always use the option that belongs to the mega-widget.

Selecting Files and Directories

One task that an application has to perform frequently is to ask the user to select files or directories. To select files, you can use the Tix *File Selection widgets*: TixFileSelectDialog and TixExFileSelectDialog. To select directories, you can use the Tix *Directory Selection widgets*: TixDirList and TixDirTree. The Tk core now offers a file selection widget, but here we'll describe the ones in Tix.

File Selection Dialog Widgets

There are two file dialog widgets inside Tix: The TixFileSelectDialog (Figure 5-23) is similar to the FileSelectionDialog widget in Motif; TixExFileSelectDialog (Figure 5-24) looks like its counterpart in MS Windows. Both widgets let the user navigate through the file system directories and select a file.

The file selection boxes share one advanced feature: ComboBoxes to store the files, directories, and patterns the user has selected in the past. If the user wants to select the same files again, he can simply open the ComboBoxes and click on his past inputs. This saves a lot of keystrokes and is especially useful when the user needs to switch among several files or directories.

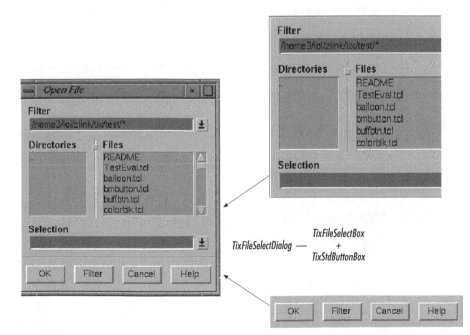

Figure 5-23: The Composition of a TixFileSelectDialog Widget

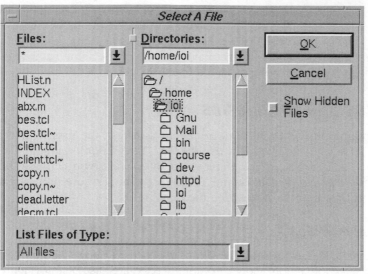

Figure 5-24: The TixExFileSelectDialog Widget

Using the TixFileSelectDialog Widget

An example of using the TixFileSelectDialog widget is in Example 5-16. At line 1, we create a TixFileSelectDialog widget and set the title of the dialog to "Select A File" using the `-title` option. We also use the `-command` option to specify that the procedure `selectCmd` should be called when the user has selected a file. `selectCmd` will be called with one parameter; the filename selected by the user. When the Tix-FileSelectDialog widget is created, it is initially not shown on the screen. Therefore, at line 3, we call its popup widget command to place the widget on the screen.

Example 5-16: Using the TixFileSelectDialog

```
tixFileSelectDialog .file -title "Select A File" -command
selectCmd
.file subwidget fsbox configure -pattern "*.txt" -directory
/usr/info
.file popup

proc selectCmd {filename} {
    puts "You have selected $filename"
}
```

The Subwidget in the TixFileSelectDialog

We may also want to set other options for the file dialog such as its file filter and working directory. To do this, we must know the composition of the TixFileSelectDialog widget. As shown in Figure 5-23, the TixFileSelectDialog contains a subwidget fsbox of the type TixFileSelectBox and a subwidget bbox of the type TixStdButtonBox.

The fsbox subwidget supports the `-pattern` and `-directory` options. At line 2 of Example 5-16, we use the `-directory` option to tell the fsbox subwidget to display files in the directory */usr/info*; we also use the `-pattern` option to specify that we only want the filenames that have the `txt` extension.

The fsbox subwidget also supports the `-selection` option, which stores the filename currently selected by the user. We can query this value through the `cget` widget command of the fsbox subwidget.

Remember that the `-pattern`, `-directory`, and `-selection` options do not belong to the TixFileSelectDialog widget. A common mistake that people make is to try to configure the nonexistent `-pattern` option of the TixFileSelectDialog, which causes much despair, long error messages, and great loss of self-confidence. *Always remember:* when you want to configure an option, find out whether it belongs to the widget or its subwidgets.

The TixExFileSelectDialog Widget

The TixExFileSelectDialog widget is very similar to the TixFileSelectDialog widget. It supports all the options and widget commands of the latter, so essentially we can just take Example 5-16 and replace the command `tixFileSelectDialog` in the first line to `tixExFileSelectDialog`.

The composition of the TixExFileSelectDialog widget is a bit different: it contains one subwidget, which is also called fsbox, of the type TixExFileSelectBox widget (Figure 5-24). Again, this fsbox widget supports all widget options and commands of the fsbox subwidget in TixFileSelectDialog, so the line 2 of Example 5-16 can work for TixExFileSelectDialog widgets without any change.

Specifying File Types for TixExFileSelectDialog

The TixExFileSelectBox widget has a ComboBox subwidget marked as "List Files of Type" (see Figure 5-24). This widget contains some pre-set types of files for the user to choose from. For example, a word processor program can include choices like "Microsoft Word Documents" and "WordPerfect Documents."

The TixExFileSelectBox widget has a `-filetypes` option for this purpose. As shown in line 5 through 9 in Example 5-17, the value for the `-filetypes` option is a list. Each item in the list should contain two parts. The first part is a list of file patterns and the second part is the textual name for this type of files.

Example 5-17: Using the tix filedialog Command

```
set dialog [tix filedialog]
$dialog -title "Select A File" -command selectCmd
$dialog subwidget fsbox configure -pattern "*.txt" -directory
/usr/info
if {[winfo class $dialog] == "TixExFileSelectDialog"} {
    $dialog subwidget fsbox configure -filetypes {
        {{*}            {*      -- All files}}
        {{*.txt}        {*.txt -- Text files}}
        {{*.c}          {*.c    -- C source files}}
    }
}
```

```
$dialog popup

proc selectCmd {filename} {
    puts "You have selected $filename"
}
```

The tix filedialog Command

TixExFileSelectDialog and TixFileSelectDialog are very similar. So which one should we use? That is just a matter of taste. However, since we know that programmers usually have bad taste, clever programmers would rather step aside and let the users exercise their own taste. To do this, we can use the `tix filedialog` command.

For any programs based on Tix, the user can choose his preferred type of file dialog by setting the X resource `FileDialog` to either `tixFileSelectDialog` or `tixExFileSelectDialog`. This can usually be done by inserting a line similar to the following into the user's `.Xdefaults` file:

```
*myapp*FileDialog: tixExFileSelectDialog
```

When we call the command `tix filedialog`, it returns a file dialog widget of the user's preferred type.

The advantage of using `tix filedialog` is it that makes coding flexible. If the management suddenly mandates that we dump the Motif look and feel in favor of the MS Windows look and feel, we don't need to dig up every line of `tixFile-SelectDialog` calls and replace it with `tixExFileSelectDialog`. Also, `tix filedialog` creates only one copy of the file dialog, which can be shared by different parts of the program. Therefore, we can avoid creating a separate file dialog widget for each of the "Open," "Save," and "Save As" commands in our application. This way, we can save resources, since a file dialog is a large widget and it takes up quite a bit of memory.

The use of the `tix filedialog` command is shown in Example 5-17. This example is very similar to what we saw in Example 5-16, except now we aren't really sure which type of file dialog the user has chosen. Therefore, if we want to do something that only one type of file dialog allows, we have to be careful. At line 4 of Example 5-17, we use the `winfo` command to see whether the type of the file dialog is TixExFileSelectDialog. If so, we set the value for the `-filetypes` option of its fsbox subwidget.

Selecting Directories with the TixDirTree and TixDirList Widgets

There are two Tix widgets for selecting a directory: TixDirTree and TixDirList (see Figure 5-25). Both of them display the directories in a hierarchical format. The display in the TixDirList widget is more compact; it shows only the parent and child directories of a particular directory. The TixDirTree widget, on the other hand, can display the whole tree structure of the file system.

The programming interfaces of these two widgets are the same and you can choose one depending on your application. As shown in the following example, you can

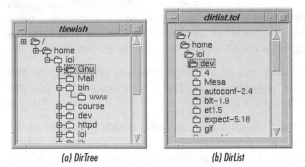

(a) DirTree   (b) DirList

Figure 5-25: The DirTree and DirList Widgets

use the `-directory` option of the TixDirList widget to specify a directory to display. In the example, we set `-directory` to be */home/ioi/dev*. As a result, the TixDirList widget displays all the subdirectories and all the ancestor directories of */home/ioi/dev*. You can use the `-command` and `-browsecmd` options to handle the user events: a double-click or Return keystroke will trigger the `-command` option and a single-click or spacebar key stroke will trigger the `-browsecmd` option. Normally, you would handle both type of events in the same manner, as we have done in Example 5-18.

Example 5-18: Using the TixDirList Widget

```
tixDirList .d -value /home/ioi/dev
     -command "selectDir" -browsecmd "selectDir"
pack .d

proc selectDir {dir} {
     puts "now you select $dir"
}
```

Tix Object-Oriented Programming

This section is intended for experienced programmers who want to create new Tix widgets. If you just want use the Tix widgets in your applications, you can skip this section.

Introduction to Tix Object-Oriented Programming

Tix comes with a simple object-oriented programming (OOP) framework, the *Tix Intrinsics*, for writing mega-widgets. The Tix Intrinsics is not a general purpose OOP system and it does not support some features found in general purpose OOP systems such as [INCR TCL]. However, the Tix Intrinsics is specially designed for writing mega-widgets. It provides a simple and efficient interface for creating mega-widgets so that you can avoid the complexity and overhead of the general purpose OOP extensions to Tcl.

The hard thing about programming with mega-widgets is to make sure that each instance you create can handle its own activities. Events must be directed to the

---

right widget, procedures must act on data that is internal to that widget, and users should be able to change the options associated with the widget. For instance, we'll show an arrow widget that needs to know what direction it's pointing; this requires each instance of the widget to have its own variable to indicate its direction.

Furthermore, each widget should respond properly to changes requested by the application programmer during the program's run. The whole reason people use Tcl/Tk is because they can alter things on-the-fly.

The advantage of an object-oriented programming system is that you can easily associate a widget with its own data and procedures (methods). This chapter shows how to do that, and how to configure data both at the time the widget is initialized and later during the program.

Widget Classes and Widget Instances

All the mega-widget classes in Tix, such as TixComboBox and TixControl, are implemented in the Tix Intrinsics framework. Also, you can write new *widget classes* with the Tix Intrinsics. In the next section, I'll go through all the steps of creating a new widget class in Tix. I'll illustrate the idea using a new class `TixArrowButton` as an example. TixArrowButton is essentially a button that can display an arrow in one of the four directions (see Figure 5-26).

Figure 5-26: Arrow Buttons

Once you have defined your classes, you can create *widget instances* of these classes. For example, the following code will create four instances of the TixArrowButton class, whose arrows point to the directions north, west, south, and east.

```
tixArrowButton .north -direction n
tixArrowButton .west  -direction w
tixArrowButton .south -direction s
tixArrowButton .east  -direction e
```

What Is in a Widget Instance?

Each widget instance is composed of three integral parts: variables, methods, and component widgets.

Variables

Each widget instance is associated with a set of variables. In the example of the TixArrowButton class, we may use a variable to store the direction of the arrow. We may also use a variable to count how many times the user has pressed the button.

Each variable can be public or private. Public variables may be accessed by the application programmer (usually via `configure` or `cget` methods), and their names usually start with a dash (–). They usually are used to represent some user-configurable options of the widget instance. Private variables, on the other hand, cannot be accessed by the application programmer. They are usually used to store information about the widget instance that is of interest only to the widget writer.

All the variables of an instance are stored in a global array that has the same name as the instance. For example, the variables of the instance `.north` are stored in the global array `.north`. The public variable `-direction`, which records the direction to which the arrow is pointing to, is stored in `.north(-direction)`. The private variable `count`, which counts how many times the user has pressed the button, is stored in `.north(count)`. In comparison, the same variables of the `.down` instance are stored in `.down(-direction)` and `.down(count)`.

Methods

To carry out operations on the widget, you define a set of procedures called *methods* (to use common object-oriented terminology). Each method can be declared as public or private. *Public methods* can be called by the application programmer. For example, if the `TixArrowButton` class supports the public methods `invoke` and `invert`, the application programmer can issue the commands to call these methods for the widget instance `.north`.

```
.north invert
.north invoke
```

In contrast, *private methods* are of interest only to widget writers and cannot be called by application programmers.

Component Widgets

A Tix mega-widget is composed of one or more component widgets. The main part of a mega-widget is called the *root widget*, which is usually a frame widget that encompasses all other component widgets. The other component widgets are called *subwidgets*.

The root widget has the same name as the the mega-widget itself. In the preceding example, we have a mega-widget called .north. It has a root widget which is a frame widget and is also called .north. Inside .north we have a button subwidget called .north.button.

Like variables and methods, component widgets are also classified into public and private component widgets. Only public widgets may be accessed by the application programmer, via the `subwidget` method of each widget instance.

Widget Class Declaration

The first step of writing a new widget class is to decide the base class from which the new class derives. Usually, if the new class does not share any common features with other classes, it should be derived from the TixPrimitive class. If it does share common features with other classes, then it should be derived from the appropriate base class. For example, if the new class supports scrollbars, it should be derived from TixScrolledWidget; if it displays a label next to its "main area," then it should be derived from TixLabelWidget.

In the case of our new TixArrowButton class, it doesn't really share any common features with other classes, so we decide to use the base class TixPrimitive as its superclass.

Using the tixWidgetClass Command

We can use the `tixWidgetClass` command to declare a new class. The syntax is:

```
tixWidgetClass classCommandName {
-switch value
-switch value
....
}
```

For instance, Example 5-19 is the declaration section of TixArrowButton.

Example 5-19: Declaration of the TixArrowButton Class

```
tixWidgetClass tixArrowButton {
    -classname  TixArrowButton
    -superclass tixPrimitive
    -method {
        flash invoke invert
    }
    -flag {
        -direction -state
    }
    -configspec {
        {-direction direction Direction e}
        {-state state State normal}
    }
    -alias {
        {-dir -direction}
    }
}
```

The first argument for `tixWidgetClass` is the *command name* for the widget class (`tixArrowButton`). Command names are used to create widgets of this class. For example, the code

```
tixArrowButton .arrow
```

creates a widget instance `.arrow` of the class TixArrowButton. The command name is also used as a prefix of all the methods of this class. For example, the `Foo` and `Bar` methods of the class TixArrowButton are `tixArrowButton:Foo` and `tixArrowButton:Bar`.

The *class name* of the class (`TixArrowButton`) is specified by the `-classname` switch inside the main body of the declaration. The class name is used only to specify options in the options database. For example, the following commands specify that the default values for the `-direction` and `-state` of TixArrowButton should be `up` and `normal`, respectively.

```
option add *TixArrowButton.direction up
option add *TixArrowButton.state      normal
```

Notice the difference in the capitalization of the class name and the command name of the TixArrowButton class: both of them have the individual words capitalized, but the command name `tixArrowButton` starts with a lowercase letter while the class name `TixArrowButton` starts with an uppercase letter. When you create your own classes, you should follow this naming convention.

The `-superclass` switch specifies the superclass of the new widget. In our example, we have set it to `tixPrimitive`. Again, pay attention to the capitalization: we should use the superclass's command name, not its class name.

Writing Methods

After we have declared the new widget class, we can write methods for this class to define its behavior. Methods are just a special type of Tcl procedures and they are created by the `proc` command. There are, however, three requirements for methods. First, their names must be prefixed by the command name of their class. Second, they must accept at least one argument and the first argument that they accept must be called **w**. Third, the first command executed inside each method must be

```
upvar #0 $w data
```

For example, the following is an implementation of the invert method for the class TixArrowButton:

```
proc tixArrowButton:invert {w} {
    upvar #0 $w data

    set curDirection $data(-direction)
    case $curDirection {
        n {
            set newDirection s
        }
        s {
            set newDirection n
        }
        # ....
    }
}
```

Notice that the name of the method is prefixed by the command name of the class (`tixArrowButton`). Also, the first and only argument that it accepts is **w** and the first line it executes is `upvar #0 $w data`.

The argument **w** specifies which widget instance this method should act upon. For example, if the user has issued the command

```
.north invert
```

on an instance `.north` of the class tixArrowButton, the method `tixArrowButton:invert` will be called and the argument **w** will have the value `.north`.

The `invert` method is used to invert the direction of the arrow. Therefore, it should examine the variable `.north(-direction)`, which stores the current

---

direction of the instance .north, and modify it appropriately. It turns out that in Tcl, the only clean way to access an array whose name is stored in a variable is the upvar #0 $w data technique; essentially, it tells the intepreter that the array data should be an alias for the global array whose name is stored in $w. We will soon see how the widget's methods use the data array.

Once the mysterious upvar #0 $w data line is explained, it becomes clear what the rest of the tixArrowButton:invert method does: it examines the current direction of the arrow, which is stored in $data(-direction), and inverts it.

Declaring Public Methods

All the methods of a class are by default private methods and cannot be accessed by the application programmer. If you want to make a method public, you can include its name in the -method section of the class declaration. In our TixArrow-Button example, we have declared that the methods flash, invert, and invoke are public methods and they can be accessed by the application programmer. All other methods of the TixArrowButton class will be private. Note that private methods need not—and must not—be declared in the -method section.

Usually, the names of private methods start with a capital letter and with individual words capitalized. The names of public methods start with a lowercase letter.

Standard Initialization Methods

Each new mega-widget class must supply these standard initialization methods. When an instance of a Tix widget is created, three methods will be called to initialize this instance. The methods are InitWidgetRec, ConstructWidget, and SetBindings, and they will be called in that order. The following sections show how these methods can be implemented.

The InitWidgetRec Method

The purpose of the InitWidgetRec method is to initialize the variables of the widget instance. For example, the following implementation of tixArrowBut-ton:InitWidgetRec sets the count variable of each newly created instance to zero.

```
proc tixArrowButton:InitWidgetRec {w} {
    upvar #0 $w data

    set data(count) 0
}
```

Earlier, we showed how each widget you create is associated with an array of the same name. Within the methods, you always refer to this array through the name data—the method then works properly in each instance of the widget.

Chaining Methods

The previous implementation is not sufficient because our TixArrowButton class is derived from TixPrimitive. The class derivation in Tix is basically an *is-a* relationship:

TixArrowButton *is a* TixPrimitive. TixPrimitive defines the method `tixPrimitive:InitWidgetRec` which sets up the instance variables of every instance of TixPrimitive. Since an instance of TixArrowButton is also an instance of TixPrimitive, we need to make sure that the instance variables defined by TixPrimitive are also properly initialized. The technique of calling a method defined in a superclass is called the *chaining* of a method. The following implementation does this correctly:

```
proc tixArrowButton:InitWidgetRec {w} {
    upvar #0 $w data

    tixPrimitive:InitWidgetRec $w
    set data(count) 0
}
```

`tixPrimitive:InitWidgetRec` is called before anything else is done. This way, we can define new classes by means of successive refinement; we can first ask the superclass to set up the instance variables, then we can modify some of those variables when necessary and also define new variables.

The tixChainMethod Call

The implementation of `tixArrowButton:InitWidgetRec` is correct but it may be cumbersome if we want to switch superclasses. For example, suppose we want to create a new base class `TixArrowWidget`, which presumably defines common attributes of any classes that have arrows in them. Then, instead of deriving TixArrowButton directly from TixPrimitive, we decide to derive TixArrowButton from TixArrowWidget, which is in turn derived from TixPrimitive:

```
tixWidgetClass tixArrowWidget {
    -superclass tixPrimitive
    ...
}
tixWidgetClass tixArrowButton {
    -superclass tixArrowWidget
    ...
}
```

Now we would need to change all the method chaining calls in TixArrowButton from:

```
tixPrimitive:SomeMethod
```

to:

```
tixArrowWidget:SomeMethod
```

This may be a lot of work because you may have chained methods in many places in the original implementation of TixArrowButton.

The `tixChainMethod` command solves this problem. It automatically finds a superclass that defines the method we want to chain and calls this method. For example, the following is a better implementation of `tixArrowButton:InitWidgetRec` that uses `tixChainMethod` to avoid calling `tixPrimitive:InitWidgetRec` directly:

```
proc tixArrowButton:InitWidgetRec {w} {
    upvar #0 $w data

    tixChainMethod $w InitWidgetRec
    set data(count) 0
}
```

Notice the order of the arguments for `tixChainMethod`; the name of the instance, `$w`, is passed before the method we want to chain, `InitWidgetRec`. In general, if the method we want to chain has $1+n$ arguments:

```
proc tixPrimitive:MethodToChain {w arg1 arg2 ... argn} {
    ...
}
```

we call it with the arguments in the following order:

```
tixChainMethod $w MethodToChain $arg1 $arg2 ... $argn
```

We'll come back to more detailed discussion of `tixChainMethod` shortly. For the time being, let's take it for granted that `tixChainMethod` must be used in the three standard initialization methods: `InitWidgetRec`, `ConstructWidget`, and `SetBindings`.

The ConstructWidget Method

The `ConstructWidget` method is used to create the components of a widget instance. In the case of TixArrowButton, we want to create a new button subwidget whose name is button, and use an image to display an arrow on this button. Assume the images are stored in the global variables `arrow(n)`, `arrow(w)`, `arrow(s)`, and `arrow(e)` for the directions north, west, south, and east. The string substitution `$arrow($data(-direction))` will give us the appropriate image for the widget instance.

```
proc tixArrowButton:ConstructWidget {w} {
    upvar #0 $w data
    global arrow

    tixChainMethod $w ConstructWidget

    set data(w:button) [button $w.button \
        -image $arrow($data(-direction))]
    pack $data(w:button) -expand yes -fill both
}
```

The `tixArrowButton:ConstructWidget` method sets the variable `data(w:button)` to be the pathname of the `button` subwidget. As a convention of the Tix Intrinsics, we must declare a public subwidget *swid* by storing its pathname in the variable `data(w: swid)`.

The SetBindings Method

In your interface, you generally want to handle a lot of events in the subwidgets that make up your mega-widget. For instance, when somebody presses the button in a

TixArrowButton widget, you want the button to handle the event. The `SetBindings` method is used to create event bindings for the components inside the mega-widget. In our TixArrowButton example, we use the `bind` command to specify that the method `tixArrowButton:IncrCount` should be called each time the user presses the first mouse button. As a result, we can count the number of times the user has pressed the button (obviously for no better reason than using it as a dumb example).

```
proc tixArrowButton:SetBindings {w} {
    upvar #0 $w data

    tixChainMethod $w SetBindings

    bind $data(w:button) <1> "tixArrowButton:IncrCount $w"
}

proc tixArrowButton:IncrCount {w} {
    upvar #0 $w data

    incr data(count)
}
```

Declaring and Using Variables

The private variables of a widget class do not need to be declared. In fact, they can be initialized and used anywhere by any method. Usually, however, general purpose private variables are initialized by the `InitWidgetRec` method and subwidget variables are initialized in the `ConstructWidget` method.

We have seen in the tixArrowButton:InitWidgetRec example that the private variable `data(count)` was initialized there. Also, the private variable `data(w:button)` was initialized in `tixArrowButton:ConstructWidget` and subsequently used in `tixArrowButton:SetBindings`.

In contrast, public variables must be declared inside the class declaration. The following arguments declare the public variables and specify various options for them:

- `-flag` declares all the public variables of the TixArrowButton class, `-direction` and `-state`.

- `-configspec` specifies the details of each public variable. For example, the following declaration

```
-configspec {
    {-direction direction Direction e}
    {-state state State normal}
}
```

  specifies that the `-direction` variable has the resource name `direction` and resource class `Direction`; its default value is `e`. The application programmer can assign value to this variable by using the `-direction` option in the command line or by specifying resources in the options database with its resource name or class. The declaration of `-state` installs similar definitions for that variable.

- `-alias` specifies alternative names for public variables. In our example, the setting

```
-alias {
    {-dir -direction}
}
```

specifies that `-dir` is the same variable as `-direction`. Therefore, when the application issues the command

```
.north configure -dir w
```

it is the same as

```
.north configure -direction w
```

The `-alias` option provides only an alternative name for the application programmer. Inside the widget's implementation code, the variable is still accessed as `data(-direction)`, *not* `data(-dir)`.

Initialization of Public Variables

When a widget instance is created, all of its public variables are initialized by the Tix Intrinsics before the `InitWidgetRec` method is called. Therefore, `InitWidgetRec` and any other method of this widget instance are free to assume that all the public variables have been properly initialized and use them as such.

The public variables are initialized according to the following criteria.

1. If the value of the variable is specified by the creation command, this value is used. For example, if the application programmer has created an instance in the following way:

   ```
   tixArrowButton .arr -direction n
   ```

   The value n will be used for the `-direction` variable.

2. If the value wasn't specified in step 1, but the value of the variable is specified in the options database, that value is used. For example, if the user has created an instance in the following way:

   ```
   option add *TixArrowButton.direction w
   tixArrowButton .arr
   ```

   The value w will be used for the `-direction` variable.

3. If the value wasn't in the options database, the default value specified in the `-configspec` secton of the class declaration will be used.

You can use a *type checker procedure* to ensure that the application has supplied a value of the correct type for a public variable. The type checker is specified in the `-configspec` section of the class declaration after the default value. The following code specifies the type checker procedure `tixArrowButton:CheckDirection` for the `-direction` variable:

```
-configspec {
```

```
    {-direction direction Direction e tixArrowButton:CheckDirection}
    {-state state State normal}
  }
  ...
}

proc tixArrowButton:CheckDirection {dir} {
  if {[lsearch {n w s e} $dir] != -1} {
    return $dir
  } else {
    error "wrong direction value \"$dir\""
  }
}
```

In this example, since no type checker has been specified for the **-state** variable, its value will not be checked.

If a type checker procedure is specified for a public variable, this procedure will be called once the value of a public variable is determined by the three steps just mentioned.

Public Variable Configuration Methods

After a widget instance is created, the user can assign new values to the public variables using the **configure** method. For example, the following code changes the **-direction** variable of the **.arr** instance to **n**.

```
.arr configure -direction n
```

In order for configuration to work, you have to define a configuration method that does what the programmer expects. The configuration method of a public variable is invoked whenever the user calls the **configure** method to change the value of this variable. The name of a configuration method must be the name of the public variable prefixed by the creation command of the class and **:config**. For example, the name of the configuration method for the **-direction** variable of the TixArrowButton class is **tixArrowButton:config-direction**. The following code implements this method:

```
proc tixArrowButton:config-direction {w value} {
    upvar #0 $w data
    global arrow

    $data(w:button) configure -image $arrow($value)
}
```

When **tixArrowButton:config-direction** is called, the **value** parameter contains the new value of the **-direction** variable, but **data(-direction)** contains the **old** value. This is useful when the configuration method needs to check the previous value of the variable before taking in the new value.

If a type checker is defined for a variable, it is called before the configuration method is called. Therefore, the configuration method can assume that the type of the **value** parameter is always correct.

Sometimes it is necessary to override the value supplied by the user. The following code illustrates this idea:

```
proc tixArrowButton:config-direction {w value} {
    upvar #0 $w data
    global arrow

    if {$value == "n"} {
        set value s
        set data(-direction) $value
    }

    $data(w:button) configure -image $arrow($value)
    return $data(-direction)
}
```

The code always overrides values of n to s. If you need to override the value, you must do the following two things:

1. Explicitly set the instance variable inside the configuration method.

2. Return the modified value from the configuration method.

If you do not need to override the value, you don't need to return anything from the configuration method. In this case, the Tix Intrinsics assigns the new value to the instance variable for you.

Configuration Methods and Public Variable Initialization

For efficiency reasons, the configuration methods are not called during the initialization of the public variables. If you want to force the configuration method to be called for a particular public variable, you can specify it in the -forcecall section of the class declaration. In the following example, we force the configuration method of the -direction variable to be called during intialization:

```
-forcecall {
    -direction
}
```

Summary of Widget Instance Initialization

The creation of a widget instance is a complex process. You must understand how it works in order to write your widget classes. The following are the steps taken by the Tix Intrinsics when a widget instance is created:

1. When the user creates an instance, the public variables are initialized as discussed earlier. Type checkers are always called if they are specified. Configuration methods are called only if they are specified in the -forcecall section.

2. The InitWidgetRec method is called. It should initialize private variables, possibly according to the values of the public variables.

3. The ConstructWidget method is called. It should create the component widgets. It should also store the names of public subwidgets into the subwidget variables.

4. The `SetBinding` method is called. It should create bindings for the component widgets.

After completing these steps, the creation of the instance is complete and the user can manipulate it using its widget command.

Loading the New Classes

Usually, you can use a separate script file to store the implementation of each new widget class. If you have several of those files, it will be a good idea to group the files into a single directory and create a `tclIndex` file for them so that the new classes can be auto-loaded.

Suppose you have put the class files into the directory `/usr/my/tix/classes`. You can create the `tclIndex` file using the `tools/tixindex` program that comes with Tix:

```
cd /usr/my/tix/classes
/usr/my/Tix4.0/tools/tixindex *.tcl
```

The `tclIndex` file must be created by the `tixindex` program. You cannot use the standard `auto_mkindex` command that comes with Tcl.

Once you have created the `tclIndex` file, you can use your new widget classes by auto-loading. Here is a small demo program that uses the new **TixArrowButton** class:

```
#!/usr/local/bin/tixwish
lappend auto_path /usr/my/tix/classes

# Now I can use my TixArrowButton class!
#
tixArrowButton .arr -direction n
pack .arr
```

Putting It Together

Here is the complete code for the TixArrowButton widget. You can also find it in the file `demos/samples/ArrowBtn.tcl` in the Tix distribution.

```
set arrow(n) [image create bitmap -data {
    #define up_width 15
    #define up_height 15
    static unsigned char up_bits[] = {
        0x80, 0x00, 0xc0, 0x01, 0xe0, 0x03,
        0xf0, 0x07, 0xf8, 0x0f, 0xfc, 0x1f,
        0xfe, 0x3f, 0xc0, 0x01, 0xc0, 0x01,
        0xc0, 0x01, 0xc0, 0x01, 0xc0, 0x01,
        0xc0, 0x01, 0xc0, 0x01, 0x00, 0x00};
}]
set arrow(w) [image create bitmap -data {
    #define left_width 15
    #define left_height 15
    static unsigned char left_bits[] = {
```

```
            0x00, 0x00, 0x40, 0x00, 0x60, 0x00,
            0x70, 0x00, 0x78, 0x00, 0x7c, 0x00,
            0xfe, 0x3f, 0xff, 0x3f, 0xfe, 0x3f,
            0x7c, 0x00, 0x78, 0x00, 0x70, 0x00,
            0x60, 0x00, 0x40, 0x00, 0x00, 0x00};
    }]
    set arrow(s) [image create bitmap -data {
        #define down_width 15
        #define down_height 15
        static unsigned char down_bits[] = {
            0x00, 0x00, 0xc0, 0x01, 0xc0, 0x01,
            0xc0, 0x01, 0xc0, 0x01, 0xc0, 0x01,
            0xc0, 0x01, 0xc0, 0x01, 0xfe, 0x3f,
            0xfc, 0x1f, 0xf8, 0x0f, 0xf0, 0x07,
            0xe0, 0x03, 0xc0, 0x01, 0x80, 0x00};
    }]
    set arrow(e) [image create bitmap -data {
        #define right_width 15
        #define right_height 15
        static unsigned char right_bits[] = {
            0x00, 0x00, 0x00, 0x01, 0x00, 0x03,
            0x00, 0x07, 0x00, 0x0f, 0x00, 0x1f,
            0xfe, 0x3f, 0xfe, 0x7f, 0xfe, 0x3f,
            0x00, 0x1f, 0x00, 0x0f, 0x00, 0x07,
            0x00, 0x03, 0x00, 0x01, 0x00, 0x00};
    }]

tixWidgetClass tixArrowButton {
    -classname  TixArrowButton
    -superclass tixPrimitive
    -method {
        flash invoke invert
    }
    -flag {
        -direction -state
    }
    -configspec {
        {-direction direction Direction e
            tixArrowButton:CheckDirection}
        {-state state State normal}
    }
    -alias {
        {-dir -direction}
    }
}

proc tixArrowButton:InitWidgetRec {w} {
    upvar #0 $w data

    tixChainMethod $w InitWidgetRec
    set data(count) 0
}
```

```
proc tixArrowButton:ConstructWidget {w} {
    upvar #0 $w data
    global arrow

    tixChainMethod $w ConstructWidget

    set data(w:button) [button $w.button \
            -image $arrow($data(-direction))]
    pack $data(w:button) -expand yes -fill both
}

proc tixArrowButton:SetBindings {w} {
    upvar #0 $w data

    tixChainMethod $w SetBindings

    bind $data(w:button) <1> "tixArrowButton:IncrCount $w"
}

proc tixArrowButton:IncrCount {w} {
    upvar #0 $w data

    incr data(count)
}

proc tixArrowButton:CheckDirection {dir} {
    if {[lsearch {n w s e} $dir] != -1} {
        return $dir
    } else {
        error "wrong direction value \"$dir\""
    }
}

proc tixArrowButton:flash {w} {
    upvar #0 $w data

    $data(w:button) flash
}

proc tixArrowButton:invoke {w} {
    upvar #0 $w data

    $data(w:button) invoke
}

proc tixArrowButton:invert {w} {
    upvar #0 $w data

    set curDirection $data(-direction)
    case $curDirection {
        n {
            set newDirection s
```

```
        }
        s {
            set newDirection n
        }
        e {
            set newDirection w
        }
        w {
            set newDirection e
        }
    }
    $w config -direction $newDirection
}

proc tixArrowButton:config-direction {w value} {
    upvar #0 $w data
    global arrow

    $data(w:button) configure -image $arrow($value)
}

proc tixArrowButton:config-state {w value} {
    upvar #0 $w data
    global arrow

    $data(w:button) configure -state $value
}
```

6

TclX

by De Clarke

Overview of the TclX Extension

Many Tcl extensions are designed to provide a particular function. Tcl-DP, for example, provides interprocess communication and support for RPC (remote procedure calls) for the design of multiprocess applications. I wrote the first draft of this text using TkWWW, a Tk which has been enhanced to use HTTP services and process HTML documents. Scotty, another enhanced Tcl, is dedicated to network service enhancements (TCP, UDP, ICMP, SNMP). TclX is different from all of these; it was not designed for a particular kind of application or problem. The purpose of TclX is to make Tcl a general purpose programming language for the Unix environment.

TclX, then, is a diverse set of enhancements to Tcl, useful for every kind of programming effort. In fact, I find Tcl without the TclX extension rather unwieldy—like your favorite Swiss Army Knife with several blades missing. TclX adds to Ousterhout's core Tcl many of the features that Unix/C programmers are accustomed to—for example:

- the `system`, `fork`, and `execl` calls
- additional file operations
- code library management

In addition to these, it extends Tcl with numerous useful string and list functions.

It's not difficult to add most other extensions on top of TclX. Almost all the extensions I have tried built easily (especially if I use T. Poindexter's very useful `tcl-my-fancy` tool). In fact, some published tools and extensions rely on TclX.

Even so, TclX does not replace C (or C++). In raw speed and access to OS internals, compiled languages always out-perform interpreters. Tcl is not suitable, for example, for massive data reduction projects, real-time factory floor control systems, or device drivers. However, for user interfaces, small-to-midsize standalone tools, and as a "glue" to unify a collection of C-based executables into one large application, Tcl (and Tk) is an amazingly productive language; TclX makes it even more productive. TclX is an excellent hybrid. It combines the ease of use and simplicity of a shell or scripting language with many of the more powerful features associated with high level languages.

I should say up front that I am assuming you are familiar with Unix as well as with some use of core Tcl. If I seem very enthusiastic about Tcl, note that this may be because I'm a database and information systems programmer; I deal mostly with GUI design, text manipulation, parsing, inference, and formatted output— all problems for which Tcl/Tk is very well suited.

I'll consider the features of TclX here not in order of importance, but more in the order in which the novice user might encounter, use, and come to appreciate them. The first mildly pleasant feature of TclX that the new user might notice is that the shell `echo` command is supported, and can be used instead of core Tcl `puts` `stdout`. `echo` can accept multiple arguments, so arguments containing whitespace need not be quoted:

```
tcl> echo Hello world!
Hello world!
```

TclX Math Functions

TclX adds the useful functions `max`, `min`, and `random`. The `max` and `min` functions accept a list argument and do what you would expect. `random`, like most other random number generators, returns a randomized value between zero and some limit, in this case the argument.

```
tcl> max 8 6 5 0 2 3 10 7 9
10
tcl> random 100
53
tcl> random 100
14
```

You can set the seed for the random function (basically a call to `srand`):

```
tcl> random seed 10
tcl> random seed [getclock]
```

The Unix `random` library function is not as random as one might really like, so it pays to feed it an unpredictable seed. Using the system clock integer (via `getclock`) is a good way to make your seed value, and hence your randomized value, unpredictable. Your process ID is another unpredictable seed value. (Even a relatively *unpredictable* seed like the clock or PID may still be easily *guessable*; I would not advise you to base any security mechanisms on this kind of seed. If your app requires secure authentication and/or privacy of data, you should make a thorough study of the literature of authentication and encryption.)

TclX also provides access to the standard list of Tcl math functions without the `expr` syntactic construct. That is, in TclX you can write expressions like:

```
tcl> set a 1
tcl> set b [tan [sin [cos $a]]]
0.565143
```

instead of

```
tcl>set b [expr {tan( sin( cos($a) ) )}]
0.565143
```

These functions date from the time when `expr` didn't have floating-point math functions. After the `expr` command was improved, the old floating-point function commands were preserved in TclX for backward compatibility and convenience.

You pay a small price in performance for using these shortcuts; these functions are Tcl procs which call `expr`, so the conversion of string to floating point number is done once per function, rather than once for the entire expression. The penalty is small, however; if you were writing an application so math-heavy that you cared about the difference, you probably shouldn't be writing it in Tcl.

TclX String Functions

TclX adds several character and string functions, permitting you to perform quite easily many operations that would be inconvenient in core Tcl.

The function `cequal` compares two strings:

```
cequal strA strB
```

It returns 1 if the two strings are identical, and 0 if they are not. This is a shorter syntax than `string compare`, and the result is more intuitive (though `string compare` is modeled on the C `strcmp`, many programmers find `strcmp` confusing at first, and `cequal` is more "sensible").

```
tcl> cequal "This" "That"
0
tcl> cequal "This" "This"
1
tcl> if {[cequal $strA $strB]} {
 . . .
```

`cequal` also gets you around a well-known "gotcha" in Tcl expressions: If a string happens to conform to the Tcl syntax for a numeric quantity, the normal equals operator (=) interprets it as a number, and finds it to be equal to another string that seems to represent the same number. Thus:

```
tcl>set str1 "0x7"
tcl>set str2 "007"
tcl>if {$str1 == $str2} {echo they are the same}
they are the same
```

To overcome this in standard Tcl you have to resort to `string compare`.

The `cindex` function does character-wise indexing into strings. Thus,

```
cindex string indexExpr
```

returns the character indexed by the `indexExpr`. For example,

```
tcl>cindex Hello 1
e
```

Note that Tcl strings and lists are indexed starting with index 0, *not* 1!

`clength` gets the length in characters of a string:

```
tcl>clength Hello
5
```

If you need to extract substrings by character indices,

> crange *string ind1Expr ind2Expr*

returns the range of characters from index `ind1Expr` through index *ind2Expr*:

```
tcl>crange "Hello World" 2 7
llo Wo
```

`csubstr` does almost the same thing as `crange`, but by start position and length, so

> csubstr *string indExpr lenExpr*

returns a range of characters starting at the index *indExpr* and *lenExpr* long. If the values of these arguments take `csubstr` beyond the end of the string, it simply returns what it can get.

```
tcl>csubstr "Hello World" 4 5
o Wor
tcl>csubstr "Hello World" 9 10
ld
```

One common application that can be tedious and repetitive to code is the parsing of ASCII input. With its list functions and string functions, Tcl and TclX are remarkably useful for parsing. TclX includes the `ctoken` function specifically for this purpose:

> ctoken *strVar sepString*

This parses a token out of a character string. The string to parse is contained in the variable *strVar*, and the string *sepString* contains all the valid separator characters for tokens in the target string. The first token is returned and the contents of *strVar* are modified to contain only the remainder of the input string following the extracted token:

```
tcl>set sepString ~_
tcl>set parse "_~This~is_a~string__to_parse~for~tokens"
tcl>ctoken parse $sepString
This
tcl>echo $parse
~is_a~string__to_parse~for~tokens
tcl>ctoken parse $sepString
is
tcl>ctoken parse $sepString
a
```

(and so on). `ctoken` ignores any leading separators. `ctoken` is basically a more intelligent `split`, with the addition of the "eat token and shorten string" step that one would otherwise have to code by hand. `ctoken` is a close analogue of the C library routine `strtok`.

Parsing problems often involve the validation or "typing" of input tokens. TclX provides ctype to address this:

```
ctype [-failIndex var] charClass string
```

returns 1 if every character in the string is of the specified *charClass*, and 0 if any character is not. It also returns 0 if the string is of zero length. If the failIndex flag and variable name are provided, then the index of the first character to fail the test for membership in type *charClass* is returned in the variable.

```
tcl>set str 87654h890
tcl>ctype digit $str
0
tcl>ctype -failindex where digit $str
0
tcl>echo $where
5
tcl>echo [cindex $str $where]
h
```

Other character classes include alnum, alpha, ascii, cntrl, lower, upper, space, etc. ctype does more than just test strings for type; it can also be used to convert decimal ASCII values to characters, and vice versa:

```
tcl>ctype ord e
101
tcl>ctype char 101
e
```

Eventually every programmer needs this conversion. It's one more wheel that the TclX user doesn't have to reinvent. Here's a practical example, part of a filter that replaces ugly 8-bit character codes left in a text file by a PC word processor:

```
case [ctype ord $c] in {
{142} {
        puts -nonewline $nfp "e"
}
{209} {
        puts -nonewline $nfp "--"
}
{213} {
        puts -nonewline $nfp "'"
}
{default} {
        puts -nonewline $nfp $c
}
}
```

Here, ctype ord is used to get the numeric character value, which is tested in a crude case statement and converted to a printable string.

TclX has yet more "fun with strings" in its bag of tricks: replicate and translit.

```
replicate string times
```

simply returns a string constructed of *times* replications of the string *string*:

```
tcl>replicate a 10
aaaaaaaaaa
tcl>replicate ab 10
abababababababababab
```

The Unix `tr` command is mirrored in

        translit *inrange outrange string*

which translates characters in *string*, changing any char in the range *inrange* to its corresponding char in *outrange*. You could use this as an alternative version of `string toupper`:

```
tcl>set str "Hello World"
tcl>translit a-z A-Z $str
HELLO WORLD
```

or you could do some simple-minded data obfuscation:

```
tcl>translit a-z b-za abc
bcd
tcl>translit a-z m-zA-L abcpqr
mnoBCD
tcl>translit m-zA-L a-z mnoBCD
abcpqr
```

The string expand function,

        cexpand *string*

expands all backslash sequences in *string* to their actual character values.

```
tcl>set str "This is a square bracket \\\[ in a string"
tcl>echo $str
This is a square bracket \[ in a string
tcl>cexpand $str
This is a square bracket [ in a string
```

Of these functions, I have found `clength`, `cindex`, `crange`, and `ctype` the most essential; when parsing user input they are invaluable. Tcl can be called essentially a string processing language, since its variables are typeless; the more powerful the string parsing and manipulation commands in your toolbox, the better you can exploit Tcl's "everything's a string" philosophy.

TclX List Commands

Lists are an important Tcl feature. The core Tcl list functions alone are quite powerful, giving Tcl somewhat LISP-like strengths. User or data file input often looks like a valid Tcl list, so Tcl's list-processing features add to its utility as a parsing language. TclX expands Tcl list functionality considerably, adding ten new commands.

In core Tcl, as a beginner, I not infrequently wrote code along these lines:

```
tcl>set dlist [list This was input from some source or other]
tcl>set var1 [lindex $dlist 0]
tcl>set var2 [lindex $dlist 1]
```

Later I became a little smarter and wrote code more like this:

```
tcl>set dlist [list This was input from some source or other]
tcl>set vlist [list var1 var2 var3 var4 var5 var6 var7 var8]
tcl>set dl [llength $dlist]
tcl>for {set i 0} {$i < $dl} {incr i} {
=>set [lindex $vlist $i] [lindex $dlist $i]
=>}
tcl>echo $var1
This
```

and so on. Using TclX, the equivalent code is:

```
tcl>set dlist [list This was input from some source or other]
tcl>lassign $dlist var1 var2 var3 var4 var5 var6 var7 var8
tcl>echo $var1
This
```

or even more concisely

```
tcl>eval lassign \$dlist $vlist
```

(Note the use of eval here, and the backslash which "escapes" the dollar sign for later parsing. This command gets parsed twice; in other words, first vlist is evaluated into the list of variable names, then the lassign is actually done and dlist is evaluated). The list assignment command,

```
            lassign list var [var...]
```

assigns each element of list to one of a list of variable names which follow the list argument. If fewer variables are provided than there are list elements in dlist, lassign returns a list of the unassigned values:

```
tcl>lassign $dlist var1 var2 var3
from some source or other
```

If too many variables were provided, those for which there are no list values are set to the null value (but they do exist):

```
tcl>lassign $dlist var1 var2 var3 var4 var5 var6 var7 var8 var9
tcl>echo $var9
tcl>info exists var9
1
```

lassign is another TclX feature that any programmer might well write as a procedure for her own private library, but is so basic and useful that it belongs in the language.

Sometimes all you need to know about a list is whether it is empty (has no members). The command

```
            lempty list
```

---

is slightly more concise than comparing the list to a null string, or checking whether [llength list] is 0.

```
tcl>set dlist ""
tcl>lempty $dlist
1
tcl>set dlist "a b cd e"
tcl>lempty $dlist
0
```

Now we come to one of my favourite commands,

> lrmdups *list*

Because I write a lot of list-processing code, I find this command very useful; it simply sorts *list* and suppresses all duplicate entries (the equivalent of a sort -u):

```
tcl>set dlist [list the quick brown fox jumped over the lazy dog]
tcl>lrmdups $dlist
brown dog fox jumped lazy over quick the
```

Core Tcl uses the lsearch command to determine whether a string is found in a list and in what position. TclX carries this concept several steps in a different direction with

> lmatch ?-*mode*? *list pattern*

Instead of returning the index of the first matching element, lmatch returns a list of all matching elements. The three possible modes are -exact, -glob (the default), and -regexp. When -exact is chosen, as you would expect, the supplied match value must be found, intact, as an element of the list. The -glob option causes lmatch to behave like core Tcl string match, and -regexp causes it to work more like the core Tcl regexp command.

```
tcl>set dlist [list The quick brown fox jumped over the lazy dog]
tcl>lmatch -exact $dlist do
tcl>lmatch -exact $dlist dog
dog
tcl>lmatch $dlist *o*
brown fox over dog
tcl>lmatch -regexp $dlist "e+"
The jumped over the
tcl>lmatch -regexp $dlist "(o+)|(h+)"
The brown fox over the dog
```

Core Tcl provides the list and lappend commands for creating lists. The TclX commands lvarcat, lvarpop, and lvarpush help you to construct and deconstruct lists by adding and removing list elements.

> lvarcat *varName* string ?*string...*?

Like the core Tcl concat command, it creates a single list out of all its *string* arguments; the difference is that it sets the variable *varName* as well. If any *string* is a list, it is deconstructed into individual elements which are appended to the output list. The output list is stored in *varName* and also returned as the command result. The variable *varName* need not preexist; lvarcat creates it if necessary.

Here I'll illustrate the difference between lappend and lvarcat.

```
tcl>set dlist1 {The quick}
tcl>set dlist2 {brown fox jumped}
tcl>set dlist3 {over the lazy {or hazily over the} dog}
tcl>lappend blist $dlist1 $dlist2 $dlist3
{The quick} {brown fox jumped} {over the lazy dog}
tcl>lvarcat xlist $dlist1 $dlist2 $dlist3
The quick brown fox jumped over the lazy {or hazily over the} dog
```

As you can see, lappend makes a list of lists, with embedded braces delimiting the original lists. lvarcat makes one list.

Somewhat similar to ctoken is

> lvarpop *varName* *?listIndex?* *?newString?*

which deletes (and returns) the list element indexed by *listIndex*. If the index is not supplied, it defaults to 0 and the command lifts off the first list element as if popping a stack. If a *newString* argument is supplied, then the original deleted item is replaced by newString. The return value is the deleted item, so this is another handy way to strip items from space-separated lists (such as command line arguments).

```
tcl>set dlist "The quick brown fox jumped over the lazy dog"
tcl>lvarpop dlist
The
tcl>echo $dlist
quick brown fox jumped over the lazy dog
tcl>lvarpop dlist 3 flew
jumped
tcl>echo $dlist
quick brown fox flew over the lazy dog
tcl>lvarpop dlist end cow
dog
tcl>echo $dlist
quick brown fox flew over the lazy cow
tcl>lvarpop dlist end-1 industrious
lazy
tcl>echo $dlist
quick brown fox flew over the industrious cow
```

This is somewhat faster and easier than using lappend, lreplace, and linsert to the same effect. This is a sample script, rather than an interactive session, to demonstrate how you could easily use lvarpop to parse command line arguments and flags.

```
#
# sample script
#        args -Eerrfile -Ooutfile -Mmyname@host infile.dat
#        args do not have to be in order
#
```

```
while {![lempty $argv]} {
        set word [lvarpop argv]
        if {[cindex $word 0] == "-"} {
                switch -- [cindex $word 1] {
                        E { set errfile [crange $word 2 end] }
                        O { set outfile [crange $word 2 end] }
                        M { set mailto [crange $word 2 end] }
                        default {
                                puts stderr "Bad flag $word"
                                echo $syntax_reminder
                                exit 1
                        }
                }
        } else {
                set infile $word
        }
}
echo Errfile: $errfile Outfile: $outfile Mail: $mailto Infile: $infile
```

If this script is called *testargs,* and the user runs it like this:

```
%  testargs in.dat -Mmyname@host -Eerr.dat -Oout.dat
```

the output will be

```
Errfile: err.dat Outfile: out.dat Mail: myname@host Infile: in.dat
```

The corresponding "push" command for lists is

```
        lvarpush varName newString ?listIndex?
```

which inserts a new item *newString* into the list just before position `listIndex`, and `listIndex` again defaults to 0 if unspecified. We had lopped off the first word of "The quick brown fox..." (in dlist): let's use lvarpush to stick it back on:

```
tcl>lvarpush dlist The
tcl>echo $dlist
The quick brown fox flew over the industrious cow
```

List processing is often set processing; in other words, the object is to determine or assign membership of entities or attributes (elements) in sets (lists). TclX's toolkit for this kind of problem starts with

```
        union listA listB
```

which simply merges the two lists and eliminates dups; in other words, it's just lvarcat plus lrmdups.

More useful to most programmers than union is

```
        intersect listA listB
```

which returns the intersection of two lists (the list of elements found in both lists):

```
tcl>set listA {bb xx aa gg yy pp}
tcl>set listB {zz nn bb oo tt yy mm}
tcl>union $listA $listB
```

```
        aa bb gg mm nn oo pp tt xx yy zz
  tcl>intersect $listA $listB
  bb yy
```

Last and (IMHO) most useful of the "set theory" commands is

```
        intersect3 listA listB
```

which returns a list of three lists: first, all the elements of listA not found in listB; second, the normal intersect of the two lists (elements they have in common); third, the elements of listB not found in listA. This function has been of repeated use to me in database applications where lists of entities and attributes must be compared, merged, and diffed.

```
  tcl>intersect3 $listA $listB
  {aa gg pp xx} {bb yy} {mm nn oo tt zz}
```

I've used TclX list functions in a network traffic mapping problem, for which I had gathered extensive summary data describing packet traffic by source and destination address. From these data I could determine for each host a list of "buddies" with whom it chatted more than with other (non-buddy) hosts. The question was whether these sets of buddies would group into larger "clubs," all of whose members tended to chat far more within the club than outside the club. The answer to this question would tell us whether our overloaded single Ethernet backbone could be partitioned rationally (using routers and bridges) to optimize bandwidth usage.

This question was a set theory problem: Can each host be assigned to a "club," and what degree of crossmembership is there between clubs? TclX list manipulation commands seemed like the right tool, and this is an excerpt from the application:

```
  #     players is the list of hosts who are "playing" this game
  #     the proc "buddies" returns a list of hosts who chat with me
  #     more than the threshold amount (parameter)
        foreach p $players {
  #     p is an IP address, which we convert to a name via an array
  #     set at the beginning of the "game" using nslookup (scotty
  #     tcl extension) and local database
            set hn $name($p)
            set myset [buddies $hn]
            set myclub -1
            set besto 0
  #     clubs is an array of lists of hosts where each list of hosts
  #     is an association or club whose members chat with each other.
  #     with which existing club does my social set (buddies) have
  #     the largest overlap?
            foreach c [array names clubs] {
                set cl $clubs($c)
                lassign [intersect3 $myset $cl] mynew overlap others
                    set ol [llength $overlap]
                    if {$ol > $besto} {
                            set besto $ol
                            set myclub $c
                }
            }
```

```
#      if there was no overlap at all then we are a new club of our own
       if {$myclub  0} {
               set newc 0
               catch {eval set newc \[max [array names clubs]\]}
               set myclub [expr $newc + 1]
               set clubs($myclub) ""
       }
#      whether new or old, we append all my buddies to the selected
#      club membership list
       foreach h $myset {
               lappend clubs($myclub) $h
               set membership($h) $myclub
       }
#      then we remove dups from this club
       set clubs($myclub) [lrmdups $clubs($myclub)]
       }
```

The TclX basic list commands are enhancements that any programmer could provide with a private library of procs, like the math functions and `lassign` command, but it's far more pleasant to have them "off the shelf" as part of the installed interpreter.

You can do even more with lists in TclX by using its "keyed list" concept. A keyed list is a list with fixed internal structure; that is, a list of lists. The commands `keylset` and `keylget` store and retrieve data from keyed lists. An example will be far more useful than a lengthy explanation here:

```
tcl> keylset person LAST Flintstone FIRST Fred PHONE 333-4444 \
         OCCUP Toon SALARY 0 NOTES "What a swell guy"
tcl> echo $person
{LAST Flintstone} {FIRST Fred} {PHONE 333-4444} {OCCUP Toon}
{SALARY 0}
{NOTES {What a swell guy}}
tcl> keylget person OCCUP
Toon
```

What we just did was to establish a set of key/value pairs and to give that set a name (`person`). We can now retrieve specific values by key (what is the "occupation" of "person"?). Database programmers will immediately recognize this construct as a tuple expressing attributes; other programmers may see a strong resemblance to a C struct. The syntax is

```
keylset listName Keyword Value ?Keyword Value ...?
keylget listName Keyword
```

A lot of my Tcl code is basically state-enginesque; that is, if it were written in C, all the structs would be global (and very large). So I just use large global arrays for 90 percent of my data storage. I have thus been sheltered from the one significant limitation of arrays in Tcl: Arrays are not first-class objects. You can't pass or return an array by value, only by name.

When you want to pass structured packages of data between procs by value, you may not want to refer to a lot of `upvar` levels and pass everything by name. Unless your code is already a state engine, you may not want to make most of your variable space global either. (To many programmers this is repugnant on general principles.) At this point you generally use a list:

```
proc foo mylist {
        global ofp
        lassign $mylist last first phone
        echo $ofp [format "%-15s %-15s %07d" Last First Phone]
        echo $ofp [format "%-15s %-15s %07d" $last $first $phone]

        ...

}
lappend person $last_name
lappend person $first_name
lappend person $phone_num
set res [foo $person]
...
```

The only clue to the meaning of the list elements is their order; that's not so painful, but this kind of code can present maintenance problems later, especially if different programmers work on different modules. If you choose good variable names, as just shown, it's almost self-documenting; but if you get sloppy and start referring to your list elements by raw index numbers:

```
if {[cequal [lindex $mylist 0] $test_name]} {
        do_something
    }
```

the code starts to lose legibility. Who can tell, without poring over (perhaps a lot of) other source, whether the name being compared is a first or a last name?

Keyed lists were introduced into TclX to provide a first-class object (one that could be passed and returned by value), yet had internal structure and was self-documenting and conducive to good coding. You could say that keyed lists are a stylistic, rather than a purely functional, enhancement. They offer you a syntactic construct that encourages good programming style.

As you saw, a keyed list is just a list of lists. There's no radical new Tcl variable type here; just some commands that allow you to create and manipulate a list of lists easily and concisely. Naturally, the story does not end with storage and retrieval. You can also delete a key and its associated value out of the list:

```
tcl> keyldel person SALARY
tcl> echo $person
{LAST Flintstone} {FIRST Fred} {PHONE 333-4444} {OCCUP Toon}
{NOTES {What a swell guy}}
```

or add a new one

```
tcl> keylset person HOBBIES "Lithography Zoetropes Oenology"
{LAST Flintstone} {FIRST Fred} {PHONE 333-4444} {OCCUP Toon}
{NOTES {What a swell guy}} {HOBBIES {Lithography Zoetropes Oenology}}
```

And, as with the array names command, you can retrieve the list of valid keys set for this keyed list:

```
tcl>keylkeys person
LAST FIRST PHONE OCCUP NOTES HOBBIES
```

Now you have a data storage convention with the benefits both of an array (named storage locations whose names are retrievable from the storage object itself) and of a list (can be passed by value). The benefits of passing by value become more obvious when we consider the challenges of a distributed (client/server) application. If I want to pass a structured package of information from the client to the server or vice versa, neither has any knowledge of the other's variable space; I have to pass by value. It would be nice if I could examine the return value I had just received to see what I was given, rather than relying on hard-coded index positions and arcane rules ("if the first word of the list is X, then position 3 is the phone number").

Let's say the client has the social security number of a person, and it wants to know what the server knows about that person. The client might contain some code like this:

```
#   I sent the server a request for info, containing some lookup
#   code like a social security number.
#   The server process returned me a keyed list which I call "answer".
    set flds [keylkeys answer]
    set patient "FIRST LAST FLOOR WARD BED CHARTNUM MEDS DIET PPHYS"
    set doctor "FIRST LAST DIVIS SPECIAL CASELOAD HOURS PAGER HOME"
#   If there are fields in the answer that are not patient fields
#   then it has to be a doctor; there are only two species in our
#   taxonomy
    if {![lempty [lindex [lintersect3 $flds $patient] 0]]]} {
            set type "Doctor"
    } else {
            set type "Patient"
    }
    echo "$type [keylget answer FIRST] [keylget answer LAST]:"
    keyldel answer FIRST
    keyldel answer LAST
    foreach k [keylkeys answer] {
            echo "$k : [keylget answer $k]"
    }
```

We'll cover the commands that actually implement servers and clients in TclX later in this chapter; this example is just to demonstrate that I can pass a structured message by value and retrieve not only its contents, but embedded information about the meaning of its contents. It also demonstrates the use of a list intersect command to compare lists of attributes, in order to determine the type of an entity (for those who like that kind of thing).

As to maintainability, you can add fields to keyed lists without disturbing procs that already use those lists, because the procs can easily be written to ignore the length of the list and order of elements. There is no temptation to indulge in raw integer indexing, so the readability of code written with keyed lists depends only on an intelligent choice of key.

A keyed list can itself be a value element in a keyed list (just as structs can contain structs in C). This makes them more powerful than mere key/value pairs.

```
tcl>keylset n LAST Smith FIRST Sybilla
tcl>echo $n
{LAST Smith} {FIRST Sybilla}
tcl>keylset person NAME $n ADDR "1 Haresfoot Crescent"
tcl>echo $person
{NAME {{LAST Smith} {FIRST Sybilla}}} {ADDR {1 Haresfoot Crescent}}
tcl> keylget person NAME.LAST
Smith
tcl>keylget person NAME
{LAST Smith} {FIRST Sybilla}
```

Here we made n a keyed list which became one element of the keyed list person. Note that we can now retrieve the subelements of NAME without resorting to [keyl-get [keylget...] ...] by means of the dot-syntax NAME.LAST. This is in fact necessary, because the keyed list commands refer to their target lists by name and not value! We could also have set the nested list values using the same dot-syntax:

```
tcl>keylset person NAME.LAST Smith
tcl>keylset person NAME.FIRST Shadrach
tcl>echo $person
{NAME {{LAST Smith} {FIRST Shadrach}}} {ADDR {1 Haresfoot Crescent}}
```

You could model fairly complex hierarchical data structures using keyed lists.

Now for the catch: If you misuse keyed lists, they can pose a performance problem. A keyed list is not an array; it should not have an arbitrarily large, dynamically generated, expanding set of keys. In C terms, think of it as a struct: The elements of a struct are predefined, not dynamically constructed at runtime. The performance penalty for abusing keyed lists can be severe.

If you want the keyed list features but you need large storage, remember that a keyed list can also be stored in an array; you can build large arrays in which each array element is a keyed list. I have used this strategy successfully in several data-processing applications.

Here's a simple example. Let's pretend we have a table of telemetry data from an instrument; it's stored in a Sybase relational database. One record is added to the table every N minutes during operation of the instrument, and each record is identified by a unique value in the field samplen. We get about 20 telemetry data points from this instrument, so the table definition consists of 20 columns plus the samplen column. We want to grab some of that table and use it in a Tcl application; we've done a SQL query to select records of interest, and now we are collecting the returned records:

```
set cols [sybCols 1]
while {1} {
set line [sybNext 1]
if {$line == ""} {break}
eval lassign \$line $cols
foreach c $cols {
keylset $inst.Status($samplen) $c [set $c]
}
```

We get the column names; for each record returned, we use the `lassign` command to assign the column values to variables of the same names. Then we turn the column names and values into the key/value pairs of a keyed list. The keyed list is stored as one element of an array. Note that the array name is dynamically constructed using a variable `inst` (name of the instrument). This does not pose a performance problem.

Let's say our query returned about 400 samples. We end up with a 400-element array. What if we had flattened the table into a single keyed list by exploiting the key namespace, like this?

```
keylset $inst.Status ${samplen}_$c [set $c]
```

This flattened list would have 400×20, or 8000 keys! The 400-element array of keyed lists in the previous example will perform quite briskly; the bloated list with 8000 dynamically constructed key names will perform very poorly.

A keyed list, in other words, corresponds well to one record of a table (class) in relational database jargon. An array of keyed lists corresponds well to the table. What would be a violation of the 3rd Normal Form in database design would also be a bad idea when using keyed lists.

TclX Unix Access Commands

TclX provides many built-in commands (not procedures) that add the functionality of C or of most Unix shells to core Tcl. These functions include date and time processing, file operations, process handling, and the "system" function. Even the simplest commands provide a performance enhancement over core Tcl because no **exec** is necessary. The more advanced commands provide functionality not needed in the original vision of core Tcl, but very much needed to make Tcl a standalone language.

This chapter is not an introduction to Unix programming. I'm assuming that you are already a Unix programmer, and therefore familiar with the Unix-style functions discussed here.

chown, chgrp, and chmod are syntactically much as you would expect. The only difference between the shell syntax and the TclX syntax is in chown, where owner and group (if both are specified) are a 2-element space-separated list rather than the owner.group (or POSIX owner:group) form familiar from the command line. (Some older Unices may not even let you specify owner and group with *chown*, but force you to use *chgrp* separately.)

```
tcl>ls -l testfile
-rw-r--r--   1 root       system        0 May 23 19:42 testfile
tcl>chown wombat testfile
tcl>ls -l testfile
-rw-r--r--   1 wombat     system        0 May 23 19:42 testfile
tcl>chown {de ourstaff} testfile
tcl>ls -l testfile
-rw-r--r--   1 de         ourstaff      0 May 23 19:42 testfile
tcl>set fd [open testfile r]
tcl>chown {de ourstaff} -fileid $fd
```

All three commands can accept symbolic as well as numeric user and group IDs, and chmod can accept both octal and symbolic protection modes. All three commands can accept a list of filenames in place of a single filename.

One essential command for controlling file access is umask, which works exactly like its csh equivalent:

    umask ?*octalMask*?

If the *octalMask* argument is omitted, the current umask is returned.

The chroot command:

    chroot *dirName*

invokes the POSIX chroot system call, setting the process's effective filesystem root (/) to the specified directory; only the superuser can use this command.

dirs, pushd, and popd also function much as a C or bash shell user would expect. dirs lists the directories currently on the directory stack; pushd *dirName* changes to the directory *dirName* and pushes it onto the stack; and popd pops the topmost (most recent) entry from the stack and cd's to it:

```
tcl>dirs
/home/de
tcl>pushd /usr/local/etc
tcl>dirs
/usr/local/etc /home/de
tcl>pushd /tmp
tcl>dirs
/tmp /usr/local/etc /home/de
tcl>popd
/usr/local/etc
tcl>popd
/home/de
```

TclX's confirming echo for pushd and popd differs slightly from what csh or bash would provide, but the functionality is the same.

An important Unix feature is the ability to deliver signals to processes, using either system calls or the kill command.

    kill ?-pgroup? ?*signal*? *idList*

sends a signal *signal* (the default is SIGTERM, or 15, if unspecified) to a process ID or list of process IDs provided as *idList*. If the -pgroup flag is present, the IDs in *idList* are accepted as process group IDs instead of individual process ids; when this flag is present *and* the process ID is 0, the current process group is assumed. (Not all Unices have process groups; they are a BSD concept, a way of grouping processes that share certain resources like stdin and stdout. POSIX-compliant systems should support process groups.) The signal can be specified as a Unix integer signal number, SIG*nnn*, or merely *SigName*, so the following are all equivalent:

```
tcl> kill HUP 151
tcl> kill SIGHUP 151
tcl> kill 1 151
```

The Unix *ln* command is implemented as

        link ?-sym? *origPath linkPath*

which works exactly like the command-line equivalent, the only difference being that the symbolic link flag is -sym instead of simply -s. (Some Unix systems do not support symbolic links, so the -sym flag is not available when TclX is built on those systems.) The unlink command

        unlink ?-nocomplain? *fileList*

requires no explanation—and is more economical by far than exec /bin/rm -f $filename.

The mkdir command:

        mkdir ?-path? *newDir*

differs from the Unix *mkdir* command only in that the -p flag has been expanded to the verbose -path. (Not every Unix supports the -p flag, but all TclX implementations should support -path.) This flag, for those who are unfamiliar with the Unix version, causes the mkdir command to create as many directories as are necessary to create the final "leaf" directory.

        rmdir ?-nocomplain? *dirList*

does exactly what you would expect.

        readdir *dirPath*

returns a list of all the files in the target directory and represents a slight increase in efficiency (no additional process is launched) over exec ls dirPath:

```
tcl>readdir /usr/local/www/de/book
outline.html over.html math.html string.html list.html unix.html
debug.html file.html tcp.html keyl.html sample.sgml
```

The nice command can change only the current process priority, with the same rules that apply to the shell *nice* command: Negative niceness values work only if you're the superuser! A major difference (from the shell version of this command) is that even the superuser cannot change the priorities of other processes using the TclX nice comand. The priority increment is expressed as a positive integer value (with no dashes to confuse the user):

```
tcl> nice 10
```

The sleep command does just what you would expect:

        sleep *sleepSeconds*

causes the TclX process to suspend itself for *sleepSeconds* seconds. (Note: This feature was implemented in Tcl release 7.5 as the after command.)

The TclX sync command implements both the shell sync command and the fsync system call (if the Unix system where TclX was built supports this call). sync with no argument schedules all cached disk writes for physical flush, and returns immediately. sync *fileId*, however, immediately flushes and syncs the file associated with *fileId*, and does not return until the flush is complete. If the current Unix system does not support `fsync`, a TclX `sync` command with a *fileId* argument just ignores the argument and does a regular `sync`.

Not all TclX Unix functions are implementations of ordinary shell commands, as we saw with `sync`. Some implement C library functions and system calls.

> alarm *delaySec*

requests a SIGALARM after *delaySec* seconds. *delaySec* can be expressed as a floating-point number, to denote fractional seconds; on systems without `setitimer`, *delaySec* is rounded up to the next integer number of seconds. Only one alarm can be active at any given time; if an `alarm` command cancels a previous alarm, the return value is the number of seconds that were remaining in the earlier alarm.

The following time-related commands were implemented in core Tcl at release 7.5 (as the `clock` command) and are documented here for those who are still running earlier revisions of Tcl.

The function `getclock` returns the system time, as an integer number of seconds; this is useful for a quick and dirty unique filename:

```
tcl>set ofp [open /tmp/checkdump.[getclock] w]
```

Because `getclock` returns an integer number of seconds, it can easily be used for relative time calculations. The additional date/time functions `convertclock` and `fmtclock` make it relatively trivial to parse and calculate datetime values.

> fmtclock *clockval* ?*formatString*? ?GMT?

converts a system clock value (as returned by `getclock`) into a formatted date/time string:

```
tcl>set now [getclock]
tcl> echo $now
801285817
tcl>fmtclock $now
Tue May 23 20:23:37 PDT 1995
tcl>fmtclock $now %H:%M:%S
20:23:37
tcl>fmtclock $now "%a %d %h %Y at %R"
Tue 23 May 1995 at 20:23
```

See the `strftime` (or equivalent function) manual page on your system for some idea of `fmtclock`'s formatting capabilities. `convertclock` provides the reverse transformation, converting a datetime string back into a system clock value. The command

> convertclock *dateString* ?GMT? ?*baseclock*?

accepts some useful keywords in *dateString*, such as `yesterday`, `tomorrow`, `3 weeks` (from now), etc.:

```
tcl>fmtclock [convertclock tomorrow]
Thu May 25 08:46:47 PDT 1995
tcl>fmtclock [convertclock yesterday]
Tue May 23 08:46:56 PDT 1995
tcl>fmtclock [convertclock "3 weeks"]
```

```
Wed Jun 14 08:47:03 PDT 1995
tcl>fmtclock [convertclock "next Tuesday"]
Tue Jun 06 00:00:00 PDT 1995
```

The *baseclock* argument, seldom used, permits you to supply a system clock value to be used as the current date. Only the date component of *baseclock* is used. You can then add relative time values to this base date value:

```
tcl>convertclock "May 1, 1980 17:57"
326077020
tcl>convertclock "12:00" {} 326077020
326055600
tcl>fmtclock 326055600
Thu May 01 12:00:00 PDT 1980
```

You can have a lot of fun with convertclock and fmtclock, doing date magic for many kinds of user applications. fmtclock can be used on the system clock values returned by file mtime and file atime as well:

```
tcl>set thresh [convertclock "-2 days"]
tcl>echo $thresh
832124172
tcl>fmtclock $thresh
Tue May 14 18:36:12 PDT 1996
tcl>fmtclock [getclock]
Thu May 16 18:36:26 PDT 1996
tcl>foreach f [glob .*] {
=>        if {[file mtime $f] > $thresh} {
=>                echo "file $f was modified in the last 2 days"
=>        }
=>}
file . was modified in the last 2 days
file .cshrc was modified in the last 2 days
file .history was modified in the last 2 days
file .netscape-preferences was modified in the last 2 days
file .netscape-cache was modified in the last 2 days
file .netscape-history was modified in the last 2 days
file .netscape-bookmarks.html was modified in the last 2 days
tcl>
```

(You could have done this with the Unix *find* command, of course, but using Tcl you can do more complicated things with files selected by mtime/atime/... than are easily done with the -exec flag on *find*.) This concludes the discussion of the system clock commands, once available only via TclX.

Another Unix feature you can use easily from a sh script, but not from core Tcl, is the times command:

```
tcl>times
0 51 0 0
```

The return value is a list containing (in order) the user time and system time of the parent (tcl script) and child (executed command) processes (see the time function for your system, or the csh time and sh times commands).

The `id` command rolls up into one syntax the `setuid/getuid` family of system calls. It converts user/group ID numbers easily into user names and vice versa, as well as setting UID and GID.

```
tcl>id convert user de
777
tcl>id convert userid 777
de
tcl>id convert groupid 666
ourstaff
tcl>id convert group ourstaff
666
tcl>id user
de
tcl>id userid
777
tcl>id group
ourstaff
```

A user with sufficient privileges can change her group or uid:

```
tcl>id group tdevils
tcl>id group
tdevils
```

The TclX `id` command implements `setuid` but not `seteuid`; both of these commands

```
        id user userName
        id userid userID
```

would set both real and effective UIDs to the user represented by *userName* or *userID*. `id process` returns the PID of the current process and its relatives:

```
tcl>id process
1452
tcl>id process parent
504
tcl>id process group
1452
tcl>
```

The `system` command is provided as an alternative to `exec`, with the advantages of the `system` library function on which it is based. Unlike `exec`, `system` does not return the executed command's stdout as its result:

```
tcl>set res [exec ls .mailrc]
tcl>echo $res
.mailrc
tcl>set res [system "ls .mailrc"]
.mailrc
tcl>echo $res
0
tcl>
```

Instead, it forwards stdout back to the interpreter, and returns the system call exit status as the result. What advantages does this function offer over **exec**? **system** uses the Unix shell, so wildcard expansion, redirection, etc., work as from the shell command line:

```
tcl>set res [exec ls .ma*]
Error: .ma* not found
tcl>set res [system "ls .ma*"]
.mailcap        .mailrc
tcl>
```

When the TclX **system** call was written, output redirection was not possible with **exec**; it is still a little more work with **exec** than with **system**. Stdout, stdin, and stderr are associated with those file descriptors for the Tcl process. The **exec** Tcl command expects a list of command elements, but the **system** call expects a single string containing the command, properly delimited with double-quotes or braces:

```
tcl>exec ls -l
total 282
-rw-r--r--    1 de       wombats                0 May 22 18:18 debug.html
-rw-r--r--    1 de       wombats                0 May 22 18:18 file.html
tcl>system ls -l
wrong # args: system command
tcl>system "ls -l"
total 282
-rw-r--r--    1 de       wombats                0 May 22 18:18 debug.html
-rw-r--r--    1 de       wombats                0 May 22 18:18 file.html
tcl>exec "ls -l"
couldn't find "ls -l" to execute
```

(This trivial inconsistency is sometimes difficult for Tcl users learning TclX; it springs from the faithfulness with which each of these commands imitates its associated C library routine.) The behavior of the **exec** command can be a bit of a nuisance when you are passing commands around as strings:

```
tcl>set dir /tmp
tcl>set cmd "ls -lg $dir"
tcl>exec $cmd
Error: couldn't execute "ls -lg /tmp": no such file or directory
tcl>eval exec $cmd
-rw-r--r-- 1 de de 5026 Oct 23 22:07 cd
-rwxr-xr-x 1 de de 69136 Oct 13 19:29 lcache00.tmp
-rw-r--r-- 1 de de 71 Oct 12 21:45 logfile.txt
...
tcl>system $cmd
-rw-r--r-- 1 de de 5026 Oct 23 22:07 cd
-rwxr-xr-x 1 de de 69136 Oct 13 19:29 lcache00.tmp
-rw-r--r-- 1 de de 71 Oct 12 21:45 logfile.txt
...
```

Remember that characters enclosed in braces are sacrosanct to Tcl, but characters enclosed in double-quotes are not: if you wish to pass to the shell any characters that are "magic" for Tcl, you must "escape" them :

```
tcl>system "echo $HOME"
Error: can't read "HOME": no such variable
tcl>system "echo \$HOME"
/no/place/like
0
```

TclX also offers the Unix `fork` and `execl` system calls. `fork` returns a zero to the child process, and the child process ID to the parent; a Tcl error is generated if the fork fails. Using TclX you can launch and control child process from your Tcl scripts.

The following example is from a CGI script (the backend to a WWW query page). The purpose of the script is to run a financial ledger; however, the ledger could take from minutes to hours to complete, and the Webserver and its client have a limited attention span. If the CGI script does not write back to stdout quickly enough, the user gets a misleading error about malformed HTML headers. This script accepts parameters from the user via the Web page, then forks off a copy of itself to run the ledger, eventually mailing the output to the user.

```
# feed the client something to keep its attention
puts stdout "Content-type: text/html\n"
puts stdout ""
#
# Log the user request, as we are about to start the job
# set now [getclock]
set afp [open /data/data7/hlogs/GL_log a]
puts $afp "WANTED [fmtclock [getclock]] $type $args "
close $afp
#
# fork off another process to exec the job
# the correct command to exec will be found in the array cmd,
# indexed by the type of ledger to be run
#
        zif {[set childPid [fork]] == 0} {
#       child process actions
        close stdout
        close stdin
        eval exec $cmd($type) &
        exit
        }
# # Meanwhile...
# parent process goes on and confirms to user that job was created,
# then exits
#
        puts stdout "<h1> Banner FIS Report: $type -- CONFIRM</h1>
        <p> <hr> <p> "
        puts stdout "Your report<br> "
        puts stdout "<b>Banner_$type $args</b><p>"
        puts stdout "will be sent to $addr when complete. If you do"
```

```
puts stdout "not receive this report within the next hour,"
puts stdout "please inform Webmaster."
puts stdout "<p> <hr> <p> </body> </html>"
flush stdout
exit
```

In a later section we'll show how we could launch our child process and continue to communicate with it over Unix pipes; alternatively, we could just wait for it to complete and run down before taking some other action:

wait ?-nohang? ?-untraced? ?-pgroup? ?processID?

This waits for the termination of a process, then returns a three-element list containing first the PID of the terminated process that we were waiting for; then (usually) the string EXIT; and lastly, the exit code. If the process terminated because of a signal, the second list item would be SIG and the third would be the name of the signal that caused the termination. If the process is stopped (assuming your Unix system supports SIGSTP) then the second list item would be STOP and the third would be the signal name (SIGSTP).

If −nohang is specified, TclX does not block waiting for a termination, but returns immediately. If a child has already terminated, it returns the three-element list just described; if not, it returns an empty list. If −untraced is specified, wait returns the status of child processes that have stopped, but whose status has not yet been reported. The -pgroup option causes TclX to wait on any process whose group process id is processID; processID (reasonably enough) defaults to the group id of the calling process.

We can use fork to create child processes, send them signals using kill, take action upon their demise with wait, and exchange information with them via pipes—all from within a Tcl script. We can also handle signals sent to us by other processes:

```
tcl>signal trap 15 "echo I got a sig15, ouch!"
tcl>id process
7896
tcl>I got a sig15, ouch!
```

Here I started another login session and issued a kill -15 7896 from the csh command line; TclX trapped the signal and took the specified action. The signal command has many options: signals can be ignored, mapped into catchable Tcl error conditions, trapped as above, or blocked and unblocked (if you're POSIX-compliant). The signal get command allows you to check on the status of your signal handling:

```
tcl>signal get HUP
{SIGHUP {default 0}}
tcl>signal get 15
{SIGTERM {trap 0 {echo I got a sig15, ouch!}}}
```

The return from signal get is a keyed list (we discussed keyed lists earlier in this chapter) in which the label is the name of the signal, and the value is itself a list indicating the action to be taken and whether the signal is blocked or not:

```
tcl>signal block HUP
tcl>signal get HUP
{SIGHUP {default 1}}
```

By giving the Tcl programmer access to all these system calls and library functions, TclX makes Tcl a "real" Unix programming language in which you can write synchronized applications, daemons, and so forth. As we'll see later, TclX also supports TCP/IP for multiprocess programming. With these features, some programmers can almost live without C—except, of course, when performance is really critical or you have to manipulate binary data.

File I/O Commands

Core Tcl supports file `open`, `close`, `puts`, `gets`, and `read`. TclX, as usual, adds a collection of convenience features and C-like functions to make file handling easier and more sophisticated.

I use `for_file` a lot. This proc does something simple and useful:

```
tcl>for_file line /etc/hosts {echo [lindex $line 0]}
```

reads the file /etc/hosts one line at a time, putting each line into the variable `line` and then executing the contents of the third (code) argument for each line. `for_file` is simpler and easier than using `open`, `gets`, etc. Obviously you can use `for_file` as an alternative to *awk* and *grep*, but TclX also offers other, more powerful, file scanning commands (to be described later).

You don't always want to read files one line at a time, so

```
read_file ?-nonewline? fileName
read_file fileName numBytes
```

opens the named file for you, reads its contents, and returns them as a single string.

```
write_file fileName string ?string. ...?
```

likewise opens the named file for you and writes the specified string(s) to it in one command.

```
tcl>cat .logout
stty rows 24
stty cols 80
clear
tcl>set res [read_file .logout]
tcl>echo $res
stty rows 24
stty cols 80
clear
```

`lgets` is a special variant of the core Tcl `gets` command:

```
lgets fileID ?varName?
```

It reads data from a file as a series of Tcl lists. `lgets` reads the next syntactically correct Tcl list (by parsing matching braces and newlines) from the open file, rather than simply the next line.

If a newline is present within a brace-delimited list, it does not terminate the input; only a newline outside curly braces terminates a single read operation. If *varName* is specified, the newly read list is put into *varName* and the return value is a count of characters read; if no *varName* is specified, the return value is the list. Let's say I create a file test.list in which I try to introduce many combinations of braces and newlines:

```
{This is the first line of the file}
Now we will type a carriage
return but no braces
{and then a list with braces and a
carriage return}
and {this is another list} with a list in it, no return
{This is a list {with a {yow a subsublist} sublist} in it, no return}
{Another nested list: {This is a nested list with a
carriage return} in it {and another sublist} ...OK, enough}
This is the last line
```

Now I read this file with lgets:

```
tcl>set fd [open test.list r]
tcl>lgets $fd listvar
36
tcl>echo $listvar
{This is the first line of the file}
tcl>lgets $fd
Now we will type a carriage
tcl>lgets $fd
return but no braces
tcl>lgets $fd
{and then a list with braces and a carriage return}
tcl>lgets $fd
and {this is another list} with a list in it, no return
tcl>lgets $fd
{This is a list {with a {yow a subsublist} sublist} in it}
tcl>lgets $fd
{Another nested list: {This is a nested list with a carriage
return} in it {and another sublist} ...OK, enough}
tcl>lgets $fd listvar
19
tcl>echo $listvar
This is the last line
tcl>lgets $fd listvar
-1
tcl>
```

This is quite powerful; a list can be a highly structured object. As we saw in the discussion of keyed lists, a structured list makes a good package in which to pass a data set to another process (for example), with minimal parsing effort at the receiving end. (See the `pipe` command later in this section, which opens file IDs for interprocess communications.) A complex list stored to a file could be a checkpoint dump for an application. Some Tcl code itself can be parsed as syntactically valid lists (beware, though, since any exceptional use of braces, such as in a comment line, could break the list syntax).

To change the name of a file,

        frename *oldPath* *newPath*

uses the `rename` system call, and spares you an `exec mv` *oldPath* *newPath*. `ftruncate` truncates a file to a maximum size:

        ftruncate *fileName* *newSize*

and on some systems can be used against open file IDs:

        ftruncate -fileid *fileID* *newSize*

The core Tcl commands `open`, `close`, `puts`, and `gets` permit you to to use file IDs for simple file I/O. TclX can do more with file IDs.

The `copyfile` command allows you to copy from one open file ID, starting at the current position and continuing for a specified maximum number of bytes, to another open file ID starting at its current position. The number of bytes copied can be specified with the `-bytes` flag, in which case an error is returned if fewer than the specified number of bytes were read from the input file. If the `-maxbytes` flag is specified, however, no error is returned even if the input stream runs out before the desired byte count is achieved. The syntax is

        copyfile -bytes *byteCount* *inputFileID* *outputFileID*
        copyfile -maxbytes *byteCount* *inputFileID* *outputFileID*

You could use this command to intersperse binary data from some input file into an output stream of mostly ASCII strings. (Tcl, in which "everything is a string," can't really handle binary data.) For example, you could pass GIF images between Tcl programs using `copyfile`.

`bsearch` uses read and seek functions to perform a binary search on an open file ID, similar to the search performed on an array by the C library function `bsearch`:

        bsearch *fileID* *keyString* ?*returnVar*? ?*compareProc*?

This command searches the opened file pointed to by *fileID*. By default, *keyString* is matched against the first (white-space separated) field of each record; if *compareProc* is specified, it is the name of a procedure which will evaluate each line of the file against the *keyString*. This procedure must accept two arguments (the *keyString* and the record read from the file), and must return a number less than 0 (if the key is less than the line value), greater than 0 (if the key is greater), or 0 if this is a match.

This file must contain lines of text sorted into ascending order with regard to the criteria for the search. In other words, if you're expecting to find a certain string in the second field of the target record, you must use the *compareProc* argument, and the contents of the file must be pre-sorted by the second field of all records.

bsearch tries to find an exact match for *keyString*. No wildcard or regexp magic characters are used. By default it returns either the text of the line where a match was found, or a null string if no match was found; but if *returnVar* is specified, then the return value is 1 or 0 for match success/failure, and the found line is returned in *returnVar*.

This is not the most trivial of commands to use, but its various options give you considerable flexibility in turning bsearch to your own purposes.

TclX offers its own version of the dup system call:

> dup *fileID* ?*targetFileID*?

An open file *fileID* is duplicated; the new file ID is returned, or *targetFileID* is opened addressing the same file as *fileID*. If *targetFileID* is specified, it would normally be stdin, stdout, or stderr, and the dup command takes care of the flush and close for you. (We should perhaps note here that stdin, stdout, and stderr are not Tcl file IDs, but magic keywords that are interpreted by puts, gets and other commands as if they were file IDs. You could use file0, file1, and file2 instead, but the keywords are easier to remember.)

The fcntl call likewise is implemented as a simple command:

> fcntl *fileID* *flagName* ?*valueInt*?

If no *valueInt* is specified, then fcntl returns the current setting of the fcntl flag *flagName* for *fileID*; if a *valueInt* is specified then TclX tries to set the fcntl flag to that value.

```
tcl>fcntl stdin READ
1
tcl>fcntl stdin WRITE
1
tcl>fcntl stdin WRONLY
0
tcl>set fd [open test.file r]
tcl>echo $fd
file3
tcl>fcntl $fd WRITE
0
tcl>fcntl $fd LINEBUF
0
tcl>fcntl $fd LINEBUF 1
tcl>fcntl $fd LINEBUF
1
tcl>fcntl $fd NOBUF 1
```

The NOBUF option is probably the most useful for most people, permitting you to turn off buffering on the target file ID.

flock and funlock are supported, to lock both entire files and ranges of bytes within files:

```
flock -read|write ?-nowait? fileIDtor ?startByte? \
       ?lengthBytes? ?originKeyWord?
```

The -nowait option prevents blocking on failure to get the lock. If the -nowait option is used, the return value is 1 for success and 0 for failure (file is already locked). If this option is not used, then the flock command hangs if the file is already locked. *startByte* and *lengthBytes* are two optional integers describing the section to be locked, *startByte* being the offset from an origin specified by *originKeyWord*. *originKeyWord* can be start (the default), current, or end.

funlock takes the same arguments but without the options:

```
funlock fileIDtor ?startByte? ?endByte? ?originKeyWord?
```

Here's a simple example:

```
tcl>set fd [open test.file w]
tcl>echo $fd
file3
tcl>flock -write $fd
tcl>
```

Now, from another process on the same system:

```
tcl> set fd [open test.file a]
tcl> if {![flock -write -nowait $fd]} {echo File is locked, oops.}
File is locked, oops.
tcl>
```

fstat uses the fstat system call, in two forms: one queries a particular file status flag, and the other returns an array containing the settings of all the supported flags. The syntax is

```
fstat fileID statusFlag
fstat fileID stat arrayName
```

For example:

```
tcl>set fd [open /dev/null r]
tcl>fstat $fd type
characterSpecial
tcl>fstat $fd nlink
1
tcl>fstat $fd size
0
tcl>set fd [open /etc/hosts r]
tcl>fstat $fd uid
3
tcl>fstat $fd gid
4
tcl>fstat $fd size
2327
tcl>fmtclock [fstat $fd mtime]
Tue May 09 09:45:43 PDT 1995
tcl>fstat $fd type
```

```
file
tcl>fstat $fd stat hostat
tcl>array names hostat
tty type size mtime ino dev atime uid ctime nlink gid mode
tcl>echo $hostat(ino)
3078
tcl>echo $hostat(nlink)
1
tcl>
```

The `pipe` command uses the `pipe` system call:

```
pipe ?readVar writeVar?
```

It creates a pipe and (if the arguments are omitted) returns a list containing the read and write file ID of the pipe. If the var names are supplied, *readVar* is set to the file ID for the read side of the pipe and *writeVar* to the write side. We can now continue our discussion of communication with child processes, with a more elaborate example using pipes (code courtesy of R. Stover, UCO/Lick Observatory). The parent process creates some pipes:

```
# Run the command given as an argument.  The return value is a
# list containing: 1) The pid of the command, 2) The handle to write
# to (this is connected to the commands standard input), and 3) The
# handle to read from (this is connected to the commands standard
# output).
proc RunProcess {cmd} {
#       First create pipes for communications
        pipe MyInPipe ChildOutPipe
        pipe ChildInPipe MyOutPipe
#       Make them all non-buffered
        fcntl $MyOutPipe NOBUF 1
        fcntl $MyInPipe NOBUF 1
        fcntl $ChildOutPipe NOBUF 1
        fcntl $ChildInPipe NOBUF 1
#       Go spawn the program we will talk to
        set childPid [ChildProcess $cmd $ChildInPipe $ChildOutPipe]
#       Close the unused sides of the pipes
        close $ChildInPipe
        close $ChildOutPipe
#       Return the pid of the child and our input and output pipes
        return "$childPid $MyInPipe $MyOutPipe"
}
```

The code that creates the child process looks like this:

```
#   This process executes a command "cmd" with the standard input and
#   standard output connected to pipes.
proc ChildProcess {cmd InPipe OutPipe} {
    if {[set childPid [fork]] == 0} {
#       The child does these things
        upvar MyInPipe ParentInPipe MyOutPipe ParentOutPipe
#       Make the input pipe the standard input
        dup $InPipe stdin
```

```
        close $InPipe
#       Make the output pipe the standard output
        dup $OutPipe stdout
        close $OutPipe
#       Close the other ends of the pipes
        close $ParentInPipe
        close $ParentOutPipe
#       Overlay ourself with the desired command
        execl $cmd
    }
    return $childPid
}
```

Here we set up a child process to execute the Unix command cmd, connecting the child's stdin and stdout to a couple of pipes set up in the calling routine before ChildProcess was called. The fork command establishes the new process; if the return value is 0 then we are the child process, and we attach our stdin and stdout to the parent's in and out pipes and execl the command that was passed to us as cmd. If we are the parent, we return to the calling routine with the PID of the child.

To make your file ID tools complete, TclX uses the select system call (so you can tell whether your pipes are readable, among other things). It's fairly simple, compared to the select function in C:

> select *readList ?writeList? ?exceptList? ?timeoutSec?*

You can wait on zero or more file handles (IDs) to be "ready" in each of three categories: ready for read, ready for write, and having an exceptional condition pending. You provide a set of file IDs in the form of three lists corresponding to these categories; these file IDs are checked, with a timeout wait determined by the floating-point *timeoutSec* argument. The return value is a three-item list, each item being the list of files found to be "ready" in one category. (This is another good example of the use of lists for passing structured data!) If you skip the "write" and "exception" lists, select will just check for files ready for reading.

Here's a possible invocation of this command:

```
tcl> select {file5 file6 file7 file 8} {file4 file9} {file10} 30.5
```

and the return value might be something like:

```
{file6 file8} {} {file10}
```

meaning that file IDs 6 and 8 are ready for reading, nothing is ready for writing, and file10 has an exception condition. If no file IDs had been ready for any operation, this select command could have taken up to 30.5 seconds to return. However, if we assume that file6 and file8 were readable at the time we issued the select command, then it would have returned immediately as shown.

File Scanning Commands

It is always possible to parse a file in TclX as follows:

```
for_file line list.html {
```

```
        do_something_with $line
    }
```

However, the TclX developers went much further than this, and provided a family of commands expressly for file scanning. These commands give you the power of *awk* and *grep* (and then some) in Tcl, and the file scan works remarkably fast. The basic mechanism is more complicated than *grep*, but once you grasp the concepts it's actually simpler to use.

For those who aren't sure what file scanning is about, here is a summary. Programmers often want to scan through an ASCII file, and perform an operation on each line like: "if the line contains `foo` do this, and if it contains `bar` do that". The Unix *awk* utility was designed for just this purpose; the *grep* family of Unix commands more simply extracts matching lines from files, given a pattern. TclX can do this concisely, without a `system` or `exec` invocation of *awk*; furthermore, you can easily add or expand an operation. (Note: a *regular expression* or *regexp* is a way of specifying complex match criteria in a single string, by using wildcards and other substitution macros; TclX uses regular expressions, just as *grep* and *egrep* do, to scan files.)

The essential concept for scanning is a *scancontext*, which is a *handle*. Tcl commonly uses handles, like the value returned by an `open` command, to manipulate files and other data sources. You use the `scancontext` command to create the handle, and then the `scanmatch` command to associate it with a regular expression and some code to execute if a match is found. You can use multiple `scanmatch` commands to set up checking and processing for several regular expressions at once. Then you issue the `scanfile` command, which actually scans the file, executes the code you established for each match, and puts match status information in a global variable `matchInfo`. So the sequence is:

```
set fileHandleVar [open fileName r]
set scanHandleVar [scancontext create]
scanmatch $scanHandleVar regExp codeToExecute
scanfile $scanHandleVar $fileHandleVar
```

Here's a simple example. The object is to pull out of a log file some records matching the current month, and to rewrite those records into a new format in an output file:

```
# set up a target dir and some date-related strings
set accdir /usr/local/bean/counting/puse
set efp [open $accdir/HOST_ERROR.LOG a]
set yd [fmtclock [convertclock yesterday]]
set ydd [lrange $yd 0 2]
set ydm [lindex $yd 1]
set yy [lindex $yd 5]
set rcode PRT001
# set up a target output file and open it
set target $accdir/$rcode.$ydm.$yy.flat
set bfp [open $target w]
# set up a file pointer for the file to scan
set fd [open /var/adm/$accfile r]
# create a scancontext
```

```
set sc [scancontext create]
# attach a scanmatch to the scancontext
scanmatch $sc "\[A-z\] $ydm \[0-9\]* \[0123456789:]* $yy" \
        {processLine $matchInfo(line)}
# scan the file using the scancontext
scanfile $sc $fd
```

Here we want to scan a printer accounting file for lines logged during a certain
month. We set up some strings and file pointers, then create a scancontext handle
(scancontext create). We then associate a regexp with that, which should
match lines like

```
Tue Jul 11 17:42:16 1995 foo.ps marvin helios.cia.org 1 535.570 666
```

where the month ($ydm) is Jul and the year is 1995. If we get a match, we call
processLine, with one argument: the text of the matching line. Here's
processLine. It's not very interesting, but note the use of lassign, a TclX command discussed earlier in this chapter; the core Tcl list commands llength,
split, and lindex are also useful here:

```
proc processLine line {
        global efp
        global bfp
        global rcode
        if {[llength $line] > 11} {
                puts $efp "Cannot parse line from printer $rcode:"
                puts $efp "  $line"
        } else {
        lassign $line wday mon day time yr file user host pages cpu uid
        set date "$wday $mon $day $time $yr"
        set toy [convertclock $date]
        set host [lindex [split $host .] 0]
        puts $bfp "$toy~$rcode~$user~$file~$host~$pages"
        }
}
```

We split the line into words, convert the date to an integer clock value to conserve
space, and write a line of output. Another utility (in this case, Sybase bcp) can now
read the data, using the tildes as field separators, and store these records in a relational database. You could do the same thing with a for_file, checking to see if
each line matches the month ydm. Or you could exec a grep command and
process the output of the exec. But as it turns out, the file scanning commands are
faster than either of those solutions.

The scancontext/scanfile mechanism is tremendously flexible and powerful
because you can create several scancontexts, each bound to any set of regexps and
conditional code. Each line of the scanned file will be checked against the regular
expressions *in the order in which you added them using* scanmatch. If a line happens to match more than one of your regexps, you can permit all the scanmatch
code to be executed, but often you want to stop if you match a particular expression. In that case you can use continue in the scanmatch code, which makes
scanfile skip all later scanmatches in the scancontext. You can thus write,

---

remarkably tersely, a complex file parsing algorithm that might otherwise take many, many lines of code (as a for_file loop with a complicated mess of if-blocks).

Some of the potential power of these commands starts to reveal itself in the match-Info array. The text of the matching line (array index `line`) is only the beginning. `scanfile` also returns in `matchInfo` the following indices:

- `offset`: byte offset into the file of the first character of the matching line
- `linenum`: the line number of the matching line
- `context`: the handle of the scancontext that yielded this match
- `handle`: the file handle of the file where the matching line was found
- `submatch0`: the characters that matched the first parenthesized subexpression in the regexp; the second will be in `submatch1` and so on
- `subindex0`: a two-element list of the start and end indices of the string matching the first parenthesized subexpression; the second will be in subindex1, and so on

Here's another, slightly smarter example (code courtesy of R. Stover, UCO/Lick Observatory). To help you visualize what these code excerpts are really doing, here's some sample data from a "services" file that controls a large data-taking system:

```
host:lichenous.cia.org
trtalk            horticultist.cia.org # traffic controller host
JAPANDTAKE        /u/developers/crate/japan/dtake
TIGERDTAKE        /u/developers/crate/tiger/dtake
DSP-TIGERDTAKE    /u/developers/host/lab/dtake
TOSSDTAKE         /u/developers/crate/toss/dtake
TOSS_CONTROLLER   nocontroller
SPROCKETDTAKE     /u/developers/crate/sprocket/dtake
LURKERDTAKE       /u/developers/crate/lurker/dtake
lockfile          /usr/local/noise/lockfile
dictdir           /usr/local/noise/info/
errorlog          /usr/local/noise/log/errorlog
runnerlog         /usr/local/noise/log/runnerlog
trafficlog        /usr/local/noise/log/trafficlog
INFOHOST          horticultist.cia.org # Host for infoman
INFOMAN           /u/developers/host/infoman/infoman
hamtalk           horticultist.cia.org # Machine for talking to hambone
hamport           /dev/ttyb            # Port for hambone spectrograph
```

And here is some code that parses this file:

```
# Read the services file and scan for all entries corresponding to
# a given host.  Return the entries in an array.
# Input:        File          The pathname of the file to scan
#               host          The host section to scan for
# Output:       savearray     The array into which the procedure
#                             func can store the matched values.
```

```
#                    The return value is 1 if all processing went OK at 0
#                    otherwise.
#
# Sample call: Services /home/ccdev/dtakeservice myHost arrayName
#
#@package: services Services Servicefile
proc Services {File host savearray} {
    global ServiceHost
    set ServiceHost ""
    set fd [open $File r]
    if {$fd == -1} {return 0}
    set sc [scancontext create]
    scanmatch $sc "host:" {ScanServiceForHost $host}
    scanmatch $sc {ScanForService $savearray}
    scanfile $sc $fd
    scancontext delete $sc
    close $fd
    unset ServiceHost
    return 0
}
```

Here the author sets up two regexps, one to look for lines containing "host:" and the other to look at all lines not containing "host:"—the lack of a regexp in the second scanmatch is shorthand for "does not match any of the regexps in the current scancontext." Here is ScanServiceForHost, which we call if the string "host:" is present in the line:

```
# Input:          host     The name of the host to scan for.
# Output:         Global ServiceHost is either set or unset.
proc ScanServiceForHost {host} {
    global ServiceHost
    upvar 1 matchInfo matchInfo
    set hline $matchInfo(line)
    set colon [string first ":" $hline]
    incr colon
    set hostval [string trim [string range "$hline" $colon end]]
    if {[string match $hostval $host] == 1} {
        set ServiceHost $host
    } else {
        set ServiceHost ""
    }
}
```

Here we find the hostname, that is, the string immediately following the string host:, and check to see whether it matches our own hostname. If so, we are the ServiceHost. But for any line that does not contain host:, we do this:

```
# Output: savearray    The services are stored in this array, with the
#                      service name used as the index.
proc ScanForService {savearray} {
    global ServiceHost
    if {$ServiceHost != ""} {
```

```
        upvar #0 $savearray save
        upvar 1 matchInfo matchInfo
        set sline [string trim $matchInfo(line)]
        if {[string length "$sline"] == 0} return
        if {[string first "#" "$sline"] == 0} return
        set sname [lvarpop sline 0]
        set service [string trim [string range "$sline" 0 end]]
        set save($sname) $service
    }
}
```

Here we use the global variable ServiceHost, which was set in ScanForServiceHost, and if it has been set (i.e., we previously encountered a line containing host: and the hostname matched our hostname), we collect the service names from the matching lines and stuff them in an array.

You would have had to use two exec calls (a grep and a grep -v) or some untidy logic with a for_file to achieve this same result by other means. The file scanning commands are a concise, modular, all-Tcl method of performing complex processing of input files. The overhead of repeated process startup (via exec) is obviated, and there are no external awk/sed script files. In my estimation, scan-context, scanmatch, and scanfile are three of the most ingenious and useful commands in TclX.

TCP/IP Communications Commands

TclX includes a basic command set suitable for creating IP-based client/server applications. While the network-oriented commands are not so elaborate as those in (for example) the 'scotty' Tcl extension, they are perfectly adequate for writing IP servers—run by inetd or standalone—and clients. Tcl7.5 (and later) provides TCP/IP server/client features; previous versions did not. At 7.4 and earlier, TclX was the simplest way to add client/server capability to Tcl.

So, why would anyone want to write clients and servers using Tcl?

Suppose I have a Sun with a licensed copy of Sybase DBlib (OpenClient) on it. I have also an AIX machine where I don't want to build any elaborate or frequently used Sybase code (so I don''t want to buy DBlib). The users of that machine would, however, like access to one trivial utility (a phone book lookup tool, let's say) that queries the Sybase data. This tool runs on all the Suns just fine. How shall I keep the AIX users happy? I could now go out and buy DBlib for AIX. Or I could run a server on the Sun machine that performs this one simple query and returns an answer to a client on *any* remote machine.

In any case where machine X has access to data or services that machine Y does not, it's possible to make a client process on Y contact a server process on X to get an answer. A machine without NFS could get access to selected files on a remote disk in this way, for example.

Alternatively, let's say that I have an SNMP monitoring tool (which I do) that has a very slow startup (it sure does). It takes more than 45 seconds just to load the Tcl code, initialize the SNMP monitor agent, etc. By that time, whatever network condition I just noticed may be over. I would like to have the monitor running as a daemon (server) so I could contact that server process and request a quick statistical snapshot of my ethernet.

Whenever a process is expensive or slow to initialize, but you want to get a quick answer out of it, one solution is to start it up and let it run as a server, making quick connections to it thereafter from client processes without all that overhead. Statistics-gathering and monitoring processes are particularly appropriate subjects for this technique.

A TclX server can accept and manage simultaneous connections. Interprocess communication takes place in the form of strings passed over an IP socket, which is read with `gets`, `lgets` or `read`, and written with `puts` or the `server_send` command.

The `server_create` command establishes a TCP/IP socket on the local host, returning a file handle associated with that socket. The file handle does not become ready for reading until there's a successful connection request. The syntax is

> server_create ?-myip *IPaddress*? ?-myport *PortNumber*? \
> ?-backlog *integerVal*?

The `-myip` option allows you to choose between multiple network interfaces on a multi-homed machine. The `-myport` option permits you to choose your IP port number. If the port number is already in use, you will get an error. The `-backlog` option limits the length of the pending connections queue (the default is 5, and on some BSD-derived systems the limit is always 5 regardless of your attempts to change it).

Once a server is established on a host, other processes can connect to it using the `server_connect` command. The basic syntax of `server_connect` is

> server_connect ?*options*...? *hostDesig serviceDesig*

where the host may be designated by a name or IP address, and the service by a name or port number.

The options enable you to configure the TCP/IP connection. You can force the socket to be buffered (`-buf`) or unbuffered (`-nobuf`). If it is unbuffered, you get only one file ID for both reading and writing. The `-twoids` option forces the return of two file IDs, the first one usable for reading and the second for writing. (You must close both of them separately to shut down the socket.) The `-myip` option works as it does with `server_create`, and is useful only for multi-homed hosts. `-myport` lets you assign a port number for the client end of the connection.

After a client attempts to connect, the server has to accept the connection using the `server_accept` command. The syntax is

> server_accept ?*options*? *fileID*

where the *fileID* is one returned previously by `server_create`. Possible options are `-buf`, `-nobuf`, and `-twoids`, as above.

Either end of the connection can now write to the other using the `server_send` command:

> server_send ?*options*? *fileID sendString*

You might wonder why the authors added this command, when `puts` would work just as well. The `server_send` command is actually better for socket writes, as it has some error detection built in to handle lost connections and other IP-layer problems. You won't need a `flush` command if you use `server_send`, even if the socket is buffered.

The options for `server_send` are `-nonewline` (the default behavior is to tack a newline onto the string sent), `-dontroute` (suppress routing and use only the direct interface), and `-outofband` (send out-of-band data).

Here are two simple Tcl scripts: a client and a server. The client is the simpler of the two, so let's start there (even though in practice we would probably write the server first). We decide in advance that the server will be listening on port 3011, so that's where the client attempts to connect.

```
# we send you a Hello and you send us a World.
#
set port 3011
#
set fp [server_connect sunny.mafia.org 3011]
#
while {1} {
        puts -nonewline stdout "What shall we say? "
        gets stdin what
        server_send $fp "$what"
        select $fp {} {}
        set err [catch {gets $fp answer} res]
        if {$err} {
                echo "No more server!\n$res"
                exit 0
        }
        echo "Server answered:  $answer"
}
```

This client gets a string from the user and sends it to the server. It then gets the server's answer and shows it to the user.

The server is almost as simple-minded:

```
# You send us a Hello and we send you a World
#
set fp [server_create -myport 3011]
#
while {1} {
#       check the socket and wait 4 seconds if it's not ready
        set res [select $fp {} {} 4.0]
        lassign $res rd wr ex
#       When the socket becomes readable, connect to the client
#       and start listening.
        if {$rd == "$fp"} {
                set cfp [clientConnect $fp]
                clientListen $cfp
        }
}
```

```
proc clientConnect {fp} {
#       accept the client connection and return the client-specific
#       file ID
        set err [catch {set cfp [server_accept $fp]} res]
        if {$err} {
                echo "error completing connection:\n$res"
                exit 1
        }
        return $cfp
}
proc clientListen {fp} {
#       Listen to the client on private file ID fp until
#       it says "Die" and we die
        while {1} {
                set err [catch {gets $fp client_said} res]
#       if the gets failed, the client has vanished
                if {$err} {
                        echo "No more client!\n$res"
                        exit 0
                }
#       if you get a null string, the client didn't say anything yet
                if {$client_said == ""} {
                        sleep 1
                        continue
                }
                if {$client_said == "Hello"} {
                        server_send $fp "World"
                        continue
                }
                if {$client_said == "Die"} {
                        server_send $fp "Shutting down"
                        close $fp
                        exit 0
                }
                server_send $fp "Say what?"
        }
}
```

The server responds to two keywords: Hello and Die. It responds to Hello by
answering "World," and to Die by exiting. (If it had been started by inetd via the
services database, the server would automatically restart when any attempt was
made to connect to 3011; but in this case the server was run manually, so it runs
exactly once.) Otherwise it just says, "Say what?" and keeps running. Here's how
the client actually looks in operation:

```
578) sunny.cia.org.de: test.client
What shall we say? howdy
Server answered:  Say what?
What shall we say? yahoo!
Server answered:  Say what?
What shall we say? Hello
Server answered:  World
```

```
What shall we say? Die
Server answered:  Shutting down
What shall we say? bye bye
No more server!
error reading "file4": Connection reset by peer
```

Obviously, far more error-checking should be done for a production application. However, this gives you a very basic model from which to build your own clients and servers.

Programming in TclX

TclX does not just add new "verbs" to your Tcl vocabulary. Certain Tcl commands enhance the process of code development, and others might influence your choice of coding strategy, offering new and more concise methods of flow control. A few more assist you to debug and streamline your code, and a set of code library management functions permit you to organize and package your code more efficiently.

Some Tcl commands are self-referential. Tcl is an "introspective" language; that is, it can look at its own internal state using commands such as info. TclX adds a few more.

infox *option* returns the value of the specified configuration option, which can come in handy when your Tcl application wants to run on many different platforms:

```
tcl>infox version
7.4a-b4
tcl>infox patchlevel
0
tcl>infox have_fchown
1
tcl>infox have_sockets
1
```

One of the nice things about Tcl is the ability to test little snippets of code interactively while writing larger modules. With TclX, you can do a lot of development without ever leaving the interpreter. You can retrieve the definition of a Tcl procedure using showproc *procName*:

```
tcl>showproc for_file
proc for_file {var filename code} {
    upvar $var line
    set fp [open $filename r]
    while {[gets $fp line] >= 0} {
        uplevel $code
    }
    close $fp
}
```

You can edit a specific procedure or procedures directly from the interpreter prompt using

```
        edprocs ?procName [procName...]?
```

The named procedures, or by default all currently defined procedures, are written to a temporary file, and the editor specified by your EDITOR environment variable is started on that file. If EDITOR is not set, you get vi. When you write and quit, the changed proc definitions are loaded back into the running interpreter.

Using

```
saveprocs fileName ?procName [procName...]?
```

you can write loaded procs out to a text file. You can combine edprocs and saveprocs for quick code development. For example,

```
tcl> source myprocs.tcl
tcl> doMyProc arg1 arg2
(... get some error message)
tcl> edprocs doMyProc
(... do some editing)
tcl> doMyProc arg1 arg2
I worked this time!
tcl> saveprocs doMyProc.tcl doMyProc
```

The ability to test and edit without leaving the interpreter can sometimes speed up your code development significantly.

TclX might even change the way you structure your code, or the approach you take to flow control. Core Tcl provides the while and for statements for loop control. TclX enhances loop design and control with the loop command:

```
loop loopVar startVal limitVal ?incrAmount? execCode
```

where *startVal*, *limitVal*, and *incrAmount* must all be integers. *incrAmount* defaults to 1 if not specified. The loop statement runs faster than a for loop, and makes for less verbose coding when the start and end values are known and the integer is always the same fixed amount. Compare

```
tcl> for {set i 0} {$i < 5} {incr i} {echo "i is $i"}
i is 0
i is 1
i is 2
i is 3
i is 4
```

to

```
tcl>loop i 0 5 {echo "i is $i"}
i is 0
i is 1
i is 2
i is 3
i is 4
```

(Using the for syntax, some programmers might more naturally have written i <= 4; I wanted to make the two loops logically identical.) If you use variables for *startVal* and *limitVal* you can change their values within the loop—but to no avail. They, and the *incrAmount*, are evaluated only once when the loop command is parsed. Note that the loop ends after the last iteration where the counter variable is less than the limit.

execCode is any syntactically correct block of Tcl code, as above. Both `break` and `continue` work within *execCode*, exactly the same as within the body of a `while` or `for` loop.

TclX also provides a couple of procs for convenient looping using arrays and the results of `glob` commands:

> for_array_keys *varName arrayName execCode*

loops once for each key of the array *arrayName*, putting the key value in *varName* and executing *execCode*:

```
tcl>set a(1) This
tcl>set a(2) is
tcl>set a(3) a
tcl>set a(4) test
tcl>for_array_keys k a {
=>echo value of a(k) is $a($k) and k is $k
=>}
value of a(k) is test and k is 4
value of a(k) is This and k is 1
value of a(k) is is and k is 2
value of a(k) is a and k is 3
tcl>
```

By the way, this also happens to illustrate the unordered nature of array indices, of which the novice Tcl programmer should beware. I personally prefer

```
tcl>foreach k [lsort -integer [array names a]] {
=>echo k is $k and its value is $a($k)
=>}
k is 1 and its value is This
k is 2 and its value is is
k is 3 and its value is a
k is 4 and its value is test
tcl>
```

More useful and interesting is the `recursive_glob` enhancement, a proc that recursively `glob`'s over a list of directories:

> recursive_glob *dirList globList*

All the directories specified in *dirList* are recursively searched (breadth-first), and each file found is compared against all the glob patterns in *globList*. This is handy, as it's somewhat onerous to achieve the same result with the core Tcl `glob` command. *Note that symbolic links are not followed!*.

In the tradition of `for_file`,

> for_recursive_glob *varName dirList globList execCode*

simply loops over the filenames returned from a `recursive_glob`, and is equivalent to

```
        foreach varName [recursive_glob dirList globList] execCode
```

... it's a just little less typing. Here's an example of the difference between `glob` and `recursive_glob`:

```
tcl>foreach f [glob *] {
=>if {[file isdirectory $f]} {
=>        lappend dirs $f
=>}
=>}
tcl>echo $dirs
tcl dbase deimos doc text
tcl>
tcl>recursive_glob $dirs {*ail*}
tcl/Mail tcl/HINTS/mail.filt.Z tcl/HINTS/mailinglist
tcl/w/wisql.monthly.mailing tcl/WOES/tpmail tcl/a/mail.acct ...
```

We used `glob` to get names of directories found in the current directory. Then we used that list of directories in the `recursive_glob` command to search the entire tree under each of those directories for matches to the regular expression.

A more exotic looping construct is `commandloop`, which passes control to stdin; an application can invoke this command to provide the user with a tcl prompt, as shown here:

```
tcl> commandloop -prompt1 {concat "Hi De> "}
Hi De> echo "hello world"
hello world
Hi De>
tcl>
```

This somewhat arcane feature can be useful when you want the user to be able to interact directly with the interpreter even in the middle of an executing script.

Debugging Tcl applications is not always a trivial exercise. TclX offers you some useful tools for debugging and performance tuning.

The `cmdtrace` command lets you trace the path of execution through your source code:

```
            cmdtrace level|on ?noeval? ?notruncate? ?procs? ?fileID?
```

The `level` argument tells TclX at which calling level (as understood by `upvar`) to start tracing. All commands executed at that level or lower will be echoed to the tracefile (or to stdout if no tracefile is specified). If the word "on" is used instead of an integer level number, then all commands executed at any level will be echoed.

If `noeval` is specified, variables are echoed unevaluated; by default they are evaluated before printing. If `notruncate` is specified, command lines longer than 60 characters are echoed in their entirety; by default, they are truncated to 60 characters with an appended ellipsis ("..."). If `procs` is specified, only commands that invoke Tcl procedures (as opposed to compiled C code) are echoed; by default, all commands are echoed.

If you wish the trace output to be saved in a file, you can specify `fileID`, a file ID such as is returned by `open`. The command

---

```
tcl> cmdtrace on [open cmd.log w]
```

begins complete command tracing and saves the output in the file cmd.log.

```
tcl> cmdtrace off
```

turns command tracing off again, and

```
tcl> cmdtrace depth
```

returns the current maximum trace level, or zero if tracing is disabled.

The `profile` command allows you to make a performance profile of your TclX application. The profiling feature collects the number of calls to each procedure, and the number of real seconds and CPU seconds spent in the procedure. The syntax is

```
profile ?-commands? on
profile off arrayVarName
```

If the `-commands` option is specified, `profile` collects data for all the commands within procedures as well as for the procedures themselves. When profiling is turned off again, an array variable must be specified; the collected information is moved into this array.

You could examine this array manually, but it might get tedious; TclX provides an output formatting command `profrep` to present the profiling data legibly.

```
profrep arrayVarName sortKey stackDepth ?outFile? ?userTitle?
```

Sorting is done according to *sortKey*, which must be `calls`, `cpu`, or `real`. The *stackDepth* parameter controls the amount of stack information reported; a value of 1 reports only by procedure, but a value of 2 reports both the procedure name and its caller, and so on. The output file specification in this case is a file name, not a file ID; if you omit this argument, `stdout` is the default. You can optionally add a title of your own choice to the formatted output written to the file.

Earlier in this chapter I mentioned a performance difficulty with large keyed lists. It would have been quite difficult to isolate this problem (in a 10,000 line Tcl/Tk application), had I not been able to use `profile` and `profrep`.

As your Tcl applications grow larger, you're challenged by more than just debugging the increasingly complex code; you begin to need ways of organizing your code into libraries, eliminating duplicate functions, and writing general purpose routines to serve more than one application—just as C programmers do. TclX provides some fairly sophisticated tools for doing this.

TclX supports the core Tcl `tclIndex` type of code library. It also introduces more powerful and flexible methods of library management, by means of *.tlib* and *.tndx* files. Collections of procedures can be stored in a "tlib" (Tcl LIBrary) file. A tlib file is a plain text file containing Tcl procedure code and some "magic" comment lines which delimit "packages" within the library. We'll discuss the function of packages later, but basically they are intended to be groups of related procedures. You can edit a tlib file with any common text editor. Tlib file names must always have the extension *.tlib*.

We should note here that a certain confusion crept in when Tcl release 7.5 began to use the term "package" for a related, but quite distinct concept. The core "package" concept means a related set of one or more shareable objects and Tcllib files which can be loaded as one "package." The "packages" defined in tlib files used by TclX, however, are like object modules (each containing some functions) loaded into a library.

For TclX to use the tlib file, there must be a corresponding index file: a library file `mumble.tlib` would have an index file `mumble.tndx`. The purpose of the index file is to speed up access to procedures in the tlib file, by establishing byte offsets for the start and end of each package in the library. TclX automatically recreates this index file if it is missing or out of date (provided, of course, that the user running TclX has write access to the library directory). When the TclX application "asks for" the library, TclX checks the dates on the index file and the tlib file, and regenerates the index file if it is older than the tlib file.

The global variable `auto_path` (analogous to the csh environment variable PATH) contains a list of directories to be searched, in order, for tlib files. On the first unknown command trap during an execution of TclX code, the indices for libraries on this path are loaded into memory. A string search commences for the name of the missing procedure. The first package containing that procedure name is loaded in its entirety (all commands in that package are loaded). In other words, say you have a tlib file named *foo.tlib*, as follows:

```
#@package: MyPackageName myproc1 myproc2 myproc3 myproc4 \
        myproc5 myproc6
myproc1 {foo faa} {
        . . .
}
myproc2 {fee fie} {
        . . .
}
```

and so forth. This tlib file is in a directory found in the `auto_path` variable. Now, in your TclX code, you have a call to `myproc1`:

```
if {$err} {
        myproc1 azuki garbanzo
}
```

`myproc1` has not been previously defined in your source, so TclX gets an unknown command trap. The interpreter responds to the trap by searching your `auto_path` and loading in the indices for all tlibs on that path. It then searches the loaded indices for the string `myProc1`, which it finds in the `MyPackageName` package. The interpreter loads in the entire package. Now it can resolve the missing command name, and execution continues.

The package concept improves efficiency, provided that you define your packages sensibly. Generally speaking, procedures do fall into "families" of related functionality; an application that loads one member of the family is likely to require one or more of the others. The loading of the entire package ensures that no further unknown command traps and delays will be involved in accessing this family of procedures.

You can also explicitly load a particular tlib file at the start of your source code, rather than relying on `auto_path`. Whichever method you use, beware of duplicate procedure names in your tlib files. The *first* package containing the procedure with the name of the missing command is the one that will get loaded.

The command `auto_packages` returns a list of all the defined packages (established by the automatic loading of .tndx files along the `auto_path`, at startup). The command `auto_commands` tells the names of all known (found in loaded indices) commands that can be auto-loaded. With the `-loaders` option it will also specify the command that will be executed to load the command.:

```
tcl> auto_packages
TclX-convertlib TclX-buildhelp TclX-ucblib TclX-Compatibility ...
tcl>auto_commands -loaders
{write_file {auto_load_pkg {TclX-stringfile_functions}}}
{sin {auto_load_pkg {TclX-fmath}}}
{assign_fields {auto_load_pkg {TclX-Compatibility}}}
{log10 {auto_load_pkg {TclX-fmath}}}  ...
```

(I have formatted this for legibility; in each case, the output is actually just one long list without newlines). The output of `auto_commands` tells you which package each command belongs to. For example, the `sin` command belongs to the package `TclX-fmath`. Note that this messy looking list is actually a valid keyed list:

```
tcl>set kl [auto_commands -loaders]
tcl>keylget kl sybNext
auto_load_pkg {UCO-Sybase}
tcl>keylget kl sin
auto_load_pkg {TclX-fmath}
```

What does it mean, that `sin` is in the TclX-fmath package? If I were to delve into the TclX distribution, I would find a tlib file `tcl.tlib`, and looking inside that file I would find a package header `TclX-fmath`:

```
#@package: TclX-fmath acos asin atan ceil cos cosh \
           exp fabs floor log log10 sin sinh sqrt tan \
           tanh fmod pow atan2 abs double int round
```

This reveals the TclX authors' assumption with regard to their math functions: An application that uses one is likely to use the rest, but an application that did no heavy math might never use any of them; so they are loaded as a package.

So how would I have known that the fmath package was in that particular file? You can find out in which tlib file the package is defined by using the `-files` flag on the `auto_packages` command (again, I have reformatted this output for legibility):

```
tcl> auto_packages -files
{UCO-trf /opt0/share/tcl/lib/ucodb/ucodb.tlib}
{TclX-ClockCompat /opt0/tcl/tclX/7.5.2/tcl.tlib}
{TclX-convertlib /opt0/tcl/tclX/7.5.2/tcl.tlib}
{UCO-PG95 /opt0/share/tcl/lib/ucodb/ucodb.tlib}
{TclX-buildhelp /opt0/tcl/tclX/7.5.2/tcl.tlib}
...
{UCO-Oracle /opt0/share/tcl/lib/ucodb/ucodb.tlib}
```

```
tcl>set kl [auto_packages -files]
tcl>keylget kl UCO-PG95
/opt0/share/tcl/lib/ucodb/ucodb.tlib
```

and as you can see, it's once again a valid keyed list.

The command

        `auto_load` *commandName*

attempts to resolve the reference to *commandName* by loading the entire package
in which `commandName` is found. It searches along `auto_path` for tlib files. This
permits you to prevent the unknown command trap by manually loading the commands you know you will be using. The command `auto_load_file` `fileName`
attempts to `source` the file `fileName`, but searches for it along `auto_path`
rather than in the current directory.

The command

        `searchPath` *dirPath* *fileName*

was developed to support TclX libraries and packages: *dirPath* is a list of directory specifications, which will be searched for *fileName*. The return value is the
full path name of the file. You may find this command useful in other contexts, not
just when dealing with libraries.

The command

        `buildpackageindex` *listOfTlibs*

allows you to force a rebuild of the index files for every tlib file in the list. You
might want to think of this as analogous to the `ranlib` Unix command. (Note: the
specified filenames must include the .tlib suffix.) You might want to do this during
interactive development, when you are editing tlib files directly from the TclX shell
prompt. Of course, you have to have write access to the directories where the tlib
files reside, because new .tndx files will be created there.

The command

        `loadlibindex` *tlibFile*

forces a load of the entire contents of tlibFile. This command allows you to load
tlib files not found on `auto_path` (or, looked at in a slightly different light, relieves
you of the need to maintain a complex `auto_path`). You might also use it condi-
tionally, to load different versions of a library depending on user choices or other
conditions identified by the application. You might write a generic database interface application which loaded different versions of high-level query routines
depending on the user's choice of database engine:

```
if {$db == "OR"} {
        loadlibindex /some/long/path/OracleProcs.tlib
} else {
        loadlibindex /some/long/path/IngresProcs.tlib
}
```

You can, in fact, use `loadlibindex` to override a previous load of the index for
a named package, for example, to write a local or experimental version over a pro-

---

duction version. However, if any procedure has actually been invoked from the previously loaded version of the package, the override will fail and the procedure definitions from the earlier load will persist. Therefore, you cannot use `loadlibindex` iteratively during interactive development. However, all the "magic" package information in a tlib file is embedded in comment lines; this means that the tlib file is just an ordinary Tcl script. You can `source` it if you need to to override previous loaded procedure definitions.

Lastly,

> `convert_lib` *tclIndexFile tlibFile ?ignoreList?*

will convert an existing old-style tclIndex file and its associated source files into a TclX package library. In this case, you can omit the .tlib extension from *tlibFile* and it will be appended for you. The optional list *ignoreList* specifies tcl source files to be ignored when the tlib file is constructed. The file names in the *ignoreList* should be only base filenames, without paths.

The TclX method of maintaining code libraries is tidy and flexible. It is functionally analogous to object libraries, in that a single file is used to store an archive of functions and subroutines, which can be loaded at will into applications. I find tlib files extremely useful for organizing procedures into general purpose and specific functions; the general purpose library *ucodb.tlib* is loaded (via `loadlibindex`) in all my database/tcl applications, but each app has also its own private tlib file full of functions and subroutines useful only to itself.

I usually maintain individual Tcl procedure modules in a CVS subdirectory, with a Makefile in the parent directory that constructs a tlib out of them. The tlib file is then checked in, acquiring a "release" number independent of the individual revision numbers of all its components. This is comfortably analogous to the normal C development style (object files and libraries), gives me individual revision control over each procedure and of the tlib file, and makes the code easy to package and export (usually each application consists only of one "main" and one or two tlib files).

I am not one of the TclX developers, nor have I any investment in TclX except as a happy user. Any errors I may have made in my descriptions or my understanding of TclX commands are my responsibility and should not reflect on Diekhans and Lehenbauer, the primary authors of TclX. I would like to thank Mark Diekhans for sanity checks throughout the disorderly evolution of this chapter; also many thanks to my colleagues Will Deich and Steve Allen, Richard Stover, and to the Tcl community at large.

7

The BLT Toolkit

by George A. Howlett
Copyright 1997 Lucent Technologies, Inc.

The BLT toolkit is a collection of widgets and utilities that makes building Tk applications easier. BLT adds new commands that extend the functionality of the Tk toolkit, providing simpler, easier ways of doing things that are hard in Tk. Figure 7-1 shows a few examples:

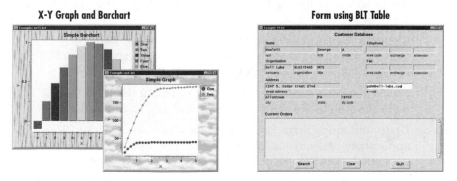

Figure 7-1: BLT meets several needs.

- Graphs are ubiquitous to scientific computing. BLT has an X-Y graph and bar chart widget that are both easy to use and customize. If you tried to build a graph with Tk's canvas widget, you would need to write hundreds (if not thousands) of lines of Tcl code. And some operations, like zooming, wouldn't be possible due to the way canvas items are scaled.

- Many find the packer (Tk's standard geometry manager) difficult to use. It requires extra frames to group and align widgets for even simple compositions. Common components, like forms, are hard to build because you can't align widgets both horizontally and vertically. The BLT table geometry manager has a more intuitive model that makes it easy to build and rearrange GUI layouts.

- Sometimes you need to make specific widgets or panels temporarily busy. For example, you may want to block the user from interacting with a canvas widget while it's redrawing itself. The BLT `busy` command blocks user interactions, such as mouse-button clicks and key strokes, until the widget is released. In addition, it will display its own busy cursor.

- When the `exec` command waits for a Unix command to complete, no Tk events are handled. This means that scrollbars can't work, widgets won't redraw themselves, and worst of all, your Tk application appears hung up or dead. The BLT `bgexec` command works like `exec`, but also allows Tk events to be handled.

The BLT toolkit doesn't require any changes to the source code of either Tcl or Tk. You simply load the BLT library, either statically or dynamically, and new BLT commands are added to the Tcl/Tk interpreter. The commands are described in Table 7-1.

Table 7-1: BLT Commands

Command Name	Description
barchart	Creates a bar chart for plotting two-dimensional data displayed as bars. Charts can be customized in a variety of ways.
bgexec	Like the `exec` command, runs a program and returns its output, but in addition allows Tk to handle events. Lets you run programs in the background while monitoring their output and exit status.
bitmap	Creates and manipulates bitmaps. Bitmaps can be defined, rotated, and scaled directly from Tcl code. You can also draw text into bitmaps to create rotated or scaled text.
busy	Makes widgets temporarily "busy" by shielding them from user interactions like mouse-button clicks and keyboard activity.
drag&drop	Drags and drops items between widgets or even separate Tk applications. Acts like a telephone operator, establishing a communication link between drag/drop sources and targets.
graph	Creates an X-Y graph. You can customize how the axes, legend, data elements, crosshairs, etc., are displayed. It's easy to add new interactive behaviors like zooming or brushing data points. Generates PostScript output, too.
htext	Creates simple hypertext, combining text and widgets in a scrollable text window. Any widget can be embedded to form a hyperlink.
spline	Computes a spline fitting a specified set of data points and produces a BLT vector of the interpolated images (Y-coordinates).

Continued

Table 7-1: Continued

Command Name	Description
table	Manages the size and placement of widgets. Widgets are arranged in a table by row and column. There is also a constraint mechanism to finely control how widgets are resized.
vector	Creates vector data objects. A vector is an ordered set of real numbers that can be manipulated three ways: through a Tcl array variable, a Tcl command, or the vector's C API. Both the graph and barchart widgets work directly with vectors, redrawing themselves automatically whenever the vector changes.
watch	Schedules user-defined Tcl procedures to be invoked before and after the execution of each Tcl command. It can be used in variety of ways to log, trace, profile, or debug Tcl code.

The standard Tcl/Tk distributions have incorporated several features from BLT. Tk's text widget has hypertext and can embed widgets directly into text, in part, because of BLT's htext widget. The new grid geometry manager is a clone of the BLT table. At the same time, BLT still provides functionality not found in Tk. For example, the BLT table has capabilities not found in the grid.

If there is a common thread in BLT, it is the philosophy that the commands should act as building blocks for applications, leveraging the power and simplicity of Tcl. Commands should perform simple functions that can be combined to create interesting new applications, letting Tcl act as the glue. It's not enough to provide just a graph widget, but a graph widget from which a wide range of user interactions can be quickly and easily constructed.

Plotting

In scientific applications, it's typical to display the results of experiments or simulations by plots. BLT has both an X-Y graph and bar chart widget for plotting two-dimensional data; the X-Y graph displays data as lines and symbols, the bar chart displays data as bars (see Figure 7-2). The two widgets share the many of the same capabilities. Indeed, it is possible to combine both bars and lines and symbols in the same graph.

Handling large data sets (tens of thousands of data points) can be a problem in Tcl. The numbers stored in Tcl lists or associative arrays must be translated back and forth from strings to binary whenever you compute with them. In BLT, there are vectors to store arrays of numbers. Vectors can be manipulated from Tcl or by writing new C code, using the vector's C language API. An advantage of the latter method is that the vector's data is available in its binary form, eliminating the redundant string conversions.

Vectors are used in several places in BLT. The spline command computes a spline based upon X-Y coordinates given as vectors, and returns the result as a new vector. The graph and bar chart widgets work intimately with vectors. They watch

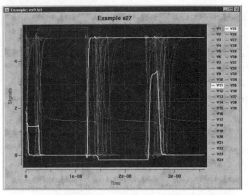
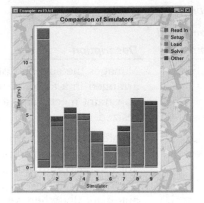

Figure 7-2: BLT X-Y Graph and Bar Chart

the vectors they use, redrawing themselves whenever a vector changes. You don't have to worry about replotting the data, because it happens automatically for you.

The BLT Graph Widget

The `graph` command creates a new graph widget. The data points are real numbers, drawn as connected lines and/or symbols inside a plotting area displayed in the center of the widget (see Figure 7-3).

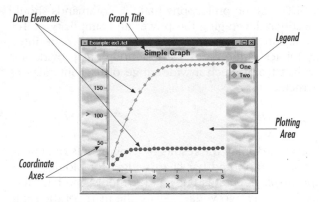

Figure 7-3: Example of the BLT Graph

```
# Create a graph widget ".g1"
graph .g1 -title "Simple Graph" -tile tileImage
pack .g1
```

The graph widget has its own set of configuration options that can be specified when creating the widget, such as the graph's title or background image (using the -tile option).

A graph is composed of several *components*: coordinate axes, data elements, legend, grid, crosshairs, postscript, and annotation markers. Instead of one big set of configuration options and operations, the graph is partitioned, where each component has its own configuration options and operations that specifically control that aspect or part of the graph. For example, the `element` component handles data elements.

Table 7-2 describes the different graph components.

Table 7-2: Components of a Graph Widget

Component	Description
axis	The graph widget can display up to four coordinate axes: two X-coordinate and two Y-coordinate axes. The axes control what region of data is displayed and how the data is scaled. Each axis consists of the axis line, title, major and minor ticks, and tick labels. Tick labels display the value of each major tick.
crosshairs	Crosshairs are used to finely position the mouse pointer in the graph. Two perpendicular lines are drawn across the plotting area, intersecting at the current location of the mouse pointer.
element	An element represents a set of data points. Elements can be plotted with a symbol at each data point and lines connecting the points. The appearance of the element, like its symbol, line width, and color is configurable.
grid	Extends the major and minor ticks of the X and Y axes across the plotting area.
legend	The legend displays the name and symbol of each data element. The legend can be displayed in any margin or in the plotting area.
marker	Markers are used annotate or highlight areas of the graph. For example, you could use a polygon marker to fill an area under a curve, or a text marker to label a particular data point. Markers come in various forms: text strings, bitmaps, connected line segments, polygons, or embedded widgets.
postscript	The graph widget can generate encapsulated PostScript output. There are several options to configure the PostScript output.

The commands to access components have operations that have the following form.

```
graphName component operation ?arg?...
```

The operation (located after the name of the component) is the function to be performed on that component. Each component has its own set of operations that manipulate that component.

For example, we can make a "Print" button that will print a PostScript file of the graph whenever it's pressed. It invokes the `postscript` component's `output` operation.

```
button .button -text "Print" -command {
    .g1 postscript output "out.ps"
}
```

To make the crosshairs follow the mouse pointer, you call the `crosshairs` component's `configure` operation whenever the mouse is moved.

```
bind .g1 <Motion> {
    g1 crosshairs configure -position @%x,%y
}
```

To turn on grid lines or crosshairs, you invoke the on operation.

```
# Turn on the display of cross hairs and grid lines.
.g1 crosshairs on
.g1 grid on
```

The graph in Figure 7-4 shows both crosshairs and grid lines.

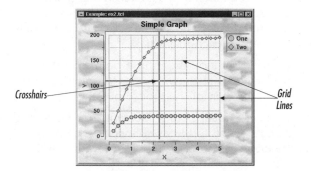

Figure 7-4: Graph with Crosshairs and Grid Lines

All components have configuration options, but the component's configuration options are specific to that component. You can use the component's cget and configure operations to query or modify its configuration.

Elements

Once you've created a graph, you can then insert data elements into it. A *data element* is a set of data points, represented in the graph by a single curve or set of symbols. To insert a new element, you simply invoke the command with its element component, the create operation, the new name of the element, and any configuration options.

```
.g1 element create "e1"
```

The X-Y coordinates of the element are specified using the element's -xdata and -ydata configuration options.

```
# Data values
set x { 0.2 0.4 0.6 0.8 1 1.2 1.4 1.6 1.8 2 2.2 2.4 2.6 2.8 3 3.2 3.4
    3.6 3.8 4 4.2 4.4 4.6 4.8 5 }
set y1 { 11 21 28 34 38 39 39 39 39 40 40 40 40 40 40 40 40 40 40 40
    40 40 40 41 41 }
set y2 { 26.2 50.5 72.9 93.3 112 128 143 156 167 175 182 187 190 191
    191 191 192 192 193 193 193 194 194 194 195 }

 # Add two new elements named "e1" and "e2" to the graph
.g1 element create "e1" -label "One" -xdata $x -ydata $y1
.g1 element create "e2" -label "Two" -xdata $x -ydata $y2
```

In the preceding example, the coordinates were hard-coded, using strings of numbers. But we could easily have generated data on-the-fly using expr, collecting the values into Tcl lists.

Chapter 7: The BLT Toolkit

```
# Generate X-Y coordinate data
set pi 3.14159265358979323846
for { set i -360 } { $i <= 360 } { incr i 5 } {
    lappend xVar $i
    set theta [expr $i*($pi/180.0)]
    lappend sinVar [expr sin($theta)]
    lappend cosVar [expr cos($theta)]
}
# Create two elements to represent cosine and sine values
.g1 element create "e1" -label "sin(x)" -xdata $xVar \
-ydata $sinVar
.g1 element create "e2" -label "cos(x)" -xdata $xVar \
-ydata $cosVar
```

As new data elements are created, they automatically get an entry in the graph's legend. The entry consists of the element's name and symbol type. The name can be replaced using the –label option. Figure 7-5 shows the results.

Figure 7-5: Computed Sine and Cosine Values

Elements have several configuration options that control their appearance. You can redefine element attributes, such as color, line width, symbol, symbol size, etc.

```
# Configure attributes of the element "e1"
.g1 element configure "e1" \
            -symbol circle \
            -color blue \
            -outline blue4 \
            -dashes { 2 4 2 } \
            -linewidth 2 \
            -pixels 1.75m
```

Several common element configuration options are listed in Table 7-3.

Table 7-3: Element Configuration Options

Element Option	Description
–dashes	Sets the dash style of the line segments connecting data points. The value is a list of up to 11 numbers (1–255) which alternately represent the lengths of the dashes and gaps on the line segment.

Continued

Table 7-3: Element Configuration Options (continued)

Element Option	Description
-data	Specifies element data using X-Y coordinate pairs.
-fill	Sets the interior color for symbols.
-color	Sets the color of the connecting line segments.
-hide	Indicates if the element should be displayed or hidden.
-label	Specifies the label displayed in the legend. If the value is the empty string (""), the element will have no entry in the legend.
-linewidth	Sets the width of the connecting line segments.
-mapx	Selects the axis on which to map the element's X-coordinates.
-mapy	Selects the axis on which to map the element's Y-coordinates.
-offdash	Sets the color of the stripes when traces are dashed (see the -dashes option).
-outline	Sets the color of the outline for symbols.
-outlinewidth	Sets the width of the outline for symbols.
-pixels	Sets the size of symbols.
-symbol	Specifies the symbol to use for the element. The value can be square, circle, diamond, plus, cross, splus, scross, triangle, or none (where no symbol is drawn).
-xdata	Specifies the X-coordinates of the element.
-ydata	Specifies the Y-coordinates of the element.

Elements can be displayed using symbols or line segments or both. The type of symbol displayed is controlled by the -symbol configuration option. The width of the line segments connecting pairs of data points is controlled by the -linewidth option. Symbol and line attributes are set in the same way. You can set the symbol's colors (-fill and -outline) or line attributes like dashed or striped lines (-dashes). Figure 7-6 demonstrates several different line and symbol styles.

Legend

The legend displays the symbol and label for each element. It's managed by the legend component. Again using the component's configure operation, you can specify the color, font, and location of the legend.

```
# Display the legend in the plotting area
.g1 legend configure \
    -position plotarea \
    -font fixed \
    -foreground navyblue
```

Several common legend configuration options are listed in Table 7-4.

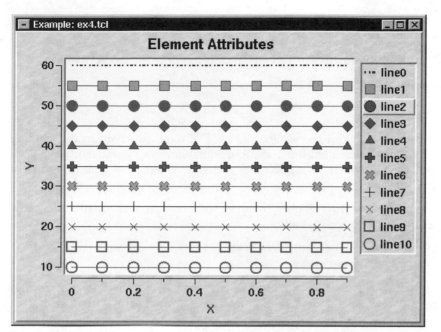

Figure 7-6: Example of Different Symbol and Line Styles

Table 7-4: Legend Configuration Options

Legend Option	Description
-activebackground	Sets the background color for active legend entries.
-activeborderwidth	Sets the width of the 3-D border around the outside of active legend entries.
-activeforeground	Sets the foreground color for active legend entries.
-activerelief	Specifies the 3-D effect desired for active legend entries.
-background	Sets the background color of the legend.
-borderwidth	Sets the width of the 3-D border around the legend.
-font	Sets the font of the element labels.
-foreground	Sets the color of the text drawn for the element labels.
-hide	Indicates if the legend should be displayed.
-position	Specifies where the legend is displayed. The legend can be automatically displayed in any margin of the graph or the plotting area.
-relief	Specifies the 3-D effect for the border around the legend.

You can highlight legend entries by making them *active*. An active entry is drawn with a 3-D border using the active attributes (indicated by the -activeback-ground, -activeforeground, -activerelief, and -activeborderwidth options). Entries are made active using the legend's **activate** operation.

```
# Make the entry for element "e1" active
.g1 legend activate "e1"
```

To display the entry normally again, you can use the **deactivate** operation.

```
.g1 legend deactivate "e1"
```

Coordinate Axes

The coordinate axes control the scale and range of data displayed in the plotting area. When a graph is created, there are four initial axes: **x**, **y**, **x2**, and **y2**. Data elements are then mapped to one X axis and one Y axis. By default, they are mapped to **x** and **y**.

You can create and use any number of axes. To create an axis, invoke the **axis** component and its **create** operation.

```
# Create a new axis called "temperature"
.g1 axis create temperature
```

You map data elements to an axis using the element's **-mapy** and **-mapx** configuration options. They specify which coordinate axes an element is mapped onto.

```
# Now map the temperature data to this axis.
.g1 element create "temp" \
    -xdata $x -ydata $tempData \
    -mapy temperature
```

While you can have any number of axes, the graph can display only four axes. They are displayed in each of the margins surrounding the plotting area.

Figure 7-7 displays all four axes. The axes **x** and **y** are displayed in the bottom and left margins. The axes **x2** and **y2** are displayed in top and right margins. Only **x** and **y** are shown by default. Note that the axes can have different scales.

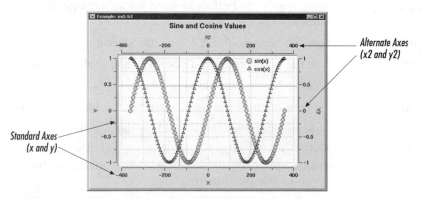

Figure 7-7: Graph Displaying All Four Axes

To display a different axis, you invoke one of the following components: **xaxis**, **yaxis**, **x2axis**, or **y2axis**. The use operation designates the axis to be displayed in the corresponding margin: **xaxis** in the bottom, **yaxis** in the left, **x2axis** in the top, and **y2axis** in the right.

```
# Display the axis temperature in the left margin.
.g1 yaxis use temperature
```

Axes have configuration options that control their appearance, particularly how ticks and tick labels are drawn. By default, the graph decides the axis tick intervals, but you can specify your own uniform or non-uniform intervals (e.g., time-series plots). You can also arbitrarily rotate tick labels. Some common axis configuration options are listed in Table 7-5.

Table 7-5: Axis Configuration Options

Axis Option	Description
-color	Sets the color of the axis and tick labels.
-command	Registers a Tcl command to be invoked when the axis formats its tick labels. The procedure will return the formatted label.
-descending	Specifies that values along the axis should be displayed in decreasing order.
-hide	Indicates if the axis should be displayed or hidden.
-justify	Specifies how the axis title should be justified. This matters only when the title contains more than one line of text.
-linewidth	Sets the width of the axis and tick lines.
-logscale	Indicates if the scale of the axis is logarithmic or linear.
-loose	Indicates if the limits of the axis should fit the data points tightly, at the outermost data points; or loosely, at the outermost tick intervals.
-majorticks	Specifies where to place major ticks. This is useful for creating non-uniform intervals of ticks.
-max	Sets the maximum limit of axis.
-min	Sets the minimum limit of axis.
-minorticks	Specifies where to place minor ticks. This is useful for creating non-uniform intervals of minor ticks.
-rotate	Specifies the angle of tick labels.
-showticks	Indicates if axis ticks should be displayed.
-stepsize	Specifies the interval between major ticks.
-subdivisions	Indicates how many minor ticks are to be displayed.
-tickfont	Specifies the font for tick labels.
-ticklength	Sets the length of major and minor ticks.
-title	Sets the title of the axis.
-titlefont	Specifies the font for axis title.

Normally, the graph automatically computes axis tick labels. But you can set your own labels by registering a procedure that will be called by the graph whenever tick labels are needed for that axis.

For example, you might want to display a degree symbol after the value for each tick on the X axis. By setting the –command option for axis x, you can have a procedure called whenever the graph needs to generate a tick label on the X axis.

```
.g1 axis configure "x" -command FormatTickLabels
```

When the FormatTickLabels procedure is called it will be passed two arguments: the name of the graph and the tick value. It returns the new tick label. In this example, it simply appends a degree symbol (represented by the octal value "\260") to the current tick value.

```
proc FormatTickLabels { widget value } {
    return "[expr round($value)]\260"
}
```

You may also want to display ticks at 90-degree intervals. By default, the range of an axis is computed from the data points mapped onto it. As new elements are added to the graph, the graph recalculates the axis scale to fit *all* the data. Tick intervals are automatically generated that nicely fit the axis range. But you can designate your own step interval with the –stepsize option.

```
# Maintain ticks intervals every 90.0 units. Don't display minor ticks.
.g1 axis configure "x" -step 90.0 -subdivisions 0
```

Figure 7-8 displays the customized ticks.

The –min and –max axis options specify the limits of the axis and therefore its scale. If you shorten the range of an axis, setting closer –min and –max limits, the graph is rescaled and the plotting area redrawn. Only the data points within the range of the axis are drawn, effectively magnifying that region of the graph.

```
# Magnify a region of data
.g1 axis configure "x" -min -80.0 -max 230.0
.g1 axis configure "y" -min 0.163 -max 1.0
```

Figure 7-9 shows the result of changing the axis limits.

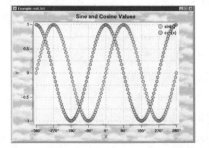

Figure 7-8: Normal View

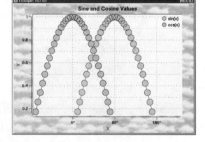

Figure 7-9: Magnified View

The size of the symbols representing data elements will also scale if you set the element's –scalesymbols options to true. This is useful when you want to give the user a visual feedback on how closely she is zooming the graph. The current axis range is used as a baseline for scaling the elements. That is, the element is drawn at 100% (its normal size) when the axis is at its default range. But if the axis range is cut in half, thereby zooming the graph 200%, the size of the symbol is also scaled 200%.

To reset the axis scale back to its default, set the axis −min and −max options to the empty string (""). The graph will automatically rescale to fit all the data points again.

```
.g1 axis configure "x" -min "" -max ""
.g1 axis configure "y" -min "" -max ""
```

Markers

Markers are used to annotate or highlight areas of the graph. They come in various forms, like text strings, bitmaps, connected line segments, polygons, or embedded widgets. For example, if you want to fill an area under a curve (like the cosine element in the preceding example), you can use a polygon marker to represent the fill area (see Figure 7-10).

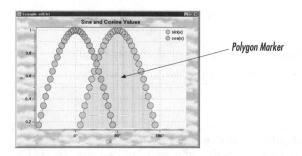

Figure 7-10: Polygon Marker Filling Area Under Curve

The coordinates of the polygon are the X-Y coordinates of the cosine data, sandwiched by two points that designate the polygon's left and right lower bounds. Marker coordinates are specified in graph (not screen) coordinates.

```
# Build a list of data values plus bottom values of the polygon
set data [.g1 element cget e2 -data]
set first { -360 -1.0 }
set last  { 360 1.0 }
set coords [concat $first $data $last]
```

```
.g1 marker create polygon -coords $coords -under true \
    -fill orange -stipple @/home/gah/bitmaps/pattern5.xbm
```

Markers have configuration options, too. Some options, like the −fill and −stipple options in the preceding example, are specific to the type of marker. There are some options that are common to all types of markers. They are listed in Table 7-6.

Table 7-6: General Configuration Options for Markers

Marker Option	Description
−coords	Specifies the coordinates of the marker. The list represents X-Y coordinate pairs. The number of coordinates is dependent upon the type of marker. Text, bitmap, and window markers require two

Continued

Table 7-6: General Configuration Options for Markers (continued)

Marker Option	Description
	values (an X-Y coordinate pair). Line markers need at least four values, polygons at least six.
-hide	Specifies if the marker is displayed or hidden.
-mapx	Specifies the axis to map the marker's X-coordinates onto.
-mapy	Specifies the axis to map the marker's Y-coordinates onto.
-name	Specifies the name for the marker. If this option isn't specified, the marker's name is uniquely generated.
-under	Indicates if the marker should be drawn above or below the data elements.
-xoffset	Specifies a screen distance to offset the marker horizontally.
-yoffset	Specifies a screen distance to offset the markers vertically.

Miscellaneous Graph Options

The graph widget also has several general options that are not specific to any component. In previous examples, we set the graph's title and background tile using the -title and -tile options. With other graph options you can set the cursor, relief, border, foreground, and background colors for both the plotting area and the surrounding area. Several common graph widget options are listed in Table 7-7.

Table 7-7: Graph Options

Graph Option	Description
-background	Sets the background color of the graph.
-borderwidth	Sets the width of the 3-D border around the graph.
-bottommargin	Specifies the size of the margin below the plotting area.
-bufferelements	Indicates to use an internal pixmap to buffer the display of data elements. This option is especially useful when the graph is redrawn frequently while the data remains unchanged (for example, moving a marker across the plot).
-cursor	Specifies the cursor.
-font	Specifies the font of the graph title.
-height	Sets the requested height of the graph window.
-invertxy	Inverts the positions of the X and Y axes.
-leftmargin	Sets the size of the margin to the left edge of the plotting area.
-plotbackground	Specifies the background color of the plotting area.

Continued

Table 7-7: Continued

Graph Option	Description
-plotborderwidth	Sets the width of the 3-D border around the plotting area.
-plotrelief	Specifies the 3-D effect for the plotting area.
-rightmargin	Sets the size of margin to the right of the plotting area.
-tile	Sets the name of an image to tile the background of the graph.
-title	Sets the title of the graph.
-topmargin	Specifies the size of the margin above the plotting area.
-width	Sets the requested width of the graph window.

By default, the graph automatically computes the size of the margins surrounding the plotting area. It considers things like the dimensions of axis tick labels and title, the location of the legend, etc. Sometimes you may want to override the computed size for a particular margin. For example, if you are displaying three graphs for comparison, the width and height of the plotting area should be the same for all graphs. You can use the -bottommargin, -leftmargin, -rightmargin, and -topmargin options to set the same size margins for each graph.

```
foreach graph { .g1 .g2 .g3 } {
    $graph configure -leftmargin 20m -topmargin 6m \
            -rightmargin 2m -bottommargin 14m
}
```

Figure 7-11 shows the three graphs with the same size plotting area.

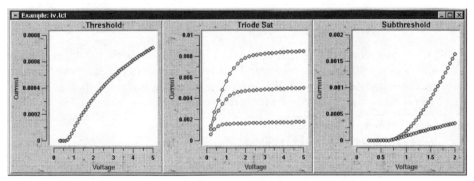

Figure 7-11: Three Graphs with Uniform Margins

Building Interactive Graphs

You've seen how the graph can be configured in a variety of ways. But the best feature of the graph widget is how easily new interactive behaviors can be added to it. This is what distinguishes a graph widget from the typical plotting program. You can add specialized behaviors to make the plotting more tightly coupled to the problem your application is solving.

For example, you may have a graph which plots many elements. If there are many traces, it becomes difficult to distinguish one trace from another. Using different line styles (colors, dashes, etc.) and symbols doesn't help. They simply clutter the graph.

Instead, let's plot all the elements with the same attributes, but let the user highlight the particular traces that she is interested in. We'll build an interactive legend; when the user clicks on an entry in the legend, the corresponding element will be highlighted. Figure 7-12 displays such a graph.

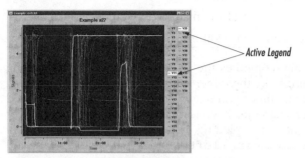

Figure 7-12: Graph with Interactive Legend

We first need to determine what entry in the legend that the user has clicked on. The `PickElement` procedure calls the legend's `get` operation to find an entry at a given screen coordinate and returns the name of the element corresponding to the entry. If the coordinate isn't over an entry, the empty string ("") is returned.

```
proc PickElement { x y } {
    .g1 legend get @$x,$y
}
```

Provided with the name of the element, you can highlight both the legend entry and the element. Both the `element` and `legend` components have `activate` operations. The `SelectTrace` following procedure highlights both the element and its legend entry using the their `activate` operations.

```
proc SelectTrace { elemName } {
    .g1 legend activate $elemName
    .g1 element activate $elemName
}
```

To revert back to the element and legend's normal appearance, you can use their `deactivate` operations.

```
proc DeselectTrace { elemName } {
    .g1 legend deactivate $elemName
    .g1 element deactivate $elemName
}
```

When the user clicks on the legend, we want to toggle the state of the entry: active or normal. To find out if an entry is active, you call the legend's `acti-`

---

vate operation with no arguments. It returns a list of the currently active entries. If the element isn't in the list, you highlight the entry; otherwise, un-highlight the entry, redrawing it normally. The procedure `ToggleTrace` performs this function.

```
proc ToggleTrace { elemName } {
    if { [lsearch [.g1 legend activate] $elemName] < 0 } {
        SelectEntry $elemName
    } else {
        DeselectEntry $elemName
    }
}
```

The last thing to do is to invoke the `bind` command to link some Tcl code with the mouse button event. Our code checks if the mouse was clicked over a legend entry. If so, the `ToggleTrace` procedure is called to toggle the appearance of the legend entry and the element.

```
bind .g1 <ButtonPress-1>  {
    set elemName [PickElement %x %y]
    if { $elemName != "" } {
        ToggleTrace $elemName
    }
}
```

The BLT Bar Chart Widget

The `barchart` command creates a new bar chart widget.

```
# Create a barchart widget ".b1"
barchart .b1 -title "Simple Barchart"
pack .b1
```

The bar chart widget has the same architecture as the graph widget. It has exactly the same set of components as the graph. The data points are real numbers. The `axis`, `element`, `legend`, `crosshairs`, `grid`, `postscript`, and `marker` components work exactly the same way (see Figure 7-13).

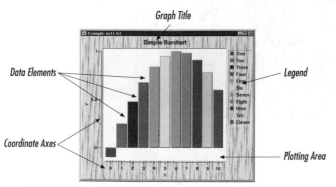

Figure 7-13: A Simple Bar Chart

The major difference is how data elements are handled and drawn. Data elements are drawn as bars, not lines or symbols. Consequently, the elements of the bar chart have different configuration options. They are listed in Table 7-8.

Table 7-8: Configuration Options for Bar Chart Elements

Element Option	Description
-background	Sets the color of the border around each bar.
-barwidth	Specifies the width of the bars drawn for the element.
-borderwidth	Sets the width of the 3-D border drawn around each bar.
-foreground	Sets the color of the interior of the bars.
-label	Sets the label for the element displayed in the legend.
-hide	Indicates if the element is displayed.
-mapx	Selects the axis to map the element's X-coordinates onto.
-mapy	Selects the axis to map the element's Y-coordinates onto.
-relief	Specifies the 3-D effect desired for bars.
-stipple	Specifies a stipple pattern with which to draw the bars.
-xdata	Specifies the X-coordinates of the element.
-ydata	Specifies the Y-coordinates of the element.

For example, you can set the relief, border width, and stipple attributes for bar chart elements. Figure 7-14 is an example of the different stipples and colors that can be specified for bar chart elements.

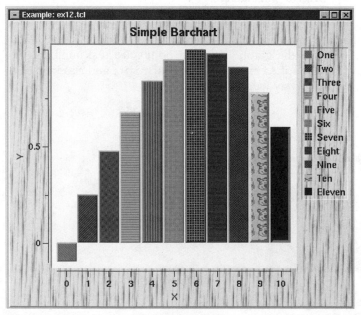

Figure 7-14: Example of Stippled Elements

Controlling How Bars Are Displayed

Data elements are added to the bar chart using the `element` component's `create` operation. The data points are specified using the `-xdata` and `-ydata` configuration options.

```
set Y { -0.1 0.25 0.48 0.68 0.84 0.95 1.0 0.98 0.91 0.78 0.6 }
set count 0
# Create an element for each value.
foreach value $Y {
    .b1 element create "e$count" -xdata $count -ydata $value
    incr count
}
```

A bar is drawn for each data point. This means that a typical bar chart can be represented in two ways. You could use as many elements as there are data points (such as in the examples we've previously seen). Alternately, you could represent all the data points in a single element consisting of many bars.

```
set Y { -0.1 0.25 0.48 0.68 0.84 0.95 1.0 0.98 0.91 0.78 0.6 }
set X { 0 1 2 3 4 5 6 7 8 9 10 }
.g1 create element "all" -xdata $X -ydata $Y
```

Drawing a single element is faster, especially if there are many data points. For example, if you use the bar chart widget as a strip chart, you may want to use a single element. Strip charts plot a single variable at several time steps. They are updated frequently (at each time point), so performance matters. Figure 7-15 is a bar chart used as a strip chart.

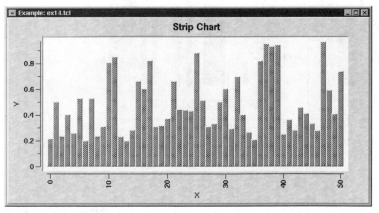

Figure 7-15: Strip Chart Using Single Element

The data points can be in any order. One bar is drawn for each X-Y coordinate pair. Since we are using just one element, all the bars will have the same attributes (colors, stipple, etc.). Elements can have different attributes, but not the bars of an individual element.

Since one bar is drawn at each data point, you can also place and group bars by their X-coordinates.

```
set X { 0 1 3 4 6 7 9 10 }
set Y { -0.1 0.25 0.68 0.84 1.0 0.98 0.78 0.6 }

for { set i 0 } { $i < [llength $y] } { incr i } {
      .b1 element create "e$i" -xdata [lindex $X $i] -ydata
[lindex $Y $i]
}
```

Note how the X-coordinate values position the individual bars. Figure 7-16 shows the results.

The height of each bar is proportional to the Y-coordinate of the data point. Data points with positive Y-coordinates are drawn with bars ascending from 0.0. Negative Y-coordinates are drawn with bars descending from 0.0. The width of each bar is, by default, 1.0 X-axis units wide. You can change this using the -barwidth option.

```
.b1 configure -barwidth 0.5
.b1 element configure elem3 -barwidth 1.5
```

Figure 7-17 shows the results. The widget's option changes the bar width globally for all elements. The element -barwidth option lets you change the width of specific elements.

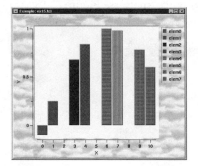 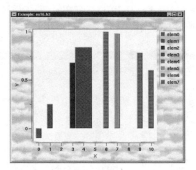

Figure 7-16: Grouped Bars   *Figure 7-17: Variable-Width Bars*

Display Modes

Sometimes bar charts are used to represent a cross-section of variables rather than a single variable. For example, let's say we want to compare the time to run particular operations over a group of programs. The data elements represent not the individual programs, but the set of times a particular operation takes across all the programs. The programs are instead represented by the X-coordinates. For all data elements, a program will have the same X-coordinate.

The bar chart will draw a bar for each data point centered at its X-coordinate. Since the X-coordinates for all the elements are the same, the bars will overlay themselves. You can see this in Figure 7-18.

You can change how bars with the same X-coordinates are drawn by setting the widget option `-barmode` to `aligned` or `stacked`.

```
.chart configure -barmode aligned
```

Figure 7-19 is the chart with the mode set to `aligned`. The data points with the same X-coordinates are displayed as thin bars side by side. The width of each bar is a fraction of its normal width (based upon the number of bars at that X-coordinate).

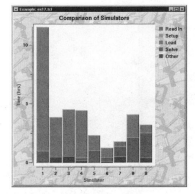

Figure 7-18: Normal Mode

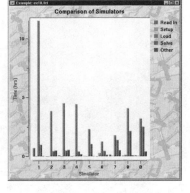

Figure 7-19: Aligned Mode

```
.chart configure -barmode stacked
```

If the mode is `stacked`, the bars are stacked by element, one on top of the next. The height of the bars at a particular X-coordinate represents the sum of the Y-coordinates. Figure 7-20 shows the same chart in `stacked` mode.

Managing Data

In the previous examples of the `barchart` and `graph` widgets, the X-Y coordinate data was managed using Tcl lists of numbers. But there are problems using lists when the data sets grow large (let's say, greater that a few hundred points).

The `barchart` and `graph` widgets must convert the data into an internal binary format (array of doubles). Yet often, the data you wish to plot is already binary, or could easily be converted into an array of doubles. It would be nice if the graphs could accept the binary data as is, rather than requiring you to redundantly translate the data into decimal strings, just to have it translated right back to binary.

It's also inefficient. The same data points are stored in two different formats: decimal strings and binary data. One copy is the Tcl list of numbers you specified as the element's X-Y coordinates. The other is the internal array of doubles the graph maintains. Even if several elements use the same Tcl list for their coordinates, each element will also maintain its own internal binary copy.

Lastly, it's slow to manipulate large lists of numbers. This is because Tcl lists are reparsed each time an element is indexed. For instance, the time to select values from

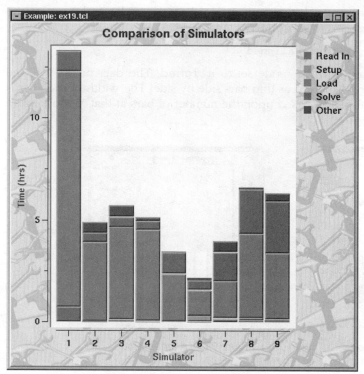

Figure 7-20: Stacked Mode

a list of 10,000 numbers using a Tcl `for` loop is on the order of minutes, not seconds. This makes data processing using lists impractical.

Tcl's associative arrays are no remedy either. There's no implied ordering to associative arrays. Especially for plotting, you want to insure the second data point comes after the first, and so on. This isn't possible since arrays are really hash tables. For example, you can't get a range of values between two indices. Nor can you sort an array. Worse, associative arrays consume memory inefficiently as they grow. This is because both the index and value are stored as strings for each data point.

BLT vectors overcome these problems by providing a convenient Tcl interface and a C application programming interface (API). Vectors are very useful for storing plotting data. The `graph` and `barchart` widgets work intimately with vectors, accessing and sharing the data in its binary form.

The BLT Vector Command

A vector is simply an order set of real numbers. Vectors have three ways in which they can be accessed and modified: a Tcl array variable, a Tcl command, and the vector's C language API.

Vectors are created using the `vector` command. You supply a name and optionally the initial size of the vector. If no size is specified, the vector will be empty. The values of all the components are initialized to 0.0.

```
# Create two new vectors.
vector q(50)
vector p
```

Vector's Tcl Array Interface

When you create a vector, a Tcl array variable of the same name is also generated. A variable by that name cannot already exist. Using the array variable, you can read, write, or delete the individual components of the vector. For example, when you set an element in the array, the corresponding vector component is also set.

```
set q(0) 9.25
set q(1) 10.23
```

When you read from the array, it returns the value of the vector component at that index.

```
# Print the second component.
puts "the 2nd value is $q(1)"
```

When you unset an array element, the vector's component is also deleted. The vector is automatically compacted. This means that all the trailing components are moved down one index. Owing to the way Tcl implements variable traces, you must have read or set the array element once, before you can unset it.

```
# Remove the first component
set q(0)
unset q(0)
```

By default, the array is indexed by integers starting from zero. Unlike normal associative arrays, where the indices can be any string, vector indices are restricted to specific forms. They are described in Table 7-9.

Table 7-9: Vector Index Formats

Index	Valid Operations	Description
integer	read/write/unset	Designates the value in the vector at the given index. The starting index is 0.
first:last	read/write/unset	Designates a range of values in the vector. Both first and last are integers.
end	read/write/unset	Designates the last element in the vector.
min	read	Returns the minimum value in the vector.
max	read	Returns the maximum value in the vector.
mean	read	Returns the mean of the vector's values.
stddev	read	Returns the standard deviation of the vector.
++end	write	Appends the specified value to the end of the vector.

You can specify a range of indices by using a colon to separate the first and last indices of the range. For example, you can set a range of components to the same value.

```
# Set the first six components of q
set q(0:5) 25.2
```

If you omit one of the indices in a range, it defaults to the first or last index of the vector. Therefore, the index ":" specifies the entire vector.

```
# Print out all the components of q
puts "q = $q(:)"
```

A vector also has special non-numeric indices. The index "end" returns the last component of the vector. The "min" and "max" indices return the current minimum and maximum values of the vector.

```
# Print the bounds of the vector q
puts "min=$q(min) max=$q(max)
```

Some non-numeric indices can only be read. It's an error to set or unset array elements with them. The index "++end" can only be set. It automatically extends the vector by one component and sets its value.

```
# Extend the vector by one component.
set q(++end) 0.02
```

The differences between the indices of vectors and normal associative arrays are summarized in Table 7-10.

Table 7-10: Vector Index Errors

Example	Description of Error
set q(fred) 1.0	Bad index. Vector arrays are indexed by integers, not arbitrary strings.
set q(0) "hello, world"	Bad value. Vector values can only be numbers.
set q(50000) 2.0	Index is out of range. You can't add new elements on-the-fly. Indices must fall within the vector's current range of indices.
% array names end	Array indices are not generated automatically for each element to conserve memory. So commands like array names and parray won't work.

Vector's Tcl Command Interface

When a vector is created, a Tcl command by the same name is also generated. The command has several operations. You can query, copy, append, or sort vectors by invoking the command, the name of the operation, and any arguments. Vector operations are listed in Table 7-11.

Table 7-11: Vector Operations

Vector Operation	Description
append	Appends values to the vector.
delete	Deletes components from the vector.
dup	Creates a copy of the vector.
length	Queries or resets the number of values in the vector.
merge	Merges the successive values from a group of vectors.
notify	Controls how vector clients are notified of changes to the vector.
offset	Changes the starting index of the vector.
populate	Creates a new vector which is a superset of the original. The new vector will be populated by additional values, evenly distributed between the pairs of original values. This is useful for generating abscissas to be interpolated along a spline.
range	Returns a list of values between two vector indices.
search	Searches for a value or range of values in the vector, returning a list of indices for all matching values.
set	Sets the values of the vector from a list of numbers or another vector.
sort	Sorts the vector.
* / + -	Performs vector arithmetic.

The length operation returns the number of components in the vector.

```
# Get the size of the vector
set size [y length]
```

The range operation returns a list of values that lie within a given range of indices.

```
# List the components in reverse order
puts "y = [y range end 0]"
```

The search operation returns a list of indices for all components matching a specified value. You can also search for a range of values by designating the minimum and maximum values of the range.

```
# Find all components equal to 50.0
set indices [x search 50.0]

# Find all components >= 50.0
set indices [x search 50.0 $x(max)]
```

If the search fails, the empty string is returned.

The delete operation deletes one or more vector components. Its arguments are the indices of the components to be deleted.

```
# Delete a single component
x delete 0

# Delete all components >= 50.0
eval x delete [x search 50.0 $x(max)]
```

If no arguments are supplied, the entire vector is deleted.

It's easy to translate between vectors and Tcl lists. Both the vector set and append operations can take lists of numbers as arguments. The set operation sets the values of a vector from one or more lists of values.

```
x set { 0.1 1.2 2.3 }
```

The append operation appends values onto the end of the vector. Each time the vector is appended, the length of vector is automatically extended.

```
x append { 2.3 4.5 10.3 }
```

The sort operation does more than simply sort the components of a vector. If you specify the names of additional vectors, those vectors are rearranged precisely as the sorted vector. For example, you can sort X-Y coordinates stored in separate vectors, while retaining the same coordinate pairings.

```
# Sort x.
x sort y
# Vector y is rearranged, same coordinate pairs as before
```

Vectors also have the built-in arithmetic operations: addition, subtraction, multiplication, and division. The right-hand operand can be either another vector or a scalar value. All arithmetic operations return a list of numbers, without changing the original vector.

```
# Add the two vectors
puts "x+y=[x + y]"
```

If you want to modify the vector, you can use the set operation.

```
# Scale the vector by 2.1
x set [x * 2.1]"
```

Vector's C Language Interface

Another way to work with vectors is from C code, using the vector's C API. You can write your own special data handling functions in C. The advantage of this method is that you can quickly process large amounts of data.

Vectors can be created, modified, and destroyed from C code, using library routines. You need to include the header file "*blt.h*". It contains the definition of the structure Blt_Vector, which represents the vector. It appears in the following code:

```
typedef struct {
    double *valueArr; /* memory holding vector components */
    int numValues;    /* Number of vector components used */
    int arraySize;    /* Number of components allocated */
```

```
        double min, max;   /* Minimum and maximum values in vector */
    } Blt_Vector;
```

Table 7-12 describes the routines available from C to manipulate vectors.

Table 7-12: BLT Vector C Library Routines

BLT Library Function	Description
Blt_CreateVector	Creates a new vector provided the new vector name and initial size. Both a new Tcl command and array variable by the same name are created.
Blt_DeleteVector	Destroys the vector. Both the Tcl command and array variable are destroyed, too.
Blt_GetVector	Retrieves a vector by name.
Blt_ResetVector	Resets the components of a vector. Calling Blt_ResetVector will cause the vector to dispatch notifications. You can also specify how the vector should free memory when it's resized or destroyed.
Blt_ResizeVector	Resets the length of the vector to a new size. If the vector is extended, the new components are initialized to 0.0.
Blt_VectorExists	Indicates if a vector by a given name exists.

For example, you may want read data from a file that is in its own special format (let's say, binary format). You can create a new vector and fill it with the values from a file using the vector's C API.

```
    #include <tcl.h>
    #include <blt.h>
    ...
        Blt_Vector vecInfo;
        double *newArr;
        FILE *f;
        struct stat statBuf;
        int numBytes, numValues;

        f = fopen("binary.dat", "r");
        fstat(fileno(f), &statBuf);
        numBytes = (int)statBuf.st_size;

        /* Allocate an array big enough to hold all the data */
        newArr = (double *)malloc(numBytes);

        numValues = numBytes / sizeof(double);
        fread((void *)newArr, numValues, sizeof(double), f);
        fclose(f);

        if (Blt_VectorExists(interp, "data"))  {
            if (Blt_GetVector(interp, "data", &vecInfo) != TCL_OK) {
                return TCL_ERROR;
```

```
        }
    } else {
        if (Blt_CreateVector(interp, "data", 0, &vecInfo) !=
            TCL_OK) {
            return TCL_ERROR;
        }
    }
    /* Update the fields of the Blt_Vector structure. */
    vecInfo.numValues = numValues;
    vecInfo.valueArr = newArr;
    /*
     * Reset the vector. Clients will be notified when Tk is
     * idle. TCL_DYNAMIC tells the vector to free the memory
     * allocated if it needs to reallocate or destroy the vector.
     */
    if (Blt_ResetVector(interp, "data", &vecInfo, TCL_DYNAMIC) !=
        TCL_OK) {
        return TCL_ERROR;
    }
```

The preceding example opens a file of binary data and stores it in an array of doubles. The array size is computed from the size of the file. If the vector `data` exists, calling `Blt_VectorExists`, `Blt_GetVector` is called to fill in a C structure representing the vector. Otherwise, the routine `Blt_CreateVector` is called to create a new vector. Just like the Tcl interface, both a new Tcl command and array variable are created when a new vector is created. It doesn't make any difference what the initial size of the vector is since it will be reset shortly. The structure fields are updated and `Blt_ResetVector` is called. `Blt_ResetVector` updates the vector so that the changes are visible from the Tcl interface, too.

Lifetime of Vectors

Vectors watch their Tcl command and array variable. If the vector's Tcl command is deleted or array variable is unset, the vector will destroy itself, freeing whatever memory it is using.

```
# Destroy the vectors x y1 y2
unset x
rename y1 ""
y2 delete
```

This *also* means that the lifetime of a vector depends on the scope of the array variable associated with it. If the vector is created inside a Tcl procedure, the scope of the vector's array variable is *local* to that procedure. The vector will be automatically destroyed when the procedure returns, because all local variables are unset at that time. If you want a vector to persist beyond the scope of a procedure, you must make certain that the variable is global using the `global` command.

```
proc doit {} {
    global x
    vector x(10)
    set x(9) 2.0
```

```
        . . .
}
```

Vectors and Graphs

While vectors are customary data structures for many applications, they have special utility with the BLT graphs. Both the `graph` and `barchart` widgets allow you to specify element data with vectors, instead of Tcl lists of numbers.

```
vector x y
barchart .b1
.b1 element create  e1  -xdata x -ydata y
```

The graph widgets work closely with vectors. When a vector changes, the vector notifies the `graph` or `barchart` to redraw itself. This happens automatically no matter how you changed the vector: using vector's Tcl command, array variable, or C API. So by using vectors, you can separate the data handling portion of your application without worrying about replotting the data.

Let's say you want to build a strip chart that displays only the last 60 time points. You can use a bar chart containing only one element and a pair of vectors to hold the X-Y coordinates.

As new data arrives, you will: 1) add the new time point to the x and y vectors; 2) remove the oldest time point if you have more than 60; and 3) redraw the chart. We can use a Tcl variable `time` to track the number of time points.

```
# Add the new time point
incr time
set x(++end) $time
set y(++end) $value

# Remove the least recent time point if when the vector is full.
if { $time > 60 } {
    x delete 0
    y delete 0
}
```

It's not necessary to update the chart when the vectors change. The chart is redrawn automatically. The bar chart sees the new values because it shares the vector's data instead of making its own internal copy. Several graphs can use the same vector, but there will be only one copy of the data.

Client Notifications

When a vector is modified, resized, or deleted, it may trigger callbacks to notify clients of the vector, such as graphs or bar charts. By default, the notification is deferred until the next idle point, when Tk reenters its event loop. This means that you can modify a vector successively and the graph or bar chart widgets using it will be redrawn exactly once, when Tk processes its idle tasks. You can change this behavior using the `notify` operation. For example, to be notified of changes immediately, you specify `always` as the argument to `notify`.

```
# Make vector x notify after every change
x notify always
```

Vectors and Splines

Vectors are used in the BLT `spline` command, too. The original X-Y coordinates are passed as vectors. The command returns the interpolated Y-coordinates in another vector. Splines are useful in plotting data. They can be used to generate smooth curves, instead of the single straight-line segments that connect data points.

A *spline* is a device used in drafting to produce smoothed curves. The points of the curve, known as *knots*, are fixed and the spline, typically a thin strip of wood or metal, is bent around the knots to create the smoothed curve. *Spline interpolation* is the mathematical equivalent. The curves between adjacent knots are formed by piece-wise functions such that the resulting spline runs exactly through all the knots.

The `spline` command interpolates the spline using cubic or quadratic polynomial functions. The spline is established from the knots, passed as two vectors.

For this example, we'll plot the function $\sin(x^3)/x^2$. We first need to create two vectors that will represent the knots or the X-Y coordinates of the data that we are trying to fit. The X-coordinates must be sorted in increasing order.

```
vector X(10) Y(10)
for {set i 1} {$i <= 10} {incr i} {
    set X($i-1) [expr $i*$i]
    set Y($i-1) [expr sin($i*$i*$i)]
}
graph .g1
pack .g1
.g1 element create "Original" -x X -y Y
```

The graph is shown in Figure 7-21.

We need a third vector. It represents the X-coordinates of the points to be interpolated by the spline. With it, you control both the number of interpolated points and their distribution. Every X-coordinate in this vector will have an interpolated Y-coordinate computed for it. This vector must also be sorted in increasing order, and its values must lie between the first and last knots.

Typically you want to include the knots in the interpolated coordinates so that the line segments forming the curve will run through the original points. Both the quadratic and cubic splines preserve the knots (i.e., an X-coordinate of any knot will always produce the corresponding Y-coordinate), so you can use the vector's `pop-ulate` operation to create a superset of the origin `x` vector.

```
# Create a superset of x in XS
X populate XS 10
```

The `populate` operation creates a new vector that contains the coordinates of the original vector, but is populated by some number of values between X-coordinates. The new values are evenly distributed.

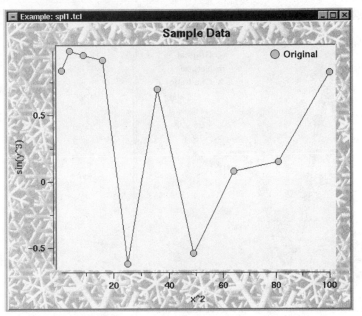

Figure 7-21: Coarsely Sampled Data Set

Based on the X-coordinates of the new points, the `spline` command generates the Y-coordinates (or the images of the spline) of the interpolated points and stores them in a fourth vector.

```
spline natural X Y XS Y1
```

The `natural` operation computes the spline using a cubic interpolant. In drafting terms, a natural spline minimizes the amount of energy required to bend the spline (strip of wood), through each of the knots. In mathematical terms, the second derivatives of the first and last points are zero. The vectors `XS` and `Y1` represent the X-Y coordinates of the interpolated points.

Alternatively, you can use the `quadratic` operation.

```
spline quadratic X Y XS Y2
```

Quadratic interpolation produces a spline that follows the line segments of the data points much more closely. The vectors `XS` and `Y2` represent the coordinates of the interpolated points. We can now plot the interpolated coordinates against the original values.

```
.g1 element create "Natural" -x XS -y Y1
.g1 element create "Quadratic" -x XS -y Y2
```

Figure 7-22 shows the results.

Designing Graphical Interfaces

Probably the most painstaking aspect of developing graphical applications is getting the placement and size of the widgets just right. Toolkits have made creating

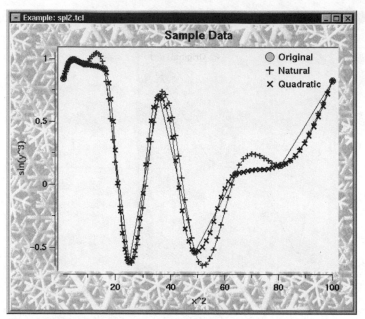

Figure 7-22: Plot of Interpolated Versus Original Data

widgets easy, but arranging the widgets into panels and forms is still hard. That's because designing graphical interfaces isn't a mathematical problem, but rather a visual problem that requires human interaction to test the look and feel of the interface. Spatial qualities like alignment, symmetry, and balance become more important than minimizing the amount of space used.

Designing graphical interfaces is an iterative process. You try out a new design, rearranging and resizing widgets, and then you test to see if it looks good and that it's usable. The interface still has to be functional, even if the window is stretched or shrunk.

In Tk, the location and size of widgets is handled by a *geometry manager*. Widgets are positioned within the boundaries of a superior widget, such as a parent `frame` widget. If the frame is resized, the geometry manager rearranges and resizes the subordinate widgets according to its own layout model and policies.

Consider a simple panel consisting of a text widget, label, and two scrollbars. We'll use Tk's standard geometry manager, the packer.

```
frame .frame
label .title
text .frame.text
scrollbar .frame.vbar
scrollbar .hbar -orient horizontal
pack .title -side top -fill x
pack .frame.vbar -side right -fill y
pack .frame.text -side left -fill both
pack .hbar -side bottom -fill x
pack .frame
```

The packer arranges widgets as if packing a suitcase. It packs (arranges) widgets one at a time, allocating the minimum amount of space needed for each widget. The widgets are stitched together in the order that they are packed. The packing order determines in what ways widgets can be arranged.

The packer has no real facility for aligning widgets. Instead, you use additional frames to create widget sub-hierarchies. For even this straightforward design, you need an extra frame to contain and align the text widget and the vertical scrollbar. Figure 7-23 below shows the results. Note how with the packer, you can't prevent the horizontal scrollbar from extending beyond the end of the text widget.

Worse, if the user resizes the application, narrowing it slightly, the vertical scrollbar disappears. Figure 7-24 shows the resized application. It's like using too small a suitcase. There's no room left for the last widgets to be packed. The packer doesn't shrink the widgets uniformly.

Overlapping scrollbars

Figure 7-23: Simple Layout with Packer 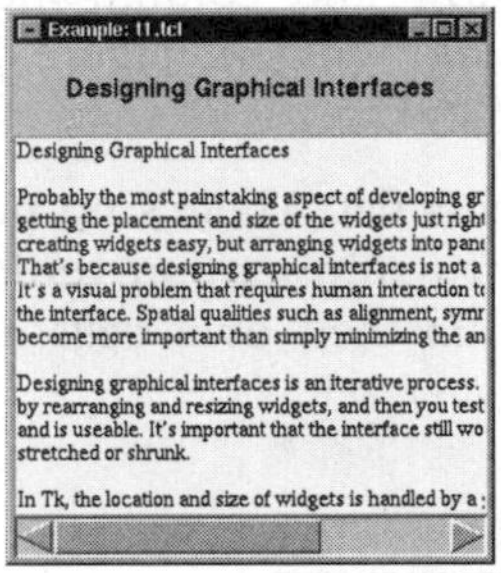   *Figure 7-24: Same Layout Resized*

It's also hard to make iterative design improvements. If you change alignments or add new widgets, it's like repacking the entire suitcase. Widget hierarchies need to be recreated, removing or adding new aligning frames.

The metaphor is wrong. The packer is designed to minimize the space used, not finely control the arrangement of widgets. Graphical interfaces are more akin to the visual layouts that a graphic artist creates. The same properties of design apply. For forms, an important spatial property is alignment. The alignment of particular widgets communicates that items are thematically related. Use of symmetry and balance not only lead to more visually pleasing layouts, but draw the user's eye across the form.

Grids are a ubiquitous tool in graphic arts. Grids help designers align and balance components. Also note that any rectilinear arrangement (such as rectangular widgets) can be described by a non-uniform grid. These observations motivated the grid model of the BLT table geometry manager.

The BLT Table Geometry Manager

To use the table geometry manager, you invoke the `table` command and the name of a container widget, such as a `frame` or `toplevel` widget. The table is associated by its container widget.

```
table .
```

The container widget (here the `toplevel` widget ".") designates the boundaries of the table. If the container widget is resized, the table is also resized and rearranged.

Let's try that simple example again, this time using the table.

```
label .title
text .text
scrollbar .vbar
scrollbar .hbar -orient horizontal
table . .title 0,0
table . .text 1,0 -fill both
table . .vbar 1,1 -fill y
table . .hbar 2,0 -fill x
```

Widgets are added to the table by arranging them (by row and column index) into cells of the table. Row and column indices start from zero. The table grows dynamically as you add widgets. Figure 7-25 represents a schematic view of the table.

The widget hierarchy is flat. There's no need for extraneous frames to group widgets because tables naturally support vertical and horizontal alignments. The scrollbars are aligned within their own cells and no longer overlap. You can see the results in Figure 7-26.

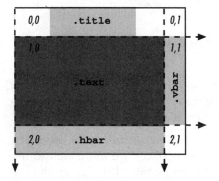

Figure 7-25: Schematic View of Layout

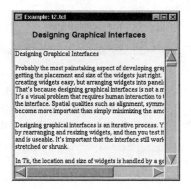

Figure 7-26: Layout Using the Table

The table arranges widgets using a grid model. It computes the sizes of the rows and columns based upon the widgets that span them. The table asks each widget, what size it wants to be. This is the widget's requested size. The widest widget in a column determines that column's width. The tallest widget in a row determines that row's height. The size of the table is the sum of the row and column sizes.

Controlling the Appearance of Widgets

You can control a widget's size and placement within its span of cells by setting options in the table. Widget-specific options are set either when adding a widget to the table, or using the table's `configure` operation. The available options are listed in Table 7-13.

Table 7-13: Widget-Specific Options

Option	Description
`-anchor`	Anchors the widget to a particular edge of the cell(s) it resides.
`-columnspan`	Specifies how many columns the widget spans.
`-columnstress`	Specifies how much emphasis the width of the widget should have when the table computes the sizes of the columns it spans.
`-fill`	Indicates if widget should occupy its entire span.
`-height`	Overrides the widget's requested height.
`-ipadx`	Sets the horizontal padding to add internally on the left and right sides of the widget.
`-ipady`	Sets the vertical padding to add internally on the top and bottom of the widget.
`-padx`	Sets the padding to the left and right exteriors of the widget.
`-pady`	Sets how much padding to the top and bottom exteriors of the widget.
`-rowspan`	Specifies how many rows the widget spans.
`-rowstress`	Specifies how much emphasis the height of the widget should have when the table computes the sizes of the rows it spans.
`-width`	Overrides the widget's requested width.

A widget may be smaller than its span of cells. This is true if the widget isn't the largest widget in that particular row or column. By default, the table centers the widget in its row or column. In our example, the width of the first column is controlled by the text widget, since it's wider than the label. The label is centered in the column. You can change the placement of the widget using the `-anchor` option.

```
table configure . .title -anchor w
```

The diagram in Figure 7-27 shows the results of anchoring the widget.

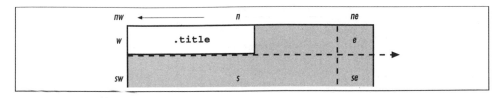

Figure 7-27: Example of Anchored Widget

The -fill option resizes the widget to fill its span either vertically or horizontally or both. For example, we want the scrollbars to be as long as the text widget. The text widget should also grow to fill its cell.

```
table configure . .vbar -fill y
table configure . .hbar -fill x
table configure . .text -fill both
```

The -padx and -pady options add extra padding around the widget. The -padx option pads the left and right sides, the -pady option pads the top and bottom.

```
table configure . .title -padx 8
table configure . .title -pady 8
```

Unlike the packer, you can add padding unevenly to opposite sides of a widget. For example, specifying -pady with only one value evenly pads the top and bottom by that amount. But if you specify a list of two values, the first value sets the padding above the widget and the second the padding below. Figure 7-28 demonstrates how the padding is distributed.

```
table configure . .title -pady { 6 2 }
```

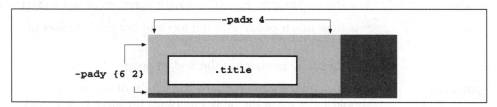

Figure 7-28: Example of Even and Uneven Padding

By default, a widget occupies a single cell of the table. You can make a widget span any number of rows or columns with the -rowspan and -columnspan options (-rspan and -cspan are synonyms). For example, we can center the label widget within the entire table by allowing it to span both columns.

```
table configure . .title -columnspan 2
```

The diagram in Figure 7-29 shows the results.

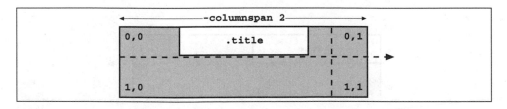

Figure 7-29: Example of Widget Spanning Multiple Cells

The -width and -height options override the widget's requested width and height. This can be particularly useful for widgets that don't let you set their requested sizes in screen units, like pixels or inches. For example, Tk's text widget's -width and -height can be only in units of characters and lines. We can force the text widget in our example to be exactly four inches wide, regardless of the screen resolution or the font used.

```
.table configure . .text -width 4i
```

Figure 7-30 shows the results.

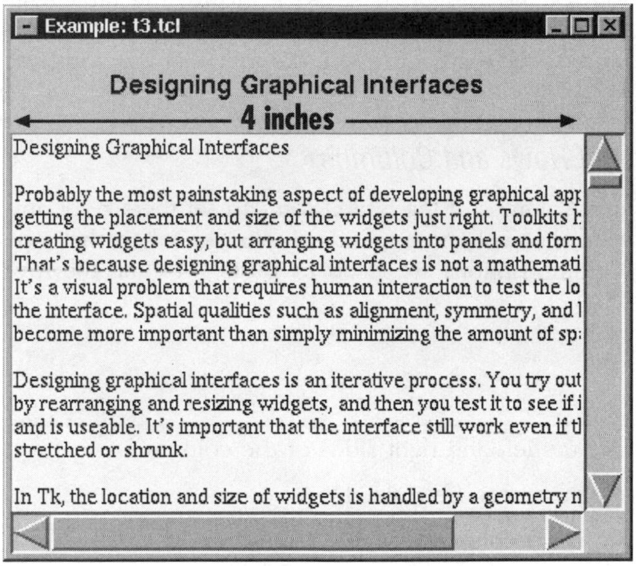

Figure 7-30: Overriding Size of Text Widget

In everyday life, it's normal to see uniformly sized buttons. When you go into an elevator, you don't expect the size of the buttons to vary according to the number of digits on the button. The same is true for dialog boxes. Why should it be harder to select a particular option, simply because it has fewer letters than the others? You can use the -width and -height options to make a set of buttons the same size.

```
toplevel .dialog
...
table configure .dialog .dialog.yes .dialog.no .dialog.cancel \
    -height .5i -width 1i
```

Compare the two dialog boxes in Figure 7-31; one with and without uniformly sized buttons.

You can adjust how the table calculates the size of rows and columns. For example, you may want the size of a particular row or column to be completely governed by the size of one particular widget, regardless if there are bigger widgets

---

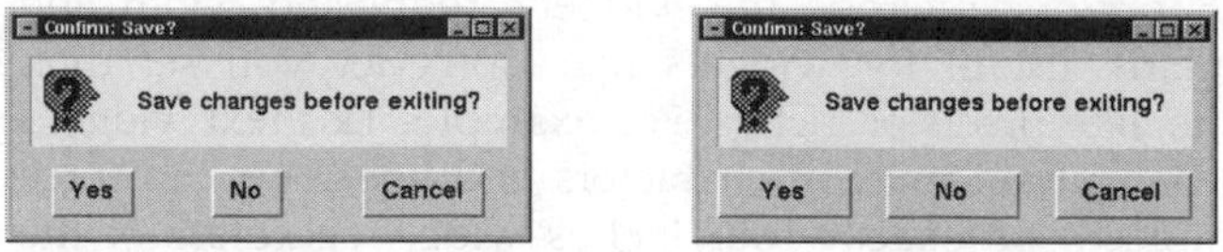

Figure 7-31: Non-Uniform and Uniform Buttons

in the span. The -rowstress and -columnstress options let you adjust how the table calculates the size of rows and columns. The value can be either normal, none, or full. If -columnstress is full, the width of column is solely determined by the width of the widget. If stress is none, the table will ignore the widget when it computes the widths of any columns which it spans. The default is normal. The widest slave spanning the column sets the width of the column.

Controlling the Appearance of Rows and Columns

You can also configure rows and columns of the table. You can set the size of any row or column or control if a row or column expands or shrinks when the container widget is resized. The column options are listed in Table 7-14 and the row options are listed in Table 7-15.

Table 7-14: Column Options

Option	Description
-padx	Sets the padding for the left and right sides of the column.
-resize	Indicates how the column can be resized.
-width	Specifies the width of the column.

Table 7-15: Row Options

Option	Description
-height	Specifies the height of the row.
-pady	Sets the padding above and below the row.
-resize	Indicates how the row can be resized.

Row and column options are set by invoking the table's configure operation. Rows are designated by "R*i*" and columns by "C*i*" respectively, where *i* is the index of the row or column. You can also use "R*" and "C*", to configure all rows or columns.

You can pad a row or column setting its -padx or -pady option. As with widgets, padding can be added unevenly. The padding will be in addition to the width or height of the column or row.

```
table configure .dialog R0 -pady 2
table configure .dialog C0 -padx { 1 2 }
```

The -height or -width options let you override the normal size of any row or column. The computed size of the row or column is ignored, regardless of the widgets it contains. This is useful when you want to set the size of a row or column to known screen distance.

```
# Make the 1st column 2 inches wide table
table configure . C0 -width 2.0i
```

You can also create *white space* with the -height or -width options. There's no requirement that a row or column contain any widgets. You can use the -width or -height options to set the dimensions of the empty areas.

Empty space is useful in balancing the layout of your widgets. For instance, we can rearrange our example so that the first column is empty.

```
table . .title 0,1 -cspan 2 \
        .text 1,1 -fill both \
        .vbar 1,2 -fill y \
        .hbar 2,1 -fill x
```

You can add several widgets at a time to the table. We'll set the width of the first column to be the same as the width of the vertical scrollbar.

```
table configure . C0 -width .vbar
```

Note that the size of the column is specified using the name of the scrollbar. The column will be set to the requested width of the widget. Figure 7-32 shows the results.

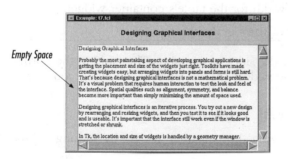

Figure 7-32: Example of White Space

When the table computes its normal size, it tries to resize its container widget so that it exactly fits the table. This can fail. The geometry manager that controls the container widget may disallow it. For example, the user may have resized the top-level window.

If the container is larger or smaller than needed, the table is stretched or shrunk accordingly. By default, the table proportionally resizes all rows and columns. You can change this for any row or column using the -resize option. The -resize option indicates whether the partition can shrink or stretch.

Some rows and columns you may want to freeze at their normal sizes. For instance, the row containing the horizontal scrollbar and the column holding the vertical scrollbar in the first example should not be resized.

```
table configure . C1 R1 -resize none
```

If -resize is set to none, the row or column is frozen at its normal size. If set to shrink, the partition can only be resized smaller than its normal size. If set to expand, the partition can only be resized larger.

Miscellaneous Table Options

The table itself has several configuration options. They are listed in Table 7-16.

Table 7-16: General Table Options

Table Option	Description
-columns	Resets the number of columns in the table.
-padx	Sets how much padding to add to the left and right sides of the table.
-pady	Sets how much padding to add to the top and bottom of the table.
-propagate	Indicates if the container widget should be resized to exactly fit the table.
-height	Sets the requested height for the table's container widget.
-width	Sets the requested width for the table's container widget.
-rows	Resets the number of rows in the table.

The -padx and -pady options pad the sides of the table. They add to the normal size of the table. They work like the widget-specific options, allowing you to pad unequally.

```
table configure . -padx { 0 0.5i } -pady 4
```

You can prevent the table from resizing the container widget by turning off the -propagate option.

```
table configure . -propagate no
```

The -height and -width options let you override the normal size of the table.

```
table configure . -width 4i -height 3i
```

Stacking Widgets

More than one widget can occupy a particular location in the table. This means that you can stack widgets. This is useful when you want to use a special frame as a background, while still maintaining alignments with other widgets in the table.

For example, in the following calendar, a frame with a 3-D sunken border is positioned under the label widgets displaying the names of the weekdays. This is different than packing the labels into the frame because we want the labels to still be aligned with the numbered days in the calendar. Note that both the widgets .cal.week and .cal.daySun are located in cell 1,0.

```
frame .cal.week -relief sunken -bd 2
table .cal .cal.week 1,0 -columnspan 7 -fill both
set column 0
foreach day { Sun Mon Tue Wed Thu Fri Sat } {
    label .cal.day$day -text $day
    table .cal .cal.day$day 1,$column -pady 2 -padx 2
    incr column
}
```

The calendar is displayed in Figure 7-33.

Figure 7-33: Two Widgets Placed into the Same Cell

Constraining Sizes

Sometimes it's desirable to *not* set a widget to a particular size. Instead, you just want to restrict the size of a widget or row to lie within an acceptable range. You can do this for toplevel widgets, using the minsize and maxsize operations of the wm command. But in Tk, there's no way to constrain the size of an arbitrary widget.

We've seen in previous examples how the -width and -height options have been used to set the dimensions of widgets, rows, and columns, and even the table itself. But the -width and -height options can also specify bounds. Instead of a single value, they can take a list of up to three values. The number of elements in the list determines how the values are interpreted. Table 7-17 describes the different formats.

Table 7-17: Bounding List Formats

Bounding List	Description
{}	Empty list. No bounds are set.
{ *size* }	Sets the size of the widget or partition. It cannot grow or shrink.

Continued

Table 7-17: Bounding List Formats (continued)

Bounding List	Description
{ *min max* }	Restricts the size of the widget or partition between minimum and maximum size limits.
{ *min max nom* }	Restricts the size of the widget or partition between a range of sizes, but also sets its nominal size. This overrides the calculated size of the widget or partition.

For example, instead of preventing the scrollbars from being resized with `-resize` option, we'll bound the size of the scrollbars between two values so that they can be resized slightly.

```
# Bound the scrollbars between 1/8 and 1/2 inch
table configure . C2 -width { 0.125 0.5 }
table configure . R2 -height { 0.125 0.5 }
```

The scrollbars will shrink to no smaller than 1/8 of an inch, or stretch no bigger than 1/2 inch. The initial size of the scrollbars is their requested size, only so long as it falls within the specified limits.

Building Forms

While the table can arrange any widget layout, it's most helpful in building forms. A typical form is composed of many widgets. It's very important to group and align the widgets to visually separate their functions. A haphazardly designed form confuses users.

The following simple form contains more than 40 widgets.

```
table . \
    .overall_label      0,1 -cspan 10 -pady 5 \
    .name_label         1,2 \
    .last_entry         2,2 -cspan 2 \
    .first_entry        2,4 \
        ...
    .zip_label          12,5 \
    .orders_title       16,2  -pady { 4 0 } \
    .text               17,2 -cspan 8 -fill both -padx 2 \
    .vscroll            17,10 -anchor center -fill both \
    .status_label       18,3 -cspan 6 -width {0 4i} \
    .search_button      18,3 -width .9i -anchor center -pady 8\
    .clear_button       18,5 -width .9i -anchor center \
    .quit_button        18,8 -width .9i -anchor center
```

Note that the widgets are all arranged using one table. Figure 7-34 displays the results. There are no extra frames needed to contain or group widgets. This form isn't possible with the packer.

One trick in creating forms is to specify enough rows and columns to align even those items that may appear visually distant. The buttons on the bottom of the form are aligned with the fields of the form although they are not directly related to those fields. Unbalanced and unaligned controls distract users.

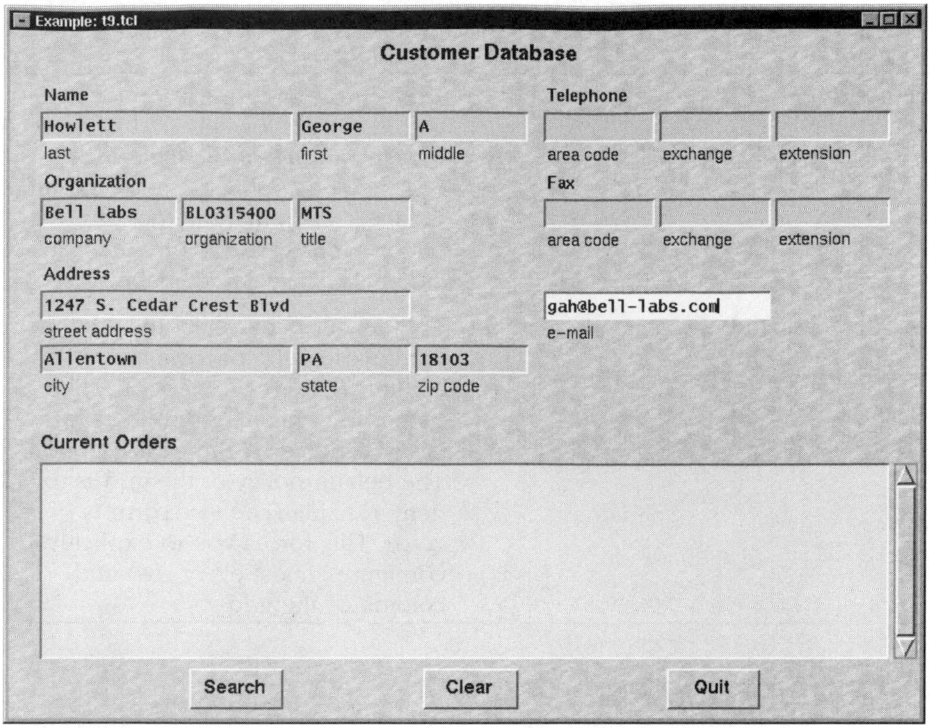

Figure 7-34: Form Containing 40+ Widgets

Comparison with Tk's Grid

Recent distributions of Tk have included a new grid geometry manager. It was based upon the table, so it employs a similar grid layout model. Much of the syntax of the grid is taken directly from the table.

There are several features of the table not found in the grid. Some of the features are reviewed in Table 7-18.

Table 7-18: Features of the BLT Table

Table Feature	Description
Override sizes of widgets	The requested size of any widget can be overridden. You can create uniformly sized buttons, or specify widget dimensions as a screen distance.
Constrain sizes	The size of any widget, row, column, or the table itself can be constrained to a range of sizes. This is especially useful for forms, where the resizing of widgets and partitions needs to be finely controlled.

Continued

Table 7-18: Features of the BLT Table (continued)

Table Feature	Description
Uneven padding	The –padx and –pady options let you disproportionately pad widgets, rows, columns, or the table itself. For example, you can pad a column of labels, such that the top and bottom appear padded by the same amount as between the labels.
Proportional resizing of rows and columns	The default behavior of the table is to allow resizing of rows and columns. The few exceptions, like partitions containing scrollbars, are easily handled by the -resize option. The default policy of the grid is to deny resizing (i.e., -weight is zero). This forces you to explicitly configure almost every row and column of the grid.

Application Wrappers

Many text-based programs could be improved by a graphical interface. Unix programs like df and vmstat commands immediately come to mind. It would be much nicer to view their numeric output as part of a graph or pie chart.

But we can't always add Tcl and Tk to these programs. There are many programs where we either don't have access to its source code, or the program is so complicated that it's easier to treat it as a black box. Instead, we can create a script that acts as a *wrapper* for the program (see Figure 7-35).

In Tcl-only applications, this is easy. The exec command lets you capture the output from commands or programs. Exec collects the command's output and returns it when the command finishes. You can exec a program, saving the result, and then parse the captured output using regexp or one of several Tcl string processing commands.

In Tk applications, we have a rash of problems. While the command runs, scrollbars stop working, none of the Tk widgets get packed or redrawn properly, the send command fails, and so on. The application appears hung up or dead. The problem is that while exec is waiting for the command to finish, Tk isn't handling events.

The BLT commands bgexec and busy simplify writing GUI wrappers. They work around the difficulties of event-driven programming inherent in GUI applications, while still retaining the simplicity of the Tcl-only model.

The BLT Bgexec Command

Suppose you want to collect directory usage for the system. We can run the Unix command du and save its output.

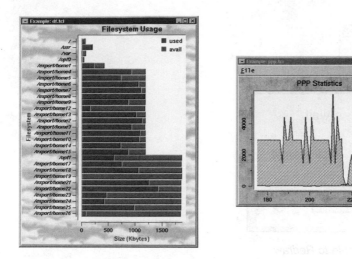

Figure 7-35: Examples of Graphical Application Wrappers

```
set dir "/usr"
set usage [exec du -s $dir]
destroy .wait
puts "Disk usage for $dir is $usage
```

The du command may take a while to complete so we'll create a simple dialog box to be displayed while du is running. Figure 7-36 shows the dialog box.

Figure 7-36: Dialog Box for Disk Usage

While du is running, another window pops up and partially covers our dialog. When the dialog is uncovered, the application appears hung up or dead. Figure 7-37 shows the result.

The problem is that while exec is waiting for du to finish, Tk isn't handling X events, like telling widgets to redraw themselves.

The bgexec command works just like Tcl's exec, except that it also allows Tk to process events. You can execute a long-running Unix command and the Tk widgets will behave normally.

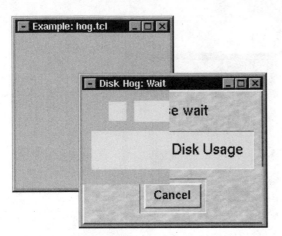

Figure 7-37: Dialog Box Unable to Redraw

```
set dir "/usr"
set usage [bgexec myStatus du -s $dir]
destroy .wait
puts "Disk usage for $dir is $usage"
```

Now when du runs, the window can be redrawn properly. When it finishes, its exit status is written to the Tcl variable myStatus. The result of the bgexec is the output from the command.

It's easy to convert from exec to bgexec because they both have exactly the same syntax for I/O redirection and pipelines. Like exec, bgexec returns an error if the exit code of the Unix command is not zero. If you think you may get an abnormal exit code, you might want to invoke bgexec from within the catch command.

```
catch { set usage [bgexec myStatus du -s $dir] }
```

The format of the bgexec command is as follows:

bgexec *statusVariable ?switches? cmd ?arg...?*

StatusVariable is the name of a global variable that will contain the exit status of the Unix command *cmd*. The status variable is linked with the command being executed. The variable isn't set until the command finishes. If you set the status variable before the command completes, it will terminate the Unix command by sending a kill signal.

For example, we can have the du command killed when the user presses the dialog's Cancel button. It simply sets the variable myStatus. Note that it doesn't matter what value the variable is set to.

```
button .wait.cancel.but -text "Cancel" -command {
    set myStatus 0
}
```

Bgexec has several switches to collect various forms of information. They are described in the Table 7-19.

Table 7-19: bgexec Switches

Switch	Description
-error	Specifies the name of a global variable to be set with the contents of stderr after the command has completed.
-keepnewline	Indicates that a trailing newline should be retained in the output.
-killsignal	Specifies the signal to be sent to terminate the Unix command.
-output	Specifies the name of a global variable to be set with the output of the command after the command has completed.
-update	Specifies the name of a global variable to be updated when data is written to stdout of the command. Unlike the -output option, the variable is updated as soon as new data becomes available.
--	This marks the end of the options. The following argument will be considered the name of a command even if it starts with a dash (-).

The -error switch tells bgexec to capture information from the standard error channel. The Tcl variable you specify will be set with the standard error information when the command terminates.

```
global myStatus myError
bgexec myStatus -error myError program arg arg
```

The -update switch specifies a Tcl variable that is written to each time output from the command becomes available. For example, if you have a command that produces its output in drips and drabs, you may want to process its output as it becomes available, rather than waiting for the command to finish.

```
global myStatus myUpdate
bgexec myStatus -update myUpdate program arg arg
```

By default, bgexec waits for the command to finish. But you can detach the command by adding an ampersand "&" to the end of the command line. bgexec returns immediately and its result will instead be a list of the spawned process ids. You can determine if the command has finished by examining the status variable.

```
global myStatus
bgexec myStatus  du -s $dir &
```

Even though the program is detached, you can still capture its output, using the -output switch. The variable specified will be set to the output of the command.

```
global myStatus myOutput
bgexec myStatus -output myOutput du -s $dir &
```

Another way to track when a detached command completes is to put a trace on the status variable. It will trigger some Tcl code to fire automatically when the command finishes.

```
proc UsageDone { part1 part2 how } {
    puts "du command completed"
}
global myStatus myOutput
bgexec myStatus -output myOutput du -s $dir &
trace variable myStatus w UsageDone
```

If at some point, you still need to wait for the command to finish, you can use the tkwait command to block until the status variable is set.

```
global myStatus myOutput
bgexec myStatus -output myOutput du -s $dir &
    . . .
tkwait variable myStatus
```

When du finishes, the variable myStatus will be written to, breaking out of the tkwait command.

Comparison with fileevent

Some Tcl programmers try to simulate what bgexec does with Tk's fileevent command. You can open a pipe to a Unix program and then monitor its standard output with file events. In your file event handler, you collect the output of the command. The assumption is that when the standard output channel closes, the program has completed. While this method sometimes works, there are some important advantages with bgexec. They are summarized in Table 7-20.

Table 7-20: Advantages of bgexec

Advantage	Description
Simpler	bgexec requires no additional Tcl code to run a program. It collects output automatically while transparently handling non-blocking I/O for you. Non-blocking I/O is better and more easily handled in C code.
Runs any command	With fileevent, we blindly assume the program has finished once standard output is closed. This means that you can't run a command that redirects standard output. Some commands like compress, immediately close and reopen stdout, fooling fileevent.
Faster	Since data is collected in C code, bgexec gets back to the Tk event loop more quickly. The less time spent out of Tk's event loop, the more responsive your program will be for user interactions.

Making Widgets Busy

In the last section, you saw how bgexec runs Unix commands in the background while Tk handles events. The example of collecting disk usage from the system demonstrated that you can wait for a long running Unix command while still executing Tcl commands.

In the process, we have introduced another problem. Suppose the user presses a button to bring up the "Disk Hog" dialog box, and now, while du is running, presses the button again. This starts a second command (see Figure 7-38). The problem is that the second bgexec will preempt the first. Any Tcl code following the bgexec command will not be executed until the second du completes.

Figure 7-38: Two bgexec Commands

The simple solution is to prevent the user from pressing the button again. We want to make the widget temporarily *busy*, so that it doesn't respond to user interactions like button and key presses.

You could use Tk's grab mechanism. The grab command restricts user interactions to a single widget hierarchy. But this makes it impossible for the user to further interact with the application, such as popping up a help window or scrolling text. The grab command does too much. Often you want only particular widgets busy, not the entire application.

You could change the -state configuration option of the widget to disabled. This effectively disables the widget. There are two flaws with this method. First, it means something very different when a widget is "disabled" than when it's busy. A busy widget is by definition active, not disabled. It misinforms the user when you indicate that a feature is disabled, when it's really running. More importantly, not all widgets have a -state option (like the canvas widget).

The BLT Busy Command

The BLT busy command makes Tk widgets busy. This means that user interactions like button clicks, moving the mouse, typing at the keyboard, and so forth, are ignored by the widget. You can set a special cursor (like a watch) that overrides the widget's normal cursor, providing feedback that the widget is temporarily busy.

When a widget is busy, all its children also become busy. It's easy then to make a panel of widgets busy by simply making the toplevel widget (like ".") busy. This is a lot easier than recursively traversing the widget hierarchy, disabling each widget and reconfiguring its cursor.

Consider how you would create an animated busy cursor, like the Macintosh watch. The watch dial spins as the application is busy processing, updating the cursor at successive intervals. To provide the same behavior in Tk, at each time step you would descend the entire widget hierarchy and reconfigure every widget's cursor. With the busy command, you need only to reconfigure the busy cursor.

You make a widget busy by invoking the busy command and its hold operation.

```
frame .top
button .top.button
canvas .top.canvas
pack .top.button .top.canvas
pack .top
    . . .
busy hold .top
update
```

The frame .top and all its children (the widgets packed into .top) are now busy. The update command insures that the busy command has a chance to update its busy cursor.

When a widget is busy, it can't gain the keyboard focus by moving the pointer or clicking the mouse on the widget. However, if focus was previously set, widgets can still receive key press events. To disable keyboard activity, move the focus to another widget.

```
busy hold .top
label .dummy
focus .dummy
update
```

When the application is no longer busy and you want to allow user interactions again, you can invoke the release operation.

```
busy release .top
```

Whenever you need to make the widget busy, simply invoke the hold operation again.

```
# Make widget hierarchy busy again
busy hold .top
```

The forget operation works like release, allowing user interactions, but it also frees the X resources used to make the widget busy. Use forget when you no longer need to make the widget busy.

```
busy forget .top
```

Binding Events to the Busy Window

Even when a widget is busy, you can still watch events using the bind command. The busy command is implemented by creating and mapping a transparent InputOnly class window that completely covers the widget. Like Tk widgets, the InputOnly window has a name in the Tk widget hierarchy. This means that you can use the `bind` command to watch events occurring anywhere in the `Input-Only` window.

Example: Animated Cursors

Let's build an animated busy cursor. An animated cursor provides a nicer visual cue than a simple dialog box that an application is busy working. You animate a cursor by simply changing the busy cursor at regular time intervals using the `after` command.

The busy cursor is set using the `configure` operation, modifying the `-cursor` option. We will cycle through a set of cursor bitmaps.

```
busy configure .top -cursor "@fc_left fc_leftm blue green"
```

The names of the bitmap files are stored in a global variable `bitmapList`. Each file contains the name of the source bitmap for a cursor. The corresponding mask bitmap has the same name, but with a "m" appended to it. Cursors can be any shape. The mask file indicates what pixels are transparent.

```
# Initialize a list of bitmap file names that make up the animated
# fish cursor. The bitmap mask files have a "m" appended to them.
set bitmapList {
    fc_left fc_left1 fc_mid fc_right1 fc_right
}
```

We'll create two procedures to start and stop the animation. The `StartAnimation` procedure changes the cursor and reschedules another update in 125 milliseconds. It maintains an index to the current bitmap in the list, passed as the argument `count`. The procedure sets the cursor, using `configure`, and then bumps the index to the next bitmap in the list. Since we're treating the list as circular, it must wrap around the index whenever we move past the end of the list.

```
proc StartAnimation { widget count } {
    global bitmapList
    set name [lindex $bitmapList $count]
    busy configure $widget -cursor [list @$name ${name}m blue green]
    incr count
    if { $count >= [llength $bitmapList] } {
        set count 0
    }
    global afterId
    set afterId($widget) [after 125 StartAnimation $widget $count]
}
```

The `StopAnimation` procedure simply cancels the scheduled `after` event.

```
proc StopAnimation { widget } {
    global afterId
    after cancel $afterId($widget)
}
```

Whenever we make a widget busy, we invoke our `StartAnimation` procedure.

```
busy hold .top
StartAnimation .top 0
update
```

When it's released, we call `StopAnimation`.

```
StopAnimation .top
busy release .top
```

But we can automatically trigger animated cursors for every busy window. When the `hold` operation is invoked, an `InputOnly` window is mapped. When either the `release` or `forget` operation is run, the `InputOnly` window is unmapped. Therefore, we can automatically start and stop the animation simply by binding to the `Map` and `Unmap` events in the `InputOnly` window. We can bind to all busy `InputOnly` windows using their class name, `Busy`.

```
bind Busy <Map> {
    StartAnimation widgetName
}
bind Busy <Unmap> {
    StopAnimation  widgetName
}
```

The only problem left is that we need to translate the name of the `InputOnly` window to the widget that was made busy. Usually, the `InputOnly` window is a sibling of the widget's window. The name of the `InputOnly` window is *widget*_Busy where *widget* is the name of the widget made busy. The exceptions to this rule are `toplevel` widgets (for example, "."). The `InputOnly` window can't be a sibling of a `toplevel` widget. Here it's a child of the widget's window. The name of the window will be *widget*._Busy, where *widget* again is the name of the widget made busy.

We can write a procedure `TranslateBusy` to translate from the `InputOnly` window name to the name of the widget.

```
proc TranslateBusy { window } {
    set widget [string trimright $window "_Busy"]
    if { $widget != "." } {
        set widget [string trimright $widget "."]
    }
    return $widget
}
```

It will be called when the `Map` and `Unmap` events are triggered.

```
bind Busy <Map> {
    StartAnimation [TranslateBusy %W] 0
}
bind Busy <Unmap> {
    StopAnimation  [TranslateBusy %W]
}
```

Now the animated busy cursors are turned on and off automatically. Whenever the hold operation is invoked, the Map event is triggered. When the release operation is called, the Unmap event is triggered.

The BLT bitmap Command

Bitmaps are used in several places in Tk. The canvas and text widgets use bitmaps for stippling. The label and button widgets use bitmaps to display symbols instead of text. The BLT graph and barchart also use bitmaps for stippling and annotation markers.

Tk has a handful of built-in bitmaps. But more commonly, bitmaps are loaded from X11 bitmap files. Any custom bitmap must be generated as a bitmap file. This makes it cumbersome to manage bitmaps, especially when you are distributing a program as a wish script, since each bitmap must be stored in its own file. Your Tcl code is more complicated because you have to worry about in what directory the bitmaps are sitting. It would be much easier to define new bitmaps right from your Tcl script.

The bitmap command lets you do just that. You can define new bitmaps from Tcl code. You can also generate and define bitmaps from text strings, rotating and scaling them as you wish.

The bitmap command has the following syntax.

bitmap *operation bitmapName ?arg..?*

Table 7-21 describes the valid operations.

Table 7-21: Bitmap Operations

Operation	Description
compose	Creates a bitmap from a text string. The bitmap can also be scaled and rotated.
data	Returns a list of both the bitmap's dimensions and its source data.
define	Defines a new bitmap. The bitmap can be scaled and rotated.
exists	Indicates if a built-in bitmap already exists.
height	Returns the height of the bitmap.
source	Returns the source data of the bitmap.
width	Returns the width of the bitmap.

You define a new bitmap with the **define** operation. The following example creates a new stipple by defining a new bitmap called light_gray.

bitmap define light_gray { { 4 2 } { 0x08, 0x02 } }

To Tk, light_gray is now another built-in bitmap that can be used with widgets in exactly the same ways. For example, we can use it to stipple a data element in a barchart widget.

    .b1 element configure e1 -stipple **light_gray**

The `define` operation requires two arguments. The first argument is the name of the new bitmap. A built-in bitmap by that name cannot already exist. The second argument is the data that defines the bitmap. It is a list of two lists.

The first sub-list contains the height and width of the bitmap. The second sub-list is the source data. Each element of the source data is a hexadecimal number specifying the pixels set in the bitmap. The format of the source data is exactly the same as the X11 bitmap. The `define` operation is very lenient about the syntax of the source data. The data values may or may not be separated by commas. They may or may not be prefixed by `0x`. All the following definitions are equivalent.

```
bitmap define light_gray { { 4 2 } { 0x08, 0x02 } }
bitmap define light_gray { { 4 2 } { 0x08 0x02 } }
bitmap define light_gray { { 4 2 } { 8 2 } }
```

The `define` option also takes switches that let you scale or rotate a bitmap as you create it. The `-scale` option scales the bitmap by a given factor. The `-rotate` option rotates the bitmap by an arbitrary number of degrees.

```
set data { { 25 25 } {
    00 00 00 00 00 00 00 00 00 c0 03 00
    78 e0 07 00 fc f8 07 00 cc 07 04 00
    0c f0 0b 00 7c 1c 06 00 38 00 00 00
    e0 03 10 00 e0 41 11 00 20 40 11 00
    e0 07 10 00 e0 c1 17 00 10 e0 2f 00
    20 e0 6f 00 18 e0 2f 00 20 c6 67 00
    18 84 2b 00 20 08 64 00 70 f0 13 00
    80 01 08 00 00 fe 07 00 00 00 00 00
    00 00 00 00}
}
bitmap define hobbes $data
bitmap define hobbes2 $data -scale 3.0
bitmap define hobbes3 $data -scale 3.0 -rotate 90.0

label .icon1 -bitmap hobbes
label .icon2 -bitmap hobbes2
label .icon3 -bitmap hobbes3
pack .icon1 .icon2 .icon3 -side left
```

The new bitmaps `hobbes2` and `hobbes3` are three times the normal size. The bitmap `hobbes3` is also be rotated by 90 degrees. The results can be seen in Figure 7-39.

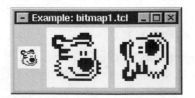

Figure 7-39: Scaled and Rotated Bitmaps

You can also generate bitmaps from text strings. The `compose` operation creates a new bitmap by drawing text into it. It also takes switches that allow you to rotate and scale the bitmap.

The `compose` operation is useful in cases where space is tight and a rotated button or label would work better. Unfortunately, the X Windowing System doesn't easily provide for rotated fonts. What you can do instead is create a rotated bitmap from the text string and then use the bitmap with the label or button widget.

```
bitmap compose title_bitmap "Simulated Data 25\260C" \
    -rotate 90.0 -font *helvetica*-bold-r-*-20-* -pady 6
label .title -bitmap title_bitmap
```

Figure 7-40 shows the results.

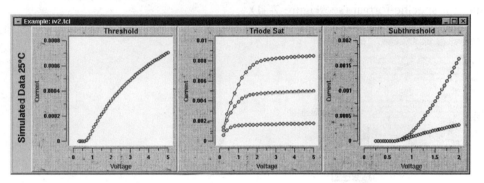

Figure 7-40: Label with Rotated Bitmap

There are a number of operations to query bitmaps.

```
% bitmap exists light_gray
1
% bitmap width light_gray
4
% bitmap height light_gray
2
% bitmap data light_gray
  {4 2} {
    08 02
  }
% bitmap source light_gray
    08 02
```

The `exists` operation indicates if a bitmap by that name is defined. You can query the dimensions of the bitmap using the `width` and `height` operations. The `data` operation returns the list of the data used to create the bitmap.

These operations are not restricted to built-in bitmaps. You can query the data of any bitmap, not just those created by the `bitmap` command. For example, you can use this feature to transfer bitmaps between Tk applications using the `send` command.

```
set data [bitmap data @/usr/X11R6/include/X11/bitmaps/ghost.xbm]
send {wish #2} bitmap define ghost $data
```

Drag-and-Drop

Drag-and-drop is the graphical metaphor of picking up data from one widget and dropping it on another. The data is represented by a bitmap or token window as it's dragged between widgets. Typically, the widgets are in separate applications. Based on the data, the target application will perform some action. The most familiar example is when a file token is dropped onto a wastebasket icon, causing the file to be removed.

Before data is actually transferred, the drag-and-drop source and target may negotiate the type and content of the data. For instance, the drag target may prefer the data in a specific format (see Figure 7-41).

Figure 7-41: Drag-and-Drop Color Selector

Most everyday examples of drag-and-drop transfer nothing more complex than simple text strings, like file names. But imagine a suite of applications where you can pick up a circuit description from a database browser. When you drop it on the circuit simulator it solves the circuit. Drop it on a graph and it plots the currents and voltages. Drop it on a schematic capture tool and it displays the circuit diagram. Drop it on a spreadsheet when you want to analyze the data. The really interesting and powerful examples are abstract and problem-specific.

We don't see many interesting examples of drag-and-drop. One reason is that negotiating data transfers is difficult. It's hard to get the source and target to understand each other when communication is limited to specific message types.

The BLT `drag&drop` command builds upon the advantages of the Tk toolkit to provide a flexible, yet powerful drag-and-drop mechanism. Using the `send` command, Tk applications have a powerful remote procedure call mechanism that simplifies negotiations.

The BLT drag&drop Command

The `drag&drop` command was developed by Michael McLennan and donated to the BLT toolkit. The `drag&drop` command provides a set of facilities for managing drag-and-drop data transfers. It acts like a telephone switchboard, registering widgets as drag-and-drop sources and targets and managing the connections between them. Widgets registered as *sources* export data, while widgets registered as *targets* import data. Note that a widget can be registered both as a source and a target.

The `drag&drop` command manages all the details of the connection for you. When the user clicks on a mouse button over a source widget, it automatically posts a token window for you (see Figure 7-42). A token window is a `toplevel` widget that represents the data to be dropped. As the user holds the button and moves the mouse, the `drag&drop` command moves the token to follow it.

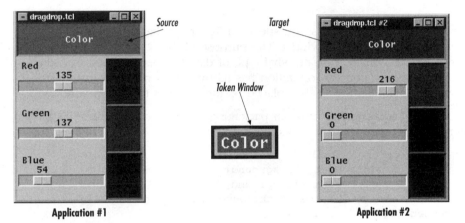

Figure 7-42: Components of Drag-and-Drop

The `drag&drop` command recognizes when the mouse pointer is moved over a valid target widget. It will change the relief of the token to be raised. When the button is released, the `drag&drop` command asks the target if it wants to accept the data. If not, a rejection symbol (shown in Figure 7-43) is displayed in the token window to indicate failure. The token window is automatically unmapped.

Figure 7-43: Token Window Rejection

The part of the drag-and-drop process that you control is the negotiation between the source and target. The `drag&drop` command lets you register Tcl scripts to package the data to be sent. You can also register scripts that specify the type of data that can be accepted by the target.

Registering a Drag-and-Drop Source

You register a widget as a drag-and-drop source, using the `source` operation.

```
drag&drop source .sample -packagecmd { PackageColor %t }
```

Once you've registered a source, you can create a token window using the `token` operation. A token window is simply a `toplevel` widget. The `drag&drop` command will automatically post and unpost this window as data is picked up and dropped.

```
set token [drag&drop token .sample]
label $token.label -text "Color"
pack $token.label
```

You can pack the token window as you would any `toplevel` widget. It can contain a canvas or small graph widget. Here, we've added a label to display color values.

The `-packagecmd` option lets you specify a Tcl script that is invoked whenever the user clicks on the source widget. The purpose of the script is to configure the token window to visually indicate what type of data has been picked up. Like the `bind` command, the `source` operation has its own percent sign substitutions. In the previous example, the "%t" is replaced by the name of the token window.

The procedure `PackageColor` is our packaging script for color values. It's passed the name of the token window as its argument.

```
proc PackageColor {token} {
    set bg [.sample cget -background]
    set fg [.sample cget -foreground]
    $token.label configure -background $bg -foreground $fg
    return $bg
}
```

Since we are picking up a color from the source widget `.sample`, the script simply changes the foreground and background colors of the label in the token window to reflect the color picked up from `.sample`.

The return value of the packaging script is the actual data to be transferred to the target. You can short-circuit the drag-and-drop operation by returning the empty string. This is useful when no source data is available to be transferred.

Source Handlers

Source handlers define the data types that can be exported. You designate source handlers using the `source` operation.

```
drag&drop source .sample handler color
drag&drop source .sample handler string
```

In more complex transfers, the source may need to process a data type. If you need to format the data in order to transfer it to the target application, you can register a Tcl script as an extra argument.

```
drag&drop source .sample handler color { MassageColor %v }
```

The "%v" is replaced by the value of the data. The return value of the script is the data to be transferred to the target.

Registering Drag-and-Drop Targets

You register widgets as drag-and-drop targets using the `target` operation.

```
drag&drop target .sample handler color { SetColor %v }
```

Unlike a source, a target must have Tcl script registered. The `drag&drop` command automatically tries to match the data types available for the source with those that can be accepted by the target.

The purpose of the target's Tcl script is to deal with the dropped data. For example, it may simply save the data in a Tcl variable. For example, the `SetColor` procedure updates the background target widget.

```
proc SetColor { value } {
    .sample configure -background $value
}
```

For our example, we defined a source for both `color` and `string` types. We might add an entry widget that is a target for string values.

```
frame .color
label .color.label -text "Color:"
pack .color.label -side left
entry .color.value -width 10
pack .color.value -side left -expand yes -fill both
bind .color.value <KeyPress-Return> { SetColor [%W get] }

# Set up the entry widget as a drag&drop target for "string"
values:
drag&drop target .color.value handler string {
    %W delete 0 end
    %W insert 0 "%v"
}
```

We'll set up the entry widget to act as a source for string values as well.

```
# Set up the entry widget as a drag&drop source for "string"
values:
drag&drop source .color.value -packagecmd {
    package_string [%W get] %t
}
drag&drop source .color.value handler string

# Establish the appearance of the token window:
set token [drag&drop token .color.value]
label $token.label
pack $token.label
```

Now if you bring up two of these applications you will notice that you can drop color samples on another color sample or on an entry widget. Color samples export both "color" and "string" types. If you grab a "string" type from an entry widget, you can only drop it on another entry widget. Entry widgets are the only targets that accept "string" types (see Figure 7-44).

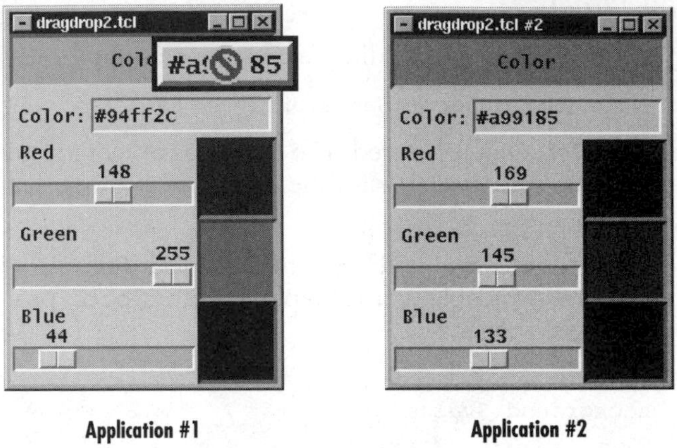

Application #1   Application #2

Figure 7-44: Example of Two Drag-and-Drop Types

Examples: Building Applications with BLT

This section will present two extended examples demonstrating how you can build more interesting and powerful applications with BLT. The theme for both examples is the same. From simple building blocks and a powerful, high-level programming language, you can quickly and easily build better applications. It's easy to add new and interesting behaviors to your programs, simply by gluing together primitive operations using Tcl. Even moderately complex components such as graphs and forms snap into your applications with just a little Tcl code.

Zooming Graphs

Zooming is a common feature for plotting data. When a graph is zoomed, a selected region of the graph is scaled and redrawn. The region appears closer or magnified, as if it was viewed through a high power lens. Zooming allows the user to more closely examine slopes of curves or the density of data in particular regions. By default, the graph widget doesn't have a zooming feature. But it's easy to create one.

We'll start off by creating a graph and filling it with data elements. We'll plot sine and cosine values again. The zooming feature is unrelated to the type of data plotted. It will work with any data set. The calculated sine and cosine values are stored in the vectors Sine and Cosine. Note that the values are themselves numeric expressions. We don't need to call expr, the vector evaluates the expressions automatically.

```
set pi 3.14159265358979323846
vector X Sine Cosine

for { set i -360 } { $i <= 360 } { incr i 5 } {
    set X(++end) $i
    set theta [expr $i*($pi/180.0)]
    set Sine(++end) sin($theta)
    set Cosine(++end) cos($theta)
```

```
}
graph .g2 -title "Zooming Graph"
.g2 element create e1 -label sin(x) -fill red -color red4 \
    -xdata X -ydata Sine -scalesymbols yes
.g2 element create e2 -label cos(x) -color green4 -fill green \
    -xdata X -ydata Cosine -scalesymbols yes
```

The user will select a zoom region on the graph, using the mouse. The graph will then zoom into the selected region, magnifying it. Figure 7-45 shows an example of a zooming graph.

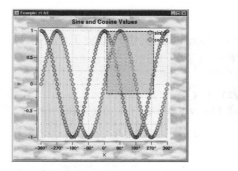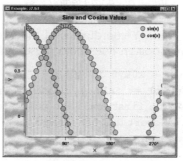

Figure 7-45: Graph Before and After Zooming

From the previous section on the graph widget, we know that changing axis limits, using the axis component's **-min** and **-max** configuration options, scales and magnifies that region of the graph.

```
# Zoom into the region [-80..230],[0.163..1.0]
.g2 axis configure x -min -80.0 -max 230.0
.g2 axis configure y -min 0.163 -max 1.0
```

Selecting a Zoom Region

We'll let the user select the axis limits by dragging out a rectangle on the graph with the mouse. The rectangle's coordinates will represent the zoom region. Rather than selecting all four corners of the rectangle, the user needs only to pick two opposing corners. The coordinates of the corners can be represented by four Tcl variables. The first corner (**$x0**, **$y0**) is selected when the user clicks on the left mouse button. The second corner (**$x1**, **$y1**) can be anywhere the mouse moves from that point. Figure 7-46 shows the selected zoom region.

The following two lines of code zoom the selected region.

```
.g2 axis configure x -min $x0 -max $x1
.g2 axis configure y -min $y0 -max $y1
```

The user can drag out a rectangle in any direction. Therefore, when setting the **-min** and **-max** options for the X-axis and Y-axis, we need to consider their relative positions. We also need to check that the two corners really form a rectangle. That

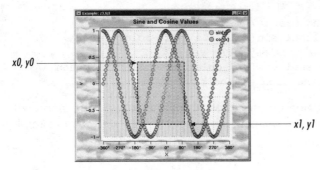

Figure 7-46: Example of Zoom Region

is, neither of the X-Y coordinates of the two corners can be the same The following procedure `ZoomIn` does both these things.

```
proc ZoomIn { x0 y0 x1 y1 } {
    if { ($x0 == $x1) || ($y0 == $y1) } {
        # The first and last points of the zoom region are the same.
        # Revert to the start.
        return
    }
    if { $x0 > $x1 } {
        .g2 xaxis configure -min $x1 -max $x0
    } elseif { $x0 < $x1 } {
        .g2 xaxis configure -min $x0 -max $x1
    }
    if { $y0 > $y1 } {
        .g2 yaxis configure -min $y1 -max $y0
    } elseif { $y0 < $y1 } {
        .g2 yaxis configure -min $y0 -max $y1
    }
}
```

We need to set up three event bindings (using the `bind` command) for selecting the zoom region. When the left mouse button is clicked in the graph window, a procedure `SelectStart` will be called. It will be passed the screen coordinates of the current position of the mouse over the graph. As the mouse is moved, holding down the left mouse button, the procedure `SelectMove` will be invoked. When the user finally releases the left mouse button, the procedure `SelectEnd` will be called.

```
bind .g2 <ButtonPress-1> { SelectStart %x %y }
bind .g2 <B1-Motion-1> { SelectMove %x %y }
bind .g2 <ButtonRelease-1> { SelectEnd %x %y }
```

`SelectStart` simply saves the X-Y coordinates that represent the first corner (x0, y0) of the zoom region. `SelectMove` displays a rectangle on the graph, representing the currently selected region. `SelectEnd` uses the current X-Y coordinates of the mouse as the second corner of the zoom region and calls `ZoomIn` to change the axis limits of the graph.

We have one problem to solve first. Our `ZoomIn` procedure expects the X-Y coordinates of the rectangular region to be *graph coordinates*. The `bind` event will give us the current *screen coordinates* of the mouse. The screen coordinates need to be converted to graph coordinates.

The graph's `invtransform` operation does just that. It returns a list of the graph coordinates transformed from a given X-Y screen coordinate. The procedure `GetCoords` breaks the converted coordinates out of the list and returns them in separate variables, whose names are passed as `xVar` and `yVar`.

```
proc GetCoords { scrX scrY xVar yVar } {
    upvar $xVar x
    upvar $yVar y
    set coords [.g2 invtransform $scrX $scrY]
    set x [lindex $coords 0]
    set y [lindex $coords 1]
}
```

`SelectStart` converts the mouse position to graph coordinates and saves them in the global variables `x0` and `y0`. It also initializes a graph marker to display the selected zoom region.

```
proc SelectStart { x y } {
    global x0 y0
    GetCoords $x $y x0 y0
    CreateRectangle
}
```

`SelectMove` converts the current mouse position to graph coordinates, this time saving them in the variables `x1` and `y1`. This point and the initial corner (`$x0` and `$y0`) represent the zoom region. The procedure `DrawRectangle` will draw a rectangle to highlight the currently selected zoom region.

```
proc SelectMove { x y } {
    global x0 y0
    GetCoords $x $y x1 y1
    DrawRectangle $x0 $y0 $x1 $y1
}
```

`SelectEnd` also converts the current mouse position to graph coordinates and stores them in `x1` and `y1`. They represent the second corner of the zoom region. It calls `ZoomIn`, passing the both corners (`$x0`, `$y0` and `$x1`, `$y1`) of the zoom region. The procedure `DestroyRectangle` will destroy the graph marker used to highlight the region.

```
proc SelectEnd { x y } {
    global x0 y0
    GetCoords $x $y x1 y1
    DestroyRectangle
```

```
    ZoomIn $x0 $y0 $x1 $y1
}
```

Highlighting the Zoom Region

There are several ways of highlighting the zoom region using the graph's marker
component. For example, we could mark the zoom region by drawing a dotted-line
rectangle around the area using a `line` marker.

```
.g2 marker create line -name ZoomRegion" \
    -coords { $x0 $y0 $x1 $y0 $x1 $y1 $x0 $y1 $x0 $y0 } \
    -dashes { 4 2 }
```

We can also display the rectangle as a stippled polygon using a `polygon` marker.

```
.g2 marker create polygon -name ZoomRegion" \
    -coords { $x0 $y0 $x1 $y0 $x1 $y1 $x0 $y1 $x0 $y0 } \
    -stipple pattern3
```

The polygon must be stippled so that the data elements underneath it can be seen.
Markers are normally drawn on top of data elements. If you want a solid-filled polygon, you can use the `-under` option to draw the polygon underneath the data elements.

```
.g2 marker create polygon -name "ZoomRegion" \
    -coords { $x0 $y0 $x1 $y0 $x1 $y1 $x0 $y1 $x0 $y0 } \
    -under yes
```

The method we choose depends on two factors; 1) how many data points we are
displaying, and 2) how fast our X server performs certain operations. If we have
thousands of data points, we don't want a solid-filled polygon. All the data points
are redrawn when the polygon is redrawn, each time the mouse is moved. The
`-under` option forces the graph to redraw itself each time the polygon is updated.
When the polygon is drawn on top of the data elements (`-under` is false), only the
marker needs to be redrawn. The data elements are cached into an off-screen
pixmap that can be quickly redrawn. If your X server draws stipples slowly, you
can to a line marker.

Our example uses a stippled polygon. Figure 7-47 shows an example of a polygon
marker.

```
bitmap define pattern3 { {2 2} {01 02} }


proc CreateRectangle { } {
    .g2 marker create polygon -name "ZoomRegion" \
        -stipple pattern3 -outline "" -fill "blue"
}
```

The procedure `CreateRectangle` only creates the marker. The marker is given
a name (ZoomRegion) that we'll use later to `configure` and `delete` the marker.
Note that the marker is not displayed on the screen until coordinates are designated

---

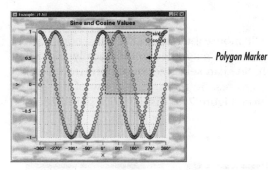

Figure 7-47: Polygon Marker Displaying Zoom Region

for it (this happens below). The `bitmap` command is used to create a stipple for the polygon.

```
proc DrawRectangle { x0 y0 x1 y1 } {
     .g2 marker configure "ZoomRegion" \
          -coords { $x0 $y0 $x1 $y0 $x1 $y1 $x0 $y1 $x0 $y0 }
}
```

The `DrawRectangle` procedure sets the coordinates of the polygon. The coordinates change as the mouse is moved with the left button held down. The coordinates of the polygon are the four corners of the zoom region. Given the two opposite corners $x0,$y0 and $x1,$y1, by symmetry, we know the other two corners. The marker's coordinates are set using the `configure` operation. The marker is redrawn automatically.

```
proc DestroyRectangle { } {
     .g2 marker delete "ZoomRegion"
}
```

`DestroyRectangle` erases the marker from the screen using the marker's `delete` operation.

Restoring the Original View

We also have to let the user zoom out, restoring the original view of the graph. As you might have guessed, we simply reset the original axis limits. The default axis limits are computed from the data elements displayed in the graph. You don't need to know those values. You can reset the default axis limits, by setting the `-min` and `-max` options to the empty string (`""`).

```
proc ZoomOut { } {
     .g2 xaxis configure -min "" -max ""
     .g2 yaxis configure -min "" -max ""
}
```

```
bind .g2 <ButtonRelease-3>   ZoomOut
```

The `ZoomOut` procedure will be called when the right mouse button is clicked.

Recursive Zooming

Our graph can now be zoomed. The left mouse button selects the zoom region. When the mouse button is released, the area is magnified automatically. Note that the user can recursively zoom the graph. She can select zoom regions from smaller and smaller subsets of the original view. To restore the original view of the graph, she simply clicks on the right mouse button. Figure 7-48 displays our graph zoomed once and then zoomed again.

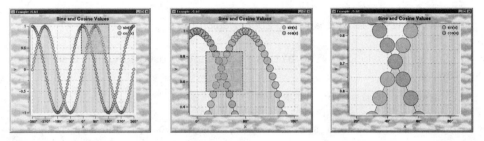

Figure 7-48: Recursive Zoomed Graph

Refinements

There's one problem with recursive zooming. It's common to click accidently on the left mouse button, after releasing it, triggering the selection of an unwanted zoom region. This is most likely to happen when there are lots of data points and the graph takes a moment to redraw itself. We want to temporarily prevent the user from selecting new zoom regions, while the graph is redrawing itself. We can use the busy command for this purpose.

```
proc ZoomIn { x0 y0 x1 y1 } {
    ...
    # Make the graph temporarily busy while it redraws itself.
    busy hold .g2
    update
    busy release .g2
}
```

When the update command is invoked, the graph redraws itself with the new axis limits. Invoking busy on the graph before update prevents accidental button presses while the graph is redrawing.

Zoom Stacks

The problem of accidental mouse clicks begs another question. What if the user doesn't like the currently selected region and would like to select another region? She can always click the right mouse button to restore the original view. What if the graph has been recursively zoomed? She loses all the previously accumulated zooming.

Instead, let's create a zoom stack. When `ZoomIn` is called, we'll stack the current axis limits. When `ZoomOut` is called, we'll reset the axis limits to their previous values. This way the user can recursively zoom in and then pop back to any of the previous zoom levels.

Tcl lists work nicely as stacks. We'll use them to build the usual *push*, *pop*, and *empty* stack procedures.

```
# Initial the zoom stack
set zoomStack {}

proc EmptyStack {} {
    global zoomStack
    return [expr { [llength $zoomStack] == 0 }]
}
```

The procedure `EmptyStack` simply checks if the list has any elements.

```
proc PushStack { xmin xmax ymin ymax } {
    global zoomStack
    set fmt {
        .g2 xaxis configure -min "%s" -max "%s"
        .g2 yaxis configure -min "%s" -max "%s"
    }
    lappend zoomStack [format $fmt $xmin $xmax $ymin $ymax]
}
```

The `PushStack` procedure will save the current axis limits just before the graph is zoomed. Its arguments are the current axis limits. But instead of pushing a list of the axis limits on the stack, you can take it a step farther, and push the exact commands that restore the axis limits.

When the procedure `PopStack` is called, it returns the commands as a string. To restore the limits, you simply execute the string using the `eval` command.

```
proc PopStack {} {
    global zoomStack
    set cmd [lindex $zoomStack end]
    set zoomStack [lreplace $zoomStack end end]
    return $cmd
}
```

You need to make only small changes to the `ZoomIn` and `ZoomOut` procedures to install the stack. In `ZoomIn`, just before the axis limits are reset, call `PushStack` to save the current axis limits.

```
proc ZoomIn { x0 y0 x1 y1 } {
    if { ($x0 == $x1) && ($y0 == $y1) } {
        return
    }
    # Push the current axis limits on the stack
    PushStack [.g2 xaxis cget -min] [.g2 xaxis cget -max] \
```

```
        [.g2 yaxis cget -min] [.g2 yaxis cget -max]
    ...
}
```

In ZoomOut, we no longer want to restore the original view, just the view at the last zoom level. It checks the stack, calling EmptyStack, and pops the last commands of the stack with PopStack. To restore the previous axis limits, you simply eval the command string.

```
proc ZoomOut { } {
    if { ![EmptyStack] } {
        busy hold .g2
        eval [PopStack]
        update
        busy release .g2
    }
}
```

Note that the graph is also busy when the user zooms out. For similar reasons, we don't want the user to accidentally click the right mouse button again when the graph is redrawing itself.

Displaying the Zoom Level

Building graphical applications is all about doing the little things right. We really should display the current zoom level; otherwise, it's difficult for the user to know where she is in the zoom stack.

You can use a `text` marker to display the zoom level. While a zoom region is being selected (as the left mouse button is held down), the next zoom stack level is displayed in the upper-left corner of the plotting area. When the user zooms out (releasing the button), the level of the restored view will be momentarily displayed. Figure 7-49 shows how this would appear.

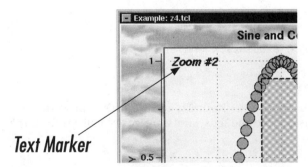

Figure 7-49: Graph Displaying Zoom Level

We'll create a procedure ShowLevel to display the level in the upper-left corner of the graph. The level is passed as an argument.

```
proc ShowLevel { level } {
    set text "Zoom #$level"
    if { [.g2 marker exists "ZoomLevel"] } {
        .g2 marker configure "ZoomLevel" -text $text
    } else {
        .g2 marker create text -name "ZoomLevel" -text $text \
            -coords { -Inf Inf } -anchor nw -bg {}
    }
}
```

The ShowLevel procedure creates a text marker in the upper-left corner of the plot area. Markers have elastic coordinates called -Inf and Inf that convert to the minimum and maximum axis values. The position -Inf, Inf is always the upper-left corner of the plotting area.

Each time ShowLevel is called it resets the text displayed for the level. You can use ShowLevel in two places. It's called by CreateRectangle when the first corner of the zoom region is selected. There it displays the *next* zoom level.

```
proc CreateRectangle { } {
    .g2 marker create polygon -name "ZoomRegion" \
        -stipple pattern3 -fill "" -outline "blue"
    # Display the level of the next zoom.
    global zoomStack
    ShowLevel [expr [llength $zoomStack] + 1]
}
```

ShowLevel is also called by ZoomOut when a zoom level is restored. It displays the current zoom level.

```
proc ZoomOut { } {
    if { ![EmptyStack] } {
        global zoomStack
        ShowLevel [llength $zoomStack]
        ...
    }
}
```

The HideLevel procedure deletes the text marker, if the current zoom level is the same as what was passed to it. We will see later where this fits into ZoomOut.

```
proc HideLevel { level } {
    global zoomStack
    if { $level == [llength $zoomStack] } {
        .g2 marker delete "ZoomLevel"
    }
}
```

HideLevel is called from DestroyRectangle, after the last corner of the zoom region has been selected.

```
proc DestroyRectangle { } {
    .g2 marker delete "ZoomRegion"
```

```
        global zoomStack
        HideLevel [expr [llength $zoomStack] + 1]
}
```

HideLevel is also called indirectly from ZoomOut. When the user pops back a zoom level, you want to display the current zoom level. But after the user is reminded of the stack level, the marker should be removed.

```
proc ZoomOut {} {
    global zoomStack
    if { ![EmptyStack] } {
        global zoomStack
        set level [llength $zoomStack]
        ShowLevel $level
        # Remember to remove the label in a bit
        after 2000 "HideLevel $level"
        ...
    }
}
```

You can use the after command to remove the text marker after two seconds.

If the user pops the zoom stack successively, faster than once every two seconds, the marker delete operation will be called again when the marker has already been destroyed. We want only to remove the marker on the last HideLevel procedure scheduled by the after command. The argument level passed to HideLevel is checked against the current zoom level to see if any intervening zoom outs have occurred.

Wrapping pppd and pppstats

One good use of an application wrapper is to simplify tasks that you perform over and over. For example, whenever I dial my internet service provider from my home computer, I have to do the following things:

- Run a dialer program such as chat or seyon that executes a script that logs in to my internet provider and starts up the Point-to-Point Protocol (PPP) service on the provider's machine.

- Start a PPP daemon (pppd) on my home computer. The pppd program establishes an Internet Protocol (IP) connection with my service provider. It will run as long as I'm connected to my provider.

- Check the throughput and quality of my connection by running the program pppstats. It reports the rate of serial packets received and sent.

To disconnect I do the following:

- Run the dialer program again, this time executing a dial-out script that hangs up the modem.

- Terminate pppd and pppstats on my home computer.

What I want is a simple GUI interface. It should have a "Connect" button that automatically dials the service provider and starts the PPP service. It should then automatically start the PPP daemon on my local machine. The interface should also have a "Shutdown" button that disconnects the modem and kills the PPP daemon. It would also be nice to display the I/O rates of serial packets as a strip chart. I can see the line throughput and know when I'm connected to a slow host.

I really don't want to rewrite these programs (`pppd`, `pppstats`, `seyon`, etc.) just to compile in Tcl and Tk. That would be too much work. All the programs work fine as is. I just want to wrap them together.

We can build an application wrapper that would call these programs, and then parse and interpret their outputs. Tcl and Tk supply many of the commands and utilities needed to do this. We can use BLT to provide the missing pieces like the `graph`, `bgexec`, and `busy` commands.

The wrapper application is really very simple. It consists of just a menu bar with two menubuttons, and a graph widget (see Figure 7-50). The graph plots the last 60 time points worth of PPP statistics.

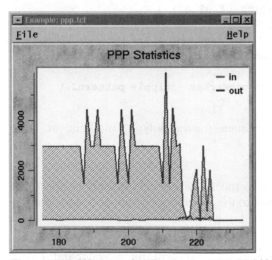

Figure 7-50: Wrapper Application for PPP Dial-Up

```
frame .mbar -relief raised -bd 2
menubutton .file -text "File" -menu .file.menu -underline 0
menubutton .help -text "Help" -underline 0
graph .graph -width 4.0i -height 3.0i -rightmargin 5
.graph axis configure y -rotate 90
.graph legend configure -position plotarea -anchor ne
table . \
    .mbar   0,0 -fill both -cspan 3 \
    .file   0,0 -anchor w -pady 2 \
```

```
    .help   0,2 -anchor e -pady 2 \
    .graph 1,0 -cspan 3 -fill both
```

You can use three vectors (x, sent, and recv) to store the statistical data. The vector x contains the time points, while recv and sent hold the number of packets received and sent at each time point. We'll plot both the packets using two data elements.

```
# Store the data in three vectors (tick is the time)
vector x recv sent

.graph element create in -color green3 -linewidth 2 \
    -xdata x -ydata recv
.graph element create out -color red2 -linewidth 2 \
    -xdata x -ydata sent
```

The area under each element will be filled using a stippled polygon. The polygons are stippled so that you can still see both elements, even if they overlap. Again, you can use the bitmap command to create the stipple.

```
bitmap define pattern1 { {4 4} {01 02 04 08} }
bitmap define pattern2 { {4 4} {08 04 02 01} }

# Add two polygon markers to fill the area under in and out elements
.graph marker create polygon -name inMarker -stipple pattern1 \
-fill green3
.graph marker create polygon -name outMarker -stipple pattern2 \
-fill red2
```

Note that we haven't specified any coordinates for the polygon markers yet.

Connecting

The connection process is triggered from the File menu. Clicking on the Connect entry dials the modem, connecting to the internet provider, and starts the PPP service. If the service is successfully started, the PPP daemon (pppd) is run and the input and output rates are plotted in the graph widget.

```
.file.menu add command -label "Connect" -underline 0 -command {
    if { [ConnectModem $startScript] == 0 } {
        StartDaemon $localAddr $remoteAddr
        StartStats
    }
}
```

To connect to the service provider, you can run one of several Unix dialer programs, like chat or seyon, to execute an automated script with the modem.

```
proc ConnectModem { file } {
    global seyonExit
    WaitDialog "Connecting to fast.net" seyonExit
    bgexec seyonExit seyon -script $file -modems /dev/cua3 -- \
        -iconic
}
```

The `ConnectModem` procedure runs `seyon`, passing it the name of a script file that automatically dials into the provider. It starts the PPP service, and then exits. The procedure `WaitDialog` displays a dialog box while `seyon` is running. Figure 7-51 shows the results

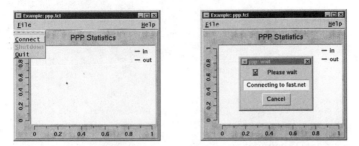

Figure 7-51: Connecting to Service Provider

We can't use `exec` to run the program. The dial-in program may take several minutes and our GUI application may need to redraw itself. This is where `bgexec` is needed instead.

```
proc ConnectModem { file } {
    global seyonExit
    bgexec seyonExit seyon -script $file -modems /dev/cua3 -- \
        -iconic
}
```

The `bgexec` command runs the `seyon` program and waits for it to complete. The global variable `seyonExit` is set when `seyon` finishes, containing the exit status of the `seyon` program.

We can also stop `seyon` before it finishes by setting this variable. For example, a dialog box will be displayed while `seyon` is connecting. When the `Cancel` button is pressed, `seyonExit` is set, killing the `seyon` program.

Starting the Daemon

Once the PPP service is established on the remote host, the PPP daemon `pppd` must be started on my home computer.

```
proc StartDaemon { localAddr remoteAddr } {
    global pppdExit pppdErrs
    bgexec pppdStatus -error pppdErrs \
        pppd $localAddr:$remoteAddr /dev/cua3 38400 &
}
```

You can use `bgexec` again, this time running the program detached in the background. The `pppd` program runs for the entire session, as long as you are connected to the PPP service. If the last argument to `bgexec` is &, the program runs in the background and the `bgexec` command will return immediately.

Handling Errors

Our program also needs to monitor pppd, noting if it should die unexpectedly. This can occur if the remote host terminates the connection (see Figure 7-52).

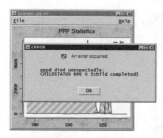

Figure 7-52: Example of Abnormal Disconnection

Bgexec is handy for precisely these situations. Bgexec automatically sets the status variable pppdExit when pppd completes or terminates. You can put a trace on this variable and have an error dialog automatically pop up. If pppd unexpectedly fails, bgexec sets pppdExit.

```
global pppdExit
trace variable pppdExit w DaemonDied

proc DaemonDied { part1 part2 how } {
    global pppdExit pppdErrs
    ErrorDialog "pppd died unexpectedly: $pppdErrs\n$pppdExit"
    # Hangup modem, terminate session
    ...
}
```

The variable pppdErrs will contain any output from the standard error I/O channel.

Displaying Statistics

I also want to collect statistics using pppstats. The pppstats program generates output in the following form.

```
in    pack    comp uncomp   err  |   out    pack  comp uncomp ip
 0      0       0     0       0   |    0      0     1    -1     0
```

The in field is the number of packets received and the out field is the number sent. Let's assume we have a ParseStats procedure that extracts the in and out values.

```
ParseStats { data inVar outVar } {
    upvar $inVar in
    upvar $outVar out
    ...
    set in [lindex $data 0]
```

```
        set out [lindex $data 6]
        ...
}
```

You could run pppstats at successive intervals using the after command.

```
after 1000 { set stats [exec pppstats]}
```

But it's simpler to let pppstats run continuously. It will output statistics at a specified interval. For instance, the following example runs pppstats continuously, writing I/O statistics every one second.

```
pppstats -i 1
```

Like pppd, pppstats runs as long the connection is established. You can use bgexec here, too. The difference is that we also need to collect output from pppstats as it becomes available so that we can plot the statistics at each time step.

```
proc StartStats { } {
    global statsExit statsUpdate
    set statsUpdate {} ; set statsExit {}
    bgexec statsExit -update statsUpdate pppstats -i 1 &
    trace variable statsUpdate w DisplayStats
}
```

The -update option tells bgexec to set the variable statsUpdate whenever output becomes available from pppstats. By tracing statsUpdate, we can update the graph automatically as new data becomes available. Figure 7-53 shows the results.

The graph plots the last 60 time points. A global variable counter maintains the time. At each new time point, you add a new data point and remove the least recent point. Since our data is stored in vectors, this is easy. You can append the new values to each vector using the ++end index. You can remove the least recent values by deleting the first component of each vector. The vectors will automatically move their components down one index.

```
set recv(++end) $inValue
set sent(++end) $outValue
set x(++end) $counter
if { $counter > 60 } {
    recv delete 0 ; sent delete 0 ; x delete 0
}
```

The DisplayStats procedure is called each time new data is output from pppstats. As pppstats outputs new values, bgexec sets statsUpdate; consequently, the trace on statsUpdate will cause DisplayStats to be invoked. DisplayStats extracts the new data points from statsUpdate, using ParseStats, and updates the respective vectors. Since the data is stored in vectors, we don''t need to reconfigure the graph to display the new data. This is handled automatically.

```
proc DisplayStats { part1 part2 how } {
    global statsUpdate counter
```

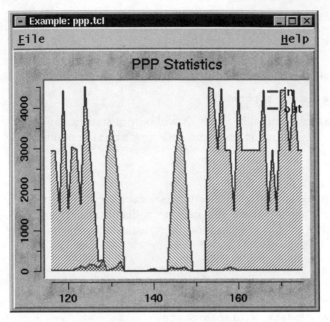

Figure 7-53: Graph Displaying PPP Statistics

```
    incr counter
    set data $statsUpdate
    set statsUpdate {}
    if { ![ParseStats $data inValue outValue] } {
        return
    }
    global recv sent x
    set recv(++end) $inValue
    set sent(++end) $outValue
    set x(++end) $counter
    if { $counter > 60 } {
        recv delete 0 ; sent delete 0 ; x delete 0
    }
    UpdateFills
}
```

Notice that the graph is never mentioned in DisplayStats. The data elements in and out are automatically updated when the vectors recv and sent are modified.

```
proc UpdateFills {} {
    global recv sent x
    set fill [concat -Inf Inf [x merge recv] Inf Inf ]
    .graph marker configure inMarker -coords $fill
    set fill [concat -Inf Inf [x merge sent] Inf Inf]
    .graph marker configure outMarker -coords $fill
}
```

The polygon markers filling the area under both elements are manually updated in the procedure `UpdateFills`. The coordinates of each polygon are the X-Y coordinates of the data element sandwiched between the bottom left and right corners of the plotting area. You can gather the current data coordinates using the vector `merge` operation. The coordinates of the X-coordinate and Y-coordinate vectors are merged into X-Y coordinate pairs.

Disconnecting

You disconnect from the PPP service by hanging up the modem. This can be done again with `seyon`, this time using a dial-out script. Another dialog box will appear while `seyon` is running (see Figure 7-54).

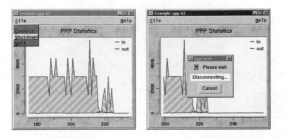

Figure 7-54: Disconnecting from the Service Provider

```
proc DisconnectModem { script } {
    global seyonExit
    set seyonExit {}
    Wait . "Disconnecting..." seyonExit
    bgexec seyonExit seyon -script $script -modems /dev/cua3 -- \
        -iconic
}
```

Before hanging up the modem, we need to terminate the running `pppstats` and `pppd` programs. The programs are terminated when the `Shutdown` menu entry is invoked.

```
.file.menu add command -label "Shutdown" -underline 0 -command {
    StopDaemon
    StopStats
    DisconnectModem $stopScript
}
```

To terminate either program, we simply set the status variable associated with the program. `Bgexec` sends a kill signal to the programs. You can kill `pppd` by setting `pppdExit` and `pppstats` by setting `statsExit`.

```
set pppdExit 0
set statsExit 0
```

We better remember to delete the variable traces before we set the variables. For example, if you set pppdExit without deleting its trace, the error dialog box will automatically pop up when pppd exits.

```
proc StopDaemon {} {
    global pppdExit
    trace vdelete pppdExit w PppdDied
    set pppdExit {}
}
proc StopStats {} {
    global statsExit statsUpdate
    trace vdelete statsUpdate w DisplayStats
    set statsExit {}
}
```

8

Tcl-DP

by Brian Smith and Lawrence A. Rowe

This chapter describes the Distributed Programming extension to Tcl/Tk called Tcl-DP. Tcl-DP lets you write client/server applications as high-level scripts using Internet protocols and sockets. As with Tcl, the goal is ease of programming for applications, not maximal performance. In particular, Tcl-DP provides the following features:

- Reliable Remote Procedure Call (RPC)
- Automatic cleanup on file close and program exit
- A name server for locating, starting, and authenticating servers
- Event handling functions
- Support for TCP, UDP, and IP-multicast transport protocols
- Socket configuration primitives
- Interfaces to DNS lookup functions that map machine names to IP addresses

The following script will give you a feel for the power of Tcl-DP. It uses Tcl-DP's RPC functions to implement a trivial "id server" that returns unique identifiers in response to GetID requests:

```
set myId 0
proc GetId {} {
    global myId
    ncr myId
    return $myId
}
dp_MakeRPCServer 4545
```

All of the code in this script except the last line is ordinary Tcl code. It defines a global variable myId and a procedure GetId that increments the variable and returns the next id. The dp_MakeRPCServer command is part of Tcl-DP; it causes the application to listen for client requests on a TCP socket (port 4545). All commands in the Tcl-DP extension begin with "dp_."

Other Tcl applications communicate with this server using scripts that look like:

```
set server [dp_MakeRPCClient server.company.com 4545]
dp_RPC $server GetId
```

The first command opens a connection to the id server and saves a reference to the connection in the variable `server`. The arguments to `dp_MakeRPCClient` identify the server's host and the port on which the server is listening. The `dp_RPC` command, whose arguments are a connection and an arbitrary Tcl command, performs a remote procedure call. `Dp_RPC` forwards this command to the server, which executes the script and returns a result (a new id in this case). The value returned by the server is the value returned by the `dp_RPC` command.

Any command or script can be substituted in place of the `GetId` command. For example, the commands

```
dp_RPC $server info tclversion
dp_RPC $server info procs dp_*
```

return the version of Tcl that is running in the server process and all the Tcl-DP procedures in the server, respectively. Next, we describe how a server can limit what machines can connect to it and what commands a client can execute.

`dp_RPC` is similar to the `send` command in Tk. The primary difference is that `send` requires both processes to be connected to an X server to communicate, while `dp_RPC` can be run without an X server. Because `dp_RPC` does not use the X server for communication, it's faster than `send`—three to five times faster for most commands.

Getting Started

This chapter is designed to be used interactively. That is, although you can just *read* the chapter, you will get more out of it by trying out the commands as you read them. In order to run Tcl-DP scripts, you must run a `wish` that has been extended with Tcl-DP. The CD-ROM provided with this book, of course, has the newest version at the time of publication. This extension can also be retrieved from the Tcl-DP home page at:

http://www.cs.cornell.edu/Info/Projects/zeno/Projects/Tcl-DP.html

The distribution includes source code, instructions, and scripts to configure, compile, and install the system, and Unix manual pages and several examples that document the system. The files *README* and *INSTALL* describe the distribution and how to make it.

Once installed, you can use the shell application called `dpwish` to try out the commands in this chapter. Type the command

% dpwish

to your shell to invoke `dpwish`, which behaves like an ordinary `wish` interpreter, reading commands from standard input and writing the results to standard output.

Since Tcl-DP is intended for communicating applications, a second `dpwish` simplifies the examples. In another window on your machine, start up a second `dpwish`. We will call the first interpreter "A" and the second "B." To help you distinguish the interpreters, we recommend that you change the prompt of each interpreter. In A, use the following Tcl commands:

```
proc PromptA {} {puts -nonewline "A% "}
set tcl_prompt1 PromptA
```

Use these commands in B:

```
proc PromptB {} {puts -nonewline "B% "}
set tcl_prompt1 PromptB
```

The prompt for A and B should now be "A%" and "B%" respectively. In the examples that follow, the prompt indicates in which dpwish the example commands are to be executed. We will refer to the processes as A and B.

The remainder of this chapter is divided into three sections. The first section summarizes Tcl-DP functions for creating client/server applications. After reading it, you will be able to write robust distributed applications using Tcl-DP. The second section describes the socket level communication primitives in Tcl-DP; it will teach you how to use sockets and event handling. The third section describes the Tcl-DP distributed object system.

We assume the user is familiar with the basic properties of Internet protocols like TCP/IP and UDP/IP, and has a superficial understanding of the Berkeley socket abstraction. Stevens* provides more information than you need to know on these topics.

Each section alternates between presenting a group of Tcl-DP functions and integrating them into an example program (a distributed whiteboard) that shows them in use.

Client/Server Architectures in Tcl-DP

The most important feature of Tcl-DP is that it simplifies the creation of client/server applications. For example, the following commands make a server:

```
A% dp_MakeRPCServer 4567
4567
```

dp_MakeRPCServer turns a process into a server listening on port 4567. The system will select a port number for you if you omit the port number or specify 0 as the port number. The chosen port number is returned, whether or not you specify it. The machine and process configuration is shown in Figure 8-1(A).

A client connects to a Tcl-DP server using the dp_MakeRPCClient command. dp_MakeRPCClient takes two arguments: 1) the machine on which the server is running; and 2) the port number on which the server will listen for client connection requests. For example, suppose the name of the machine that A is running on is *mayo.sandwich.com*. The following command will make B a client of A.

```
B% set server [dp_MakeRPCClient mayo.sandwich.com 4567]
file4
B%
```

---

* Stevens, Richard W., *UNIX Network Programming*, Prentice Hall International, Englewood, Cliffs, NJ, 1990, ISBN 0-13-949876-X.

Figure 8-1: Ports and Server Processes

The return value of dp_MakeRPCClient, *file4* in this example, is an identifier for the connection between the client and the server. The exact value of the identifier may be slightly different on your machine. It may appear that you can write a client only if you know the server's address, but Tcl-DP provides a name service that we'll describe later that makes the process more flexible.

When A receives the connection request on port 4567, it opens a new file in the server that handles incoming dp_RPC requests. This leaves port 4567 free for accepting requests from other clients. Figure 8-1(B) shows the machine and process architecture after the connection is established.

You can execute a Tcl command in the remote interpreter using this identifier as an argument to the dp_RPC command. For example, the following command prints "hello" in A's window:

```
B% dp_RPC $server puts hello
```

The extra arguments to dp_RPC (after $server) can be any Tcl command. For example, the following RPC creates a procedure in A that returns the first line in a file.

```
B% dp_RPC $server proc ReadFirstLine {filename} {
        set f [open $filename r]
        set firstline [gets $f]
        close $f
        return $firstline
```

If B executes the following command, the variable x in B will contain the first line of the file */etc/passwd* on A.

```
B% set x [dp_RPC $server ReadFirstLine /etc/passwd]
root:r.shdrfURbfwu:0:0:Operator:/:/bin/csh
```

This example shows an important feature of dp_RPC: the value returned by the dp_RPC call is the value returned by the command executed on A. As another example, the following sequence of commands creates a variable x in A, computes eight times its value, and assigns the result to the variable y in B:

```
B% dp_RPC $server set x 5
5
B% set y [dp_RPC $server expr {8*$x}]
40
```

The curly braces in the dp_RPC call are needed to prevent the Tcl interpreter in B from substituting the local value of x, which contains the first line of */etc/passwd*.

If an error occurs while executing an RPC, dp_RPC sets the errorInfo and errorCode variables in the originating interpreter and returns with an error. For example, the following call to dp_RPC triggers an error since ReadFirstLine requires a filename as a parameter.

```
B% set line1 [dp_RPC $server ReadFirstLine]
no value given for parameter "filename" to "ReadFirstLine"
```

The error is signaled using the standard Tcl mechanisms, exactly as if you had called ReadFirstLine locally. For example, the error can be trapped using the Tcl catch command:

```
if [catch {dp_RPC $server ReadFirstLine /does/not/exist} line1] {
    # Handle error any way you want...
    puts "Caught error: $errorInfo"
    puts "line1: $line1"
}
Caught error: couldn't open "/does/not/exist":
No such file or directory
    while executing
"open $filename r"
    invoked from within
"set f [open $filename r]..."
    (procedure "ReadFirstLine" line 2)
    invoked from within
"ReadFirstLine /does/not/exist"
    invoked from within
"dp_RPC $server ReadFirstLine /does/not/exist"
line1: couldn't open "/does/not/exist": No such file or directory
```

The examples thus far have shown how a client uses dp_RPC to execute a command in a server. Now suppose the server needs to execute a command in a client. This function might be used, for instance, to build an application that supports a publish/subscribe paradigm. Clients contact the server to subscribe to a database, and servers issue callbacks to the clients when the database is updated. The server can use dp_RPC to issue such a callback, but in order to do so, the server needs a connection identifier such as $server. Where does the server get the identifier for a client? The answer is from the dp_rpcFile variable.

Whenever Tcl-DP processes an RPC, it sets a global variable, named dp_rpcFile, to the connection identifier of the incoming RPC for the duration of the call. Servers can use dp_rpcFile to identify the source of the call, which can be used to contact the client later.

For example, suppose you want to write a server that supports the publish/subscribe paradigm. The server must maintain a list of all clients that have subscribed. The following code uses a Subscribe procedure that clients may call to subscribe to the database that will build this list.

```
A% set clientList {}
A% proc Subscribe {} {
    global dp_rpcFile clientList
    if {[lsearch $clientList $dp_rpcFile] == -1} {
        lappend clientList $dp_rpcFile
```

```
        }
    }
```

After one or more clients have subscribed, the server can use the following code to broadcast a message to all its subscribers:

```
A% proc Publish {msg} {
       global clientList
       foreach c $clientList {
          dp_RPC $c puts $msg
       }
   }
```

This example brings up a subtle point that can cause your client/server application to deadlock. To illustrate, suppose A contains the following procedure:

```
A% proc Greeting {msg} {
       global dp_rpcFile
       puts $msg
       dp_RPC $dp_rpcFile puts "Pleased to meet you"
   }
```

Now suppose B issues the following call:

```
B% dp_RPC $server Greeting "Hello there"
```

The expected behavior is that "Hello there" will appear in A's window, and "Pleased to meet you" will appear in B's. Instead, both A and B hang because, while waiting for dp_RPC to return, B blocks. But, while processing the Greeting call, A issues a dp_RPC to B which causes it to block. Since B is stopped waiting for A, and A is stopped waiting for B, the system is *deadlocked*, as shown in Figure 8-2.*

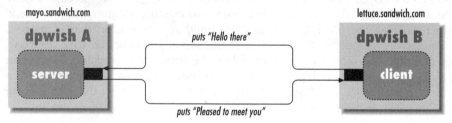

Figure 8-2: Deadlock

Tcl-DP provides three mechanisms to prevent deadlock:

- the -events option of dp_RPC
- the -timeout option of dp_RPC
- the dp_RDO procedure

We will discuss each mechanism in turn.

---

* If you run this example, your processes won't actually deadlock because Tcl-DP uses a default value for the -events option of dp_RPC, which is discussed later, that prevents deadlock.

The first way to prevent deadlock is to force processes to respond to inbound RPC requests while waiting for previously issued requests to return. If this feature was used in the preceding example, B would process the `puts` "Pleased to meet you" call from A while waiting for the `dp_RPC` call to return. Thus, A's RPC to B would return, allowing the remote call to `Greeting` to return, so that B's RPC to A would return. The key to implementing this strategy is to get B to process incoming RPCs while waiting for an outstanding RPC to return.

`dp_RPC` will process inbound RPCs while waiting for an outbound RPC to complete if it is called with the `-events` option. In other words, if we used the following code to call Greeting on A, the system won't deadlock:

```
B% dp_RPC $server -events rpc Greeting "Hello there"
```

The `-events` option with a value of RPC allows B to process inbound `dp_RPC` calls, but B will be unresponsive to other Tk events, like events from the window system (e.g., requests to redraw the screen) and timer events (created using the after command in Tk).

To make B responsive to other events while in an RPC, the `-events` option can be passed a list of event types that B should continue to process while waiting for the RPC to return. Table 8-1 lists the event types that can be processed with `-events`. For example, to force B to continue processing events generated by the X window system while waiting for a response from A, the `x` event type is used:

```
B% dp_RPC $server -events x Subscribe
```

To process timer events, use `timer` as the event type:

```
B% dp_RPC $server -events timer Subscribe
```

To process multiple event types, such as RPCs and X events, pass a list to `-events`.

```
B% dp_RPC $server -events {rpc x} Subscribe
```

Finally, to process all events, use the event type `all`:

```
B% dp_RPC $server -events all Subscribe
```

Table 8-1: Event Types that dp_RPC Recognizes

Event Type	Meaning
x	Events from the X window system (created with Tk's bind command)
file	Events that occur on a file or socket (created with Tcl-DP's dp_filehandler command)
rpc	Same as the file event type
timer	Timer events (created with Tk's after command)
idle	Events that correspond to when-idle events (such as display updates, window layout calculations, and tasks scheduled with dp_whenidle)
all	Same as the list {x file timer idle}
none	Don't process any events; block

A second way to prevent deadlock is to use the -timeout option to dp_RPC. If the dp_RPC call does not return within the specified timeout, which is given in milliseconds, dp_RPC returns with an error. Since it can trigger an error, -timeout is typically used in combination with Tcl's catch command. For example, the following code calls the Subscribe procedure on A, but prints a message on the screen if A does not respond within 100 milliseconds.

```
B% if [catch {dp_RPC $server -timeout 100 Subscribe}] {
       puts "Couldn't register with server"
   }
```

As an alternative to catching the error, you can use the -timeoutReturn option to specify a fragment of Tcl code to be executed if the dp_RPC call times out. The code is called with the connection id of the failed callback appended. The previous example could be expressed like this.

```
B% proc HandleTimeout {file} {
       puts "Couldn't register with server"
   }
B% dp_RPC $server -timeout 100 -timeoutReturn HandleTimeout Subscribe
```

The third way to prevent deadlock in Tcl-DP is to use a non-blocking RPC rather than a blocking RPC. The command dp_RDO, which stands for "remote do," initiates the RPC but does not wait for a response from the remote interpreter. Instead, it simply sends a message containing the request to the remote interpreter and immediately processes the next command in the script.

dp_RDO is ideal for procedure calls that are used for their side effects rather than their return values. The Subscribe procedure is an example of such a procedure. The purpose in calling Subscribe is not to get a return value (in fact, it does not return a value), but rather to modify a global variable in the server. Whenever a procedure is called that does not return a useful value, it can be called with dp_RDO instead of dp_RPC. For example, the following command calls the Subscribe procedure using dp_RDO:

```
B% dp_RDO $server Subscribe
```

Besides preventing deadlock, dp_RDO is also more efficient than dp_RPC. The difference can be dramatic. Depending on the distance to the remote site, the load on the network, and the responsiveness of the server, dp_RPC can take anywhere from 2 to 200 milliseconds (or more!) to complete. In contrast, dp_RDO typically returns within a fraction of a millisecond. Moreover, dp_RDO reduces load on the network, client, and server, since the server does not send back a response, the client does not process a response, and the network does not transport the response.*

Another consequence of using dp_RDO is that the client and server can run in parallel. For example, in its initialization code, a typical client of our server will create a user interface and subscribe to the server database. A typical calling sequence might look like:

```
B% dp_RPC $server Subscribe
B% CreateUserInterface
```

---

* That is, assuming the application does not request a return value using the -callback option.

By replacing the dp_RPC call in the second line with dp_RDO, the client can create the user interface while the server executes the Subscribe code.

dp_RDO has two important options: -callback and -onerror. The -callback option is used when the return value from the remote procedure call is of interest to the client, but you want to use the parallelism provided by dp_RDO. For example, suppose we modify the Subscribe procedure to return a subscription code that the client uses to identify itself to the server.

```
A% set code 0
0
A% proc Subscribe {} {
       global dp_rpcFile clientList code
       if {[lsearch $clientList $dp_rpcFile] == -1} {
           lappend clientList $dp_rpcFile
       }
       incr code
       return $code
   }
```

You might think that the client can not use dp_RDO to call Subscribe because it needs to return a value to the caller. The -callback flag to dp_RDO is designed to handle this case. The argument to -callback is a Tcl script that is evaluated in the client with the return value from the remote call appended. For example, the following code calls the modified Subscribe procedure using dp_RDO and sets the local variable scode to the subscription code:

```
B% dp_RDO $server -callback {set scode} Subscribe
B% CreateUserInterface
```

When Subscribe completes, the Tcl fragment set scode is evaluated in B with the new identifier appended.

One problem that can arise using -callback is synchronizing the client and server. For example, suppose the client, after creating the user interface, must execute a procedure on the server, that takes the identifier returned from the Subscribe function as an argument. You might try to write this code to call the procedure:

```
B% proc Setup {} {
       global server scode
       dp_RDO $server -callback {set scode} Subscribe
       dp_RDO $server puts $scode
   }
B% Setup
can't read "scode": no such variable
```

This code fails on the second dp_RDO because the client has not processed the callback of the first dp_RDO, which sets the scode variable. This problem is called a client/server *synchronization problem*. To understand the solution to the synchronization problem, we must take a brief detour into the implementation of Tcl-DP.

Tcl-DP uses TCP sockets for dp_RDO and dp_RPC. In Unix, sockets are represented by files that are *readable* when the socket has data waiting to be read. Tk contains a mechanism, called *file handlers*, that automatically invokes a C callback function whenever a file is *readable*. The callback is issued from the `Tk_DoOneEvent` function, which invokes callbacks in response to X window events, file events, and timer events.

Tcl-DP uses file handlers and TCP sockets to implement the RPC mechanisms. In particular, `dp_MakeRPCClient` creates a socket and a file handler on the socket that reads strings that come in on the socket, evaluates them as Tcl commands, and returns the result. But the file handler associated with a Tcl-DP socket is not invoked until the client calls `Tk_DoOneEvent`.

The implementation of `-onerror` and `-callback` use `dp_RDO`. In the preceding example, A uses `dp_RDO` to set `scode` in B. Since the response by A is passed to B using `dp_RDO`, `scode` is not set until the client calls `Tk_DoOneEvent`. So, to solve the synchronization problem, we have to call `Tk_DoOneEvent` until the server's response is received.

Tcl-DP provides two Tcl commands to call `Tk_DoOneEvent`: `dp_update` and `dp_waitvariable`. `dp_update` calls `Tk_DoOneEvent` repeatedly until no X, timer, or file events are pending. `Dp_waitvariable` calls `Tk_DoOneEvent` until a specified variable changes value. The solution to the synchronization problem can use `dp_waitvariable`:

```
B% proc Setup {} {
       global server scode
       dp_RDO $server -callback {set scode} Subscribe
       dp_waitvariable scode
       dp_RDO $server puts $scode
   }
B% Setup
```

`dp_waitvariable` calls `Tk_DoOneEvent` repeatedly until `scode` changes value, which happens when the server sends back the subscription identifier.

In addition to the `-callback` option, `dp_RDO` has a `-onerror` option that specifies a Tcl fragment that will be evaluated if the remote procedure call terminates with an error. This option can be used, for example, to trap errors that occur in the remote execution of `dp_RDO`. To see `-onerror` in action, try the following fragment:

```
B% dp_RDO $server -onerror puts Greeting arg1 arg2
```

Since the `Greeting` procedure only takes one argument, this `dp_RDO` call will trigger an error, which will be printed on the screen using `puts`.

We cannot finish our basic discussion without describing how to close connections. Since the connection identifier is an ordinary file descriptor, the Tcl `close` command can be used to terminate the connection. For example, the command

```
B% close $server
```

shuts down the connection between B and A.

An Extended Example

To show how the functions described in this section are used in an application, we will show you how to build a simple distributed whiteboard. Before showing how this application works across a network, it is simplest to learn how the nondistributed version works.

The Tk code for a standalone whiteboard, which can be found in the file *wb.tcl* in the *examples/whiteboard* subdirectory in the Tcl-DP distribution, is shown in Example 8-1.

Example 8-1: A Simple Tcl/Tk Whiteboard

```
1    #!/usr/local/bin/wish -f
2    wm grid . 1 1 1 1
3
4    # Create menu bar:
5    frame .menubar -relief ridge
6    menubutton .menubar.file -text "File" -menu.menubar.file.menu
7    pack .menubar.file -side left
8    menubutton .menubar.object -text "Objects" -menu \
9        .menubar.object.menu
10   pack .menubar.object -side left
11   pack .menubar -side top -fill both
12   menu .menubar.file.menu
13   .menubar.file.menu add command -label "Exit"-command exit
14   menu .menubar.object.menu
15   .menubar.object.menu add command -label "Clear"-command \
16       ".c delete all"
17   .menubar.object.menu add command -label "Circle"-command \
18       "CreateCircle"
19
20   # Create canvas, procs, bindings
21   canvas .c -background green
22   pack .c -fill both
23
24   proc CreateRect {x y} {
25       .c create rectangle $x $y $x $y -width 4 -outline white
26   }
27   proc CreateCircle {} {
28       set i [.c create oval 150 150 170 170 -fill skyblue]
29       .c bind $i <Any-Enter> ".c itemconfig $i -fill red"
30       .c bind $i <Any-Leave> ".c itemconfig $i -fill SkyBlue2"
31       .c bind $i <2> "PlotDown .c $i %x %y"
32       .c bind $i <B2-Motion> "PlotMove .c $i %x %y"
33   }
34   proc Clear {} {.c delete all}
35   proc PlotDown {w item x y} {
36       global plot
37       $w raise $item
```

```
38          set plot(lastX) $x
39          set plot(lastY) $y
40      }
41   proc PlotMove {w item x y} {
42          global plot
43          $w move $item [expr $x-$plot(lastX)] [expr$y-$plot(lastY)]
44          set plot(lastX) $x
45          set plot(lastY) $y
46      }
47
48   bind .c <B1-Motion> {CreateRect %x %y}
```

This code creates a canvas and a menubar, as shown in Figure 8-3. The functions CreateRect and CreateCircle create rectangles and circles on the canvas. The function Clear deletes all objects on the canvas. The functions PlotDown and PlotMove work together to move a previously created circle.

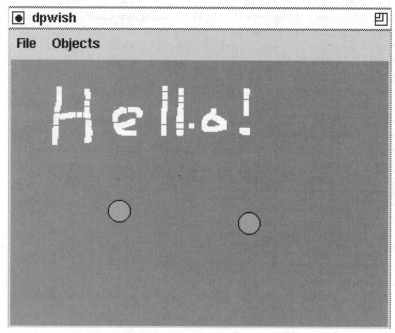

Figure 8-3: A Simple Whiteboard

The whiteboard is used as follows. To create rectangles, press the left button down in the main window and move the mouse while holding the button down. A trail of small, 4-by-4 pixel squares will follow the mouse on the canvas. Internally, this response is implemented by binding (at line 48) the Button-1-motion event to call the CreateRect function.

To create a circle, select the Circle menu item in the Object menu. You can move the circle to a new position by pressing the middle button down while the mouse is over the circle and moving the mouse. To clear the whiteboard, select the Clear menu item in the Object menu.

This code can be adapted to a shared whiteboard by broadcasting every change to the canvas, whether through bindings or procedure calls, to the other whiteboards. To handle the broadcasts, we will use a centralized server process as a reflector. Each client connects and subscribes to the whiteboard. The clients and server form a"star," with the server at the center as shown in Figure 8-4. When a client wants to execute a whiteboard command, it sends the command to the server, which broadcasts the command to all the clients, where they are executed.

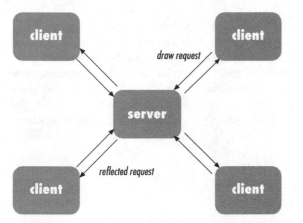

Figure 8-4: Architecture of the Shared Whiteboard Example

The Tcl-DP code to create the server is shown in Example 8-2. The call to dp_MakeRPCServer on line 2 initializes the server and listens for connections from clients on port 4544. A client connects to the whiteboard by executing dp_MakeRPCClient and calling the Subscribe procedure. The server maintains a list of all clients connected to it in the global variable clients and a history of all whiteboard commands in the global variable log. When a new client is added, the commands in the log are sent to the new client so that its display is brought up to date with the other clients. The command Publish is called when a client executes a whiteboard command. It writes the command to the log and broadcasts the command to all the clients.

Example 8-2: Tcl-DP Shared Whiteboard Server

```
1       #!/usr/local/bin/dpwish -f
2       dp_MakeRPCServer 4544
3
4       set clients {}
5       set log {}
6
7       proc Subscribe {} {
8           global dp_rpcFile clients log
9           lappend clients $dp_rpcFile
10          foreach cmd $log {
11              eval dp_RDO $dp_rpcFile $cmd
12          }
13      }
```

```
14
15   proc Publish {args} {
16       global clients log
17       lappend log $args
18       foreach i $clients {
19           eval "dp_RDO $i $args"
20       }
21   }
```

The modified client code is shown in Example 8-3, with the modified code in bold-face. Lines 2–5 connect the client to the server. The DoCmd procedure defined in lines 6–9 uses dp_RDO to call Publish in the server, which sends whiteboard commands to the clients. The CreateRect, CreateCircle, and Clear routines use DoCmd. It is interesting to note that the client does not directly execute the commands creating rectangles and circles when the user requests them; instead, the client simply sends the commands to the server's log file and waits to be updated by the server.

Example 8-3: Tcl-DP Shared Whiteboard Client

```
1    #!/usr/local/bin/dpwish -f
2    puts "Enter hostname of server:"
3    gets stdin host
4    set server [dp_MakeRPCClient $host 4544]
5    dp_RDO $server Subscribe
6    proc DoCmd {args} {
7        global server
8        eval dp_RDO $server Publish $args
9    }
10   wm grid . 1 1 1 1
11
12   # Create menu bar:
13   frame .menubar -relief ridge
14   menubutton .menubar.file -text "File" -menu.menubar.file.menu
15   pack .menubar.file -side left
16   menubutton .menubar.object -text "Objects" -menu \
17       .menubar.object.menu
18   pack .menubar.object -side left
19   pack .menubar -side top -fill both
20   menu .menubar.file.menu
21   .menubar.file.menu add command -label "Exit"-command exit
22   menu .menubar.object.menu
23   .menubar.object.menu add command -label "Clear"-command DoCmd
24       .c delete all"
25   .menubar.object.menu add command -label "Circle" \
26       -command "DoCmd CreateCircle"
27
28   # Create canvas, procs, bindings
29   canvas .c -background green
30   pack .c -fill both
31
32   proc CreateRect {x y} {
```

```
33              DoCmd .c create rectangle $x $y $x $y -width 4 \
34                    -outline white
35    }
36    proc CreateCircle {} {
37              set i [.c create oval 150 150 170 170 -fill skyblue]
38              .c bind $i <Any-Enter> "DoCmd .c itemconfig $i -fill red"
39              .c bind $i <Any-Leave> "DoCmd .c itemconfig $i \
40                    -fill SkyBlue2"
41              .c bind $i <2> "DoCmd   plotDown .c $i %x %y"
42              .c bind $i <B2-Motion> "DoCmd plotMove .c $i %x %y"
43    }
44    proc Clear {} {DoCmd .c delete all}
45    proc plotDown {w item x y} {
46              global plot
47              $w raise $item
48              set plot(lastX) $x
49              set plot(lastY) $y
50    }
51    proc plotMove {w item x y} {
52              global plot
53              $w move $item [expr $x-$plot(lastX)] [expr$y-$plot(lastY)]
54              set plot(lastX) $x
55              set plot(lastY) $y
56    }
57
58    bind .c <B1-Motion> {CreateRect %x %y}
```

Security

One problem with this server is that any client can connect, and a connected client can execute any command. Tcl-DP uses two mechanisms to handle these two different security holes.

The first level of defense is an optional "login" procedure that can be supplied with the dp_MakeRPCServer command. This procedure allows a server to specify a Tcl procedure that will be executed when a client connects to the server. The procedure is called with the file handle and IP address of the new client (e.g., *file4* and 128.32.133.117) as arguments. For example, the following server logs all connection requests to a file.

```
A% set logFile [open /tmp/connect.log w]
A% proc LogConnection {file addr} {
     global logFile
     puts $logFile "Connection accepted from $addr on $file"
   }
A% dp_MakeRPCServer 4545 LogConnection
```

The login procedure can be used to prevent illegal connections. If the connection is determined to be illegal, the login procedure should return an error. For example, the following server allows connections only from hosts in the 128.32.134 subnet.

```
A% proc CheckConnection {file addr} {
     if {[[string match $addr 128.32.134.*] != 1]} {
```

```
                error "Host not authorized"
        }
    }
A% dp_MakeRPCServer 4545 CheckConnection
```

The default login procedure for Tcl-DP is `dp_CheckHost`, which provides a simple access control list mechanism, similar to `xhost` in the X window system, for limiting connections to a set of IP host addresses. The access control list is modified by the `dp_host` command. For example, the following Tcl-DP commands allow connections from machines in the 128.32.134 subnet except 128.32.134.117, or from the machine named *mayo.sandwich.com*. Once executed, the `dp_host` restrictions apply to every server that Tcl-DP subsequently creates.

```
A% dp_host -
A% dp_host +128.32.134.*
A% dp_host -128.32.134.117
A% dp_host +mayo.sandwich.com
A% dp_MakeRPCServer 4567
```

By default, connections from any host are allowed (equivalent to `dp_host +`). The `dp_host` command and its associated `loginFunc` are implemented entirely in Tcl. They can be found in the file *$dp_library/acl.tcl* in the distribution. This code can be used as an example for building more complex login security functions. For example, a server could maintain a list of authorized users and passwords and require a client to explicitly log in. Or a server could use a system like PGP or Kerberos to authenticate clients.

The login procedure can prevent rogue users from accessing a server, but even innocent users can accidentally run commands with horrible side effects. Such mistakes are particularly disastrous if the server is running as root. For example, we all want to stop someone from accidentally running

```
B% dp_RDO $server exec rm -rf /
```

To prevent such catastrophes, `dp_MakeRPCServer` takes a second optional argument, called the *check command*, which checks each command from a `dp_RPC` or `dp_RDO` call before it is run. The return code from the check command specifies whether to disallow the command, to continue checking sub commands, or to allow the command to be executed with no further checking. If the procedure returns a normal value, the command is allowed and no further checking is performed. If the option `-code  break` is used with the return, the command is disallowed. If `-code  continue` is used, the command is allowed but nested commands are checked. Notice that the nested checking allows commands like

```
B% dp_RPC $server eval rm -rf /
```

to be caught.

To illustrate the use of check commands, the following code defines a procedure that allows `puts` to be run on standard error, `set` to be run with one argument, `Subscribe` to be run with no further checking, and `eval`, `catch`, and `if` to be run with embedded command checking. All other commands are disallowed.

```
A% proc CheckCmd {cmd args} {
```

```
        case $cmd in {
            Subscribe return;
            puts{
                set file [lindex $args 0]
                if {[string compare $file stderr] != 0]} {
                    return -code break
                }
                return;
                }
        set{
                if {[llength $args] != 1} {
                    return -code break
                }
                return;
                }
            eval {return -code continue}
            catch {return -code continue}
            if  {return -code continue}
        }
        return -code break;
    }
```

We will now use both features to make the whiteboard program more secure. We will allow only clients whose IP-address is in the *whiteboard-clients* file to connect, and we will verify that the clients are executing legal commands. The modified code is shown in Example 8-4.

Example 8-4: Extra Commands for Secure Tcl-DP Shared Whiteboard Server

```
 1  # Set the list of allowed clients from whiteboard-clients
 2  set f [open whiteboard-clients r]
 3  dp_host -
 4  while {[get $f host] != -1} {
 5          dp_host +$host
 6  }
 7  close $f
 8
 9  # The only allowed commands are Subscribe and Publish
10  proc WhiteboardCmdCheck {cmd args} {
12      case $cmd in {
13          Subscribe return
14          Publish return
15      }
16      return -code break;
17  }
18
19  dp_MakeRPCServer 4545 dp_CheckHost WhiteboardCmdCheck
```

Of course, the server can still execute commands in the client. This capability can cause problems in environments where the user cannot verify that a server is authentic. For example, a client can innocently connect to a server and the server can remove all files in the client environment. To allow inbound RPCs to be checked on any socket (client side or server side), use the `dp_SetCheckCmd` function. For example, to add client-side command checking, the client can execute the following command:

```
dp_SetCheckCmd $server ClientCheckCommand
```

where `ClientCheckCommand` is a command checking procedure similar to `WhiteboardCmdCheck` in Example 8-4. Alternatively, the client check command can be specified when the connection is made:

```
set server [dp_MakeRPCClient $host 4544 ClientCheckCommand]
```

Cleanup

In distributed programs like the whiteboard example, clients and servers crash or shut down without warning. These crashes can cause unexpected, often fatal, errors to occur. For example, if a whiteboard client dies unexpectedly, the server wants to remove the client from the `clients` variable. The `dp_atclose` command is designed to handle such cleanup actions automatically.

`dp_atclose` associates a list of Tcl commands with a file. Just before the file is closed, which happens automatically if a connection is broken, each command in the list is called. The first argument to `dp_atclose` is a file identifier (e.g., `$server`) that specifies the target file or connection, and the second argument is a command. Valid commands are `append`, `remove`, `appendUnique`, `insert`, and `list`. `append` adds a new callback to the end of the list. `remove` deletes a previous appended callback. `appendUnique` adds a callback to the end of the list, but only if it is not already part of the list. `Insert` places a callback at the beginning of the list, and list returns the current callback list. Table 8-2 lists the valid commands and arguments for `dp_atclose`. Tcl-DP has another cleanup command, `dp_atexit`, that is similar to `dp_atclose`. `dp_atexit` callbacks execute just before the program exits.

Table 8-2: Arguments for dp_atclose and dp_atexit

Command	Arguments	Description
append	callback	Invokes callback when file closes
appendUnique	callback	Invokes callback precisely once when file closes

Table 8-2: Continued

Command	Arguments	Description
list	-	Returns file closing callback list
remove	callback	Removes callback from file closing callback list
insert	callback	Inserts callback at beginning of callback list

We can use `dp_atclose` in the whiteboard program to remove a client that has crashed from the `clients` variable by making the following change to the `Sub-scribe` command. The modified code is shown in italics:

Continued

```
A% proc Subscribe {} {
    global dp_rpcFile clients log
    lappend clients $dp_rpcFile
    dp_atclose $dp_rpcFile append \
        "set clients [ldelete $dp_rpcFile $clients]"
    foreach cmd $log {
        eval dp_RDO $dp_rpcFile $cmd
    }
}
```

The Name Server

As distributed applications get more complex, the tasks of starting and stopping servers, locating a server and the port on which it is listening, and keeping track of the server state become more of a problem. For example, in our whiteboard program, we want to start the client application and have it connect to a running server if one is available or start one if it is not running. The problem is how do we locate a running server or start one if it is not running? The Tcl-DP *name server* solves this problem.

The name server associates a name with each process that is patterned after Unix file-names. For example, the name of the whiteboard server might be */demo/whiteboard*.

When the server starts up, it uses the procedure `NS_SrvcInit` to contact the name server and declare its name. The prefix for all name server commands is "NS_." For example, the following command tells the name server that the whiteboard server is running on *mayo.sandwich.com*, port 4500:

```
A% NS_SrvcInit /demo/whiteboard mayo.sandwich.com 4500
```

Registering a name with the name server adds it to the list of servers that the name server knows about. We call a registered name a *service*. When a whiteboard client wants to locate the whiteboard server, it issues an `NS_GetServiceConn` call to find the service. `NS_GetServiceConn` takes the name of a service as an argument, contacts the name server, and returns a host and port number where the server can be contacted. For example, the code

```
B% set whiteboardServer [NS_GetServiceConn /demo/whiteboard]
```

queries the name server to get the host and port number of the whiteboard server, which can be passed to `dp_MakeRPCClient`.

If the server is not running when `NS_GetServiceConn` is called, the name server can start the process for you if the service is registered as an *autostart* service. Only processes marked as autostart in the file *$dp_library/ns/nsconfig* can be started automatically. For example, adding the following lines to this file makes the whiteboard an autostart service:

```
ns_Register addService /demo/whiteboard mayo.sandwich.com \
            "dptcl -f /home/tcldp/ns/wbServer.tcl"
ns_Register aliasService /demo/whiteboard /wbServer
```

The name server can associate several names, called aliases, with a single process. A call to NS_GetServiceConn searches through service names and their aliases for a match. The name server supports pattern matching on service names similar to Unix filename matching to locate servers. The interface to this pattern matching function is NS_FindService. NS_FindService returns a list of all the matching names, similar to the way the Tcl glob command returns a list of filenames that match a pattern. For example, the following call locates all servers in the demo tree:

```
B% set demoServers [NS_FindService /demo/*]
```

The use of the slash ("/") character to give a hierarchical structure to the process names is only a convention. NS_FindService uses the Tcl string match command to search for matches. Consequently, you can establish any naming scheme you like, but we encourage you to use the naming convention presented earlier (i.e., use slash characters) to ensure uniformity.

The name server is a network-wide service built using Tcl-DP. It runs on a well known host and port number in your network. The exact host and port are specified in the file *$dp_library/ns/nsconfig.tcl*. This immediately brings to mind two questions: Who starts the name server, and what happens if the machine that runs the name server crashes? The answer to the first question is that the name server is typically started by an entry in */etc/rc.local* when a designated machine boots. The answer to the second question is that backup copies of the name server can be run at the same time as the primary server. The machines on which the backup server are run are specified in the file *$dp_library/ns/nsconfig.tcl*. All name server functions accessible from the client, such as NS_GetServiceConn and NS_Find-Service, locate the primary server and connect to it. If the primary name server crashes, the backups elect a new primary name server. More details on the design and implementation of the name server are available elsewhere.*

Tcl-DP Communication Services

This section shows you how to use Tcl-DP's interfaces to TCP, UDP, and IP-multicast. It also shows you how to query and set various properties of sockets, like buffer sizes and blocking properties, to gain more control over the properties of the communication channel. Finally, this section will show you how to access the Internet Domain Name Service (DNS) using Tcl-DP. The DNS maps internet addresses (e.g., 128.32.149.117) to host names (e.g., *toe.cs.berkeley.edu*).

Review of Berkeley Sockets

Before discussing Tcl-DP's mechanisms for connecting two processes, we will briefly review Berkeley sockets. Sockets come in several varieties, distinguished by the communication protocol (e.g., TCP or UDP), how the socket is identified, and whether or not the socket is the connection initiator. In this section, we will discuss the primitives used for *connected* (i.e., TCP) sockets. We will discuss the primitives associated with unconnected (UDP and IP-multicast) sockets later.

---

* P. T. Liu, B. L. Smith, and L. A. Rowe, "Tcl-DP Name Server," Proc. 3rd Tcl/Tk Workshop, Toronto, Canada, July 1995. Available from USENIX Association.

TCP Sockets

Connecting two processes using TCP is a three-step process, illustrated in Figure 8-5. First, one process, say A, creates a *listening* socket with an associated *name* so that other processes can contact it. The name can be either a Unix filename or an Internet address and port number. Second, another process (B) creates another socket and *connects* to A's listening socket. Third, A *accepts* the connection, which creates a new socket so that other processes can contact A using A's listening socket.

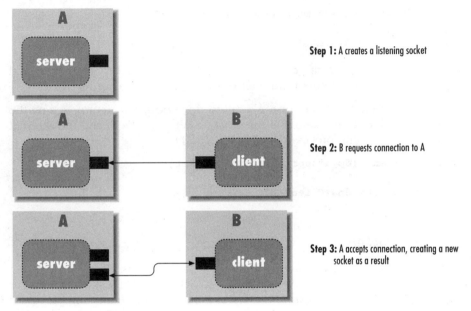

Step 1: A creates a listening socket

Step 2: B requests connection to A

Step 3: A accepts connection, creating a new socket as a result

Figure 8-5: Connecting Processes Using TCP

In Tcl-DP, dp_connect is used for steps one and two, and dp_accept for step three. Dp_connect will create a listening socket if the -server flag is provided. For example, the following command creates a listening socket on port 1905 and assigns the socket identifier (*file4*) to the variable listeningSocket.

```
A% set info [dp_connect -server 1905]
file4 1905
A% set listeningSocket [lindex $info 0]
file4
```

The third parameter to dp_connect is the port number. Only one socket can be associated with a given port at any time. If another socket is already open on that port, dp_connect will return an error. You can have the operating system select an unused port by specifying a port number of 0 to dp_connect. No matter who selects the port number, dp_connect will return a list of two values: the identifier for the socket and its port number.

After creating the listening socket, the server typically waits for a connection to arrive by calling dp_accept, which will return when another process attempts to connect to the socket. For example, the following code causes A to block while waiting for a client:

```
A% set newClient [dp_accept $listeningSocket]
```

Another process connects to A using another form of dp_connect. In this form, the hostname of the machine on which the server is running, and the port number of the server socket, are passed as parameters to dp_connect. If the hostname of A is *mayo.sandwich.com*, the following code will connect machine B to A:

```
B% set info [dp_connect mayo.sandwich.com 1905]
file4 3833
B% set s2 [lindex $info 0]
```

As with the previous call to dp_connect, a handle to the socket (e.g., *file4*) and the operating system selected port number of the socket (3833) are returned.

B's attempt to connect to A will cause A's call to dp_accept to return, setting the newClient variable to the handle of the new socket (e.g., *file5*) and the Internet address of the connecting process (e.g. 128.83.218.21).

```
A% set newClient [dp_accept $listeningSocket]
file5 128.83.218.21
A% set s1 [lindex $newClient 0]
file5
```

Unix Domain Sockets

The previous example created *Internet domain* sockets. That is, B uses an Internet address and port number to rendezvous with A's socket. On Unix systems, another naming scheme, called Unix *domain* sockets, can be used for connecting processes if they reside on the same machine. In this case, a file name (e.g., */tmp/mysocket*) is used to name the socket. The following example shows a connection using Unix domain sockets.

Server code:

```
% set f [dp_connect -server /tmp/mysocket]
file4
% set s1 [dp_accept $f]
```

Client Code:

```
% set s2 [dp_connect /tmp/mysocket]
file4
```

Regardless of whether Unix or Internet domain sockets are used, processes communicate using the handles of the sockets as arguments to Tcl-DPfunction. In the examples, these handles are stored in the variables s1 and s2.

Sending and Receiving Data

The simplest way to send data from one application to another is to use the Tcl functions gets, read, and puts. For example, in the following fragment B sends the string "Hello world" to A:

```
B% puts $s2 "hello world"
```

To receive the string, A calls gets:

```
A% gets $s1
hello
```

Another interface for sending and receiving data is dp_send and dp_receive. dp_send takes the same arguments as puts and serves the same function. dp_receive is similar to the Tcl read command, except it takes an optional -peek flag indicating that the data should be read from the socket, but not consumed, so that a subsequent call to dp_receive will see the same data. In addition, if the connection is ever broken, dp_send and dp_receive automatically close the socket.

TCP sockets provide a stream interface, which can cause unexpected results if you want to use them to send messages between processes. For example, suppose B sends several messages to A. When A reads its socket, the messages might be concatenated or only part of a message may be present. The following code fragment shows this effect in action. If B executes the following commands

```
B% dp_send $s2 "message 1"
B% dp_send $s2 "message 2"
```

when A calls dp_receive, it gets both messages at once:

```
A% dp_receive $s1
message 1
message 2
```

Since some applications want to preserve message boundaries and want the reliability of TCP, Tcl-DP provides two functions—dp_packetSend and dp_packet-Receive—that provide message-oriented delivery. For example, suppose B uses dp_packetSend instead of dp_send in the example just shown:

```
B% dp_packetSend $s2 "message 1"
B% dp_packetSend $s2 "message 2"
```

When A calls dp_packetReceive, it gets one message per function call.

```
A% dp_packetReceive $s1
message 1
A% dp_packetReceive $s1
message 2
```

It is possible that only part of the message is available at the time dp_packetReceive is called. In this case, dp_packetReceive will buffer the partial result internally and return an empty string. A subsequent call to dp_packetReceive will return the entire packet.

To preserve message boundaries, dp_packetSend attaches a binary header onto the message, which dp_packetReceive strips. The presence of this header means that applications must be careful about intermixing calls to dp_packet-Send and dp_packetReceive with dp_send and dp_receive, and other data transmission functions.

File Handlers

So far, the socket functions we have seen block if no data is present on the socket. That is, the function call will not return until some data arrives. Blocking can cause problems in some situations, for example, if a program needs to read data from several connections at once. To address this problem, Tcl-DP provides a mechanism called *file handlers* that arranges for a Tcl function to be called whenever the file becomes *readable* or *writable*. A socket becomes readable when another process attempts to connect to it, in the case of a listening socket; or when it has data waiting at its input, in the case of a data socket. A data socket becomes writable whenever a call to `dp_send`, `puts`, or `dp_packetSend` will not block.*

The file handler callback procedure takes two parameters. The first parameter, called the *mode*, indicates whether the socket has become readable or writable. It will be `r` if the socket is readable, or `w` if the socket is writable. The second parameter is the handle of the socket. For example, the following fragment arranges for A to accept a new connection whenever one is requested on its listening socket. The filehandler callback procedure `MyAccept` calls `dp_accept` to accept the connection, prints a message on the screen, and adds the new socket to the `socketList` variable.

```
A% proc MyAccept {mode file} {
      global socketList
      set info [dp_accept $file]
      set newSocket [lindex $info 0]
      puts "Accepted connection from [lindex $info 1]"
      lappend socketList $newSocket
   }
A% dp_filehandler $listeningSocket r MyAccept
```

The call to `dp_filehandler` specifies that the callback procedure for `MyAccept` is to be called whenever `listeningSocket` becomes readable. The second parameter to `dp_filehandler` (`r` in the example above) indicates that the file handler should be called only when the socket is readable. If `w` is used for this parameter, the function will be called when the socket becomes writable.

If an error occurs when a file handler callback executes, the file handler is automatically removed to prevent the program from going into an infinite loop if the file handler does not consume the data at the socket. You can manually remove a file handler by calling `dp_filehandler` without the `mode` or `callback` parameters.

Another way of detecting if a file is readable or writable is to use the `dp_isready` command. `dp_isready` takes a file handle as a parameter and returns a list of two Boolean values (0 or 1). The first element of the return value indicates whether the file is readable. If it is 0, then any call that attempts to read data from the file (e.g., `gets` or `dp_receive`) will block. The second element of the return value indicates whether the file is writable. If it is 0, then any call that attempts to write data to the file (e.g., `puts` or `dp_send`) will block.

---

* Such calls can block if they are communicating over a particularly slow connection, since the system will buffer only a limited amount of data. The amount of data buffered can be adjusted using the `dp_socketOption` command.

For example, if a call to read data on `s1` would block, `dp_isready` returns 0 1:

```
A% dp_isready $s1
0 1
```

If B sends some data to A:

```
B% dp_send $s2 "hi there"
```

a call to read data on `s1` would not block, so `dp_isready` returns 1 1:

```
A% dp_isready $s1
1 1
A% dp_receive $s1
hi there
```

A typical situation where the second (write) value would be zero is when you've sent a lot of data on a socket and you need to wait for the receiving side to consume it.

Example: A Simple FTP Server

Suppose you wanted to implement a simple FTP style server using Tcl-DP. One way to implement it is to create a new TCP connection for each file transfer, which would be a four-step process, as illustrated in Figure 8-6.

1. The client opens the output file and creates a listening socket (the *connect socket*).

2. The client sends the following information to the server: the client's hostname, the port number of the connect socket, and the filename to transfer.

3. The server opens the input file and a TCP connection to the client's connect socket, which gives the server a *data socket*. It then enters a loop where it repeatedly reads the input file and sends the data over to the client. It then closes the data socket and input file.

4. Meanwhile, the client accepts the connection on the connect socket, closes it, and enters a loop where it receives data from the server and writes it to the output file. If `dp_receive` ever returns an error, it means the connection was broken, presumably because the transfer is complete.* Since `dp_receive` automatically closes the file when the connection is broken, the client only has to close the output file before returning.

The Tcl-DP code in Examples 8-5 and 8-6 implement this protocol. The client uses `dp_RPC` to implement step 2 by calling the `SendFile` function in the server.

Example 8-5: Server Code for Tcl-DP FTP Example

```
9    dp_MakeRPCServer 1905
10   proc SendFile {host port filename} {
11       set inFile [open $filename r]
12       set info [dp_connect $host $port]
```

---

* Of course, the connection could be lost for other reasons, like the server crashing. A better implementation of the client and server would handle this case but complicate the example.

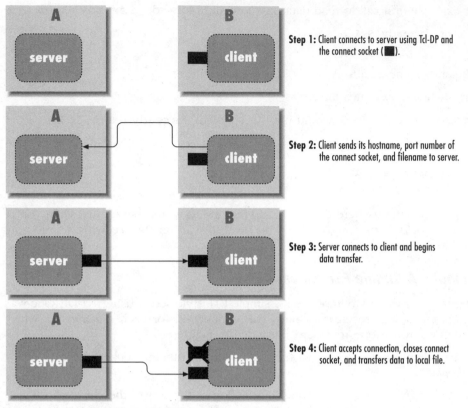

Step 1: Client connects to server using Tcl-DP and the connect socket (▬).

Step 2: Client sends its hostname, port number of the connect socket, and filename to server.

Step 3: Server connects to client and begins data transfer.

Step 4: Client accepts connection, closes connect socket, and transfers data to local file.

Figure 8-6: Mechanics of an FTP-Style File Transfer Using Tcl-DP

```
13        set socket [lindex $info 0]
14        while {![eof $inFile]} {
15                set data [read $inFile 8192]
16                dp_send $socket $data nonewline
17        }
18      close $inFile
19      close $socket
20    }
```

Example 8-6: Client Code for Tcl-DP FTP Example

```
1    proc Connect {serverHost} {
2        return [dp_MakeRPCClient $serverHost 1905]
3    }
4    proc GetFile {server remoteFilename localFilename} {
5        set outFile [open $localFilename w]
6        set cInfo [dp_connect -server 0]
7        set cSocket [lindex $cInfo 0]
8        set cPort [lindex $cInfo 1]
9        dp_RDO $server SendFile [dp_hostname] $cPort$remoteFilename
```

```
10     set dInfo [dp_accept $cSocket]
11     close $cSocket
12     set dSocket [lindex $dInfo 0]
13     while {1} {
14             if [catch {dp_receive $dSocket} data] {
15                 break;
16             }
17             puts -nonewline $outFile $data
18             puts -nonewline "#"
19             flush stdout
20     }
21     puts ""
22     close $outFile
23   }
24   set s [dp_MakeRPCClient server.company.com 1905]
25   GetFile $s /tmp/motd server-motd
```

TCP Socket Options

A socket has many parameters that affect its behavior. Tcl-DP sets these parameters to reasonable default values when the socket is created. *Socket options* give you control over these options. They can be used to specify whether function calls block, how data is buffered, and the reliability of the connection. They are accessed using dp_socketOption, which takes two or three parameters, similar to configure requests on Tk widgets. The first parameter is the socket identifier (e.g., file4), the second is the *property* of the socket you want to examine or modify, and the third parameter, if present, is the new value for the property. If the third parameter is not supplied, the current value of the property is returned. The following paragraphs discuss the properties relevant to TCP sockets, which are summarized in Table 8-3.

Table 8-3: TCP Socket Properties Set By the dp_socketOption Command

Property	Legal Values	Default	Description
sendBuffer	1-64K*	> 8192	Size of TCP send buffer
recvBuffer	1-64K	> 8192	Size of TCP receive buffer
noblock	yes, no	no	Will calls on the socket will block?
autoClose	yes, no	yes	Will the socket automatically close and remove file handlers if the connection is broken?
linger	>=0	0	Blocking time on close to ensure data delivery
reuseAddr	yes, no	yes	Allow local address reuse?

* The range varies from system to system, as does the default This is a typical vaule.

- **Buffer Sizes**: When a process writes data to a socket, the operating system copies that data into an internal buffer, called the *send buffer*, where it remains until its transfer is acknowledged by the receiver. As long as there is sufficient free space in the send buffer, calls like dp_send that write data to the socket will not block. Similarly, the receiver's operating system has an internal buffer (the *receive buffer*) where it stores incoming data until the client executes a call like dp_receive to read it.

  You can set or query the size of the send and receive buffers for each socket using the sendBuffer and recvBuffer properties. For example, the following code prints out the current size of the send and receive buffers and then sets them both to 32 KBytes.

  ```
  A% puts "Send buffer size: [dp_socketOption $s1 sendBuffer]"
  Send buffer size: 8192
  A% puts "Receive buffer size: [dp_socketOption $s1recvBuffer]"
  Receive buffer size: 8192
  A% dp_socketOption $s1 sendBuffer 32768
  32768
  A% dp_socketOption $s1 recvBuffer 32768
  32768
  ```

  Each operating system imposes certain restrictions on the maximum size of the buffers (it's rarely greater than 64 KBytes). In some cases, when and how you can resize them is also restricted. The best way to figure it out for your personal configuration is by experimentation.

- **Blocking Behavior**: By default, calls that write data to a socket will block if there is not enough room left in the send buffers, and calls that read data from a socket will block if there is no data waiting to be read. These behaviors can be changed by using the noblock property. Noblock is a Boolean valued property (yes or no).

  The first line of code queries the current value of the noblock property. The second line makes the socket non-blocking, so that subsequent calls to dp_receive do not block. If no data is available on the socket, the call to dp_receive returns an empty string.

  ```
  A% dp_socketOption $s1 noblock
  no
  A% dp_socketOption $s1 noblock yes
  A% dp_receive $s1
  ```

- **Automatic Socket Cleanup**: By default, dp_send and dp_receive automatically close a socket and remove its file handlers when the connection is broken. If an application programmer wants to close the file manually, this behavior can be suppressed by setting the autoClose property of the socket. autoClose is a Boolean valued property (yes or no).

- **Linger**: When a socket is closed and unsent data is present in the kernel buffers associated with that socket, the operating system will wait until all the unsent data has been delivered before closing the connection. Since this could take forever (e.g., if the network partitions), a timeout value is used to ensure that the socket eventually closes. The linger socket option is used to set this timeout. The linger time is measured in *clock ticks*, a system-dependent measurement of time. On most Unix systems, a clock tick is 10 milliseconds. The default `linger` time is zero, which means that the connection is immediately closed and any unsent data is discarded.

- **Reusing Port Numbers**: When a process with an open socket crashes, the operating system prevents other processes from opening a socket with the same port number until enough time has passed that any old packets floating around in the network that are destined for the dead process have expired. If the boolean property `reuseAddr` is set to `yes`, processes can reuse the port number in question immediately.

UDP

TCP sockets provide reliable, in-order data delivery with a stream interface. In contrast, UDP sockets provide no guarantees on whether data will get through, but preserve message boundaries. That is, when a message is sent by one application to another using UDP, either the entire message will get through and the receiver will receive it in as a single unit, or the message will not get through at all. There is a chance that a message may be duplicated using UDP, but such duplication is rare.

To create a UDP socket using Tcl-DP, you call `dp_connect` with the `-udp` flag and port number of the socket. For example, the following command creates a UDP socket with port number 2020 in process A.

```
A% set info [dp_connect -udp 2020]
file3 2020
A% set udpA [lindex $info 0]
file3
```

As with TCP sockets, an identifier for the socket (`file3`) and the port number of the socket (`2020`) are returned. If you can pass in a port number of 0, the system will choose (and return) an unused port number.

For the examples that follow, we will need another UDP socket in process B:

```
B% set info [dp_connect -udp 4100]
file3 4100
B% set udpB [lindex $info 0]
file3
```

You can use the `dp_sendTo` command to send a message using UDP. `dp_sendTo` takes three parameters: the socket identifier (`file3`), the message ("`hello`"), and the destination address. The last parameter is created using the `dp_address` command.

`dp_address` creates, deletes, and queries *addresses*. To create an address, you must specify the host address and a port number. For example, assuming process A is running on *mayo.sandwich.com*, the following command creates an address for the socket on port 2020:

```
B% set dest [dp_address create mayo.sandwich.com 2020]
addr0
```

The return value of `dp_address create` can then be used as a parameter to `dp_sendTo`, as shown here:

```
B% dp_sendTo $udpB "Hello there" $dest
```

Process A can read the message using dp_receiveFrom:

```
A% set x [dp_receiveFrom $udpA]
addr0 {Hello there}
```

dp_receiveFrom returns a list of two values. The first is the address of the sender and the second is the message. The address can be used for replies:

```
A% dp_sendTo $udpA "Pleased to meet you" [lindex $x 0]
```

An important feature of UDP sockets is that they are *connectionless*. That is, a pair of TCP sockets is needed for each pair of processes that communicate. The two sockets are *connected*. In contrast, a single UDP socket can be used to communicate with an unlimited number of other processes, since the destination address is specified in the message. Since many operating systems place rather stringent limits on the number of open sockets in a process, but almost no limit on the number of addresses that can be created, UDP sockets are useful in applications that communicate with many other processes.

The standard functions close, dp_atclose, dp_isready, dp_filehandler, and dp_socketOption can be used with UDP sockets. The following properties can be set on UDP sockets using dp_socketOption:

- **Buffer Sizes**: Setting the buffer size of UDP sockets determines the maximum message size. For example, if the send or receive buffer is 8 KBytes and you try to send a 12-KByte message, the message will not get through and you will get an error message:

```
B% dp_socketOption $udpB sendBuffer
9000
B% dp_sendTo $udpB [format %12000d 10] $dest
error writing file3: Message too long
B% dp_socketOption $udpB sendBuffer 15000
15000
B% dp_sendTo $udpB [format %12000d 10] $dest
B%
```

  If the receive buffer is too small, the message will be dropped silently.

  As with TCP sockets, each system imposes certain restrictions on the maximum size of the buffers.

- **Blocking Behavior**: dp_receiveFrom normally blocks if there is no data waiting to be read. This behavior can be changed by using the noblock property. noblock is a Boolean-valued property (yes or no). dp_sendto never blocks.

IP-Multicast

IP-multicast sockets are similar to UDP sockets, in that they transmit whole messages unreliably using dp_sendTo, dp_receiveFrom, and dp_address, but they have the advantage that they can efficiently send data to several clients with one function call and a single address.

To use IP-multicast, you must first understand the concept of a *group address*. A group address looks like an ordinary IP address, except the range is 224.0.0.1 to 239.255.255.255 and it is not associated with a single machine, but with a group of machines. When a process sends a message to a group address, all machines that have created a multicast socket with that group address will receive it.* To become part of a group, a machine creates a socket by calling dp_connect with the -mudp flag, passing in three additional parameters: the group address, the port number, and the *time-to-live* (ttl). We will explain the meaning of the ttl parameter shortly.

For example, suppose you have a pool of Unix machines on your network that can be used for general purpose computing. You decide to use Tcl-DP to build a load monitor that reports the load on each machine in the pool to every other machine in the pool once a second so that you can find an unloaded machine. The code in Example 8-7 shows an implementation of this service that uses IP-multicast to send the load average of each machine to every other machine. The procedure GetLoad returns the load average on each machine, obtained from parsing the results of the Unix uptime command. The procedure SendReport sends a message containing the hostname and load average on the local machine to every machine in the group, and then schedules another call to SendReport using Tk's after command. SendReport takes two parameters: an IP-multicast socket and a group address. The ReceiveReport procedure is called by a file handler whenever the IP-multicast socket becomes readable (i.e., when a report has been received). ReceiveReport updates the global array load, which contains the load average of each machine in the pool. The multicast group address and port number, 225.28.199.17 and 2120, respectively, were chosen arbitrarily.

Example 8-7: A Load Monitor Using IP-Multicast

```
proc GetLoad {} {
    set info [split [exec uptime] ,]
    lindex [lindex $info 3] 2
}

proc SendReport {socket address} {
    set msg "[dp_hostname] [GetLoad]"
    dp_sendTo $socket $msg $address
    after 1000 SendReport $socket $address
}

proc RecvReport {mode socket} {
    global load
    set info [dp_receiveFrom $socket]
    set x [lindex $info 1]
    set hostName [lindex $x 0]
    set hostLoad [lindex $x 1]
    set load($hostName) $hostLoad
}

set socket [lindex [dp_connect -mudp 225.28.199.17 212016] 0]
set address [dp_address create 225.28.199.17 2120]
dp_filehandler $socket r RecvReport
SendReport $socket $address
```

---

* Unless, of course, the message is lost in the network. In this case, only some of the machines will receive the message.

Given this structure, you can find the most lightly loaded machine by searching through the `load` array. Alternatively, you could use Tk to build an interface that graphically displayed the contents of this array.

Note that, in the preceding example, each machine also receives load average reports from itself. For some applications this behavior, which is called *loopback*, may be undesirable. Loopback can be turned off using the `loopBack` socket option.

IP-multicast sockets and UDP sockets can be used to send data to each other. That is, you can use a UDP socket to send to a multicast address, and a multicast socket to send to a UDP socket. For example, the following code uses a UDP socket to report the load average to the multicast group (assuming the procedure SendReport is defined as above).

```
set udp [lindex [dp_connect -udp 0] 0]
set address [dp_address create 225.28.199.17 2120]
SendReport $udp $address
```

IP-Multicast Socket Options

IP-multicast sockets have the same socket options as UDP sockets, and four other properties that can be set using **dp_socketOption**:

- **Loop Back**: When a message is sent to a group address, the sender also receives a copy of the message. This property, called *loopback*, can be toggled by setting the `loopBack` property of the socket using `dp_socketOption`. `loopBack` is a Boolean-valued property (`yes` or `no`).

- **Time to Live (TTL)**: When an IP-multicast message is sent, one of the fields in the packet is called the time-to-live, or `ttl`, field. When the packet is routed through a gateway, the `ttl` field is decremented. If the `ttl` field is ever zero, the gateway drops the packet. The `ttl` field thus limits the lifetime of a packet, preventing packets from forever wandering through the network.

  The default value for `ttl` is specified when the socket is created and can be changed later by setting the `ttl` property on the socket. For example, the following fragment sets the `ttl` of socket to `128`:

  ```
  dp_socketOption $socket ttl 128
  ```

  The `ttl` property can be used to limit the range of a multicast. For example, to send only to hosts on your local area network, use a `ttl` value of 0. To reach all hosts within two network hops, set `ttl` to 2.

- **Adding and Dropping Membership**: A single IP-multicast socket can belong to several groups at once. When an IP-multicast socket is created, an initial group and port number are specified. You can join other groups by calling `dp_socketOption` with the `addMbr` command. For example, the following three lines of code create a socket that belongs to three groups:

  ```
  set socket [lindex [dp_connect -mudp 225.28.199.17 2120 16] 0]
  dp_socketOption $socket addMbr 224.2.12.187
  dp_socketOption $socket addMbr 235.102.89.5
  ```

The same port number is used for all three addresses. You can use `dropMbr` to remove yourself from a group:

```
dp_socketOption $socket dropMbr 235.102.89.5
```

The Domain Name Service

One use of the dp_address command is to specify the source or destination of addresses for UDP and IP-multicast sockets. Another use is to find out information about hosts and services using the dp_address info command. For example, suppose you create the following address:

```
A% set a [dp_address create fw.cs.cornell.edu 0]
addr1
```

You can find information about that address using the **dp_address** info command:

```
A% dp_address info $a
128.84.154.8 0 {alvin.cs.cornell.edu fw.cs.cornell.edu
alvin.csalvin fw.cs fw}
```

The return value shows that the IP address of *fw.cs.cornell.edu* is *128.84.154.8*, and that it is known by several names, including alvin, alvin.cs, and fw.cs.cornell.edu. The **dp_address** command can be used to create a function that returns the IP address given a host's name, or vice versa, as shown in the following two functions:

```
A% proc InetAddress {hostname} {
        set addr [dp_address create $hostname 0]
        set x [dp_address info $addr]
        dp_address delete $addr
        lindex $x 0
   }
A% proc Hostname {inetAddr} {
        set addr [dp_address create $inetAddr 0]
        set x [dp_address info $addr]
        dp_address delete $addr
        lindex [lindex $x 2] 0
   }
A% InetAddress alvin.cs.cornell.edu
128.84.154.8
A% Hostname 128.84.154.8
alvin.cs.cornell.edu
```

By the way, as shown in the next to last line of each of the preceding procedures, you should execute the `dp_address delete` command to free up the memory associated with an address when you are finished with it.

Learning More

This concludes our tour of the Tcl-DP extension to Tcl/Tk. There are a few other features in Tcl-DP that we haven't discussed, but we have covered the main ones here. We hope you have gained an appreciation for how simple it is to build distributed programs using Tcl-DP and that you have enough background now to explore on your own. To learn more, study the examples in the *examples* subdirectory, post articles to the *comp.lang.tcl* newsgroup, and read the manual pages in the *doc* subdirectory.

Tcl-DP is the result of the efforts of many, many people. Some of the major contributors are Steve Yen, Pekka Nikander, Tim MacKenzie, Lou Salkind, R. Lindsay Todd, Peter Liu, Ulla Bartsich, Mike Grafton, Jon Knight, Gordon Chaffee. You can help, too. If you add a new feature to Tcl-DP or port it to a new platform, please send mail to *tcl-dp@cs.cornell.edu* so that we can incorporate the changes into the source.

9

TSIPP: A 3D Graphics Toolkit

by Mark Diekhans

TSIPP is a Tcl interface to the SIPP 3D graphics rendering library. It provides a high-level Tcl command interface for creating three-dimensional scenes and rendering them to files or the Tk photo image. While TSIPP is a fun way to generate artistic images, its main goal is for use as a visualization tool. Using 3D graphics for displaying data associated with a scientific or engineering problem is a powerful aid in understanding the data. TSIPP provides a simple-to-use, yet flexible and rich interface for generating 3D graphics within a Tk-based application. TSIPP has also proven itself to be valuable in the teaching of computer graphics.

SIPP is an acronym for SImple Polygon Processor. It is a C library designed to provide a simple-to-use yet powerful interface for the C programmer to create 3D images. It was developed by Jonas Yngvesson and Inge Wallin of the Linkoping Institute of Technology, Sweden. SIPP makes it very easy to define and render sophisticated 3D scenes from a C program. TSIPP—for Tcl-SIPP—is a Tcl interface on top of the SIPP library developed by Mark Diekhans. It provides Tcl commands for defining scenes and generating and displaying images. Scenes can be quickly defined using high-level Tcl commands; yet, the majority of the computation still takes place in the compiled SIPP library, so the performance is not negatively impacted by programming at the Tcl level. While TSIPP does not provide the speed of a hardware assisted rendering package, its portability and ease of use make it an appropriate tool for many applications.

This chapter is an introduction to TSIPP. It is geared toward people who have no experience with computer graphics. Knowledge of basic geometry will be sufficient for using most of the features of TSIPP discussed here. Complete documentation is available as part of the TSIPP distribution.

Generating a Simple Image

TSIPP provides impressively complex shapes and textures as primitives, letting you start to create graphics at a high level right away. To illustrate this point, I'll develop a fairly nice-looking (if uninspiring) picture with a few lines of code.

The following script defines a scene containing a single ellipsoid, then renders the image directly to a viewing program. It is run using the `tsipp` program, a version of the TclX shell that has the TSIPP commands linked in.

```
set shader [SippShaderBasic 0.5 0.6 0.2 {0.6 0.3 0.5}]

set ellip [SippEllipsoid {2.0 3.0 2.0} 32 $shader]
SippObjectAddSubobj WORLD $ellip

SippLightSourceCreate {15.0 15.0 15.0} {0.9 0.9 0.9} POINT
SippCameraParams STDCAMERA {0.0 0.0 10.0} {0.0 0.0 0.0} \
{0.0 1.0 0.0} 0.4

set pbm [SippPBMOpen "| xv -8 -owncmap -" w]
SippRender $pbm 256 256 PHONG
SippPBMClose $pbm
```

Run the script either by passing it as an argument to the `tsipp` command or by starting the script with a line like

```
#!/usr/local/bin/tsipp
```

and making the script executable. A monochrome version of the color image that was generated by the preceding script is shown in Figure 9-1.

While the TSIPP commands are more complex than the standard Tcl command set, they are actually fairly straightforward. We will now go through each of the commands.

Figure 9-1: Ellipsoid: Full Rendering

The appearance of an object's surfaces is determined by the shading algorithm and parameters that are associated with the surface. At rendering time, the shading algorithm calculates the color of each displayed pixel of the surface. The calculation is based on the shading parameters and the light that strikes the surface. Under TSIPP, the shading algorithm and parameters are grouped together in an entity called a shader. In this example, the command

```
set shader [SippShaderBasic 0.5 0.6 0.2 {0.6 0.3 0.5}]
```

defines a shader that is to be associated with the surfaces of the object. This command creates an instance of the basic shader, a commonly used shading algorithm in TSIPP that creates surfaces with a single color. The shader creation commands allocate and fill a data structure that describes the shader, and return a handle to it. You save this handle in a variable and pass it to subsequent commands that create graphical objects.

The first parameter, 0.5, is the ambient light amount. This value, between 0.0 and 1.0, indicates how much of the surface color is visible when no other light is illuminating it. It simulates ambient room light in the real world. Lowering the value will generate a surface where areas not directly illuminated by the light source are much darker than the ones directly illuminated. This leads to a high-contrast, shadowy object. A higher value will generate an object where areas not directly illuminated are almost as bright as those that are.

The second parameter, 0.6, is the fraction of light that is specularly reflected. Reflection is either specular or diffuse. Light specularly reflected leaves the object in a single direction relative to the angle it hits the object. This creates the highlighted appearance of shiny surfaces. Diffused light leaves the object in all directions, creating a dull, uniform surface. The large fraction of the light that is specularly reflected, the larger the highlights on the surface.

The third parameter, 0.2, is the shininess factor. A value of 0.0 results in a very dull surface, 1.0 a very shiny surface. By adjusting the amount of specular reflection and the shininess factor for an object, you can make the surface appear to be made of a shiny metal or a dull, nonreflective material.

The fourth parameter, {0.6 0.3 0.5}, is the color for the surface. It is expressed as a Tcl list of red, green, and blue intensities, each in the range 0.0 to 1.0.

An optional fifth parameter, which was not specified, is used to define translucent surfaces.

When you define the color of a surface, the quickest approach is to create a script containing a single, simple object, such as this example. Adjust the shader for the surface until the desired appearance is achieved; then apply the shader parameters to a bigger scene.

Several other shading algorithms are available, including ones to define surfaces that have the appearance of wood, marble, or granite.

The command

```
set ellip [SippEllipsoid {2.0 2.0 3.0} 32 $shader]
```

creates an ellipsoid object and returns a handle to the object. The handle uniquely identifies the object and is passed to commands to manipulate the object. There are many other commands available to create primitive objects including cones, blocks, cylinders, and spheres.

The first argument, {2.0 2.0 3.0}, is the dimensions of the ellipsoid. It is a Tcl list consisting of the X, Y, and Z radius. These values are floating-point world units. All sizes and distances in SIPP are in world units. World unit values are a measure of length in the SIPP virtual world. They don't directly map to the number of pixels in the display size, which is also influenced by the location of the camera (view point) and size of image created. The important thing to realize is that a world unit is always the same, no matter how it is used within the SIPP virtual world. Think of it as a millimeter or a mile, whatever makes sense for your particular scene. However, if an object is scaled, its size in world units also changes. This will become clearer later on in the chapter.

The second argument, 32, is the resolution. This value controls the number of polygons that will be used to construct the ellipsoid's surface. It is the number of polygons that will be created around the object's equator. Increasing this value improves the appearance of the ellipsoid, leading to smoother object edges, but also increases rendering time and memory requirements. You'll find it more efficient to develop a scene with low numbers of polygons per object while you're writing and prototyping your program, and then increase the value for a final rendering.

The third argument, $shader, is the handle of the shader that was created in the previous command. All surfaces of the object will be rendered with the algorithm and attributes specified by this shader.

Objects may be combined into a hierarchical tree to form composite objects. These in turn may be combined to form even more complex objects. The power of building composite objects will be demonstrated in the next example.

For an object to be rendered and displayed, it must be a descendent of the world object. This object is specified by the special object handle WORLD. The command

```
SippObjectAddSubobj WORLD $ellip
```

adds the ellipsoid as a sub-object of the world object.

In order to provide for anything other than flat, ambient lighting, light sources need to be specified. The command

```
SippLightSourceCreate {15.0 15.0 15.0} {0.9 0.9 0.9} POINT
```

creates a light source at a point in the world; in this case, the point with the X, Y, and Z coordinates of 15.0, 15.0, 15.0. The second parameter is the color of the light. In this case, since the red, green, and blue components are all the same, it specifies a white light of 90% intensity. The keyword POINT specifies a point light source. The other type of light that may be created by this command is a directional light, which will be discussed later. A handle to the light is returned, but since no future manipulation is to be done on the light, it is ignored.

The last remaining attribute of the scene is the point from which the scene will be viewed. Often referred to as the eye point, in SIPP this point is called the camera. A camera is defined by four parameters: the point in space at which it is located, a point that it is looking at, the direction that is considered up, and its focal ratio. The effects of these attributes will be discussed in more detail later in this chapter. For now, the important thing to understand is that the camera parameters are adjusted to give the desired view of the scene. They control both the angle that the scene is viewed from and how much of the scene is visible. A misplaced camera is a common source of blank images being generated. The camera must be aimed at a point containing the objects in the scene, and be far enough away to view the desired portions of the scene yet close enough that the objects appear sufficiently large.

A preexisting camera is defined and is addressed by the handle STDCAMERA. In this example, the command

```
SippCameraParams STDCAMERA {0.0 0.0 10.0} {0.0 0.0 0.0} \
{0.0 1.0 0.0} 0.4
```

is used to adjust the location and parameters of **STDCAMERA**. The location is set to the X, Y, and Z coordinates of 0.0, 0.0, 10.0. The camera is set to be looking at the center point coordinate: 0.0, 0.0, 0.0. The fourth parameter is a vector that specifies which direction is up. The value of 0.0, 1.0, 0.0 has the positive Y axis as the up direction. The fifth parameter, 0.4, is the focal ratio of the camera. A large focal ratio will result in the camera having a wide angle view of the scene, while a small ratio will result in the telescopic view.

Now that the objects and parameters for the scene have been specified, all that is left to do is specify where the generated image is to be written, and then do the actual rendering of the scene. TSIPP lets you write images in a great variety of ways. Files, pipes to processes, in-memory storage areas, and Tk widgets can be used to store or display images. Collectively, they are referred to as image store. For now, only files and processes will be considered.

The command

```
set pbm [SippPBMOpen "| xv -8 -owncmap -" w]
```

is used to open a PBM format file. PBM files are a very common file format defined by the Portable Bit Map toolkit. While a disk file can be created and later displayed, in this case, an image viewer is launched directly. By starting a filename with |, we create a process with the PBM file as its `stdin`. It this case, John Bradley's popular image viewing and manipulation program, *xv*, is executed. The *xv* parameter -8 instructs *xv* to map the image down to a maximum of 256 colors (8 bits). The -owncmap option tells *xv* to use a private color map for the image. This results in the maximum number of colors being available for displaying the image, but requires the mouse pointer to be in the window to display the correct colors. If you're lucky enough to have a 24-bit color display, these parameters may be omitted. Some viewers will determine the color mapping automatically. The *xv* parameter - tells *xv* to read the image from `stdin` instead of a disk file. If the command

```
set pbm [SippPBMOpen example-1.1.pbm w]
```

is used, the image is written to a PBM file named *example-1.1.pbm*.

The second parameter to the `SippPBMOpen` command, w, indicates that the file is to be opened for write access. The command returns a PBM file handle.

It's now time to actually render the image. This is generally the biggest consumer of computer time in the process of producing an image. The command

```
SippRender $pbm 256 256 PHONG
```

renders the image. The first argument specifies the file to render the image to. The next two values are the width and height of the image to produce. Start small while designing an image as, the larger the image, the longer it takes to render. The argument, PHONG, specifies that the Phong rendering algorithm is to be used to generate the image. Phong produces the most realistic images of all the available algorithms, but is also the slowest.

The *xv* viewer window will appear after the rendering has completed, displaying the generated image.

The final command

```
SippPBMClose $pbm
```

closes the open file. Since the PBM file is a pipe to the viewer process, this command waits for the viewer to be exited before returning.

Generating line images is much faster than generating fully rendered images and is useful for designing the placement of objects in a scene. In order to generate a line image, replace the `SippRender` command in the preceding example with the command

```
SippRender $pbm 256 256 LINE
```

The resulting image is shown in Figure 9-2.

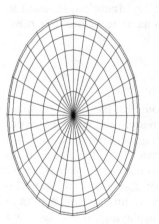

Figure 9-2: Ellipsoid: Wire Frame Rendering

Notice that lines of hidden surfaces are hidden in this line image. While having hidden lines removed from the image is generally best for anticipating how an image will eventually look, sometimes it's desirable or just plain interesting to display these lines. By issuing the command

```
SippShowBackFaces 1
```

before the call to `SippRender`, you can display hidden lines. Due to the number of lines in an ellipsoid, it would not adequately show the effect of leaving in hidden lines, so I will show the effect using a cube. Figure 9-3 is a cube rendered in LINE mode with hidden line elimination. Figure 9-4 is the same cube with `SippShow-BackFaces` turned on. In most cases, you should not enable the showing of back faces during a full rendering of an image; it will greatly increase the time required to render the scene.

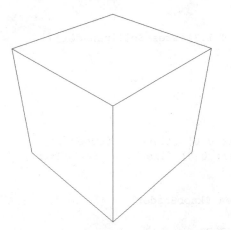

Figure 9-3: Cube: Wire Frame Rendering

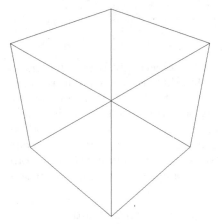

Figure 9-4: Cube: Wire Frame Rendering Displaying Hidden Lines

Building Compound Objects

The TSIPP primitive object creation commands offer a range of basic shapes that can be used in constructing a scene; however, manipulating a lot of simple objects independently is tedious. Building complex scenes can be made easier by creating composite objects from the standard primitive objects. Procedures to create composite objects can be used to form libraries of reusable objects.

The following procedure, MBrickObject, creates a composite object and returns its handle. The composite object it returns is no different to the caller of this function than an object created with the built-in object primitives. Operations that are done to the composite object, like scale, rotation, and moves, effect all of the objects that compose it.

```
proc MBrickObject {cubeShader ellipShader knobShader final} {
    set cubeSide 4.0
    set cube [SippCube $cubeSide $cubeShader]

    set res [expr $final ? 50 : 10]
    set ellip [SippEllipsoid {1.3 1.8 1.3} $res $ellipShader]
    SippObjectMove $ellip {0.0 1.7 0.0}
    SippObjectAddSubobj $cube $ellip
    SippObjectUnref $ellip

    set res [expr $final ? 30 : 5]
    set cubeHalf [expr $cubeSide / 2]
    set moveList [list [list $cubeHalf 0 0] [list 0 0 $cubeHalf] \
                    [list -$cubeHalf 0 0] [list 0 0 -$cubeHalf]]

    foreach move $moveList {
        set knob [SippSphere 0.5 $res $knobShader]
        SippObjectMove $knob $move
        SippObjectAddSubobj $cube $knob
        SippObjectUnref $knob
    }

    return $cube
}
```

This procedure defines the physical attributes of the object, given the shaders to associate with the various elements of the object. In addition, the Boolean parameter final specifies if this is a test or final image. If final is 0, then component objects are defined with a small number of polygons. This results in a faster rendering, but rounded objects that are roughly defined and unrealistic. This mode is used when doing experimental rendering while defining a scene. Once the scene is laid out, you can specify final as 1. This results in a large number of polygons being used to define the objects. Rounded objects will appear smooth, but rendering will take longer and require more memory.

The creation of the cube part of the composite object is straightforward:

```
set cubeSide 4.0
set cube [SippCube $cubeSide $cubeShader]
```

with the size, cubeSize, being saved for use in later calculations. The cube serves as the root of the mbrick object; all other objects will be sub-objects of it. The handle returned for the cube object will be used as the handle for the entire mbrick object.

Next, a ellipsoid is created and positioned so that it appears to be embedded in the cube. The commands

```
set res [expr $final ? 60 : 12]
set ellip [SippEllipsoid {1.3 1.8 1.3} $res $ellipShader]
```

determine the resolution to use and creates an ellipsoid of the appropriate dimensions. The ellipsoid that was just created is centered in world space, as is the cube. However, it is desired that the ellipsoid appear to protrude from the top of the cube. The command

```
SippObjectMove $ellip {0.0 1.7 0.0}
```

moves the object 1.7 world units in the Y direction. No movement takes place in the X and Z directions.

At this point, the ellipsoid exists as an independent object. If the cube is moved or scaled, the ellipsoid will remain unchanged. The commands

```
SippObjectAddSubobj $cube $ellip
SippObjectUnref $ellip
```

add the ellipsoid as a sub-object of the cube. The `SippObjectUnref` command is used to free the handle associated with the ellipsoid. To understand this, you have to know a little bit about SIPP internals. Each object takes up resources that SIPP would like to conserve, so it keeps track of where each object is being used and deletes the object as soon as it can. The ellipsoid object has a reference count of 1 when we create it, and this count is incremented to 2 when we make it a sub object of the cube. We don't need it anywhere else, so we can decrement its reference count right now; then when the cube is deleted, SIPP can also delete the ellipsoid.

The next elements to add to the composite object are four spherical knobs that are embedded in the sides of the cube. When creating multiple copies of the same object in a scene, a common approach is to set up a loop that creates the objects and moves them to different locations. The first step is to set up the attributes used in creation of the objects. The command

```
set res [expr $final ? 30 : 5]
```

determines what polygon resolution to use for each sphere.

The commands

```
set cubeHalf [expr $cubeSide / 2]
set moveList [list [list $cubeHalf 0 0]  [list 0 0 $cubeHalf] \
                   [list -$cubeHalf 0 0] [list 0 0 -$cubeHalf]]
```

build a list of the distances to move each sphere that is created. Each list contains X, Y, and Z coordinates measured in world units. The coordinates represent the distances from the center of the WORLD object (which is also the center of the cube) to the four sides of the cube.

The distance list, moveList, is used to control the loop:

```
foreach move $moveList {
    set knob [SippSphere 0.5 $res $knobShader]
    SippObjectMove $knob $move
    SippObjectAddSubobj $cube $knob
    SippObjectUnref $knob
}
```

Building Compound Objects   **385**

Each iteration through the loop creates a new sphere, using the `SippSphere` command with a radius of 0.5 world units. It then moves the sphere to one of the side planes of the cube and adds it as a sub-object of the cube. Lastly, the handle associated with a sphere is unreferenced.

This loop results in four identical spheres that have their own unique definitions. While easy to set up, it means the internal data structures that define the sphere are duplicated. It is possible to create the sphere only once and then use the `SippObjectInstance` command to create duplicates of the sphere that share resources, but can be moved independently. The code for a loop like this is more complex and it will not be used in this procedure. If the object being duplicated is complex, using `SippObjectInstance` can save considerable memory.

The final step is to return the handle to the composite object that has just been created:

```
return $cube
```

Since all other objects that were created are sub-objects of the cube, its handle serves as the handle for the entire composite object.

The `MBrickObject` procedure defines the physical structure of the `mbrick` object, parameterized by shaders for the each of the component objects. To show how this procedure might be used, we'll define another procedure, `MBrick`, that creates the `mbrick` object with a specified set of shaders and surface parameters. Its only argument is the final Boolean to pass through to the `MBrickObject` procedure.

```
proc MBrick {final} {
    set cubeShader [SippShaderGranite 0.1 0.3 1.0 100.0 \
            {1.0 0.1 0.1} {0.1 0.1 0.1}]
    set ellipShader [SippShaderBasic 0.4 0.6 0.2 {0.0 0.0 1.0}]
    set knobShader [SippShaderBasic 0.4 0.6 0.2 {0.0 1.0 0.0}]

    set obj [MBrickObject $cubeShader $ellipShader $knobShader \
            $final]

    SippShaderUnref $cubeShader
    SippShaderUnref $ellipShader
    SippShaderUnref $knobShader
    return $obj
}
```

The command

```
set cubeShader [SippShaderGranite 0.1 0.3 1.0 100.0 \
                        {1.0 0.1 0.1} {0.1 0.1 0.1}]
```

defines a shader for the cube part of the object. The resulting surface is intended to resemble red brick. To achieve this appearance, we choose the granite shading algorithm. The first argument is the ambient light, which we set low to give a dark appearance. The second argument is the fraction of light that is specularly reflected. This is set low to give a non-metallic appearance. The third argument, c3, the shininess factor, is set to 1.0, for a very dull surface.

The fourth argument is a factor that determines the scaling of an area of an object to an area of the generated granite texture. A large value of 100.0 is specified, yielding a fine-grained appearance. The granite appearance is generated by mixing areas of two different colors, which are specified with the fifth and sixth arguments. The first color, {1.0 0.1 0.1}, generates a red surface; the second color, {0.1 0.1 0.1}, is a dull black.

For the ellipsoid and spherical knobs, the familiar basic shader algorithm is used:

```
set ellipShader [SippShaderBasic 0.4 0.6 0.2 {0.0 0.0 1.0}]
set knobShader [SippShaderBasic 0.4 0.6 0.2 {0.0 1.0 0.0}]
```

Both of the shaders are defined to generate a metallic appearance. The ellipsoid is blue and the knobs are green.

Next we create the object with the previously defined procedure, supplying these shaders and saving the new composite object's handle.

```
set obj [MBrickObject $cubeShader $ellipShader $knobShader $final]
```

Shaders also have a reference count associated with them. Now that the shaders have been associated with the surfaces of the objects, you can delete the handle associated with the shader. This invalidates the handle, while leaving the shaders associated with the object. This allows the memory occupied with the shaders to be reclaimed when the composite object is released.

```
SippShaderUnref $cubeShader
SippShaderUnref $ellipShader
SippShaderUnref $knobShader
```

Lastly, the handle of the composite object is returned.

```
return $obj
```

The first scene that is created using the `mbrick` object just creates one instance of the object. The following commands define the light source and camera for this scene.

```
SippLightSourceCreate {15.0 15.0 15.0} {0.9 0.9 0.9} POINT
SippCameraParams STDCAMERA {-4.0 4.0 10.0} {0.0 0.0 0.0} \
{0.0 1.0 0.0} 0.4
```

The same light source is used as in the previous example. This time, the camera is not positioned looking straight at the object on the Z axis. Instead it's positioned a little bit to the left and up from a point 10 world units back on the Z axis.

Next, call the `MBrick` procedure to create the composite object and add it to the WORLD object:

```
SippObjectAddSubobj WORLD [MBrick 0]
```

The handle to the `mbrick` object is not saved, so no more operations can be performed on the object. The handle to the light source was not saved either. This approach is most often used for a script that is going to execute and then exit the interpreter. When building applications that do multiple renderings, handles are usually maintained in variables so objects and lights can be manipulated or deleted.

The following commands generate a line rendering of the scene:

```
SippShowBackFaces 1
set pbm [SippPBMOpen "| xv -8 -owncmap -" w]
SippRender $pbm 256 256 LINE
SippPBMClose $pbm
```

The resulting image is shown in Figure 9-5. Line rendering of compound objects with hidden line elimination is less than ideal in TSIPP, as forward-facing edges of objects that are hidden by other objects are still drawn. For instance, the complete ellipse can be seen even though part of it is embedded in the cube. It's often more useful to just show all hidden lines, as enabled here with the `SippShowBack-Faces` command.

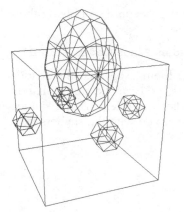

Figure 9-5: Write Frame Rendering of MBrick Object

The preliminary image shown in Figure 9-6 is generated by removing the `Sipp-ShowBackFaces` command and specifying `PHONG` rendering mode instead of `LINE` on the `SippRender` command. Note that the construction of the rounded objects from polygons is quite obvious with the low resolution.

To generate the final image, shown in Figure 9-7, the following commands are used after defining the light and camera:

```
SippObjectAddSubobj WORLD [MBrick 1]
set pbm [SippPBMOpen "| xv -8 -owncmap -" w]
SippRender $pbm 256 256 PHONG 3
SippPBMClose $pbm
```

Specifying a non-zero value to the Boolean argument to the `MBrick` procedure uses a larger number of polygons to define the ellipsoid and spheres. The fifth argument to `SippRender` is the oversampling factor to use in generating the image. Oversampling is a technique used to reduce aliasing, which is the jagged look that lines take on when they are made out of diagonal sequences of pixels. Oversampling generates the image internally as a larger image and then averages the values of pixels together to generate the final image. The value of 3 means that an image three times as large will be generated internally and that each final pixel is the result of averag-

Figure 9-6: Preliminary Rendering of MBrick Object

ing together 3 by 3 matrix of pixels. Specifying this option as a value greater than 1 greatly increases the rendering time; however, memory utilization increases only slightly, since only one line of the final image is kept in memory at a time.

Figure 9-7: Final Rendering of MBrick Object

The next example demonstrates how to duplicate an object in the construction of a scene. The following procedure defines a compound object consisting of four mbrick objects.

```
proc FourMBricks {final} {
    set moveList [list [list  0  0 -6] \
```

```
                    [list  6  0  0] \
                    [list  0  0  6] \
                    [list -6  0  0]]

    # Create mbrick objects.

    foreach move $moveList {
        if ![info exists objList] {
            set obj [MBrick $final]
        } else {
            set obj [SippObjectInstance $prevObj]
        }
        SippObjectMove $obj $move
        lappend objList $obj
    }

    # Create base for mbricks to sit on.

    set shader [SippShaderBasic 0.5 0.4 0.3 {0.5 0.6 0.8}]
    set obj [SippBlock {20.0 0.1 20.0} $shader]
    SippShaderUnref $shader
    SippObjectMove $obj {0 -2.05 0}
    lappend objList $obj

    # Create surfaceless object to containing all other objects.

    set topObj [SippObjectCreate]
    SippObjectAddSubobj $topObj $objList
    SippObjectUnref $objList
    return $topObj
}
```

The first step in defining the scene is to create four mbrick objects. This is done by creating one object and then duplicating it using SippObjectInstance. The moveList variable is assigned a list of lists. Each sublist contains the X, Y, and Z coordinates to move each object. The list is used to drive a foreach loop that creates each of the objects. The first time through the loop, the MBrick function is called to create the initial object. Subsequent times through the loop, SippObjectInstance is used to make a copy of the previous object.

SippObjectInstance creates a new object that shares all of the sub-object and surface description of the original object. This results in considerable memory savings. The disadvantage is that any modification to sub-objects of the object being duplicated will affect all duplicates. Normally, this is not a problem, as compound objects tend to be treated as atomic units once they are created. When SippObjectInstance creates the new object, it clears all transformations (moves, scales, and rotations) that were performed on the original object. In this example, this results in the new object being at the world center. Transformations that were performed on sub-objects are not modified. Clearing the transformations on the new object generally makes it easier to calculate the location to move the new object to. SippObjectInstance has an option, -keeptransf, that retains all of the transformations if this behavior is not desired.

Each time through the loop, we moved the new object to its location and added it to a list of objects. Each object could have been added to the container object as it was created. However, in this example, a list was built of all the object handles to simplify the loop and demonstrate the manipulation of lists of objects.

The next step is to create a plane for the objects to sit on. The plane is simply a thin block object, not a true plane, as there are no two-dimensional objects in TSIPP. The command

```
set obj [SippBlock {20.0 0.1 20.0} $shader]
```

creates a block object with a width and depth of 20.0 world units and a height of 0.1 world units. The object is then moved down -2.05 world units so that the `mbrick` objects appear to rest on its surface.

An empty object is created to contain all of the objects in this compound object using the `SippObjectCreate` command. While any of the objects could have been selected as the container, it's often cleaner and more extensible to create an empty object. Since the object has no surfaces associated with it, it will not affect the appearance of scene in any way. All objects are added as sub-objects of this empty object. While they could be added one at a time, this program demonstrates that the `SippObjectAddSubobj`, and most of the TSIPP object commands, are capable of operating on a list of objects as well as a single object. All of the handles for the sub-objects can be unreferenced in a similar manner.

Finally a handle to the compound object is returned. While the `mbrick` objects could have been added directly to the `WORLD` object, creating a compound object is very little additional overhead and provides greater flexibility for the procedure to be used in constructing other scenes.

The following commands are issued to render the scene:

```
FourMBricks $final
SippLightSourceCreate {15.0 15.0 15.0} {0.9 0.9 0.9} POINT
SippCameraParams STDCAMERA {-8.0 8.0 22.0} {0.0 0.0 0.0} \
{0.0 1.0 0.0} 0.4

set pbm [SippPBMOpen $output w]
SippRender $pbm 256 256 PHONG [expr $final ? 1 : 3]
SippPBMClose $pbm
```

This time, the camera is moved back farther from the world center so all four objects are in view. The resulting final image is Figure 9-8. In Figure 9-9, the same scene is rendered with the camera at {0.0 15.0 20.0}.

Defining Surface Shaders

All examples so far have used the basic shader. TSIPP offers a variety of other shaders that produce either solid or patterned appearances on the surfaces.

The Phong shader, not to be confused with the PHONG option to the `SippRender` command, produces a solid color appearance on an object's surface using the Phong illumination model. The sphere in Figure 9-10 is created using a shader specified by

```
SippShaderPhong 0.4 0.4 0.6 100 {0.5 0.0 1.0}
```

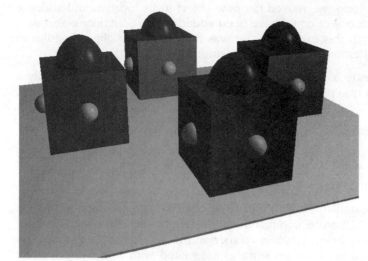

Figure 9-8: Multiple MBrick Objects

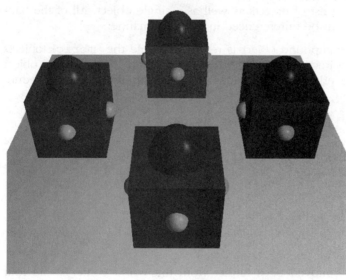

Figure 9-9: Another View of Multiple MBrick Objects

The first argument, 0.4, is the fraction of the surface color that is visible as ambient light when no other light source is illuminating the surface. The second argument, 0.4, is the fraction of light diffusely reflected from the surface, with the next argument, 0.6, being the fraction specularly reflected. The fourth argument, 100, is an integer value that specifies how shiny the surfaces are. The normal range used for this value is 1 to 200, where 1 yields a very dull surface and 200 yields a very shiny one. The fifth argument, {0.5 0.0 1.0}, is the color of the surface, expressed in the standard TSIPP format: a list of red, green, and blue color values in the range of 0.0 to 1.0.

Figure 9-10: Phong Sphere

The next set of shaders are built upon the basic shader. They generate patterns known as textures rather than consistent colors. The shaders all share a standard set of arguments: *ambient*, *specular*, and *c3*. *ambient* is the amount of ambient light reflected from the surface in the range 0.0 to 1.0; *specular* is the fraction of light that is specularly reflected; and *c3* is the shininess factor, with 0.0 being the dullest and 1.0 being the shiniest. These attributes of light were defined in the previous section. These shaders also take one or more color arguments, which are the standard list of red, green, and blue intensities. These arguments are all familiar from the `SippShaderBasic` command. Most of the shaders have another argument, *scale*. This value is the amount the texture is scaled before associating with a surface. A large scale factor results in a very fine pattern, while a small number results in a coarse pattern.

The sphere in Figure 9-11 is produced using the wood shader and is specified with the command

```
SippShaderWood 0.4 0.0 0.99 10.0 {0.770 0.568 0.405} \
{0.468 0.296 0.156}
```

This shader produces a wood-like appearance by generating rings of one color mixed in a base color. The first three arguments are the standard ambient, specular, and c3 parameters. The fourth argument, `10.0`, is the scale factor. The next argument, `{0.770  0.568  0.405}`, is the base color and `{0.468  0.296 0.156}` is the ring color.

The command `SippShaderMarble` also generates a pattern with a pattern color on a base color similar to the wood shader, only it has the appearance of marble. The command

```
SippShaderMarble 0.4 0.5 0.05 8.0 {0.90 0.80 0.65} {0.30 0.08 0.08}
```

is used to define the surface of the sphere in Figure 9-12. The first three arguments are the standard basic shader arguments. The fourth argument, `8.0`, is the scale

Figure 9-11: Wood Sphere

factor; the fifth argument, {0.90 0.80 0.65}, is the base color. The next argument, {0.30 0.08 0.08}, is the color of the strips that are interspersed with the base color.

Figure 9-12: Marble Sphere

The command SippShaderGranite creates a shader that is similar to the marble shader, only the two colors are mixed without treating one color as a base. The sphere in Figure 9-13 is generated with the granite shader using the same arguments as were used to create the marble sphere in Figure 9-12. The shader for this sphere was defined with the command

```
SippShaderGranite 0.4 0.5 0.05 8.0 {0.90 0.80 0.65} {0.30 0.08 0.08}
```

Figure 9-13: Granite Sphere

The only difference between the granite and marble shader is that the granite shader mixes the two colors in equal amounts, rather than the first one being the base.

The bozo shader generates a surface pattern by choosing colors from a list using a random noise function. The surface of a bozo object can be defined using commands like

```
set colors {{1.0 0.0 0.0} {0.2 0.4 0.0}}
SippShaderBozo 0.4 0.5 0.05 8.0 $colors
```

Figure 9-14: Bozo Sphere

The first three arguments are the ambient, specular, and c3 parameters. The fourth argument is the scale factor. The final argument is a list of colors to choose from. Since a single color is represented as a list, this is in fact a list of lists, each containing three numbers.

The sphere in Figure 9-15 was shaded using the command

```
SippShaderPlanet 0.4 0.0 0.5
```

Figure 9-15: Planet Sphere

This shader generates a surface that resembles an Earth-like planet. The planet's features are oceans, continents, and clouds. The *ambient*, *specular*, and *c3* arguments are specified in this example. The planet shader is not scalable and hence has no scale factor. It is possible to create objects other than spheres with the planet surface. A cube generated with the planet shader is shown in Figure 9-16. The planet shader is rather slow, so images containing objects shaded with it are time-consuming to generate.

The bumpy shader produces surfaces that have bumps, holes, or both. This shader does not generate the color of the surface; instead, it relies on other shaders. The sphere in Figure 9-17 is generated with the shader created by the commands

```
set granite [SippShaderGranite 0.4 0.3 1.0 100.0 {1.0 0.1 0.1} \
                        {0.1 0.1 0.1}]
SippShaderBumpy $granite 14.0 HOLES
```

First, the granite shader is created to generate the color of the surface. This is passed as the first argument to the bumpy shader. The second argument is the texture scale factor. The third argument, HOLES, tells the shader to generate only holes in the surface. If the command

```
SippShaderBumpy $granite 14.0 BUMPS
```

Figure 9-16: Planet Cube

Figure 9-17: Granite Sphere with Holes

is used, it results in the sphere in Figure 9-18, with only bumps and no holes. The command

```
SippShaderBumpy $granite 14.0 HOLES BUMPS
```

generates the sphere in Figure 9-19 with both bumps and holes. If neither of the arguments HOLES or BUMPS is supplied, both are assumed.

All of the TSIPP shader commands, except for `SippShaderBumpy`, have an optional final argument that specifies the opacity. This parameter specifies how much light from objects behind the surface will be allowed to pass through. The parameter may be specified as a single value or a list of three values, one for each

---

Figure 9-18: Granite Sphere with Bumps

Figure 9-19: Granite Sphere with Holes and Bumps

color. A value of 1.0 is totally opaque and a value of 0.0 is totally transparent. The following code creates a translucent sphere in front of a cube, as in the scene in Figure 9-20.

```
set granite [SippShaderGranite 0.4 0.3 1.0 100.0 {1.0 0.1 0.1} \
                              {0.1 0.1 0.1}]
set cube [SippCube 0.5 $granite]
SippObjectMove $cube {0.0 0.0 -1.5}

set glass [SippShaderBasic 0.4 0.6 0.2 {0.0 0.0 1.0} 0.6]
set sphere [SippSphere 1.0 25 $glass]
```

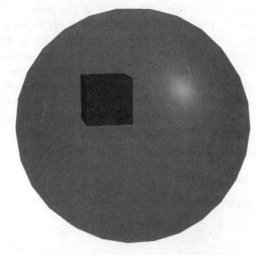

Figure 9-20: Translucent Sphere

Primitive Object Creation Commands

TSIPP provides a wide range of primitive object creation commands. So far, commands to create spheres, cubes, and ellipsoids have been discussed. This section introduces the other primitive objects and their attributes.

In the examples that follow, the command

```
set shader [SippShaderBasic 0.4 0.6 0.2 {0.0 0.0 1.0}]
```

is used to specify the surface shader, which generates objects with a blue metallic appearance.

The torus in Figure 9-21 was generated with the command

```
SippTorus 4.0 2.0 20 10 $shader
```

Figure 9-21: Torus Object

The first argument, 4.0, specifies the radius of the torus. The second argument, 2.0, specifies the radius of the tube of the torus. The third and forth arguments specify the number of polygons used to define the torus. The third argument, 20, is the number of polygons that will be used around the circumference of the torus. The forth argument, 10, is the number of polygons used around the circumference of the tube of the torus. As with the previously discussed objects, adjusting the polygon resolution of a torus is a tradeoff of speed versus quality. The primary attribute that affects the appearance of a torus is the ratio of the tube radius to the ring radius. The command

```
SippTorus 4.0 3.0 20 10 $shader
```

creates the torus in Figure 9-22, which has a much fatter tube.

SippCone command creates a cone object. The command

Figure 9-22: Fat Torus Object

```
SippCone 2.0 0.0 4.0 20 $shader
```

creates the cone in Figure 9-23. This first argument, 2.0, is the radius of the bottom of the cone; the second argument is the radius of the top of the cone. In this case, with 0.0 as the top radius, a full cone is generated. The third argument, 4.0, is the length; and the fifth, 20, is the polygon resolution. If the top radius is greater than zero, a truncated cone is generated. The command

```
SippCone 2.0 1.0 4.0 20 $shader
```

generates the truncated cone in Figure 9-24.

While the SippCone command could be used to generate a cylinder, it's more straightforward to use the SippCylinder command. The cylinder in Figure 9-25 is generated with the command

Figure 9-23: Cone Object

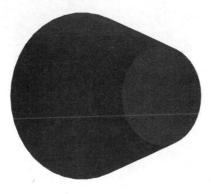

Figure 9-24: Truncated Cone Object

```
SippCylinder 1.0 4.0 10 $shader
```

This specifies a cylinder with a radius of 1.0 world units and a length of 4.0. A polygon resolution of 10 indicates the number of polygons around the rim of the cylinder.

The `SippPrism` creates a prism object by extending a two-dimensional polygon. The defining polygon can be thought of as the shape of the top and bottom of the prism. The following commands create the prism in Figure 9-26:

```
set pnts {{-0.5 0.0} {-1.0 0.5} {1.0 1.0} {-1.0 2.0} {-2.0 0.5}}
SippPrism $pnts 0.01 $shader
```

Primitive Object Creation Commands   **401**

Figure 9-25: Cylinder Object

Figure 9-26: Prism Defining Polygon

The variable `pnts` contains a list of X and Y coordinates that define a polygon. Each coordinate within the variable is expressed as a list. The second argument, 0.01, is the Z length of the prism. A very short length has been chosen to show the shape of the defining polygon. The image in Figure 9-27 is generated with the command

```
SippPrism $pnts 2.0 $shader
```

which specifies a length of 2.0 world units. Figure 9-28 is the same prism with a length of 5.0 world units.

With the previously introduced `SippCube` command, simple cube objects can be created. To create block objects where sides are of different sizes, the `SippBlock` command is available. Figure 9-29 is created with the command

Figure 9-27: Short Prism Object

Figure 9-28: Long Prism Object

```
SippBlock {1.0 3.0 1.5} $shader
```

The first argument, {1.0 3.0 1.5}, is a list of the X, Y, and Z world unit lengths of the size of the block.

A teapot is a classic object in computer graphics demonstration images. TSIPP provides the SippTeapot command to generate just such objects. The teapot in Figure 9-30 was generated with the commands

```
set obj [SippTeapot 10 $shader]
SippObjectRotateX $obj D-90
SippObjectMove $obj {0.0 -0.25 0.0}
```

Figure 9-29: Block Object

Figure 9-30: Teapot Object

where 10 is the polygon resolution to use. The exact number of polygons that will result from any given value is complex to determine. The easiest approach to determining a good value is experimentation.

When the teapot object is initially created, it is oriented on its side. The `SippObjectRotateX` and `SippObjectMove` commands rotate and move the teapot so it's upright relative to the positive Y axis and centered at the world origin.

It is also possible to define separate objects for various parts of a teapot. This allows different shaders to be used on each part. The following commands, with the same arguments as `SippTeapot`, are available.

- SippTeapotBody—The teapot body object.

- SippTeapotLid—The teapot lid object.

- SippTeapotHandle—The teapot handle object.

- SippTeapotSpout—The teapot spout object.

TSIPP also provides commands for defining objects based on Bezier curves or patches. While an explanation of Bezier curves and patches is beyond the scope of this chapter, the commands `SippBezierCurve` and `SippBezierPatch` are documented in the TSIPP manual page for those wanting to use them.

All of the TSIPP primitive object creation commands have an optional final parameter that has not been discussed; the texture mapping algorithm to use for the object. This is a symbolic value that indicates how the textures generated by the shader are to be applied to the surface of the object. What it describes is a relationship, or mapping, of a coordinate on the object's surface to a coordinate in the pattern generated by the surface's shader. The texture mapping is not applicable to shaders that don't generate patterns, like the basic or Phong shaders. With shaders that generate patterns, like the marble, wood, or planet shaders, the texture mapping algorithm makes a big difference in how the pattern appears on the surface of the object. Note that the texture patterns I'm talking about are not the same as the differences in surface appearance caused by the light that strikes the surface. The texture mapping algorithm affects only the generated pattern, not the appearance of light and shadows on the surface. To better understand the behavior of this parameter, the best approach is to experiment with it. Try the marble or wood shader with an ellipsoid object.

The following values are valid for the texture mapping algorithm argument:

- `NATURAL`—This value uses a texture mapping algorithm that is natural for a particular object. The natural mapping algorithm may be one of the other mappings or one unique to the object. See the manual page for the definition of `NATURAL` mapping for a particular object type.

- `CYLINDRICAL`—The texture is mapped as if applied to a cylinder surrounding the object and centered on the Z axis.

- `SPHERICAL`—The texture is mapped as if applied to a sphere surrounding the object.

- `WORLD`—The texture is mapped one-to-one to three-dimensional world coordinates of the object at creation time. This is the default when an explicit texture mapping algorithm is not specified.

Understanding how the texture mapping algorithm will affect the appearance of a particular object with a particular shader is often nonintuitive. The best approach is to experiment. The image in Figure 9-31 is a truncated cone shaded with the marble shader. The shader is applied using the `CYLINDRICAL` texture mapping algorithm. This object is generated with the commands

```
set shader [SippShaderMarble 0.4 0.5 0.05 8.0 {0.90 0.80 0.65} \
                             {0.30 0.08 0.08} {1.0 1.0 1.0}]
SippCone 2.0 1.0 4.0  $shader CYLINDRICAL
```

Figure 9-31: Cone with Cylindrical Texture Mapping

By using SPHERICAL instead of CYLINDRICAL the image in Figure 9-32 is generated. A texture mapping of WORLD results in the image in Figure 9-33. Specifying NATURAL texture mapping for cones results in the same appearance as CYLINDRICAL. In most cases, you will want to use either NATURAL or WORLD mappings.

Object Transformations

I've already demonstrated the use of the SippObjectMove command to change the location of objects in world space. In addition to moving objects, there are several commands that perform transformations on objects. These fall into two categories: rotations and scales.

Figure 9-32: Cone with Spherical Texture Mapping

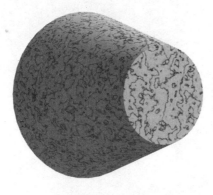

Figure 9-33: Cone with World Texture Mapping

Rotations of an object occur around an axis in space. Three commands, `SippOb-jectRotateX`, `SippObjectRotateY`, and `SippObjectRotateZ` perform rotations around the X, Y, and Z axes, respectively. If the truncated cone in Figure 9-34 is rotated with the command

```
SippObjectRotateX $obj D35.5
```

it rotates the object, specified by the handle stored in the variable `obj` 35.5 degrees around the X axis. The prefix `D` on the angle indicates degrees. If the prefix was omitted or `R`, the angle would be in radians. The resulting cone is shown in Figure 9-35.

The command `SippObjectRotate` is used to rotate an object around an arbitrary axis rather than one of the standard ones. The rotation axis is defined by a point and a vector (a direction). The command

```
SippObjectRotate $obj {0 0 0} {1 2 1} R40
```

when applied to the truncated cone in Figure 9-34 (shown with the rotation axis), results in the image Figure 9-36.

It's often easier to think of an axis being defined between two points rather than as a point and a vector. The `SippMkVector` command can be used to convert a pair of points to a vector. Thus, the preceding command could be expressed as

```
SippObjectRotate $obj {x y z} [SippMkVector {x y z} {x2 y2 z2}]
```

The other transformation is *scaling*. Scaling is changing the size of an object. An object can be scaled in its entirety or along one or more of the X, Y, or Z directions. The command

```
SippObjectScale $obj 0.5
```

applied to the truncated cone in Figure 9-34 results in a cone half the size, as in Figure 9-37. By applying the command

Figure 9-34: Original Cone Object

Figure 9-35: X-Axis Rotation

Figure 9-36: Arbitrary Axis Rotation

```
SippObjectScale $obj {1.5 0,5 1.0}
```

to the original cone, the size is 1.5 times larger in the X dimension and half the size in the Y dimension, resulting in Figure 9-38.

Lights, Shadows, and Cameras

Light sources play an important part in the appearance of a computer-generated scene. They simulate natural types of lighting, producing both light and dark areas and specular reflections. TSIPP supports three types of lights: point, directional, and spotlight. All previous examples have used point light sources.

Figure 9-37: Scaling to Half Size

Lights, Shadows, and Cameras

Figure 9-38: Doubling in X Direction

Point lights are located at a particular point in space and simulate a relatively close light, like a room light. Directional lights illuminate from a particular direction, but don't have a specified location in space. They simulate distant light, like the sun. Both types of lights are created with the `SippLightSourceCreate` command. The image in Figure 9-39 is illuminated with a light specified by the command

```
SippLightSourceCreate {30.0 30.0 30.0} {0.9 0.9 0.9} POINT
```

Figure 9-39: Distant Point Light

This creates a point light at world coordinate {30.0 30.0 30.0} with a color of {0.9 0.9 0.9}. This is a white light at 90% intensity. Using lights of different colors can produce some very interesting effects in a scene, but the results would not be visible in a book limited to grayscale images, so colored light is left for the reader to experiment with. Contrast this image with the one in Figure 9-40. That image was created with the command

```
SippLightSourceCreate {3.0 3.0 3.0} {0.9 0.9 0.9} POINT
```

Figure 9-40: Close Point Light

which gives a point light located much closer to the object. Note that this results in the light illuminating a much smaller area with a smaller highlight.

The image in Figure 9-41 is the same ellipsoid illuminated with a directional light. This light was created with the command

```
SippLightSourceCreate {1.0 1.0 1.0} {0.9 0.9 0.9} DIRECTION
```

For a directional light, the first argument is a vector, not a point. It indicates the direction that the light comes from. In this case, {1.0 1.0 1.0} describes a light above and to the right of the viewer. This is the same direction as the two point light examples. The appearance of the object illuminated by a directional light is very similar in appearance to a distance point light, as in Figure 9-39. Directional lights are generally simpler to use when there is no need to have a light appear to be at a specific location.

For more interesting lighting effects, a scene may be illuminated by multiple lights. Figure 9-42 is illuminated with two point lights created with the commands

```
SippLightSourceCreate {10.0 10.0 10.0} {0.9 0.9 0.9} POINT
SippLightSourceCreate {-10.0 10.0 10.0} {0.9 0.9 0.9} POINT
```

In all of the previous examples, lights have been created and then left unchanged in the scene. This is the normal approach for static image generation, but for generating animations and in interactive applications, it is necessary to manipulate a light once it is created. The `SippLightSourceCreate` command returns a

Figure 9-41: Directional Light

handle that is used to manipulate the light. The command `SippLightSourcePut` changes the location of a point light or the direction of a directional light. A light's color and intensity can be changed with the `SippLightColor` command. Lights can also be turned off and back on with the `SippLightActive` command. The `SippLightDestruct` command is used to delete a light that is no longer needed. It can also be used to delete all defined lights.

Spotlights provide a more flexible and powerful type of TSIPP illumination. They may be used to simulate highly focused lights or other types of lighting and can generate shadows.

Figure 9-42: Two Point Lights

Spotlights project a cone of light at a specified angle. There are two main types of spotlights: sharp and soft. For sharp lights, the edges of the cone are sharply defined where it strikes surfaces. For soft lights, the edges gradually blend with the color of the surface. The following commands are used to illuminate the ellipsoid in Figure 9-43:

```
SippSpotLightCreate {10.0 10.0 10.0} {0 0 0} D7 {0.9 0.9 0.9} SHARP
SippLightSourceCreate {-1.0 1.0 1.0} {0.3 0.3 0.3} DIRECTION
```

Figure 9-43: 7 Degree Sharp Spotlight

The world space location of the spotlight is given by the first argument, `{10.0 10.0 10.0}`. The second argument, `{0 0 0}`, is the point at which the spotlight is pointing. The next argument is the angle of the cone of illumination, which can be thought of as the opening of the spotlight. As with other angles in TSIPP, the D prefix indicates that this argument is 7 degrees. The dim directional light is used to illuminate areas of the ellipsoid that are not struck by the spotlight. Without it, these areas would appear to be flat, with no curvature. The object would be visible only because of the ambient light associated with the surface. If the angle is changed to 12 degrees, the image in Figure 9-44 results.

A soft spotlight is created by specifying `SOFT` instead of `SHARP`. Figure 9-45 is generated with a 7 degree soft spotlight.

An optional sixth parameter is used to indicate whether the spotlight is going to create a shadow when shadows are globally enabled. It is a Boolean parameter, where a nonzero value or the string `true` enables shadows and a zero or `false` disables shadows.

If the handle returned by `SippSpotLightCreate` is saved, it can be used to modify the attributes of the spotlight. The commands `SippSpotLightPos` and `SippSpotLightAt` alter the position or point that the light is aimed at. The illu-

Figure 9-44: 12 Degree Sharp Spotlight, Moved

Figure 9-45: 7 Degree Soft Spotlight

mination cone angle can be modified with `SippSpotLightOpening` and the shadow generation for the light can be enabled or disabled with `SippSpot-LightShadows`. `SippLightDestruct`, `SippLightColor`, and `SippLigh-tActive` also work for spotlights.

TSIPP can generate shadows for light cast by spotlights. The shadows must both be explicitly enabled for a light and globally enabled with the `SippShadows` command. The image in Figure 9-46 is created with the following code:

```
SippObjectAddSubobj WORLD [FourMBricks $final]
```

```
    SippSpotLightCreate {15.0 15.0 15.0} {0.5 3.0 6.0} D20 {0.9 0.9
0.9} \
        SOFT true
    SippSpotLightCreate {-15.0 15.0 15.0} {0.0 0.0 0.0} D60 {0.4
0.4 0.4} \
        SHARP true

    SippShadows true [expr $size*2]

    SippCameraParams STDCAMERA {-8.0 8.0 22.0} {0.0 0.0 0.0} {0.0
1.0 0.0} 0.4

    set pbm [SippPBMOpen $output w]
    SippRender $pbm $size $size $mode [expr $final ? 1 : 3]
    SippPBMClose $pbm
```

Figure 9-46: 7 Degree Soft Spotlight, Large Scene

The first argument to SippShadows is a Boolean that either globally enables or globally disables shadows. If shadows are enabled, a second argument is required. This is the size allocated for a structure used in shadow generation known as a depth map. This depth map size allocated is a tradeoff between speed and memory utilization and image quality. The size for the depth maps is normally the size of the largest dimension of the image that is being generated. For instance, specifying a size of 250 pixels results in 250 by 250 depth map, where each entry is of type float. If the shadows in the resulting image are aliased (jagged) or malformed, increasing the size of the depth maps used in the rendering should improve the appearance. Care must be taken, however, because memory requirements can go up quickly with the number and size of depth maps.

I've already discussed how to set up the parameters of the predefined camera, identified by the handle STDCAMERA. It is possible to create multiple cameras, although only one may be active at a given time. Multiple cameras can be useful for rendering a scene from different views, such as is done when generating stereo images. The command `SippCameraCreate` takes the same arguments as `SippCamera-Params`, but it creates a new camera and returns a handle to it. A camera is set as the active one by passing its handle to `SippCameraUse`. `SippCameraDestruct` is used to delete a camera that is no longer needed.

Just as when you position a real camera, the camera parameters control what parts of the scene will be visible. The most common parameter to adjust is the point that the camera is located at. Moving the camera location while keeping the same distance from the scene will show the scene from different perspectives. To demonstrate, let's view the same scene from three different angles, all with the camera looking at the virtual world center, approximately 7.0 units from the center. Figure 9-47 is the scene viewed looking down the Z axis, with the camera at 0.0, 0.0, 7.0. Moving the camera toward the right to 5.0, 0.0, 5.0, which maintains a similar distance from the scene, results in the image in Figure 9-48. If the camera is then moved to 4.0, 5.0, 3.0, the result is the image in Figure 9-49.

Figure 9-47: Camera at 0.0 ,0.0, 7.0, Looking at 0.0, 0.0, 0.0, Focal Ratio 0.2

It is often necessary to adjust the distance of the camera to the objects in the scene or change the focal length of the camera. Of primary importance is to position the camera so that it is not inside any object in the scene. The farther from the scene, the more of the scene is in view, but the smaller the objects. In Figure 9-50, the camera is moved back and the point being looked at is adjusted so a different part of the scene is in the center of the camera's view. This reveals a spherical object that was present all along but not visible. In Figure 9-51, the camera is kept at about the same distance as Figure 9-49, but the focal ratio is changed from 0.2 to 0.3. The results are similar to moving the camera away from the scene.

The adjustment of the camera very much depends on the desired appearance of the final image. Start by generating line images with the camera being somewhat dis-

Figure 9-48: Camera at 5.0, 0.0, 5.0, Looking at 0.0, 0.0, 0.0, Focal Ratio 0.2

tant. Once a desired angle of view is established, move the camera closer. If the camera is to be placed amongst objects in the scene, use the focal ratio, rather than the distance from the objects, to determine how much of the scene is within view.

Creating, Storing, and Manipulating Images

In the previous examples, images have been written to a PBM format file by the `SippRender` command. While the file was piped directly to a viewer, it could have been written to a disk file. TSIPP provides other methods of displaying and storing images. An image can be written to or read from a file, an area in memory, or a Tk

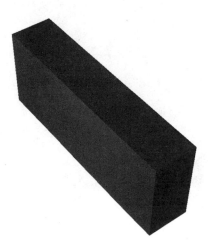

Figure 9-49: Camera at 4.0 5.0 3.0, Looking at 0.0 0.0 0.0, Focal Ratio 0.2

Figure 9-50: Camera at 6.0, 7.5 4.5, Looking at 1.0, 0.0, 0.0, Focal Ratio 0.2

photo image. These targets are collectively referred to as image store. They are identified by a handle that can be passed to a number of TSIPP commands.

The file format used so far in the examples is the PBM Plus format. This format is often used because of the great number of tools that read and manipulate it. The PBM Plus toolkit is a set of utilities for manipulating PBM Plus files and converting them to dozens of different graphics file formats.

There are really two PBM Plus format files produced by TSIPP: PBM for line renderings and PPM for all other renderings. PBM (Portable Bit Map) is a monochrome

Figure 9-51: Camera at 4.0, 5.0, 3.0, Looking at 1.0, 0.0, 0.0, Focal Ratio 0.3

image format, storing one bit of data per image pixel. PPM (Portable Pixel Map) is a full color image format, storing three bytes of data per image pixel. Currently, TSIPP does not support the reading of PBM and PPM files.

Both images can be written in two encoding formats: plain, which is an ASCII character encoding; and raw, which is a binary encoding. The format is specified by the -plain or -raw flag to the SippPBMOpen command. Raw is the default and preferred format, as it is smaller and faster to write.

While the PBM Plus formats are useful for simple photos, they don't compress images and allow only one image per file. Because of these limitations, TSIPP also supports the RLE file format, as defined by the Utah Raster Toolkit. RLE is an acronym for Run Length Encoding, which is a compression technique that is particularly effective for computer generated images. RLE files are usually considerably smaller than PPM files. RLE files can also store multiple images, which supports the storage of animations. TSIPP also supports the reading of RLE files, a feature not supported for the PBM Plus format. This allows images to be rendered, saved to a file, and then brought back into a TSIPP application for future manipulation or display.

You can open RLE files via the SippRLEOpen command and close via the SippRLEClose command. To query information about the current image and state of the file, use SippRLEInfo. RLE files are rendered to in the same manner as PBM Plus files, by passing an RLE file handle to the SippRender command. The following code copies one RLE file to another:

```
set in [SippRLEOpen in.rle]
set out [SippRLEOpen out.rle w]
while {![SippRLEInfo $in EOF]} {
    SippCopy $in $out
}
SippRLEClose $in
SippRLEClose $out
```

The SippCopy command copies a single image from one image store to another. The SippRLEInfo checks for end of file. The EOF argument indicates a Boolean test for whether the RLE file is at the end. Always perform this check before each access to the image; not as a status return as with standard Tcl file access. SippRLEInfo can also return the width and height of the current image by using the XSIZE or YSIZE arguments. While the preceding code fragment is not particularly useful, the target of the SippCopy command could be a Tk photo image that is used to display the images from the RLE file.

In certain applications you want to be able to store images in memory for later display or writing to a file. TSIPP provides a type of image store known as a pixel map. It can be used as the target of the SippRender command just like any other image store. The following code renders an image to a pixel map and then copies the pixel map to an RLE file:

```
set pix [SippPixMapCreate]
SippRender $pix $size $size $mode [expr $final ? 1 : 3]

set rle [SippRLEOpen $output w]
```

```
SippCopy $pix $rle
SippRLEClose $rle

SippPixMapUnref $pix
```

The `SippPixMapCreate` command creates a new pixel map image store and returns a handle to it. The width and height of the pixel map are not set until an image is stored in it. The image is rendered to the pixel map with `SippRender`, just as with any other image store. The image is now available for copying to another image store in a fraction of the time required to generate the image. In this example, the image is copied directly to an RLE file using the `SippCopy` command. When we are finished with the image in the pixel map, the `SippPixMapUnref` command is used to release the pixel map and the memory associated with it. Like the other unreference commands, the `SippPixMapUnref` deletes the handle associated with the pixel map. If there are no other references to the pixel map, it is released. In the current version of TSIPP, a handle is the only reference supported, so this always deletes the pixel map.

Building an Application with TSIPP and Tk

While generating an image file with TSIPP can also be useful for noninteractive applications, TSIPP can be useful for building interactive applications using Tk. The Tk photo image is used to display the images generated by TSIPP. See the Tk `image` and `photo` manual pages for details on how to use photo images.

The following code is a simple program to render the `MBrick` object defined in previous examples to a photo image. It is run using the `tksipp` program, a version of the `wish` program with the TSIPP commands linked in.

```
SippLightSourceCreate {15.0 15.0 15.0} {0.9 0.9 0.9} POINT
SippCameraParams STDCAMERA {-4.0 4.0 10.0} {0.0 0.0 0.0} \
{0.0 1.0 0.0} 0.4
SippObjectAddSubobj WORLD [MBrick $final]

proc DoRender {} {
    global photoImg final
    .buttons.render configure -state disabled
    .buttons.abort configure -state normal
    SippRender $photoImg 256 256 PHONG [expr $final ? 1 : 3]
    .buttons.abort configure -state disabled
    .buttons.render configure -state normal
}

set photoImg [image create photo -height $size -width $size]
label .photo -image $photoImg -background [SippColor tox {0 0 0}]

frame .buttons
button .buttons.render -text Render -command DoRender
button .buttons.abort -text Abort -command SippAbortRender \
-state disabled
button .buttons.exit -text Exit -command {exit 1}
```

```
pack .photo
pack .buttons
pack .buttons.render -side left
pack .buttons.abort -side left
pack .buttons.exit -side left
```

First, a photo image is created and its image name is saved. Next, a label widget is created on which to display the image. The widget background is set to black. While the string `black` could have been used to specify the background color, in this instance, the command `SippColor` is used for specifying the color in the TSIPP format of a list of red, green, and blue values. The option `tox` converts a color list to a standard X11 color specification, which is suitable for specifying a color in Tk. The option `tosipp` converts an X11 color to a TSIPP color list.

Three buttons are created. A render button is set up to call a procedure `DoRender`. This starts the rendering of the scene that is already defined. An abort button is set up to call the command `SippAbortRender`, but it is set to disabled. The function of this command and its relationship to the rendering process will be discussed in the next paragraph. An exit button is also defined to exit the program.

Graphical user interfaces generally require that long executing tasks be broken up into small pieces. This allows the program to be controlled by the event loop and continue to handle events like redisplays or button presses while the task is being processed. Graphics rendering is a computationally intensive process that requires the program to maintain a great deal of state information. This makes it difficult to break the SIPP rendering loop up into small steps. The solution used by TSIPP is to call the Tk `update` command periodically during the rendering loop. The `update` command processes all pending events before returning to the rendering loop. This is how the abort button in the example works. It simply calls the `SippAbortRender` command, which causes the rendering loop to be terminated upon completion of the `update`.

The handling of arbitrary events during the render process has the danger of allowing the application to modify the SIPP data structures while the rendering loop is using them. To prevent this, only a small set of the TSIPP commands, like `SippAbortRender` and `SippInfo`, are allowed during the rendering process. All other commands return errors. One interesting way you can use the periodic `update` is to have an `after` handler that updates a flashing widget that indicates rendering is in progress. If your application does not respond quickly enough during renderings, the update period can be changed with the `-update` option to the `SippRender` command.

The `DoRender` procedure defined in the example first changes the state of the render button to disabled and the state of the abort button to normal, allowing only the abort or exit buttons to be pressed. Then `SippRender` is used to render to the photo image. The script is blocked at this point until the rendering completes. Tcl commands can be executed during the rendering processes as a result of events, but the script will resume execution at the statement following the `SippRender` command when the rendering is finished or aborted. When the rendering completes, the buttons are restored to their original state. Figure 9-52 shows the resulting image.

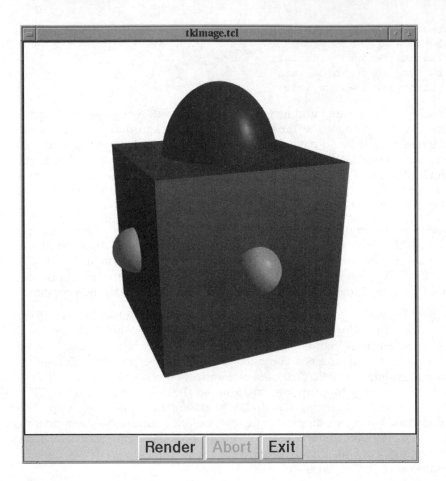

Figure 9-52: Rendering to a Tk Photo Image

Summary

In this chapter we have used TSIPP to construct several simple images as well as introduced most of the functionality available in TSIPP. Someone with limited experience in the algorithmic aspects of computer graphics will probably want to spend time experimenting with TSIPP as a way of building on this brief tutorial. One of the key advantages of working in Tcl over lower-level compiled languages is the speed of development. Tcl gives one the ability to quickly try adusting TSIPP parameters and observe the results. The best way to use TSIPP to learn more about computer graphics or to determine if it is approriate for your applications is to try it.

10

The Tree Widget

by Allan Brighton

Much of the information that computers deal with is hierarchical, or can be viewed as a hierarchy. A Unix file system is one of the most common examples. The Tk widget hierarchy is another. One of the best ways to display an overview of this kind of data is in the form of a tree.

This chapter describes a widget for displaying dynamic trees in a Tk. A tree, in our case, is made up of nodes and the lines connecting them, where a node can be any combination of text and graphics. Since the Tk canvas widget already offers us a powerful and flexible drawing interface, the tree widget makes use of this by simply managing the positions of items in a canvas window. Using canvas items for the tree nodes and lines has some great advantages. The tree nodes can be made up of any combination of canvas items, including text, bitmaps, images, and other graphics. You design the lines connecting the tree nodes, so you can make them in any color, style, or thickness you like.

The tree widget is *dynamic* in that you can add and delete nodes or change a node's layout at any time. For example, a directory browser might add subdirectories to a tree when the user clicks on a node. A second click could cause the subtree to disappear again. Clicking on the root of the directory tree could cause the tree to grow by adding the selected directory's parent.

Since the tree nodes can be any canvas items, including other windows (canvas window items), you could display an entire widget hierarchy in one tree. Each node could consist of a label indicating the name of the widget, with the widget itself above it.

The following examples demonstrate how you might implement a directory browser using the tree widget. If you are not familiar with all the commands for canvases, keep the reference page handy—we use a lot of them in the examples that follow. For a quick overview of the tree widget subcommands, see Table 10-1 at the end of this chapter.

A Simple Tree

Before we get into any more detail, let's look at an example of a simple tree application: a directory tree. The program uses the Unix *ls* command to recursively build up a tree of directories. It's only a simple demonstration, so there are no menus and no bindings yet. Don't be confused by the apparent overloading of names like `tree`, `canvas`, and `frame` in the examples. This is simply a way of naming variables in Tcl, so that it is easy to remember what they refer to. Rather than writing out the complete pathname for a widget, I use a variable, like `$tree` or `$canvas` to refer to it.

```
# create a canvas with horizontal and vertical scrollbars in the
# given frame with the given name

proc MakeCanvas {frame canvas} {
    set vscroll [scrollbar $frame.vscroll -command "$canvas yview"]
    set hscroll [scrollbar $frame.hscroll -orient horiz \
-command "$canvas xview"]
    canvas $canvas -xscrollcommand "$hscroll set" \
-yscrollcommand "$vscroll set"
    pack $vscroll -side right -fill y
    pack $hscroll -side bottom -fill x
    pack $canvas -fill both -expand 1
    bind $canvas <ButtonPress-2> "$canvas scan mark %x %y"
    bind $canvas <B2-Motion> "$canvas scan dragto %x %y"
    return $canvas
}


# add the directories under $dir to the tree (recursively)

proc ListDirsRec {canvas tree dir} {
    foreach i [exec ls $dir] {
        if {[file isdir $dir/$i]} {
            AddDir $canvas $tree $dir $dir/$i $i
            ListDirsRec $canvas $tree $dir/$i
        }
    }
}


# add the given directory to the tree
#
# Args:
#   canvas  - tree's canvas
#   tree    - the tree
#   parent  - pathname of parent dir
#   dir     - pathname of new dir being added
#   text    - text for tree node label (last component of dir)

proc AddDir {canvas tree parent dir text} {
    $canvas create text 0 0 -text $text -tags $dir
    set line [$canvas create line 0 0 0 0]
    $tree addlink $parent $dir $line
```

```
}

# main

wm geometry . 400x275
set canvas [MakeCanvas . .c]
set tree [tree $canvas.t -layout vertical]

set dir [file dirname [pwd]]
AddDir $canvas $tree {} $dir [file tail $dir]
ListDirsRec $canvas $tree $dir
```

Figure 10-1 shows the window produced by the preceding code when run from the *demos* directory in the tree-4.1 distribution (the *rootnode* directory is a dummy directory created for test purposes).

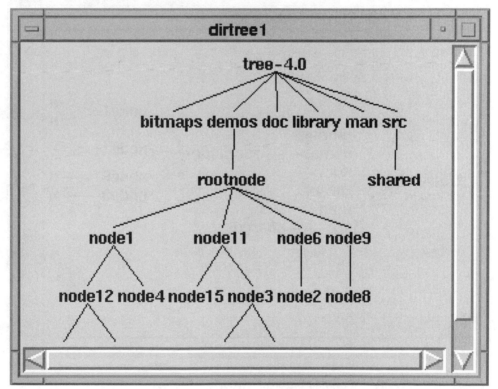

Figure 10-1: A Simple Directory Tree

Creating the Tree

The first thing you need to do to use the tree widget is to create a canvas widget. The MakeCanvas procedure in the previous code creates a canvas with two scrollbars and the usual Tk bindings, so you can scroll by dragging the middle mouse button. As we will see later on, the [INCR TK] tree interface takes care of this part for us.

The tree widget itself is created toward the end of the example with the following command:

```
set tree [tree $canvas.t -layout vertical]
```

Like all Tk widgets, the `tree` command returns the pathname of the widget being created, in this case `.c.t`. In the example, the new tree's pathname is saved in a variable so that it can be referred to later as `$tree`. Note that the tree is created here as a child of the canvas window. This is a requirement of the tree widget.

The default layout of the tree is `horizontal` or left to right. In this example the layout was set to `vertical`. You can change the layout at any time by using the `configure` subcommand:

```
$tree configure -layout horizontal
```

This produces a tree as shown in Figure 10-2.

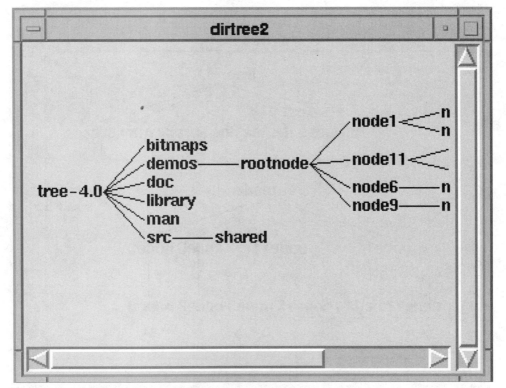

Figure 10-2: Directory Tree with Horizontal Layout

Adding Nodes To the Tree

A tree node can be made up of one or more canvas items, like text, bitmap, image, or other graphics. The following code creates a simple tree node consisting only of a label displaying the string given by `$text`. The example first creates a canvas text item and the line that attaches it to the tree and then adds the new node to the tree with the `addlink` subcommand.

```
$canvas create text 0 0 -text $text -tags $dir
set line [$canvas create line 0 0 0 0]
$tree addlink $parent $dir $line
```

When the tree widget is created, a single, invisible root node is also created. This node is given an empty tag and can be referred to as " " or {}. To start adding nodes to the tree, you use the tree subcommand addlink.

The addlink subcommand takes three arguments, which are the canvas tags or ids of the *parent* node, the *node* you are adding to the tree, and the *line* connecting them. If the new node should be the root of the tree, then *parent* is specified as the empty tag {}.

Note that canvas items are referred to by their *tags* or *ids*. Each canvas item has a unique id, which is the return value from the canvas create command. In addition, each item can be assigned one or more tags, where a tag is any string not starting with a digit. It is also possible to group canvas items together by assigning them all a common tag and using that tag to refer to the group of items. So, for example, if you wanted to create a tree node consisting of an image, a label, and a circle, you would create the three items somewhere in the canvas in correct relation to each other and assign them all a common tag (with the -tags canvas option).

In the previous example, the tree node consists only of a canvas text item displaying the last component of the directory name $text. We use the full pathname $dir as the canvas tag, since it uniquely describes the node. We could also have used some other unique value, like the the directory's i-node number.

The label is created at the arbitrary position (0, 0). The tree widget will move it to its final position, so we can place it anywhere we like. Likewise, the line connecting the parent and child nodes is created as a canvas line with length 0 at position (0, 0), since the tree widget positions the line as needed. The advantage of creating the line yourself rather than having the tree widget do it for you is that you can specify the color, thickness, and other properties of the line when you create it.

The line does not need to (and should not) have the same tag as the node. It is enough to specify the line's id, as returned from the canvas create command. In fact, in the previous example, we could also have specified the canvas id for the node's label rather than using the $dir tag, but that would work only as long as the node is made up of a single canvas item.

More Complex Nodes

To illustrate how to include multiple canvas items in a node using tags, let's modify the previous example to add a bitmap image to each node. To do that we modify the AddDir procedure from the example above and add a new procedure LayoutNode to arrange the items in the node:

```
# add the given directory to the tree
#
# Args:
#   canvas   - tree's canvas
#   tree     - the tree
#   parent   - pathname of parent dir
```

```
#  dir      - pathname of new dir being added
#  text     - text for tree node label (last component of dir)

proc AddDir {canvas tree parent dir text} {
    set bitmap @../bitmaps/dir.xbm
    $canvas create text 0 0 -text $text \
-tags [list $dir text $dir:text]
    $canvas create bitmap 0 0 -bitmap $bitmap \
-tags [list $dir bitmap $dir:bitmap]
    set line [$canvas create line 0 0 0 0]
    LayoutNode $canvas $tree $dir
    $tree addlink $parent $dir $line
}



# layout the components of the given node depending on whether
# the tree is vertical or horizontal

proc LayoutNode {canvas tree dir} {
    set text $dir:text
    set bitmap $dir:bitmap

    if {[$tree cget -layout] == "horizontal"} {
        scan [$canvas bbox $text] "%d %d %d %d" x1 y1 x2 y2
        $canvas itemconfigure $bitmap -anchor se
        $canvas coords $bitmap $x1 $y2
    } else {
        scan [$canvas bbox $bitmap] "%d %d %d %d" x1 y1 x2 y2
        $canvas itemconfigure $text -anchor n
        $canvas coords $text [expr "$x1+($x2-$x1)/2"] $y2
    }
}
```

Figure 10-3 shows what the new tree looks like.

In the preceding example, we start by creating each node's bitmap and label at position (0, 0). We then call the LayoutNode procedure to either center the label below the bitmap (for vertical trees) or center the bitmap to the left of the label (for horizontal trees).

We could also center the bitmap above the label (for vertical trees) or center the label to the right of the bitmap (for horizontal trees). The result should be the same.

Only the relative positions of the canvas items in the node are important. The tree widget later moves all of the items that make up a node as a unit to their final position in the tree. The LayoutNode procedure was written so that it could be called again for each node if the tree's layout is changed. For example, we could now toggle the tree's layout between vertical and horizontal with the following procedure:

```
# Toggle the layout of the tree between vertical and horizontal
```

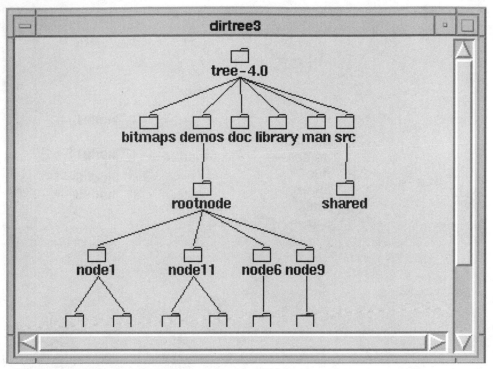

Figure 10-3: Directory Tree with More Complex Nodes

```
proc ToggleLayout {canvas tree} {
    if {[$tree cget -layout] == "horizontal"} {
        $tree config -layout vertical
    } else {
        $tree config -layout horizontal
    }

    # change the layout of the nodes so that the bitmap is on top for
    # vertical trees and at left for horizontal trees
    foreach i [$canvas find withtag text] {
        set dir [lindex [$canvas gettags $i] 0]
        LayoutNode $canvas $tree $dir
        $tree nodeconfigure $dir
    }
}
```

What this procedure does is loop through all of the tree nodes and change the layout of the items in each node depending on the layout of the tree (horizontal or vertical). To do this, we use the cget tree subcommand here to get the value of the -layout option and then set the option with the config subcommand. The nodeconfigure tree subcommand is then called for each node to tell the tree widget to recalculate the node's size and position. Figure 10-4 shows the same tree now with the *layout* set to horizontal.

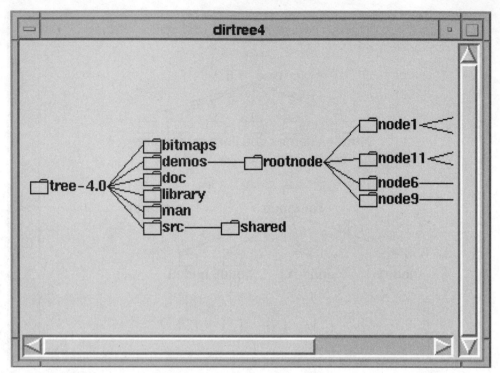

Figure 10-4: Sample Tree After Calling ToggleLayout

Using Canvas Tags to Reference Nodes

In the previous example, the canvas items that make up a tree node were each given a list of three tags:

```
        $canvas create text 0 0 -text $text \
 -tags [list $dir text $dir:text]
        $canvas create bitmap 0 0 -bitmap $bitmap \
 -tags [list $dir bitmap $dir:bitmap]
```

The first tag `$dir` (the directory pathname for the node) is shared by all of the items that make up a single node and is used to reference that node. the `Toggle-Layout` procedure depends on this tag being the first in the list of tags for a node. The second tag identifies all of the node labels (`text`) or all of the bitmaps (`bitmap`) in the tree. The third tag is a combination of the first two and identifies the label or bitmap of a particular tree node. This is used in the `LayoutNode` procedure to change the position of the label and bitmap of each node.

The advantage of assigning multiple tags to the canvas items in this way is flexibility. In the case of the directory tree, given a directory path name, you can access any tree node as a whole (by specifying the directory pathname as the tag) or the bitmap or label separately (by appending `:text` or `:bitmap` to the tag. You can also access all tree nodes at once. For example:

```
        $canvas find withtag text
```

returns a list of all the canvas items having the tag `text`. Since each of the tree nodes we created also has a label with this tag, the return value is a list of all of the labels in the tree:

```
% $canvas find withtag text
1 4 7 10 13 16 19 22 25 28 31 34 37 40 43 46 49 52 55 58 61 64 67
%
```

The numbers in the list are the canvas ids for the tree node labels.

Changing the Distance Between Sibling Nodes

In the horizontal tree just shown, the layout looks a bit crowded. You can change this by specifying a border space around the individual nodes with the `-border:` option to `addlink`:

```
proc AddDir {canvas tree parent dir text} {
    ...
    $tree addlink $parent $dir $line -border 2m
}
```

Although this option is set separately on each node, it usually looks best when all of the nodes have the same border size, as shown in Figure 10-5.

By default there is no border around a node.

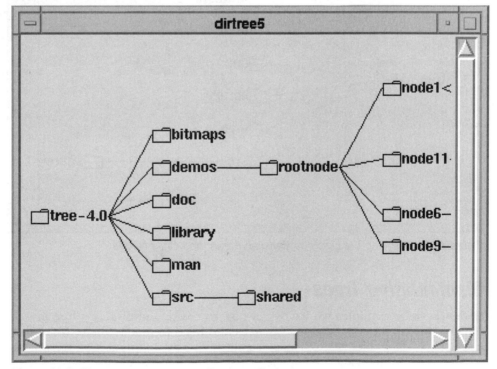

Figure 10-5: Changing the Distance Between Nodes

You can also change the distance between parent and child nodes. Unlike the -border option in the last example, which is applied to each node, the -parentdistance option is set once for the entire tree, either as an option when creating the tree or through the configure widget subcommand. The default parentdistance is 30 pixels, however, you can use any of the standard Tk units, such as c for centimeter as shown here:

```
proc AddDir {canvas tree parent dir text} {
    ...
    $tree addlink $parent $dir $line -border 2m
}
...
set tree [tree $canvas.t -layout horizontal -parentdistance 3c]
...
```

The resulting tree is shown in Figure 10-6.

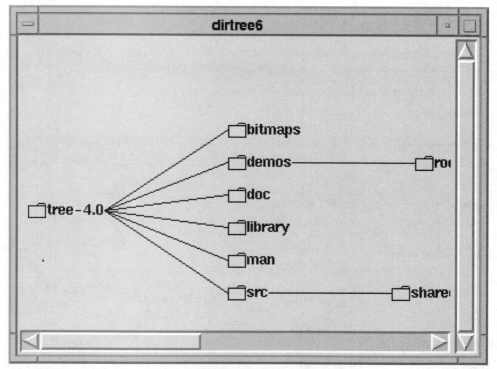

Figure 10-6: Changing the Distance Between Parent and Child Nodes

Manipulating Trees

In the previous examples we have seen how to create and display a tree in a Tk canvas. Most applications that display trees also need to modify them dynamically and possibly allow the user to manipulate them directly. In this section we will discuss ways to examine and modify the tree structure and handle user input.

Selecting Tree Nodes

Let's extend the sample directory tree application to allow the user to select tree nodes with the mouse and perform operations on them. Since the tree nodes are made up of canvas items, we use the canvas widget's commands to handle the user input. First we add some bindings so that clicking with mouse button 1 on a tree node highlights the label or bitmap and prints out the pathname of the selected directory. The bindings and the procedures that implement them are listed in the following example:

```
# set the bindings for the tree canvas

proc SetBindings {canvas} {
    # bind mouse button <1> to select the label or bitmap
    $canvas bind text <1> "focus %W; SelectNode $canvas"
    $canvas bind bitmap <1> "SelectBitmap $canvas"
}


# select the current node's label

proc SelectNode {canvas} {
    $canvas select from current 0
    $canvas select to current [string length [$canvas itemcget \
        current -text]]
    DeSelectBitmap $canvas
    puts "selected label: [GetPath $canvas]"
}


# de-select all node labels

proc DeSelectNode {canvas} {
    $canvas select clear
}


# highlight the node's bitmap

proc SelectBitmap {canvas} {
    catch {focus {}}
    set path [lindex [$canvas gettags current] 0]
    DeSelectNode $canvas
    DeSelectBitmap $canvas
    $canvas itemconfigure current -background \
        [$canvas cget -selectbackground] \
        -tags "[$canvas gettags current] selected"
    puts "selected bitmap: [GetPath $canvas]"
}


# stop highlighting the node's bitmap
```

```
proc DeSelectBitmap {canvas} {
    $canvas itemconfigure selected -background [$canvas cget \
-background]
    $canvas dtag selected
}



# return the pathname (dir) for the item currently selected
# (bitmap or text)

proc GetPath {canvas} {
    set id [$canvas select item]
    if {"$id" == ""} {
        return [lindex [$canvas gettags selected] 0]
    }
    return [lindex [$canvas gettags $id] 0]
}
```

After defining the procedures, we still need to insert a call to `SetBindings` to set up the canvas bindings for selecting tree nodes (canvas text items and bitmaps).

```
# set up bindings for selecting tree nodes
SetBindings $canvas
```

The code to select a node's label is fairly straightforward. You use the canvas features to select the text item under the mouse, given by the special canvas tag `current`. Since there is no predefined way of selecting a bitmap, we simply set the bitmap's background color to the same color used to display selected text and give it the tag `selected`. Note that `current` is a special, predefined tag in Tk, while `selected` is just an arbitrary name we use here.

The `GetPath` routine checks for either a selected label or a selected bitmap and returns the first tag in the list of tags for the item, which is in this case the directory pathname.

Figure 10-7 shows the tree with one of the nodes selected.

On my machine, clicking on the node labeled *rootnode* produced the following output:

```
selected label: /diskb/tcl/tree-4.1/demos/rootnode
```

You could of course use other methods to select a node, like drawing a border around it or changing the bitmap or image used to display it.

Editing Trees Interactively

Suppose we want to allow the user to navigate the tree by double-clicking on the tree nodes. We could define the following behavior:

- A double-click on the root node's bitmap inserts the node's parent (in our case, the parent directory) and siblings (subdirectories of the new root) to the tree. Double-clicking on other nodes makes the selected node the new root of the tree.

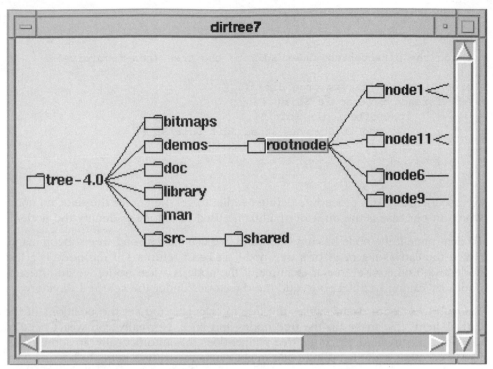

Figure 10-7: Selecting a Tree Node

- A double-click on a node's label adds any subnodes (subdirectories here) to the tree, or if the subnodes are already in the tree, removes them.

To implement this behavior we add two new bindings that call some new Tcl procedures. These procedures make use of a number of `tree` subcommands that we haven't discussed yet, but I will explain them shortly.

```
$canvas bind text <Double-Button-1> \
"ToggleChildren $canvas $tree"
$canvas bind bitmap <Double-Button-1> \
"ToggleParent $canvas $tree"
```

First, the `ToggleChildren` procedure adds child nodes to a node if none are present or removes them if they are present:

```
# If the current selection is a leaf, add its subnodes, otherwise
# remove them

proc ToggleChildren {canvas tree} {
    set path [GetPath $canvas]
    if [$tree isleaf $path] {
        ListDirs $canvas $tree $path
        $tree draw
    } else {
        $tree prune $path
    }
```

```
    }

# add the directories under $dir to the tree (non-recursive)

proc ListDirs {canvas tree dir} {
    foreach i [exec ls $dir] {
        if {[file isdir $dir/$i]} {
            AddDir $canvas $tree $dir $dir/$i $i
        }
    }
}
```

We use the `GetPath` procedure defined earlier to get the tag for the selected node, which in our case is the directory pathname used to uniquely identify the node.

To determine if the node has any subnodes, we use the `isleaf` tree subcommand. Given the canvas tag or id of a tree node, `isleaf` returns 1 if the node is a leaf node and 0 otherwise. In our example, if the node is a leaf node, we add its subnodes by calling `ListDirs` to add the directories under the selected directory.

The call to `$tree draw` causes the tree to calculate and set the positions of the canvas items that make up the tree nodes and lines. Normally you won't need to use this subcommand, since the tree widget does this automatically. In some cases, however, other event-handling code might cause the canvas items to become visible before they are in their proper positions. This call makes sure that everything is in the right place before it becomes visible.

If the node is not a leaf, then it has subnodes and we want to remove them from the tree. This is exactly what the `prune` tree subcommand does. It deletes any subnodes of the given node and the corresponding canvas items, but otherwise leaves the node intact. The *pruned* nodes are not saved anywhere, so if you want to add them to the tree again, you have to add them in the same way as before, with the `addlink` subcommand.

The `ToggleParent` procedure is somewhat more complicated. It makes the selected node the root of the tree, unless it already is the root, in which case a new root and its subnodes are inserted before the selected node:

```
# If the selected node is the root of the tree, add its parent
# and siblings
# to the tree, otherwise make the selected node the new root of
# the tree.

proc ToggleParent {canvas tree} {
    set path [GetPath $canvas]
    if [$tree isroot $path] {
        set dir [file dirname $path]
        if {$dir != $path} {
            AddDir $canvas $tree "" $dir [dir_tail $dir]
            set tail [file tail $path]
            foreach i [exec ls $dir] {
                if {[file isdirectory $dir/$i]} {
                    if {$i == $tail} {
```

```
                    $tree movelink $path $dir
            } else {
                    AddDir $canvas $tree $dir $dir/$i "$i"
            }
        }
    }
        $tree draw
    }
    } else {
        $tree root $path
    }
}


# return the last component of the directory name
# (/ is a special case)

proc dir_tail {dir} {
    if {$dir == "/"} {return $dir}
    return [file tail $dir]
}
```

The `ToggleParent` procedure first checks if the selected node is the root node. The `isroot` tree subcommand is similar to `isleaf` used in the preceding example. It returns 1 if the given node is the root of the tree and 0 otherwise.

If the node is the root of the tree and the directory is not /, we add the node's parent and sibling directories to the tree. To do this, we first add the new root to the tree and then add one level of subdirectories. When we come to the node that was originally selected, instead of recreating it, we move it to its new position under the new root node using the `movelink` tree subcommand.

The `movelink` subcommand works much like the Unix *mv* command when both arguments are directories. It unhooks the node named by the first argument and inserts it as a child of the node named by the second argument. As when moving directories, moving a node with `movelink` causes the entire subtree to move with it.

In the case where the selected node was not the root of the tree, we simply use the tree `root` subcommand to make the given node the new root of the tree. The canvas items for any nodes that are no longer accessible from the root node are automatically deleted.

Figure 10-8 shows the tree again after navigating around the directory hierarchy. Compare this with the tree in Figure 10-7.

Pruning Trees, Moving Nodes, and Removing Nodes

In the previous example we used the `prune` and `movelink` tree subcommands. The `prune` subcommand removes the subnodes from the given node. The `movelink` command moves the given node to a new position in the tree. One other command that we have not discussed yet, `rmlink`, is used to remove the named node and all of its subnodes from the tree. The `rmlink` tree subcommand

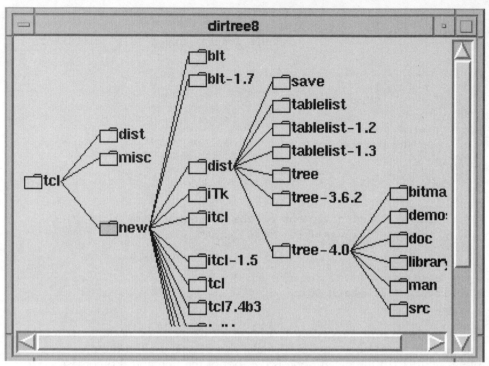

Figure 10-8: Navigating Through the Tree

is similar to the `prune` subcommand, except that the given node is also removed from the tree. The example below adds key bindings to the previous example so that CTRL-D removes the selected node and its subtree.

```
bind $canvas <Control-d> "HideNode $canvas $tree"

# remove the selected node and its subnodes from the tree

proc HideNode {canvas tree} {
    set path [GetPath $canvas]
    if {"$path" != "" && ![$tree isroot $path]} {
        $tree rmlink $path
    }
}
```

In the preceding example, we call `GetPath` to get the name of the directory for the selected node. If no node was selected, this could return an empty string. We also check that the selected node is not the root of the tree, since we don't want to remove it.

Note: Don't confuse the displayed root of the tree, which can have any tag, with the invisible *pseudo root*, which has the empty tag and cannot be selected, because it is not displayed. The invisible root node usually has one child node, the visible root node. However, you could add more subnodes to it to display multiple trees in one canvas. This kind of display could be useful for displaying a class hierarchy where there might not be a single root.

Traversing the Tree

There are a number of tree subcommands for querying and traversing the tree being displayed. Each of the following subcommands takes as an argument the canvas tag or id of a tree node and returns the tags of one or more tree nodes as a result:

- **subnodes:** Returns a Tcl list of the given node's subnodes.
- **parent:** Returns the name of the parent of the given node. If the node has no parent (i.e., is a root node), an empty string is returned.
- **child:** Returns the tag of the first child of the given node. If the node has no children, an empty string is returned. The `sibling` subcommand can be used to get the names of the other child nodes in sequence.
- **sibling:** Returns the name of the next sibling of the given node. If the node has no siblings, an empty string is returned.
- **ancestors:** Returns a Tcl list of the given node's ancestors, for example: `{parent grandparent ...}`.

Let's use the preceding commands to implement key bindings for our sample tree so that you can use the cursor (arrow) keys to navigate the tree.

```
# add bindings for the arrow keys

bind $canvas <Left> "SelectNext $canvas $tree %K"
bind $canvas <Right> "SelectNext $canvas $tree %K"
bind $canvas <Down> "SelectNext $canvas $tree %K"
bind $canvas <Up> "SelectNext $canvas $tree %K"


# select the current node's parent, child or sibling
# depending on the value of direction (Left, Right, Up or Down)

proc SelectNext {canvas tree direction} {
    set id [$canvas select item]
    set path [lindex [$canvas gettags $id] 0]

    if {[$tree cget -layout] == "vertical"} {
        case $direction in {
            Left          {set next_node Prev_Sibling}
            Right         {set next_node Next_Sibling}
            Up            {set next_node Parent}
            Down          {set next_node Child}
        }
    } else {
        case $direction in {
            Left          {set next_node Parent}
            Right         {set next_node Child}
            Up            {set next_node Prev_Sibling}
            Down          {set next_node Next_Sibling}
        }
    }
}
```

```
        case $next_node in {
            Parent {
                set node [$tree parent $path]
                if {"$node" == ""} {
                    ToggleParent $canvas $tree
                    set node [$tree parent $path]
                }
            }
            Child {
                set node [$tree child $path]
                if {"$node" == ""} {
                    ListDirs $canvas $tree $path
                    set node [$tree child $path]
                    $tree draw
                }
            }
            Next_Sibling {
                set node [$tree sibling $path]
                if {"$node" == ""} {
                    set node [$tree child [$tree parent $path]]
                }
            }
            Prev_Sibling {
                set next [$tree child [$tree parent $path]]
                while {"$next" != ""} {
                    set node $next
                    set next [$tree sibling $next]
                    if {"$next" == "$path"} {
                        break;
                    }
                }
            }
            default {return}
    }

    if {"$node" != ""} {
        set next [$canvas find withtag $node:text]
        $canvas select from $next 0
        $canvas select to $next [string length [$canvas itemcget \
                                    $next -text]]
    }
}
```

The preceding `SelectNext` procedure takes as arguments the name of the tree and canvas widgets and a *direction*, which is one of the arrow key names Up, Down, Right, or Left. The action taken depends on the key pressed, the selected node, and the layout of the tree. For example, if the tree layout is horizontal, pressing Left traverses the tree by selecting the current node's parent, adding it to the tree first if necessary. Pressing Right traverses the tree in the other direction, adding subtrees as needed. The Up and Down arrow keys don't add any nodes; they only traverse the selected node's siblings.

Reconfiguring Tree Nodes

When you make any changes to the canvas items that make up a tree node, like rearranging the layout, adding items, or removing items, the tree widget needs to be told to recalculate the node's size. Normally the tree widget stores the dimensions of a node once when it is added to the tree and assumes that they will remain the same. If you change a node's dimensions, you need to notify the tree widget of this, so it can recalculate the layout. (Otherwise, the layout may be incorrect.) The `nodeconfigure` subcommand causes the tree to recalculate a node's size and also allows you to change the node's options. `nodeconfigure` accepts the same options as the `addlink` command:

`-border` *width*

specifies the width of the nodes border. This determines the distance between the individual nodes in the tree. The default is 0.

`-remove` *command*

specifies a Tcl command to be evaluated when the node is removed from the tree. This option is necessary when a node contains a window like a listbox or button, so that these can also be properly deleted. The default action, when a node is to be removed, is to use the canvas `delete` command to delete the canvas items with the given tag or id.

The `-remove` option is used in the next example, where we add Tk windows to tree nodes.

Using Tk Windows in Tree Nodes

In the examples so far, the trees have displayed only directories. Normally you would also want to see a list of the files in a selected directory. We could display files in the tree along with the directories, say with a different bitmap, but that might clutter up the tree too much, since there tends to be many more files than directories. So instead, we could display a list of files in the selected directory in a separate listbox. In fact, we could make the listbox a part of a tree node and display it there when needed. Whether this is a good idea or not probably depends on the application, but for the sake of example, let's add some bindings to the example directory tree application to do it. In order to be useful, the example also has to allow resizing of the listbox and add code to get the name of a selected file.

The following code adds a binding to tree node labels (canvas text items) to open or close a listbox listing the files in the selected directory:

```
$canvas bind text <2> \
"focus %W; SelectNode $canvas; ShowFiles $canvas $tree"


# Display the file names in the selected directory in a scrolling
# list beneath the node, or remove the list if it is already there

proc ShowFiles {canvas tree} {
    set dir [GetPath $canvas]
```

```
set frame [UniqueName $canvas $dir]

# create the frame and list if not already there
if {[llength [$canvas find withtag $dir:list]]} {
    RemoveListFrame $canvas $tree $frame $dir
} else {
    MakeListFrame $canvas $tree $frame $dir
}
}
```

In the ShowFiles procedure, we first get the directory name for the selected node and then check to see if the tree is already displaying a list of files in that directory. If the tag $dir::list exists in the canvas, then there must be a listbox open in the node, so we remove it by calling RemoveListFrame. Otherwise, we create one by calling MakeListFrame.

```
# generate and return a unique name for a listbox widget
# in the canvas for the given directory.

proc UniqueName {canvas dir} {
    global dirtree
    if {[info exists dirtree($canvas.$dir)]} {
        return $dirtree($canvas.$dir)
    }
    if {[info exists dirtree(listboxcnt)]} {
        incr dirtree(listboxcnt)
    } else {
        set dirtree(listboxcnt) 0
    }
    set dirtree($canvas.$dir) $canvas.list$dirtree(listboxcnt)
    return $dirtree($canvas.$dir)
}
```

Since every widget needs to have a unique name, we generate a name for the node's listbox in the procedure UniqueName. The listbox created for a node has a name like $canvas.list0, $canvas.list1, and so on (canvas window items must be children of the canvas).

The global array variable dirtree is used here and in a number of other procedures for storing local, private information. dirtree(listboxcnt) holds a count of the listboxes created and is used to generate the unique names. dirtree($canvas.$dir) holds the name of the listbox created for the given canvas and directory.

The following MakeListFrame procedure takes care of filling out the contents of the new frame in the tree. It creates the listbox and scrollbar, packs them in the frame, and then fills the listbox with the list of files in the selected directory. We need to set the size of the listbox frame in the canvas create call, since the canvas controls the size of canvas window items.

```
# make the list frame for displaying the files in dir

proc MakeListFrame {canvas tree frame dir} {
```

```
global dirtree

# make the list frame and set up resizing
frame $frame \
    -borderwidth 3 \
    -cursor bottom_right_corner
scrollbar $frame.scroll \
    -relief sunken \
    -command "$frame.list yview" \
    -width 10
listbox $frame.list \
    -yscrollcommand "$frame.scroll set" \
    -relief sunken \
    -bg  [$canvas cget -bg] \
    -selectmode single

pack $frame.scroll -side right -fill y
pack $frame.list -side left -expand yes -fill both

# fill the list with the files in the selected dir
foreach i [exec ls $dir] {
    if {[file isfile $dir/$i]} {
        $frame.list insert end $i
    }
}

# insert the list frame in the canvas
$canvas create window 0 0 -tags "$dir $dir:list list" \
    -window $frame -width 3c -height 2c

# arrange the items in the tree node and change the bitmap
# to show an "open" directory
LayoutNode $canvas $tree $dir
$canvas itemconfigure $dir:bitmap -bitmap "@bitmaps/open_dir.xbm"
$tree nodeconfigure $dir -remove "destroy $frame"

# add bindings for resizing the listbox in the canvas
SetFileListBindings $canvas $tree $frame $frame.list \
                    $frame.scroll $dir
}
```

We call LayoutNode to arrange the items in the node and change the bitmap to display an open directory while the listbox is displayed. The call to the tree sub-command nodeconfigure arranges to have the listbox automatically deleted when the node is deleted. Finally, we call the SetFileListBindings procedure to add some bindings for resizing the listbox frame.

The RemoveListFrame procedure is called to remove the listbox frame from a node while the node is still displayed. It undoes the work of MakeListFrame by destroying the listbox frame and unsetting the dirtree array values. Again, node-configure is used to notify the tree of the change in the node dimensions and options. Here we also reset the -remove option (which was previously set by

---

MakeListFrame), since we no longer need to have the `destroy $frame` command evaluated to delete the listbox frame when the node is deleted.

```
# remove the list frame for displaying the files in dir

proc RemoveListFrame {canvas tree frame dir} {
    global dirtree
    $canvas delete $dir:list
    destroy $frame

    $canvas itemconfigure $dir:bitmap -bitmap @bitmaps/dir.xbm
    $tree nodeconfigure $dir -remove "" -border 2
    set dirtree(list) ""
    set dirtree(dir) ""
}
```

The `LayoutNode` procedure from earlier examples has been extended here to handle the layout when a listbox frame is part of the node. We also add some bindings to the listbox frames in the `SetFileListBindings` procedure so that you can resize them by dragging on the corner of the frame with mouse button 1. As in the previous version of `LayoutNode`, the layout of the tree (horizontal or vertical) determines the layout of the node.

```
# layout the components of the given node depending on whether
# the tree is vertical or horizontal
# (Also take the file listbox into consideration if it is open)

proc LayoutNode {canvas tree dir} {
    set text $dir:text
    set bitmap $dir:bitmap
    set list [$canvas find withtag $dir:list]

    if {[$tree cget -layout] == "horizontal"} {
        scan [$canvas bbox $text] "%d %d %d %d" x1 y1 x2 y2
        $canvas itemconfigure $bitmap -anchor se
        $canvas coords $bitmap $x1 $y2
        if {"$list" != ""} {
            scan  [$canvas bbox $text $bitmap] "%d %d %d %d" \
                                               x1 y1 x2 y2
            $canvas itemconfigure $list -anchor nw
            $canvas coords $list $x1 $y2
        }
    } else {
        scan [$canvas bbox $bitmap] "%d %d %d %d" x1 y1 x2 y2
        $canvas itemconfigure $text -anchor n
        $canvas coords $text [expr "$x1+($x2-$x1)/2"] $y2
        if {"$list" != ""} {
            scan  [$canvas bbox $text $bitmap] "%d %d %d %d" \
                                               x1 y1 x2 y2
            $canvas itemconfigure $list -anchor n
            $canvas coords $list [expr "$x1+($x2-$x1)/2"] $y2
        }
```

```
        }
    }
```

In `SetFileListBindings`, we set up the bindings for a new listbox displaying the files in a node's directory.

```
    # set the bindings for a file listbox in the tree canvas

    proc SetFileListBindings {canvas tree frame list scroll dir} {
        global dirtree
        bind $frame <ButtonPress-1> \
            "ResizeList $canvas $tree $frame $list %x %y $dir first"
        bind $frame <Button1-Motion> \
            "ResizeList $canvas $tree $frame $list %x %y $dir"
        bind $frame <ButtonRelease-1> \
            "ResizeList $canvas $tree $frame $list %x %y $dir last"

        # set/clear the resize cursor
        bind $list <Any-Enter> "$frame config -cursor {}"
        bind $list <Any-Leave> \
            "$frame config -cursor bottom_right_corner"
        bind $scroll <Any-Enter> "$frame config -cursor {}"
        bind $scroll <Any-Leave> \
            "$frame config -cursor bottom_right_corner"

        bind $list <;1>;  "set dirtree(list) %W; set dirtree(dir)
    $dir; [bind Listbox <;1>;]"
        bind $list <;Double-Button-1>; ChooseFile
    }
```

The first group of bindings allows the user to resize the list frame in the canvas by dragging with mouse button 1. The next group of bindings arranges to display special cursors at the edges of the listbox window to indicate that resizing is allowed. The last two bindings set up a selection mechanism, so that a single-click with mouse button 1 selects a filename in the list and a double-click calls the `Choose-File` procedure to do something with the file. We use the global array variable `dirtree` here again to save information about which directory and listbox are currently selected.

```
    # event proc called to resize the file listbox in the canvas
    # while the user is dragging its corner

    proc ResizeList {canvas tree frame list x y dir {when any}} {
        global dirtree

        case $when {
            first {
                set dirtree(tlx) $x
                set dirtree(tly) $y
            }
            last {
                $tree nodeconfigure $dir
```

```
            }
        any {
                set w   [$canvas itemcget $dir:list -width]
                set h   [$canvas itemcget $dir:list -height]
                set nw [expr $w+($x-$dirtree(tlx))]
                set nh [expr $h+($y-$dirtree(tly))]
                $canvas itemconfigure $dir:list -width $nw -height
$nh
                set dirtree(tlx) $x
                set dirtree(tly) $y
        }
    }
}
```

The `ResizeList` procedure is called when the user presses (`when = first`), drags (`when = any`), or releases (`when = last`) mouse button 1 on the border of a node's listbox frame. We use the global array variable `dirtree` here again to save the X and Y mouse coordinates between events so we can resize the canvas window by the difference each time.

Windows in tree nodes are not managed by a geometry manager such as the *packer*. You have to set and get the window size with canvas commands and not with the `-width` or `-height` widget options. We set the default size of the list-box frame when we created the canvas window item:

```
$canvas create window 0 0 -tags "$dir $dir:list list" \
    -window $frame -width 3c -height 2c
```

And now, when we want to resize the listbox frame interactively, we use the canvas `itemconfigure` subcommand:

```
set w   [$canvas itemcget $dir:list -width]
set h   [$canvas itemcget $dir:list -height]
    ...
$canvas itemconfigure $dir:list -width $nw -height $nh
```

It is important that the canvas knows the size of the window, so that the tree can get the correct information from the canvas about the size of the tree nodes.

```
# Return the path name of the file currently selected in the
# current node's listbox, or the empty string if none are
selected.

proc GetFilename {} {
    global dirtree
    set dir $dirtree(dir)
    set list $dirtree(list)
    if {"$dir" == "" || "$list" == ""} {return ""}

    set sel [$list curselection]
    if {![llength $sel]} {return ""}
    return $dir/[$list get [lindex $sel 0]]
}
```

GetFilename uses the information saved in the global array `dirtree` to determine the pathname of the file selected in some node's listbox. The directory and listbox name are kept in the array and the last component of the file pathname is taken from the listbox selection.

When a user double-clicks on a file in a node's listbox, the `ChooseFile` procedure is called:

```
proc ChooseFile {} {
    set file [GetFilename]

    # for test purposes, just print the file name here
    puts "got $file"
}
```

In a real application, you might start an editor to view the selected file. In this case, we simply print the pathname of the file.

Figure 10-9 shows the sample application now after some file lists have been opened and resized.

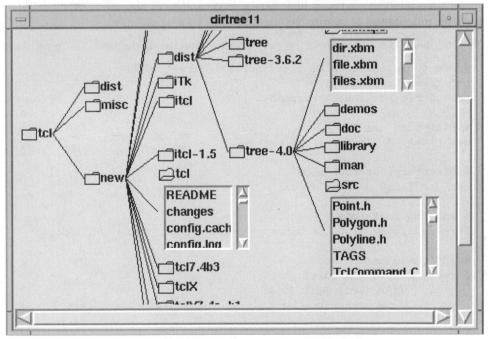

Figure 10-9: Directory Tree with Embedded Listbox Windows for Files

An [INCR TK] Interface to the Tree Widget

The sample directory tree application developed in the previous section only made use of standard Tcl, Tk, and the tree extension. In practice, I almost always use a *wish* with at least the [INCR TCL] (Chapter 2), [INCR TK] (Chapter 3), TclX (Chapter 6), and BLT (Chapter 7) extensions added. In particular, I prefer to organize Tcl code in an object-oriented way using [INCR TCL] classes. The [INCR TCL] extension, discussed in the chapter on [INCRTCL], adds classes and inheritance to Tcl. The [INCR TK] extension is based on [INCR TCL] and also includes features that make it easy to create *mega-widgets* or combinations of widgets that behave like the standard Tk widgets.

The tree widget release also contains a sample [INCR TK] Tree mega-widget, as a *wrapper* for the basic tree widget. In order to use the [INCR TK] version of the tree widget, you use the capitalized widget name `Tree` instead of `tree`. The [INCR TK] tree widget accepts all of the standard tree options and subcommands and passes them on to the underlying tree widget. In addition, the [INCR TK] widget takes care of creating the canvas, tree, and scrollbars, defines a standard layout for tree nodes, handles node selection, and offers methods for common operations on trees. A number of the Tcl procedures described in the previous section are also available as methods in the [INCR TK] Tree widget.

The advantage of using an object-oriented widget extension like [INCR TK] is that it makes it easy to develop complex widgets at the Tcl level. [INCR TK] provides built-in `cget` and `configure` methods (subcommands in Tk) and option handling that make mega-widgets act just like standard Tk widgets. You can extend widgets through inheritance or simply use them as is in your application.

The following is an example of a simple directory tree using the [INCR TK] `Tree` class:

```
# create an instance of the [incr Tk] "Tree" widget
set tree [Tree .tree]
pack $tree -fill both -expand 1

# bitmap to use for nodes
set bitmap "../bitmaps/dir.xbm"

# directory for root node
set dir [file dirname [pwd]]

# add the root node
$tree add_node {} $dir -bitmap @$bitmap -text [file tail $dir]

# add the subnodes
foreach i [exec ls $dir] {
    if {[file isdir $dir/$i]} {
        $tree add_node $dir $dir/$i -bitmap @$bitmap -text $i
    }
}
```

Figure 10-10 shows the window created by the preceding simple application.

As the previous example shows, using the [INCR TK] Tree widget can save you a bit of coding. The mega-widget version takes care of arranging the node's label and bitmap and creating the tree lines. Besides creating the widget components (frame, canvas, scrollbars, and tree), the [INCR TK] Tree widget also sets up bindings for

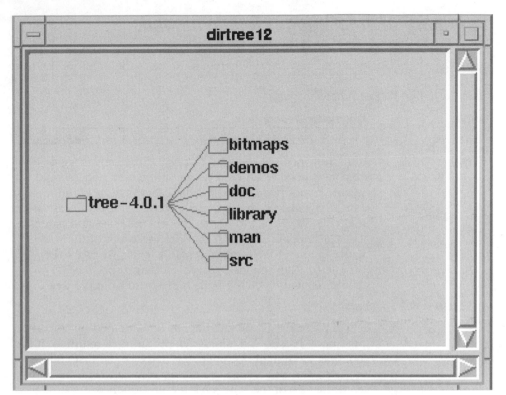

Figure 10-10: A Simple [INCR TK] Directory Tree

selecting nodes with mouse button 1. All the basic tree subcommands are accepted and some additional *methods* are implemented.

The `add_node` method, for example, adds a tree node with an optional label and/or bitmap. The arguments are:

- the canvas tag for the parent node
- the tag for the node being added to the tree
- an optional `-text` *node-label*
- an optional `-bitmap` *node-bitmap*

The `add_node` method sets up the node's layout and basic bindings for selection. All tree labels get the common tag `text` and the bitmaps share the tag `bitmap`. So if you want to perform some action when the user double-clicks on a node, you could add some code like this to your application:

```
$canvas bind text <;Double-Button-1>; "some_action..."
$canvas bind bitmap <;Double-Button-1>; "some_action..."
```

The [INCR TK] Tree widget also offers methods for getting the currently selected node and for toggling the tree's layout. In addition, options are available to control the fonts used for tree labels and the colors used for lines and bitmaps. For a list of methods and options, see the manual page *itclTree(n)*.

Summary of Tree Widget Subcommands

Table 10-1 summarizes all of the tree widget subcommands. The syntax is always *pathName subcommand arguments*, where pathName is the name of the tree.

Table 10-1: Tree Widget Subcommands

Name	Arguments/Description
addlink	*parent child line ?-border width? ?-removecommand?*
	Add a new node to the tree. *parent* is the canvas tag or id of the parent node or an empty string if the new node should become a root node. *child* is the canvas tag or id of the items that make up the new child node. *line* is the canvas tag or id of a canvas line to use to connect the child and parent nodes. The optional *width* specifies the width of the node's border in any of the forms acceptable to Tk_GetPixels (default: 0). The optional remove *command* specifies Tcl code to be evaluated when the node is removed from the tree.
child	*tagOrId*
	Return the name of the child of the node named by *tagOrId*. If the node has no children, an empty string is returned. If the node has more than one child, the name of the first child is returned. The pathName *sibling* command can be used to get the names of the other children in sequence.
configure	*?option value ...?*
	Query or modify the configuration options of the tree widget. This command works in the same way as the configure subcommands for all the Tk widgets. The options specified may be any of those accepted by the tree command.
cget	*?option?*
	Returns the widget's value for the given option, which may be any of the options accepted by the tree command.
draw	Forces the tree to be drawn in the canvas. The tree normally redraws itself automatically when needed, but this command can be used to force it to redraw itself immediately before any of the canvas items become visible.
isleaf	*tagOrId*
	Return true ("1") if the named node is a leaf (has no children) and false ("0") otherwise.
isroot	*tagOrId*
	Return true ("1") if the named node is a root node and false ("0") otherwise. Note that it is possible to have multiple visible root nodes that are all internally managed as children of the invisible pseudo root node. The invisible root node can be referenced with the empty tag "".

Table 10-1: Tree Widget Subcommands (continued)

Name	Arguments/Description
movelink	*child parent* Move the subtree whose root is the node named by *child* so that it becomes a subtree of the node named by *parent*.
nodeconfigure	*tagOrId ?option value?* Recalculate the node's size and position and set node options. This command accepts the same options as the addlink command and should be used whenever a node has changed size or to set the node's options.
parent	*tagOrId* Return the name of the parent of the node named by *tagOrId*. If the node has no parent (i.e., is a root node), an empty string is returned.
ancestors	*tagOrId* Returns a Tcl list of the given node's ancestors, for example: {*parent grandparent* ...}.
prune	*tagOrId* The subnodes of the node named by *tagOrId* are removed from the tree and deleted from the canvas. The named node is left in the tree.
rmlink	*tagOrId* Removes the node named by *tagOrId* and all its subnodes from the tree. The canvas items corresponding to the removed nodes are also deleted.
root	*tagOrId* The node named by *tagOrId* becomes the new root of the tree. Any nodes that are not subnodes of the named node are deleted.
sibling	*tagOrId* Returns the name of the next sibling of the node named by *tagOrId*. If the node has no sibling, an empty string is returned.
subnodes	*tagOrId* Returns a list containing the names of the subnodes of the node named by *tagOrId*. Only the child node, if any, and its siblings are in the list.

General Information About the Tree Widget

The tree widget was developed by the author of this chapter, Allan Brighton (abrighto@eso.org), in an effort to learn about Tcl/Tk while between consulting jobs. Since then, it has been used in numerous Tcl/Tk-based applications to display hierarchical information. It is freely available from the Tcl archives under the same basic copyright as Tcl/Tk.

The layout algorithm is based on an article in IEEE Software, July 1990, "Drawing Dynamic Trees," by Sven Moen of Brown University.

11

Oratcl: An Oracle Interface for Tcl

by Tom Poindexter

Introduction

Oratcl is an extension for Tcl that provides access to Oracle, the relational database management system from Oracle, Inc. With Oratcl, a Tcl program can retrieve data from the database server, insert new rows, and update or delete existing rows. Oratcl can also access advanced Oracle features, like reading or writing long data, and execute PL/SQL procedures on the database server. Oratcl is compatible with Oracle Server Version 6 and Version 7. Oracle's OCI (Oracle Call Interface) libraries are required to build Oratcl. Oratcl was written using the Sybtcl extension as a model, thus, Oratcl shares many similarities with Sybtcl.

While there is nothing that Oratcl can do that can't be accomplished with C and OCI or Pro*C (Oracle's embedded SQL preprocessor for C), Oratcl promotes rapid development due to Tcl's environment. Interactive applications can be developed quickly using Tcl/Tk. Database administration procedures like site specific backup/restore that are often cobbled together with Shell, Awk, and SQL*Plus (Oracle's command-line SQL processor) can be written in a single language. Other uses of Oratcl reported by users include: an Oracle sever database administration tool; email gateway address translation; and ad-hoc user report generation.

Oratcl adds several new commands to Tcl. All Oratcl commands are prefixed with "ora" to differentiate Oratcl commands from other Tcl commands. Oratcl also adds a global array variable, `$oramsg`, that provides the Tcl program with information about the execution of various Oratcl commands. Various indexes in the `oramsg` array are set with information about the success or failure of Oratcl commands. The `oramsg` array can be accessed anytime after an Oratcl command.

Here is a short example of Oratcl using the sample tables shipped with the Oracle product. In this example, we will connect to the Oracle server and select rows from the `emp` table:

```
tclsh> oralogon scott/tiger
```

```
oratcl0
tclsh> oraopen oratcl0
oratcl0.0
tclsh> orasql oratcl0.0 "select empno, ename from emp"
0
tclsh> orafetch oratcl0.0
7379 SMITH
tclsh> orafetch oratcl0.0
7499 Allen
tclsh> oralogoff oratcl0
```

The Oratcl distribution also includes two handy applications: Wosql, an Oracle SQL processor; and the Insert-Update-Delete Maker, a tool to build custom table maintenance applications. These tools will be discussed later in this chapter.

Basic Oratcl Commands

Every database programmer needs to make a connection to a database, query it for rows, check the results, and commit changes. Those operations are discussed in the following sections.

Server Connections and Cursors

Oracle allows connection to a database server either on a local host via pipes, or over a network connection with Oracle''s SQL*Net. Oracle client programs, like Oratcl, communicate with the Oracle database server; the server in turn performs the database access and returns the results to the client. In order for Oratcl to access the database, you must connect to the database server with a user id and password. `oralogon` is the command in Oratcl to make the connection.

```
oralogon connect-str
```

`Oralogon` requires a single parameter, the Oracle connect string. Oracle allows a connect string to take several forms:

- **(null string)**: Oracle will use the operating system id as a userid, if the server has been administered to use this facility. A single / may also be used.

- **name/password**: a *userid* name and *password*, separated by a /.

- **name/password@server**: a *userid* name and *password*, attaching to an Oracle server named *server* on the local host.

- **name/password@n:host:server**: a *userid* and *password*, attaching via network type *n* (typically "T", for TCP/IP), on host *host*, to an Oracle server named *server*.

- **name/password@serveralias**: a *userid* name and *password*, attaching to an Oracle server named *serveralias* that is defined in */etc/sqlnet* or a user's *.sqlnet* file.

If a server is not specified on a connect string, the server name is taken from the user's environment variable ORACLE_SID. Upon a successful connection, `oralo-`

gon returns a connection "handle" in the form of a string. A connection handle is similar in purpose to a file descriptor or the value returned by the Tcl `open` command. The Oratcl connection handle is used with other Oratcl commands that operate at a connection level. Several connections to the same or different Oracle servers can be open at the same time; each connection uses a separate handle. Oratcl handle strings are in the format `oratcl0`, the numeric suffix incrementing for each new handle opened. Normally, the handle would be saved into some Tcl variable for later access:

```
set handle [oralogon $id/$passwd]
```

If you plan to use the same handle for the life of your program, be sure to specify the variable as `global` before using the variable in a Tcl procedure, and in all other procedures where you will be using Oratcl commands. In the case of several simultaneous connections, you would save each handle into separate variables:

```
global localserver remoteserver
set localserver  [oralogon ${userid}/${password}]
set remoteserver [oralogon ${remoteid}/${remotepw}@${server}]
```

If a connection cannot be made to the Oracle server, either because of an invalid user id/password combination, server unavailable, and so forth, `oralogon` will cause a Tcl crror to be raised. Information on why a connection cannot be made is available in `$oramsg(errortxt)`. In the rest of this chapter, `$handle` will be used to signify a valid connection from `oralogon`.

Oracle further requires that one or more *cursors* be used to perform SQL queries and retrieve rows. Cursors are opened over a logon connection; a single logon connection can support multiple cursors. The Oratcl command `oraopen` opens an Oracle cursor:

```
tclsh> set handle [oralogon $id/$passwd]
oratcl0
tclsh> set query_cursor [oraopen $handle]
oratcl0.0
tclsh> set update_cursor [oraopen $handle]
oratcl0.1
```

In the rest of this chapter, `$cursor` will be used to signify a valid cursor opened with `oraopen`.

Oratcl cursors and connection handles should normally be closed when the database connection is no longer needed, just as you would normally close an open file descriptor. Oratcl provides the `oraclose` and `oralogoff` commands to close a cursor or connection handle, respectively.

```
oraclose $query_cursor
oraclose $update_cursor
oralogoff $handle
```

`oraclose` ensures that the cursor to the Oracle server is cleanly terminated. Each Oratcl cursor and connection handle occupy slots in an internal data structure. Properly closing a cursor or logon handle frees its corresponding slot, allowing the slot to be available for another new connection or cursor. Alternatively, `oralo-`

`goff` will also close all open cursors that have been opened on a handle at one time, in addition to terminating the logon connection.

Sending SQL

So far, we've demonstrated connecting to a Oracle server, accessing databases in the server, and disconnecting. Now it's time for some real action. Oratcl provides two commands that do most of the data manipulation: `orasql` and `orafetch`.

```
orasql $cursor $sql-statement
```

`orasql` is the command that sends a single SQL statement to the Oracle server for execution. Any valid Oracle SQL statement can be sent using `orasql`:

- Data manipulation commands: `select, insert, update, delete`
- Data definition commands: `create, alter, drop, grant`, etc.
- Oracle transaction control commands: `commit, rollback, savepoint`, etc.
- Oracle session control commands: `set role, alter session`

`orasql` passes the SQL statement in its entirety to the Oracle server, aside from normal Tcl variable and command substitution. It's very convenient to use Tcl's variable substitution to construct an SQL command:

```
puts "search for what name?"
gets stdin searchname
orasql $cursor "select * from emp where ename like '${searchname}'"
```

`orasql` will cause a Tcl error to be raised if the Oracle server rejects the SQL statement, either for improper syntax or if the SQL statement references tables or column names that do not exist.

SQL Quoting Issues

It's prudent to enclose any `orasql` command that may have user input inside of Tcl's `catch`. Additionally, where limited external input is used to construct a SQL statement as in the precedingexample, it may be necessary to preprocess the input. If the user were to enter:

```
O'Reilly
```

in response to the prompt, the resulting SQL statement would become invalid because the single quote after the "O" would specify the end of the literal string, leaving "Reilly" as an invalid SQL statement. In such a case, you might want to consider the SQL quoting and wildcard characters ("%","_") when building an SQL statement with string literals. To quote the quote character in SQL, you specify two quote characters. `Regsub` is handy to ensure that a literal string is properly quoted:

```
regsub -all ' $searchname '' searchname
```

Assuming a valid SQL statement was sent to the server, `orasql` will return "0" if the SQL is executed properly. Should a Tcl error be raised because of an invalid

SQL statement, `$oramsg(rc)` will contain the Oracle error number, and `$oramsg(errortxt)` will contain the description of the error.

Retrieving Rows

When SQL is executed, the server holds any data rows generated by the query until requested by the program. To retrieve data rows from the server as the result of an SQL statement, Oratcl provides the `orafetch` command.

```
orafetch $cursor ?tcl-statements?
```

`orafetch` retrieves the next row available, and returns the results in the form of a Tcl list. List elements correspond to the columns selected in the same order as specified in a "select" statement. The columns returned can then easily be picked apart with standard Tcl list oriented commands: `lindex`, `lrange`, and so forth. `orafetch` can also execute Tcl commands for every row returned; the tcl-statements option will be discussed after the basic usage.

```
orasql $cursor "select * from emp"
set row [orafetch $cursor]
puts "number of columns: [llength $row]"
puts "first column is: [lindex $row 0]"
```

`orafetch` converts all SQL datatypes to printable strings, in keeping with the Tcl model that all data are strings. This is not normally a problem for rows returned in Oratcl, except for the Oracle datatypes `raw` or `long raw`, in which the hexadecimal representation is returned.

Each execution of `orafetch` will return the next row from the current set. In addition to returning rows, `orafetch` sets the variable `$oramsg(rc)` to a status indicating what was returned. Typical values after executing `orafetch` include:

0 —a row was returned

1403 —end of rows reached

In the case of executing a SQL "select" statement, each row returned would be further processed in some fashion. For example, to print a list of employee names and hire dates from the `emp` database:

```
puts [format "%-15.15s %s" "Employee" "Hire date"]
orasql $cursor "select ename, hiredate from emp"
set row [orafetch $cursor]
while {$oramsg(rc) == 0} {
    puts [format "%-15.15s %s" [lindex $row 0] [lindex $row 1]]
    set row [orafetch $cursor]
}
```

Since it is very common programming construct to retrieve and process all the rows from a query, `orafetch` can accept an optional argument that is a block of Tcl statements to be executed for each row returned in a result set. `Orafetch` internally takes care of the "while" loop, retrieving rows and checking for the end-of-rows condition. The preceding example can be rewritten as:

```
puts [format "%-15.15s %s" "Employee" "Hire date"]
orasql $cursor "select ename, hirehdate from emp"
orafetch $cursor { puts [format "%-15.15s %s" @1 @2] }
```

Columns from each row are specified using a special substitution notation, prefixed with "@". @1 refers to the first column, @2 refers to the second column, and so on. @0 is the entire row as a Tcl list, just as `orafetch` would normally return. There is no limit to the number of times a column may be specified, or the number of Tcl statements executed in the block.

There are a few extra rules to remember when using the `tcl-statements` option. First, don't try to reference a column beyond the number of columns that are returned. Second, columns are substituted into the tcl-statements in a way to ensure that the tcl-statements after substituting the column data are still valid Tcl commands, a proper Tcl list for example. Since the data returned in the column may contain Tcl quoting characters, the entire substitution may be enclosed with Tcl quoting, with adjacent spaces inserted. If you need to format the columns for printing, use the Tcl `format` command as in the preceding example, or assign the column values into Tcl variables with the `set` command. Last, if any commands in the tcl-statements block fail, `orafetch` will raise a Tcl error.

The Tcl commands `break` and `continue` may be used in the `tcl-statements` block the same way they are used in `while` or `for`. Break will cause the `orafetch` command to return and Tcl will then execute the next command. Any further rows remaining in the query can be retrieved with a subsequent `orafetch` command. Continue will cause any remaining Tcl commands to be skipped and continue processing the tcl-statements with the next row. The following example counts authors names that begin with "A" through "L", printing only the first five:

```
orasql $cursor "select ename from emp order by ename"
set num_rows 0
orafetch $cursor {
    incr num_rows
    if {[string compare @1 M] == 1} {
      # employee name greater than "L", break out of orafetch
      break
    }
    if {$num_rows > 5} {
      # more than five rows in query, don't print any more
      continue
    }
    puts @0
}
puts "number employees with names beginning A-L: $num_rows"
```

Column Information

Besides retrieving data from the Oracle server, Oratcl also can retrieve information about the names of columns returned, their datatypes, and lengths. `oracols` returns a Tcl list of the names of the columns returned by `orafetch`.

```
oracols $cursor
```

`oracols` can be used after an `orasql` or `orafetch` command. The names of the columns returned are in the same order as the data values returned by `orafetch`. The names are the actual column names as defined in the tables from which the columns are retrieved, or any column alias name that may have been coded as part of the "select" statement.

```
tclsh> orasql $cursor {
       select ename "Last Name", hiredate, sal from emp
                             where empno=7499
}
0
tclsh> orafetch $cursor
ALLEN 20-FEB-81 1600
tclsh> oracols $cursor
{Last Name} HIREDATE SAL
```

Besides getting column names, `oracols` also sets the column datatypes and lengths in the `oramsg` global array. `$oramsg(coltypes)` is a Tcl list of the datatypes corresponding to the columns. `$oramsg(collengths)` is a Tcl list of the column lengths. Datatype values can be any of Oracle's datatypes:

- char
- varchar2
- number
- long
- rowid
- date
- raw
- long_raw
- mslabel
- raw_mlslabel
- unknown

For "char" datatypes, the length returned is the maximum length defined in the table, not the column lengths of the last row retrieved. Additionally, number datatypes have elements in `$oramsg(colprecs)` and `$oramsg(colscales)`— Tcl lists of the precision and scale. Nonnumeric types have null elements within the precision and scale lists. In the following example, the select column "empno" has a column name "EMPNO," type of "number," with a length of 40 (numeric digits) .

```
tclsh> orasql $cursor {select from empno, ename, hiredate, sal from emp}
REG_ROW
tclsh> oracols $cursor
EMPNO ENAME HIREDATE SAL
tclsh> puts $oramsg(coltypes)
number varchar2 date number
tclsh> puts $oramsg(collengths)
```

```
40 10 75 40
tclsh> puts $oramsg(colprecs)
4 {} {} 7
tclsh> puts $oramsg(colscales)
0 {} {} 2
```

Session and Transaction Management

Sometimes it is desirable to stop processing rows before all rows have been retrieved. Oratcl provides the `oracancel` command for such a case.

```
oracancel $cursor
```

`oracancel` informs the server that pending rows from the last `orasql` command are to be discarded. `orasql` always performs an implicit `oracancel` before each execution of SQL; `oracancel` may be used explicitly at any time.

Oratcl also provides transactional level commands that operate on a connection handle basis. In normal Oracle processing, uncommitted changes to a database are only visible to the user making the changes; all other users of the database are unaware of changes until those changes are committed to the database.

```
oracommit $handle
```

`oracommit` will cause Oracle to commit all changes to the database, making those changes visible to other users. Oracle causes all cursors that have been opened through the same logon connection to be committed:

```
orasql $cursor {insert into dept values
                        (96, 'DEVELOPMENT', 'DENVER') }
oracommit $handle
```

```
oraroll $handle
```

`oraroll` will cause Oracle to roll back all changes to the database, reverting any changes since the last commit. As with `oracommit`, all cursors that have been opened through the same logon connection are rolled back:

```
tclsh> orasql $cursor { select loc from dept where deptno=10 }
tclsh> orafetch $cursor
{NEW YORK}
tclsh> orasql $cursor { update dept set loc='DENVER' where deptno=10 }
tclsh> orasql $cursor { select loc from dept where deptno=10 }
tclsh> orafetch $cursor
DENVER
tclsh> oraroll $handle
tclsh> orasql $cursor { select loc from dept where deptno=10 }
tclsh> orafetch $cursor
{NEW YORK}
```

In a transaction-oriented program, it is often desirable that changes be committed immediately. Oratcl allows changes to be committed automatically on each SQL statement by using the `oraautocom` command:

```
oraautocom $handle on
```

When auto commit is turned on, each change to the database through `orasql` (insert, update, delete) is committed immediately. The default value for `oraauto-com` is "off." If auto commit is enabled with `oraautocom`, it can later be disabled by specifying "off" as the parameter for `oraautocom`.

Advanced Oratcl Commands

Oracle includes several advanced features in its database server product. Executing server-side stored procedures, and reading and writing larger binary objects ("long columns") are supported by Oracle. Oratcl in turn supports these features with specialized commands.

PL/SQL

PL/SQL is a procedural language that can be executed on the Oracle database server. PL/SQL procedures are often used for transactional processing, where an entire group of SQL statements is treated as an atomic unit. PL/SQL procedures can be executed as a block of statements sent to the server or stored in the database for later execution (stored procedures). Changes made to the database in a PL/SQL procedure can be treated as a unit, committed or rolled back as a group, in case any one SQL statement does not execute successfully. PL/SQL procedures can take arguments and return values.

Oratcl supports the use of PL/SQL procedures through the `oraplexec` command.

```
oraplexec $cursor pl-block  ?:varname1 value1 :varname2 value2  ....?
```

`oraplexec` requires an open cursor and a string that contains a block of PL/SQL code. The `pl-block` is an *anonymous* block of PL/SQL code (*anonymous* is Oracle terminology for PL/SQL code that is not stored in the database or otherwise named.) When a PL/SQL procedure requires arguments, the `oraplexec` command should specify the same number of PL/SQL bind variables as arguments on the `oraplexec` command. Bind variable names are denoted with a preceding colon (:), and cause the following value to be bound to the corresponding variable. As many `:varname value` pairs are required on the `oraplexec` command as are coded in the PL/SQL block.

Assume the following PL/SQL procedure has been created in the Oracle database, which will compute and return the total amount of monthly pay based on job classification. The procedure takes two arguments: the first being the job type as an input argument, and the second is the total salary returned as an output argument:

```
create procedure total_monthly_job_pay
   (job_type in  varchar2,
    tot_sal  out number)
as
   tot_fixed number;
   tot_var   number;
```

```
begin
    select sum(sal) into tot_fixed
        from emp
        where job = job_type;
    select decode(sum(comm),NULL,0,sum(comm)) into tot_var
        from emp
        where job =job_type;
    tot_sal := tot_fixed + tot_var;
end;
```

The `oraplexec` command to execute the total_monthly_job_pay procedure would be:

```
set anon_pl {
    begin
        total_monthly_job_pay (:type, :total);
    end;
}
oraplexec $cursor $anon_pl :type SALESMAN   :total 0
```

In this example, the `anon_pl` string is an anonymous block that takes two bind variables, and calls the stored procedure. The `:type` variable in the block is assigned the value "SALESMAN," and is received as `job_type` by the stored procedure. Even though `tot_sal` is an output-only variable in the procedure, `oraplexec` requires a value ("0") be associated with the bind variable `:total`.

`oraplexec` will return all bind variables after execution of the PL/SQL block, with values that have been returned by the procedure. The return values are also buffered as a single data row, so that `orafetch` will also return the values.

```
tclsh> orafetch $cursor
SALESMAN 7800
```

Long Columns

Another advanced feature of Oracle supported by Oratcl is the storage and retrieval of `long` or `long raw` data columns. Long and `long raw` datatypes are similar, each datatype holding up to two gigabytes. Long datatypes usually imply printable text, whereas `long raw` datatypes are completely arbitrary. Sounds, graphics, and MPEG streams are examples of data that can be stored in `long raw` columns. Because `long` and `long raw` datatypes may contain binary zeros (thus unable to be represented as a Tcl string), Oratcl provides commands to read and write long data to and from files.

```
orawritelong $cursor rowid table column filename
orareadlong  $cursor rowid table column filename
```

`orawritelong` is the Oratcl command to write a file into a `long` or `long raw` data column. `orawritelong` requires the row be identified by the Oracle *rowid* as well as the table and column names. The rowid can be determined by issuing a "select," returning the Oracle rowid pseudo column. (Every row in an Oracle table can be referenced by its absolute position in the Oracle database, in other words, the *rowid*. Oracle allows this value to be retrieved on a "select" statement, or used as a constraint in a "where" clause.)

In this example, assume that the table "emppix" is designed to store images of employees in the `long raw` column "photo." Assume a table, `emppix`, has been created as

```
create table emppix (
  empno number(4,0),
  photo long raw
)
```

```
# find the rowid associated with an employee
orasql $cursor {select rowid from emppix where empno=7499}
set rowid [orafetch $cursor]
# write the employee's photo from the file "image.gif"
orawritelong $cursor $rowid emppix photo image.gif
```

`orawritelong` returns the number of bytes written to the column.

`orareadlong` is the compliment of `orawritelong`; it retrieves the long data from the database and writes the contents into a file. Like `orawritelong`, the row must be identified by an Oracle rowid, table, and column. Long columns can be retrieved by `orafetch`, just as ordinary columns, but there are a few problems with this approach. First, `long raw` columns are converted to a printable hexadecimal notation, which may require another conversion step to reconstruct the actual data values. Second, the column would be stored as an ordinary Tcl variable, with the risk that not enough memory could be allocated to hold the value. `orareadlong` eliminates these problems by retrieving the data in smaller chunks, and writes the data directly to an operating system file.

```
# get the rowid for the employee
orasql $cursor {select rowid from emppix where empno=7499}
set rowid [orafetch $cursor]
# read the value from the row and write it to a file
orareadlong $cursor $rowid emppix photo image.gif
```

Oracle Version 6 limits the maximum length of a long column to 65,536 bytes. Oracle Version 7 limits the maximum length to 2,147,483,647 bytes.

Server Information and Feedback

Besides the Oracle specific commands that are added to Tcl by Oratcl, a global array is maintained and used by Oratcl for information from the server, and to control various aspects of Oratcl. `oramsg` is the name of the array, and it should always be referenced as `global` before accessing it in any Tcl procedure. We've already touched lightly on some of the elements in `$oramsg`. Now we will examine each element in detail. The `nullvalue` and `maxlong` elments can be set by the programmer, the remainder of the elements in `$oramsg` are informational only. Oratcl resets the informational elements on every Oratcl command. Any element not explicitly set by a particular Oratcl command is set to a null string.

The first to be discussed are the elements that can be set by the Oratcl user and how they affect Oratcl processing.

`$oramsg(nullvalue)`

Nullvalue controls how Oratcl represents columns containing NULL when retrieved with `orafetch`. The default value for `$oramsg(nullvalue)` is `default` which converts numeric datatypes to 0 and all other datatypes to a null string `""`. For example, you might want to set `nullvalue` to an unlikely string to differentiate a NULL from a column that consists of whitespace characters.

```
tclsh> set oramsg(nullvalue) "<null>"
tclsh> orasql $cursor {select 'literal string',NULL from dual}
REG_ROW
tclsh> orafetch $cursor
{literal string} <null>
```

`$oramsg(maxlong)`

`maxlong` limits the amount of `long` or `long raw` data that is retrieved from the server for `orafetch`. The default limit is 32768 bytes; `maxlong` can be set to the maximum allowed by Oracle, 2147483647. Any change to `maxlong` becomes effective on the next execution of `orasql`.

`$oramsg(handle)`

Since the `oramsg` array is shared among all open connections, this element reports the handle or cursor of the last Oratcl command executed.

`$oramsg(rc)`

`rc` has been has already been mentioned for both `orasql` and `orafetch`. The `rc` value is the return code from the OCI library function calls. Here's a quick review of some common values:

- 0: Function completely without error
- 900-999: Invalid SQL statement, missing keywords, invalid column names, etc.
- 1000-1099: Logon denied, insufficient privileges, etc.
- 1400-1499: SQL execution errors
- 1403: End of rows reached on `orafetch`
- 1406: A long column retrieved by `orafetch` was truncated

Oracle has an exhaustive set of return codes. See the *Oracle Error Messages and Codes* manual for detailed information.

`$oramsg(errortxt)`

`errortxt` is a descriptive message associated with an `rc` code. The description that Oracle provides is usually one line per error. For more information of a failure, check the *Oracle Errors Messages and Codes* manual.

`$oramsg(collengths)`

`collengths` is a Tcl list of column lengths that correspond to the column names that are returned by `oracols`. The column lengths are either the number of digits for numeric datatypes, or the maximum length that character datatypes are defined in the database.

`$oramsg(coltypes)`

`coltypes` is a Tcl list of column datatypes that correspond to the column names that are returned by `oracols`. As with `collengths`, `coltypes` is only set after `oracols` has been executed.

`$oramsg(colprecs)`

`colprecs` is a Tcl list of the precision of numeric columns that correspond to the column names that are returned by `oracols`. For nonnumeric columns, the corresponding list element is a null string. Oracle libraries for Version 6 cannot retrieve the numeric column precision infomation, so Oratcl returns zeros if that version of Oracle is used.

`$oramsg(colscales)`

`colscales` is a Tcl list of the scale of numeric columns that correspond to the column names that are returned by `oracols`. For nonnumeric columns, the corresponding list element is a null string. Column scales have the same limitations as `colprecs` for Oracle Version 6—zeros are returned.

`$oramsg(sqlfunc)`

`sqlfunc` is a numeric code of the last SQL command performed. Codes for common SQL commands are:

- 3: insert
- 4: select
- 5: update
- 9: delete

A complete list of SQL command types are documented in the *Oracle Call Interface* manual.

`$oramsg(ocifunc)`

`ocifunc` is a numeric code of the last OCI function performed. A complete list of function types are in the *Oracle Call Interface* manual.

`$oramsg(rows)`

`rows` is the number of rows affected by an insert, update, or delete SQL command, or the cumulative number of rows fetched by `orafetch`.

Handling Errors

Oratcl commands will raise a Tcl error condition when a Oratcl command is invalid or when the Oracle server reports an error in an SQL statement. Oratcl was designed with this conservative error-handling approach so that inadvertent operations to a database would be reported.

The Tcl interpreter normally halts script processing when a Tcl error is raised. The Tcl command `catch` allows errors to be trapped and error-handling code to be executed. For example, the `oralogon` command will normally raise a Tcl error when either an Oracle userid or password is invalid, or when the Oracle server is unavailable. Catching the error allows the script to continue, and information about the error to be extracted from the `$oramsg` array:

```
if [catch {oralogon ${userid}/${passwd} } handle] {
    puts "cannot access server, reason: $oramsg(errortxt)"
    exit
}
```

In addition to raising an error on invalid or improperly formed SQL statements, `orasql` will also raise a Tcl error if the Oracle server reports a logical error. Logical errors include attempting to insert a duplicate row into a table that has unique indexes, or perhaps a PL/SQL procedure or referential integrity trigger executing a Oracle "raise application error" statement.

Applications

Oratcl includes serveral applications in the distribution.

Wosql—An X11 SQL Processor

Oratcl combined with the power of Tcl/Tk provides a basis for developing powerful database applications and tools. One common tool usually provided by database vendors is a general SQL processor, passing SQL statements to the server and printing rows that are returned. Oracle provides 'SQL*Plus,' a command-line SQL processor. Oratcl includes Wosql, a SQL processor that runs as an X11 application. Wosql is written to use commands from Extended Tcl (TclX), so its interpreter needs Tcl, Tk, TclX, and Oratcl.

Wosql is similar to other X11 applications in that it provides a menubar, scrolling edit and result panes, and various pop-up windows (see Figure 11-1).

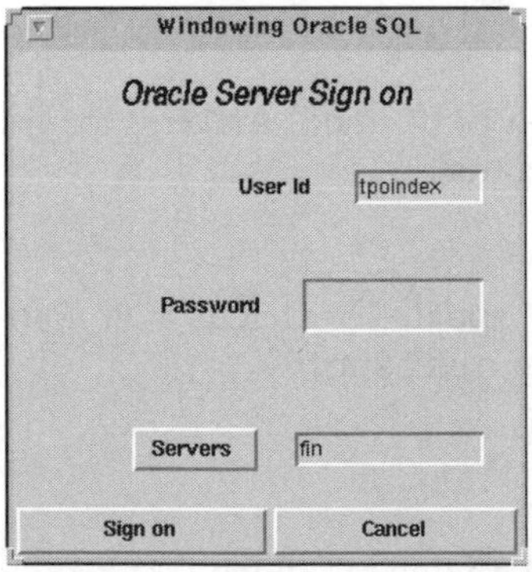

Figure 11-1: Wosql Sign-On Window

After starting wosql, the server sign on window appears to collect the Oracle user id, password, and server to which it should connect. The server entry is prepopulated with the default (ORACLE_SID environment variable); pressing the "server"

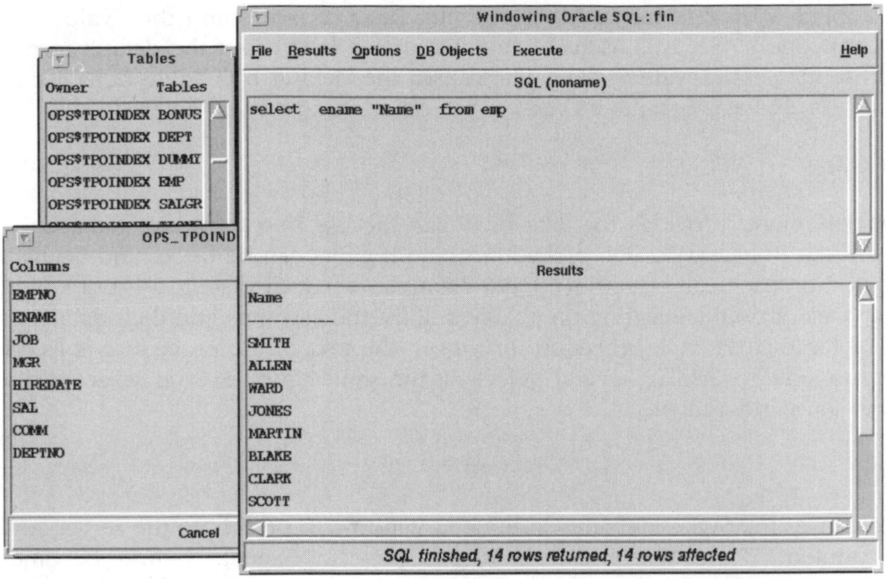

Figure 11-2: Wosql Main Window

button will list all servers from the */etc/oratab, /etc/sqlnet*, and the user's personal
.sqlnet files. Pressing "Sign on" connects to the the Oracle server (see Figure 11-2).

SQL statements are entered into the top pane (a Tk edit widget); pressing the "Execute" button will send the SQL off to the server, and results will be printed in the
lower pane (a Tk listbox). Menubar items provide additional functionality.

File

The File menu controls the SQL edit pane. "New" clears the SQL edit and Results
windows for a new query. "Open" prompts for a file containing SQL statements
through a file selection dialog window. "Save" and "Save as" save the SQL edit
window into the current filename, or prompts for a new file name. "Quit" disconnects from the server and exit Wisqlite.

Results

The Results menu controls the Results window. "Append results" or "Clear results"
selects whether the Results window should be cleared on each new SQL execution or
appended to the end of the list. "Save as" allows the Results window to be saved to a
file, overwriting any previous contents. "Print" sends the Results window to the printer
(via the Unix *lp* command.) "Font" changes the font size of the Results window.

Options

The Options menu controls several Wosql processing options as well as starting
specialized dialogs. "Autocommit" allows toggling of the auto commit feature.
"Commit Now" issues an immediate commit of changes. "Rollback Now" rolls back
any changes since the last commit. "Write Long Col..." and "Read Long Col..." opens
a dialog box to write or read a file into a LONG datatype column. "Procedure

---

Applications   **467**

Exec..." opens a dialog box in which to enter bind variables and their values for PL/SQL execution. "Set Null Value..." opens a dialog box to set the default format for representing NULL values. "Default" causes the default null value behavior as described for `$oramsg(nullvalue)`. Any other string can be entered.

DB Objects

The Objects menu provides for data dictionary access into the current database. Tables, views, indexes, PL/SQL procedures, and triggers can be listed, and detailed information on each can be retrieved. For example, when displaying a list of tables, clicking "Ok" or double-clicking on a table will list the columns and their datatypes in that table; for a PL/SQL procedure or trigger, the text of the procedure is listed. It's also possible to display several objects at the same time, as each object is displayed in its own window.

Execute

Execute causes the SQL statements in the edit window to be sent to the server, and results printed. While Wosql is retrieving rows, the Execute button becomes "Cancel"; pressing it will halt retrieval of additional rows. The SQL edit window has a few keyboard bindings worth mentioning. "Control-Return" and "Shift-Return" are bound to the Execute/Cancel button, so a user doesn't have to move a hand from the keyboard to start the query. Also, a buffer of 10 previous commands can be accessed by holding "Control" or "Shift" and pressing either the Up or Down arrow keys. For Example, "Shift-Down" will access the most recent command. Also worth noting is that the SQL text doesn't require a terminating ";" as 'SQL*Plus' requires. The "#" character at the beginning of a line indicates a comment.

Help

The last menu item is Help. It's admittedly rather sparse on information.

Insert-Update-Delete (IUD) Maker

IUD Maker is an application generator for Oracle tables (see Figure 11-3). It builds an Oratcl script that performs selection, insert, update, and delete operations on rows of a single table. IUD Maker begins by prompting for database logon userid and password, and then requests that a table be selected from a list of all tables available to the user.

After selecting a table, IUD Maker presents a list of all the columns in the target table with their datatypes. Highlighting a column and pressing "Add to Search" causes that column to be used for searching and browsing in the target application. "Add to Detail" makes the selected column appear in the detail listing. "Add all columns to Detail" populates the detail list with all columns in the table. Pressing "Generate" will build an IUD application named by writing a file named *owner.tablename*.iud.

The IUD table application can then be started (see Figure 11-4). The generated application also prompts for Oracle logon information. After a successful sign-on, the IUD application is ready for user interaction.

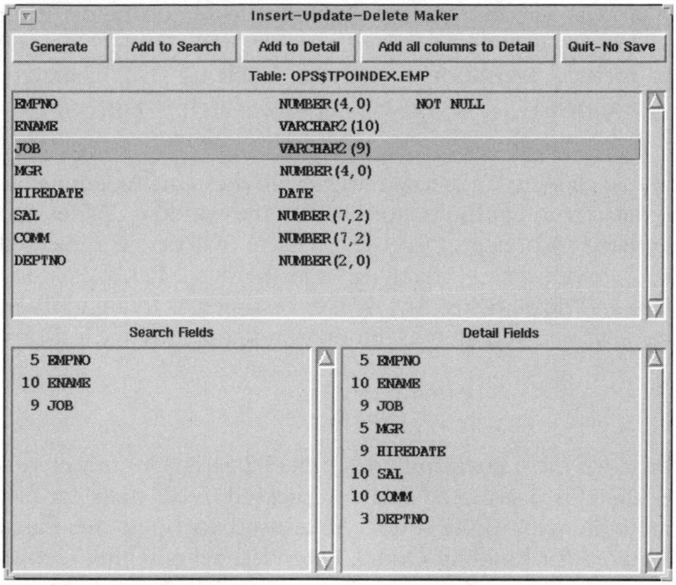

Figure 11-3: IUD Maker

At the top of the application window, search criteria can be entered for the browse columns (ones that were chosen as search columns in IUD Maker.) Pressing "Search" will retrieve rows that match the search criteria. Rows will be retrieved and

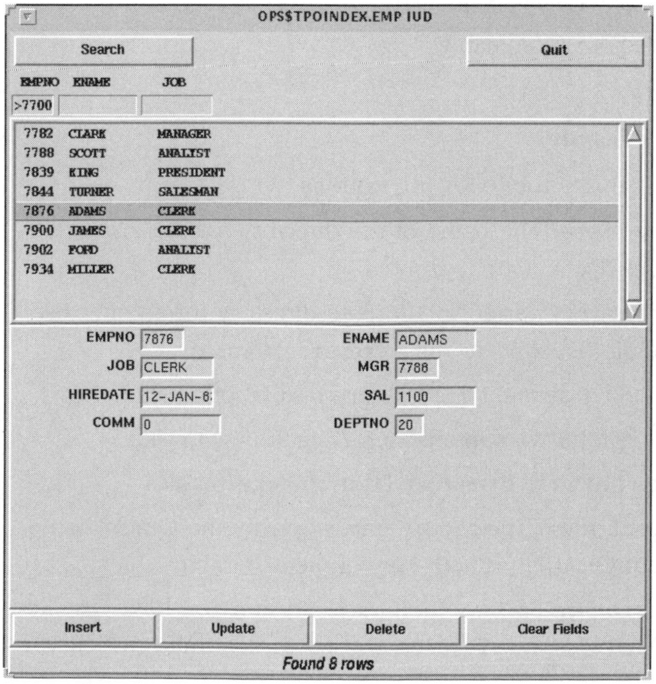

Figure 11-4: IUD Application

---

columns formatted in the browse window to line up with the search fields. If all search fields are empty, the browse list will contain all rows from the table. Numeric column search fields may include a relational operator (such as ">"); character column search fields always append "%" to the end of any search string and perform a "like" column match.

After you retrieve rows, double-clicking on a row retrieves all the detail columns for the row and populates the detail fields in the bottom half of the window. Values can be changed, and the row updated by pressing "Update." "Delete" will delete a selected row. "Insert" inserts a new row with data currently held in the detail fields. Pressing "Clear Fields" clears all search and detail fields. Any SQL errors, such as trying to insert rows with duplicate primary keys, are reported at the bottom status message.

Building Oratcl

Oratcl builds "out of the box" for most environments. Oratcl 2.41 is the current version at the time of writing. Oratcl is distributed as a compressed (GNU gzip) tar file. A `configure` shell script built with GNU Autoconf is used to build the initial Makefile. Although not required for building Oratcl, Extended Tcl is highly recommended. Wosql requires commands from TclX. `Configure` will search for Tcl, Tk, and TclX (Extended Tcl) source directories in sibling directories from where Oratcl was un-tarred.

Oratcl can be built as an extended Tcl or Wish intepreter, or as a dynamic shared library (on systems where an Oracle shared library is supported).

A dynamic Oratcl library can be loaded at runtime with the Tcl command:

```
load libOratcl[info sharedlibextension]
```

or by using the "package require" command:

```
package require Oratcl
```

before using any Oratcl commands.

The `configure` script recognizes the following options:

- `--prefix=directory name`: The name of the directory for the installation of bin, lib, and man files. Defaults to */usr/local*.

- `--exec_prefix-directory name`: An alternate directory for architecture-specific files in bin and lib. Defaults to the `--prefix=` value.

- `--enable-shared`: Build a dynamic load library instead of executables.

- `--without-tk`: Don't build a wish interpreter. Default is with Tk.

- `--without-tclx`: Don't include Extended Tcl in the executables.

- `--with-oracle-directory=directory name`: Specify the Oracle home directory, default is your ORACLE_HOME environment variable.

- `--with-oracle-version=x`: Specifiy the Oracle version you have installed, currently "6" or "7." Otherwise, `configure` will try to determine which version you have.

The other requirement for the `configure` script is finding the Oracle home directory, since Oratcl needs the Oracle OCI libraires to link executables. `Configure` looks in the directory defined by the ORACLE_HOME environment variable. The resulting Makefile will build a Tcl command-line interpreter and a Tcl/Tk Wish interpreter, each with or without TclX. The Makefile target "all" will compile *oratcl.c*, build a library that contains the Oratcl commands in addition to the required Oracle OCI objects, then build the two interpreters, leaving the executables in the distribution directory. The target "install" will copy the executables to the installation *bin* directory, and the Oratcl man page to the installation man directory. If Oratcl was built with TclX, the target "install-wosql" will configure Wosql with the proper `#!interpreter` line and copy Wosql to the installation bin directory.

The *README* file contains notes on a particular release of Oratcl: which Tcl/Tk versions are required, tested configurations, and general information. The file *INSTALL* contains detailed information on building Oratcl, including configure options recognized. Both *README* and *INSTALL* should be perused prior to building Oratcl. The file *CHANGES* is a history of features added and bugs fixed in Oratcl. The subdirectory "samples" contains additional sample Oratcl scripts.

Oratcl can be found at `ftp.neosoft.com` in the directory */pub/tcl/NEW/oratcl-2.41.tar.gz*. Newer versions will be named the same, except for incrementing the major or minor version numbers. Current Usenet discussion of Oratcl takes place in `comp.lang.tcl` or `comp.databases.oracle`. Tom Poindexter can be reached at *tpoindex@nyx.net* and maintains information about Oratcl at *http://www.nyx.net/~tpoindex*.

Command Summary

Command	Function / Return value
`oralogon` *connect-str*	Connects to an OracleServer.
	Returns: a connection handle.
`oraopen` *handle*	Opens a cursor.
	Returns: cursor handle.
`oraclose` *cursor-handle*	Closes a cursor.
	Returns: nothing.
`oralogoff` *handle*	Closes a server connection.
	Returns: nothing.
`orasql` *cursor-handle sql-statements*	Executes SQL statements on the server.
	Returns: Data availability status.
`orafetch` *cursor- handle ?tcl-statements?*	Retrieves data rows from an SQL `select` statement.
	Returns: row data as a Tcl list.
`oracancel` *cursor-handle*	Cancels pending SQL and results.
	Returns: nothing.

Continued

Command Summary (continued)

Command	Function / Return value
oracommit *handle*	Commits database changes. Returns: nothing.
oraroll *handle*	Rolls back database changes. Returns: nothing.
oraautocom *handle on |off*	Turns auto commit on or off. Returns: nothing.
oracols cursor-*handle*	Returns column names. Returns: column names as a Tcl list.
oraplexec *cursor-handle pl-sql-block :varname value ...*	Executes a PL/SQL stored procedure. Returns: output variables.
orawritelong *cursor-handle rowid table column filename*	Writes data from a file to a long or long raw column. Returns: number of bytes written to column.
orareadlong *cursor-handle rowid table column filename*	Reads text or image data from a column and writes to a file. Returns: number of bytes read from column.

12

Sybtcl: A Sybase Interface for Tcl

by Tom Poindexter

Introduction

Sybtcl is an extension for Tcl that provides access to Sybase, the relational database management system from Sybase, Inc. Sybtcl makes it possible for a Tcl program to retrieve data from the database server, insert new rows, and update or delete existing rows. Sybtcl can also access advanced Sybase features, for example, reading or writing text or image data and executing stored procedures on the database server. Sybtcl is compatible with Sybase Server Version 4.2 through System 11. Sybase's DB-Lib ("Open Client") libraries are required to build Sybtcl.

Sybtcl promotes creative uses and rapid development due to Tcl's environment. Interactive applications can be developed quickly using Tcl/Tk. Database administration procedures like site specific backup/restore that are often cobbled together with Shell, Awk, and Isql (Sybase's command-line SQL processor) can be written in a single language. Other uses of Sybtcl reported by users include: real-time server performance monitoring; interface to HTTP servers to provide World Wide Web users with access to campus telephone listings; a C++ code generation tool providing database access for a cross-platform GUI environment; and ad-hoc user report generation.

Sybtcl adds several new commands to Tcl. All Sybtcl commands are prefixed with "syb" to differentiate Sybtcl commands from other Tcl commands. Sybtcl also adds a global array variable, $sybmsg, that provides the Tcl program with information about the execution of various Sybtcl commands. Various indexes in the sybmsg array are set with information about the success or failure of Sybtcl commands. The sybmsg array can be accessed anytime after a Sybtcl command.

Here is a short example of Sybtcl using the "pubs2" sample database shipped with the Sybase product. In this example, we will connect to the Sybase server, access the "pubs2" database, and selects rows from the "authors" table:

```
tclsh> sybconnect mysybaseuserid mypassword MYSERVER
sybtcl0
tclsh> sybuse sybtcl0 pubs2
tclsh> sybsql sybtcl0 "select au_fname, au_lname from authors"
REG_ROW
tclsh> sybnext sybtcl0
Abraham Bennet
tclsh> sybnext sybtcl0
Reginald Blotchet-Halls
tclsh> sybclose sybtcl0
```

Basic Sybtcl Commands

Let's start by making a connection and doing some simple queries and stores.

Connecting to the Dataserver

Sybase uses the client/server model exclusively. The Sybase database server accepts connections from clients wishing to access the database. Sybase client programs, like Sybtcl, communicate using a protocol (provided by DB-Lib) to the server; the server in turn performs the database access and returns the results to the client. In order for Sybtcl to access the database, you must connect to the database server with a user id and password. Sybconnect is the command in Sybtcl to make the connection.

```
sybconnect userid password ?server? ?application? ?interface-file?
```

sybconnect requires two parameters: the Sybase user id and password. Three optional parameters may be specified. server is a specific Sybase server to which the connection is made. If the server is not specified on the sybconnect command, Sybtcl will attempt to connect to the default Sybase server (from the shell environment variable DSQUERY). application is any string that is passed to the server and is used by the server for system administration display, associating a name with a particular Sybase server process. Sybtcl reads server location information, a hostname and TCP port number, from a file named *interfaces* in the Sybase home directory (environment variable $SYBASE.) An alternate server interface file may be specified with the interface-file parameter on sybconnect.

Upon a successful connection, sybconnect returns a connection "handle" in the form of a string. A connection handle is similar in purpose to a file descriptor or the value returned by the Tcl open command. The Sybtcl connection handle is used with all other Sybtcl commands. Several connections to the same or different Sybase servers can be open at the same time; each connection uses a separate handle. Sybtcl handles are in the format sybtcl0, with the numeric suffix incrementing with each new connection. Normally, the handle would be saved into some Tcl variable for later access:

```
set handle [sybconnect $sybuserid $sybpassword]
```

If you plan to use the same handle for the life of your program, be sure to specify the variable as global before using the variable in a procedure, and in all other procedures where you will be using Sybtcl commands. In the case of several simultaneous connections, you would save each handle into separate variables:

```
global select_handle update_handle other_handle
# open two connections, using the same sybase user id and password
set select_handle [sybconnect $sybuserid $sybpassword]
set update_handle [sybconnect $sybuserid $sybpassword]
# open a connection to SERVER2, using the same user id and password
set other_handle [sybconnect $sybuserid $sybpassword SERVER2]
```

If a connection cannot be made to the Sybase server, either because of an invalid user id/password combination, server unavailable, and so forth, sybconnect will cause a Tcl error to be raised. Information on why a connection cannot be made is available in $sybmsg(dberrstr). In the rest of this chapter, $handle will be used to signify a valid connection from sybconnect.

Database Usage

In the Sybase architecture, a single dataserver may be responsible for managing several databases. Sybtcl provides the sybuse command to either report the database currently in use, or to cause another database to be accessed.

```
sybuse $handle ?database?
```

The result from sybuse will report the name of the database currently in use when executed without the optional database parameter. Each database user in Sybase is assigned a default database and uses that database upon a successful login to the Sybase server. Other databases may be accessed if permission has been granted by the Sybase administrator. sybuse can be used to change to another database by specifying the optional database parameter:

```
puts "currently using database: [sybuse $handle]"
sybuse $handle $newdatabase
puts "switched database to $newdatabase"
```

Connection Termination

Sybtcl connection handles should normally be closed when the database connection is no longer needed, just as you would normally close an open file descriptor. Sybtcl provides the sybclose command to close a handle:

```
sybclose $handle
```

Executing sybclose ensures that the connection to the Sybase server is cleanly terminated. Each Sybtcl connection occupies a slot in an internal data structure. Properly closing a handle frees its corresponding slot, allowing the slot to be available for another new connection with sybconnect.

Sending SQL

So far, we've demonstrated connecting to a Sybase server, accessing databases in the server, and disconnecting. Now it's time for some real action. Sybtcl provides two commands that do most of the data manipulation: sybsql and sybnext.

`sybsql` is the command that sends a SQL statement to the Sybase server for execution. Any valid Sybase SQL statement can be sent using `sybsql`:

- ordinary SQL like select, insert, update, delete, create, grant
- any of Sybase's Transact-SQL statements like execute, begin, declare, etc.
- any Sybase database administration commands: dump, checkpoint, etc.

As with any other Transact-SQL statement, multiple SQL statements may be executed in a single `sybsql` command:

```
sybsql $handle $sql-statement ?async?
```

`sybsql` passes the SQL statement in its entirety to the Sybase server, aside from normal Tcl variable and command substitution. It's very convenient to use Tcl's variable substitution to construct an SQL command:

```
puts "search for what name?"
gets stdin searchname
sybsql $handle \
    "select * from authors where au_lname like '${searchname}'"
```

`Sybsql` will cause a Tcl error to be raised if the Sybase server rejects the SQL statement, either for improper syntax or if the SQL statement references tables or column names that do not exist.

SQL Quoting Issues

Again, it's prudent to enclose any `sybsql` command that may have user input inside of Tcl's `catch` command. Additionally, where limited external input is used to construct a SQL statement as in the previous example, it may be necessary to pre-process the input. If the user were to enter:

```
O'Reilly
```

in response to the prompt, the resulting SQL statement would become invalid because the single quote after the "O" would specify the end of the literal string, leaving "Reilly" as an invalid SQL statement. In such a case you might want to consider the SQL quoting and wildcard characters (%,_,[]) when building a SQL statement with string literals. To quote the quote character in SQL, you specify two quote characters. `Regsub` is handy to ensure that a literal string is properly quoted:

```
regsub -all ' $searchname '' searchname
```

Sybase extends the ANSI SQL wildcard characters by including "[ ]", matching any character or range of characters appearing between the brackets. Of course, this wildcard specification can also be interpreted by Tcl as a command execution. If your SQL statement includes "[ ]", be sure to either quote the brackets, either with a backslash, or enclose the entire SQL statement in brackets. For example, to select authors with last names beginning with A through M, either quoting method would suffice:

```
sybsql $handle "select * from authors where au_lname like '\[A-M\]%'"
sybsql $handle {select * from authors where au_lname like '[A-M]%'}
```

Normally, `sybsql` will wait until the SQL statement has finished processing on the server before returning. An optional flag `async` may be specified on `sybsql`. `async` causes the `sybsql` command to return immediately. The `sybpoll` command can then check on the progress of the SQL command. `async` is useful during long-running SQL commands to allow the Tcl program to continue processing, `sybpoll` giving the user feedback or allowing other processing to continue. Specific use of `sybpoll` will be discussed later.

Assuming a valid SQL statement was sent to the server, `sybsql` can return different values depending on the result of the command:

- REG_ROW: At least one row of data is available from the first result set in the case of executing a "select" or a stored procedure that returned rows.
- NO_MORE_ROWS: The SQL executed properly, but no rows were returned by the first result set, or possibly "insert," "update," or "delete" was executed (again, no rows returned).
- PENDING: The "async" flag was specified, and `sybpoll` can be executed to check if the SQL command has finished on the server.

These result codes are also stored in the `sybmsg` global array element `nextow`.

Retrieving Rows

In Sybase terminology, *result sets* are the term for each separate set of rows returned from separate "select" statements. One execution of the `sybsql` command can contain more than one SQL "select" statements in the `sql-statements` argument. Thus, multiple results sets may be generated by one `sybsql` command. Note that `sybsql` doesn't return actual data rows, just the indication that rows are available.

Sybase buffers result rows in the dataserver until requested. To retrieve data rows from the server as the result of an SQL statement, Sybtcl provides the `sybnext` command:

```
sybnext $handle ?tcl-statements?
```

`sybnext` retrieves the next row available, and returns the results in the form of a Tcl list. List elements correspond to the columns selected in the same order as specified in a "select" statement. The columns returned can then easily be picked apart with standard Tcl list-oriented commands, `lindex`, `lrange`, and so forth:

```
sybsql $handle "select * from titles"
set row [sybnext $handle]
puts "first column is: [lindex $row 0]"
```

`sybnext` converts all SQL datatypes to printable strings, in keeping with the Tcl model that all data are strings. This is not normally a problem for rows returned in Sybtcl, except for the Sybase datatypes `binary` and `varbinary`, in which the hexadecimal representation is returned.

Each execution of `sybnext` will return the next row from the current result set. In addition to returning rows, `sybnext` sets the variable `$sybmsg(nextrow)` to a status indicating what was returned. Possible values are:

- `REG_ROW`: The row returned was from a "select" SQL statement.
- `NO_MORE_ROWS`: The last row from the current result set has been previously returned. The `sybnext` command returns a null string. If another result set is expected (mutliple SQL statements in the preceding `sybsql` command), the next `sybnext` command will return the first row from the next result set.
- `n`: An integer *compute row id*, indicating that the row retrieved was from a Transact-SQL "compute" statement. Compute statements are numbered beginning with 1 and increase with each compute statement appearing in the query.
- `NO_MORE_RESULTS`: The final result set from the last `sybsql` command has been retrieved. The `sybnext` command returns a null string.

If the SQL was executed with the `async` option on `sybsql`, then `sybnext` will wait until results are available before returning. Also, if the SQL statement was in error, the `sybnext` command will fail, since this is the first opportunity to report the error.

Figure 12-1 represents the possible branches when SQL statements are executed with `sybsql` and retrieved with `sybnext`:

In the case of executing a SQL "select" statement, each row returned would be further processed in some fashion. For example, to print a list of authors' names and birthdates from the "pubs2" database:

```
puts [format "%-30.30s %s" "Author" "Birthdate"]
sybsql $handle "select name, birthdate from authors"
set row [sybnext $handle]
while {$sybmsg(nextrow) != "NO_MORE_ROWS"} {
    puts [format "%-30.30s %s" [lindex $row 0] [lindex $row 1]]
    set row [sybnext $handle]
}
```

Since it is very common programming construct to retrieve and process all the rows from a query, `sybnext` can accept an optional argument that is a block of Tcl statements to be executed for each row returned in a result set. `sybnext` internally takes care of the `while` loop, retrieving rows and checking for the end-of-rows condition. The preceding example can be rewritten as:

```
puts [format "%-30.30s %s" "Author" "Birthdate"]
sybsql $handle "select name, birthdate from authors"
sybnext $handle { puts [format "%-30.30s %s" @1 @2] }
```

Columns from each row are specified using a special substitution notation, prefixed with "@". @1 refers to the first column, @2 refers to the second column, and so on. @0 is the entire row as a Tcl list, just as `sybnext` would normally return. There is no limit to the number of times a column may be specified, or the number of Tcl statement executed in the block.

There are a few extra rules to remember when using the Tcl-statements option. First, don't try to reference a column beyond the number of columns that are returned. Second, columns are substituted into the Tcl-statements in a way to ensure that the Tcl-statements after substituting the column data are still valid Tcl commands, a proper Tcl list for example. Since the data returned in the column may

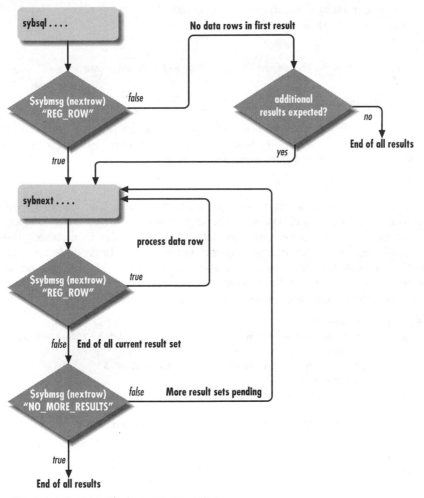

Figure 12-1: sybsql/sybnext Processing

contain Tcl quoting characters, the entire substitution may be enclosed with Tcl quoting, with adjacent spaces inserted. If you need to format the columns for printing, use the Tcl `format` command as in the previous example, or assign the column values into Tcl variables with the `set` command. Last, if any commands in the Tcl-statements block fail, `sybnext` will raise a Tcl error.

The Tcl commands `break` and `continue` may be used in the Tcl-statements block the same way they are used in `while` or `for`. `Break` will cause the `sybnext` command to return. Any further rows remaining in the query can be retrieved with a subsequent `sybnext` command. `Continue` will cause any remaining Tcl commands to be skipped and continue processing with the next row. The following example counts authors names that begin with "A" through "L," printing only the first five:

```
sybsql $handle "select au_lname from authors order by au_lname"
set num_rows 0
sybnext $handle {
    incr num_rows
```

```
    if {[string compare @1 M] == 1} { break }
    if {$num_rows > 5} { continue }
    puts @0
}
puts "number authors with names beginning A-L: $num_rows"
```

Column Information

Besides retrieving data from the Sybase server, Sybtcl also can retrieve information about the names of columns returned, their datatype, and length. `sybcols` returns a Tcl list of the names of the columns returned by `sybnext`.

```
sybcols $handle
```

`sybcols` can be used after a `sybsql` or `sybnext` command. The names of the columns returned are in the same order as the data values returned by `sybnext`. The names are the actual column names as defined in the tables from which the columns are retrieved, or any column alias name that may have been coded as part of the "select" statement. Sybase does impose two exceptions to this rule: the name returned by an aggregate function (sum, count, min, max, avg) is a null string, and the name returned by a "compute" statement is the function statement.

```
tclsh> sybsql $handle {
  select lastname = au_lname from authors where au_id ='756-30-7391'
  select count(*) from titles
  select royaltyper from titleauthor where au_ord = 3
  compute min(royaltyper)
}
REG_ROW
tclsh> sybnext $handle {puts @0; puts [sybcols $handle]}
Karsen
lastname
tclsh> sybnext $handle {puts @0; puts [sybcols $handle]}
18
{}
tclsh> sybnext $handle {puts @0; puts [sybcols $handle]}
30
royaltyper
tclsh> sybnext $handle {puts @0; puts [sybcols $handle]}
30
min(royaltyper)
```

In this example, the first select statement contains a column alias, so "lastname" is returned from `sybcols`. The second select is a SQL aggregate function, and Sybase returns a null string for that column. The third select statement is a column from a table, and its name is printed, "royaltyper." The last SQL statement is a Sybase "compute" statement, and the full function name is printed, "min(royaltyper)."

Besides getting column names, `sybcols` also sets the column datatypes and lengths in the `sybmsg` global array. `$sybmsg(coltypes)` is a Tcl list of the datatypes corresponding to the columns, and `$sybmsg(collengths)` is a Tcl list of the data lengths of each column. Datatypes can be any of Sybase's datatypes:

- char
- text
- binary
- image
- tinyint
- smallint
- int
- float
- real
- bit
- money
- decimal
- numeric
- smallmoney
- datetime
- smalldatetime

The column lengths are the internal data lengths (int = 4, real = 8, etc.); for "char" datatypes, the length returned is the maximum length defined in the table, not the column lengths of the last row retrieved.

```
tclsh> sybsql $handle {select from title, type, price, pubdate from \
                       titles}
REG_ROW
tclsh> sybcols $handle
title type price pubdate
tclsh> puts $sybmsg(coltypes)
char char money datetime
tclsh> puts $sybmsg(collengths)
80 12 8 8
```

Asynchronous SQL Processing

For SQL statements that have been executed using the `async` option on `sybsql`, the `sybpoll` command can be used to check on the status of the command. `sybpoll` allows the Tcl program to check if executing `sybnext` will cause the program to block until results are available:

```
sybpoll $handle  ?timeout?  ?all?
```

The `timeout` value, an integer number, is the maximum number of milliseconds `sybpoll` should wait before returning. The default value for `timeout` is "0," which means that `sybpoll` will return immediately with the status of the results. A `time-out` value of "-1" means that `sybpoll` will wait to return until results are avialable. "`all`" may also be specified, in which all connection handles that have pending results are checked for status. The results from `sybpoll` are either a null string, which means results for the handle are not yet available, or a list of handles that have results available. Once the first set of results for a handle have been read with `syb-next`, that handle is considered to be "ready" in any additional `sybpoll` commands.

```
# open two sybase connections with the same user id and password
set handle1 [sybconnect $id $password $server]
set handle2 [sybconnect $id $password $server]
# execute queries on each connection....
sybsql $handle1 {exec long_running_query} async
sybsql $handle2 {exec another_long_query} async
# wait for at least one query to finish...
set available [sybpoll $handle1 -1 all]
# could be one or both handles ready
foreach ready $available {
  if {[string compare $ready $handle1] == 0} {
    puts "results from handle1"
  }
  if {[string compare $ready $handle2] == 0} {
    puts "results from handle2"
  }
  # get results for the ready handle
  sybnext $ready {puts @0}
}
puts "handle not yet processed (if any) [sybpoll $handle 0 all] "
```

Note that when the `all` option is used, the handle (or list of handles) returned may not be the same as the handle used on the `sybpoll` command, since the handle used for the `sybpoll` command may not be available yet.

Another use of `sybpoll` is to allow the Tcl program to continue processing while a query is being performed. The following example provides a one-second clock tick as feedback while the query is executing:

```
sybsql $handle {select long_running_query ...} async
puts "started query"
flush stdout
set timer 0
set avail [sybpoll $handle 1000]
while {[string length $avail] == 0} {
  incr timer
  puts -nonewline " $timer"
  flush stdout
  set avail [sybpoll $handle 1000]
}
puts "\n$timer total seconds to complete"
sybnext $handle {puts @0}
```

Canceling Results

Sometimes it is desirable to stop processing rows before all rows have been retrieved from a query. Sybtcl provides the `sybcancel` command for such a case:

```
sybcancel $handle
```

The `sybcancel` command informs the server that all pending rows from the last `sybsql` command are to be discarded. `sybsql` always performs an implicit `sybcancel` before each execution of SQL; `sybcancel` may be used explicitly at any time.

Advanced Sybtcl Commands

Sybase includes several advanced features in its database server product. Sybase provides server-side execution of stored procedures, and reading and writing to larger binary objects ("text/image" columns). Sybtcl supports usage of these features.

Stored Procedures

Stored procedures, blocks of Transact-SQL code that execute on the server, are an important part of Sybase. Stored procedures are used for transactional processing, where an entire group of SQL statements are treated as an atomic unit. Changes made to the database in a stored procedure are "commited" as a unit, or may be "rolled back," in case any one SQL statement does not execute successfully. Sybase stored procedures can return information in a variety of methods:

- Return rows from "select" statements as result sets.
- Other text such as Sybase "print" messages, normally used for textual messages generated inside a stored procedure.
- Parameterized "output" variables, a form of call-by-reference, where parameters passed to a stored procedure are updated with values generated by the procedure.
- An integer value as a stored procedure return code when the stored procedure finishes.

Sybtcl fully supports the use of stored procedures, and all methods of returning information back to the calling Tcl program as listed above. `sybsql` is used to execute a stored procedure, just as you would send a "select" or "insert" statement to the server:

```
sybsql $handle {exec history_proc '5023'}
```

As mentioned before, `sybnext` is used to retrieve any rows generated within the stored procedure via "select."

Stored Procedure Output Parameters

Output parameter values are not rows in the regular sense; instead, they are the list of the stored procedure parameters after modification by the stored procedure. Sybtcl provides an additional command to retrieve the output value(s):

```
sybretval $handle
```

Use of `sybretval` follows some very strict rules, due to programming constraints with the Sybase DB-Lib interface. The return values can be accessed by **sybret-**

val only after any data rows have been retrieved with `sybnext`. If rows are generated by the procedure, `sybnext` must be called until "`$sybmsg(nextrow) ==` NO_MORE_ROWS" to access the return values. If no rows were generated, `sybsql` will return NO_MORE_ROWS, and `sybretval` can be called. The return code from the stored procedure (from the Transact-SQL "return" statement) is made available in `$sybmsg(retstatus)` after sybnext has exhausted any regular rows; `sybretval` should be called at this time to retrieve the output values.

Messages from the stored procedure "print" statements are accumulated in `$sybmsg(msgtext)` as they are generated. Should the stored procedure execute more than one "print" statement, newlines are used as delimiters between the messages. Any execution errors in the stored procedure are also reported in `$sybmsg(msgtext)`.

```
# create a stored procedure to multiply integers as an
# output variable and the sum of the integers as the return code
tclsh> sybsql $handle {
    create proc mult_sum
        @x int, @y int, @product int output
    as
    begin
        print "multiplying %1! times %2!", @x, @y
        select @product = @x * @y
        select @x = @x + @y
        return(@x)
    end
}
NO_MORE_ROWS

# execute the stored procedure
tclsh> sybsql $handle {
    declare @result int
    exec mult_sum 3, 5, @result output
}
NO_MORE_ROWS

tclsh> puts $sybmsg(msgtext)
multiplying 3 times 5
tclsh> puts $sybmsg(retstatus)   ;# get the sum as the return code
8
tclsh> sybretval $handle    ;# get the product as an output variable
15
```

Text/Image Column I/O

Another advanced feature of Sybase supported by Sybtcl is the storage and retrieval of text or image data columns. Text or image datatypes are similar, each datatype holding up to two gigabytes. Text datatypes usually imply printable text, whereas image datatypes are completely arbitrary. Sounds, graphics, and MPEG streams are examples of image data. Because image and text datatypes may contain binary zeros (thus unable to be represented as a Tcl string), Sybtcl provides commands to read and write text or image data to and from files:

```
sybwritetext $handle table.column column-number filename ?nolog?
sybreadtext  $handle filename
```

sybwritetext is the Sybtcl command to write a file into a text or image data column. The Sybase DB-Library imposes a specific order of processing to write data into an image column, and Sybtcl must follow the same order. sybwritetext requires that a preceding "select" statement be executed before writing to the text/image column. Thus, when inserting a new row into a table, the nontext/image columns must be inserted first with an "insert" SQL statement. A following SQL "update" then sets the image column to NULL. Next, a "select" statement is executed to reference the text/image column. The select statement should reference the text/image column and be constrained to return a single row using a "where" clause. Finally, the data for the text/image column can be inserted with syb-writetext. The sybwritetext command also requires the table and column names of the text/image column and the relative column position from the preceding "select" statement. The following example illustrates inserting an image file ('image.gif') into a table:

```
# set maximun text/image size that can be written (sybase limit)
set sybmsg(maxtext) 2147483647
# insert the key value for this row
sybsql $handle {insert into au_pix(au_id) values('123-45-6789')}
# update the image column to null
sybsql $handle {update au_pix set pic = NULL where \
    au_id = '123-45-6789'}
# select the image column
sybsql $handle {select pic from au_pix where au_id = '123-45-6789'}
# write the image data file to the image column
sybwritetext $handle au_pix.pic 1 image.gif
```

sybwritetext will return the number of bytes written to the column. syb-writetext will normally log updates to the server transaction log. In cases where logging is not necessary or undesirable, the nolog option may be specified. The Sybase administrator must have previously set the database option for select into/bulkcopy in order for the nolog option to function.

sybreadtext is the compliment of sybwritetext; it retrieves the text/image data from the database and writes the contents into a file. Like sybwritetext, it must be preceded by a SQL select that returns one text or image column.

Text and image columns can be retrieved by sybnext, just as ordinary columns, but there are a few problems with this approach. First, image columns are converted to a printable hexadecimal notation, which may require another conversion step to reconstruct the actual data values. Second, the column would be stored as an ordinary Tcl variable, with the risk that not enough memory could be allocated to hold the value. sybreadtext eliminates these problems by retrieving the data in smaller chunks, and writing the data directly to an operating system file.

```
# set maximum size of text/image column to be written
set sybmsg(maxtext) 2147483647
```

```
sybsql $handle {select copy from blurbs where au_id = '486-29-1786'}
sybreadtext $handle blurb.txt
```

`sybreadtext` limits the amount of text/image data retrieved, but the upper limit can be set prior to retrieval by setting the `sybmsg` array element `maxtext`. The default is 32,768, which is the total amount of data that can be written to a file. The maximum value that `sybmsg(maxtext)` may be set is 2,147,483,647.

Server Information and Feedback

A global array is maintained and used by Sybtcl for information from the server, and to control various aspects of Sybtcl. `sybmsg` is the name of the array, and you should always reference it as `global` before accessing it in any Tcl proc. We've already touched lightly on some of the elements in `$sybmsg`. Now we will examine each element in detail. The first to be discussed are the elements that can be set by the Sybtcl user and affects Sybtcl processing.

`$sybmsg(nullvalue)`

Nullvalue controls how Sybtcl represents columns containing NULL when using `sybnext`. The default value for `$sybmsg(nullvalue)` is "default" which converts numeric datatypes to "0" and all other datatypes to a null string. One possible use is to set `nullvalue` to an unlikely value to differentiate a NULL from a column that consists of whitespace characters.

```
tclsh> set sybmsg(nullvalue) <null>
tclsh> sybsql $handle {select 'not null string',
convert(integer,NULL)}
REG_ROW
tclsh> sybnext $handle
{not null string} <null>
$sybmsg(floatprec)
```

`floatprec` controls how Sybtcl returns columns containing `float` or `real` datatypes when using `sybnext`. The default value for `$sybmsg(floatprec)` is a null string, which causes float values to be returned with 17 digits of precision. `floatprec` can be set to an integer between 1 and 17, representing the total number of digits of precision:

```
tclsh> sybsql $handle {select convert(float,355.0/113.0)}
REG_ROW
tclsh> sybnext $handle
3.1415920000000002
tclsh> set sybmsg(floatprec) 4
tclsh> sybsql $handle {select convert(float,355.0/113.0)}
REG_ROW
tclsh> sybnext $handle
3.142
```

`$sybmsg(dateformat)`

dateformat alters how date values are returned by `sybnext`. The default value for `$sybmsg(dateformat)` is a null string, which causes Sybtcl to convert dates to Sybase's native date string. `dateformat` can be set to any string, and within the string certain symbols are replaced with various components of the date value. While any character can appear in the `dateformat`, there is no quoting facility to prevent unwanted substitution.

- **YYYY:** four-digit year, 1900–
- **YY:** two-digit year, 00–99
- **MM:** two-digit month, 1–12
- **MONTH:** name of month, "January"–"December"
- **MON:** month abbreviation, "Jan"–"Dec"
- **DD:** two-digit day of the month, 1–31
- **hh:** two-digit hour, 0–23
- **mm:** two-digit minute, 0–59
- **ss:** two-digit second, 0–59
- **dy:** three-digit day of the year, 0–365
- **dw:** single-digit day of week, 1–7 (Mon–Sun)

```
tclsh> sybsql $handle {select convert(datetime,'December 25, 1996')}
REG_ROW
tclsh> sybnext $handle
{Dec 25 1996 12:00:00:000AM}
tclsh> set sybmsg(dateformat) "dw MON DD, YY"
tclsh> sybsql $handle {select convert(datetime,'December 25, 1996')}
REG_ROW
tclsh> sybnext $handle
{02 Dec 25 96}
```

`$sybmsg(maxtext)`

`maxtext` limits the amount of text or image data that is retrieved from the server for both `sybnext` and `sybreadtext`. The default limit is 32,768 bytes; `maxtext` can be set to the maximum allowed by Sybase, 2,147,483,647. Any change to `maxtext` becomes effective on the next execution of `sybsql`.

The remainder of the elements in `$sybmsg` are informational only. Sybtcl resets the informational elements on every Sybtcl command. Any element not explicitly set by any particular Sybtcl command is set to a null string:

`$sybmsg(handle)`

Since the `sybmsg` array is shared among all open connections, this element reports the handle of the last Sybtcl command executed.

`$sybmsg(nextrow)`

`nextrow` has been has already been mentioned for both `sybsql` and `sybnext`. Here's a quick review of the possible values:

- **REG_ROW:** At least one row is available after executing `sybsql`, or a regular row from a select was returned by `sybnext`.

- **NO_MORE_ROWS:** No rows were returned in the first result set by `sybsql`, or the end of the current result set was reached by `sybnext`.

- **n (numeric integer):** Last row returned by `sybnext` was from a "compute" statement.

- **NO_MORE_RESULTS:** The final set of result sets have already been returned by `sybnext`.

`$sybmsg(retstatus)`

retstatus is the return code from a stored procedure. If `retstatus` is non-null, any output variables from a stored procedure are now available to be retrieved with the `sybretval` command.

`$sybmsg(collengths)`

collengths is a Tcl list of column lengths that correspond to the column names that are returned by `sybcols`. The column lengths are either the internal size for numeric datatypes, or the maximum length that character datatypes are defined in the database.

`$sybmsg(coltypes)`

coltypes is a Tcl list of column datatypes that correspond to the column names that are returned by `sybcols`. Both `collengths` and `coltypes` are only set after `sybcols` has been executed.

`$sybmsg(msgno)`

msgno is a message number generated by the Sybase server. If the server generated several messages during execution of Transact-SQL statements, each message number is separated by newline characters.

`$sybmsg(msgtext)`

msgtext is the message text generated by the Sybase server during execution of a SQL command or stored procedure, and corresponds to the message numbers in `msgno`. As in `msgno`, separate messages are separated by newlines. Messages from stored procedures that execute "print" also accumulated in `msgtext`.

```
$sybmsg(dberr)
$sybmsg(dberrstr)
$sybmsg(oserr)
$sybmsg(oserrstr)
$sybmsg(severity)
$sybmsg(svrname)
$sybmsg(procname)
$sybmsg(line)
```

Sybase provides several error feedback values, all of which are available in Sybtcl. dberr and dberrstr are error numbers and messages generated by the DB-Lib routines that Sybtcl uses. oserr and oserrstr are operating system errors detected by DB-Lib. Refer to Sybase documentation for interpretation. `svrname` is the name of the Sybase server that generated the last error message. This is not necessarily the same as the server from the `sybconnect` connection, as stored procedures on one server may access tables and stored procedures on another server. `severity` is the level of error severity reported by the server. `procname` is the name of the stored procedure that generated an error message. `line` is the line number of a SQL statement or stored procedure that generated a message.

While most errors can be easily read by examining `$sybmsg(dberrstr)` or `$sybmsg(msgtext)`, Sybase manuals contain the definitive reference for error codes and messages.

Handling Errors

Sybtcl commands will raise a Tcl error condition when a Sybtcl command is invalid or when the Sybase server reports an error in a SQL statement. Sybtcl was designed with this conservative error-handling approach so that inadvertent operations to a database would be reported.

The Tcl interpreter normally halts script processing when a Tcl error is raised. The Tcl command `catch` allows errors to be trapped and error-handling code to be executed. For example, the `sybconnect` command will normally raise a Tcl error when either a Sybase userid or password is invalid, or when the Sybase server is unavailable. Catching the error allows the script to continue, and information about the error to be extracted from the `$sybmsg` array:

```
if [catch {sybconnect $sybuserid $sybpassword $sybserver} handle] {
    puts "cannot connect to server, reason: $sybmsg(dberrstr)"
    exit
}
```

In addition to raising an error on invalid or improperly formed SQL statements, `sybsql` will also raise a Tcl error if the Sybase server reports a logical error. Logical errors include attempting to insert a duplicate row into a table that has unique indexes, or perhaps a stored procedure or referential integrity trigger executing a Sybase "raiserror" statement.

Applications

Sybtcl includes several applications that are built on Tcl/Tk and Sybtcl.

Wisqlite—An X11 SQL Processor

Sybtcl combined with the power of Tcl/Tk provides a basis for developing powerful database applications and tools. One common tool, usually provided by database vendors is a general SQL processor, passing SQL statements to the server and printing rows that are returned. Sybase provides 'isql,' a command-line SQL processor. In the process of writing and debugging Sybtcl, I wrote another SQL processor, one that uses the X Window System via the Tk extension. I originally called it *Wisql* (for Windowing ISQL); I've since renamed it to *Wisqlite*, as one of the early users of Sybtcl enhanced my original Wisql into a very comprehensive SQL processor. Wisql is described in the next section. I still maintain Wisqlite for those who prefer a leaner tool and to provide a smaller sample of using Sybtcl. Wisqlite is also written to use commands from Extended Tcl (TclX), so its interpreter needs Tcl, Tk, TclX, and Sybtcl.

Wisqlite is similar to other X11 applications in that it provides a menubar, scrolling edit and result panes, and various pop-up windows.

After starting Wisqlite, the server sign-on window appears to collect the Sybase user id, password, and server to which it should connect (see Figure 12-2). The server entry is pre-populated with the default (DSQUERY environment variable); pressing the "server" button will list all servers from the *$SYBASE/interfaces* file.

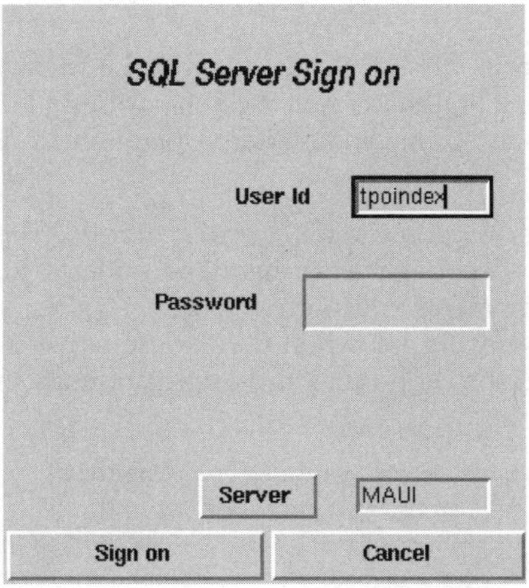

Figure 12-2: Wisqlite Sign-On Window

SQL statements are entered into the top pane of the Main window (a Tk edit widget, see Figure 12-3); pressing the "Execute" button will send the SQL off to the server, and results will be printed in the lower pane (a Tk listbox). Menubar items provide additional functionality.

File

The File menu controls the SQL edit pane. "New" clears the SQL Edit and Results windows for a new query. "Open" prompts for a file containing SQL statements through a file selection dialog window. "Save" and "Save as" save the SQL Edit window into the current filename, or prompts for a new filename. "Quit" will disconnect from the server and exit Wisqlite.

Results

The Results menu controls the Results window. "Append results" or "Clear results" selects whether the Results window should be cleared on each new SQL execution or appended to the end of the list. "Save as" allows the Results window to be saved to a

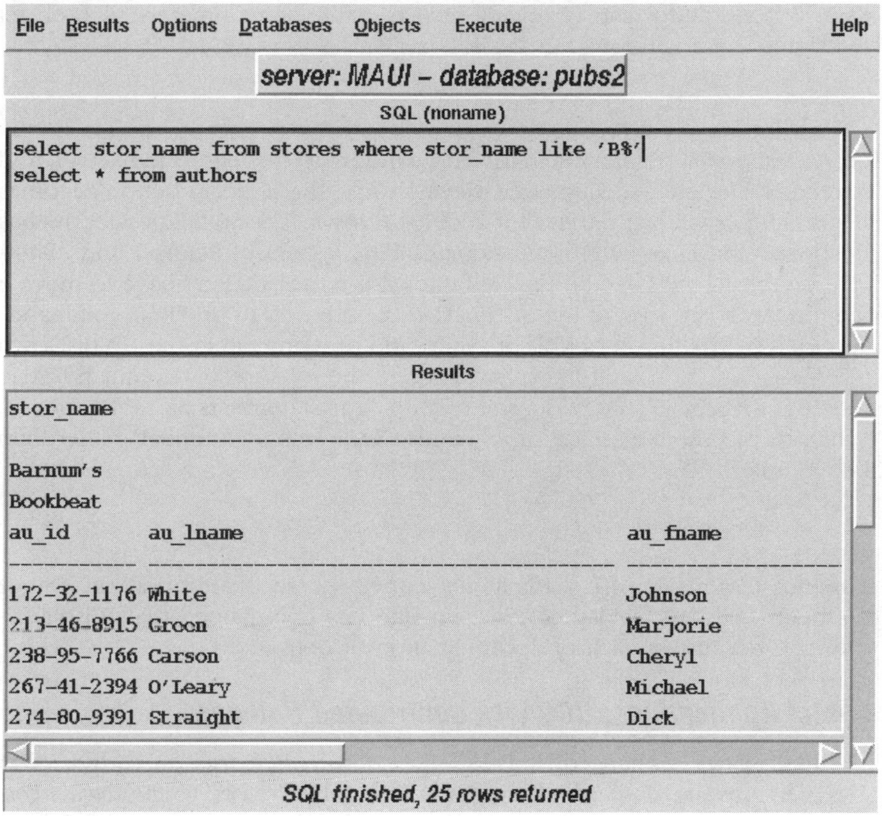
File Results Options Databases Objects Execute Help
server: MAUI – database: pubs2
SQL (noname)
select stor_name from stores where stor_name like 'B%'
select * from authors
Results
stor_name
Barnum's
Bookbeat
au_id au_lname au_fname
172-32-1176 White Johnson
213-46-8915 Green Marjorie
238-95-7766 Carson Cheryl
267-41-2394 O'Leary Michael
274-80-9391 Straight Dick
SQL finished, 25 rows returned

Figure 12-3: Wisqlite Main Window

file, overwriting any previous contents. "Print" sends the Results window to the printer (via the Unix *lp* command). "Font" changes the font size of the Results window.

Options

Currently, only one option is available in Wisqlite, and that is to set the default format for representing NULL values. "default" causes the default null value behavior as described for `$sybmsg(nullvalue).` Any other string can be entered.

Databases

The Databases menu allows the user to select a particular database to use. All of the databases that are available are listed.

Objects

The Objects menu provides for data dictionary access into the current database. Tables, views, stored procedures, rules, and triggers can be listed, and detailed information on each can be retrieved. For example, when displaying a list of tables, clicking "Ok" or double-clicking on a table will list the columns and their datatypes in that table; for a stored procedure, rule, or trigger, the text of the procedure is listed. It's also possible to display several objects at the same time, as each object is displayed in its own window.

Execute

Execute causes the SQL statements in the edit window to be sent to the server, and results printed. While the execution is retrieving rows, the Execute button becomes "Cancel"; pressing it will halt retrieval of additional rows. The SQL Edit window has a few keyboard bindings worth mentioning. First, "Control-Return" and "Shift-Return" are bound to the Execute/Cancel button, so a user doesn't have to move a hand from the keyboard to start the query. Also, a buffer of 10 previous commands can be accessed by holding "Control" or "Shift" and pressing either the Up or Down arrow keys. For example, "Shift-Down" will access the most recent command. Also worth noting is that the SQL text doesn't require "go" statements as 'isql' requires. The "#" character at the beginning of a line also indicates a comment, rather than the C-like delimiters "/* ... */".

Help

The last menu item is Help. It's admittedly rather sparse on information. (Since Sybtcl has been released in May of 1992, no one has complained that Wisqlite is too hard to use because of lack of documentation or help text!)

Other Sybtcl Applications: UCO/Lick Contributed Software

The original Wisql was enhanced by De Clarke (*de@ucolick.org*), an early user of Sybtcl. De is a software engineer at the UCO/Lick Observatory (*http://www.ucolick.org*). De's UCOwisql was designed for use both by experienced Sybase DBA/programmers and novice users alike.

UCOwisql adds context-sensitive help, and GUI screens for data editing and simple report generation for people with no SQL knowledge (see Figure 12-4). The "EZ" screens offer a point-and-click approach to building SQL statements. UCOwisql is included in the Sybtcl distribution; the latest version can be retrieved from *ftp://ftp.ucolick.org/pub/src/UCOSYB/wisql.tar.gz*.

The EZrpt window allows the user to select columns to print, assert constraints (the "where" clause), and apply complex sorting ("order by"). Additional single buttons allow the user to preview the generated SQL, count the number of rows in the target table, and transfer the SQL statement to the main window for execution.

The EZedit window allows simple editing (insert, update, and delete SQL commands) of a single table (see Figure 12-5). The user can review and modify rows in tabular format, or one row at a time. Context-sensitive help and SQL previewing are implemented in both "EZ" tools, and there are hooks to a data dictionary facility for table/column-sensitive help. UCOWisql can mail results as well as save them, and has hooks for sending results directly into the Xess X11 spreadsheet (this requires the tclXess extension.)

Another handy application, also included in the Sybtcl distribution is De's "syperf," which uses the VUW widgets ("Vumeters") extension to build a Sybase server performance monitor. A Sybase administrator can use this tool to view server statistics

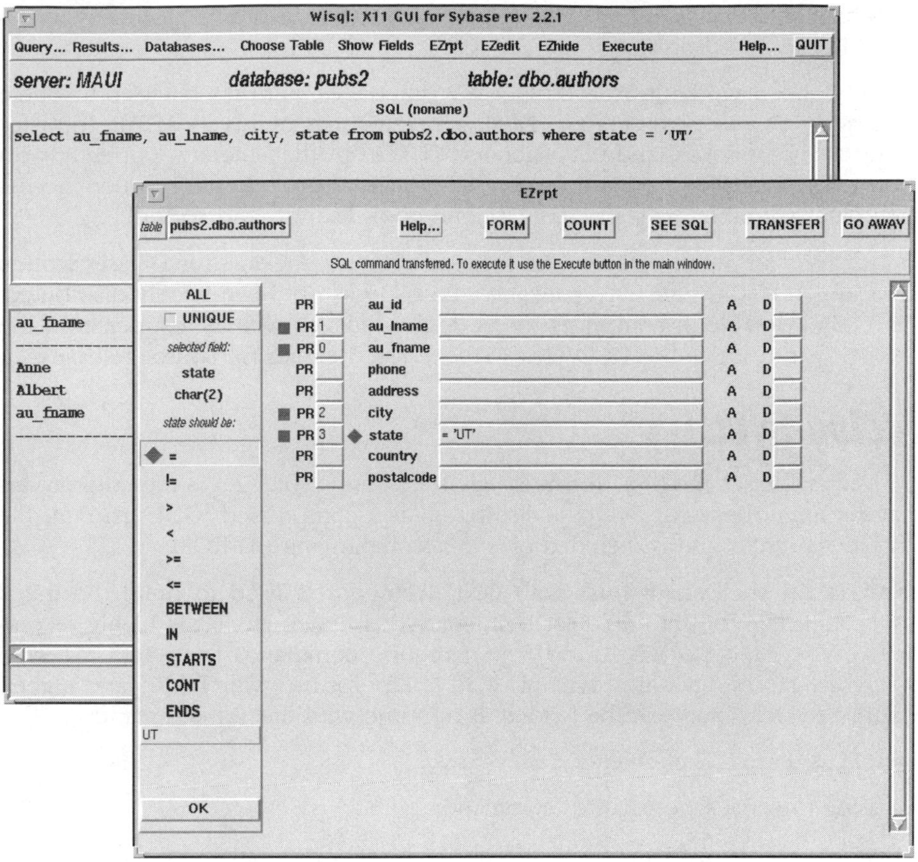

Figure 12-4: UCO Wisql EZreport

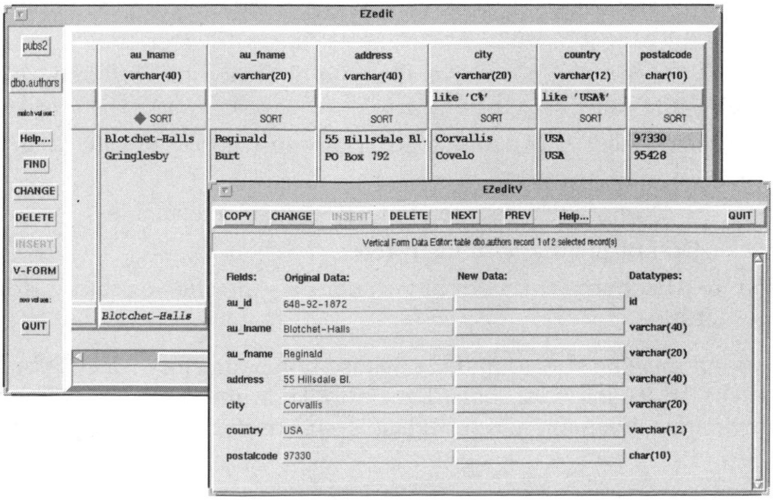

Figure 12-5: UCO Wisql EZedit

in stripchart and dial form, as well as user processes in tabular form. Syperf is included in the Sybtcl distribution.

De has also been working on Sybase/WWW interfaces, and has released a source kit consisting of two parts: (1) an HTML generator that builds an HTML form for querying a Sybase table, and (2) a generic CGI script that interacts correctly with this form. These tools have been used at UCO/Lick to provide public query access to such database tables as start charts, phone book listings, and so forth.

UCO/Lick uses an online (OLTP) GUI forms/data-entry package for Sybase, written by De using Tcl/Tk/Sybtcl. This package ("Fosql") has not been widely distributed, but is freely available. It comprises forms design tools as well as a superset of the UCOwisql features. See the UCO/Lick FTP site listed earlier for source releases.

Building Sybtcl

Sybtcl builds "out of the box" for most environments. Sybtcl 2.4 is the current version at the time of writing. Sybtcl is distributed as a compressed (GNU gzip) tar file via Internet sources and is included on the accompanying CD-ROM.

A `configure` shell script built with GNU Autoconf is used to build the initial Makefile. Although not required for building Sybtcl, Extended Tcl is highly recommended. Wisqlite, UCO Wisql, and Syperf require commands from TclX. Alternatively, Sybtcl can be built as a dynamic load library for use with Tcl 7.5 and higher. A dynamic Sybtcl library can be loaded at run-time with the Tcl command:

```
load libSybtcl[info sharedlibextension]
```

or by using the "package require" command:

```
package require Sybtcl
```

before using any Sybtcl commands.

The `configure` script can accept several configuration options:

- `--prefix=directory name`: The primary directory for installing Sybtcl, including ./bin, ./lib, and ./man. This should be the same directory where Tcl was installed. Default is /usr/local.
- `--exec-prefix=directory name`: An alternate directory for ./bin and ./lib files. The default is the same as `--prefix`.
- `--enable-shared`: Builds a dynamic load library instead of a static library and executables.
- `--without-tclx`: Do not include Extended Tcl in static executables.
- `--without-tk`: Do not build a *wish* interpreter.
- `--with-sybase-directory=directory name`: Specific directory for Sybase "home" location.

The `configure` script must be able to find the Sybase home directory, since Sybtcl needs the Sybase DB-Lib to link with. `configure` looks in the directory defined by the SYBASE environment variable, or the exlicit `--with-sybase-directory` directive. Information about the Tcl version is gathered from the *tclConfig.sh* file created by Tcl 7.5 and higher, normally in *$prefix/lib*. The resulting Makefile will build a Tcl command-line interpreter and a Tcl/Tk Wish interpreter or a dynamic load library depending if `--enable-shared` was specified. The target "install" will copy the executables or dynamic library to the installation *bin* and *lib* directories, and the Sybtcl man page to the installation man directory. If Sybtcl was built with TclX, the target "install-wisqlite" will configure Wisqlite with the proper `#!interpreter` line and copy Wisqlite to the installation *bin* directory.

The *README* file in the Sybtcl distribution contains notes on each particular release of Sybtcl, which Tcl/Tk versions that are required, tested configurations, and general information. The file *INSTALL* contains detailed information on building Sybtcl, including configure options recognized. Both *README* and *INSTALL* should be perused prior to building Sybtcl. The file *CHANGES* is a history of features added and bugs fixed in Sybtcl. The subdirectory *samples* contains additional sample Sybtcl scripts. UCOWisql and the other UCO/Lick tools are located in *samples/uco*.

Sybtcl is available on the Internet at *ftp.neosoft.com* in the directory */pub/tcl/NEW/sybtcl-2.4.tar.gz*. Newer versions will have the same file name, except for incrementing the major and/or minor version numbers. Usenet discussion of Sybtcl currently takes place in *comp.lang.tcl*, or *comp.databases.sybase*. Tom Poindexter can be reached at *tpoindex@nyx.net* and maintains information about Sybtcl at *http://www.nyx.net/~tpoindex*.

Command Summary

Command	Function / Return value
sybconnect *id password ?server?* *?application? ?interface file?*	Connects to a Sybase Server. Returns: a connection handle.
sybclose *handle*	Closes a connection.
	Returns: nothing.
sybuse *handle ?database?*	Reports active database, or causes the named database to be used.
	Returns: current database in use.
sybsql *handle sql-statements ?async?*	Executes SQL statements on the server.
	Returns: data availability status.
sybpoll *handle ?timeout? ?all?*	Polls connection for data availability during asynchronous SQL execution.
	Returns: connection handle ready for processing.
sybnext *handle ?tcl-statements?*	Retrieves data rows from an SQL `select` statement.
	Returns: row data as a Tcl list.
sybcancel *handle*	Cancels pending SQL and results.
	Returns: nothing.

Continued

Command Summary (continued)

Command	Function / Return value
sybcols *handle*	Returns column names.
	Returns: column names as a Tcl list.
sybretval *handle*	Retrieves output variables from a stored procedure.
	Returns: output variables.
sybwritetext *handle table.column column-num filename ?nolog?*	Writes data from a file to a text or image column.
	Returns: number of bytes written to column.
sybreadtext *handle filename*	Reads text or image data from a column and writes to a file.
	Returns: number of bytes read from column.

13

Expect

by Don Libes

Consider *telnet*. It was designed for a human to be doing the typing—so you can't automate a *telnet* session in a shell script. There are many programs that share this drawback, but they can all be automated with *Expect*. Expect is an extension that enables Tcl to control interactive processes like *telnet*. Using Expect, you can use Tcl to write scripts that automate *telnet* as well as *rlogin, ftp, passwd, su, crypt, fsck*, and lots of other programs.

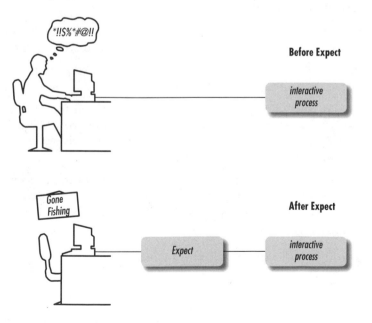

Expect is a well-behaved Tcl extension and can be used with any other Tcl extensions. For example, you can use Expect and Tk to create a GUI for an existing command-line oriented application. Expect can also handle character-graphic applications as well.

Expect also includes some useful utilities that don't have anything to do with interaction automation, but simply make Tcl a much more complete and useful environment. For instance, Expect includes commands to deal with signals. Expect also comes with a Tcl debugger that enables signal stepping, breakpoints, and other helpful aids.

A complete discussion of Expect can be found in my book, *Exploring Expect*.* It is 600 pages of techniques, tricks, and insights which explain how to apply Expect to a huge collection of problems. At the end of this chapter, I will mention some additional problems which Expect can solve. This chapter is only an introduction to Expect, but it is enough to give you a good taste of what Expect is all about.

The Basic Expect Commands

Expect defines about 40 commands, but in this chapter I will focus on a small subset of the most useful commands. These commands will allow you to get started and solve many problems.

The basic Expect commands are `spawn`, `send`, `expect`, and `interact`.

The `spawn` command starts an interactive process. For example, the following command starts a *telnet* process.

```
spawn telnet $host
```

The hostname is supplied by the host variable. `spawn` and all the other commands in Expect work just like other Tcl commands. So you can do variable substitution, use them in `if/then/else` commands, and so on.

Once an interactive process has been started, you can send commands to it; in fact, you can send any string. The following line shows how you would send the username in response to a prompt.

```
send "libes\r"
```

The string "libes\r" ends with a "\r" which is the Tcl notation for a return character. This is exactly what is sent when you manually press return while using *telnet*. Expect follows this philosophy at all times—commands merely automate what is normally done manually.

In order to read responses, prompts, and anything else from the process, use the `expect` command. If you know exactly what you expect, you can literally say that. For example, the following command waits for the string "Password":

```
expect "Password:"
```

Of course you can `send` or `expect` from variables as well.

```
send "$username\r"
expect "$prompt"
```

In addition, you can wait for patterns. This is useful if you have only some vague idea of what you want to wait for. The following command waits for the string

---

* *Exploring Expect*, by Don Libes, O'Reilly & Associates, ISBN 1-56592-090-2.

"200" and a prompt with any number of other characters in between. Here, the "*"
acts as a wildcard.

```
expect "200*$prompt"
```

Using these simple commands, it is possible to do something very useful—automate
the *passwd* program. The following commands do this automation.

```
spawn /bin/passwd $user
expect "Password:"
send "$pass\r"
expect "Password:"
send "$pass\r"
expect eof
```

The script is easy to understand. First, the *passwd* program is started with the username as its argument. Expect then waits for the program to prompt for the password. The password is sent in response along with a carriage return just like a real
user would do. Since the *passwd* program prompts twice, the script watches for it
twice as well. Finally, the script waits for the program to end. This is done using
the **expect** command with the keyword "eof."

Now it may not seem very useful to automate a single use of the *passwd* command. But suppose you are setting passwords for 5000 students at the beginning
of each semester. All of a sudden, an automated *passwd* command sounds very
attractive.

You could wrap these commands in a simple script and then call it 5000 times from
another script. To make this into a standalone script, all that is necessary is to get
the username and password from somewhere. For example, you could read it from
the command line in this way:

```
set user [lindex $argv 0]
set password [lindex $argv 1]
# password interaction as before
```

A more secure alternative is to generate the password. A password generator can
be found in *Exploring Expect*. If you take this approach, you can have Tcl do the
looping as well, merely by embedding the interaction in a loop:

```
foreach $user $list {
    # first, generate password
    # then, do password interaction as above
}
```

Changing Accounts On Multiple Machines

Suppose you have accounts on a number of machines and they don't share password files. For example, you have an account on your personal workstation,
another on a machine at MIT, and another account at Stanford. Obviously, the
machines have different password databases.

It's irritating to use different passwords on each. If you have enough accounts,
you'll need to write down your passwords somewhere. But that's not very secure.

The alternative is to use the same password. But then you'll need to change all your accounts simultaneously.

By hand, this is a hassle. With Expect, it's easy. Just write a loop and in the loop have Expect remotely log in to each host and run the password program. I know people who do this with over a hundred hosts!

The Expect software includes a large set of examples. One example is called *passmass*. *passmass* carries out the remote logins and password interactions that I just described—so you don't actually have to write any code for this particular problem. It's already been done. But it's still pretty interesting to look at. The *passmass* script is very similar to the previous example (setting 5000 passwords in a loop). The primary difference is that the hostname changes each time through the loop rather than the user name.

To connect to a remote host, the script uses *telnet* or *rlogin*. Once connected, it carries out the password interaction as before. It looks like this:

```
foreach $host $list {
    spawn telnet $host

    # login interaction
    expect "Username:"
    send "$user\r"
    expect "Password:"
    send "$oldpassword\r"
    expect "$prompt"

    # run password program
    send "passwd\r"
    # now repeat password interaction as before
}
```

Digression—Expect Philosophy

Let's focus on the simple password interaction for a moment. It is worth comparing this approach to its alternatives. We know that this automation could be solved in a different way. The traditional approach is to edit the source to *passwd* (should you be so lucky as to have it) and modify it so that given an optional flag, it reads its arguments from the command line.

If you lack the source and have to write *passwd* from scratch, of course then you will have to worry about how to encrypt passwords, lock and write the password database, and so forth. However, even if you only modify the existing code, you will find it surprisingly complicated code to look at. The *passwd* program does some very tricky things. If you do get it to work, pray that nothing changes the next time your system is upgraded. If the vendor adds NIS+, Kerberos, shadow passwords, a different encryption function, or some other new feature, you will have to revisit the code, change the code, test the code, debug the code, and install the code. And you will have to do this each time. Some sites use several password programs simultaneously (e.g., *passwd*, *yppasswd*, *nispasswd*), in which case you will have to modify each of them each time the system changes.

Rewriting code is fun for hackers, but most of us don't have the time. The Expect approach caters to the rest of us. Instead of rewriting, Expect scripts reuse existing code. Virtually everything has interfaces already, so why not reuse them? And if they're not good interfaces, well, that's what Expect is for—to make lousy interfaces better.

Waiting for Different Patterns Simultaneously

Expect can wait for multiple patterns at the same time. This is useful when a program may return different results. For example, when automating a login, it is necessary to recognize the different prompts. In fact, the *passmass* script I just mentioned has to recognize different prompts when contacting different hosts.

The following example matches three different patterns. These are specified as pairs of patterns and actions. If the pattern matches, the action is executed.

```
expect {
    "unknown host" {
        exit
    }
    "Username:" {
        send "$password\r"
    }
    "$prompt" {
    }
}
```

The first pattern matches the "unknown host" error from *telnet* or *rlogin*. Assuming the host is correct, the second pattern checks for the username prompt in which case a password is returned. The third pattern tests for a shell prompt. A shell prompt could appear without sending the password if host equivalencing is in effect, so the script must be ready for it. Notice that the action is empty since there is nothing to do. As soon as one pattern is matched successfully, the **expect** completes and control passes to the next command in the script.

Multiple patterns provide two things: flexibility and robustness. By providing alternatives, scripts can handle different situations. Most importantly, errors in the underlying programs can be detected and handled. In fact, the example just shown did just that in response to the "unknown host" message. The **exit** command is a simplistic response, but obviously it could be replaced with more sophisticated responses.

Timeout

If the patterns do not immediately match, **expect** continues waiting for some time. Perhaps more output is on its way from the process. By default, Expect waits for 10 seconds. But this is controllable. To change it, set the variable *timeout*. For example, suppose you are automating dialing a long-distance number. This could easily take more than 10 seconds. With modem initialization, 90 seconds might be more appropriate.

The following commands show how a modem might be dialed with this new timeout:

```
spawn tip modem
expect "connected"
```

```
send "ATD1234567890\r"
set timeout 90
expect "CONNECTED"
```

In this example, the "connected" string comes from the *tip* program. The "CON-
NECTED" string comes from the modem after it has established a connection with
the remote modem.

The *timeout* pattern is a keyword which matches if the timeout period has passed
without any other patterns matching. This can be used to handle the lack of any
response. For example, the modem example can be extended as follows:

```
set timeout 90
expect {
    "CONNECTED" {
        # connected, go on
    }
    timeout {
        # no answer, do something else
    }
}
```

Testing Modems and Other Things

Many people use Expect not only to automate modems, but to test them. For example, we run a script once an hour that tests all of our outgoing modems. The test
dials out and then dials back in, thereby testing our incoming modems as well. The
test even logs in to a workstation just to make sure everything works.

In a script, it's very easy to make a note of which modem is in use, which port was
allocated, and so on. So if a modem test fails, we get a complete log of every piece
of equipment involved and how far the test got before it failed. By comparison,
users don't keep track of these things—and this isn't surprising. A typical user com-
plaint is "the modems don't work!" In contrast, our modem tester will say "5:03
3/24/96, modem 5 of bank 2 on host modem.time.nist.gov responded to a reset
(ATZ) but did not produce a dial tone, retried 3 times." The script also maintains a
history—it knows that certain conditions (busy lines, for instance) are transient, but
will report them if they persist.

With our modem testing script, our time spent diagnosing flaky modems and other
communications devices has dropped to near zero. And when we find a new condition that we've never encountered before, we add it to the modem tester so that
we don't have to diagnose the problem twice. This same approach can be applied
to many devices and programs.

Partial Automation

It is often useful to automate only part of an interaction. For instance, you might
like to automate an initial *ftp* login including changing to a particular directory. This
simple sequence could be automated this way:

```
spawn ftp $host
expect "Name"
```

```
send "anonymous\r"
expect "Password:"
send "libes@nist.gov\r"
expect "ftp>"
send "cd pub/expect/scripts\r"
interact
```

The `interact` command passes control from the script to a user. After the initial interaction in this script, the user can take over.

Partial automation is useful when some of the interaction is well-defined and some isn't. For example, an *fsck* script can automatically provide the right answers to preselected questions. But if something unusual arises, the interaction can be handled manually.

Or perhaps a situation is complex or rare enough that it isn't worth the time to script it. With **interact**, you can script only the parts that have the most payback.

interact works in the opposite direction as well. You can take control over for a while and then, when convenient, return control back to the script. For example, suppose you are debugging a program that fails only after a large number of inter-actions. You could write a debugger script that drives the program to failure and then steps out of the way and allows you to experiment with it. Then you could hand control back and direct the script to carry out some more operations before taking control again.

Dangerous, Unfriendly, Or Otherwise Unlikable User Interfaces

The `interact` command is just shorthand for the simplest and most common types of filtering that can be done in interactions. It is possible to build arbitrarily sophisticated mechanisms using the tools in Expect.

For example, commands can be filtered out of interfaces to prevent users from entering commands that you would prefer they not enter. Programs can also be wrapped even more tightly. The *adb* program, for instance, can crash a Unix system with a slip of the finger or, more likely, inexperience. You can prevent this from happening by securely wrapping the *adb* program in a script. Not only does this increase the safety of your system, but your system administrators no longer all have to be masters of its intricacies.

The Unix *dump* program is another program with an unlikable interface. For exam-ple, *dump* often guesses incorrectly about the length of a tape and will prompt for a new tape even if one is not needed. An Expect script can be used to respond to *dump* so that it can continue automatically.

Expect can, in general, be applied to interfaces that you simply do not like for what-ever reason. For example, you might like to automate sequences of your favorite game, perhaps because you have long since mastered some of it and would like to practice the end game without laboriously replaying the beginning each time.

It is possible to customize exactly how much of the underlying programs show through. You can even make interactions entirely invisible so that users do not have

---

to be irritated by underlying programs that they have no interest in anyway. Their attitude is "Use any tool. Just get the job done." And they are right.

Graphical Applications

All of the interactive applications mentioned so far have been command-line based. Expect can also automate character-graphic programs like *vi* and *emacs*. While both of these editors have their own control languages, Expect provides a useful way to test the systems. And many character-graphic programs do not have built-in languages. For example, typical menuing systems are not programmable. If you seem to be spending half your day threading your way through the same sets of menus again and again, you should automate the process with Expect.

Expect can also be combined with Tk, a toolkit for the X Window System. The combination of Expect and Tk is called Expectk.* Using Expectk, it is possible to take an existing interactive application and give it a Motif-like X interface without changing any of the underlying program. No recompiling is necessary, and because the underlying programs are not changed, there is no need to retest them again. All your efforts can be focused on the graphical user interface. Making it look pretty is all you have to do.

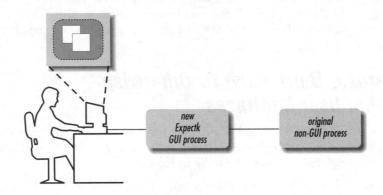

While Expectk will allow you to *build* X applications, it is limited in the amount it can *automate* existing X applications. Currently, Expect can automate *xterm* and other applications that specifically provide automation support, but Expect cannot automate any arbitrary X application.

Both character-graphic and Tk-based automation are covered in detail in *Exploring Expect*.

Job Control

Just as you can personally interact with multiple programs at the same time, so can Expect. Analogous to the way you use **fg** and **bg** to switch between processes in a shell, Expect can also switch its attention. Of course, Expect does it a lot more quickly than you can. The result is that Expect can act as "glue" for programs that were never designed to operate with other programs. An amusing example is the

---

* Expectk is pronounced "ek spec tee kay."

original chess program distributed with V7 and BSD Unix written by Ken Thompson. It was designed to interact with a user—it prompts for moves and echoes user input in algebraic notation. Unfortunately, it does not accept its own output as input. Even if it did, there is no way to pipe both inputs and outputs between two processes simultaneously from the shell. With a few lines of Expect, it is possible to make one chess process play another, including both the communication and the massaging of the output so that it is acceptable as input.

This same technique can be applied to any pair of programs that were not originally designed to talk to one another. For example, you can write a little script to interactively read mail on one system (that is not on the Internet) and download it using *ftp* to another system simultaneously.

Background Processes—cron, at, and CGI

Expect is useful for automating processes in the background such as through *cron*. By using Expect with *cron*, you can not only automate the interactions but also automate starting the process in the first place. For example, you might want to copy over files each night between two networked but otherwise unrelated systems. And you can be arbitrarily selective about choosing files. You might want to copy over only executables that are less than 1 Mb and were created on a Saturday unless the current load exceeds 2.5 and the previous transfer took less than 5 seconds, or some other such complicated set of rules. There are no Ftp clients that have such complex front ends. But you can write Expect scripts to make whatever decisions seem appropriate while driving *ftp*.

It is even possible to have a *cron* process interactively contact you while it is in the background. For example, an *ftp* script may need a password to continue what it is doing. It can search the network for you and then ask you for it. Or you can have it look for a set of users. After getting the password, Expect will go back and use it to complete the task. By having Expect query for passwords, you do not need to embed them in scripts.

The *find_help* procedure demonstrates how an Expect script might search for someone to help after encountering a problem from within a *cron* script.

```
proc find_help {
    global help

    foreach host $help(hosts)
        spawn rlogin $host
        expect ...prompt...
        foreach user "$help(users) no-such-user" {
            send "write $user\r"
            expect {
                "not logged on" continue
                "connected" break
            }
        }
        if {$user != "no-such-user"} {
            send "While doing XYZ, I encountered the problem: ..."
            send " . . . more problem description . . ."
```

```
                send "Should I retry or give up?"
                expect {
                        "r" {set action "retry"; break}
                        "g" {set action "give up"; break}
                }
        }
        close; wait
    }
    catch {
        close; wait
        return $action
    }
}
```

Doing backups from *cron* is another common reason to use Expect. If the backup program needs another tape, an Expect script can tell it to go on (for example, if your tapes are physically longer than the backup program thinks), or it can, again, contact you for assistance.

Expect works fine in CGI scripts to handle forms and other dynamic pages on the Web. Many Expect scripts can be run directly with one change—the following line should be inserted before any other output:

```
puts "Content-type: text/html\n"
```

You can get other good tips and advice on background scripts from reading the Background chapter in *Exploring Expect*.

Signal Handling and Debugging

Expect was the first popular Tcl extension. An unintentional side effect of being on the leading edge is falling into all the holes first. Two such holes in Tcl are signal and debugging support. Many Expect scripts need signal handling—and debugging is always nice—so Expect has long included support for both.

Signal handling works very similarly to that of the shell. The following example shows how to have a command invoked when the user presses ^C.

```
trap intproc SIGINT
```

More sophisticated results can be accomplished. For example:

```
trap {
    if [expr $test] return
    send_user "bye bye"
    exit
} SIGINT
```

Exploring Expect contains a chapter on signal handling. It includes a thorough explanation of all of the signals you are likely going to run into, with examples demonstrating how to handle all of them.

The book also includes a chapter on Tcl and Tk debugging techniques and tips as well as a complete explanation of the debugger. This same debugger is also now available as a Tcl extension itself.

The debugger is very similar to traditional line-oriented debuggers. For example, you can single step through a script. This is done by entering **s** at the debugger prompt. You can also set breakpoints, look at the stack, and so on. Here are the most commonly used commands:

Name	Description
s	step into procedure
n	step over procedure
r	return from procedure
b	set, clear, or show breakpoint
c	continue
w	show stack

There are no special commands to look at values because you can simply call existing Tcl commands like `puts`. In fact, you can call any Tcl command, which means you can define new procedures, load extensions, and so forth, all while debugging.

For example, imagine debugging a procedure to convert degrees between Fahrenheit and Celsius:

```
proc convert {to degrees} {
    if {$to == "c"} {
        expr {($degrees - 32)/1.8}
    } else {
        expr {32 + 1.8 * $degrees}
    }
}
```

Here's how it would look if you invoked the debugger on the call "convert f 100" (meaning: convert 100 degrees to Fahrenheit). The debugger passes control to the user after printing out the next line to be executed. Here, it shows the `convert` command is about to be called. (The "1" before the colon indicates the number of calls to Tcl_Eval in progress.)

```
1: convert f 100
dbg1.2> s
```

I typed "**s**" which causes the debugger to step to the first command in **convert**.

```
2: if {$to == "c"} { ....
dbg2.3> puts $to
f
```

At this point, I displayed the value of "to". I could call any Tcl command at this point. For example, I could change "**to**" to another string by calling **set**. Or I could do expression evaluation, and so on. The debugger interprets commands in the context of the current procedure.

The debugger has its own prompt. The left-most number refers to the stack level and the right is just the usual history number. You can display the stack with the "**w**" command (for "where").

```
dbg2.4> w
  0: expect test.tcl
*1: convert f 100
  2: if {$to == "c"} { . . .
```

Here we see three levels. The last line (2: . . .) is the command about to be executed. The line above is the command currently being executed. It is marked with an asterisk to indicate what the scope is for commands typed interactively. You can move the scope up and down with u and d. Finally, the command "0:" indicates how the script was invoked. It's not a Tcl procedure, but it make sense to show it as the end of the stack.

Another s command single steps to the expr command.

```
dbg2.5> s
3: expr {32 + 1.8 * $degrees}
dbg3.6>
```

Using Expect with Other Programs

Most of the examples in this chapter use programs that are common to all Unix systems. But Expect is not restricted to these programs. You can apply Expect to other programs. Even (gasp!) programs that *you* have written.

In the previous section, I described how you might automate *ftp*. But if you have a different program on your system to do file transfer, that's fine. Expect can use it. Expect does not have a built-in mechanism for file transfer, remote login, rebooting your colleague's workstation, or a million other useful things. Instead, Expect uses whatever local utilities you already have. This means that you do not have to learn a new file transfer protocol or a new host-to-host security system. If you use *.rhosts*, then that is what Expect will use when it does remote host operations. If you use Kerberos, then Expect will use that. And so on.

Using Expect On Non-Unix Systems

Expect makes use of a number of features that are present in all Unix systems. The family of standards known as "POSIX" describes most but not all of these features. So while Expect can run on any Unix or Unix-like system, it may have trouble providing all of its features on non-Unix systems that nonetheless claim strict POSIX compliance. While Expect works just fine on some non-Unix POSIX systems and can work in a limited way on all POSIX systems, I prefer to be conservative in my claims, so I use the phrase "Unix systems" when referring to the systems on which Expect runs.

Fortunately, Expect can be used to control other operating systems indirectly. Since Expect is capable of making network connections (through *telnet*, *rlogin*, *tip*, etc.), it can remotely contact other computers even while running on a Unix computer. In this way, it is very common to use Expect scripts to control non-Unix computers like Lisp machines, PostScript printers, modems, pagers, and so on.

Obtaining Expect and the Examples

Expect includes a number of examples, several of which are useful as tools in their own right. Indeed, quite a few have manual pages of their own and can be installed along with Expect. For example, *autoexpect* is an example that watches you interact and creates an Expect script to repeat the interactions. While tiny, this little script can substantially reduce your own time in creating Expect scripts.

You can find *autoexpect* and the other examples in the *example* directory of the Expect distribution. Following is a list of just a few of the examples that come with Expect. The *README* file in the *example* directory contains a complete list as well as full explanations about each of the examples:

- *autoexpect:* watch you and then create an Expect script to repeat the interaction
- *chess.exp:* play one *chess* game against another
- *dislocate:* allow disconnection from and reconnection to background processes
- *dvorak:* emulate a Dvorak keyboard
- *ftp-rfc:* retrieve an RFC from the Internet via anonymous Ftp
- *kibitz:* let several people control a program at the same time for remote assistance, group editing, etc.
- *lpunlock:* unhang a printer waiting for a lock
- *mkpasswd:* generate a good random password and optionally run *passwd* with it
- *passmass:* set a password on many machines simultaneously
- *rftp:* allow recursive **get**, **put**, and **list** from *ftp*
- *rlogin-cwd: rlogin* with the same current working directory
- *rogue.exp:* find a good game of *rogue*
- *timed-read:* limit the amount of time a read from the shell can take
- *timed-run:* limit the amount of time for which a program can run
- *tkpasswd:* change passwords in a GUI
- *tknewsbiff:* pop up a window (or play sounds, etc.) when news arrives in selected newsgroups
- *tkterm:* emulate a terminal in a Tk text widget
- *unbuffer:* disable output buffering that normally occurs when program output is redirected
- *weather:* retrieve a weather forecast from the Internet

These and additional examples are available with the Expect distribution. The *README* file in the distribution also describes the location of the Expect archive, which holds even more scripts. You can also contribute your own scripts to the archive. Particularly large or sophisticated applications (such as those which combine Expect with other extensions) can be found separately in the Tcl archive.

Expect now comes as a standard utility from many Unix vendors and you can also find Expect on dozens of CD-ROM software distributions. But the simplest way of ensuring that you have the latest version is to get it through the Web. The Expect home page is *http://expect.nist.gov*. The Expect home page provides pointers to the distribution, an FAQ, and lots of other information. For starters, you need a copy of Expect and a copy of Tcl. You may also want to get a copy of Tk. These can all be found from the Expect home page.

If you are restricted to using *ftp*, you can retrieve the same information from the site *potomac.nist.gov*.* To get Expect from *potomac.nist.gov* via *ftp*, retrieve the file *mel/div826/subject/expect/README*. This will tell you what other files you need to retrieve and what to do after that. The distributions for Expect, Tcl, and Tk, can all be found there.

If you are not directly on the Internet but can send mail, you can request email delivery of the files. Send a message to *library@cme.nist.gov*. The message body should be:

```
send pub/expect/README
```

Support

A number of companies and individuals sell support for Tcl. These are described in the Tcl FAQ. Cygnus Support and Computerized Processes Unlimited sell support for Expect as well, and it is likely that other companies and individuals would also offer support if approached.† This is not to mean that you will need support if you use Expect; however, it is not uncommon to find that management requires software be commercially supported before it is acceptable. As an aside, it may well be cost effective to have a professional support service solve your problems for you. Support can include modifications at your request, round-the-clock consulting by phone, site visits, and other services.

Cygnus Support
1937 Landings Drive
Mountain View, CA 94043
+1 (415) 903-1400
info@cygnus.com

Computerized Processes Unlimited
4200 S. I-10 Service Rd., Suite 205
Metairie, LA 70006
+1 (504) 889-2784
info@cpu.com

---

* All hostnames and filenames in this chapter are subject to change.

† Identification of specific companies and products does not imply recommendation or endorsement by the National Institute of Standards and Technology, nor does it imply that the products are necessarily the best available for the purpose.

14

Embedded Tk

by D. Richard Hipp

If you've ever tried to build a large-scale, compute-intensive, or commercial application using Tcl/Tk, you probably had a difficult time of it. A pure Tcl/Tk script is terrific for writing small programs or for prototyping, but it is often inadequate for really big problems. This is due to several factors:

- Execution speed is usually too slow for serious computation.
- Complex data structures are difficult to implement in Tcl.
- The lack of structure and typing in the Tcl language complicates the development of large codes.
- Tcl/Tk source is easily read by the end user, making it hard to protect proprietary algorithms.
- A script will run only on machines where the correct version of Tcl/Tk has been installed. This makes scripts more difficult to distribute.

The usual way to avoid these troubles is to code in C or C++ rather than Tcl/Tk. C is fast and well-structured. Compiled C code is difficult for users to read. And statically linked C programs will run on any binary-compatible computer, independent of other software.

But programming a graphical user interface in pure C is time-consuming and error-prone. The job can be made somewhat easier by using Tcl/Tk's C interface, and having your C program call the Tcl/Tk library routines directly. Many people have done this, some successfully. The task is still tough, though, because unlike its scripting language, Tcl/Tk's C interface is not easy to use. Properly initializing the Tcl/Tk interpreter takes skill and finesse, and calling the interpreter from C is a dull chore.

And so the problem remains: Do you go for the speed and structure of C or the power and simplicity of Tcl/Tk?

The Embedded Tk system (hereafter "ET") was created to resolve this conundrum. ET is a simple preprocessor and small interface library that make it easy to mix Tcl/Tk and C in the same program. With ET, you can put a few commands of Tcl/Tk code

---

in the middle of a C routine. ET also makes it very easy to write C functions that work as new Tcl/Tk commands—effectively allowing you to put pieces of C code in the middle of your Tcl script. These features give you the speed and structure of C with the power and simplicity of Tcl/Tk. As an added benefit, an application written using ET will compile into a standalone executable that will run on any binary-compatible computer, even if the other computer doesn't have Tcl/Tk installed.

An Example: "Hello, World!"

The ET system is designed to be easy to use. To see this, let's look at the classic "Hello, World!" program, coded using ET.

```
void main(int argc, char **argv){
  Et_Init(&argc,argv);
  ET( button .b -text {Hello, World!} -command exit; pack .b );
  Et_MainLoop();
}
```

If you compile and link these five lines, you'll get a standalone executable that pops up a "Hello, World!" button, and goes away when the button is clicked.

Let's take this program apart to see how it works. The first thing it does is call the `Et_Init` procedure. This procedure performs the tedious and confusing work needed to start up the Tcl/Tk interpreter, initialize widget bindings, create the main window ".", and so forth. The last line is a call to another procedure `Et_MainLoop` that implements the event loop. (If you don't know what an event loop is, don't worry. We'll have more to say about event loops in "A Quick Review of Event-Driven Programs" later in this chapter.) The most interesting part of the example is the middle line, the one that looks like a call to a function named `ET`. The `ET` function is special. It looks and is used like a regular C function, but takes a Tcl/Tk script as its argument instead of a C expression. Its function is to execute the enclosed Tcl/Tk. In this particular example, the `ET` function creates the "Hello, World!" button.

Because of the `ET` function, we can't give the "Hello, World!" source code directly to a C compiler and expect it to work. We have to run it through a preprocessor first. Like this:

```
et2c hello.c > hello_.c
```

The *et2c* preprocessor converts the `ET` function into real, compilable C code. The preprocessor also takes care of some other housekeeping details, like adding prototypes to the top of the file so that we don't have to bother with a `#include`. After it has been preprocessed, the source code can be compiled like any other C program:

```
cc -O -o hello hello_.c et.o -ltk -ltcl -lX11 -lm
```

Notice that you must link the program with ET's *et.o* library file, and with libraries for Tcl/Tk and X11. (See "Using ET To Build MS Windows and Macintosh Applications" later in this chapter for instructions on building applications for Microsoft-Windows or Macintosh.)

And that's all there is to it!

How To Avoid Reading the Rest of This Chapter

If you're restless to start programming and are the type of person who prefers to learn at the keyboard rather than from a book, this section is for you. It contains a terse overview of the features of ET. Peruse this section, glance quickly at the examples, and you'll be ready to start coding. You can use the rest of the chapter as a reference guide when you run into trouble.

On the other hand, if you are new to graphical interface programming, are a little unsteady with C, or just have a more deliberate and cautious attitude toward life, then you may prefer to lightly skim or even skip this section and focus instead on the tutorial-like text that follows.

The ET system consists of two things: the *et2c* preprocessor and the *et.o* library. The preprocessor takes care of translating ET source code (which looks a whole lot like C) into genuine C code that your compiler will understand. The *et.o* library contains a few support routines.

Among the support routines in *et.o* are `Et_Init` and `Et_MainLoop` for initializing the ET package and implementing the event loop, respectively. A third routine, `Et_ReadStdin`, allows standard input to be read and interpreted by the Tcl/Tk interpreter at runtime. The *et.o* library defines three global C variables as a convenience. `Et_Interp` is a pointer to the Tcl/Tk interpreter used by ET. `Et_Main-Window` is the main window. `Et_Display` is the `Display` pointer required as the first argument to many Xlib routines. ET also provides two global Tcl variables, `cmd_name` and `cmd_dir`. These contain the name of the executable and the directory where the executable is found.

The *et2c* preprocessor is used to convert an ET source file into real C code. It creates the illusion of giving the C language some new statements, like `ET_INSTALL_COMMANDS` and `ET_PROC`, and some special new functions like `ET`.

The `ET` function is used as if it were a regular C function, except that its argument is a Tcl/Tk script. The job of the `ET` is to execute the script. `ET` returns either `ET_OK` or `ET_ERROR` depending upon whether the script suceeded or failed. Similar routines `ET_STR`, `ET_INT`, and `ET_DBL` also take a Tcl/Tk script as their argument, but return the string, the integer, or the double-precision floating-point number that was the result of the last Tcl/Tk command in the argument script.

Wherever the string `%d(x)` occurs inside an `ET` function, the integer C expression `x` is converted to ASCII and substituted in place of the `%d(x)`. Similarly, `%s(x)` can be used to substitute a character string, and `%f(x)` substitutes a floating-point value. The string `%q(x)` works like `%s(x)` except that a backslash is inserted before each character that has special meaning to Tcl/Tk.

The special construct `ET_PROC( newcmd ){...}` defines a C function that is invoked whenever the `newcmd` Tcl/Tk command is executed. Formal parameters to this function, `argc` and `argv`, describe the arguments to the command. The formal parameter `interp` is a pointer to the Tcl/Tk interpreter. If a file named *aux.c* contains one or more `ET_PROC` macros, the commands associated with those macros are registered with the Tcl/Tk interpreter by invoking `ET_INSTALL_COM-MANDS(aux.c)` after the `Et_Init` in the main procedure.

The statement ET_INCLUDE(script.tcl) causes the Tcl/Tk script in the file script.tcl to be made a part of the C program and executed at the point where the ET_INCLUDE macro is found. The external Tcl/Tk script is normally read into the C program at compile time and thus becomes part of the executable. However, if the -dynamic command-line option is given to the *et2c* preprocessor, loading of the external Tcl/Tk script is deferred to runtime.

Finally, at the top of its output files, the *et2c* preprocessor inserts #defines that make ET_OK and ET_ERROR equivalent to TCL_OK and TCL_ERROR. This often eliminates the need to put "#include <tcl.h>" at the beginning of files that use ET.

And that's everything in ET! All the rest is just detail.

A Quick Review of Event-Driven Programs

Before we delve into the details of ET, it may be helpful to review the concept of an *event loop* and an *event-driven program*. Many ET users have never before written an event-driven graphical user interface (GUI) and may be unfamiliar with how such programs operate. If you are such a user, you may profit from this quick review. But if you are already familiar with event-driven programs, feel free skip ahead to "The Main Body of An ET Application."

The only inputs to a GUI are "events." An event is a notification that something interesting has happened. Events arrive whenever the mouse moves, or a mouse button is pressed or released, or a key of the keyboard is pressed, and so forth. An event-driven GUI differs from more familiar command-line programs in that its inputs (e.g., events) do not arrive in any predictable sequence. Any kind of events can arrive at any time, and the GUI program must be prepared to deal with them.

The code for an event-driven GUI can be divided into two parts: the *initialization* code and the *event loop*. The initialization code runs first and does nothing more than allocate and initialize the internal data structures of the application. As soon as the initialization code completes, the application enters the event loop. Within the event loop, the program waits for the next event to arrive, reads the event, and processes it appropriately. The loop then repeats. The event loop does not exit until the program terminates.

This is a schematic view of a typical GUI program:

```
main(){
  /* Initialization code */
  while( /* More work to do */ ){
    /* Wait for the next event to arrive */
    /* Read the next event */
    /* Take appropriate action for the event just read */
  }
}
```

Don't worry about the details here. Most of the event loop processing is handled automatically by Tcl/Tk and ET. The important things to know are that the event loop exists, it runs after the initialization code, and that it doesn't terminate until the program exits.

If you've never written an event-driven program before, and you are like most people, then you will have a little trouble at first. To help you get started, here are some important points to remember:

1. *The initialization code does not interact with the user.*

   The initialization code does only one thing—initialize. It creates the main windows of the application (but it doesn't draw the windows—that happens in the event loop!) and it sets up internal data structures. But the initialization code should never wait for input or respond to an event. Waiting and reading inputs and responding to events should happen only in the event loop.

2. *All user-initiated processing occurs in callbacks.*

   Everything that a GUI program does is in response to some event. Any C procedure or Tcl/Tk command that is called in response to an event is referred to as a *callback*. Because all inputs to a GUI program are in the form of events, the only place for user-initiated processing to occur is within the callback routines.

3. *Don't let a callback compute for more than a fraction of a second.*

   A callback should do its job quickly and then return. Otherwise, the event loop will not be able to respond to new events as they arrive, and the program will appear to "hang." If you have a callback that needs to execute for more than a few hundred milliseconds, you should either invoke the "update idletasks" Tcl/Tk command periodically within the callback, or you should break the callback's calculations up into several separate routines that can be invoked by separate events.

4. *Don't leak memory.*

   Once started, GUI programs tend to run for a long time—hours, days, weeks, or even months. Hence, you should take special care to avoid memory leaks. A memory leak occurs when you allocate a chunk of memory from the heap using `malloc` but don't return that memory to the heap using `free` when you are done with it. Because the memory was not released by `free` it can never be reused. When this happens, the amount of memory required by your application will constantly increase, until at some point it will consume all memory available, and then die. Memory leaks are probably the most common bug in GUI programs (which is why I mention them).

The Main Body of An ET Application

The `main` routines for ET applications all look pretty much alike. Here's a template:

```
void main(int argc, char **argv){
    Et_Init(&argc,argv); /* Start the Tcl/Tk interpreter */
    /* Create new Tcl/Tk commands here */
    /* Initialize data structures here */
    /* Create windows for the application here */
    Et_MainLoop(); /* The event loop */
}
```

When you need to write an ET application, but you aren't sure where to begin, this template is a good starting point. Type in the preceding template and make sure you can successfully compile and run it. (The program that results from compiling the template creates a blank window that doesn't respond to any mouse or keyboard inputs. It's the equivalent of *wish /dev/null*.) After you get the template running, slowly begin adding bits of code, recompiling and testing as you go, until you have a complete application.

Let's take a closer look at each line of the template, so that you can better understand what is going on.

The first line of `main` is a call to the `Et_Init` procedure. The `Et_Init` procedure initializes the ET system and the Tcl/Tk interpreter. It must be called before any other ET function or statement. The parameters are the `argc` and `argv` formal parameters of `main`. `Et_Init` uses these parameters to look for command-line options. ET currently understands four:

- `-display` designates the X server to use. The value of this option will override your *DISPLAY* environment variable.

- `-name` changes the application name for the program. By default, the application name is the same as the filename of the executable itself. The application name is used to derive the Tcl/Tk interpreter name for use with the Tcl/Tk `send` command. The application name is also used for processing X11 resources, and as the default text on the application's title bar.

- `-geometry` changes the starting size and/or position of the program.

- `-sync` turns on synchronous mode in the X server. This makes the program run a lot slower, but is sometimes useful when debugging. It is very rarely used.

Notice the "&" before the `argc` parameter to `Et_Init`. The number of command-line arguments is passed to `Et_Init` by address, not by value. This is so `Et_Init` can change the value of `argc`. Whenever `Et_Init` sees one of the command-line options, it removes that option from the option list in `argc` and `argv`. Hence, after `Et_Init` returns, only application-specific command-line options remain.

For example, suppose you invoke an ET program like this:

```
myapp -quiet -display stego:0 file1.data
```

The values of `argc` and `argv` passed into the `Et_Init` function are:

```
argc = 5
argv = { "myapp", "-quiet", "-display", "stego:0", "file1.data", 0 }
```

The `Et_Init` function will see the *-display stego:0* part and act upon it accordingly. It will then remove those fields from the argument list, so that after `Et_Init` returns, the values are these:

```
argc = 3
argv = { "myapp", "-quiet", "file1.data", 0 }
```

In this way, the initialization code that follows `Et_Init` never sees the ET-specific command-line arguments.

After the `Et_Init` procedure comes the initialization code. Normally, you begin the initialization by creating and registering all the new Tcl/Tk commands you will need. The details are described "Writing Tcl/Tk Routines In C" later in the chapter. Basically it involves replacing the comment in the template with one or more `ET_INSTALL_COMMANDS` statements. Once you've created the new Tcl/Tk commands, you may need to construct internal C data structures, or create linkages between C variables and Tcl variables using Tcl's `Tcl_LinkVar` function. Command-line options that haven't been removed by `Et_Init` are often processed here as well. Finally, you will probably want to create the initial windows for the application. The `ET` function (see "The ETO Function and Its Siblings") and `ET_INCLUDE` procedure (see "Including External Tcl/Tk Scripts In a C Program") are both good for this.

Of course, this is only a suggested outline of how to initialize your application. You should feel free to do something different if your program requires it. The only ground rule is that the initialization code shouldn't try to interact with the user. Instead, use callback routines to respond to user inputs.

The last line of `main` is a call to the `Et_MainLoop` procedure. `Et_MainLoop` implements the event loop. It will not return until the program is ready to exit.

Writing Tcl/Tk Routines In C

One of the first things people tend to do with ET is create new Tcl/Tk commands, written in C, that do computations that are either too slow or impossible with a pure Tcl. This is a two-step process. First you have to write the C code using the `ET_PROC` construct. Then you have to register your new Tcl/Tk command with the Tcl/Tk interpreter using the `ET_INSTALL_COMMANDS` statement. We will consider each of these steps in turn.

The Decimal Clock Sample Program

To help illustrate the concepts, this section introduces a new sample program: the *decimal clock*. The decimal clock displays the current time of day as a decimal number of hours. For instance, 8:30 a.m. displays as "`8.500`." 11:15 p.m. shows as "`23.250`," and so forth. A screenshot of this program is shown in Figure 14-1.

Figure 14-1: Typical Appearance of the Decimal Clock

We'll begin by looking at the main procedure for the decimal clock program.

```
void main(int argc, char **argv){
  Et_Init(&argc, argv);
  ET_INSTALL_COMMANDS;
  ET(
```

```
      label .x -bd 2 -relief raised -width 7
      pack .x
      proc Update {} {
        x config -text [DecimalTime]
        after 3600 Update
      }
      Update
    );
    Et_MainLoop();
  }
```

As you can see, the main procedure is just a copy of the program template from "The Main Body of An ET Application" section, with some of the comments replaced by actual initialization code. The first initialization action is to invoke the special ET statement ET_INSTALL_COMMANDS. Don't worry about what this does just yet—we'll return to it a little later. The second initialization action is a single ET function containing seven lines of Tcl/Tk. This Tcl/Tk code does three things:

- It creates a label widget in which to show the decimal time.
- It creates a new Tcl/Tk procedure named Update that updates the label widget to show the current time, and then arranges to call itself again after 0.001 hours (3.6 seconds).
- It invokes the Update procedure once in order to initialize the text of the label widget, and to start the periodic updates.

Like all well-behaved ET programs, the main procedure for the decimal clock concludes by entering the event loop.

The ET_PROC Statement

The core of the decimal clock program is a new Tcl/Tk command, DecimalTime, that returns the current time of day as a decimal number of hours. This new command is written in C, using the special ET_PROC construct of ET. The code looks like this:

```
  #include "tcl.h"
  #include <time.h>
  ET_PROC( DecimalTime ){
    struct tm *pTime; /* The time of day decoded */
    time_t now; /* Number of seconds since the epoch */
    now = time(0);
    pTime = localtime(&now);
    sprintf(interp->result,"%2d.%03d",pTime->tm_hour,
    (pTime->tm_sec + 60*pTime->tm_min)*10/36);
    return ET_OK;
  }
```

The magic is in the ET_PROC keyword. The *et2c* preprocessor recognizes this keyword and converts the code that follows it into a compilable C function that implements the Tcl/Tk command. In general, you can create new Tcl/Tk commands using a template like this:

```
ET_PROC( name-of-the-new-command ){
   /* C code to implement the command */
}
```

You could, of course, construct appropriate C functions by hand, but that involves writing a bunch of messy details that detract from the legibility of the code. The `ET_PROC` mechanism is much easier to write and understand, and much less subject to error.

Though they do not appear explicitly in the source code, every function created using `ET_PROC` has four formal parameters.

- `argc`: This parameter is an integer that holds the number of arguments on the Tcl command that invokes the function. Its role is exactly the same as the `argc` parameter to the `main` function of a standard C program.

- `argv`: Like `argc` before it, this parameter works just like the `argv` parameter to `main`. The variable `argv[0]` contains the name of the command itself ("DecimalTime" in this example), `argv[1]` contains the name of the first argument, `argv[2]` contains the name of the second argument, and so forth up to `argv[argc]` which is a null pointer.

- `interp`: This parameter is a pointer to the Tcl/Tk interpreter. It has type "`Tcl_Interp*`." The `interp` parameter has many uses, but is most often used to set the return value of the Tcl/Tk function. (Note that you have to `#include` either `<tcl.h>` or `<tk.h>` somewhere in your source file in order to use the `interp` parameter, since one of these header files are needed to define the fields of the `Tcl_Interp` structure.)

- `clientData`: This is a pointer to the `Tk_Window` structure that defines the main window (e.g., the "." window) of the application. It has a type of "`void*`" and will need to be typecast before it is used. On the other hand, it is seldom used, so this isn't normally a problem.

The decimal clock example uses the `interp` formal parameter on the sixth line of the `ET_PROC` function. In particular, the `DecimalTime` function writes its result (e.g., the time as a decimal number) into the `result` field of `interp`. It's okay to write up to about 200 bytes of text into the `result` field of the `interp` parameter, and that text will become the return value of the Tcl/Tk command. If you need to return more than about 200 bytes of text, then you should set the result using one of the routines from the Tcl library designed for that purpose: `Tcl_SetResult`, `Tcl_AppendResult`, or `Tcl_AppendElement`. (These routines are documented by Tcl's manual pages under the name "SetResult.") If all this seems too complicated, then you can choose to do nothing at all, in which case the return value defaults to an empty string.

Another important feature of every `ET_PROC` function is its return value. Every `ET_PROC` should return either `ET_OK` or `ET_ERROR`, depending on whether or not the function encountered any errors. (`ET_OK` and `ET_ERROR` are `#define` constants inserted by *et2c* and have the save values as `TCL_OK` and `TCL_ERROR`.) It is impossible for the `DecimalClock` function to fail, so it always returns `ET_OK`, but most `ET_PROC` functions can return either result.

Part of Tcl's *result protocol* is that if a command returns `ET_ERROR` it should put an error message in the `interp->result` field. If we had wanted to be pedantic, we could have put a test in the `DecimalTime` function to make sure it is called with no arguments. Like this:

```
ET_PROC( DecimalTime ){
  struct tm *pTime; /* The time of day decoded */
  time_t now; /* Number of seconds since the epoch */
  if( argc!=1 ){
    Tcl_AppendResult(interp,"The ",argv[0],
      " command should have no argument!",0);
    return ET_ERROR;
  }
  /* The rest of the code is omitted ... */
}
```

New Tcl/Tk commands that take a fixed format normally need to have some checks like this, to make sure they aren't called with too many or too few arguments.

The ET_INSTALL_COMMANDS Statement

We've seen how the `ET_PROC` constuct will *create* a new Tcl/Tk command. But that command must still be *registered* with the Tcl interpreter before it can be used. Fortunately, ET makes this very easy.

ET uses the `ET_INSTALL_COMMANDS` keyword to register `ET_PROC` commands with the Tcl interpreter. The *et2c* preprocessor converts the `ET_INSTALL_COM-MANDS` keyword into a sequence of C instructions that register every `ET_PROC` in the current file. In the `main` procedure of the decimal clock example, the `ET_INSTALL_COMMANDS` keyword that immediately follows the `Et_Init` function is used to register the `DecimalTime` command. As it turns out, `Decimal-Time` is the only `ET_PROC` function in the same source file, but even if there had been 100 others, they would have all been registered by that single `ET_INSTALL_COMMANDS` statement.

The `ET_INSTALL_COMMANDS` keyword can also be used to register `ET_PROC` functions in separate source files, simply by putting the name of the source file in parentheses after the `ET_INSTALL_COMMANDS` keyword. Like this:

```
ET_INSTALL_COMMANDS( otherfile.c );
```

A larger program will typically have many `ET_INSTALL_COMMANDS` statements immediately following the `Et_Init` function, one statement for each file that contains `ET_PROC` functions. One recent commercial project used 33 `ET_INSTALL_COMMANDS` statements following the `Et_Init` function!

Summary of Writing Tcl/Tk Commands In C

Before leaving this section, let's briefly summarize the steps needed to create new Tcl/Tk commands in C using ET. First, you create one or more commands using the `ET_PROC` construct, as follows:

```
ET_PROC( name-of-the-new-command ){
   /* C code to implement the command */
   return ET_OK; /* Don't forget the return value! */
}
```

Then, you register these commands with the Tcl interpreter using an `ET_INSTALL_COMMANDS` statement after the `Et_Init` function call within `main`. Like this:

```
ET_INSTALL_COMMANDS( name-of-file-containing-ET_PROCs.c );
```

And that's all you have to do!

The `ET_PROC` construct lets you put a C routine in the middle of Tcl/Tk. The next section will take a closer look at `ET` which allows you to put Tcl/Tk in the middle of a C routine.

The ET() Function and Its Siblings

If you've been keeping up with the examples, you've already seen the `ET` function used twice to insert a few lines of Tcl/Tk in the middle of a C procedure. But the `ET` function can do a lot more, as this section will show.

Moving Information from Tcl/Tk To C

The first thing to note about `ET` is that, just like a real C function, it has a return value. `ET` returns an integer status code which is either `ET_OK` or `ET_ERROR` depending on whether the enclosed Tcl/Tk was successful or failed. (`ET` might also return `TCL_RETURN`, `TCL_BREAK`, or `TCL_CONTINUE` under rare circumstances.)

The status return of `ET` is nice, but in practice it turns out to be mostly useless. What you really need is the string value returned by the enclosed Tcl/Tk script. That's the purpose of the `ET_STR` function.

The `ET_STR` function works a lot like `ET`. You put in a Tcl/Tk script as the argument, and the script gets executed. But instead of returning a status code, `ET_STR` returns a pointer to a string that was the result of the last Tcl/Tk command in its argument.

The `ET_STR` function turns out to be a very handy mechanism for querying values from Tcl/Tk. For instance, suppose your program has an entry widget named ".entry" and some piece of C code needs to know the current contents of the entry. You can write this:

```
char *entryText = ET_STR(.entry get);
```

Or imagine that you need to know the current size and position of your main window. You might use code like this:

```
int width, height, x, y;
sscanf(ET_STR(wm geometry .),"%dx%d+%d+%d",&width,&height,&x,&y);
```

Does your C routine need to know the value of a Tcl variable? You could use the cumbersome `Tcl_GetVar` function, but it's much easier to say:

```
char *zCustomerName = ET_STR(set CustomerName);
```

Possible uses for `ET_STR` seem limitless.

But, there are two subtleties with `ET_STR` that programmers should always keep in mind. The first is that the Tcl/Tk script in the argument is executed at Tcl's global variable context level. This means that all of the Tcl/Tk variables `ET_STR` creates, and the only Tcl/Tk variables it can access, are global variables. This limitation also applies to the regular `ET` function, and to two other functions we haven't talked about yet: `ET_INT` and `ET_DBL`. ET provides no means for C code to access or modify local variables. On the other hand, this has not proven to be a serious hardship in practice.

The second subtlety with `ET_STR` is more dangerous, but fortunately applies to `ET_STR` only. Recall that `ET_STR` returns a *pointer* to a string, not the string itself. The string actually resides in memory that is held deep within the bowels of Tcl/Tk. The danger is that the next Tcl/Tk command may choose to change, deallocate, or reuse this memory, corrupting the value returned by `ET_STR`. We say that the return value of `ET_STR` is "ephemeral."

One way to overcome the ephemerality of `ET_STR` is by making a copy of the returned string. The `strdup` function is good for this. (Unfortunately, `strdup` is missing from a lot of C libraries. You may have to write your own string duplicator.) In place of the previous examples, you might write

```
char *entryText = strdup( ET_STR(.entry get) );
```

or

```
char *zCustomerName = strdup( ET_STR(set CustomerName) );
```

The `strdup` function uses `malloc` to get the memory it needs, so if you use this approach, be sure to `free` the value when you are done to avoid a memory leak!

The other way to overcome the ephemerality of `ET_STR` is simply not to use the returned string for very long. You should be safe in using the returned string as long as you don't invoke any other Tcl/Tk commands, or return to the event loop. Code like this

```
sscanf(ET_STR(wm geometry .),"%dx%d+%d+%d",&width,&height,&x,&y);
```

is okay since we need the return value only for the duration of the `sscanf` function and `sscanf` doesn't use Tcl/Tk.

In addition to `ET` and `ET_STR`, the ET system provides two other functions named `ET_INT` and `ET_DBL`. Both take a Tcl/Tk script for their argument, as you would expect. But `ET_INT` returns an integer result and `ET_DBL` returns a floating-point value (a `double`). In a sense, these two functions are extensions of `ET_STR`. In fact, `ET_INT` does essentially the same thing as

```
int v = strtol( ET_STR(...), 0, 0);
```

and `ET_DBL` is equivalent to

```
double r = strtod( ET_STR(...), 0);
```

Because `ET_INT` and `ET_DBL` return a value, not a pointer, their results are not ephemeral nor subject to the problems that can come up with `ET_STR`.

Moving Information from C To Tcl/Tk

We've seen how `ET_STR`, `ET_INT`, and `ET_DBL` can be used to pass values from Tcl/Tk back to C. But how do you go the other way and transfer C variable values into Tcl/Tk? ET has a mechanism to accomplish this too, of course.

Within the argument to any ET function (or `ET_STR` or `ET_INT` or `ET_DBL`), the string "`%d(x)`" is special. When ET sees such a string, it evalutes the integer C expression "`x`", converts the resulting integer into decimal, and substitutes the integer's decimal value for the original string. For example, suppose you want to initialize the Tcl/Tk variable named `nPayment` to be 12 times the value of a C variable called `nYear`. You might write the following code:

```
ET( set nPayment %d(12*nYear) );
```

As another example, suppose you want to draw a circle on the canvas `.cnvs` centered at (x,y) with radius r. You could say:

```
id = ET_INT( .cnvs create oval %d(x-r) %d(y-r) %d(x+r) %d(y+r) );
```

Notice here how the `ET_INT` function was used to record the integer object ID returned by the Tcl/Tk canvas `create` command. This allows us to later delete or modify the circle by referring to its ID. For example, to change the fill color of the circle, we could execute the following:

```
ET( .cnvs itemconfig %d(id) -fill skyblue );
```

If you want to substitute a string or floating-point value into an ET argument, you can use `%s(x)` and `%f(x)` in place of `%d(x)`. The names of these substitution phrases were inspired by the equivalent substitution tokens in the standard C library function `printf`. Note, however, that you cannot specify a field-width, precision, or option flag in ET like you can in `printf`. In other words, you can use conversions like `%-10.3f` in `prinf` but not in ET. The ET function will accept only specification, such as `%f`.

But the ET function does support a conversion specifier that standard `printf` does not: the `%q(x)` substitution. The `%q` works like `%s` in that it expects its argument to be a null-terminated string, but unlike `%s` the `%q` converter inserts extra backslash characters into the string in order to escape characters that have special meaning to Tcl/Tk. Consider an example.

```
char *s = "The price is $1.45";
ET( puts "%q(s)" );
```

Because `%q(s)` was used instead of `%s(s)`, an extra backslash is inserted immediately before the "$". The command string passed to the Tcl/Tk interpreter is therefore:

```
puts "The price is \$1.45"
```

This gives the expected result. Without the extra backslash, Tcl/Tk would have tried to expand "$1" as a variable, resulting in an error message like this:

```
can't read "1": no such variable
```

In general, it is always a good idea to use `%q(...)` instead of `%s(...)` around strings that originate from outside the program—you never know when such strings may contain a character that needs to be escaped.

Summary of the ET() Function

And that's everything there is to know about the `ET` function and its siblings. In case you missed something amid all the details, here's a 10-second review of the essential facts:

- The `ET` executes Tcl/Tk code and returns a success/failure code.
- `ET_STR`, `ET_INT`, and `ET_DBL` do the same, but return a string, an integer, or a double which was the result of the last Tcl/Tk command executed.
- The return value from `ET_STR` is ephemeral.
- The strings `%s(...)`, `%d(...)`, and `%f(...)` insert string, integer, and double C expressions into the argument of `ET` and its siblings.
- The string `%q(...)` works like `%s(...)` but adds backslashes before characters that are special to Tcl/Tk.

Now let's move on and talk about a similar construct, `ET_INCLUDE`, that allows you incorporate whole files full of Tcl/Tk into your application.

Including External Tcl/Tk Scripts In a C Program

In the sample programs seen so far in this chapter, Tcl/Tk code in an `ET` function was used to construct the main window. This works fine for the examples, since their windows are uncomplicated and can be constructed with a few lines of code. But in a real application, or even a more complex example, the amount of Tcl/Tk code needed to initialize the program's windows can quickly grow to hundreds or thousands of lines. It is impractical and irksome to put this much code into an `ET` statement, so the `ET` system provides another way to get the job done: the `ET_INCLUDE` statement.

The `ET_INCLUDE` statement is similar in concept to the `#include` statement in the C preprocessor. Both take a filename as their argument, and both read the named file into the original source program. The `ET_INCLUDE` statement expects its file to be pure Tcl/Tk code, though. Its job is to turn the Tcl/Tk source into a form that the C compiler can understand, and to arrange for the Tcl/Tk to be executed when control reaches the `ET_INCLUDE` statement.

An example may help to clarify this idea. In the decimal clock program (way back at the beginning of "Writing Tcl/Tk Routines In C") there are seven lines of Tcl/Tk in an `ET` function used to create the application's main window. Now suppose we move those seven lines of Tcl/Tk into a separate file named *dclock.tcl*. Then we could replace the `ET` function with an `ET_INCLUDE` statement that references the new file like this:

```
void main(int argc, char **argv){
   Et_Init(&argc, argv);
   ET_INSTALL_COMMANDS;
   ET_INCLUDE( dclock.tcl );
   Et_MainLoop();
}
```

When the *et2c* preprocessor sees the `ET_INCLUDE` statement, it locates the specified file, reads that file into the C program, and makes arrangements for the text of the file to be executed as if it had all appeared within an `ET` function.

Well, *almost* like an `ET` function. There are a couple of minor differences. The `ET_INCLUDE` does not understand the various `%s(...)` substitutions as `ET` does. Also, `ET_INCLUDE` is a true procedure, not a function. It doesn't return a value like `ET` so you can't use an `ET_INCLUDE` in an expression.

It is important to understand the difference between an `ET_INCLUDE` statement like this:

```
ET_INCLUDE( dclock.tcl );
```

and the `source` command of Tcl/Tk, used as follows:

```
ET( source dclock.tcl );
```

The `ET_INCLUDE` statement reads the Tcl/Tk into the program at compile time, effectively making the Tcl/Tk code part of the executable. The Tcl `source` command, on the other hand, opens and reads the file at runtime, as the application executes. This makes the executable a little smaller, but it also means that the file containing the Tcl/Tk must be available to the executable whenever it runs. If you move just the executable, but not the Tcl/Tk file, to another computer, or even another directory, then it will no longer work because it won't be able to locate and read the Tcl/Tk file.

The ability to read an external Tcl/Tk script and make it part of the executable program is an important feature of ET. But while you are developing and testing a program, it is sometimes convenient to turn this feature off and to have the application read its scripts at runtime instead of compile time. That way, you can make changes to the Tcl/Tk script and rerun your program with the changes, but without having to recompile. You can do this using the `-dynamic` option to the *et2c* preprocessor. Whenever you run *et2c* with the `-dynamic` command-line option, it effectively turns instances of the statement

```
ET_INCLUDE( filename.tcl );
```

into the statement

```
ET( source filename.tcl );
```

This feature has proven very helpful during development. But be careful to turn it off before doing your final build, or else you won't be able to move your executable to other machines!

There is just one other feature of the `ET_INCLUDE` statement that we need to discuss before moving on, and that is the algorithm it uses to locate the Tcl/Tk source code files. Just like the C preprocessor's `#include` statement, the `ET_INCLUDE` mechanism can include files found in other directories.

The *et2c* preprocessor always looks first in the working directory for files named by an `ET_INCLUDE` statement. If the file is found there, no further search is made. But if the file is not found, then *et2c* will also look in all directories named in *-I* command-line options. For example, if you run *et2c* like this:

```
et2c -I../tcl -I/usr/local/lib/tcl app.c >app_.c
```

and the *app.c* file contains a line of the form:

```
ET_INCLUDE( setup.tcl );
```

then *et2c* will search for the *setup.tcl* first in the "." directory, then in *../tcl* and in */usr/local/lib/tcl*. It will use the first instance of *setup.tcl* that it finds.

Global Variables In ET

The *et.o* library for ET defines three global C variables that are sometimes of use to programmers. In addition, `Et_Init` creates two new global Tcl/Tk variables that many programs find useful. This section will describe what all of these variables do, and suggest ways that they can be used.

Global C Variables Created By ET

Perhaps the most useful of the global variables available in ET is `Et_Interp`. This variable is a pointer to the Tcl/Tk interpreter, the one created by `Et_Init` and used to execute all Tcl/Tk commands within the program. The `Et_Interp` variable has the same value as the `interp` formal parameter found in every `ET_PROC` function.

The `Et_Interp` variable is useful because you may often want to call C routines in the Tcl/Tk library, and most of these routines require a pointer to the interpreter as their first parameter. For instance, suppose in the initialization code you want to create a link between the global C variable `nClients` and a Tcl/Tk variable by the same name. Using the `Et_Interp` variable as the first parameter to the Tcl function `Tcl_LinkVar`, you could write:

```
Tcl_LinkVar(Et_Interp,"nClients",(char*)&nClients,TCL_LINK_INT);
```

Having done this, any changes to the C `nClients` variable will be reflected in the Tcl/Tk variable, and vice versa.

Perhaps the second most useful global varible is `Et_Display`. This variable contains the `Display` pointer required as the first argument to most Xlib routines. It is used by daring, down-to-the-bare-metal programmers who like to call Xlib directly.

Here's an example. Suppose you want to create a new Tcl/Tk command, `PitchedBell`, that makes the X terminal emit a beep with a pitch specified by its sole argument. Once such a command is implemented, then the following Tcl/Tk code would emit a single tone at the pitch of concert A:

```
PitchedBell 440
```

Here a short piece of Tcl/Tk code that plays the opening bar of Beethoven's Fifth Symphony:

```
foreach pitch {784 784 784 659} {
  PitchedBell $pitch
  after 200
}
```

You probably get the idea. Here's the code that implements the `PitchedBell` command:

```
#include <tk.h> /* Will also pickup <Xlib.h> */
ET_PROC( PitchedBell ){
  XKeyboardControl ctrl; /* For changing the bell pitch */
  if( argc!=2 ){
    interp->result =
      "Wrong # args. Should be: ''PitchedBell PITCH''";
    return ET_ERROR;
  }
  ctrl.bell_pitch = atoi( argv[1] );
  XChangeKeyboardControl(Et_Display,KBBellPitch,&ctrl);
  XBell(Et_Display,0);
  XFlush(Et_Display);
  return ET_OK;
}
```

After checking to make sure it has exactly one argument, the `PitchedBell` command uses the `XChangeKeyboardControl` function of Xlib to change the bell pitch. It then rings the bell using the `XBell` Xlib function, and finally flushes the Xlib message queue using `XFlush` to force the bell to be rung immediately. All three of these Xlib functions require a `Display` pointer as their first argument, a role that is perfectly filled by the `Et_Display` global variable.

The third and final global C variable in ET is `Et_MainWindow`. This variable is a pointer to the Tcl/Tk structure that defines the application's main window. Back in the days of Tk3.6, several Tcl/Tk library functions required this value as a parameter. But the Tcl/Tk library interface changed in the move to Tk4.0, so that the main window pointer is no longer required. Hence, the `Et_MainWindow` variable isn't used much anymore. It has been kept around as a historical artifact.

Tcl/Tk Variables Created By ET

Besides the three global C variables, ET also provides two Tcl/Tk variables that are of frequent use: `cmd_name` and `cmd_dir`. The `cmd_name` variable contains the name of the file holding the executable for the application, and `cmd_dir` is the name of the directory containing that file.

The `cmd_name` and `cmd_dir` variables are useful to programs that need to read or write auxiliary data files. In order to open an auxiliary file, the program needs to know the file's pathname, but it is not a good idea to hardcode a complete pathname into the program. Otherwise, the auxiliary file can't be moved without recompiling the program. By careful use of `cmd_name` and/or `cmd_dir`, we can arrange to have auxiliary files located in a directory relative to the executable, rather than at some fixed location. That way, a system adminstrator is free to move the auxiliary file to a different directory as long as the executable moves with it.

For example, suppose you are writing a program named *acctrec* that needs to access a data file named *acctrec.db*. Furthermore, suppose the data file is located in a directory *../data* relative to the executable. Then to open the data file for reading, a program could write:

```
char *fullName = ET_STR( return $cmd_dir/../data/$cmd_name.db );
FILE *fp = fopen(fullName,"r");
```

Using this scheme, both the executable and the data file can be placed anywhere in the file system, as long as they are in the same position relative to one another. They can also be renamed, as long as they retain the same base name. This flexibility is a boon to system adminstraters, and also makes the program less sensitive to installation errors.

Reading from Standard Input

There's one last feature of ET that we haven't discussed: the `Et_ReadStdin` procedure. If this procedure is called (with no arguments) in between the calls to `Et_Init` and `Et_MainLoop`, ET will make arrangements to read all data that appears on standard input and interpret that data as Tcl/Tk commands.

You can use the `Et_ReadStdin` to implement the interactive *wish* interpreter for Tcl/Tk. The code would look like this:

```
main(int argc, char **argv){
   Et_Init(&argc,argv);
   Et_ReadStdin();
   Et_MainLoop();
}
```

Let's call this program *etwish* in order to distinguish it from the standard *wish* that comes with Tcl/Tk. The *etwish* program differs from *wish* in two ways. First, *wish* reads a set of 15 or so Tcl/Tk scripts from a well-known directory when it first starts up. Thus, to install *wish*, you have to have both the *wish* executable and the 15 startup scripts. But with *etwish*, the 15 startup scripts are compiled into the executable (using `ET_INCLUDE` statements inside the `Et_Init` function), so the external scripts are no longer required. This does make the *etwish* executable slightly larger (by about 64K bytes), but it also makes the program much easier to install and administer.

The second difference between *wish* and the *etwish* program just shown is that *etwish* is always interactive. It will not read a script from a file given as a command-line argument like standard *wish* will. But we can remove that difference using a little more code.

```
main(int argc, char **argv){
   Et_Init(&argc,argv);
   if( argc>2 && (strcmp(argv[1],"-f")==0 || strcmp(argv[1],"-
file")==0) ){
      ET( source "%q(argv[2])" );
   }else if( argc>1 ){
      ET( source "%q(argv[1])" );
   }else{
      Et_ReadStdin();
   }
   Et_MainLoop();
}
```

This revised program serves as a great template for building customized editions of *wish* that have one or more new Tcl/Tk commands written in C. All you have to do is code the new commands using the `ET_PROC` mechanism and insert a single `ET_INSTALL_COMMANDS` statement right after the `Et_Init`.

Compiling ET Applications

We've already discussed the basics of compiling ET applications back in "An Example: 'Hello, World'" when we put together the "Hello, World!" example. Basically, all you do is preprocess your source files with *et2c* and then run the results through the C compiler. But that synopsis omits a lot of detail. This section fills in the missing information.

Compiling ET Itself

But before we begin talking about how to compile ET applications, we need to first mention how to compile ET itself—the *et2c* preprocessor and the *et.o* library. (If you have one of the platforms supported by the CD-ROM in the back of this book, then you already have precompiled versions of *et2c* and *et.o* and can skip this step.)

The source code to the *et2c* preprocessor is contained in a single file named *et2c.c*. The preprocessor is written in highly portable K&R C and should compile without change on just about any 32-bit architecture. All you have to do is this:

```
cc -O -o et2c et2c.c
```

Compiling the *et.o* library is a little more problematic, but still not difficult. There are three steps. First you have to select an appropriate source code file. There are different versions of the source code (sometimes radically different) depending on which version of Tcl/Tk you are using. For Tk Version 3.6, choose *et36.c*. For Tk Version 4.0, choose *et40.c*. For Tk Version 4.1 on Unix and X11, choose *et41.c*. Your ET distribution may also have other options, such as versions for MS Windows or Macintosh, or versions with built-in support for various Tcl extensions.

Let's suppose, for the sake of discussion, that you selected the source file *et41.c*. The next step is to preprocess this file using *et2c*. This step is a little tricky because we have to use the *-I* option to *et2c* to tell the preprocessor where to find the Tcl/Tk startup scripts.

Recall that the stardard Tcl/Tk interpreter program, *wish*, reads and executes a series of Tcl/Tk scripts when it first starts up. These scripts set up default widget bindings, create procedures for handling menus, and so forth. The names of the directories from which these scripts are loaded are hardcoded in the *wish* executable. There are about 15 different startup scripts (the number varies from one version of Tcl/Tk to the next) and *wish* will not run without them.

But ET applications don't read the startup scripts at runtime. Instead, a series of ET_INCLUDE statements inside the Et_Init function bind the startup scripts into an ET executable at compile time. This feature is what enables ET applications to run on machines that do not have Tcl/Tk installed.

It is because of 15 or so startup scripts included by ET_INCLUDE statements in the ET library that we have to preprocess the library source code using *et2c*. But we also have to tell *et2c* what directories to use when searching for the startup scripts. If Tcl/Tk has already been installed on your system, then you can find out the names of the startup script directories by executing the following *wish* script:

```
#! wish
puts $tk_library
```

```
puts $tcl_library
```

Let's suppose that the startup scripts are located in the directories */usr/local/lib/tcl* and */usr/local/lib/tk*. Then the command to preprocess the ET library source code would be the following:

```
et2c -I/usr/local/lib/tcl -I/usr/local/lib/tk et41.c >et.c
```

After preprocessing the library source code, all that remains is to compile it. The library references the <tk.h> header file, which in turn references <tcl.h>, so you may have to add some *-I* options to the compiler command line to specify the directories where these header files are located. The following is typical:

```
cc -c -o et.o -I/usr/include/tcl -I/usr/include/tk et.c
```

Compiling the Application Code

Once you get *et2c* and *et.o* compiled, the hard work is done. To build your application, simply run each source file through the *et2c* preprocessor before compiling it, and add the *et.o* library with the final link. For example, the steps to compile a program from two source files, *appmain.c* and *appaux.c*, are the something like the following on most systems:

```
et2c appmain.c >temp.c
cc -c temp.c -o appmain.o
et2c appaux.c >temp.c
cc -c temp.c -o appaux.o
cc appmain.o appaux.o et.o -ltk -ltcl -lX11 -lm
```

If you're using a Makefile, you might want to redefine the default rule for converting C source code into object code to incorporate the *et2c* preprocessor step. Like this:

```
.c.o:
        et2c $temp.c
        cc -c -o $@ temp.c
```

The *et2c* does not harm files that don't use ET constructs, so this rule will work for every file in your project.

Turning Off Script Compression In the Preprocessor

The *et2c* preprocessor attempts to save memory and improve performance of your application by removing comments and unnecessary spaces from the Tcl/Tk code inside ET functions and loaded by ET_INCLUDE statements. This mechanism works well most of the time, but it is not foolproof. It is theoretically possible for a valid Tcl/Tk script to be corrupted by *et2c*'s compression attempts. If you experience trouble, and suspect that *et2c* is messing up your Tcl/Tk code, then you can turn script compression off using the -nocompress command-line option.

Compiling Using An Older K&R Compiler

If it is your misfortune not to have an ANSI C compiler, you can still use ET. The source code to et2c is pure K&R C and should work fine under older compilers. The source code to *et.o* is another matter. To compile the library using an older compiler you need to first give a –K+R option to et2c and then give a –DK_AND_R option to the C compiler:

```
et2c -K+R -I/usr/local/lib/tcl -I/usr/local/lib/tk et40.c >et.c
cc -DK_AND_R -I/usr/include/tcl -I/usr/include/tk -c et.c
```

When compiling application code with an older compiler, just give the –K+R option to *et2c*. It is not necessary to give the –DK_AND_R option to the C compiler when compiling objects other than *et.c*.

Other ET Sample Programs

Besides the very simple "Hello, World!" and decimal clock programs presented earlier, ET is distributed with a number of nontrivial sample programs. This section will briefly overview what several of these example programs do, and why ET was important to their implementation. We won't try to explain the details of how the programs work, though. You can figure that out for yourself by looking at the source code.

The Color Chooser

There is a color chooser tool for X11 called *color*. The sources to *color* are in the files *color.c* and *color.tcl*. A screen image of the program is shown in Figure 14-2.

The X11 Window System supports displays with over 280 quadrillion distinct colors (48 bits per pixel). But from this vast number, a few hundred colors are assigned

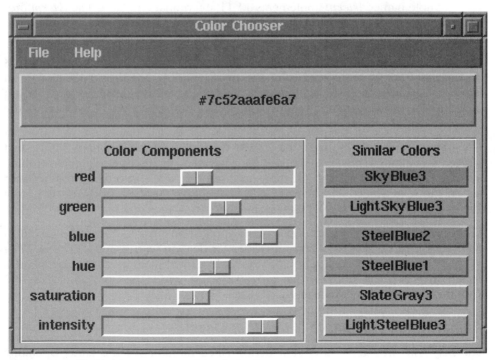

Figure 14-2: Typical Appearance of the Color Program

Other ET Sample Programs   531

English names like "blue" or "turquoise" or "peachpuff." All the rest are given arcane hexadecimal designations like "#b22cd8517f32." It is best to use colors with English names whenever possible.

The purpose of the *color* program it to help select colors with English names. At the top of the application is a large swatch showing one of the 280 quadrillion X11 colors, together with either its English name (if it has one) or its hexadecimal value. Sliders on the lower-left side of the window allow the user to vary the color of the swatch by changing various color components. On the lower-right side of the window are six smaller swatches that show colors with English names that are similar to the color in the main swatch. Moving any of the six color component sliders causes the colors in all swatches, and the other sliders, to update in real time. Clicking on any of the smaller swatches transfers its color to the main swatch, updating all of the sliders and swatches appropriately.

In theory, there is nothing to prevent the *color* program from being coded in pure Tcl/Tk, but in practice, such an implementation would be much too slow. For this reason, two key routines are coded in C. The ET_PROC command ChangeComponent is called whenever one of the color component sliders is moved. This routine moves the other sliders, changes the color of the main swatch, then computes close colors for the smaller swatches. Another ET_PROC command named ChangeColor is called whenever the user clicks on one of the smaller swatches. This routine changes the color of the main swatch, then updates the sliders and the smaller swatches accordingly.

The VT100 Terminal Emulator

The example named *tkterm* implements a VT100 terminal emulator. The *tkterm* program can be used as a direct replacement for the more familiar emulator programs *xterm* or *rxvt*.

The sources for *tkterm* are contained in three separate files. The main procedure is in *tkterm.c*. Tcl/Tk for constructing the main window for the application is in *tkterm.tcl*. Finally, the file *getpty.c* takes care of the messy details of allocating a pseudo-TTY for the emulator and invoking a shell in the pseudo-TTY. (Much of the code in *getpty.c* was copied from *rxvt*.)

The *tkterm* program simulates the VT100 display using an ordinary Tcl/Tk text widget. C routines in *tkterm.c* interpret the characters and escape sequences coming into the program and use ET functions to insert characters into their proper places within the text widget. The *tkterm.c* file is almost 1000 lines long, and is mostly devoted to interpreting the VT100 escape codes.

The *tkterm* program is an example of an application that could not be coded in pure Tcl/Tk, since Tcl/Tk has no provisions for dealing with pseudo-TTYs or TTYs in "raw" mode. But even if it could, we would probably still want to use some C code, since it seems unlikely that a Tcl/Tk script would be able to process the VT100 escape sequences efficiently.

A Real-Time Performance Monitor for Linux

The *perfmon* program is a system performance monitor for the Linux operating system. It uses bar graphs to shows the amount of memory, swap space, and CPU time currently being used. The display is updated 10 times per second. There are two source code files for this application: *perfmon.c* and *perfmon.tcl*.

The main display of the *perfmon* program is implemented using a Tcl/Tk canvas widget. But for efficiency's sake, the logic that computes the current memory, swap space, and CPU usages is all coded in C. The C code obtains the system performance data by reading the files */proc/stat* and */proc/meminfo*. It then processes this information into the desired preformance measurements and makes appropriate changes to the Tcl/Tk bar graphs using ET function calls.

On a 90MHz Pentium and with an update frequency of 10 times per second, the *prefmon* program uses a negligible amount of the CPU time. So in addition to being a nifty desktop utility for a Linux workstation, this example demonstrates that Tcl/Tk applications can be very efficient.

An ASCII Text Editor and a File Browser

The two programs *tkedit* and *browser* implement are an ASCII text editor and a Unix file browser utility, respectively. Source code to these programs is in the files *tkedit.c, tkedit.tcl, browser.c* and *browser.tcl*.

Both of these programs could just as well have been implemented as pure Tcl/Tk scripts, with no loss of features or performance. (In fact, the browser can be used as pure script by invoking the *browser.tcl* using *wish*.) But sometimes you want a program to be a real executable, not a script. For instance, you may want to be able to run the program on machines that do not have Tcl/Tk installed. Or perhaps you want the programs to run on machines that have a different, incompatible version of Tcl/Tk installed.

The *tkedit* and *browser* programs are examples of how to convert a pure Tcl/Tk script into a standalone program using ET. The idea is very simple. Your C code simply initializes ET, invokes your script using a single `ET_INCLUDE` statement, and then enters the event loop. Like this:

```
void main(int argc, char **argv){
   Et_Init(&argc,argv);
   ET_INCLUDE( browser.tcl );
   Et_MainLoop();
}
```

Compiling this code results in a standalone application that can be run on any binary-compatible machine.

Using ET To Build MS Windows and Macintosh Applications

ET, like Tcl/Tk, was originally written to support the open X11 windowing system only. But nowadays, people often need to write applications for popular proprietary windowing systems like Windows 95 or Macintosh. Beginning with Release 4.1, Tcl/Tk supports these proprietary products, and so does ET. (Actually, only Windows 95 is supported as of this writing. The author has no access to a Macintosh system on which to develop and test a Macintosh port.)

On a Macintosh, ET applications that don't call Xlib directly should compile with little or no change. The Mac won't support the `Et_ReadStdin` routine, or the `Et_Display` global variable, but then again, neither of these make much sense on a Mac. The application will compile in much the same way as it does for X11, except that you should use the *et41mac.c* source file to the *et.o* library.

More change is required to support Windows 95, however. The Windows version of ET doesn't contain either `Et_Init` or `Et_MainLoop`; instead, these functions will be invoked automatically. An ET program for Windows should contain a single `Et_Main` procedure definition to do all its setup, and nothing more. Hence, if your application used to look like this:

```
void main(int argc, char **argv){
  Et_Init(&argc,argv);
  /* Your setup code here */
  Et_MainLoop();
}
```

then under Windows, it will look like this instead:

```
void Et_Main(int argc, char **argv){
  /* Your setup code here */
}
```

Besides that, and the obvious fact that `Et_Display` is not supported, a Windows ET application should work just like an X11 ET application. It is compiled in the same way, except that you should use the *et41win.c* source file for the *et.o* library.

Summary and Acknowledgements

Over the past two years, many people have used ET to build programs from a mixture of Tcl/Tk and C. Projects have ranged in size from student programming assignments up to large-scale (100,000+ lines) commercial development efforts. In all cases, ET has proven to be an effective alternative to other GUI toolkits.

The original implementation of ET grew out of a programming contract from Lucent Technologies (formerly AT&T Bell Laboratories). Lucent Technologies was in turn funded under a contract from the United States Navy. Many thanks go to Richard Blanchard at Lucent Technologies and to Charlie Roop, Dave Toms, and Clair Guthrie at PMO-428 for allowing ET to be released to the public domain.

The author can be reached at:
D. Richard Hipp
Hipp, Wyrick & Company, Inc.
6200 Maple Cove Lane
Charlotte, NC 28269
704-948-4565
drh@vnet.net

15

Building Groupware with GroupKit

by Mark Roseman and Saul Greenberg

"Hmmm, that's interesting. Hey Linda, take a look at this."

"What do you have there Carl? Oh," Linda asked, glancing at the schematic on the screen.

"I want to get the signal here," Carl pointed, "over to this other part here, but I'm not sure the best way to do it with all this stuff in between."

"Why don't you route it this way?" Linda suggested, drawing a rough path along the schematic, "this should be the most effective."

"Oh, and then I can move this chip over to here instead," Carl replied as he dragged the chip to its new location.

Linda moved a couple of other components over. "That looks like it should pretty much do it."

"Great, that'll work. Thanks for your help."

They both turned back to their own work. A pretty typical situation that repeats itself thousands of times daily in workplaces everywhere.

Except that Linda and Carl are thousands of miles apart.

What Is Groupware?

Linda and Carl are using a technology called groupware, which lets people who are far apart but connected by a network collaborate together on the same documents—like the schematic in this example—at the same time. Although groupware had its beginnings with the visionary work of Douglas Engelbart in the 1960s, only recently have networks and workstations become powerful and ubiquitous enough to truly support it. Some examples of groupware systems in use today include shared electronic whiteboards, multiuser text editors, tools to support group brainstorming, and of course a wide variety of multiplayer games.

Groupware actually refers to any technology that lets people work together. So things like email and Usenet news are also rudimentary groupware technologies. The difference is that email and Usenet don't allow people to work together at the same time or "synchronously," but instead support different time or "asynchronous" work. Another distinction between types of groupware is whether the system supports people working in the same place (like a team meeting room) or at a distance, like different sites on the Internet. We're mostly concerned with groupware for geographically distributed groups working together synchronously.

Unfortunately, building groupware applications can be extremely difficult. Implementing even the simplest system is a lengthy and tedious process. Every application must worry about creating and managing socket connections, parsing and dispatching interprocess communication, locating other users on a network and connecting to them, keeping shared resources consistent between users, and so on. Using conventional programming tools, a lot of low-level code must be written before getting to the specifics of the application. Groupware is an application domain crying out for better programming tools.

What Is GroupKit?

GroupKit is an extension to Tcl/Tk that makes it easy to develop groupware applications to support real-time, distance-separated collaborative work between two or more people. Using Tcl's built-in socket commands for its low-level networking, GroupKit provides an application framework that handles most details of building groupware automatically for you, so you can spend time just writing your application rather than its groupware infrastructure.

GroupKit grew out of our frustrations in building groupware systems without proper tools to support the job. By moving the common elements of groupware into a Tcl/Tk extension, we can now create programs in three days that originally took three months to write, and whose complexity shrunk from several thousand lines of code to only a few hundred lines. We've also found that it is often easy to take an existing single-user Tcl/Tk program and convert it to a multiuser program. With GroupKit, we're finding that writing groupware is only slightly harder than writing an equivalent single-user program.

The GroupKit distribution you'll find on the CD-ROM consists of the GroupKit extension itself (which is implemented as a mixture of Tcl and C), documentation, and approximately 30 example groupware applications.

Using GroupKit Applications—An End User's View

Before delving into the details of how to build GroupKit applications, we'll first walk through how an end user would run some of the existing applications included in the distribution. This will give you a chance to make sure things are set up on your own system, as well as introduce some important concepts about groupware programs.

We'll assume that GroupKit has already been compiled and installed on all participating systems, with a registrar process running. If GroupKit has not yet been installed, you can install it yourself by following the step-by-step installation instructions in the *README* file in the software distribution. In your own account, you'll need to make sure that your Unix *PATH* variable points to where the GroupKit binaries have been installed (type `which open.reg` at your shell prompt to check).

Starting a Session Manager

In GroupKit, you don't run programs directly, but invoke them via another program called a session manager. The session manager is used to locate other people in your work community running GroupKit programs, and connect your programs up to them, or to start up programs of your own. Running your programs together with other people is called a conference or session. GroupKit actually comes with several different session managers, but we'll use one called the Open Registration session manager, "open.reg." Start it by typing the following in a Unix shell window:

```
open.reg &
```

The first time you start up, the session manager may ask you some questions about yourself, like your name, and store this in a file called *.groupkitrc* in your home directory. It should then show the window in Figure 15-1 (if you have problems, make sure that you have a registrar process running). The "Conferences" pane on the left shows the names of any running conferences. Selecting one will show who is in the conference in the "Participants" pane on the right. The "Conferences" menu contains a list of known GroupKit applications and lets you start up new groupware sessions.

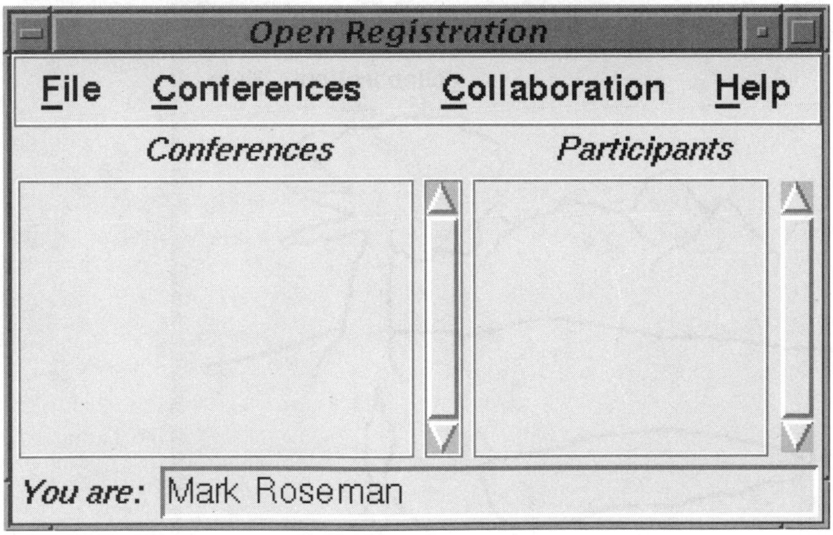

Figure 15-1: Open Registration Session Manager

Creating a New Conference

Assuming there are no conferences already running which we could join, let's create a new conference. We'll use a program called "Simple Sketchpad," which acts like a shared whiteboard, allowing several users to simultaneously draw freehand on a canvas.

To create it, pull down the "Conferences" menu in the session manager and select "Simple Sketchpad." A dialog box will appear, shown in Figure 15-2. This dialog

---

Using GroupKit Applications—An End User's View   **537**

box allows you to give your conference a name (by default it is just the name of the application) which will identify it to other users. When you've picked a name, click the "Create" button.

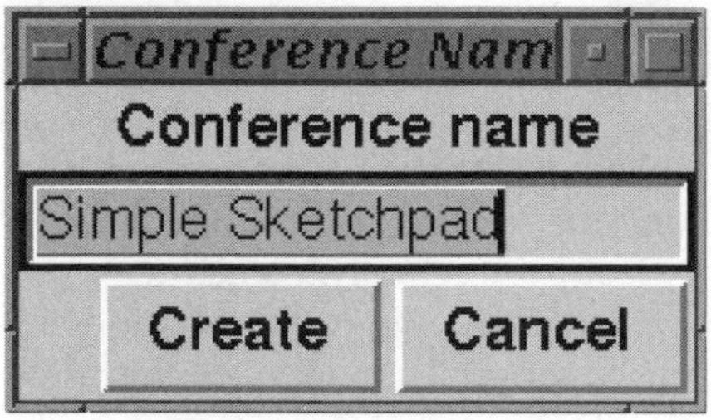

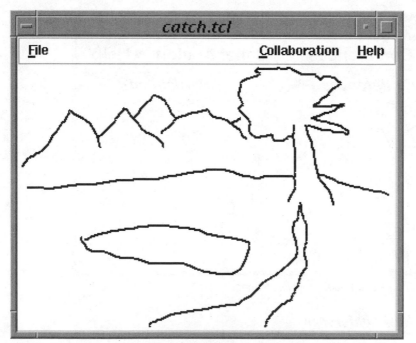

Figure 15-2: Conference Naming Dialog

At this point, you'll see the name of the conference added to the "Conferences" pane in the session manager, and the Simple Sketchpad program will come up in its own window, as shown in Figure 15-3. You can draw on the canvas using the left mouse button. The menus let you clear the canvas, exit the program, find out about other participants in the conference, and get information about both Group-Kit and the Simple Sketchpad conference. Try it!

Figure 15-3: Simple Sketchpad Conference

Joining An Existing Conference

We'll now have another user join the conference you've created. Find someone else on another machine nearby, and get them to start up their own copy of the open.reg session manager. They should see the conference you've created, and clicking on it will show that you are a participant in it. If you are just trying GroupKit out by yourself, create another open.reg on the same machine, and pretend you are a different person by changing your name to a new one in the entry box on the bottom.

To join the conference from their session manager, the other participant can double-click the name of the conference. This will add their name to the list of participants, and also bring up a window with their own copy of the Simple Sketchpad program. You'll also see that any drawing that was done in the first copy of the program appears in the new copy.

You'll now find that both people can draw at the same time, and that any drawings made by one user immediately appear on the screen of the other user. You'll also see a small cursor called a telepointer, which tracks the location of the other user's mouse cursor as he or she moves around the window. More than two people can be in this conference and others can join and participate through their own session managers.

When done, you can select "Quit" from the "File" menu of the Simple Sketchpad program to leave the conference. Your copy of the program will disappear, and you'll see your name removed from the list of conference participants in the session manager. When the last person leaves, they are asked to either save the contents of the conference (which gets stored in a background GroupKit process and would allow restarting at a later time, with the drawing intact), or to delete the conference.

It's also possible to invite other users into a GroupKit conference. In your session manager, select a conference, and then choose "Invite..." from the Collaboration menu. This will give you a list of all users who are currently running a session manager of their own. Choosing from that list will pop up a message on their screen, asking if they would like to join the conference. If they decide to join, their session manager will automatically join them to the conference.

What's Really Happening Inside

To understand what is going on, lets take a step back. As you've noticed, GroupKit consists of a number of different processes, which are illustrated in Figure 15-4. There is a central process called the registrar, a typical Unix daemon that should already be running on your system. Its job is to keep track of what conferences are running and who is joined to them. Each user runs a session manager, such as open.reg, which connects up to the registrar. The session managers are used to create conferences (like our Simple Sketchpad) which again run as separate processes. As other users join conferences through their own session managers, GroupKit opens up network connections between the conference processes, so that every process in a conference has a connection to every other process in a conference.

Other Applications

There are a number of other sample applications included with the GroupKit distribution which you should try out. Some of these are illustrated in Figure 15-5 and include:

- **Brainstorming Tool**: Allows users to brainstorm by typing in brief one-line textual ideas; all ideas appear in a listbox visible by everyone.

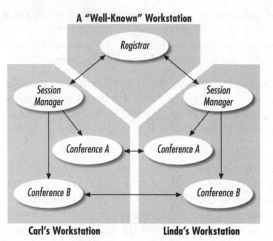

Figure 15-4: GroupKit Process and Communications Architecture

- **File Viewer**: Lets you load up the contents of a text file and browse through it. A multiuser scrollbar shows what parts of the file other people are looking at.

- **Hello World**: A simple program that creates a button; when pressed, the button changes on all users' screens to say hello from whoever pushed the button.

- **Text Chat**: A program similar to Unix talk, but which allows more than two participants. Text typed by each user is immediately seen by all others.

- **Post It**: Type in a message, which can be sent to other users where it appears as a sticky note.

- **Tic Tac Toe**: The classic game, allowing you to play against other users.

- **Tetrominoes**: Rotate and move the different shaped polygons to get them to fit inside their containers.

Important Concepts

There are several important points about GroupKit that have been illustrated so far.

- GroupKit supports real-time distributed multipoint conferences between many users.

- GroupKit systems include both session managers for managing conferences, like the Open Registration system, and conference applications which are the actual groupware tools, like Simple Sketchpad.

- Every user in a GroupKit conference session runs their own copy of the conference application in a process on their own machine. These processes are connected to each other over the network.

- GroupKit is not a media-space system, which would include things like audio or video conferencing. Many of the conference applications will strongly ben-

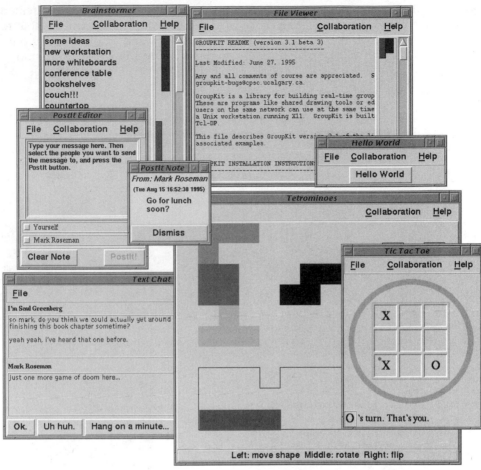

Figure 15-5: Some Example GroupKit Conference Applications

efit from having some kind of voice connection, such as provided by a telephone. Alternatively, if you have some sort of computer-based media space
system available, it would be possible to integrate it with GroupKit, so that starting a GroupKit conference also starts the media-space system.

An Example GroupKit Program

Now that we've seen what GroupKit programs look like and how their run-time
architecture is set up, we can start building our own conference application. There
are a lot of pieces in GroupKit to explain, so what we'll do is develop a relatively
sophisticated groupware program over the space of the chapter, starting with a min-
imalist single-user version and gradually adding features that illustrate GroupKit's
programming constructs.

The program we'll build is a brainstorming tool called "Note Organizer." This tool
can help a group generate and organize ideas; for example, to plan a paper, software project, advertising campaign, and so forth. As a brainstorming tool, the pro-

gram will allow users to enter ideas (a few words), each which will be represented as a text item in a Tk canvas widget. To organize the ideas, users will be able to drag them around on the canvas, grouping related ones and so on. Being groupware, everyone in the group will be able to generate and move ideas around at the same time, and see what everyone else is doing. The program will look like the one in Figure 15-6.

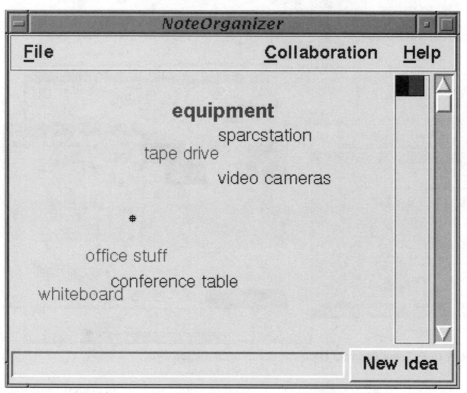

Figure 15-6: Screen Dump of Note Organizer

Here is how we'll approach building this example. We'll start off by creating a single-user version of the program that allows you to create ideas, but not to move them around. This will run as a normal "wish" script, without using GroupKit at all. We'll then take that program and modify it slightly so that it will run within Group-Kit, before putting any code in to "share" the ideas. The next step will be to share ideas, so that when one participant creates an idea on their canvas, it appears on other participants' canvases also. We can then begin to get more sophisticated, by letting users drag ideas around the display, which will introduce some techniques that are useful when building groupware systems. Finally, we'll have the program do appropriate things when people enter and leave the session, and also add some groupware widgets that will help keep track of what people are doing when they are in the session with us. That will complete the application as illustrated in Figure 15-6. If you'd like to skip ahead and see what the entire program will look like, the complete listing of the final version appears at the end of this chapter.

Single-User Version

So let's start out with just a single-user version, and only worry about creating the ideas but not moving them around yet. The code—which is standard Tcl/Tk—is shown here. The program sets up some global variables to keep track of where the ideas are to be placed on the canvas, and the font to use when drawing the ideas. It then creates the canvas to hold the ideas, an entry widget to type in the ideas, and a button used to copy the idea from the entry to the canvas. When pressed, the button calls the addNewIdea proc, which gets the idea out of the entry, calls doAddIdea and clears the entry in preparation for the next idea. The doAddIdea procedure actually puts the idea into the canvas, by creating a text item at the location found in the notes(x) and notes(y) global variables. It then adjusts these variables so as to place the next note below the one just added, starting a new column when it gets far enough down the canvas.

```
set notes(x) 20
set notes(y) 20
set notes(notefont) -adobe-helvetica-medium-r-normal--17-*

proc buildWindow {} {
    frame .main
    canvas .notepad -scrollregion "0 0 800 3000" \
                    -yscrollcommand ".scroll set"
    scrollbar .scroll -command ".notepad yview"
    frame .controls
    entry .newidea
    button .enteridea -text "New Idea" -command addNewIdea
    pack .main -side top -fill both -expand yes
    pack .notepad -side left -fill both -expand yes -in .main
    pack .scroll -side right -fill y -in .main
    pack .controls -side top -fill x
    pack .newidea -side left -fill x -expand yes -in .controls
    pack .enteridea -side left -in .controls
}

proc addNewIdea {} {
    set idea [.newidea get]
    doAddIdea $idea
    .newidea delete 0 end
}

proc doAddIdea {idea} {
    global notes
    .notepad create text $notes(x) $notes(y) -text $idea -anchor nw \
        -font $notes(notefont)
    incr notes(y) 20
    if {$notes(y)>600} {
        set notes(y) 20
        incr notes(x) 100
    }
}

buildWindow
```

You should be able to run that program just fine under Tk's normal wish. Type ideas in the entry box and press the button to add them to the canvas.

Running the Example In GroupKit

Now let's start turning this program into groupware. The first thing that every GroupKit program must do is initialize GroupKit, which is done by putting the following line at the beginning of your program:

```
gk_initConf $argv
```

The second thing you should do is add GroupKit's standard menu bar, which contains menu items to exit the program, find out what other users are working on the program with you, and display an *about* box. Add these lines before creating the main interface of your program, in other words, just before creating the canvas widget:

```
gk_defaultMenu .menubar
pack .menubar -side top -fill x
```

As before, we'll start our conference application using the Open Registration session manager. But first we have to tell the session manager about our new program. To do this, add the following line to the bottom of your *.groupkitrc* file (which was created in your home directory the first time you ran the session manager). Of course, change the /home/you to the name of the directory where you put the note organizer script. Note that each user has their own *.groupkitrc* file, which is initially copied from a template set up by whoever installed GroupKit on your system.

```
userprefs prog.NoteOrganizer.cmd \
    "exec gkwish -f /home/you/noteorg.tcl"
```

Either quit and restart your session manager, or choose "Reinitialize" from the "File" menu. You should now find an item named "NoteOrganizer" under the Conferences menu. Use it to create the Note Organizer conference as before, and then join the conference from another session manager.

If you run multiple copies, you'll quickly find that if you enter ideas in one copy of the program they don't appear on remote copies. That's because we haven't actually told the program to display ideas on all screens—GroupKit won't take care of that automatically. You will find though that items in the menu bar work fine, like the "Show Participants" item which provides information on other users in the conference.

Just One More Thing...

So now let's fix our program so when ideas are entered in one copy of the program they are sent to other users. First, quit both running copies of the program (when you quit the last one it will ask you if you want to delete the conference or keep it around; you should delete it). Now, go back into your program and change the second line in addNewIdea from:

```
doAddIdea $idea
```

to:

```
gk_toAll doAddIdea $idea
```

and then restart the program from the first session manager. After joining the conference from the second session manager, you should find that ideas entered in one copy of the program now appear in the other copy as well. That wasn't so bad!

So at this point, you've seen what is involved in getting a simple groupware program up and running in GroupKit. You've been exposed to GroupKit's session manager, learned how to tell the session manager about your new program, and how to initialize a GroupKit program. Finally, you've seen the gk_toAll command, which is one of GroupKit's programming constructs that can make it easy to turn a single-user program into a multiuser one.

So what does the gk_toAll do? That command arranges for the Tcl command following it (i.e., doAddIdea $idea) to be executed not only in the local program (where the idea was typed in), but also in every other copy of the program running in the conference. So, if you had not just two, but three, four, or ten people joined in the conference, all of their conference processes would execute that same command. This is illustrated in Figure 15-7.

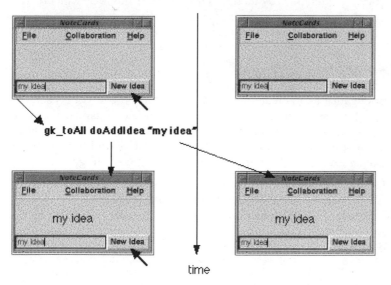

Figure 15-7: The gk_toAll Command

The gk_toAll command is an example of a Remote Procedure Call (RPC) that GroupKit provides. GroupKit has other RPCs that differ in who the commands get sent to, as shown in the sidebar. RPCs are a fairly straightforward but effective way to turn a single-user program into a multiuser one.

You'll find when you're using RPCs that you often need to "factor" your code, splitting a routine into two parts, as you saw in the "addNewIdea" and "doAddIdea" procs. This separates the code that invokes a routine (usually called from the user interface, and which is executed only by a single user) from the code that actually performs the operation (which is executed by everyone in the conference). Not only is this a useful style to adopt for groupware, but it is good coding practice generally. Factoring your code makes it easier to change your user interface, or invoke the core of your program in entirely new ways such as from a Tcl script.

Coordinating Multiple Users

Now that our Note Organizer can create ideas that show up on everyone's screens, let's start looking at how we can move the ideas around to organize them. To accomplish this in a single-user program, we would change the doAddIdea procedure to attach a binding to each canvas item after it is created, and reposition the item when the mouse moved, as illustrated in the following code fragment.

```
set canvasid [.notepad create text $notes(x) $notes(y) -text $idea \
                      -anchor nw -font $notes(notefont)]
.notepad bind $canvasid <B1-Motion> "noteDragged $canvasid %x %y"

proc noteDragged {id x y} {
    .notepad coords $id [.notepad canvasx $x] [.notepad canvasy $y]
}
```

As before, we could use `gk_toAll` to execute that callback in all users' programs by changing the line in noteDragged to:

```
gk_toAll .notepad coords $id [.notepad canvasx $x] \
        [.notepad canvasy $y]
```

This will work most of the time, but is very fragile and can break if users are entering ideas very quickly. Here's why. The preceding code assumes that copies of an idea on different users' screens all have the same canvasid. But that is not always true.

Tk assigns canvasids in the order in which items are created. But if two users create ideas at almost the same time, they may end up being created in a different order on each user's screen. If the first user enters `foo`, the `gk_toAll` adds the idea to the local canvas and then sends it across the network. If at the same time a second user enters `bar`, their `gk_toAll` puts it on their canvas and sends it across the network. This will result in the first user adding `foo` then `bar`, while the second user adds `bar` and then `foo`. The two items will be created in different orders on the different systems, and therefore the canvasids won't match. This will be a problem when it comes to moving the items around, because we need to correctly refer to the item to move. This is shown in Figure 15-8.

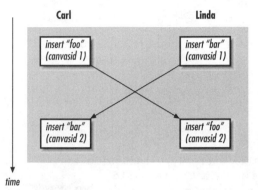

Figure 15-8: Ideas Created In Different Orders On Different Machines

To make matters worse, because the `doAddIdea` routine (which creates the text items on the canvas) also chooses the position on the canvas, if the ideas cross paths, not only will they have different canvasids, but they will appear in different places on different users' screens.

Problems like these are fairly common in most groupware applications. They can be solved, but only if the programmer is aware of the nuances of these situations. Let's address these problems one at a time.

Uniquely Referring to Ideas via Unique User Numbers

The normal way you'd uniquely refer to an idea would be to give it a unique id number, such as via a counter held in a global variable that increments by one every time you have a new idea. As we saw with the canvasids, that can create some problems in a groupware application, where the counter is not global across all processes.

What we'll do is slightly modify that scheme, so that each conference process will keep a global counter, but those counters will be unique from those of other conference processes. We will do this by prefacing each counter with a special Group-Kit id number guaranteed to be unique for that conference process.

GroupKit generates a user number for every user in a conference process. It stores that number (and a lot of other information) in a data structure called an *environment*. We'll discuss environments in a moment, but for now just assume that the following code fragment will return the user's unique id number:

```
set myid [users get local.usernum]
```

We can now generate a unique id for every idea, by combining our user number (held in myid) with a global counter. We can then send that combined id to doAdd-Idea, and tag the canvas item with the combined id. Finally we can use this unique id when we're moving the idea around. This is shown here:

```
set notes(counter) 0

proc addNewIdea {} {
    global notes
    set idea [.newidea get]
    set myid [users get local.usernum]
    set id ${myid}x$notes(counter)
    incr notes(counter)
    gk_toAll doAddIdea $id $idea
    .newidea delete 0 end
}

proc doAddIdea {id idea} {
    global notes
    .notepad create text $notes(x) $notes(y) -text $idea \
        -anchor nw -font $notes(notefont) -tags $id
    .notepad bind $id <B1-Motion> "noteDragged $id %x %y"
    ...
}

proc noteDragged {id x y} {
    gk_toAll .notepad coords $id [.notepad canvasx $x] \
        [.notepad canvasy $y]
}
```

Correctly Placing Ideas

So that takes care of uniquely referring to ideas. We will now fix the problem where ideas could end up being initially placed in different locations on different screens. This problem is really being caused because the receiver (doAddIdea) and not the sender (addNewIdea) is deciding where the idea should go. The following code fragment changes this so that the sender specifies the location, although we'll still let the receiver update the position for the next idea.

```
proc addNewIdea {} {
    ...
    global notes
    gk_toAll doAddIdea $id $notes(x) $notes(y) $idea
    ...
}

proc doAddIdea {id x y idea} {
    ...
    .notepad create text $x $y -text $idea -anchor nw \
        -font $notes(notefont) -tags $id
    ...
```

```
    }
```

What happens now when ideas are entered at the same time by different users? If you trace through the order that messages will get executed, you'll see that both ideas will end up entered in exactly the same place, overlapping each other! When you think about it, this actually makes some sense. Imagine the real-life setting where users place real paper notes on a large board. If two people place notes at the same time, they'll both reach for the same place. Seeing their problem, they can then choose to move one of the notes somewhere else. In our computer version, users can do the same thing—see the overlapping ideas and move one of them out of the way. While it's probably possible to build very elaborate algorithms into software to recover from situations like these, it is often best just to let people deal naturally with these situations.

Choosing What Information To Share

So far we've tried to keep the canvases of all users completely synchronized. This is known as a "What You See Is What I See" (WYSIWIS) view, where all participants see exactly the same thing. It is also possible to have some differences between displays, creating a "relaxed-WYSIWIS" view. GroupKit supports both paradigms, but choosing which information to share and which to keep private to a user is a design decision you have to make for your own application.

To illustrate relaxed-WYSIWIS, we'll add to our program the notion of a "selected" idea, just as you'd select text in an editor or an object in a drawing program. We'll display the selected idea in a larger font. For this application, we'll decide that each participant has his or her own selection. Users can select an idea by clicking on it. The code that actually manipulates the selection will keep track of the selected object by adding a "selected" tag to the canvas item. Here is the code:

```
set notes(selectedfont) -adobe-helvetica-bold-r-normal--20-*

proc doAddIdea {id x y idea} {
    ...
    .notepad bind $id <1> "selectNote $id"
    ...
}

proc selectNote id {
    global notes
    catch {.notepad itemconfig selected -font $notes(notefont)}
    catch {.notepad dtag selected selected}
    .notepad addtag selected withtag $id
    .notepad itemconfig $id -font $notes(selectedfont)
}
```

In this example, we made the conscious design decision to not share selection between users. However, it would of course be possible to have the selection shared, so that there is a single selection, shared among all users. This could be built by adding the appropriate gk_toAll RPC when changing the selection.

We now successfully have dealt with the problems of coordinating multiple users. Generating unique ids based on the users' unique user numbers let us refer to objects uniquely, while letting the sender decide on the idea's position resulted in ideas appearing in the correct location on all screens. Finally, we showed that it may be desireable to have some information, such as selection, that is not shared between all users.

Using Environments To Find Out Information About Users

At this point we can correctly create and move ideas, with the ideas appearing in the correct place on every user's screen. Let's now extend the program to identify who entered each idea. GroupKit keeps track of a designated color for each user which we can use to do this (participants can specify their personal color in their *.groupkitrc* file or via the "Pick Color" menu item in their session manager).

GroupKit stores each user's color (as well as other information) in a data structure called an environment. Environments are structured as a tree, where each node can contain either other nodes or a value. A node is referred to by its position in the tree, with each level of the tree separated by a dot. So for example, `local.usernum` refers to the node `usernum` which is a child of `local` which is a child of the root node of the environment. This is similar to how Tk refers to windows in the window hierarchy.

As you've gathered, information about the local user is stored underneath the `local` key in the environment called `users`, so `local.color` is the node holding your own color. You can retrieve its value by the call `[users get local.color]`. Information about remote users is stored under a remote key, and further divided up by each remote user's unique user number, as shown in Figure 15-9. So, for example, you can retrieve the color of the remote user having unique id 3 by specifying `users get remote.3.color`.* More examples of how to use environments are described in the sidebar "Using Environments."

Let's add this into our program now. When we create an idea, we'll send our user number along with the idea. When creating the text item to display the idea, we'll change its color to be that of the user who created it. We'll also add a canvas tag to the text item identifying the user who created it, which we'll come back to later. Here are the changes in the code:

```
proc addNewIdea {} {
    ...
    gk_toAll doAddIdea $id [users get local.usernum] $notes(x) \
                           $notes(y) $idea
    ...
}

proc doAddIdea {id usernum x y idea} {
    ...
```

---

* For convenience, there is also a GroupKit called "gk_getUserAttrib" which returns information about a user, and works for both the local user and remote users. So, for example, "gk_getUserAttrib $usernum color" would return the user's color.

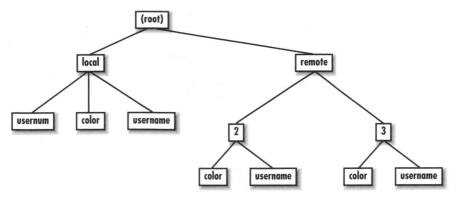

Figure 15-9: Users Environment

Using Environments

Environments have a number of different commands used to manipulate them. If you're familiar with Extended Tcl's keyed lists (see Chapter 6), you'll find some similarities. Some of the commands include:

1. **gk_newenv *envname*:** Create a new environment, which also creates a Tcl command called envname used to access the environment.

2. ***envname* set *key value*:** Set the value of the node located at key.

3. ***envname* get *key*:** Get the value of the node located at key.

4. ***envname* keys *key*:** List the children of the node located at key.

5. ***envname* delete *key*:** Delete the node located at key (and all nodes below it).

6. ***envname* exists *key*:** Check if a node located at key exists in the environment.

7. ***envname* destroy:** Destroy an environment, all data in it, and its Tcl command.

GroupKit maintains a number of environments internally. You've seen the users environment which holds information about all the users in the conference, including their color (the key "color"), their full name ("username"), their userid ("userid"), and host ("host"). You can also store your own information in the users environment, to be used by your application. The other environment you've encountered briefly is the userprefs environment, which is used within the *.groupkitrc* file to specify where different conferences exist. Environments are also used extensively throughout the session management subsystem in GroupKit.

```
        if {$usernum==[users get local.usernum]} {
            set color [users get local.color]
        } else {
            set color [users get remote.$usernum.color]
        }
        .notepad create text $x $y -text $idea -anchor nw \
            -font   $notes(notefont) -fill $color \
            -tags [list $id user$usernum]
        ...
    }
```

Environments provide a convenient way to find out information on other users. They also have other features that can help in building groupware, which we'll return to later. In the meantime however, we'll look at another GroupKit feature called *conference events*.

Conference Events

As you've noticed, GroupKit automatically takes care of users joining and leaving conferences, without your intervention. However, it's often useful to be notified when people come and go. To do this, GroupKit provides a set of three conference events.

Conference events are similar to bindings that you can attach to widgets. But rather than executing a piece of callback code when something happens to a widget (e.g., the user presses a button), conference events execute a piece of code you provide as users join and leave the conference.

To specify handlers for conference events, you use the gk_bind command, which works very similarly to Tk's bind command, right down to its use of "percent substitutions" to pass event parameters to your callback code. The general format of the gk_bind command* is:

```
    gk_bind event-type callback-code
```

New Users

The first of the conference events is the newUserArrived event, which signifies a new user has just joined the conference. We can extend our program to watch for new users arriving and displaying a dialog box with the code shown here. When this event is generated, information about the new user has already been stored in the users environment which was described previously. One of the pieces of information available besides color is the user's name, so we'll display that in our dialog box. The percent substitution "%U" refers to the user's unique user number, a parameter of this conference event. Here, we'll embed the callback code directly in the gk_bind command. As with Tk bindings, we could also have the binding call a separate procedure to handle the event.

---

* While the gk_bind command creates a binding that will execute whenever a conference event occurs, it is also possible to later remove a binding, so that it will not execute when the event occurs in the future. The gk_bind command actually returns a "binding id," which can be later passed to the gk_delbind command to remove the binding.

```
gk_bind newUserArrived {
    set newuser %U
    set name [users remote.$newuser.username]
    toplevel .new$newuser
    pack [label .new$newuser.lbl -text "$name just arrived."]
    pack [button .new$newuser.ok -text Ok \
          -command "destroy .new$newuser"]
}
```

Users Leaving

The second conference event is generated when a user leaves the conference. Again, the %U refers to the user's unique user number. The information for this user in the users environment is still available at the time this event is generated. In our program, we may choose to respond to this event by changing the color of any ideas generated by the leaving user to black, as illustrated in the following code (remember that we tagged all ideas created by that user with the word "user" appended with their user number).

```
gk_bind userDeleted {
    catch {
        .notepad itemconfig user%U -fill black
    }
}
```

Updating Latecomers and Saving Conference Results

The final conference event generated by GroupKit is the updateEntrant event, used to update latecomers to a conference already in progress. Unlike the previous two events, GroupKit sends this event to only one of the existing conference processes, chosen arbitrarily. The process receiving this event should respond to it by sending whatever information is necessary to the latecomer to bring them up to date. In our program, this would mean sending them a copy of all of the ideas that have been generated so far (see Figure 15-10).

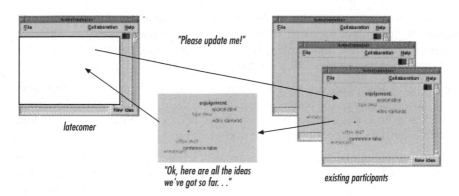

Figure 15-10: Updating Latecomers

This information is normally sent via the gk_toUserNum RPC, described earlier. This call needs the user number to send the message to, again extracted from the event via the "%U" substitution.

```
gk_bind updateEntrant {
    foreach item [.notepad find all]
        set x [lindex [.notepad coords $item] 0]
        set y [lindex [.notepad coords $item] 1]
        foreach tag [.notepad gettags $item] {
            if {[string range $tag 0 3]=="user"} {
                set usernum [string range $tag 4 end]
            } else {
                if {$tag!="selected"} {set id $tag}
            }
        }
        set idea [.notepad itemcget $item -text]
        gk_toUserNum %U doAddIdea $id $usernum $x $y $idea
    }
}
```

The updateEntrant event is also used to make conferences persist (that is, make them stick around after the last user has left, so that they can be rejoined later). You've noticed that when you quit the last program in the conference, you're asked if you'd like to delete the conference or have it save its contents (persist). If you ask it to persist, GroupKit sends an updateEntrant event to your program, but rather than asking it (via the %U parameter) to update a new user, GroupKit passes a special user number that causes your program to send messages to a special persistence server that records them. When a user next joins the conference, the messages stored in the server are played back, exactly as if they were sent from the last user.

It is also possible to create your own events, specific to your application. This can be useful as your programs get large, as a way of communicating changes between different parts of your program. See the *gk_notifier(n)* manual page for more information.

Groupware Widgets and Awareness

Our program is starting to get quite sophisticated, allowing ideas to be created and moved around on multiple screens, displaying different users' ideas in different colors, responding to new and leaving users, updating latecomers to the conference, and even persisting when all users have left the conference.

As a conference participant, you may sometimes find it hard to follow when several people are working at the same time. Ideas are being rapidly moved around, and it's unclear who's doing what and when. Also, because the canvas is quite tall, it can become hard to track where people are working.

GroupKit provides a number of different awareness widgets to help with these sorts of problems. Keeping track of where people are working and what they are doing is a common problem in a number of different groupware programs, so our widgets can be easily added to many different applications.

Telepointers

You've probably noticed yourself that when people get together around a white-board to discuss some sort of problem, that along with a lot of drawing, there's also a lot of pointing or gesturing to objects drawn on the whiteboard as well. In fact, some studies of how people use drawing surfaces like whiteboards found that gesturing is actually more common than drawing. GroupKit's telepointers provide a way to communicate this important gesturing information in groupware applications.

Telepointers, also known as multiple cursors, are used to provide very fine-grained information about where other users are working in the application. As other users move around the application, you'll see a small cursor which follows their mouse cursor. Just tracking those cursors—which you're usually just peripherally aware of—provides a surprising amount of information about who's doing what in an application, what objects people are working with, and how active different people are (see Figure 15-11). Telepointers can be attached to any Tk widget.

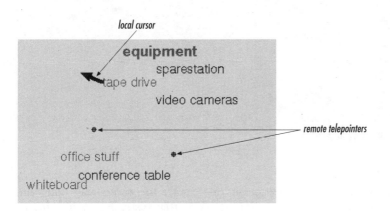

Figure 15-11: GroupKit's Telepointers

Adding telepointers to our example is quite straightforward, requiring only two lines of code. The first line initializes the telepointers, and the second attaches the telepointers to our canvas widget.

```
gk_initializeTelepointers
gk_specializeWidgetTreeTelepointer .notepad
```

MultiUser Scrollbars

While telepointers are good at answering questions like "what are people who are working close to me doing exactly?", multiuser scrollbars answer questions like "where are other people working in this large document?" They provide a more coarse-grained sense of awareness.

Figure 15-12 illustrates GroupKit's multiuser scrollbars. They consist of two parts: a conventional Tk scrollbar on the right, and a set of bars showing where users are located in a document to its left. The conventional scrollbar is used normally, to scroll your own view in the document. As you scroll, you'll also notice one of the bars to the left scrolling with you. That bar is showing your position in the document. As other users scroll their own views, the other bars on their display will change to show their new positions. Clicking on each bar will display a pop-up reminding you which user the bar is associated with. Multiuser scrollbars allow you to quickly find where others are working in a large document and—by aligning your view with theirs—join them.

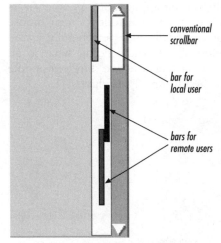

conventional scrollbar

bar for local user

bars for remote users

Figure 15-12 Multiuser Scrollbars

Multiuser scrollbars are added to applications in exactly the same way that conventional scrollbars are. In fact, the only difference is that instead of using the Tk `scrollbar` command, you use the GroupKit `gk_scrollbar` command.

```
proc buildWindow {} {
    ...
    gk_scrollbar .scroll -command ".notepad yview"
    ...
}
```

GroupKit also comes with a number of other widgets. You've already seen the menu bar, which includes items like an Exit command, an about box for Group-Kit, and an item which brings up a dialog box giving you information about the different users in the conference with you. There's also a widget called the "mini view," which is similar to the multiuser scrollbar, but when combined with a text-based program can show a miniature of the document along with the scrollbar. There's also a widget that is included to make it easier to build online help into your application.

At this point we've completed our Note Organizer program; you'll find the complete program listing at the end of this chapter. The next section will go on to talk about a very different approach to building groupware applications with GroupKit.

Shared Environments

When writing the Note Organizer application, we've used a very direct style of programming; when we wanted to move an idea around, we literally sent a message to the other users' canvas widgets to move the idea. This approach works very well for small, highly graphical applications, but doesn't always scale up well to larger applications, particularly if you'd like to allow different users to customize how they work with their applications. This section discusses an alternative approach to programming in GroupKit, using some features of environments.

To understand how environments can be used to build groupware programs, we'll have to first describe a paradigm called "Model-View-Controller" (MVC), which was first introduced in Smalltalk as a way to construct (single-user) user interfaces. The MVC paradigm suggests that an application should be divided into three distinct components:

1. A "model" represents the underlying data structure that is to be displayed.

2. A "view" looks at the contents of the model and creates an on-screen visual representation of it.

3. A "controller" reacts to user input events and sends changes to the model.

Under this paradigm, the controller never changes the on-screen view directly. Instead, it changes the model, and the changes to the model are picked up in the view which does cause a change on screen. This is illustrated in Figure 15-13.

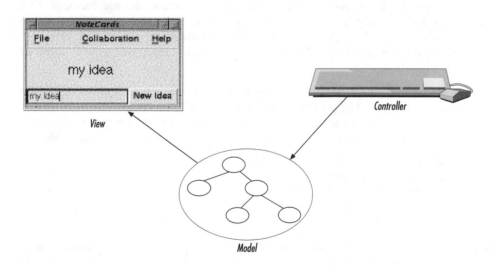

Figure 15-13: Model-View-Controller Paradigm

This approach can be a bit hard to follow at first, since input events only indirectly affect what is displayed on screen, but has a number of advantages. First, by clearly separating out your underlying data from the view of that data and how it is manipulated, it encourages you to build a very clear data model, which can help you

---

understand exactly what it is your program is manipulating. By doing this separation, you also find it easier to modularize your code, rather than trying to do everything in one place. Finally, the paradigm makes it easier to have multiple views on the same data structure, for example, allowing you to view a table of numbers as either a spreadsheet or a graph.

So how does this relate back to GroupKit? Recall that we can use GroupKit's environments to store a fairly arbitrary set of data (like names and colors in the `users` environment) arranged in a tree structure, where we can associate a string value with any node in the tree. This can serve as an underlying data structure for a wide variety of applications, and so is an appropriate choice for our Model under the MVC paradigm. Environments can also generate events (similar to the conference events used for announcing new users, etc.) when they are changed. These events can be received by other portions of your program, like a View which updates the screen to match the change in the Model. Finally, parts of your program that handle user input (the Controller portion) can react to these changes by modifying the environment.

We've taken environments one step further, and allowed them to be shared between all the users in a conference. When any user makes a change to their own copy of the environment, that change is automatically propagated to all other users' copies. So while a user's input event may change his or her own environment, which generates an event to update his or her on-screen view, the change *also* gets sent to every other user's environment, generating the same event and updating their view—instant groupware.

These shared environments and the MVC paradigm really shine on larger applications, but here we'll just present a toy example to illustrate the mechanisms. Our data model will be held in an environment called `stocks` and consist of a single piece of information, the value of the fictional GroupKit Inc. stock. Our view will consist of an on-screen label showing the value, and an entry widget will allow us to change the value.

After initializing GroupKit, we begin by creating the `stocks` environment, using the `gk_newenv` command. The `-share` flag tells GroupKit to create this as a shared environment,* and the `-bind` flag specifies that events should be generated when the environment is changed. We'll then give our GroupKit stock an initial value.

```
gk_initConf $argv
gk_defaultMenu .menubar
pack .menubar -side left -fill x
gk_newenv -share -bind stocks
stocks set groupkit 1
```

Next, we'll create our view, using a label widget. The `stocks bind changeEnv-Info` attaches a binding to the environment, so that whenever a change is made to it, the following code will be executed. There are also events for when a piece of

---

* Shared environments bring up the issue of concurrency control—what happens when two users do things at the same time? The default (specified with the "-share" flag) is to completely ignore this, which can lead to copies of the environments being out of sync. If you instead specify the "-serialize" flag, the copies will be guaranteed to be synchronized with each other, although this can cause some delays when running over slow networks. It is also possible to add other concurrency control policies into environments, though we're not going to get into that here.

information in the environment is first added (`addEnvInfo`), and when an item is removed (`deleteEnvInfo`).* The event parameter %K refers to the name of the key in the environment that changed; we could have omitted they key here since there is only one key in the environment.

```
label .view -text "GroupKit Inc. value is [stocks get groupkit]"
pack .view -side top
stocks bind changeEnvInfo {
    if {%K=="groupkit"} {
        .view config \
        -text "GroupKit Inc. value is [stocks get groupkit]"
    }
}
```

Finally, we create the controller, using an entry widget. When we hit the "Return" key in the entry, its value is retrieved and stored in the stocks environment. The view code should then notice the change and update the display. Finally, because it is a shared environment, the change will show up in all other users' environments, updating their views as well.

```
pack [entry .controller] -side top
bind .controller <Return> {stocks set groupkit [.controller get]}
```

We could easily replace either the controller or view with ones that behaved differently, without changing any other parts of the program (or they could even display several views, since multiple bindings on an event are allowed). Different users could also use different versions of the programs in the same conference. This works because only the models (the shared environment `stocks`) of different users directly communicate with each other, and not the views or controllers. For example, here is a view that uses a canvas widget to display a horizontal bar whose length depends on the value of the stock held in the environment:

```
pack [canvas .barview] -side top
.barview create rectangle 0 0 [expr [stocks get groupkit]*5] 10 \
                            -anchor nw -tags bar
model bind changeEnvInfo {
    if {%K=="groupkit"} {
        .barview coords bar 0 0 [expr [stocks get groupkit]*5] 10
    }
}
```

In summary, GroupKit's shared environments can serve as an easy way to implement the Model-View-Controller paradigm, and extend it to support multiuser applications. Environments can take care of the housekeeping chores in updating and synchronizing multiple copies of a data structure (like the multiple copies of the canvas widget used in the Note Organizer — though the canvas data structure had the advantage of having its view built-in!), and can help to modularize your appli-

---

* There is actually one other event generated by environments, the "envReceived" event. When a new user joins an already running session, GroupKit's environments will respond to an "updateEntrant" event by sending the entire contents of the environment to the new user. The "envReceived" event is generated at this point. The typical response by the programmer is to walk through the environment and create objects in your view to match what is already in the environment.

---

cation. It's a judgement call whether to use shared environments or the more direct RPCs in your application (they can be mixed for different parts, of course). In general, if your application becomes larger, if you're dealing with information that can be changed in various ways by your program, or if it can be viewed in different ways, then environments are usually an appropriate choice.

Other GroupKit Features

There's a lot more to GroupKit than we can cover here. In this section, we'll briefly mention a few more things, and also provide a set of pointers to more information.

Session Management

In this chapter, you've learned the basics of building a GroupKit conference application, such as the Note Organizer. To run it, you've used the open.reg session manager included with the GroupKit distribution. GroupKit actually comes with a number of different session managers, and also provides facilities for building your own, just as you can build your own conferences. Session management can and should be heavily influenced by the working style of a community of users (for example, should just anyone be able to join an existing conference?), and GroupKit makes it possible to meet the diverse needs of different groups.

Class Builder

GroupKit also comes with a mega-widget framework called the "GroupKit class builder," which allows you to build new types of widgets (and was used for those in GroupKit, such as the multiuser scrollbars). The class builder bears a strong resemblance to the Tix extension (see Chapter 5) and is in fact based on an earlier version of Tix.

High-Level Event Package

The `gk_bind` command used to send conference events is actually built on a more general high-level event package. This package can be used to broadcast arbitrary messages from one part of your application, which can be intercepted by other parts. Such high-level events are useful to help structure large programs, groupware or not. The `gk_notifier` object is the basis of these high-level events.

For More Information

The GroupKit distribution contains a set of manual pages describing the various commands and widgets, and their options. You'll also find a user's manual (in Postscript) format. But as usual, the best way to learn GroupKit is to look at other people's programs. The distribution contains approximately 30 example conferences and session managers, written by ourselves and also contributed by other users of GroupKit. These examples are a great starting point for your own programs.

The most up-to-date information about GroupKit can be found on our World Wide Web page, accessible at *http://www.cpsc.ucalgary.ca/projects/grouplab/groupkit*. There you'll find information on current projects, and pointers to various papers that have been written about GroupKit. The latest version of the software can be found on our ftp site, *ftp.cpsc.ucalgary.ca*, in the directory */pub/projects/grouplab/software*. Finally, we run a mailing list, which you can join by sending email to *groupkit-users-request@cpsc.ucalgary.ca*. The sidebar "Further Reading" describes a number of sources for more information on groupware in general.

Further Reading

There are a number of excellent sources of information about groupware, as well as Computer Supported Cooperative Work (CSCW), which is the academic discipline that encompasses groupware. A recent collection is "Readings in Groupware and Computer-Supported Cooperative Work: Assisting Human-Human Collaboration", written and edited by Ron Baecker and published by Morgan-Kaufmann in 1993. It includes not only technical groupware information, but also case studies of cooperative work, information on the psychology of groups, and other foundational areas whose understanding is critical to building successful groupware. Other good collections include "Computer-Supported Cooperative Work and Groupware" (edited by Saul Greenberg; published by Academic Press in 1991), and "Intellectual Teamwork: Social and Technical Foundations of Cooperative Work" (edited by Jolene Galegher, Rob Kraut, and Carmen Egido, published by Lawrence Erlbaum Associates in 1990).

The premier academic conference is the CSCW conference, sponsored by the ACM, which has been held every second year since 1986. Besides the conventional proceedings (available from ACM Press), recent years (since 1992) have also included video proceedings. The European CSCW conferences have been held in odd years since 1989. Other conferences having a large concentration of groupware or CSCW papers include the annual ACM SIGCHI conference (dealing with user interface and human factors issues), as well as the ACM Organizational Computing Systems conference (formerly Office Information Systems). Communications of the ACM has also run special issues devoted to CSCW (December 1991, January 1993, January 1994). Dedicated journals include Computer Supported Cooperative Work (Kluwer) and Collaborative Computing (Chapman and Hall), though groupware articles can also be found in Transactions on CHI (ACM) and Transactions on Information Systems (ACM).

Finally, a couple of pointers on the Internet. Yahoo maintains a page of groupware information you can access via "Computers and Internet:Software:Groupware". Pal Malm has collected together a number of systems and projects into the "unofficial CSCW Yellow Pages." Another good page of pointers is maintained by Tom Brinck.

- *http://www.yahoo.com*

- *ftp://gorgon.tft.tele.no/pub/groupware/cscw_yp.ps.Z*

- *http://www.crew.umich.edu/~brinck/cscw.html*

Complete Program Listing

Here is the complete code for the Note Organizer program that was built up during this chapter.

```
gk_initConf $argv
pack [gk_defaultMenu .menubar] -side top -fill x

set notes(x) 20
set notes(y) 20
set notes(counter) 0
set notes(notefont) -adobe-helvetica-medium-r-normal--17-*
set notes(selectedfont) -adobe-helvetica-bold-r-normal--20-*

proc buildWindow {} {
    frame .main
    canvas .notepad -scrollregion "0 0 800 3000" \
                    -yscrollcommand ".scroll set"
    gk_scrollbar .scroll -command ".notepad yview"
    frame .controls
    entry .newidea
    button .enteridea -text "New Idea" -command addNewIdea
    pack .main -side top -fill both -expand yes
    pack .notepad -side left -fill both -expand yes -in .main
    pack .scroll -side right -fill y -in .main
    pack .controls -side top -fill x
    pack .newidea -side left -fill x -expand yes -in .controls
    pack .enteridea -side left -in .controls
    gk_initializeTelepointers
    gk_specializeWidgetTreeTelepointer .notepad
}

proc addNewIdea {} {
    global notes
    set idea [.newidea get]
    set myid [users get local.usernum]
    set id ${myid}x$notes(counter)
    incr notes(counter)
    gk_toAll doAddIdea $id [users get local.usernum] $notes(x) \
                      $notes(y) $idea
    .newidea delete 0 end
}

proc doAddIdea {id usernum x y idea} {
    global notes
    if {$usernum==[users get local.usernum]} {
        set color [users get local.color]
    } else {
        set color [users get remote.$usernum.color]
    }
    if {$color==""} {
        set color black
```

```
        }
        .notepad create text $x $y -text $idea -anchor nw \
    -font $notes(notefont) -fill $color -tags [list $id user$usernum]
        .notepad bind $id <B1-Motion> "noteDragged $id %x %y"
        .notepad bind $id <1> "selectNote $id"
        incr notes(y) 20
        if {$notes(y)>600} {
            set notes(y) 20
            incr notes(x) 100
        }
}


proc selectNote id {
    global notes
    catch {.notepad itemconfig selected -font $notes(notefont)}
    catch {.notepad dtag selected selected}
    .notepad addtag selected withtag $id
    .notepad itemconfig $id -font $notes(selectedfont)
}


proc noteDragged {id x y} {
    gk_toAll .notepad coords $id [.notepad canvasx $x] \
                                 [.notepad canvasy $y]
}


gk_bind newUserArrived {
    set newuser %U
    set name [users remote.$newuser.username]
    toplevel .new$newuser
    pack [label .new$newuser.lbl -text "$name just arrived."]
    pack [button .new$newuser.ok -text Ok \
        -command "destroy .new$newuser"]
}


gk_bind userDeleted {
    catch {
        .notepad itemconfig user%U -fill black
    }
}


gk_bind updateEntrant {
    foreach item [.notepad find all] {
        set x [lindex [.notepad coords $item] 0]
        set y [lindex [.notepad coords $item] 1]
        foreach tag [.notepad gettags $item] {
            if {[string range $tag 0 3]=="user"} {
                set usernum [string range $tag 4 end]
            } else {
                if {$tag!="selected"} {set id $tag}
            }
        }
        set idea [.notepad itemcget $item -text]
```

```
        gk_toUserNum %U doAddIdea $id $usernum $x $y $idea
    }
}

buildWindow
```

16

TkReplay: Record and Playback Tools

by Charles Crowley

Using TkReplay for Demonstrations and Regression Tests

TkReplay is a program that allows you to record your interaction with another Tcl/Tk application and replay it later. Normally you run a Tcl/Tk program interactively; you click on buttons, enter text, drag objects with the mouse, and so forth. But sometimes you may want to record an interactive session with a Tcl/Tk program and play it back later. The two main reasons to do this are for program demonstrations and for regression testing.

One kind of demonstration is an automated tour of the program, to show all of its features. A demonstration like this would be useful in marketing a program, or for showing its overall capabilities. A demonstration can also be used to explain, in detail, how to use a particular feature of the program. Demonstrations of specific functions can be incorporated into an online help or tutorial system. Such demonstrations can be used as part of the documentation of the program. Instead of just describing how to perform a task, the help system can also demonstrate how to do it. It is more effective to see the program do something than to just read about how to do it.

TkReplay can also be used in program testing. When you make a change to a program (adding a new feature or fixing a bug), you will want to test the program to make sure the change works. This is normal testing. But you also will want to test the program to make sure everything else that was working before the change still works after the change. This is called *regression testing*. A regression test suite is a collection of tests that exercise all of the features of a program. Regression testing should be done after every change, on all features of the program. This means that the regression tests will be done over and over again, once after each program modification. Automatic regression testing is fairly easy to implement with noninteractive programs. It is basically a matter of creating a set of test input files and then using a comparison program to compare the output with what is expected.

Automatic regression testing is much harder with interactive programs. TkReplay allows you to do it by recording a script of an interaction and replaying it. Recording a test script is not useful if you only use the script once, but if you use it over and over again, you can save a lot of time.

TkReplay allows you to record the regression tests and run them automatically. This means that you are more likely to run the tests every time, and to run every test. This will help you find problems sooner and isolate them more easily, since a problem that comes up must have been caused by a change you made since the last regression tests.

TkReplay works by connecting to a running Tcl/Tk application using either the `send` command or a socket. Once connected, it rebinds all the Tk events for every widget so it can record them. See the section "How TkReplay Works" for more detailed information. TkReplay works on Unix, Macs, and PCs, although you must use sockets on the latter two.

The TkReplay Main Screen

Before I go over the examples, let us look briefly at TkReplay's user interface. Figure 16-1 shows the important parts of TkReplay's main window.

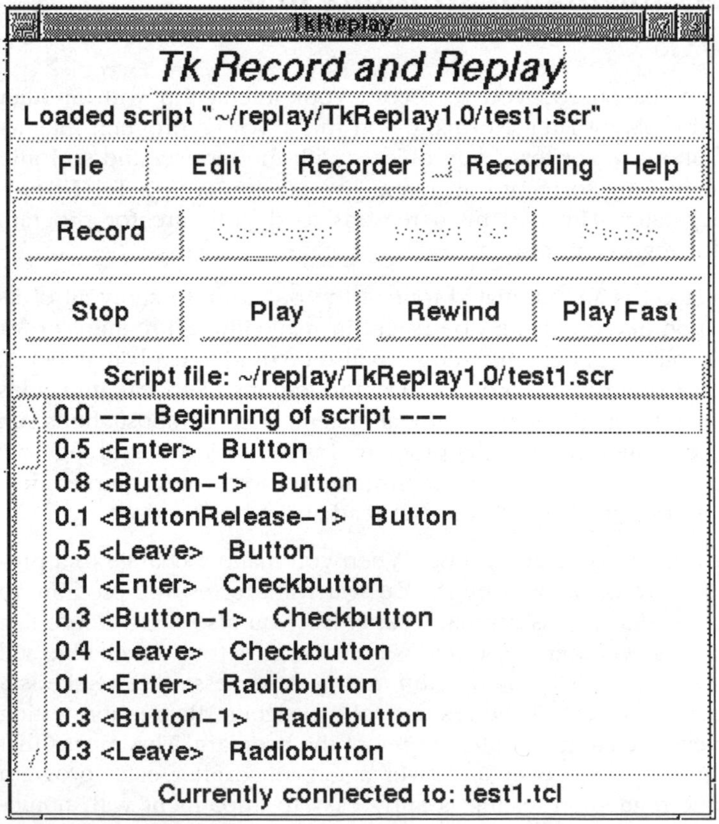

Figure 16-1: TkReplay Main Window

The *message line* provides information to the user about TkReplay's actions. If a message is especially important, it will pop up in a dialog box and require you to click on Okay. The *menu bar* contains all of the menu buttons, and also contains a checkbutton labeled Recording. This will be on when TkReplay is recording and is called the *recording light*. The next two rows of buttons are similar to the buttons on a tape recorder and are the *recorder buttons*. The Recorder menu also contains all these commands.

The next part of the screen shows the *current script*. It is useful to think of TkReplay as a tape recorder for events. The script is like the tape; you can record the script, play it, rewind it, and move around in it. Of course, since it is implemented in software, the TkReplay scripts can do more things than magnetic tape can. For example, one script can call another as a subscript.

The script has the same name as the file that contains it. The items in the script are called *events*. The script shown in Figure 16-1 is a record of a user clicking on three buttons: first a plain button, then a checkbutton, and finally a radio button. The events recorded are more detailed than you might expect. For example, you might think of pressing a button as a single event, but, actually each button press comprises four events:

- mouse pointer enters button widget
- press mouse button 1
- release mouse button 1
- mouse pointer leaves button widget

The script records the timing of these events. For example, the mouse pointer entered the button window, but the user waited 0.8 seconds to press the button. The next two buttons were pressed in 0.3 seconds. Scripts can be edited to smooth out these variations, which occur when a script is recorded (see the section "Editing Demonstration Scripts").

A record of each event is kept internally and the script listbox shows some* of the information kept about each event. For each event it shows the time (in seconds) that TkReplay will delay before it replays the event, the type of the event, and the type of widget the event occurred in. The delay is the amount of time that went by between this and the previous event (when the script was recorded).

The last line in the window indicates which applications TkReplay is connected to. The program in which events are being recorded or replayed is called the *target application*. In order to record or replay events in the target application, TkReplay must redefine some commands and define some procedures in the target application. This process is called *connecting* to the target application.

Figure 16-2 shows the TkReplay menus. The File menu enables you to save and load scripts, as well as connect to running applications and start new applications. The Edit menu lets you edit the script currently loaded into TkReplay. The Recorder menu lets you start and stop recording, and has some other features.

---

* The section "The Format of Script Files" describes all of the information kept about each event.

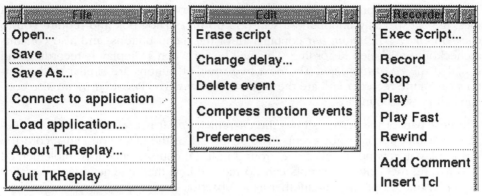

Figure 16-2: TkReplay Pull-Down Menus

First Example: Replaying a Script

In this example, you will replay a script that I have recorded. The script is stored in the file *test1.scr* and is a script for the program named *test1.tcl*. This section contains the steps to run the example.

Note: All examples should be run in the TkReplay distribution directory. This directory contains all the necessary files for these examples.

1. Start the target application: `wish test1.tcl`.

   The example program *test1.tcl* has examples of many of the Tk widgets: buttons, entry, scale, listbox, scrollbar, text, and canvas.

2. Start the TkReplay program: `wish tkreplay.tcl`.

   TkReplay will try to dynamically load a package called WarpPointer that allows it to move the mouse pointer. If it cannot load this package, it will display a message and change to pointing with a small window containing a red arrow.

3. Connect TkReplay to the target application: choose *test1.tcl* from the Connect to application submenu of the "File" menu.

   Before you can record (or play back), you have to connect TkReplay to the target application. When it connects to the target application, TkReplay uses the `send` command* to execute some code in the target application. This code sets up the record and replay facility. Connecting can take as long as 10 to 20 seconds. You will see a "watch" cursor while it is connecting and get a completion message when it is connected. In addition, the message line will display the name of the widget in the target application that is currently being processed.

4. Load the script: choose "Open..." from the "File" menu. Choose *test1.scr* from the list of files by double-clicking on it. (You will have to scroll down the list to find *test1.scr*.)

   It will take a few seconds to load the script and you will see it appear in the script list window below the recorder buttons.

---

* It can use sockets instead of the `send` command. See the section "Problems You May Have In Replaying" for more information ().

5. Replay the script: click on the Play button.

The replay will take a minute or two. The mouse will move to the widgets as events happen in them (or a small window with a red arrow in it will point to the widget). The event that is being replayed will be highlighted in the listing of the script in the TkReplay window.

Problems You May Have In Replaying

It can be very frustrating if you have tried the example I just presented and find that it's not working the way it should. In the following sections I'll give you some quick fixes you can apply to common problems.

You Are Running on a PC Or Macintosh, So send Does Not Work

The examples are set up to use the Tk send command, which only works on Unix systems. TkReplay can also use sockets for communication, but you have to set things up a little differently if you want to use sockets. The TkReplay distribution will contain a *README* file telling you what to do to make these scripts work using sockets.

You Get An Error Message That the X Server Is Insecure

By default, TkReplay uses the Tk send command which only works on secure X servers. You can either make your server secure or you can use sockets instead of send (see the *README* file in the TkReplay distribution).

The Mouse Does Not Move

The basic *wish* program does not have a command to move the mouse pointer (usually called pointer warping). Demonstrations look better when the pointer moves, so I have included WarpPointer, a loadable extension to *wish*,* which provides a command to move the mouse pointer.

If you cannot or do not want to use the WarpPointer extension, TkReplay includes an option to point with a small window containing a red arrow. This window is used to point to the widget where an event is being replayed. See the section "Replaying Mouse Pointer Motions" for information on this.

The Mouse Movement Is Jerky

It takes a little time for TkReplay to find the next event and send it to the target application. For short mouse movements, the time to find the next event is longer than the time the mouse movement takes, so the mouse motion appears jerky.

Stopping a Replay In the Middle

When a script is playing, it constantly moves the mouse to the widgets as they are replayed. As a result, it is not easy to regain control and halt the replay in the

---

* WarpPointer works only with the X Window System and Unix.

middle of a script.* To deal with this problem, TkReplay recognizes two user events that will halt a replay: pressing the left mouse button and pressing the Escape key. Each of these will halt the replay after the end of the current event. This may take a little while if TkReplay has to move the mouse some distance, or if the delay before the event is long. But the replay will halt as soon as the current event completes. After a halt you can start the replay again from where you left off just by pressing Play (or Play Fast) again.

Replaying Faster

Each event that is replayed has a time delay field. TkReplay delays for this amount of time before the event is replayed. You can use the the Play Fast button to speed up a replay. Play Fast causes TkReplay to ignore the delays and replay the script as fast as it can.

Try doing this with the example you just replayed: rewind the script (press Rewind) and press Play Fast (assuming, of course, that TkReplay is still running and is still connected to *test1.tcl*).

Changing the Mouse Speed

Another way to make a replay go faster is to speed up the mouse movements. I have recorded a script to demonstrate the mouse speeds.

1. Be sure that TkReplay and *test1.tcl* are running and that TkReplay is connected to *test1.tcl*.

2. Load the script: choose "Open..." from the "File" menu and then choose *test1.speed* from the list of files by double-clicking on it. Note all the delays are 0.0 so the mouse movement time will show up better.

3. Open the user preferences dialog box: choose "Preferences..." from the "Edit" menu.

4. Select the slowest mouse speed: click on the Slow radiobutton.

5. Replay the script: click on the Play button.

6. Change the mouse speed to Medium, Fast,Very fast, and Warp, in turn, and play the script after each change. (Warp speed jumps the mouse directly to where it is going with no visible motion in between.)

You will see that the script plays several times faster on the fastest mouse speed.

More Automatic Replaying

TkReplay has command-line options that allow you to request many of the setup actions we performed manually in the previous example. First, exit from TkReplay and *test1.tcl* so you can see how it works starting from scratch. The command:

---

* User interface experts recommend against letting a program move the mouse. I felt that TkReplay was a special case where it was justified since it is replaying an interaction that used the mouse. But to see why they make such a recommendation, try to press the Stop button while a script is being replayed. The mouse keeps being grabbed away from you.

```
wish tkreplay.tcl -app test1.tcl
```

starts wish and then executes and connects to the application *test1.tcl*. The command:

```
wish tkreplay.tcl -script test1.scr
```

starts *wish* and loads the script *test1.scr*. Finally you can use the command:

```
wish tkreplay.tcl -app test1.tcl -script test1.scr -play
```

to start *wish*, execute the application *test1.tcl*, connect to *test1.tcl*, load the script *test1.scr*, and play the script.

Replaying Mouse Pointer Motion

TkReplay does not record every mouse movement when it records a script. It does record the mouse position when the mouse pointer enters or leaves a widget, and when a mouse button is pressed or released. A script can be replayed without any mouse motion. The script records the effects of the mouse motions during recording, so there is no need for the mouse to actually move during replay. When a regression test is being replayed, it is common to not show any movement of the mouse pointer. However, for demonstrations, it is useful to show the mouse moving around from widget to widget. This helps to direct the user's attention to the widget where events are occurring. You can request that TkReplay show the mouse movements during replay. It will not show all the original mouse movements if they were irregular, but will move the mouse smoothly between the mouse pointer locations it has recorded for events.

This mouse motion can be a cause of jerkiness in the replay if the mouse has entered and left a widget without doing anything. The enter and leave events are always recorded, and so the mouse moves to that widget even though no important events occur there. These extraneous widget enter and leave events can be edited out of a script.

A checkbutton on the Preferences dialog box allows the user to decide whether the mouse pointer will be moved during replay. This option is ignored if the Warp-Pointer extension is not loaded.

TkReplay provides an alternative way of pointing to widgets if you cannot (or do not want to) use mouse movement. TkReplay will create a small window with a red arrow it in and move this arrow so it points to the widget where the next event will occur. You can turn on the red arrow option from the Preferences box also. You can use both mouse motion and the red arrow, either one, or neither of them.

Second Example: Recording a Script

Now that you have seen how a script is replayed, we will look at how a script is recorded.

1. Be sure you have exited TkReplay and *test1.tcl*.

2. Load *wish*, start *test1.tcl*, and connect to it: `wish tkreplay.tcl -app test1.tcl`.

---

3. Start recording: click on the Record button.

4. Do some things with *test1.tcl*: click on some buttons, enter some text, scroll some lists, etc.

5. Stop recording: click on the Stop button.

6. Rewind the script: click on the Rewind button.

7. Replay the script: click on the Play button. (Just to see that it recorded as you expected.)

8. Save the script as *xx.scr*: choose "Save as..." from the "File" menu and type in the file name *xx.scr*. (You can, of course, choose any name you want.)

When you start recording, the "recording light" in the menu bar goes on. When you perform some actions using *test1.tcl*, you see the events appear in the listbox showing the script you are recording. When you are done recording, stop the recording, rewind the script, and play it. At the end, save the file so you can use it again.

You can replay the script you just saved in one step:

```
wish tkreplay.tcl -app test1.tcl -script xx.scr -play
```

If you want the replay to go as fast as possible, try this.

```
wish tkreplay.tcl -app test1.tcl -script xx.scr \
                -mousespeed warp -playfast
```

Recording Comments in a Script

Sometimes, it is useful to provide commentary for the person replaying the script. This is used in demonstrations to describe what is being demonstrated, and in regression tests to inform the tester what to look for.

Adding a comment is done by pressing the Comment button while recording a script. Redo the recording you just made, but, right after you start recording, press the Comment button. A dialog box will come up requesting you to enter the comment. Enter as much text as you want in the text widget. After you have entered the text, press the Text Done button, which records the comment and text in the script. Then continue recording by doing other actions. When you want to remove the comment from the screen, press the Dismiss Comment button. During replay, the comment will be displayed when you first requested it (with the Comment button), and will continue to be displayed until it gets to the point in the replay where you pressed the Dismiss Comment button. Stop recording, rewind the script, and play it to see how the comment behaves during replay.

The Comment dialog box has a checkbutton labeled Wait for user to check Okay. If this is checked, during replay, the comment will appear and the replay will pause until the user clicks the Okay button. This is for comments that you want to be sure are read by the user before you continue.

Third Example: A Demonstration

This example illustrates the use of TkReplay to play a demonstration. It is a demonstration of a simple text editor (called *Ste*) based on the Tk text widget. I have recorded a demonstration that shows its features. The demonstration has comments to explain what it is doing.

1. Start *wish*, load *ste.tcl* with one argument (the name of the text file is *ste.ex0*), and load the script *ste.demo.scr*:

```
wish tkreplay.tcl -app "ste.tcl ste.ex0" -script ste.demo.scr.
```

2. This demonstration will pop up comments in the upper-left corner of the screen, so rearrange the windows so that area is clear and TkReplay and *Ste* do not overlap each other.

3. Replay the script: click on the Play button.

The argument to `-app` is in double quotes because it consists of the name of the wish script (*ste.tcl*) and an argument to the wish script (*ste.ex0*). These are separated by spaces, but I want them to be a single argument on the command line, so I use double quotes around them.

Fourth Example: A Regression Test

To show a regression test, we will use the same example program, *Ste*. I have recorded a test that adds a line of text, does some simple editing (with cut, copy, and paste), and saves the file. Then it compares the contents of the file with the correct version. If they are the same, we have tested the cut, copy, paste, and save operations.

1. Enter: `wish tkreplay.tcl -app "ste.tcl ste.ex1" -script ste.test.scr -play`.

2. When the dialog box pops up, click on Okay.

You will see the edits being performed, and then some Tcl code will be executed that will perform the comparison. A standard Tk dialog box will pop up showing you the results of the comparison. The replay will be suspended until you click Okay in this dialog box.

Events and Pseudoevents

Each user action is called an *event* and is recorded in the script. Each user event in a Tcl/Tk program causes an event handler (a piece of Tcl code) to be executed in response to the event. The documentation for the `bind` command lists all the events that are defined in Tk. During recording, the text of those event handlers is stored (in an array), and during replay is executed again. Some events in a TkReplay script are called *pseudoevents* because they are not the result of a user action intended for the target program. Rather, they are user actions intended for the TkReplay program itself and are used to control the replay. TkReplay defines nine pseudoevents.

- **Pause**: Stop the replay. Generated by pressing the Pause button. Pressing the Play button starts replaying the script again from where it was paused.

- **Execute Script**: Execute a subscript at this point in the replay. Generated by selecting the "Exec script..." command on the "Recorder" menu.

- **Execute Tcl:** Execute a piece of Tcl code at this point in the replay. Generated by selecting the "Insert Tcl" command on the "Recorder" menu.

- **Load Application:** Load an application for replay. Generated by selecting the "Load application..." command on the "File" menu.

- **Connect to Application:** Connect to an application for replay. Generated by selecting a name from the cascade submenu of the "Connect to application" command on the "File" menu.

- **BeginComment:** Create a comment box. Generated by selecting the "Add Comment" command on the "Recorder" menu or by pressing the Comment button.

- **EndComment:** Remove the comment box. Generated when the user dismisses a comment box during a recording.

- **Beginning of script:** A marker for the beginning of the script. All scripts have this as their first event. The beginning of the script pseudoevent is inserted automatically into scripts by TkReplay. The user cannot insert one.

- **End of script:** A marker for the end of the script. All scripts have this as their last event. The end of script pseudoevent is inserted automatically into scripts by TkReplay. The user cannot insert one.

These pseudoevents are recorded in scripts just like any other event but they are handled directly by TkReplay and are not sent to a connected target application.

Loading and Saving Scripts

At all times, there is exactly one script loaded into TkReplay. This is called the *current script*. If you start TkReplay with no `-script` command-line argument, then the script is given the default name "Unnamed." The current script is shown in the script listbox in the TkReplay main window. The script name (taken from the file name it was loaded from) is displayed above the script listbox.

After you record a script, you will want to save it for later replay. "Save" on the "File" menu will save the current script under its current name. If you want to change the name of the script and then save it, choose "Save as..." from the "File" menu. A file selection box comes up that allows you to enter the new name.

To load an existing script for replay, choose "Open..." from the "File" menu. Open brings up a file selection box that allows you to select the name of the file you want to load in. Opening a script erases the current script.

The File Selection Box

"Open...", "Save As...", "Load application...", and "Exec Script" all bring up a file selection box. Figure 16-3 shows the box.

The top line is a message that tells you whether it is a load, save, load app, or exec script. Next in the window is a scrolled list of the files in the current directory. The directories are listed first (in alphabetical order) and have a slash appended to each directory name. The regular files are listed (also in alphabetical order) after the directories. When you click on a filename in the listbox it is inserted into the text entry box. You can also type the filename into the text entry box, or edit the filename already there.

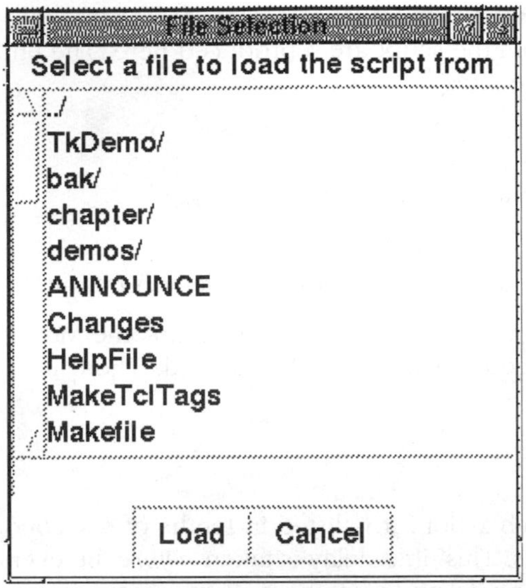

Figure 16-3: TkReplay File Selection Box

Clicking the left mouse button selects the file or directory name and copies it in the text entry box. Double-clicking on a filename in the listbox chooses that file. Double-clicking on a directory name in the listbox changes the file list to the files in that directory. The `../` entry is always first and lets you go up one level in the directory hierarchy.

Clicking the button (titled Load, Save, Load App, or Call Script) selects the filename in the text box. Clicking on the Cancel button cancels the operation.

Editing Demonstration Scripts

It is difficult to record a demonstration exactly the way you want it the first time you try. After you have a recording that contains all the parts you want, you can edit the saved script to remove unneeded actions, change the time delays, and smooth out the flow of the mouse. It is easiest to do this with a text editor. In this section, I describe the types of edits you might want to make. In the section "Editing Scripts" I will describe how to make these edits.

I have recorded a script *test1.preedit* that contains a number of typical problems with a first recording. I will use it as an example in this section. The final version is in *test1.postedit*. You should play each of them now to see the difference. They both assume you have loaded and connected to *test1.tcl*.

Removing Unneeded Enter and Leave Events

Sometimes, during a recording, you inadvertently enter a widget, but don't do anything in it. This shows up in the script as an Enter event followed immediately by a Leave event (with perhaps some Motion events in between, depending on whether the widget binds the Motion events). If you delete these two events (and the Motion events between them) the demonstration will flow more smoothly.

Look at *test1.preedit*. On lines 5 and 6, we have events that enter and then immediately leave a radiobutton. The lines from the script are reproduced here. The end of each line has been edited to make the lines fit.

```
InsertAction {11} {test1.tcl} {Bind,Radiobutton,<Enter>} \
                {{W .r2button} ...}
InsertAction {4} {test1.tcl} {Bind,Radiobutton,<Leave>} \
                {{W .r2button} ...}
```

These lines can be deleted because they are not relevant to the demonstration.

If the widget binds to Motion events, you might get an Enter event, some Motion events, and then a Leave event. This sequence can also be deleted. There is no example of this in *test1.preedit*.

Editing the Time Delays

The time delay is the second field in each action. It is listed in tenths of a second. For example, 30 represents three seconds. This time delay is taken *before* the event on this line occurs. Look for especially long delays (anything over two seconds) and see if you think they are really necessary. You do not have to leave in delays for program actions to complete (like a window to open), because TkReplay waits for them automatically. The main reason for a long delay is to allow the user to read a comment you have put up.

You might want to lengthen some delays to emphasize the action. For example, you could leave a button down for one or two seconds to emphasize that it is being pushed.

In *test1.preedit*, there are a number of unnecessarily long delays. The first few are on lines 1, 3, 5, 7, 8, 12, ... We can shorten all these delays without compromising the demonstration.

Editing Consecutive Motion Events

Often a script will have a number of Motion (that is, mouse motion) events in a row. This is because Motion events are reported regularly as the mouse is moved. During the replay, these extra Motion events can slow down the demonstration and make it appear jerky. It is often better to eliminate all but the last of a sequence of Motion events. TkReplay moves the mouse smoothly from place to place so there is usually no need for intermediate motion events. Choosing Compress Motion Events on the Edit menu eliminates all but the last event in all sequences of Motion events. You can also do this with a text editor, but the command is faster and more reliable.

Try loading *test1.preedit* and executing the `Compress motion events` command. You will find that it drastically shortens the script. You might also try playing the script before and after it is compressed.

There are a few cases where you do not want to eliminate all extra motion events. This is when the mouse motion is causing something visible to happen. For example, in my demonstration of the text editor *Ste*, I show how to "scan" the file by holding down the middle mouse button and moving the mouse up and down. If I eliminate all these events, the scanning will not happen at all. Even if I eliminate all but the last event in one direction, the demonstration will not play smoothly since the scan happens too fast. What I did for that demonstration was to record the actual Motion events and then fix them up in the script. I eliminated ones that were too close together, and spaced the others out evenly. I did this by editing the "y" mouse location fields in the events.

When we ran `Compress motion events` on *test1.preedit*, we eliminated a lot of useless Motion events, but we also made it so that the scale widget was moved from 0 to 39 in a single mouse movement. This might be too fast to observe, so we should put back a few of the intermediate events but space them evenly. You can see the result of this in *test1.postedit* on lines 11 to 15.

To summarize, you will want to eliminate extra Motion events unless they are Motion events with a button held down (for example "B1-Motion"). For these, you may want to even out the locations of the events and eliminate ones that are too close together.

Creating Regression Tests

Regression tests are quite different from demonstrations since you just want the effect of the actions and don't care about things like the mouse movements. In addition, you will want to check to be sure the results are what they should be.

Regression Test Checks

Regression tests are generally a series of individual test cases. For each test case, the program performs some actions and then checks the results. TkReplay lets you perform checks through pseudoevents that consist of arbitrary Tcl code inserted into your script. The Tcl code checks to see if the results are correct.

While recording the script, you choose Insert Tcl when you want to perform a check. This brings up a dialog box where you can enter the code. Do not worry about getting the code exactly right since it is simple to edit it later with your favorite text editor. In fact, you might just enter a Tcl comment describing what the code should do and enter all the actual code when you edit the script later. The code must check the results of the test case. This might be getting some text out of a widget and comparing it with the expected result, comparing two files, checking to see if a list contains the right things, and so forth. You can display the results of the test to the user, write them out to a file, or do both. Writing to a file will create a record of the test results. You can insert comments and headers by adding `Insert Tcl` commands in the script that write these comments and headers to the test results file.

In the example regression test script *ste.test.scr*, I made some edits, saved the file, and compared the results with what they should have been.

Writing Regression Test Checks

Here is the regression test check code pseudoevent from *ste.text.scr*.

```
InsertAction {30} {ThisApp} {ExecTcl} {{
set editedText [tkrsend ste.tcl .ste0.textframe.text get 1.0 end]
set fid [open ste.ex1.check]
set checkText [read $fid]
close $fid
```

```
if {[string compare $editedText $checkText] == 0} {
    set result "Test 1 was passed."
} else {
    set result "Test 1 failed. <$editedText>!=<$checkText>"
}
tk_dialog .rtest "Results of test 1" "\
[set result]
Click on Okay to continue the tests" "" 0 Okay
} 1}
```

This is a single Tcl command which inserts the event (the "action") into the script. The first line inserts an event of type `ExecTcl` with a delay of 3 seconds. The last line contains the constant 1, which tells TkReplay to execute this code within TkReplay. If the constant were 0, TkReplay would send this code to the application for execution. It is important which place the code is executed. Since we are executing this code within TkReplay, we have to send a message to the application to get the contents of the text widget. This is done on the second line. Note that we have to know the name of the text widget. The rest of the Tcl code compares the contents of the text widget with what it is supposed to be and reports the results.

The call to `tkrsend` is used so that TkReplay will communicate with the application using either sockets or the `send` command, whichever is being used in this configuration of TkReplay.

In this example, we report the results with a dialog box. It is more common to write the results to a text file for later analysis. But, because we did use a dialog box, this code *must* be executed within TkReplay and not the application. The reason is that user events in the application are ignored during replay, so we would not be able to click on the Okay button of the dialog box. If we wrote the results to a file, then we could execute this code in the application. In that case, we could access the text widget directly and not have to send the command over to the application.

Editing Regression Test Scripts

When you replay a regression test script, you will probably want to change the user preferences so that neither the mouse pointer nor the red arrow will move.

You will also want to edit your regression test script to eliminate unnecessary events. This will include most Motion events and unnecessary Enter and Leave events. Take care deleting Enter and Leave events, however, since they sometimes do important processing, and eliminating them will prevent the script from replaying correctly.

Editing Scripts

TkReplay has some simple facilities for editing scripts, but any substantial modifications are more easily done with a text editor. We'll describe TkReplay's facilities first.

Editing Scripts Within TkReplay

The Edit menu contains the script editing commands. If you are going to do several editing commands at a time, it is helpful to "tear off" the Edit menu so it stays on the screen while you are editing. The "Erase script" command erases the entire script. The "Compress motion events" command was described earlier in the section on "Editing Demonstration Scripts." It compresses a sequence of Motion events by deleting all consecutive Motion events except the last one.

The next two editing commands are executed on the event that is currently selected in the script list. Click on an event to select it. You can select only one event at a time.

The "Change delay" command brings up a dialog box for changing the delay before the event. Type in a new delay and press the button Apply or the Return key to change the delay. Pressing the Cancel button will dismiss the dialog box without changing the event.

The "Delete event" command deletes the selected event.

The Format of Script Files

In order to edit script files, you need to know how they are structured. Look at the file *ste.demo.scr* with a text editor to see the format. The first thing you will note is that many of the lines are quite long. There is one event per line and most events have a lot of detail. Here is a sample line:

```
InsertAction {4} {test1.tcl} {Bind,Checkbutton,<Leave>} \
    {{W .cbutton} {x 83} {y 31} {Args {}}}
```

The actual line in a script file would not have a \- continuation. We put the continuation here so it fits on this page. Each line contains five items:

1. The fixed string `InsertAction`: Each line is a Tcl command, a call to the procedure `InsertAction`.

2. The time delay (`{4}` in the sample line): In tenths of a second and inside curly braces.

3. The name of the Tk program the action came from (`{test1.tcl}` in the sample line): In most scripts this is the same for every line, but it is possible to connect to two Tk programs at a time and record a script with events from both of them. See the section "Connecting to Two Target Applications."

4. Event identifier (`{Bind,Checkbutton,<Leave>}` in the sample line): This uniquely identifies the event handler script to execute when replaying the event. It consists of:

   a. `Bind`: a fixed string

   b. Bind tag: `Button`, `CheckButton`, `Text`, `Entry`, etc. This can be a widget class name, a widget name, or any bind tag. These tags define sets of widgets and can be defined by Tk (for widget names and widget classes) or by the Tk programmer (for other bind tags).

c. Event specification: The Tk event sequence, like a mouse button press, motion event, enter, leave, key, etc. This field is a little more complex for text and canvas widgets.

5. Event details (`{{W .cbutton} {x 83} {y 31} {Args {}}}` in the sample line): This is a list of pairs. Each pair contains an event variable name and a value for that event variable. The most common event variables are:

a. `W`: the name of the widget the event occurred in.

b. `x`: the x coordinate of the event, relative to W.

c. `y`: the y coordinate of the event, relative to W.

d. `Args`: some extra arguments, widget dependent.

Script files are read in by sourcing them as Tcl scripts.

Editing Scripts with a Text Editor

Sometimes it's hard to get exactly the behavior you want by interacting with TkReplay. Nothing prevents you from tweaking the scripts by hand, and this is the best recourse for certain subtle changes.

Editing Within a Single Event

You should not change the `InsertAction` field.

You can change the time delay field to another time. Just remember that it is in tenths of a second, not in seconds.

You should not change the Tk program field or the event identifier field.

You should not change most of the subfields in the event details field. You can change the `x` and `y` (or `X` and `Y`) subfields in order to change the location of the event. This is useful for modifying the path of the mouse inside a widget.

Editing the Events As Whole Lines

You can remove parts of the demonstration by deleting lines from the script. Or you can insert a `#` in front of them to make them into comments. This makes it easy to insert them again if you discover it was a mistake to leave them out.

You can move events around by moving them with a text editor. This will change the order in which things occur. Sequences of events form logical units, so you should be careful as you delete events or move them around. A useful unit is the sequence of events between the Enter event for a widget and the corresponding Leave event. If you move or delete events in these units, you should not have any problems.

Calling Scripts from Scripts

When you are recording a script, you can insert a pseudoevent that calls another script as a subscript. During replay the subscript is loaded in and executed. When it has finished, the original script is loaded back in and resumes replaying from where it called the subscript. Scripts can be nested any number of levels; that is, a subscript can call another subscript, and so on.

Subscripts make script handling easier since you only have to record and edit small scripts. It allows you to record your scripts in small sections and combine them with other scripts in various ways. Let's look at an example using *test1.tcl*.

```
    wish tkreplay.tcl -app test1.tcl -script test1.subscripts.scr \
  -play
```

The script *test1.subscripts.scr* puts up some comments and calls three subscripts (*test1.buttons.scr*, *test1.etc1.scr*, and *test1.etc2.scr*). I have added comments to emphasize the change in scripts, but in your demonstrations you can just go from one subscript to the next without delays. The only indication of the subscript calls is that the contents of the script listbox change.

Using Subscripts To Organize Large Scripts

Large scripts are unwieldy to manage. If any part becomes obsolete, you have to modify the entire script. It is easier to organize your demonstrations and regression tests using subscripts.

Here is how I created the subscript demonstration.

1. Start TkReplay with `wish -app test1.tcl`.

2. Record the buttons part of the demonstration.

3. Use Save As... to save it as *test1.buttons.scr*.

4. Erase the script.

5. Record the middle part of the demonstration.

6. Use Save As... to save it as *test1.etc1.scr*.

7. Erase the script.

8. Record the last part of the demonstration.

9. Use Save As... to save it as *test1.etc2.scr*.

10. Erase the script.

11. Start recording, put in a comment, exec script *test1.buttons.scr*, then subscript *test1.etc1.scr* and subscript *test1.etc2.scr*.

12. Use Save As... to save the demonstration as *test1.subscripts.scr*.

The scripts that just call subscripts are simple enough that you can just create them yourself in a text editor rather than recording them. Or you can copy one such script and modify it to call different subscripts.

Using Subscripts In the Tk Widget Demo

As an example of using subscripts, I have created a set of scripts that use each part of the Tk widget demo. To try these scripts, start up the Tk widget demo (found in the *lib/demos* directory). The scripts are all in the *TkDemo* subdirectory of the TkReplay distribution directory.

Each script whose name ends in a digit exercises one of the Tk demos. The digits are the numbers in the lists in the main window of the Tk demo program. These are the only scripts that contain actual user input events. For convenience, we'll call these *digit subscripts*. All the other scripts consist solely of calls on the digit subscripts. Scripts ending in *.all* combine all the demos in the group. The script *Tk.all.all* combines all the *.all* demos and uses two levels of subscripts. The script *Tk.sample* performs one demo per group. It uses the same digit subscripts as *Tk.all.all*, but combines them in a different way (and uses fewer of them).

Connecting To Two Target Applications

TkReplay allows you to connect to more than one target application at a time. Just connect to each one in sequence. Once recording is turned on, events from all the target applications will be recorded. As an example, I have recorded a script with two target applications.

```
wish tkreplay.tcl -app test2.tcl -app test3.tcl \
-script twotargets.scr -play
```

How TkReplay Works

TkReplay records a script by getting control whenever a user event occurs. When it gets control, TkReplay records the event in the script and then does the normal event processing that should happen when that event occurs. When replaying a script, TkReplay reads the events in the script and then replays the event processing that was recorded.

In order to get control at the right times, TkReplay redefines the binding of every tag of every widget. This has two effects on the user. First, the rebinding is done while connecting to the application, which is why connecting takes a while. Notice the longer delay on the Text widget, which has many bindings. Second, the response to each event takes longer because TkReplay's binding is called first, and then TkReplay calls the original binding. This is why response is slow after connecting to an application.

While a script is replaying, user input events in the target application are ignored by TkReplay. Only the events recorded in the script are allowed to occur. The exception to this is that the left mouse button and the Escape key are detected and cause the demonstration to pause.

What Exactly Is Replayed?

An event is "replayed" by calling the Tcl script (the "event handler") that the event would have triggered. The event itself (for example, a mouse button press) does not actually occur. This could be done, but it would require an X server extension (the XTest extension). As a result, if you use TkReplay to record another instance of TkReplay the resulting recording will contain no user events. Since the user events do not actually occur when replaying a script, the second TkReplay will see no events to detect and record.

An exception to this is mouse Motion events. The WarpPointer extension makes calls to the X procedure `XWarpPointer`, which generates actual Motion events.

Since we are replaying, they are ignored and serve only to move the mouse, not to trigger Enter or Leave events. In any case, the Motion events caused by *wish* are not exactly those that occurred during recording. In fact, TkReplay will cause different Motion events to occur for the same script depending on the mouse speed selected.

The Tcl event handler script is executed at replay time. The effects of the script are not recorded at record time and are not simulated at replay time. Instead, the script executes once at record time and then again at replay time. The results of the script can be different these two times, if the situation is different. For example, if a directory is read in and displayed in a list, the contents of that directory at replay time are displayed, not the contents at recording time. If these are different, then the replay may not work as expected. See the section "Tips for Making Recordings" for more information on this.

Extending TkReplay To Work with Other Widgets

As it is written, TkReplay works only with the basic Tk widgets. It will work with mega-widgets as long as they are composed of basic Tk widgets. If you want to work with a new widget, TkReplay needs know what commands create the widgets. There is a list of all the widget creation commands in *rebind.tcl* (search for the string `WidgetCreateCommands`). Each widget creation command on the list is renamed and defined to a new procedure that creates the widget and then rebinds all its bindings. If you add the widget creation command of a new widget, then it will also be redefined, and you should be able to record and replay interactions with interfaces using it.

If you have a new widget that has its own internal binding system (like the pad++ widget (see *http://www.cs.unm.edu/pad*++), then you will have to do more work. Use the code that deals with the canvas widget in *rebind.tcl* (search for the strings `RedefineCanvasCommand`, `RebindCanvasBinding`, and *RebindSpecialCases*). If the binding system is similar to Tk's, then you should be able to copy and modify those lines for the new widget.

I have included a few options in the preferences dialog box, but it is possible to make many other changes with simple modifications to the source code. Each place where a modification is likely has been marked with a comment starting with the string `USER OPTION`.

Limitations of TkReplay

TkReplay can record and replay almost all Tk applications, but it does have problems in some areas.

Timing Issues

On replay, TkReplay takes an unpredictable amount of time to do the processing required to read and replay scripts. The time is unpredictable since you do not know the machine you are running on, the load it will encounter, the state of the virtual memory, and so forth. This time is implicitly added to the delay that occurs before each event. As a result, the replay is slower than the recording. Any events that depend on precise timing will not replay correctly. The time between a button press and release will be longer than when it was recorded.

Some interactions depend on how long a button is held down. For example, when you hold down a scroll button it begins to *autoscroll*. While recording, TkReplay records how many autoscrolls occur, and replays exactly that number on replay, so the amount of scrolling is the same. Other time delay dependent interactions are handled the same way.*

Correct Replay Depends On the Environment

TkReplay assumes that all significant input to a program comes from user events. This is not always true, and to the extent that it is not true, TkReplay will not be able to record and replay accurately. Let's take a simple example. During recording, you type a filename into a file selection dialog box in the target application. Suppose that you then delete the file and replay the program. Of course, it will not be able to read the file since it has been deleted. The state of the file system is really an input to the program. If that state is not sufficiently the same, then the script cannot be replayed successfully.

We can easily come up with an example of a program that will not replay correctly. An example is the program *spoiler.tcl*. This program looks at the current time and names a button *.even* or *.odd* depending on whether the minute value is divisible by two. The script *spoiler.scr* was recorded *spoiler.tcl* in an odd minute, and so it has recorded the button name as *.odd*. Wait until the minute is even (use `date` to see the minute), and then *startspoiler.tcl*. Then, start TkReplay, connect *tospoiler.tcl*, and open the script *spoiler.scr*. When you try to replay it, it will fail because the button name will be wrong.

Of course, this program was designed to thwart TkReplay, but it is possible that a program might do similar things for legitimate reasons and therefore will not work with TkReplay.

Tips for Making Recordings

Watch out for a few things that will cause your scripts not to replay correctly. The biggest problem is when the state of the system is not the same when you replay as it was when you made the recording. The replay repeats the events exactly as you recorded them and will fail if the events do not do the right thing in the changed conditions at replay time.

Here are some of the problems that can occur.

1. Scrolled lists may not be in the same position on replay as they were when you made the recording. For example, suppose a script scrolls a list down, but does not scroll it back up again. If you replay the script twice, the scrolled list will not be at the beginning of the list when the second replay starts. Or suppose you record several small scripts, one at a time, and one scripts scrolls a list down, while the next script scrolls it back up. If you

---

* This is done by redefining the `after` command.

replay these scripts in a different order, the scrolled list will not be where the script expects it to be.

Solution: There are two solutions to the scrolled list problem. One is always to open the window afresh before you use the scrolled list. This way the list will be created each time and will always be at the beginning. Sometimes, this is not possible. A better solution is to click very near the top of the scrollbar several times before you begin using it. If it is scrolled down, this will ensure that it is scrolled back to the top. If it is already at the top, these extra clicks on the scrollbar slider will just be ignored. This way you can assume the scroll bar is at the top of the list.

2. The same thing can happen for scales as scripts. They can be in a different starting position at replay time, because different subscripts were played.

Solution: The same as for scrolled lists.

3. Sometimes, a program dynamically changes the contents of a window. For example, there may be some entry fields that are not commonly used. Normally a button named *.w.moreoptions* with label "Show More Options" is put in the window. When that button is pressed, it is replaced by a new frame containing the seldom used fields. If this part of the window is in one state when you record a script and another when you replay it, the windows you want events to occur in will not exist.

Solution: Here you use a variation of the procedure used for scrolled lists. Try to click in the places that will bring things back to a standard configuration, if they are not already there, but will be ignored if things are already in the standard configuration.

4. Most programs make lists of files in a directory as part of a file selection box. If the current directory is different on replay from what it was when recording, a different list will display and clicking in the list will have different effects. Or if the current directory is the same, but the contents of that directory have changed, you will get similar problems. TkReplay records that, for example, the 15th item in the list was selected, not what is in that item. Even if the list changes, the 15th item will still be chosen.

Solution: This problem is hard to fix. You just have to be sure the current directory and the files in the directory are the same. You could insert Tcl code to check this and issue a warning if the current directory or the files in it are not as you expect them to be. Another solution is to type in the file-name directly rather than selecting it from a scrolled list.

5. Program generates other dynamic lists. For example, a program might make a list of all the processes currently running in the system. These dynamically generated lists may be different at replay time from what they were at record time.

Solution: The same solutions apply to all dynamic lists as to file lists. Try to be sure the lists are the same. Check them with Tcl code to be sure. Type the names in directly instead of choosing them from a list.

The TkReplay Distribution

You can get the latest distribution of TkReplay from my software distribution page: *http://www.cs.unm.edu/~crowley/software.html*. Please send comments and bug reports to Charles Crowley at *crowley@cs.unm.edu*.

TkReplay works on Unix, Macs, and PCs that support *wish*.

17

Configuration Management

One of the least glamorous but most important parts of any serious programming project is configuration management. In case you are not familiar with the term, *Configuration Management* refers to the process of maintaining your software in such a way that you can track the contents of your software releases and reliably recreate these releases. This can be especially tricky when managing multiple versions and multiple extensions. This chapter shows you how to keep your Tcl environment under control.

Getting the Software

The first task of configuration management is getting some software to configure. There are several ways of doing this.

1. On the CD with this book.

   Perhaps the simplest method is to copy the software from the CD that accompanies this book. The extension sets discussed in the book have been pre-built for a number of Unix platforms, and the source distributions are included as well.

2. From the Internet.

   The most up-to-date versions of Tcl, Tk, and their extension sets are stored at the various Internet FTP sites. Information on the most current sites are available in the Tcl newsgroup *comp.lang.tcl*. At the time of publication, the official Tcl FTP site is *ftp.smli.com:/pub/tcl* and the contributed sources archive is at *ftp.neosoft.com:/pub/tcl*.

   O'Reilly and Associates will keep its web and ftp sites up to date with Tcl/Tk and all the software on the CD. The official web site for this book is at *http://www.ora.com/info/tcltk*.

3. From a CD-ROM vendor.

   A number of CD-ROM vendors sell copies of the Tcl archives.

Before you go to a lot of trouble to obtain and install Tcl, Tk, or one of the extension sets, double-check your system and see if anyone else at your site has already installed it. In addition to saving yourself some work, you might make contact with someone who shares your interest in Tcl.

Building and Installing

Note: There is a *README* file on the CD indicating how to install the binaries on that disk.

There are five basic steps in building Tcl and Tcl extensions. This sounds like a lot of work, but in practice everything goes pretty smoothly. Tcl and Tk can usually be built and installed in less than an hour. Most of the time is spent compiling, so of course faster machines will take less time than slower machines. The steps are:

- **Unpacking:** Loading the software into your source directory, usually by extracting from a compressed tar file. If any patches are available, you will want to apply them at this time.

- **Configuring:** Tcl, Tk, and most extensions use the *autoconf* program from the Gnu project. Configuration files generated by *autoconf* can test for and adopt to a wide variety of operating system and compiler dependencies.

- **Building:** Once you have configured your system, you will then compile the source code, build libraries, and link executables like *tclsh* and *wish*.

- **Testing:** One of the great features of Tcl and Tk is its extensive array of regression tests. There are over 1700 individual tests between the two packages. Most extension packages follow the Tcl's lead and provide regression test suites of one kind or another. Even those that don't provide a test suite contain at least a set of demo programs that can be run and verified manually.

- **Installing:** Once you have built and tested the software to your satisfaction, it is ready to be installed.

We'll go through these steps in detail later. First, let's review the directory structure where Tcl is built and installed.

Directory Structures—A Quick Review

The traditional Unix directory structure is shown in Figure 17-1.

This should be familiar to anybody who's been working with Unix for any time at all. Executable programs are placed in *bin/*, libraries are placed in *lib/*, include files are placed in *include/*. Documentation (in the form of manual pages) are placed in *man/*, and miscellaneous files are placed in *etc/*. The location of the source code (if provided) varies the most, but it is frequently placed in *src/*.

The standard Tcl and Tk distributions follow this convention, as do nearly all of the extension sets. Figure 17-2 shows the details, using */usr/local* as an example. In addition to the usual directories, Tcl and Tk add their own subdirectories under *lib*.

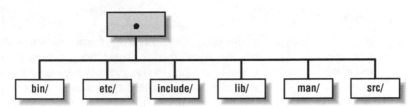

Figure 17-1: Traditional Unix Installation Area

This is where the various run-time routines are stored. In addition, the Tk library directory has a demo directory where the standard example programs are stored.

With this background, let's follow the steps previously outlined to build and install Tcl. We'll use Tcl 7.5 in our example; Tk and the extensions are similar.

Unpacking the Distribution

Tcl, Tk, and most of the extensions are usually distributed in the form of tape archive ("tar") files which have been compressed with either the *compress* or *gzip* programs. The usual filename format is composed of the package name and version, followed by *.tar* (the usual *tar* extension), followed by either a *.Z* (if compressed using *compress*) or *.gz* (if it was compressed using *gzip*). Thus, we can tell that the file *tcl7.5.tar.gz* contains version 7.5 of Tcl, and that it is a gzipped tar file.

To extract the files, we must first uncompress the archive, and then use *tar* to extract the files. It is usually easiest to combine these two steps into a Unix pipeline, uncompressing the file on-the-fly and feeding the expanded output directly to *tar* for extraction. Here are some examples of extracting Tcl 7.5. The parameters we pass to *tar* are "x" (extract), "v" (verbose), and "f -" (read from the standard input, since we are feeding *tar* the output of the decompression program).

```
compress -d tcl7.5.tar.Z | tar xvf - # for compressed files
gzip -d tcl7.5.tar.gz | tar xvf - # for gzipped files
```

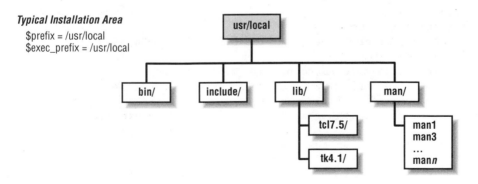

Figure 17-2: A Typical Installation Area from the Tcl Point of View

---

If you are using the GNU version of tar, you can take advantage of its built-in decompression of both types of files:

```
tar xzvf tcl7.5.tar.Z
```

Most extensions place their files under the proper subdirectory name, meaning that the directory will be created when the file is untarred. You do not have to create the directory yourself, so be sure and untar the file in the parent directory. In our example, this will be */usr/local/src*. Since we have specified the verbose option, tar will print the names of the files as it extracts them.

```
$ cd /usr/local/src
$ gzip -cd ../dist/tcl7.5.tar.gz | tar xvf -
tcl7.5/
tcl7.5/unix/
tcl7.5/unix/bp.c
tcl7.5/unix/tclAppInit.c
tcl7.5/unix/tclLoadAix.c
tcl7.5/unix/tclLoadAout.c
...
```

Patching the Installation

Whenever you get a new version of Tcl or an extension, check to see if there are any patch files that need to be installed. If so, you will need to apply these using the patch program. If you do not have *patch*, it can easily be obtained from the Net. The official GNU version is stored at *ftp://prep.ai.mit.edu/pub/gnu*. Look for a file named something like *patch-x.y.tar.gz*, where *x* and *y* represent the latest version.

To patch the distribution, apply the patches in order (*patch* will check the current patch level—if you make a mistake, *patch* will warn you and give you a chance to change your mind). We'll apply the first patch now. Note that we need to redirect the patch file into the patch program.

```
$ cd /usr/local/src/tcl7.5
$ patch <../dist/tcl7.5p1.patch
Hmm...  Looks like a new-style context diff to me...
The text leading up to this was:
--------------------------
|Prereq: "7.5"
|*** ../tcl7.5/generic/patchlevel.h     Thu Apr 11 17:13:11 1996
|--- generic/patchlevel.h        Tue Jul 23 08:48:36 1996
--------------------------
Good.  This file appears to be the "7.5" version.
Patching file generic/patchlevel.h using Plan A...
Hunk #1 succeeded at 17.
Hmm...  The next patch looks like a new-style context diff to
me...
The text leading up to this was:
--------------------------
|*** ../tcl7.5/./unix/tclUnixChan.c     Thu Apr 18 17:05:40 1996
|--- ./unix/tclUnixChan.c        Tue Jul 23 08:49:54 1996
--------------------------
```

```
Patching file ./unix/tclUnixChan.c using Plan A...
Hunk #1 succeeded at 9.
Hunk #2 succeeded at 26.
Hunk #3 succeeded at 52.
Hunk #4 succeeded at 71.
...
done
```

You will receive an entertaining commentary on the state of the source, and (hopefully) a bunch of messages like "Hunk *x* succeeded at *y*." If you get any messages like "Hunk *x* failed," there is some problem with the distribution, the patches, or some part of your installation process. Any patches which fail are saved in *.rej* files for inspection. Files which have been patched are backed up in *.orig* files. When you're finished, search for both types of files to make sure your patches have been applied successfully.

```
$ $ find . -name '*.rej' -print
(shouldn't see any)
$ find . -name '*.orig' -print
./unix/tclUnixChan.c.orig
./unix/tclUnixInit.c.orig
./unix/tclUnixNotfy.c.orig
./unix/tclUnixTime.c.orig
...
```

When in doubt, it's not a bad idea to get a fresh distribution and start from scratch.

Configuring

Tcl and Tk are portable to literally dozens of systems, so once you have loaded the source code, you will need to configure it for your system. Most Tcl packages use the GNU *autoconf* system for this. *Autoconf* has a number of features that make it easier for programmers to develop portable programs and for users to install these systems in an easily configurable manner. The most common option is "--prefix *path*" which is used to specify the directory where the package is to be installed. We will also create shared libraries by specifying the "--enable-shared" option. More details on *autoconf* can be found in O'Reilly's book, *Porting Unix Software*. Specific options can be seen by using the "--help" option.

When *configure* runs, it executes a series of tests to determine your system setup. When it finishes, it creates a makefile that is properly configured for your system.

```
$ cd /usr/local/src/tcl7.5
$ ./configure --enable-shared --prefix=/usr/local/

creating cache ./config.cache
checking for ranlib... ranlib
checking whether cross-compiling... no
checking for getcwd... yes
checking for opendir... yes
checking for strstr... yes
checking for strtol... yes
...
```

```
checking for -ldl... yes
updating cache ./config.cache
creating ./config.status
creating Makefile
creating tclConfig.sh
```

If you wish to delete the files that autoconf has created and return to a pristine state, you can run *make distclean*.

Building

Once you have configured the system, you can build the system by running *make*. This compiles the source files, and builds the libraries and executables (in this case, *libtcl.so* and *tclsh*).

```
$ make
cc -c -O -KPIC -I./../generic -I. -DNO_GETWD=1 -DNO_WAIT3=1
-DHAVE_UNISTD_H=1 -DHAVE_SYS_TIME_H=1 -DTIME_WITH_SYS_TIME=1
-DHAVE_TZNAME=1 -DHAVE_TIMEZONE_VAR=1 -Dstrtod=fixstrtod
-DSTDC_HEADERS=1 -DNO_UNION_WAIT=1 -DNEED_MATHERR=1 -Dvfork=fork
-DGETTOD_NOT_DECLARED=1         -DTCL_SHLIB_EXT=\".so\"
./../generic/panic.c
cc -c -O -KPIC -I./../generic -I. -DNO_GETWD=1 -DNO_WAIT3=1
-DHAVE_UNISTD_H=1 -DHAVE_SYS_TIME_H=1 -DTIME_WITH_SYS_TIME=1
-DHAVE_TZNAME=1 -DHAVE_TIMEZONE_VAR=1 -Dstrtod=fixstrtod
-DSTDC_HEADERS=1 -DNO_UNION_WAIT=1 -DNEED_MATHERR=1 -Dvfork=fork
-DGETTOD_NOT_DECLARED=1         -DTCL_SHLIB_EXT=\".so\"
./../generic/regexp.c
...
cc tclAppInit.o -L/usr/local/src/tcl7.5/unix -ltcl7.5 -ldl
-lsocket -lnsl -lm -lc -R /usr/local/lib -o tclsh
```

Testing

Once the system is built, it is ready to be tested. The makefile has a "test" target that builds any necessary test programs, and then executes the tests.

```
$ make test
cc -c -O -KPIC -I./../generic -I. -DNO_GETWD=1 -DNO_WAIT3=1
-DHAVE_UNISTD_H=1 -DHAVE_SYS_TIME_H=1 -DTIME_WITH_SYS_TIME=1
-DHAVE_TZNAME=1 -DHAVE_TIMEZONE_VAR=1 -Dstrtod=fixstrtod
-DSTDC_HEADERS=1 -DNO_UNION_WAIT=1 -DNEED_MATHERR=1 -Dvfork=fork
-DGETTOD_NOT_DECLARED=1         -DTCL_SHLIB_EXT=\".so\" -DTCL_TEST
./tclAppInit.c
...
append.test
assocd.test
async.test
case.test
clock.test
cmdAH.test
...
```

```
upvar.test
while.test
```

If everything is functioning properly, the list of executed tests will be all that is displayed. If an error is detected, you will be notified and given some details about the expected and actual results.

```
append.test
==== append-1.1 append command
==== Contents of test case:
    catch {unset x}
    list [append x 1 2 abc "long string"] $x
==== Result was:
{12abclong string} {12abclong string}
---- Result should have been:
{z12abclong string} {12abclong string}
---- append-1.1 FAILED
```

If you wish to see more detail about the tests as they are executed, you can run *tcltest* independently, set the variable VERBOSE to 1, and source the test file you are interested in. If you have not yet performed the installation process, you will need to set the TCL_LIBRARY environment variable to point to the copy of the library in the distribution. If you specified shared libraries, you will likewise need to set LD_LIBRARY_PATH to point to the preinstallation location of the shared libraries you have just built.

```
$ cd /usr/local/src/tcl7.5/tests
$ TCL_LIBRARY=../library; export TCL_LIBRARY
$ LD_LIBRARY_PATH=../unix:$LD_LIBRARY_PATH; export LD_LIBRARY_PATH
$ ../unix/tcltest
% set VERBOSE 1
1
% source append.test
...
==== append-4.12 lappend command
==== Contents of test case:
    set x "x \{\{\{"
    lappend x abc
==== Result was:
x {{{abc
++++ append-4.12 PASSED
...
```

This can be also used to see how many tests are being executed, and how many are passing and failing.

```
$ echo "set VERBOSE 1; source all" | ../unix/tcltest | grep
"^++++.*PASSED" | wc -l
3425
$ echo "set VERBOSE 1; source all" | ../unix/tcltest | grep "^---
-.*FAILED" | wc -l
0
```

You can use these features to generate some nice test metric reports, if your organization is into that kind of thing.

Most extensions have a set of tests that can be run via *make test*, but even the ones that don't will have a demo or example directory. If this is the case, you can change to that directory and verify a proper build by running the demo programs.

Installing

Once you have tested the programs to your satisfaction, you are ready to install the software. Installing the software consists of copying any programs, libraries, documentation, and any other support files to the installation area. The default installation area is */usr/local*. If you wish to specify another area, use *configure*'s prefix option (*configure—prefix=/your/path*). The install targets in the makefile will create any directories which do not exist, and copy the necessary files to the installation area. This usually includes executables (usually a *wish* or *tclsh* with the extension built in), libraries and header files, run-time support files, and documentation in the form of man pages.

```
$ make install
$ make install
Making directory /usr/local/lib
Making directory /usr/local/bin
Installing libtcl7.5.so
Installing tclsh
Installing tclConfig.sh
Making directory /usr/local/include
Making directory /usr/local/lib/tcl7.5
Installing tcl.h
Installing ./../library/init.tcl
Installing ./../library/ldAout.tcl
...
```

If you want to be able to view these man pages with *man*, be sure and add the man directory (*$prefix/man*) to your MANPATH environment variable, which specifies the directories that *man* will scan when looking for man pages. A path which looks in */usr/local* as well as the standard manual directory would be specified like this:

```
MANPATH=/usr/local/man:/usr/man; export MANPATH    # bourne shell
setenv MANPATH /usr/local/man:/usr/man    # csh
```

If your MANPATH variable is already set (by your shell startup files, for example), you can append the new directories like this:

```
MANPATH=/usr/local/man:$MANPATH; export MANPATH    # bourne shell
setenv MANPATH /usr/local/man:$MANPATH    # csh
```

What's Been Installed

Finally, let's take a look and see the results of installing Tcl. First, we have created the usual directories, *bin*, *include*, *lib*, and *man*. The program *tclsh7.5* has been placed in *bin*, and the library *libtcl7.5.so** has been placed in *lib*. A header file (*tcl.h*) that corresponds with the library file has been placed in *include*. Various supporting files have been place in the directory *lib/tcl7.5*. Note that this directory is strictly reserved for files from the Tcl 7.5 release. Don't try to mix files from other releases or extensions in this directory, and certainly avoid putting any of your own files there.

The file *tclConfig.sh* was created when Tcl was configured. It is a shell script with numerous pieces of useful configuration information, such as necessary include files and paths to required libraries. We will use it later when we build our own customized shells.

Additionally, notice that the install procedure has placed version numbers on the binary (*tclsh7.5*) and library (*libtcl7.5.so*). This is done to preserve backward compatibility, so that installing a new *tclsh* or *wish* will not cause existing Tcl programs to break due to versioning problems.

```
$ ls -FR
bin/ include/  lib/       man/       src/
./bin:
tclsh7.5*
./include:
tcl.h
./lib:
libtcl7.5.so*  tcl7.5/           tclConfig.sh
./lib/tcl7.5:
init.tcl       ldAout.tcl    parray.tcl    tclAppInit.c   tclIndex
./man:
man1/   man3/   mann/
```

If desired, you can manually link the versioned filenames to names without the version numbers. The benefit of doing this is that users can always get the latest *wish* or *tclsh* without changing the command name. A potential problem is that a script could suddenly stop working if the symbolic link is moved to an incompatible *wish* or *tclsh*. I recommend not making the links if you are in a large shop, since changing the link will invariably catch some people by surprise, breaking their scripts unexpectedly. Even if you do make the links (so that you can always type *wish* or *tclsh* on the command line), use the versioned filename in any scripts you write so that you aren't affected by version changes.

```
$ cd /usr/local
$ ln -s bin/tclsh7.5 bin/tclsh       # create symbolic links
$ ln -s lib/libtcl7.5.a lib/libtcl.a # -- think before doing this
```

Combining Extensions

Now that we've been through the process of building Tcl, let's see what it takes to combine several extensions. We'll do this with both Tcl (a customized *tclsh*) and Tk (a customized *wish*). It takes three steps:

---

* Since we built with --enable-shared, we have a shared library. If we had not specified this flag, we would have a statically linked library (*libtcl7.5.a*).

1. Our own version of *tclsh*.

2. Our own version of *wish*.

3. Our own version of *wish* that incorporates two extensions: BLT and Tix.

For brevity's sake, we'll skip adding any extensions to our version of *tclsh*. The procedure is exactly the same as adding extensions to *wish*.

Creating Your Own tclsh

The first step is to create the directory. It's best to put it next to the Tcl and Tk source directories. In our case this will be */usr/local/src*.

```
$ cd /usr/local/src
$ mkdir mytclsh
```

We need only two files in the directory. The first, *tclAppInit.c*, is the standard template that is provided with the Tcl distribution. We copy it from the Tcl library directory, where it was placed when Tcl was installed.

```
$ cd mytclsh
$ cp /usr/local/lib/tcl7.5/tclAppInit.c .
```

Now we need to create a makefile to build the executable. The easiest way is to steal a few lines from the Tcl makefile. This has the added advantage of being properly configured to link with the proper libraries for your system.

Example 17-1 shows the makefile that we have created. The first several lines indicate the top-level directory where we will install *mytclsh* (the same location where *tclsh* currently resides). Next, we specify the location of include files, and what libraries are needed for this system. Look at the LIBS entry in the Tcl makefile (*../tcl7.5/Makefile*) to see what *configure* has determined for your system. We then specify a rule to make *tclAppInit.o* (the *.c.o:* rule), and a target to link *mytclsh*. We also specify targets for installing and cleaning up the directory. Note that we have collated the various library and include macros into the macros MYINCL and MYLIB. This is not so important now, but you will see that it makes the makefile much more tidy when combining several extensions.

Example 17-1: mytclsh/Makefile
```
# mytclsh/Makefile
prefix =          /usr/local
exec_prefix =     ${prefix}
# the location of any include files we need
TCLINC =          -I../tcl7.5/generic
OTHERINC =
# the location of any libraries we need
TCLLIB =          -L../tcl7.5/unix -ltcl7.5
OTHERLIB =        -lm
MYINCL = $(TCLINC) $(OTHERINC)
MYLIBS = $(TCLLIB) $(OTHERLIB)
all: mytclsh
.c.o:
```

```
        $(CC) -c $(MYINCL) $<
mytclsh: tclAppInit.o
        $(CC) -o mytclsh tclAppInit.o $(MYLIBS)

install: mytclsh
        cp -p mytclsh $(prefix)/bin
clean:
        rm -f *.o mytclsh
```

A philosophical note: We have specified the include and library directories to be
../tcl7.5/generic and *../tcl7.5/unix* rather than *$prefix/include* and *$prefix/lib*, where
these files are placed when Tcl is installed. There are good reasons to do it either
way, but we choose to do it this way for three reasons:

1. This allows us to build *mywish* using an experimental (and possibly not-yet-
   installed) version of Tcl.

2. Some of the extension packages neglect to install their header files into the
   installation area, copying only their libraries and support files. Even if we link
   from the installation area (*$prefix/lib*), we are forced to include the header
   file from the source directory. It seems a little more consistent to get both
   files from the same source. (This phenomenon is probably because including
   the file is not necessary for compiling *tclAppInit.c* with a C compiler, since
   the package initialization routines return the default type for C functions. It
   causes problems when *tclAppInit.c* is compiled with a C++ compiler, where
   all functions must be declared before use.)

3. Everybody else is doing it. This is a lame reason (ask your mother), but most
   of the extension packages (including Tk) also include and link from the Tcl
   source directory. Whether this is some historical accident or whether the
   extension writers are privy to some secret insider information, there is safety
   in numbers.

Now all that's left to do is to make and install the executable.

```
$ make
cc -c -I../tcl7.5/generic  tclAppInit.c
cc -o mytclsh tclAppInit.o -L../tcl7.5/unix -ltcl7.5 -lm
$ make install
cp -p mytclsh /usr/local/bin
```

You can test *mytclsh* using the Tcl regression test suite.

```
$ cd ../tcl7.5/tests
$ ../../mytclsh/tclsh
% source all
...
```

Creating Your Own Wish

Now that we have our own *tclsh*, let's create our own *wish*. The process is pretty
much the same, but is a little more complicated because we have more libraries to
worry about. Instead of using *tclAppInit.c*, we use *tkAppInit.c*, which we have

---

Combining Extensions   **597**

copied from the Tk library directory. The makefile is shown in Example 17-2. Note that a makefile that includes Tk is usually a little more sensitive to machine or site dependencies, since it uses the X11 libraries (this example was done on a Sun box). If you are unsure of the location of the required libraries, check the Tk makefile (*../tk4.1/unix/Makefile*) or in *$prefix/lib/tkConfig.sh*, which contains the configuration information determined during the configuration step performed previously. We can make and test the executable in the same way that we did for *mytclsh*.

```
$ make
cc -c -I../tk4.1/generic -I../tcl7.5/generic -I/usr/local/include
tkAppInit.c
cc -o mywish tkAppInit.o -L../tk4.1/unix -ltk4.1 -L../tcl7.5/unix
-ltcl7.5 -L/usr/local/lib -lX11 -lm
$ cd ../tk4.1/tests
$ ../../mywish/mywish
% source all
...
```

Example 17-2: mywish/Makefile (No Extensions Yet)
```
# mywish/Makefile
prefix =            /usr/local
exec_prefix =       ${prefix}
# the location of any include files we need
TKINC =             -I../tk4.1/generic
TCLINC =            -I../tcl7.5/generic
XINC =              -I/usr/local/include
OTHERINC =
# the location of any libraries we need
TKLIB =             -L../tk4.1/unix -ltk4.1
TCLLIB =            -L../tcl7.5/unix -ltcl7.5
XLIB =              -L/usr/local/lib -lX11
OTHERLIB =          -lm
MYINCL = $(TKINC) $(TCLINC) $(XINC) $(OTHERINC)
MYLIBS = $(TKLIB) $(TCLLIB) $(XLIB) $(OTHERLIB)
.c.o:
        $(CC) -c $(MYINCL) $<

mywish: tkAppInit.o
        $(CC) -o mywish tkAppInit.o $(MYLIBS)
install: mywish
        cp -p mywish $(prefix)/bin
clean:
        rm -f *.o mywish
```

Combining Extensions In Your wish

Now that we've demonstrated that we can build a plain *wish*, let's get serious and add some extensions to it. For this example, we'll add BLT and Tix to *mywish*.

The first thing is to make sure that BLT and Tix have been built. They use the same procedure as we went through for Tcl (configure, make, make install), so we'll assume that the extensions have been built and reside at the same directory level as Tcl and Tk (i.e., in *../blt2.1* and *../Tix4.1*).*

Adding the extensions is a fairly straightforward process. We need to add initialization code to *tkAppInit*.c, and we need to specify the proper include and link elements in the makefile. While not strictly necessary for C programs, it's good style to include the appropriate extensions declarations. Of course, it's not an option if you are compiling with C++. Example 17-3 shows where we added the include directives near the top of *tkAppInit.c*.

Example 17-3: Adding Include Directives to tkAppInit.c

```
/*
 * tkAppInit.c --
 *
 * Provides a default version of the Tcl_AppInit procedure for
 * use in wish and similar Tk-based applications.
 *
 * Copyright (c) 1993 The Regents of the University of California.
 * Copyright (c) 1994 Sun Microsystems, Inc.
 *
 * See the file "license.terms" for information on usage and redis-
 * tribution of this file, and for a DISCLAIMER OF ALL WARRANTIES.
 */

#ifndef lint
static char sccsid[] = "@(#) tkAppInit.c 1.21 96/03/26 16:47:07
#endif /* not lint */

#include "tk.h"
#include "blt.h" /* added for mywish */
#include "tix.h" /* added for mywish */
```

Once we have added the declarations, we need to initialize the packages. Following the standard Tcl protocol, we do this by adding package initialization calls to the function *Tcl_AppInit* (yes, even for Tk programs) (see Example 17-4).

Example 17-4: Adding Package Initialization Calls to tkAppInit.c

```
    /*
     * Call the init procedures for included packages.   Each
     * call should look like this:
     *
     * if (Mod_Init(interp) == TCL_ERROR) {
     *      return TCL_ERROR;
     * }
```

---

* One of the benefits of having the directories reside at the same level is that it enables all directory references to be made relative to the parent directory, allowing you to avoid the trouble of hardcoding absolute path names.

```
    *
    * where "Mod" is the name of the module.
    */

    if (Blt_Init(interp) == TCL_ERROR) {
        return TCL_ERROR;
    }

    if (Tix_Init(interp) == TCL_ERROR) {
        return TCL_ERROR;
    }
```

Once we have added the appropriate initializations to *tkAppInit.c*, the only thing that remains is to add the appropriate include and link specifications to the makefile (this is why we went to the trouble of adding the seemingly redundant MYINCL and MYLIB macros earlier). Example 17-5 shows the revised makefile. Note that the order of the libraries in MYLIB is important, and follows the dependency order of the libraries. The extensions go first, since they depend on Tcl and Tk. Next comes Tk, since it depends upon Tcl. Finally come the X and system libraries.

Example 17-5: The Revised mywish//Makefile
```
# mywish/Makefile (with Tix and BLT)
prefix =            /usr/local
exec_prefix =       ${prefix}
# the location of any include files we need
BLTINC =            -I../blt2.1
TIXINC =            -I../Tix4.1b1/include
TKINC =             -I../tk4.1/generic
TCLINC =            -I../tcl7.5/generic
XINC =              -I/usr/local/include
OTHERINC =
# the location of any libraries we need
BLTLIB =            -L../blt2.1/src -lBLT
TIXLIB =            -L../Tix4.1b1/unix-tk4.1 -ltix
TKLIB =             -L../tk4.1/unix -ltk4.1
TCLLIB =            -L../tcl7.5/unix -ltcl7.5
XLIB =              -L/usr/local/lib -lX11
OTHERLIB =          -lm
MYINCL = $(BLTINC) $(TIXINC) $(TKINC) $(TCLINC) $(XINC) $(OTHERINC)
MYLIBS = $(BLTLIB) $(TIXLIB) $(TKLIB) $(TCLLIB) $(XLIB) $(OTHERLIB)

.c.o:
        $(CC) -c $(MYINCL) $<
mywish: tkAppInit.o
        $(CC) -o mywish tkAppInit.o $(MYLIBS)
install: mywish
        cp -p mywish $(prefix)/bin
clean:
        rm -f *.o mywish
```

Revision Control

If you are doing serious software development, either commercially or in support of internal projects, you probably already have a configuration management or revision control system in place. If this is the case, then it is a good idea to get your Tcl source under control as well.

Tcl, Tk, and most of the extensions follow the directory naming scheme *product-version*. For example, various Tcl distributions (both directories and tar files) have been called *tcl7.3*, *tcl7.4*, and *tcl7.5*, while the corresponding versions of Tk have been named *tk3.6*, *tk4.0*, and *tk4.1*. While all CM systems have facilities to "stack" these version on top of each other in a version tree, the strategy which seems to work best is to create the directories in a flat structure (i.e., untarring all the distributions from the same parent directory, giving a structure like this:

```
$ cd .../src
$ ls -F
tcl7.3/    tcl7.5/    tk3.6/
tcl7.4/    tk3.6/     tk4.0/
```

If you are using a revision control system, you should check in your modified files at these points:

1. Add the directory immediately upon unpacking the distribution. This will capture the pristine state of the distribution.

2. Update the directory after configuration. This will add files generated by *configure*. It will also capture any files modified by the configuration process (under normal circumstances, no files are modified, so this shouldn't happen).

3. Update the directory after applying any patches that have been distributed.

4. Of course any modifications you make yourself should be captured.

5. Some shops will also make a snapshot of the destination directory after installation, either to facilitate system reinstallations, or out of plain paranoia.

Properly done, configuration management of Tcl and Tcl extensions should be a relatively low-maintenance procedure.

A Hint for Serious Shops

If you are in a Very Serious Software Shop, you will probably have a Change Control Board and a Release Librarian who jointly supervise building and releasing software loads. If this is the case, they will probably have a cataloging system where every product provided for both internal and external consumption gets a catalog number. If this is the case, ask for a separate catalog number for Tcl, Tk, every extension you build, and any composite *wish*s or *tclsh*s you build yourself. This will make it easy to track versions through your own build process and to communicate unambiguously with your release librarian's staff.

An Example

Suppose you were using Tcl, Tk, and the extensions BLT and Tcl-DP. You might have catalog "generic" numbers assigned like

Package	Catalog No.
Tcl	8347
Tk	8348
BLT	8349
Tcl-DP	8350
Our-Wish	8351 (this is a custom wish with BLT and Tcl-DP)

When you applied versions to the generic catalog numbers, you would end up with something like this:

Release No.	Item
8347-73-01	Tcl 7.3 (after configuration—that's the "01")
8347-74-01	Tcl 7.4
8348-36-01	Tk 3.6
8348-40-01	Tk 4.1
8349-17-01	BLT 1.7
8349-18-01	BLT 1.8
8350-32-01	Tcl-DP 3.2
8350-33-01	Tcl-DP 3.3
8351-10-01	Our-Wish (Tcl 7.3, Tk 3.6, BLT 1.7, Tcl-DP 3.2)
8351-11-01	Our-Wish (Tcl 7.4, Tk 4.1, BLT 1.8, Tcl-DP 3.2)
8351-12-01	Our-Wish (Tcl 7.4, Tk 4.1, BLT 1.8, Tcl-DP 3.3)

You can then unambiguously specify the contents of various wishes, saying, for example, "8351-11-01 consists of 8347-73-01, 8348-36-01, 8349-17-01, and 8350-32-01. 8351-12-01 is the same, except we replace 8350-32-01 with 8350-33-01." *

Specifying Interpreters

There are two ways that the interpreter is commonly specified in Tcl scripts. The first (traditional) way is fine for many cases, but can cause problems in other circumstances.

The Traditional Method

The traditional method for specifying the interpreter or shell to be used for a script is to have the first line of the start with "#!" followed by the name of the program

---

* Believe me, your life will never be the same after attending a meeting where people talk this way.

that will be used as the shell. For example, to specify a *wish* script (where *wish* resides in */usr/local/bin*), the file would start with

```
#!/usr/local/bin/wish -f*
```

When the file is executed, the kernel notices that the file begins with "#!" and does two things:

1. The kernel appends the current filename to the command line.

2. The specified shell is invoked with the modified command line.

If the file is named *myprog.tcl*, the following command would be executed:

```
#!/usr/local/bin/wish -f myprog.tcl
```

Since the first character of the line is a comment (it starts with "#"), it is ignored by the Tcl interpreter. This feature is the reason so many languages that grew up on Unix use "#" to introduce comments.

This works in general, but has two problems:

- The path to the interpreter is hardcoded. This makes it difficult to test a new interpreter without installing it first, and causes problems if your file resides on a heterogenous network, where a specific executable might not work for all computers on the network.

- On many systems, the command name is limited to 31 characters, and multiple parameters are not allowed. Thus, the following shell specifications would not work:

```
#!/my/long/directory/path/to/my/customized/wish
#!/usr/local/bin/wish -sync -f
```

The first specification would fail because the path was too long (you might get an error like "/my/long/directory/path/to/my/c: not found"). The second would fail on some systems, since the -sync and -f parameters would not be properly passed to *wish*.

A Better Way

This method gets around the problems just mentioned by exploiting a difference in the way that Tcl and the Bourne shell handle comments and continuation characters. Instead of specifying the Tcl interpreter directly on the "#!" line, we start the file this way (using *wish* as an example):

```
#!/bin/sh
# \
exec wish "$0" "$@"
```

On the surface, this is reasonably unintuitive, so let's examine the code line by line, and then step through what happens when the file is executed.

---

* The "-f" is not needed for *wish* Versions 4.1 and later.

Line 1: This line specifies that the Bourne shell (*/bin/sh*) will be invoked when the program is executed.

Line 2: This is a comment, both in Tcl and in the Bourne shell. Note that last character of the line is a backslash. In Tcl, this means that the next line will be a continuation of this comment. The Bourne shell scanner ignores the backslash, since it is in a comment.

Line 3: In Tcl, this is a continuation of the comment started in the previous line and is therefore ignored. Since the Bourne shell did not continue the comment, this line uses the **exec** command to run wish. The "$0" "$@" is the shell's syntax to pass along the parameters given to the shell without stripping any user-specified quoting.

Now, let's see exactly what happens when a program (called *myprog.tcl*) is invoked.

1. When the program is invoked, the "#!" is honored by the Unix kernel as previously described, and invokes the Bourne shell with the command

   ```
   /bin/sh myprog.tcl
   ```

2. The shell starts executing the file. Lines 1 and 2 do nothing, since they are comments.

3. When the shell executes line 3, it overlays the current process (that's what **exec** does) with wish, using the command line

   ```
   wish myprog.tcl
   ```

   The "$0" has been replaced with the script name (myprog.tcl). If there had been any parameters passed to the program, they would have been replaced in the "$@" construct.

4. *Wish* reads the file and executes it. Lines 1 and 2 are skipped since they are comments. More importantly, line 3 is also skipped, since it is merely a continuation of the comment specified in line 2. This is the "magic" that allows the file to be treated both as a shell script and as a Tcl script.

5. The rest of the file is executed normally by the Tcl interpreter.

This method has several benefits:

- The interpreter is found by searching the user's path. If you want to test a new version of *wish*, for example, you can simply add the new *wish*'s directory to the beginning of your path and run your program normally. Current users will not be disturbed, since their path will continue to point to the current production *wish*.

- There are no limitations on the length of the path, or on any parameters you wish to pass to the program.

You can add any additional shell commands or environment variables needed for proper execution. We once used this feature to work around a problem situation where many users had some bad shared libraries in their shared library path. This was on a SunOS system, which used the environment variable LD_LIBRARY_PATH to specify the path to search for shared libraries. We simply made sure the proper shared libraries would be loaded by changing the third line to

```
#  \
LD_LIBRARY_PATH=/our/good/path:$LD_LIBRARY_PATH
#  \
exec wish "$0" "$@"
```

18

Development Tools

In this chapter, we will look at several packages that help you developing Tcl and Tk applications.

The Tk Demo Directory

One of the best kept secrets of the Tk world is the Tk demo directory. It contains about a dozen sample programs, and is an excellent starting point for exploring Tk.*
We'll look at two of the more useful programs for doing development.

The Tk Widget Demonstration Program

This program is a collection of demo programs for the various widgets in the Tk library. When run, it displays a list of the demos that can be run (see Figure 18-1).

Here, we have clicked on the checkbutton demo, and clicked on the "see variables" button (see Figure 18-2).

Finally, you can click the See Code button. An editing window containing the code is displayed. You can edit the program and click the Rerun Demo button to see the results of your modifications (see Figure 18-3).

rmt—The Tk Remote Controller

This program is a remote controller for Tk applications. It allows you to attach to running programs, and interactively send commands to them. To attach to a program, select "File/Select Application" from the menu bar. A list of running interpreters is displayed, from which you can select your application. In this example, we will talk to the widget program mentioned earlier (see Figure 18-4).

---

* A special request of site administrators: Make sure your users know about this directory—mention its location in your site documentation (maybe even include the *README* file). When I was preparing this chapter, I was surprised at how many people at my own site were unaware of this directory.

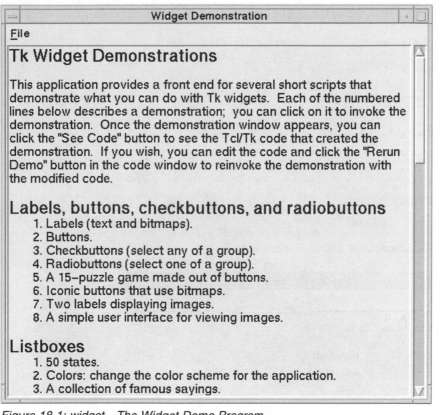

Figure 18-1: widget—The Widget Demo Program

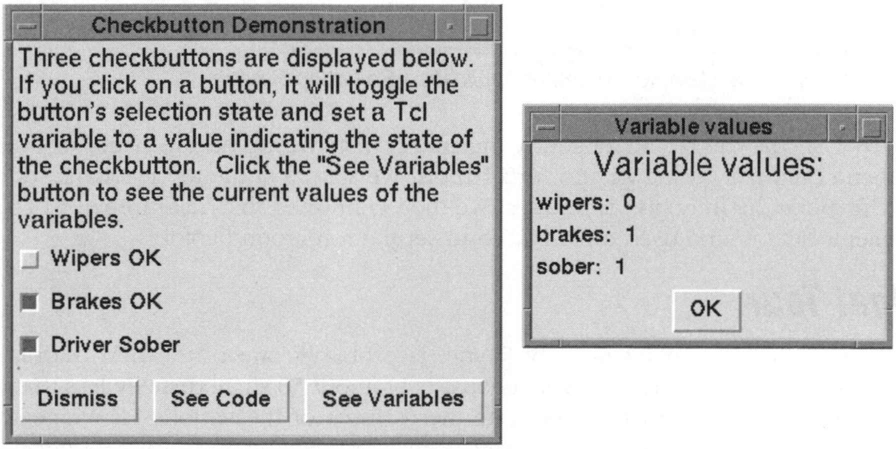

Figure 18-2: The Checkbutton Demonstration Program

Once we have selected the application (notice that the prompt changes), we can type any Tcl command. The command is sent to the remote interpreter (using Tk's send command), and the response (if any) is displayed. We'll use it to query and change some configuration options in the *widget* program.

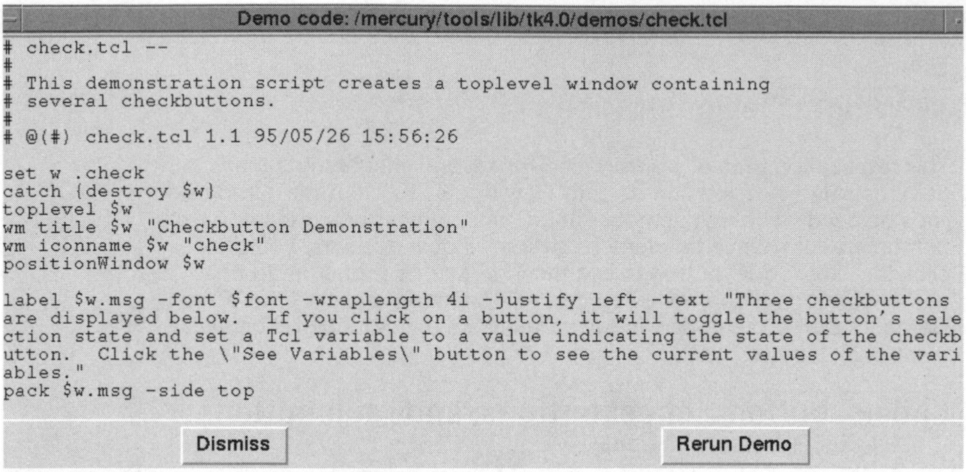

```
# check.tcl --
#
# This demonstration script creates a toplevel window containing
# several checkbuttons.
#
# @(#) check.tcl 1.1 95/05/26 15:56:26

set w .check
catch {destroy $w}
toplevel $w
wm title $w "Checkbutton Demonstration"
wm iconname $w "check"
positionWindow $w

label $w.msg -font $font -wraplength 4i -justify left -text "Three checkbuttons
are displayed below.  If you click on a button, it will toggle the button's sele
ction state and set a Tcl variable to a value indicating the state of the checkb
utton.  Click the \"See Variables\" button to see the current values of the vari
ables."
pack $w.msg -side top
```

Dismiss   Rerun Demo

Figure 18-3: Checkbutton Demo Source Code

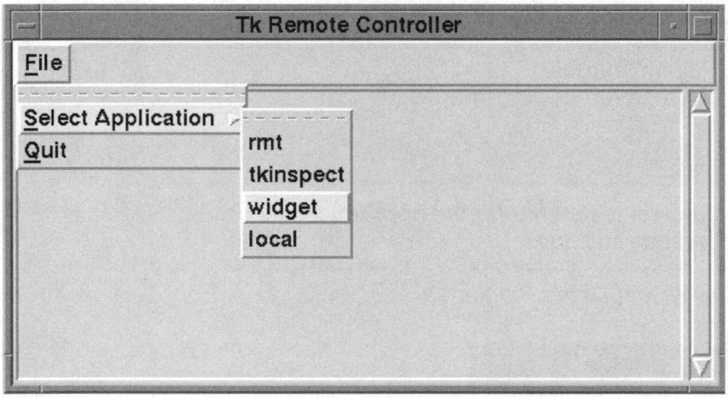

Figure 18-4: rmt—The Remote Controller Application Selection Screen

Figure 18-5 shows the results of four commands. First, we found the name of the "File" menu button by using `winfo children`. We started at the top level and followed the hierarchy through `.menuBar`. We then confirmed that `.menuBar.file` was a menu button, and used `configure` to set the foreground color.

Widget Tour

The Widget Tour, written by Andrew Payne, is probably one of the best tutorial introductions to using the Tk widgets. It consists of about 50 small (usually less than 10 to 20 lines) programs that demonstrate the features of the various Tk widgets. You can edit the programs and view the results by clicking the "apply" button. Figure 18-6 shows the program demonstrating the ease of manipulating listboxes.

tkshowkeys

It is often necessary to know particular key names for binding purposes. Here is a small script that displays this information. To use it, move the mouse over the window and press a key. The key name will be displayed as you press it.

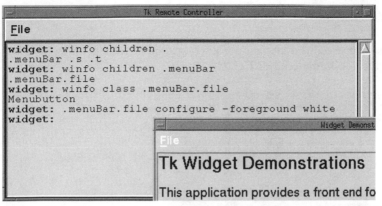

Figure 18-5: Using rmt To Control the Widget Demonstration (inset).white

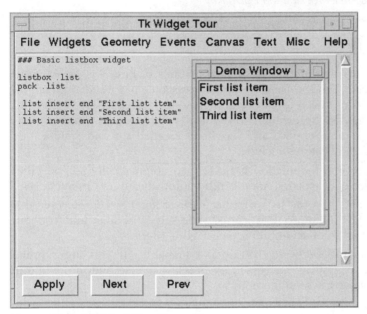

Figure 18-6: A Widget Tour Demo Program

```sh
#!/bin/sh
# The next line is a comment in Tcl, but not sh \
        exec wish $0 -f ${1+"$@"}

set m { This program shows the X11 key symbols for keys. \
Move your mouse on this window and press some keys.  The key \
symbols will appear below.}

pack [message .msg -text $m -aspect 500]
pack [label .key -text "key is:"] -anchor w
pack [button .q -text Quit -command {destroy .}]

wm title . "tkshowkeys"
```

```
bind .msg <Any-Key> {.key configure -text "key is: %K"}
focus .msg
```

In Figure 18-7, I have pressed the key on my keyboard labelled "PgDn," which we can see is mapped to the key identifier F25.

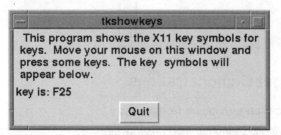

Figure 18-7: tkshowkeys After Pressing the PgDn Key

Emacs Tcl Mode

As Emacs aficionados are aware, one of the nice features of Emacs is its ability to support language specific "modes," which provide assistance in formatting, compiling, and running programs. There are several Tcl modes available—we'll concentrate on the one that has the best integration with the X version of Emacs. It was originally written by Gregor Schmid, and has been cleaned up and significantly enhanced by Mark Ulferts. Features include:

- C-mode style formatting. Indentation is performed automatically as you enter your code, and blocks of existing code can be automatically reformatted.

- Sending a file or parts of a file to a running *wish* or another Tcl interpreter. If an interpreter is not running, one is started. The screen is split, and you can type commands in an interactive buffer (see Figure 18-8).

- A pull-down menu to access all Tcl mode commands. If you are running XEmacs, this menu can also be accessed by pressing mouse button 3 while in the source code window. (see Figure 18-9).

- If you are running under XEmacs, color highlighting and different fonts for the various syntactic parts of Tcl.

Installing and Configuring

Unlike most of the other tools we discuss here, you may need to perform a little bit of individual setup to use this mode. We don't have enough room to talk about all the details of installing Emacs files, but there should be enough to get you up and running. In case of any difficulties, I recommend consulting a good Emacs book and your local Emacs expert.

With that disclaimer, there are basically three things you need to do:

1. If it's not already installed, you need to copy the file *tcl-mode.el* somewhere. We'll assume it's in the directory *~/emacs*.

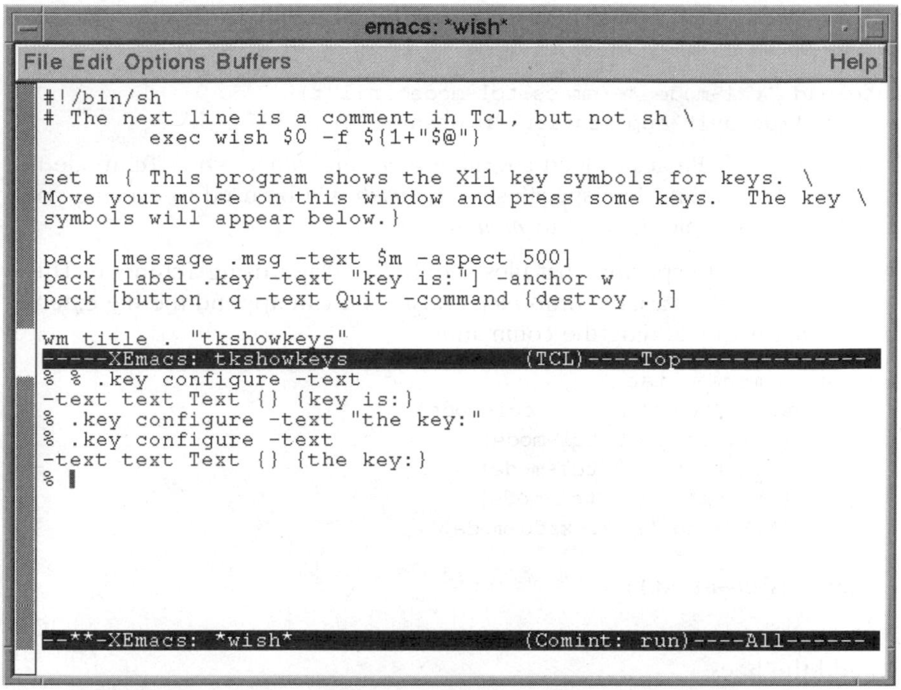
emacs: *wish*
File Edit Options Buffers
Help
#!/bin/sh
The next line is a comment in Tcl, but not sh \
exec wish $0 -f ${1+"$@"}
set m { This program shows the X11 key symbols for keys. \
Move your mouse on this window and press some keys. The key \
symbols will appear below.}
pack [message .msg -text $m -aspect 500]
pack [label .key -text "key is:"] -anchor w
pack [button .q -text Quit -command {destroy .}]
wm title . "tkshowkeys"
-----XEmacs: tkshowkeys (TCL)----Top--------------
% % .key configure -text
-text text Text {} {key is:}
% .key configure -text "the key:"
% .key configure -text
-text text Text {} {the key:}
%
--**-XEmacs: *wish* (Comint: run)----All------

Figure 18-8: A Split Screen in Emacs Tcl-Mode

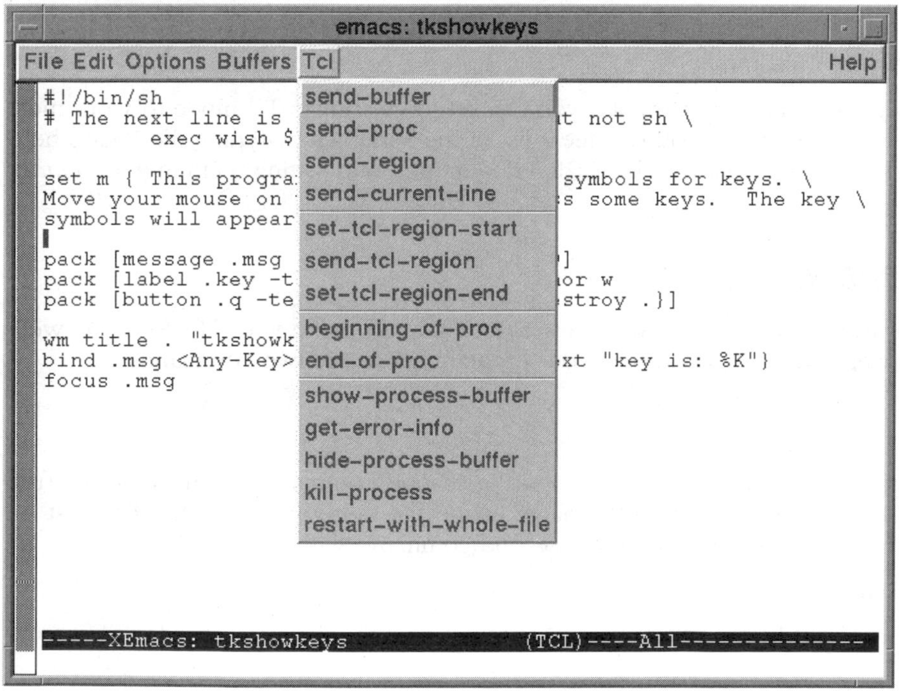
emacs: tkshowkeys
File Edit Options Buffers Tcl
Help
#!/bin/sh
The next line is
t not sh \
exec wish $
set m { This progra
symbols for keys. \
Move your mouse on
s some keys. The key \
symbols will appear
pack [message .msg
pack [label .key -t
or w
pack [button .q -te
stroy .}]
wm title . "tkshowk
bind .msg <Any-Key>
xt "key is: %K"}
focus .msg
send-buffer
send-proc
send-region
send-current-line
set-tcl-region-start
send-tcl-region
set-tcl-region-end
beginning-of-proc
end-of-proc
show-process-buffer
get-error-info
hide-process-buffer
kill-process
restart-with-whole-file
-----XEmacs: tkshowkeys (TCL)----All--------------

Figure 18-9: Using the Tcl Mode Menu to Issue a Command

2. Next, we need to tell Emacs how to access the mode file. Add these lines to the file *.emacs* in your home directory:

```
(autoload 'tcl-mode "~/emacs/tcl-mode" nil t)
(setq tcl-default-application "mywish")
```

The first line tells Emacs to load the file *~/emacs/tcl-mode* when Tcl mode is requested. The second line specifies which *wish* will be used to execute your code. In this example, it is set to *mywish*.

3. Finally, we need to specify what files should be edited using Tcl mode. This is controlled by the variable *auto-mode-alist*. You can append the file extensions to that list by adding the command:

```
(setq auto-mode-alist
    (nconc '(("\\.itk"   . tcl-mode)
        ("\\.itcl"  . tcl-mode)
        ("\\.tcl"   . tcl-mode)
        ("\\.tk"    . tcl-mode)
        (".Xdefaults" . xrdb-mode)
        )
    auto-mode-alist))
```

If you have a file that does not end in one of the extensions that Emacs recognizes, you can add the lines:

```
#;; Local Variables:
#;; mode: Tcl
#;; End:
```

near the end of your file. Emacs will see these lines and recognize them as instructions to enter Tcl mode.

There are several other variables you can set to customize Tcl mode to work most efficiently at your site. You can see a list of the variables by typing the Emacs help key (usually **C-h**) followed by **m** (describe mode), and setting them in your *.emacs file* as shown in the example.

Tcl and vi

If you are a vi user, there are a few tricks that can make your life easier as well. Whenever you are ready to test your program, issue the two commands

```
:w
:!%
```

The first command writes the file, and the second command executes the file (the percent sign is expanded to the name of the file being edited). The file must be executable. If it is not, replace the second command with

```
:!wish %
```

As vi users are fond of saying, it's simple, effective, and runs everywhere.*

---

* Or as one reviewer noted: "crude but effective, much like Vi users themselves."

zapinterps

Occasionally, you may have a program die which has a *wish* interpreter registered with the windowing system. This can result in a stale interpreter reference that can be returned from the `winfo interps` command. This handy program by Jim Curran fixes that. It consists of two programs: a Tcl program to query the registered interpreters and figure out which references are stale, and a C program which removes the interpreter name from the registry.

To clean up all stale references, run the command:

```
zapinterps.tcl
```

If you have a need to zap a particular interpreter by name, you can call the lower-level program directly:

```
unregister interp-names...
```

19

Debugging

One of the first thing that new Tcl programmers notice is that Tcl doesn't come with a traditional debugger like *gdb* or *dbx*. For programmers used to programming in traditional compiled languages like C or C++, this seems odd, since a debugger is usually considered one of the base parts of a programmer's toolkit. But don't worry! Several debugging techniques are available, including at least two graphical debuggers. This chapter discusses various strategies for debugging and how to leverage various extension sets in your debugging efforts.

Print Statements

The simplest and most obvious approach to debugging is to simply insert print statements in your code. This is a time-honored method of debugging, as we can see from this forty-year-old report on FORTRAN:

> *In order to produce a program with built-in debugging facilities, it is a simple matter for the programmer to write various PRINT statements, which cause "snapshots" of pertinent information to be taken at appropriate points in his or her procedure, and insert these in the deck of cards comprising the original FORTRAN program. After compiling this program, running the resulting machine program, and comparing the resulting snapshots with hand-calculated or known values, the programmer can localize the specific area in his or her FORTRAN program which is causing the difficulty.*[*]

Of course, Tcl programmers need not concern themselves with recompilation or adding punched cards to their program, but the concept remains the same:

```
proc addlink {parent child} {
    puts "addlink: $parent $child"
    ...
```

---

[*] The FORTRAN Automatic Coding System, J. W. Backus, et al., 1957.

In some cases, this is easier to do on the calling end, since it is easy to copy a line and convert it to a print statement. For example, if you were interested in tracing the command:

```
addlink $parent $child
```

you could simply copy the line, and wrap it in a puts statement:

```
puts "addlink $parent $child"
addlink $parent $child
```

Of course, you want to be careful if the command you are tracing has side effects. For example, if you wanted to see the results of sending a command to a remote *wish* shell, this would be the wrong way to do it,

```
puts "set response [send $otherwish $cmd]"
set response [send $otherwish $cmd]
```

since the **send** command would be executed twice, very likely causing confusion at the other end.

For small tasks, this is a quick and easy way to see what's going on in your program. Now, let's take a look at some other methods.

BLT Tracing

The BLT toolkit has several useful debugging commands. The first of these is:

```
blt_debug ?level?
```

This command causes Tcl commands to be traced during execution. As each command is executed, it is printed twice to standard error, both before and after substitutions have taken place. The parameter *level* indicates at what level to stop tracing. A level of 0 (the default) indicates that no tracing is performed.

One problem with tracing can be controlling the large amount of output for sections of code that you are not concerned about. There are several ways of reducing this output and increasing the signal to noise ratio.

1. You can simply turn tracing on and off in your program by wrapping it around the code you wish to trace:

```
blt_debug 1
buggy code ...
blt_debug 0
```

2. You can bring up another *wish* and use the **send** command to turn tracing off and on. This is especially handy when you want to debug some code associated with a particular command, like pressing a button or selecting something from a list. For example, if you were running a *wish* program called *myinterp*, you could run another *wish* to control debugging output:

```
# wait for non-buggy code to execute
send myinterp {blt_debug 1}
# after the buggy code executes
send myinterp {blt_debug 0}
```

3. Usually, you want to set *level* to as low a value as possible, in order to reduce the amount of output. In some cases, you may want to temporarily increase the level in order to see some detail about one particular piece of code. In this case, it is sometimes desirable not to arbitrarily turn off tracing when you have finished, but to set the debug level back to its previous value.

```
set old_debug_value [blt_debug]
blt_debug 1
# buggy code...
blt_debug $old_debug_value
```

BLT also includes the more general form of command tracing, `blt_watch`. This command allows you to specify particular procedures to be called before and after each command is executed. These are specified as parameters when the watch is created.

```
blt_watch create name -precmd prestring -postcmd poststring
```

If provided, *prestring* is executed before every command that follows in the script, and *poststring* is executed after each command. As the interpreter executes *prestring* and *poststring*, it appends several arguments containing useful trace information. For `-precmd`, these are:

1. The current execution level.

2. The command string being executed.

3. A list containing the command after variables have been substituted and the arguments have been split into words.

For `-postcmd`, these are

1. The current execution level.

2. The command string being executed.

3. A list containing the command after variables have been substituted and the arguments have been split into words.

4. The return code of the command just executed.

5. The result of the command just executed.

This example from the *blt_watch* man page performs command tracing in a manner similar to that of *blt_debug*:

```
proc preCmd {level commmand argv} {
    set name [lindex $argv 0]
    puts stderr "$level $name -> $command"
}

proc postCmd {level command argv retcode results} {
    set name [lindex $argv 0]
    puts stderr "$level $name -> $argv= ($retcode) $results"
}

blt_watch create trace -postcmd postCmd -precmd preCmd
```

There are a number of other options for managing, activating, and deleting watches detailed in the man page.

tdebug

tdebug, written by Gerd Schmid, takes a different and highly interesting approach. *tdebug* attaches to a running *wish* program, and adds the debugging code on-the-fly to the running program.

When you start *tdebug* (by running *TdChoose.tcl*) and select an interpreter, you are presented with a list of the procedures currently defined in the interpreter you have attached to (see Figure 19-1).

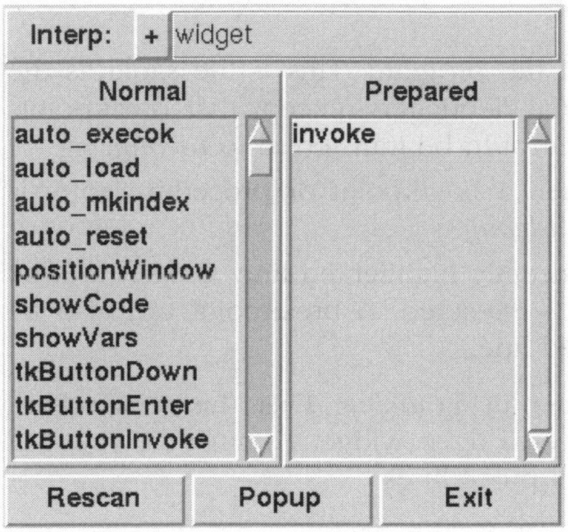

Figure 19-1: tdebug Selection Window

Clicking on a procedure in the "Normal" column prepares it for debugging. This is the equivalent of setting a breakpoint, in that whenever that procedure is entered, control of execution will be transferred to *tdebug*, and you will be able to interact with the program using the control panel (see Figure 19-2).

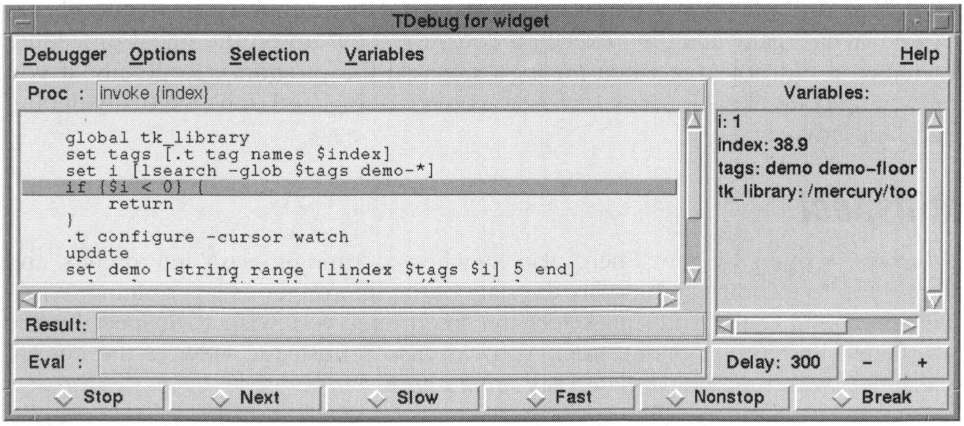

Figure 19-2: tdebug Control Panel

The control panel contains several elements, the most important of which are the source and variable windows. The source window has the current statement highlighted, and the value of all variables in the procedure (including global variables referenced in the procedure) are displayed in the variable window. You can perform any of these actions:

- **Next**: Execute the `next` command. If there are nested statements (e.g., an `if` command, or a command nested in square brackets), these are executed in turn. The result (if any) of each command is shown in the result window.
- **Slow**: Resume executing, tracing each command, pausing briefly after each command. The delay can be adjusted by the "-" and "+" buttons on the right side of the window.
- **Fast**: This is similar to the `slow` command, except that there is no pause after executing each instruction.
- **Nonstop**: Resume normal execution of the program. This is the same as the `continue` command in most traditional debuggers, except that breakpoints and procedure entries do not cause control to be transferred to *tdebug*.
- **Stop**: This re-enables breakpoints. When a breakpoint or procedure entry is reached, control is again transferred to *tdebug*.
- **Break**: This adds a breakpoint at the currently highlighted line. Control will be transferred to *tdebug* before this line is executed. A breakpoint can also be added by double-clicking on the desired line.

There are a few caveats to keep in mind when using *tdebug*. First, this version handles only code in procedures. If you desire to trace widget commands, you will need to code your button commands to call procedures

```
button .b -command {say_hello}
proc say_hello {} {
    puts hello
}
```

rather than to perform the commands directly:

```
button .b -command {puts hello}
```

Also, there are a few cases that it cannot handle. For example, a procedure that is created dynamically and then executed does not show up on the initial procedure list (since it did not exist when *tdebug* examined the program). Hopefully, if you are writing code like this you know what you are doing, and don't need any debugging help anyway.

tkinspect

Tkinspect, written by Sam Shen, also attaches to running *wish* interpreters and allows you to examine and modify the state of the interpreter as it is running. When you first bring it up, you can select the interpreter you wish to inspect by the "File/Select Interpreter" menu item. You can also refresh the view of the current interpreter with the "File/Update Lists" menu item.

When you attach to an interpreter, you will see four lists: one each for procedures, global variables, windows, and menus. Clicking on an item in the list causes *tkin-*

spect to display the current value of the selected item. The item is displayed in the proper syntax to reconfigure the item. You can move your mouse into the window and, if desired, edit any of the item's parameters. You can display a pop-up menu by clicking the right mouse button over the display window. The most useful command is send value, which sends the `configure` command to the interpreter being inspected, thereby applying any of the changes you have made. In Figure 19-3, we have changed the foreground color of a label widget to white, and sent it to the program we were inspecting (in this case, the widget demo program). In the inset we can see that the foreground has been changed.

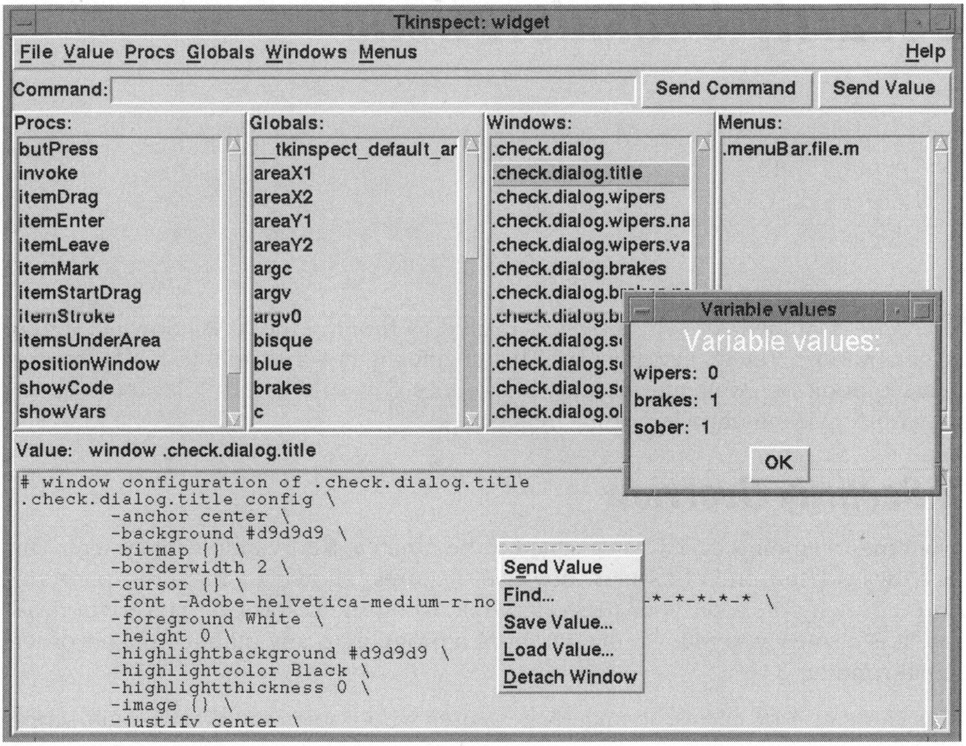

Figure 19-3: tkinspect—Modifying the Foreground Color of a Widget

20

Security Considerations

There are a number of security issues related to running the X Windowing System in general and Tcl/Tk in particular. This chapter is not a substitute for a comprehensive book on computer security, but it does cover the issues relevant to securing your environment when using Tcl and Tk.

X Security Overview

From the beginning, X11 was designed to be a networked windowing system. This has always been one of its most powerful features, allowing you to run programs on other computers on your network, while using the display on your own desktop. It is also easy to redirect the output of a program to any other computer or terminal running X11.

This can cause problems, though. A new user who copies someone's login scripts could inadvertently have his or her display variable set to another display. A prankster can run programs to "melt" another person's display or to cause roaches to run around the screen, or can fill the screen with annoying pictures.

There are also several things a malicious user or a system cracker can do. He or she can attach to your display and watch the output of your screens or what you are typing at the keyboard (several programs have been posted to the Usenet which do this). If you are using Tk, he or she can use the **send** command to send any arbitrary command to one of your Tk programs (and via the **exec** command, any arbitrary shell command).

Fortunately, there are steps you can take to set up a secure X environment. In addition, Tk verifies the security of your X setup, and refuses to honor **send** commands if your setup is insecure. The file *tkSend.c* contains this explanation of the check that is made.*

---

* Don't fall into the trap of thinking that Tk creates the problem—it just makes it obvious that there is a problem.

```
/*
 * See if the server appears to be reasonably secure.  It is
 * considered to be secure if host-based access control is
 * enabled but no hosts are on the access list;  this means
 * that some other form (presumably more secure) form of
 * authorization (such as xauth) must be in use.
 */
```

Testing Your Security

This section covers how to test and see what your current level of security is. You can be either:

- **insecure**: The `send` command detects an insecure setup and reports it.
- **secure**: Your system is secure and `send` works.
- **insecure**: but `send` still works because your wish was built with security disabled.

Does Your send Command Work?

First, let's check to see if your `send` command works. The program *test-send* (Example 20-1) will tell you this. It starts a second *wish* (named "victim"), attempts to send to it, and reports the results.

Example 20-1: test-send

```
#!/bin/sh
# the next line restarts using wish \
exec wish "$0" "$@"

# start a wish and give it some time to come up.  We give this wish
# an explicit name ("victim") so that we can send to it.
set pid [exec wish -name victim &]
exec sleep 1

# now, let's try to send to it.  If the send fails, the "catch"
# will be true and we will get the reason.
if {[catch {send victim {puts "in victim"}} ret]} {
    puts "send failed: $ret"
} else {
    puts "send succeeded"
}

# clean up victim and exit
exec kill $pid
exit
```

Let's look at a couple of examples. First, let's see the results of running on an insecure display (in this case, one which has allowed access to all hosts with the command *xhost +*).

```
$ xhost +
access control disabled, clients can connect from any host
$ test-send
% send failed: X server insecure (must use xauth-style authoriza-
tion); command ignored
```

This is the same error you will see (usually in a pop-up dialog box) when you run
a Tk program that tries to use **send** on an insecure system.

Now, let's turn xhost access off (with **xhost -**). Now, assuming that everything
else is secure, we can run the program again and see that it works. The "victim"
shell prints the message, and **send** reports no errors.

```
$ xhost -
access control enabled, only authorized clients can connect
$ test-send
% in victim
send succeeded
```

There's the possibility that this might fail on your system. If so, it's because you
haven't got the other elements of X security in place. Don't worry, we'll cover this
in the next section.

Have You Disabled send Security?

There's another case to consider as well. It is possible (but not recommended) to
disable security checking in **send** when building Tk. The program *test-nosec*
(Example 20-2) will check this. It is similar to *test-send* except that it intentionally
allows access (via the *exec xhost +* line) before sending to the victim shell. If you
have a normally compiled **send**, you will see output like this:

```
$ test-nosec
% send failed, your wish is checking for security!
```

If your wish was built with security disabled, you will see output like this:

```
$ test-nosec
% in victim
```

send succeeded, your wish is insecure!

```
#!/bin/sh
# the next line restarts using wish \
exec wish "$0" "$@"

# this program checks to see if your wish was built with NO_SECURITY
# first, make the display insecure by allowing all hosts to access
exec xhost +

# start a wish and give it some time to come up.  We give this wish
# an explicit name ("victim") so that we can send to it.
set pid [exec wish -name victim &]
exec sleep 1

# now, let's try to send to it.  If the send fails, the "catch"
```

Example 20-2: test-security

```
# will be true and we will get the reason.
if {[catch {send victim {puts "in victim"}} ret]} {
    puts "send failed, your wish is checking for security!"
} else {
    puts "send succeeded, your wish is insecure!"
}

# clean up victim and exit
exec kill $pid
exit
```

Setting Up Security

Like many things in X, display security can seem like a complicated thing to the casual observer.* The short form of X security is:

1. Host-based security (*xhost*) is bad—turn it off.

2. User-based security (*xauth*) is good—turn it on.

3. Security is more important on some computers than others. A university workstation on the Internet is probably at more risk of unfriendly attack than a non-networked PC locked in someone's study—plan your security strategy accordingly.

Host-Based Security with xhost

Host-based security was the first form of security added to X. It restricts access to your display based upon the host computer on which the client program is running. This may have been adequate at one time, but is usually not acceptable now, because it is common to allow login access to all workstations on a network. So, allowing access by your colleague's workstation (in order to let him or her access your display) also allows access by anyone who can log into your colleague's system.

Basic xhost Commands

There are two basic *xhost* commands: **xhost +** to enable access, and **xhost –** to disable access. Each form of the command can be given an optional list of hosts, in order to enable or disable access for a particular host. Running *xhost* with no parameters shows the current system status. For example, to allow access to any program running on any machine:

```
$ xhost +
access control disabled, clients can connect from any host
```

To allow access to any program running on either of the hosts **jasper** or **ruby**:

```
$ xhost + jasper ruby
```

---

* Actually, X security can seem confusing even to someone who has spent hours reading manuals and trying to configure it.

```
jasper being added to access control list
ruby being added to access control list
```

To disallow general access:

```
$ xhost -
access control enabled, only authorized clients can connect
```

To disallow access to any programs running on **ruby**:

```
$ xhost - ruby
ruby being removed from access control list
```

To see the current xhost state:

```
$ xhost
access control enabled, only authorized clients can connect
jasper.ora.com
```

Notice that turning off general access is not sufficient if access has already been granted to specific hosts—these must be turned off individually.

Turning Off All xhost Access

So, in order to turn off all *xhost* access, you must do two things:

1. Turn all general xhost access via `xhost -`
2. Turn off *xhost* access for each of the hosts already granted access via `xhost - hostname...`

As an example, let's clean up access for this display,* which currently allows general access, in addition to host-specific access for **jasper** and **ruby**. First, let's see what our current state is.

```
$ xhost
access control disabled, clients can connect from any host
ruby.ora.com
jasper.ora.com
```

This is pretty bad. Access control is disabled, leaving us wide open. First, let's turn that off.

```
$ xhost -
access control enabled, only authorized clients can connect
```

This is better, but running *xhost* again shows us that we still have two hosts that client programs can connect from.

```
$ xhost
access control enabled, only authorized clients can connect
ruby.ora.com
jasper.ora.com
```

---

* The script in Figure 20-3 does this automatically. I use this in my X start-up scripts, just in case there were any `xhost +` commands in any of the default start-up scripts.

Let's turn access off to each of these. We can do it one by one, or several on the command line.

```
$ xhost - ruby
ruby being removed from access control list
$ xhost
access control enabled, only authorized clients can connect
jasper.ora.com
$ xhost - jasper
jasper being removed from access control list
```

Let's check our status one last time, to make sure that we didn't overlook anything.

```
$ xhost
access control enabled, only authorized clients can connect
```

The output of the final command is what you want to see. It means that all host base access has been disabled and that you can now proceed to set up user-based authorization (see Example 20-3).*

Example 20-3: no-xhost—Turn Off All xhost Access

```
#!/bin/sh
# the next line restarts using tclsh \
exec tclsh "$0" "$@"

# turn off general xhost access
exec xhost -

# run xhost to get host-specific information
set XHOST [open "|xhost"]

# throw away the "access control enabled"
gets $XHOST

# loop through each host in the access list and disable it
while {[gets $XHOST hostname] > -1} {
    exec xhost - $hostname
}

close $XHOST
```

User-Based Security with xauth

Once we have disabled xhost-based access, we need to enable user-based access. The basic procedure is this:

1. Start your X server with xauth enabled. Depending on your system setup, this may be done for you automatically, or you may need to pass some special flags to your X server.

---

* However, it doesn't tell you whether there is already a client connection from an untrusted sight, so once you have finished setting up your configuration you should restart your X session. Remember, if the X server was insecure at any time, there is the possibility that your security was violated.

2. The X server is given a special password in binary format (usually referred to as a "magic cookie").

3. Upon connection, any program which can provide the magic cookie to the server will be allowed access. Any program which cannot provide the magic cookie is denied access.

How It Works

The "magic cookie" is stored in a file in your home directory (usually *$HOME/.Xauthority*) which must be readable only by yourself (if other people can read it, they can copy your magic cookies and attach to your X server). When the X server is started, it reads the cookie from that file. Any X client programs that request a connection to the server must supply the cookie to the server in order to receive the connection. This will be no problem for client programs run by you, since the client can access the data in the authorization file. Users who do not have access to the authorization file will not be able to supply the cookie to the server and will be denied access.*

Starting Your X Server

The hardest thing about using *xauth* is making sure that your X server has been started with *xauth* enabled. If you did not enable *xauth* when you started your server, you will go through all the following steps, and they will appear to work. You can run the *xauth* program, set your access permissions and save them, and so on, and everything will appear to be normal. However, your authorization will fail, because you didn't start the X server with authorization enabled.

A special note to X terminal users: Since you don't have any control over how your X terminal starts up (start-up options are preconfigured by your administrator), you will need to get your system administrator to make any changes you need.

If you finish setting up *xauth* and it doesn't work, it is most likely because your X server was not started with *xauth* enabled.

To start your X session with user authorization, you need to pass the `-auth filename` parameter when you start X. Here are some typical ways of doing this. If none of these work, then it's time to ask your system administrator.

- **X Display Manager (XDM)**: You are most likely running XDM if your login screen has a window with entry fields for your login name and password, and a message that says something like "Welcome to the X Window System." Normally, XDM has *xauth* turned on by default, so there is nothing special you need to do.†

- **Open Windows**: Sun very wisely made Open Windows use *xauth* by default. If you start your X server by running *openwin* you will not need any extra parameters.

---

* Xauth has quite a few other features and options. For more information, consult the *X Window System Administrator's Guide* by Linda Mui and Eric Pearce.
† A good overview of setting up XDM is "The X Administrator: Taming the X Display Manager" by Miles O'Neal, X Resource Journal, Issue 4, Fall 1992.

- **xinit:** *xinit* is the standard "low-level" program for starting X servers. Other methods of starting an X server (such as *openwin*) frequently end up calling *xinit* after setting things up. If you are running *xinit* directly, you can pass the authorization parameter directly to the X server by putting the "-auth" parameter behind a "—" delimiter.

  ```
  xinit -- :0 -auth ~/.Xauthority
  ```

- **startx:** *startx* is a shell script that is distributed with the standard X distribution. It is expected that the site administrator will customize this script for his or her site, so hopefully *xauth* is already included. If not, you can pass parameters to the X server in a manner similar to *xinit*:

  ```
  startx -- -auth ~/.Xauthority
  ```

Am I Running with xauth?

Unfortunately, there's no straightforward way to tell if *xauth* has been turned on. About the best you can do is to view your processes with the `ps` command, look for the X server processes, and see if it has been run with *-auth*. This will vary from system to system, but will probably look something like one of these examples:

- On a system with an AT&T-like `ps` command (e.g., HP/UX or Solaris), run `ps -ef` and look for a line like:

  ```
  mh 285 132 80 Apr 15 console 400:33 X :0 -auth
  /homes/mharriso/.Xauthority
  ```

- On a system with a BSD-like `ps` command (e.g., SunOS or FreeBSD), run `ps aux` and look for a line like:

  ```
  mh 12 2.2 5 5652 console  S   Apr 15 9:42 X :0 -auth
  /homes/mh/.Xauthority
  ```

- Sometimes your X server has a different name. Here are the results from a Solaris system running CDE (the Common Desktop Environment):

  ```
  mh 233 207 0 Apr 26 ? 5:17 /usr/openwin/bin/Xsun :0 -nobanner -
  auth /var/dt/A:0-a0003F
  ```

The key things to remember:

1. Use the `ps` command to see what is running.

2. You are looking for the X server. The X server can have various names, but it will usually either be called "X" or begin with "X" and be followed by the name of the customized version, such as "Xsun."

3. If you see `-auth` you are most likely running with *xauth* enabled.

4. If you do not see `-auth`, you are almost certainly not running with *xauth* enabled.

Configuring xauth

Once you have your server running with user authorization enabled, you need to configure it. Again, there are various levels of security that you can set—take your own circumstances into account.

The various levels of security include:

1. **Somewhat Reasonable Security**: You can set your cookie once, and reuse the same cookie for each X session. This has the advantage of being simple, but if someone gets hold of your *.Xauthority* file, they will be able to use this to interact with your future X sessions. This is about the same level of security as your login password, since it changes infrequently relative to the number of times you log in. Still, an unfriendly person with root access (or someone who had unsupervised access to your terminal for 30 seconds) could just make a copy of your file for future use.

   This also creates the problem that an unfriendly person can write a program to guess the value of your cookie, since he or she will be able to run it over longer periods of time. This is not *quite* as bad as it sound, since an exhaustive search for the cookie would take $3*10^{38}$ tries (the cookie is 128 bits long).

2. **Better Security**: This method uses the same basic approach as the previous method, but generates a new authorization key for each session. Thus, if an unfriendly person obtained the contents of your *.Xauthority* file, the information would become useless as soon as you started your next X session.

3. **Best Security**: This is identical to method 2, except that it uses a cryptographically "strong" hash function called MD5 (see the sidebar) to make the cookie much harder to guess.

MD5

MD5 is a program that generates strong 128-bit checksums (also known as "message digests," hence the name) of a given input. It is useful for verifying that files have not changed, that a message has not been modified in transit, or for generating unique one-time values. This last purpose is what we used it for in this chapter—we generated some unique system and time-dependant output, and used MD5 to generate a checksum for it.

It was designed by well-known cryptologist Ronald Rivest of MIT, and is described in detail in Internet RFC 1321.

MD5 is available from many FTP sites on the Internet. The official copy is available from *rsa.com*. CERT (the Computer Emergency Response Team) maintains a copy at *ftp.cert.org*. We have also included it on the CD accompanying this book.

The basic steps in all three of these methods are essentially the same. You run the *xauth* command

```
xauth add display-name proto-name hex-key
```

Where *display-name* is the name of your X display, *proto-name* is the name of the security scheme you are using (usually "MIT-MAGIC-COOKIE-1"), and *hex-key* is a even-numbered sequence of random hex digits. The only difference between the three methods is the content of *hex-key*.

You will need to run *xauth* twice, in order to add both local access and network access to your display. First, let's do the simplest approach. We will arbitrarily pick the value "0102030405060708" as our random key.* For convenience, we can specify "." as the *proto-name*, as this is a synonym for "MIT-MAGIC-COOKIE-1."

```
$ xauth add `hostname`:0 . 0102030405060708
$ xauth add `hostname`/unix:0 . 0102030405060708
$ xauth list
ruby.ora.com:0  MIT-MAGIC-COOKIE-1  0102030405060708
ruby/unix:0  MIT-MAGIC-COOKIE-1  0102030405060708
```

You can also use `localhost:0` instead of `hostname`:0.

To use the second scheme, we need to come up with a random collection of hex digits. This Perl program† will work.

```
$ randomkey=`perl -e 'for (1..4) { \
    srand(time+$$+$seed); \
    printf("%4.5x", ($seed = int(rand(65536)))); } \
  print "\n";'`
$ xauth add `hostname`:0 . $randomkey
$ xauth add `hostname`/unix:0 . $randomkey
$ xauth list
ruby.ora.com:0  MIT-MAGIC-COOKIE-1  0cd1302a1d0c5bc09d0a
ruby/unix:0  MIT-MAGIC-COOKIE-1  0cd1302a1d0c5bc09d0a
```

Finally, to use MD5 to generate a truly difficult-to-guess key, we send it the output of a number of system commands‡ that give unpredictable output, and use the results of MD5 as our key.

```
$ randomkey=`(ps -ael; nfsstat -m; nfsstat -r; who; netstat -m;
date) | md5`
$ xauth add `hostname`:0 . $randomkey
$ xauth add `hostname`/unix:0 . $randomkey
$ xauth list
ruby.ora.com:0  MIT-MAGIC-COOKIE-1 07e89019fd03bd20d008
ruby/unix:0  MIT-MAGIC-COOKIE-1 07e89019fd03bd20d008
```

If you use one of the per-session methods, add the lines to your X start-up file, such as *.xinitrc* or *.xsession*. Finally, make sure that your *.Xauthority* file is not readable or writable by anyone other than yourself. This is done automatically by the *xauth add*, but it doesn't hurt to double-check occasionally.

---

* Don't use this as your random key!

† Thanks to Ben Gross and Baba Buehler for these examples.

‡ This is pretty system-specific—you may need to customize this for your system. Use commands that report system status, or that are date and time dependent.

```
$ ls -l .Xauthority
-rw-------  1 mh                    150 Oct 19 17:24 .Xauthority
```

Xauth has quite a few other features and options. For more information, consult the X Window System Administrator's Guide by Linda Mui and Eric Pearce.

Which One Should I Use?

Again, this decision depends upon your circumstances. If you are at a site that is particularly open to outside attack (a university computer center, for example), then use the strongest methods to protect yourself that you can. If you're on a relatively isolated site, the weaker methods may be adequate.

However, once any of these methods are set up, they are all equally simple to use in daily practice. The most troublesome part of setting up *xauth* is getting the procedural issues (such as how to start X) straightened out, and getting the supporting software (like MD5) in place. Once these things are done, there is relatively little else to do. Ask your administrator to help set these things up for all the users in your site—good security will pay off for everyone in the long run.

Disabling Tk Security

It is possible to build Tk with security disabled. This is usually not advisable, but based on your own analysis of your situation, it might be needed. There is only one scenario I can think of where this is a reasonable thing to do: if you (1) cannot configure your X setup to be secure, and (2) if you are running on a single-user computer that is not attached to a network (a non-networked laptop PC, for example).

If you decide this is acceptable, you can edit the Tk makefile, and change the lines that read

```
# To turn off the security checks that disallow incoming sends when
# the X server appears to be insecure, reverse the comments on the
# following lines:
SECURITY_FLAGS =
#SECURITY_FLAGS = -DTK_NO_SECURITY
```

to

```
#SECURITY_FLAGS =
SECURITY_FLAGS = -DTK_NO_SECURITY
```

The **send** command from the resulting build will not make its usual security checks.

Application Security

Finally, there are several things you can do in your application to enhance security. To disable the **send** command altogether, you can simply delete the command before your program starts by renaming to the empty string:*

---

* Be sure to do this before the main window is created, in order to avoid a gap in which send will work.

```
rename send {}
```

In a similar way, other commands that you do not wish to be available at runtime can be deleted during start-up. A program could be disallowed disk access by removing the file-related commands, for example.

Safe Interpreters

Starting with Tcl 7.5, there is an `interp` command that can be used to create multiple interpreters within your program. Any of these interpreters can be designated as a "safe" interpreter. A safe interpreter has restricted functionality, so that it can execute scripts from untrusted sources without fear.

For example, if you were receiving a command from an untrusted remote source (a client operating on a remote internet site, for example), you wouldn't want to do something like this:

```
set cmd [gets $REMOTE]        ;# read a command from a remote user
eval $cmd                     ;# and execute it
```

Evaluating *cmd* would leave your program at the mercy of whoever sent you the script. They could destroy your application, delete your files, or worse.

Instead, let's create a safe interpreter and use that to evaluate the command.

```
% interp create -safe
interp0
% set cmd {exec echo "dangerous command, beware!"}
% interp0 eval $cmd
invalid command name "exec"
```

Since a safe interpreter does not include the `exec`* command, the evil script is rendered harmless.

Of course, you can only remove functionality up to a point before the interpreter becomes useless. To counteract this, you can alias commands in the safe interpreter to commands in the master interpreter that can perform the desired action after performing any necessary checks on the command or its parameters. For example, you may allow access to a set of data files. In this case, you might alias a "safe" command `open_data_file` to a trusted command that would verify the parameters and allow access to only a limited set of non-classified data files.

Computer security is a tricky business—witness the regular reports of computer break-ins on the evening news. Keep these things in mind when writing programs that deal with scripts from untrusted sources:

1. Always keep in mind which scripts or data come from an untrusted source. Never `eval` or `subst` this data, since that would allow a potential back door into your program.

2. Be careful when creating command aliases. The code that the safe command is aliased to is executing in "dangerous" mode, so review and inspect your

---

* The interp man page specifies the exact set of commands that are included for safe interpreters.

code thoroughly. Do you ever allow unrestricted system access, such as opening a filename that you have not verified?

3. Try to think like a criminal. Think of ways to break your own system and correct them.

4. Read the *Risks Digest*, usually found in the Usenet newsgroup *comp.risks*. This forum, moderated by Peter G. Neumann, is an excellent place to learn not just about security issues, but about "safe" computing in general.

Appendix **A**

Getting Help

There are many resources available for you to learn more about Tcl, and many places where you can seek help.

Tcl Newsgroups

One of the best Tcl resources available is the Usenet newsgroup *comp.lang.tcl*. All of the extension authors are active participants in this newsgroup (as well as John Ousterhout and the members of the Tcl group at Sun), and there are many people discussing their Tcl-related work, questions, etc. It's a sure bet that you will find plenty of ideas and inspiration here.

There is also a moderated newsgroup *comp.lang.tcl.announce*, which is used only for announcements related to Tcl, like upgrades, new extensions and packages, training, and the like. Since it is moderated, it has a very high signal to noise ratio.

FAQ (Frequently Asked Questions) Lists

One of the traditions of Usenet is the Frequently Asked Questions list. Originally started to reduce the number of repetitive newsgroup postings, FAQs have in some cases expanded to near-encyclopedic works covering every aspect of the topic being discussed. There are a number of Tcl-related FAQs that are posted regularly to both *comp.lang.tcl* and *comp.lang.tcl.announce*. They are also archived on the Web at the sites mentioned here.

At press time, these FAQs are currently available:

- **The Tcl Introductory FAQ (Larry Virden):** The original Tcl FAQ. It includes a comprehensive catalog of Tcl-related programs and extensions.
- **Tcl Usage FAQ (Joe Moss):** Questions about using Tcl the language (as distinct from Tk).

- **Tcl Bibliography (Glenn Vandenburg):** A comprehensive bibliography of all articles about Tcl/Tk or that contain references to Tcl/Tk.
- **Tk Usage FAQ (Thomas J. Accardo):** Questions about using the Tk toolkit.
- **Tcl Commercial Uses FAQ (Gerald Lester):** A list of Tcl-related products, services, and training.
- **Tcl Windows FAQ (Eric Johnson):** Answers questions related to using Tcl on Microsoft Windows.

Tcl Archive Sites

There are two primary FTP sites for obtaining Tcl-related software, including the extensions in this book. These are:

- *ftp://ftp.smli.com/pub/tcl/:* The official Tcl site for obtaining releases from Sun.
- *ftp://ftp.neosoft.com/pub/tcl/:* The official site for Tcl contributed software. It also mirrors the Sun site, and has a searchable WWW interface (described later).

Web Pages

Many sites on the World Wide Web discuss Tcl. These are some of the larger sites which have many pointers to other sites.

- *http://www.sunlabs.com/research/tcl:* The official Sun Tcl page.
- *http://www.sco.com/Technology/tcl/Tcl.html:* A very comprehensive collection of pointers to Tcl resources on the Web.
- *http://www.neosoft.com/tcl/:* The WWW interface to the Tcl contributed software archive.
- *http://www.tcltk.com/:* A source of general Tcl/Tk information.
- *http://web.cs.ualberta.ca/~wade/HyperTcl/:* A searchable index of Tcl resources.
- *http://www.teraform.com/~lvirden/tcl-faq/:* The official release area for the FAQs.
- *http://www.yahoo.com/Computers_and_Internet/Programming_Languages/Tcl_Tk/:* Yahoo's index of Internet Tcl resources.

Index

A

Accelerators, 155
Accounts, changing. *See* Multiple machines
adb program, 503
Aggregate function, 480. *See also* SQL
alarm command, 235
Animated cursors, 315–317
Annotation markers, 268
ANSI C compiler, and embedded Tk, 530
API. *See* Application programming interface
Application building
  Embedded Tk, 511–534
  Mega-Widget usage, 106–108
Application security, 630–632
Application wrappers, 308–320
Applications. *See* Graphical applications;
    Target applications
Array indices, 258
Asynchronous SQL processing, 481–482
at, 505–506
autoexpect, 509
auto_load command, 263
auto_packages command, 262
auto_path variable, 261
Autoloading [incr Tcl], 62
Automatic replaying, 570–571
Automatic socket cleanup, 370
Automation
  Expect, 497–510
  TkReplay, 565–586
Autoscroll, 584
Awk comparison, 248
Axis
  limits, 329, 331
  tick labels, 275, 279
  values, 333

B

Background processes, 505–506
Backslash sequences, 222, 456, 476
BLT
  applications, building, 324–342

bar chart widget, 281–285
  bars, display control, 283–284
  display modes, 284–285
Bgexec command, 308–312
bitmap command, 317–320
busy command, 313–317
drag&drop command, 320–324
graph widget, 268–281
  coordinate axes, 274–277
  elements, 270–272
  graph options, 278–279
  legend, 272–274
  markers, 277–278
graphs, 293
spline command, 294
table geometry manager, 265, 297–308
toolkit, 265–342
tracing, 615–617
vector command, 286–295
Bandwidth usage, 227
Bar chart widget. *See* BLT
Bar charts, 284
Barchart command, 281
Bars. *See* BLT
Base class, 33, 35, 41, 42, 46, 60, 72, 97, 105
  component, 103
  constructors, 43
  context, 36
  design, 94–99
Base date value, 236
Berkeley socket abstraction, 345
Berkeley sockets, review, 362
Bgexec command. *See* BLT
Binary data, 285
Bind variable, 468
Bindings, 445. *See* Key bindings
Bitmap command, 329. *See also* BLT
Bitmap files, 315. *See also* X11 bitmap files
Bitmap image, 427
Black-box reuse, 47
Blocking behavior, 370
Blocking RPC, 350
Body command, 23, 24
Boolean, 386, 415

MDIWindow, 164
Media-space system, 540, 541
Mega-Widgets, 4, 111, 448. *See also*
    Fileconfirm mega-widget; Tix Mega-
    Widgets
  building, [incr Tk] usage, 69–110
  classes, 99
  components, accessing, 168–172
  configuration options
  construction, 73
    Tix, 201
  creation, 119–122
  defining, 88–93
  example, 82–94
  framework, 560
  ignoring, 80–81
  keeping, 76–78
  overview, 71–82
  path name, 114
  usual options, 79–80
    defining, 93–94
  renaming, 78–79
  restricted access, 172
  set, 111–114
  summary, 108
  Tix, 164–216
Member functions, 8
Membership, adding/dropping, 374–375
Memory, leakage, 515
Memory utilization, 389, 415
Menu bar, 567
Menubar commands, 155
Message line, 567
Messagedialog, 146, 149, 156
Message-oriented delivery, 365
Methods, 8
min command, 218
mkdir command, 234
Model-View-Controller (MVC), 557, 558
  paradigm, 558, 559
Modems, testing, 502
Mosaic, 5
Motif 2.0, 172
Motif prompt dialog, 149
Motif-like X interface, 504
Motif-style file selection widget, 151
Motion events, 575, 576, 578. *See also*
    Consecutive motion events
Mouse movement, 569
Mouse pointer motion, replaying, 571
Mouse speed, 570
MPEG streams, 484

MS Windows building, ET usage, 533–534
mtime variable, 36
Multi-file text editor, 154
Multiple inheritance, 38–42
Multiple machines, accounts changing,
    499–500
Multiple users, coordination, 546–550
Multiprocess programming, 241
MultiUser scrollbars, 555–556
Multiuser text editors, 535
MVC. *See* Model-View-Controller

N

Name collisions, 10
Name resolution, 51–52
Name server, 361–362
names command, 229
Namespaces, 48–59. *See also* filebrowser
    namespace; folder namespace; Global
    namespace
  context, 98
  creation, 48–51
  objects, usage, 52–54
  path, 53
  quick reference, 67–68
  usage, 55–56
Network interfaces, 253
New conference, creation, 537–538
nice command, 234
Niceness values, 234
NOBUF option, 244
Nodes. *See* Complex nodes; Reference
    nodes; Sibling nodes
  adding. *See* Tree
  border, 441
  moving, 437
  removing, 437–438
No-match string, 152
Non-blocking RPC, 350
Non-classified data files, 631
Noninteractive applications, 420
Non-networked PC, 623
Non-numeric indices, 288
Non-uniform intervals,
  axis ticks, 275
Non-Unix systems, Expect usage, 508
Note Organizer, 559, 562
NoteBook widget, 180. *See also*
    Tabnotebook: TexNoteBook
Notification messagedialog, 158

About the Author

Mark Harrison has been involved in computer networking since 1980, when he had a college job answering email for Radio Shack's computer service department. He has worked in several areas of computing, including multilingual human interfaces and compiler design, and now works in the telecommunications industry as a senior architect for Advanced Intelligent Network (AIN) products at DSC Communications Corporation. He lives in Richardson, Texas, with his wife and two children, both of whom have Usenet accounts. His interestes include juggling, playing classical music, and collecting rare books.

Colophon

Edie Freedman designed this book's cover, and Hanna Dyer designed the CD label, using QuarkXPress running on a PowerMacintosh. The extension cord image was photographed by Kevin Thomas and retouched using Adobe Photoshop. The cords were purchased at Winchester True Value Hardware, in Winchester, Massachusetts. The photo is copyright 1997, O'Reilly & Associates, Inc.

Edie Freedman also designed the page layout. Book production was completed by Benchmark Productions, Inc., Boston, MA. Online copyediting was achieved using revision tools in Microsoft Word 6. The page layout was produced with Quark XPress 3.3. The body text of the book is set in the Adobe ITC Garamond typeface; the examples are set in Constant Willison. Heading and captions are set in the Helvetica Condensed Bold Oblique typeface. The illustrations that appear in the book were created in Macromedia Freehand 7.0 and Adobe Photoshop 4.0 by Robert Romano.

Whenever possible, our books use RepKover™, a durable and flexible lay-flat binding. If the page count exceeds RepKover's limit, perfect binding is used.

 # More Titles from O'Reilly

Tools

Programming with GNU Software

By Mike Loukides & Andy Oram
1st Edition January 1997
260 pages, ISBN 1-56592-112-7

 This book and CD combination is a complete package for programmers who are new to UNIX or who would like to make better use of the system. The tools come from Cygnus Support, Inc., a well-known company that provides support for free software. Contents include GNU Emacs, *gcc*, C and C++ libraries, *gdb*, RCS, and *make*. The book provides an introduction to all these tools for a C programmer.

Applying RCS and SCCS

By Don Bolinger & Tan Bronson
1st Edition September 1995
528 pages, ISBN 1-56592-117-8

 *Applying RCS and SCCS* is a thorough introduction to these two systems, viewed as tools for project management. This book takes the reader from basic source control of a single file, through working with multiple releases of a software project, to coordinating multiple developers. It also presents TCCS, a representative "front-end" that addresses problems RCS and SCCS can't handle alone, such as managing groups of files, developing for multiple platforms, and linking public and private development areas.

lex & yacc

By John Levine, Tony Mason & Doug Brown
2nd Edition October 1992
366 pages, ISBN 1-56592-000-7

 This book shows programmers how to use two UNIX utilities, *lex* and *yacc*, in program development. The second edition contains completely revised tutorial sections for novice users and reference sections for advanced users. This edition is twice the size of the first, has an expanded index, and covers Bison and Flex.

Managing Projects with make

By Andrew Oram & Steve Talbott
2nd Edition October 1991
152 pages, ISBN 0-937175-90-0

 *make* is one of UNIX's greatest contributions to software development, and this book offers the clearest description of *make* ever written. Even the smallest software project typically involves a number of files that depend upon each other in various ways. If you modify one or more source files, you must relink the program after recompiling some, but not necessarily all, of the sources.

make greatly simplifies this process. By recording the relationships between sets of files, *make* can automatically perform all the necessary updating. This book describes all the basic features of *make* and provides guidelines on meeting the needs of large, modern projects.

Software Portability with imake, 2nd Edition

By Paul DuBois
2nd Edition September 1996
410 pages, ISBN 1-56592-226-3

 *imake* is a utility that works with *make* to enable code to be compiled and installed on different UNIX machines. *imake* makes possible the wide portability of the X Window System code and is widely considered an X tool, but it's also useful for any software project that needs to be ported to many UNIX systems.

This Nutshell Handbook—the only book available on *imake*—is ideal for X and UNIX programmers who want their software to be portable. The book is divided into two sections. The first section is a general explanation of *imake*, X configuration files, and how to write and debug an *Imakefile*. The second section describes how to write configuration files and presents a configuration file architecture that allows development of coexisting sets of configuration files. Several sample sets of configuration files are described and are available free over the Net.

The second edition covers X Window System X11 R6.1. New material includes a discussion of using *imake* for Windows NT and covers some quirks that occur when imake is used under OpenWindows/Solaris.

O'REILLY™

TO ORDER: **800-998-9938** • *order@oreilly.com* • *http://www.oreilly.com/*
OUR PRODUCTS ARE AVAILABLE AT A BOOKSTORE OR SOFTWARE STORE NEAR YOU.
FOR INFORMATION: **800-998-9938** • **707-829-0515** • *info@oreilly.com*

Tools *(continued)*

Porting UNIX Software

By Greg Lehey
1st Edition November 1995
538 pages, ISBN 1-56592-126-7

If you work on a UNIX system, a good deal of your most useful software comes from other people—your vendor is not the source. This means, all too often, that the software you want was written for a slightly different system and that it has to be ported. Despite the best efforts of standards committees and the admirable people who write the software (often giving it away for free), something is likely to go wrong when you try to compile their source code.

This book deals with the whole life cycle of porting, from setting up a source tree on your system to correcting platform differences and even testing the executable after it's built. The book exhaustively discusses the differences between versions of UNIX and the areas where porters tend to have problems. The assumption made in this book is that you just want to get a package working on your system; you don't want to become an expert in the details of your hardware or operating system (much less an expert in the system used by the person who wrote the package!). Many problems can be solved without a knowledge of C or UNIX, while the ones that force you to deal directly with source code are explained as simply and concretely as possible.

Exploring Expect

By Don Libes
1st Edition December 1994
602 pages, ISBN 1-56592-090-2

Written by the author of Expect, this is the first book to explain how this new part of the UNIX toolbox can be used to automate Telnet, FTP, passwd, rlogin, and hundreds of other interactive applications. Based on Tcl (Tool Command Language), Expect lets you automate interactive applications that have previously been extremely difficult to handle with any scripting language.

The book briefly describes Tcl and how Expect relates to it. It then describes the Expect language, using a combination of reference material and specific, useful examples of its features. It shows how to use Expect in background, in multiple processes, and with standard languages and tools like C, C++, and Tk, the X-based extension to Tcl. The strength in the book is in its scripts, conveniently listed in a separate index.

X User Tools

By Linda Mui & Valerie Quercia
1st Edition November 1994
856 pages, Includes CD-ROM, ISBN 1-56592-019-8

X User Tools provides for X users what *UNIX Power Tools* provides for UNIX users: hundreds of tips, tricks, scripts, techniques, and programs—plus a CD-ROM—to make the X Window System more enjoyable, more powerful, and easier to use. This browser's book emphasizes useful programs culled from the network, offers tips for configuring individual and systemwide environments, and includes a CD-ROM of source files for all—and binary files for some—of the programs.

UNIX Power Tools

By Jerry Peek, Mike Loukides, Tim O'Reilly, et al.
1st Edition March 1993
1162 pages, Includes CD-ROM
Random House ISBN 0-679-79073-X

Ideal for UNIX users who hunger for technical—yet accessible—information, *UNIX Power Tools* consists of tips, tricks, concepts, and freeware (CD-ROM included). It also covers add-on utilities and how to take advantage of clever features in the most popular UNIX utilities.

This is a browser's book...like a magazine that you don't read from start to finish, but leaf through repeatedly until you realize that you've read it all. You'll find articles abstracted from O'Reilly Nutshell Handbooks®, new information that highlights program "tricks" and "gotchas," tips posted to the Net over the years, and other accumulated wisdom.

The goal of *UNIX Power Tools* is to help you think creatively about UNIX and get you to the point where you can analyze your own problems. Your own solutions won't be far behind.

"Let me congratulate you all for writing the best and the most complete book written for UNIX. After glancing and skimming through the book, I found [it] to be a very powerful reference/learning tool. The best part...is the humor.... Thanks for providing a good/solid/funny UNIX book."
—Shawn Gargya, scgargya@vnet.ibm.com

UNIX Basics

Learning the UNIX Operating System

By Grace Todino, John Strang & Jerry Peek
3rd Edition August 1993
108 pages, ISBN 1-56592-060-0

If you are new to UNIX, this concise introduction will tell you just what you need to get started and no more. Why wade through a 600-page book when you can begin working productively in a matter of minutes? It's an ideal primer for Mac and PC users of the Internet who need to know a little bit about UNIX on the systems they visit. This book is the most effective introduction to UNIX in print. The third edition has been updated and expanded to provide increased coverage of window systems and networking. It's a handy book for someone just starting with UNIX, as well as someone who encounters a UNIX system as a "visitor" via remote login over the Internet.

Learning GNU Emacs, 2nd Edition

By Debra Cameron, Bill Rosenblatt & Eric Raymond
2nd Edition September 1996
560 pages, ISBN 1-56592-152-6

Learning GNU Emacs is an introduction to Version 19.30 of the GNU Emacs editor, one of the most widely used and powerful editors available under UNIX. It provides a solid introduction to basic editing, a look at several important "editing modes" (special Emacs features for editing specific types of documents, including email, Usenet News, and the World Wide Web), and a brief introduction to customization and Emacs LISP programming. The book is aimed at new Emacs users, whether or not they are programmers. Includes quick-reference card.

Learning the bash Shell

By Cameron Newham & Bill Rosenblatt
1st Edition October 1995
310 pages, ISBN 1-56592-147-X

Whether you want to use *bash* for its programming features or its user interface, you'll find *Learning the bash Shell* a valuable guide. If you're new to shell programming, it provides an excellent introduction, covering everything from the most basic to the most advanced features, like signal handling and command line processing. If you've been writing shell scripts for years, it offers a great way to find out what the new shell offers.

Learning the Korn Shell

By Bill Rosenblatt
1st Edition June 1993
360 pages, ISBN 1-56592-054-6

This Nutshell Handbook is a thorough introduction to the Korn shell, both as a user interface and as a programming language. The Korn shell is a program that interprets UNIX commands. It has many features that aren't found in other shells, including command history. This book provides a clear and concise explanation of the Korn shell's features. It explains *ksh* string operations, co-processes, signals and signal handling, and command-line interpretation. The book also includes real-life programming examples and a Korn shell debugger called *kshdb*, the only known implementation of a shell debugger anywhere.

Using csh and tcsh

By Paul DuBois
1st Edition August 1995
242 pages, ISBN 1-56592-132-1

Using csh and tcsh describes from the beginning how to use these shells interactively to get your work done faster with less typing. You'll learn how to make your prompt tell you where you are (no more pwd); use what you've typed before (history); type long command lines with few keystrokes (command and filename completion); remind yourself of filenames when in the middle of typing a command; and edit a botched command without retyping it.

Learning the vi Editor

By Linda Lamb
5th Edition October 1990
192 pages, ISBN 0-937175-67-6

This book is a complete guide to text editing with *vi*, the editor available on nearly every UNIX system. Early chapters cover the basics; later chapters explain more advanced editing tools, such as *ex* commands and global search and replacement.

O'REILLY™

TO ORDER: **800-998-9938** • **order@oreilly.com** • **http://www.oreilly.com/**
OUR PRODUCTS ARE AVAILABLE AT A BOOKSTORE OR SOFTWARE STORE NEAR YOU.
FOR INFORMATION: **800-998-9938** • **707-829-0515** • **info@oreilly.com**

UNIX Basics *(continued)*

sed & awk, 2nd Edition

By Dale Dougherty & Arnold Robbins
2nd Edition Winter 1997
450 pages (est.), ISBN 1-56592-225-5

sed & awk, one of the most popular books in O'Reilly & Associates' Nutshell series, describes two text processing programs that are mainstays of the UNIX programmer's toolbox. The book lays a foundation for both programs by describing how they are used and by introducing the fundamental concepts of regular expressions and text matching. This new edition covers the *sed* and *awk* programs as they are now mandated by the POSIX standard. It also includes a discussion of the GNU versions of both programs, which have extensions beyond their UNIX counterparts. Many examples are used throughout the book to illustrate the concepts discussed.

SCO UNIX in a Nutshell

By Ellie Cutler & the staff of O'Reilly & Associates
1st Edition February 1994
590 pages, ISBN 1-56592-037-6

The desktop reference to SCO UNIX and Open Desktop®, this version of *UNIX in a Nutshell* shows you what's under the hood of your SCO system. It isn't a scaled-down quick reference of common commands, but a complete reference containing all user, programming, administration, and networking commands.

UNIX in a Nutshell: System V Edition

By Daniel Gilly &
the staff of O'Reilly & Associates
2nd Edition June 1992
444 pages, ISBN 1-56592-001-5

You may have seen UNIX quick-reference guides, but you've never seen anything like *UNIX in a Nutshell.* Not a scaled-down quick reference of common commands, *UNIX in a Nutshell* is a complete reference containing all commands and options, along with generous descriptions and examples that put the commands in context. For all but the thorniest UNIX problems, this one reference should be all the documentation you need. Covers System V, Releases 3 and 4, and Solaris 2.0.

What You Need to Know: When You Can't Find Your UNIX System Administrator

By Linda Mui
1st Edition April 1995
156 pages, ISBN 1-56592-104-6

This book is written for UNIX users, who are often cast adrift in a confusing environment. It provides the background and practical solutions you need to solve problems you're likely to encounter—problems with logging in, printing, sharing files, running programs, managing space resources, etc. It also describes the kind of info to gather when you're asking for a diagnosis from a busy sys admin. And, it gives you a list of site-specific information that you should know, as well as a place to write it down.

Volume 3M: X Window System User's Guide, Motif Edition

By Valerie Quercia & Tim O'Reilly
2nd Edition January 1993
956 pages, ISBN 1-56592-015-5

The *X Window System User's Guide, Motif Edition* orients the new user to window system concepts and provides detailed tutorials for many client programs, including the xtermterminal emulator and the twm, uwm, and mwmwindow managers. Later chapters explain how to customize the X environment. Revised for Motif 1.2 and X11 Release 5.

What You Need to Know: Using Email Effectively

By Linda Lamb & Jerry Peek
1st Edition April 1995
160 pages, ISBN 1-56592-103-8

After using email for a few years, you learn from your own mistakes and from reading other people's mail. You learn how to include a message but leave in only the sections that make your point, how to recognize if a network address "looks right," how to successfully subscribe and unsubscribe to a mailing list, how to save mail so that you can find it again. This book shortens the learning-from-experience curve for all mailers, so you can quickly be productive and send email that looks intelligent to others.

O'REILLY™

TO ORDER: **800-998-9938** • **order@oreilly.com** • **http://www.oreilly.com/**
OUR PRODUCTS ARE AVAILABLE AT A BOOKSTORE OR SOFTWARE STORE NEAR YOU.
FOR INFORMATION: **800-998-9938** • **707-829-0515** • **info@oreilly.com**

UNIX Programming

Programming Python

By Mark Lutz
1st Edition October 1996
906 pages, ISBN 1-56592-197-6

This O'Reilly Nutshell Handbook describes how to use Python, an increasingly popular object-oriented scripting language freely available over the Net. Python is an interpreted language, useful for quick prototyping and simple programs for which C++ is too complex and unwieldy. The Python interpreter is available on most popular UNIX platforms, including Linux, as well as Windows, NT, and the Mac.

Programming Python, the only source of user material available for this scripting language, complements online reference material provided with Python releases. It has been both reviewed and endorsed by Python creator Guido van Rossum, who also provides the foreword. You'll find many useful running examples, which become more complex as new topics are introduced. Examples that describe Graphical User Interface (GUI) use TK as well as Python. The appendix contains a short language tutorial. Includes a CD-ROM containing Python software for all major UNIX platforms, as well as Windows, NT, and the Mac.

Pthreads Programming

By Bradford Nichols, Dick Buttlar & Jacqueline Proulx Farrell
1st Edition September 1996
284 pages, ISBN 1-56592-115-1

The idea behind threads programming is to have multiple tasks running concurrently within the same program. They can share a single CPU as processes do, or take advantage of multiple CPUs when available. In either case, they provide a clean way to divide the tasks of a program while sharing data. The POSIX threads standard, which is the subject of this book, is supported by the Distributed Computer Environment (DCE), as well as Solaris, OSF/1, AIX, and several other UNIX-based operating systems.

In this book you will learn not only what the pthread calls are, but when it is a good idea to use threads and how to make them efficient (which is the whole reason for using threads in the first place). The author delves into performance issues, comparing threads to processes, contrasting kernel threads to user threads, and showing how to measure speed. He also describes in a simple, clear manner what all the advanced features are for, and how threads interact with the rest of the UNIX system.

UNIX Systems Programming for SVR4

By David A. Curry
1st Edition July 1996
620 pages, ISBN 1-56592-163-1

Any program worth its salt uses operating system services. Even a simple program, if practical, reads input and produces output. And, most applications have more complex needs. They need to find out the time, use the network, or start and communicate with other processes. Systems programming really means nothing more than writing software that uses these operating system services.

UNIX Systems Programming for SVR4 gives you the nitty gritty details on how UNIX interacts with applications. If you're writing an application from scratch, or if you're porting an application to any System V.4 platform, you need this book.

The first part of the book presents simple functions and concepts supported by numerous code fragment examples and short demonstration programs. These examples become building blocks for the application program examples that appear later in the book to illustrate more advanced, complex functions.

UNIX Systems Programming for SVR4 is thorough and complete and offers advice on:

- Working with low-level I/O routines and the standard I/O library
- Creating and deleting files and directories, changing file attributes, processing multiple input streams, file and record locking, and memory-mapped files
- Reading, printing, and setting the system time and date
- Determining who is logged in, times users log in and out, how to change a program's effective user ID or group ID, and writing set user ID programs
- Changing system configuration parameters for resource limits
- Creating processes, job control, and signal handling
- Using pipes, FIFOs, UNIX-domain sockets, message queues, semaphores, and shared memory for interprocess communication
- Reading and setting serial line characteristics including baud rate, echoing, and flow control
- Network programming with Berkeley sockets, Transport Layer Interface (TLI), a less popular but more flexible inter-face to network programming, and the data link provider interface

UNIX Programming (continued)

Power Programming with RPC

By John Bloomer
1st Edition February 1992
522 pages, ISBN 0-937175-77-3

A distributed application is designed to access resources across a network. In a broad sense, these resources could be user input, a central database, configuration files, etc., that are distributed on various computers across the network, rather than found on a single computer. RPC, or remote procedure calling, is the ability to distribute the execution of functions on remote computers outside of the application's current address space. This allows you to break large or complex programming problems into routines that can be executed independently of one another to take advantage of multiple computers. Thus, RPC makes it possible to attack a problem using a form of parallel processing or multiprocessing.

Written from a programmer's perspective, this book shows what you can do with Sun RPC, the de facto standard on UNIX systems. It covers related programming topics for Sun and other UNIX systems and teaches through examples.

POSIX Programmer's Guide

By Donald Lewine
1st Edition April 1991
640 pages, ISBN 0-937175-73-0

Most UNIX systems today are POSIX compliant because the federal government requires it for its purchases. Even OSF and UI agree on support for POSIX. Given the manufacturer's documentation, however, it can be difficult to distinguish system-specific features from those features defined by POSIX.

The *POSIX Programmer's Guide*, intended as an explanation of the POSIX standard and as a reference for the POSIX.1 programming library, helps you write more portable programs. This guide is especially helpful if you are writing programs that must run on multiple UNIX platforms. This guide also helps you convert existing UNIX programs for POSIX compliance.

"POSIX Programmer's Guide belongs on the shelf of every Unix system programmer. Posix texts will be written, and Posix reference manuals will be produced, but it is rare to find such an interesting compromise between the two."
—Ed Gordon, BDataSystems, *IEEE Software Magazine*

POSIX.4

By Bill O. Gallmeister
1st Edition January 1995
568 pages, ISBN 1-56592-074-0

Real-world programming (typically called real-time programming) is programming that interacts in some way with the "real world" of daily life. Real-world programmers develop the unseen software that operates most of the world that surrounds you, software typically characterized by deadlines—and harsh penalties if the deadlines aren't met. When you've just rear-ended another car, it's no consolation that a sudden flurry of input slowed down your brake processor, so it couldn't react quickly enough when you hit the pedal.

This book covers the POSIX.4 standard for portable real-time programming. The POSIX.4 standard itself is a massive document that defines system interfaces for asynchronous I/O, scheduling, communications, and other facilities. However, this book does more than explain the standard. It provides a general introduction to real-time programming and real-time issues: the problems software faces when it needs to interact with the real world and how to solve them. If you're at all interested in real-time applications—which include just about everything from telemetry to transaction processing—this book will be an essential reference.

POSIX. 4 includes problem sets, answers, and reference manual pages for all functions and header files.

Programming with curses

By John Strang
1st Edition 1986
78 pages, ISBN 0-937175-02-1

Curses is a UNIX library of functions for controlling a terminal's display screen from a C program. It can be used to provide a screen driver for a program (such as a visual editor) or to improve a program's user interface.

This handbook will help you make use of the curses library in your C programs. We have presented ample material on curses and its implementation in UNIX so that you understand the whole, as well as its parts.

How to stay in touch with O'Reilly

1. Visit Our Award-Winning Web Site

http://www.oreilly.com/

★ "Top 100 Sites on the Web" —*PC Magazine*
★ "Top 5% Web sites" —*Point Communications*
★ "3-Star site" —*The McKinley Group*

Our web site contains a library of comprehensiveproduct information (including book excerpts and tables of contents), downloadable software, background articles, interviews with technology leaders, links to relevant sites, book cover art, and more. File us in your Bookmarks or Hotlist!

2. Join Our Email Mailing Lists

New Product Releases

To receive automatic email with brief descriptions of all new O'Reilly products as they are released, send email to: **listproc@online.oreilly.com**
Put the following information in the first line of your message (*not* in the Subject field):
subscribe oreilly-news "Your Name" of "Your Organization" (for example: subscribe oreilly-news Kris Webber of Fine Enterprises)

O'Reilly Events

If you'd also like us to send information about trade show events, special promotions, and other O'Reilly events, send email to: **listproc@online.oreilly.com**
Put the following information in the first line of your message (*not* in the Subject field):
subscribe oreilly-events "Your Name" of "Your Organization"

3. Get Examples from Our Books via FTP

There are two ways to access an archive of example files from our books:

Regular FTP

* ftp to:
  ftp.oreilly.com
  (login: anonymous
  password: your email address)
* Point your web browser to:
  ftp://ftp.oreilly.com/

FTPMAIL

* Send an email message to:
  ftpmail@online.oreilly.com
  (Write "help" in the message body)

4. Visit Our Gopher Site

* Connect your gopher to:
  gopher.oreilly.com

* Point your web browser to:
  gopher://gopher.oreilly.com/

* Telnet to:
  gopher.oreilly.com
  login: gopher

5. Contact Us via Email

order@oreilly.com
To place a book or software order online. Good for North American and international customers.

subscriptions@oreilly.com
To place an order for any of our newsletters or periodicals.

books@oreilly.com
General questions about any of our books.

software@oreilly.com
For general questions and product information about our software. Check out O'Reilly Software Online at **http://software.oreilly.com/** for software and technical support information. Registered O'Reilly software users send your questions to: **website-support@oreilly.com**

cs@oreilly.com
For answers to problems regarding your order or our products.

booktech@oreilly.com
For book content technical questions or corrections.

proposals@oreilly.com
To submit new book or software proposals to our editors and product managers.

international@oreilly.com
For information about our international distributors or translation queries. For a list of our distributors outside of North America check out:
http://www.oreilly.com/www/order/country.html

O'Reilly & Associates, Inc.
101 Morris Street, Sebastopol, CA 95472 USA
TEL   707-829-0515 or 800-998-9938
          (6am to 5pm PST)
FAX   707-829-0104

Titles from O'Reilly

Please note that upcoming titles are displayed in italic.

WEB PROGRAMMING
Apache: The Definitive Guide
Building Your Own Web
 Conferences
Building Your Own Website
CGI Programming for the World
 Wide Web
Designing for the Web
HTML: The Definitive Guide,
 2nd Ed.
JavaScript: The Definitive Guide,
 2nd Ed.
Learning Perl
Programming Perl, 2nd Ed.
Mastering Regular Expressions
WebMaster in a Nutshell
Web Security & Commerce
Web Client Programming with
 Perl
World Wide Web Journal

USING THE INTERNET
Smileys
The Future Does Not Compute
The Whole Internet User's Guide
 & Catalog
The Whole Internet for Win 95
Using Email Effectively
Bandits on the Information
 Superhighway

JAVA SERIES
Exploring Java
Java AWT Reference
Java Fundamental Classes
 Reference
Java in a Nutshell
*Java Language Reference, 2nd
 Edition*
Java Network Programming
Java Threads
Java Virtual Machine

SOFTWARE
WebSite™ 1.1
WebSite Professional™
Building Your Own Web
 Conferences
WebBoard™
PolyForm™
Statisphere™

SONGLINE GUIDES
NetActivism   NetResearch
Net Law   NetSuccess
NetLearning   NetTravel
Net Lessons

SYSTEM ADMINISTRATION
Building Internet Firewalls
Computer Crime: A
 Crimefighter's Handbook
Computer Security Basics
DNS and BIND, 2nd Ed.
Essential System Administration,
 2nd Ed.
Getting Connected: The Internet
 at 56K and Up
Linux Network Administrator's
 Guide
Managing Internet Information
 Services
Managing NFS and NIS
Networking Personal Computers
 with TCP/IP
Practical UNIX & Internet
 Security, 2nd Ed.
PGP: Pretty Good Privacy
sendmail, 2nd Ed.
sendmail Desktop Reference
System Performance Tuning
TCP/IP Network Administration
termcap & terminfo
Using & Managing UUCP
Volume 8: X Window System
 Administrator's Guide
Web Security & Commerce

UNIX
Exploring Expect
Learning VBScript
Learning GNU Emacs, 2nd Ed.
Learning the bash Shell
Learning the Korn Shell
Learning the UNIX Operating
 System
Learning the vi Editor
Linux in a Nutshell
Making TeX Work
Linux Multimedia Guide
Running Linux, 2nd Ed.
SCO UNIX in a Nutshell
sed & awk, 2nd Edition
Tcl/Tk Tools
UNIX in a Nutshell: System V
 Edition
UNIX Power Tools
Using csh & tsch
When You Can't Find Your UNIX
 System Administrator
Writing GNU Emacs Extensions

WEB REVIEW STUDIO SERIES
Gif Animation Studio
Shockwave Studio

WINDOWS
Dictionary of PC Hardware and
 Data Communications Terms
Inside the Windows 95 Registry
Inside the Windows 95 File
 System
Windows Annoyances
*Windows NT File System
 Internals*
Windows NT in a Nutshell

PROGRAMMING
Advanced Oracle PL/SQL
 Programming
Applying RCS and SCCS
C++: The Core Language
Checking C Programs with lint
DCE Security Programming
Distributing Applications Across
 DCE & Windows NT
Encyclopedia of Graphics File
 Formats, 2nd Ed.
Guide to Writing DCE
 Applications
lex & yacc
Managing Projects with make
Mastering Oracle Power Objects
Oracle Design: The Definitive
 Guide
Oracle Performance Tuning, 2nd
 Ed.
Oracle PL/SQL Programming
Porting UNIX Software
POSIX Programmer's Guide
POSIX.4: Programming for the
 Real World
Power Programming with RPC
Practical C Programming
Practical C++ Programming
Programming Python
Programming with curses
Programming with GNU Software
Pthreads Programming
Software Portability with imake,
 2nd Ed.
Understanding DCE
Understanding Japanese
 Information Processing
UNIX Systems Programming for
 SVR4

BERKELEY 4.4 SOFTWARE DISTRIBUTION
4.4BSD System Manager's
 Manual
4.4BSD User's Reference Manual
4.4BSD User's Supplementary
 Documents
4.4BSD Programmer's Reference
 Manual
4.4BSD Programmer's
 Supplementary Documents
X Programming
Vol. 0: X Protocol Reference
 Manual
Vol. 1: Xlib Programming Manual
Vol. 2: Xlib Reference Manual
Vol. 3M: X Window System User's
 Guide, Motif Edition
Vol. 4M: X Toolkit Intrinsics
 Programming Manual, Motif
 Edition
Vol. 5: X Toolkit Intrinsics
 Reference Manual
Vol. 6A: Motif Programming
 Manual
Vol. 6B: Motif Reference Manual
Vol. 6C: Motif Tools
Vol. 8 : X Window System
 Administrator's Guide
Programmer's Supplement for
 Release 6
X User Tools
The X Window System in a
 Nutshell

CAREER & BUSINESS
Building a Successful Software
 Business
The Computer User's Survival
 Guide
Love Your Job!
Electronic Publishing on CD-
 ROM

TRAVEL
Travelers' Tales: Brazil
Travelers' Tales: Food
Travelers' Tales: France
Travelers' Tales: Gutsy Women
Travelers' Tales: India
Travelers' Tales: Mexico
Travelers' Tales: Paris
Travelers' Tales: San Francisco
Travelers' Tales: Spain
Travelers' Tales: Thailand
Travelers' Tales: A Woman's
 World

International Distributors

UK, Europe, Middle East and Northern Africa (except France, Germany, Switzerland, & Austria)

INQUIRIES
International Thomson Publishing
Europe
Berkshire House
168-173 High Holborn
London WC1V 7AA, United Kingdom
Telephone: 44-171-497-1422
Fax: 44-171-497-1426
Email: itpint@itps.co.uk

ORDERS
International Thomson Publishing
Services, Ltd.
Cheriton House, North Way
Andover, Hampshire SP10 5BE,
United Kingdom
Telephone: 44-264-342-832
 (UK orders)
Telephone: 44-264-342-806
 (outside UK)
Fax: 44-264-364418 (UK orders)
Fax: 44-264-342761 (outside UK)
UK & Eire orders: itpuk@itps.co.uk
International orders: itpint@itps.co.uk

France

Editions Eyrolles
61 bd Saint-Germain
75240 Paris Cedex 05
France
Fax: 33-01-44-41-11-44

FRENCH LANGUAGE BOOKS
All countries except Canada
Phone: 33-01-44-41-46-16
Email: geodif@eyrolles.com

ENGLISH LANGUAGE BOOKS
Phone: 33-01-44-41-11-87
Email: distribution@eyrolles.com

Australia

WoodsLane Pty. Ltd.
7/5 Vuko Place, Warriewood NSW 2102
P.O. Box 935, Mona Vale NSW 2103
Australia
Telephone: 61-2-9970-5111
Fax: 61-2-9970-5002
Email: info@woodslane.com.au

Germany, Switzerland, and Austria

INQUIRIES
O'Reilly Verlag
Balthasarstr. 81
D-50670 Köln
Germany
Telephone: 49-221-97-31-60-0
Fax: 49-221-97-31-60-8
Email: anfragen@oreilly.de

ORDERS
International Thomson Publishing
Königswinterer Straße 418
53227 Bonn, Germany
Telephone: 49-228-97024 0
Fax: 49-228-441342
Email: order@oreilly.de

Asia (except Japan & India)

INQUIRIES
International Thomson Publishing Asia
60 Albert Street #15-01
Albert Complex
Singapore 189969
Telephone: 65-336-6411
Fax: 65-336-7411

ORDERS
Telephone: 65-336-6411
Fax: 65-334-1617
thomson@signet.com.sg

New Zealand

WoodsLane New Zealand Ltd.
21 Cooks Street (P.O. Box 575)
Wanganui, New Zealand
Telephone: 64-6-347-6543
Fax: 64-6-345-4840
Email: info@woodslane.com.au

Japan

O'Reilly Japan, Inc.
Kiyoshige Building 2F
12-Banchi, Sanei-cho
Shinjuku-ku
Tokyo 160 Japan
Telephone: 81-3-3356-5227
Fax: 81-3-3356-5261
Email: kenji@oreilly.com

India

Computer Bookshop (India) PVT. LTD.
190 Dr. D.N. Road, Fort
Bombay 400 001
India
Telephone: 91-22-207-0989
Fax: 91-22-262-3551
Email: cbsbom@giasbm01.vsnl.net.in

The Americas

O'Reilly & Associates, Inc.
101 Morris Street
Sebastopol, CA 95472 U.S.A.
Telephone: 707-829-0515
Telephone: 800-998-9938 (U.S. & Canada)
Fax: 707-829-0104
Email: order@oreilly.com

Southern Africa

International Thomson Publishing
Southern Africa
Building 18, Constantia Park
138 Sixteenth Road
P.O. Box 2459
Halfway House, 1685 South Africa
Telephone: 27-11-805-4819
Fax: 27-11-805-3648